BUSINESS IN BRITAIN IN THE TWENTIETH CENTURY

Terry Gourvish

Business in Britain in the Twentieth Century

Edited by
RICHARD COOPEY AND PETER LYTH

OXFORD
UNIVERSITY PRESS

OXFORD

UNIVERSITY PRESS

Great Clarendon Street, Oxford OX2 6DP

Oxford University Press is a department of the University of Oxford.
It furthers the University's objective of excellence in research, scholarship,
and education by publishing worldwide in

Oxford New York

Auckland Cape Town Dar es Salaam Hong Kong Karachi
Kuala Lumpur Madrid Melbourne Mexico City Nairobi
New Delhi Shanghai Taipei Toronto

With offices in

Argentina Austria Brazil Chile Czech Republic France Greece
Guatemala Hungary Italy Japan Poland Portugal Singapore
South Korea Switzerland Thailand Turkey Ukraine Vietnam

Oxford is a registered trade mark of Oxford University Press
in the UK and in certain other countries

Published in the United States
by Oxford University Press Inc., New York

© Oxford University Press, 2009

British Library Cataloguing in Publication Data

Data available

Library of Congress Cataloging in Publication Data

Data available

Typeset by SPI Publisher Services, Pondicherry, India
Printed in Great Britain
on acid-free paper by
CPI Antony Rowe, Chippenham, Wiltshire

ISBN 978–0–19–922600–9

1 3 5 7 9 10 8 6 4 2

In honour of Terry Gourvish

Contents

List of Figures   ix
List of Tables   ix
Terry Gourvish: An Appreciation   xi

Introduction. British Business in the Twentieth Century:
Decline and Renaissance?
Richard Coopey and Peter Lyth   1

1. Strategic Games, Scale, and Efficiency, or Chandler goes to Hollywood
   Leslie Hannah   15

2. Industrial Policy in Twentieth Century Britain
   Geoffrey Owen   48

3. Business in the Regions: From 'Old' Districts to 'New' Clusters?
   Andrew Popp and John Wilson   65

4. Elites, Entrepreneurs, and British Business in the Twentieth Century
   Youssef Cassis   82

5. Invisible Entrepreneurs? Women and Business in Twentieth
   Century Britain
   Katrina Honeyman   97

6. From a Solution to a Problem? Overseas Multinationals in Britain
   during Economic Decline and Renaissance
   Peter Scott   116

7. British Management since 1945: 'Renaissance' and Inertia, Illusions
   and Realities
   Nick Tiratsoo   137

8. Not 'Decline and Revival': An Alternative Narrative on British
   Post-War Productivity
   Jim Tomlinson   153

9. Marketing Management in Britain: What is the Evidence for 'Failure'?
   Robert Fitzgerald   168

10. British Retail Banking in the Twentieth Century: Decline and
    Renaissance in Industrial Lending
    Lucy Newton   189

11. The Decline and Renewal of British Multinational Banking
    Geoffrey Jones and Lucy Newton   207

12. Back to the Future: The Aircraft and IT Industries in Britain since 1945
    Richard Coopey and Peter Lyth   225

13. Industrial Research and the Employment of Scientists in British
    Industry before the 1970s
    Sally Horrocks   252

14. Increasing Value? Modern British Retailing in the Late
    Twentieth Century
    Carlo Morelli   271

15. Predicting, Providing, Sustaining, Integrating? British Transport
    Policy since 1945
    Mike Anson and Gerald Crompton   287

16. The Film Industry in Twentieth Century Britain: Consumption
    Patterns, Government Regulation, and Firm Strategy
    Peter Miskell   306

17. British Sport Transformed: Sport, Business, and the Media since 1960
    Dilwyn Porter   330

18. Ethics, Religion, and Business in Twentieth Century Britain
    David Jeremy   356

Index   385

List of Figures

6.1. New U.S. entrants to the UK, by mode of entry, 1908–62 (average per year)   124

16.1. Annual revenues from cinema admissions in Britain (at 1936 prices)   321

18.1. Company liquidations and violations from 1890 to 2002   360

List of Tables

2.1. Value added as % of total value added in 2006   62

5.1. Service employment by gender, UK, 1956–97 (percentages)   100

5.2. Employees in service industry group by gender, UK, 1984–98, thousands (percentages)   101

5.3. Female self-employed, UK, 1956–2001   103

5.4. Self-employed in service industry group by gender, 1984–98, thousands (percentages)   104

6.1. Location quotients for each main assisted region's share of foreign-owned manufacturing employment relative to their share of UK manufacturing employment   127

6.2. Alternative local linkage scenarios for inward direct investment   131

8.1. Labour productivity in manufacturing, 1960–95   154

8.2. Causes of decline?   155

8.3. Anglo-German labour productivity differences, 1938–89 (UK = 100)   156

8.4. Manufacturing labour productivity in Britain and West Germany, 1951–89 (% per annum per person engaged)   158

8.5. Manufacturing labour productivity, 1973–9   158

8.6. Employment in manufacturing, 1973–9   159

8.7. Changes in output and labour productivity, 1973–9 (1973 = 100)   160

8.8. Whole economy labour productivity, 1973–9 (output/hour worked; 1993 = 100)   161

8.9. Labour productivity in manufacturing within the golden age (average annual rates of growth in output per hour worked between cyclical peaks)   163

13.1. Treasury estimates of government funded 'scientific research', 1925   260

13.2. Vickers Group R&D expenditure noted in archives compared to expenditure reported to FBI survey, 1930 and 1935   260

13.3. Expenditure on R&D by manufacturing industry, £ million at current prices   263

13.4. Proportion of R&D carried out within private manufacturing industry
and financed by the British government by sector, 1959–70   264

13.5. Distribution of private manufacturing industry funded R&D by sector,
1959–70   264

16.1. Worldwide sources of revenue for distributors of feature films (percentages)   322

18.1. Cases of gross unethical behaviour in British business, 1890s–1990s   361

18.2. Companies, directors, accountants in Britain, 1900–2000   371

Terry Gourvish

An Appreciation

This is a book of essays in honour of Terry Gourvish. Terry has been at the very heart of business history in Britain for the last four decades. The corpus of work he has produced stands as testament to the scale of his contribution during this period. This includes major works on the history of the railways, the Channel Tunnel, brewing, and many edited collections on a wide range of topics. It is not easy to pigeonhole Terry in terms of scholarship. There is no single theoretical position to celebrate, for example. In many ways, the central theme of this book – the refutation of the simplistic ascription of some overarching theory to the question of British business history – is an apt reflection of Terry's approach. While bandwagons have rolled inexorably past, he has consistently refused to take the easy ride offered. Instead he has marched steadfastly down the road of erudition, with frequent sojourns in dusty archives, and produced a series of works of consistent quality, which many other scholars have been grateful to have to hand for the foundation of their own efforts. Terry's hallmark is in exhaustive interrogation of the records, and the presentation of findings in a comprehensive, but always readable and engaging style. The result of this is clear. While ephemeral work based on this or that fashionable theory will end up as dust in the winds of history, Terry's work will stand. Historians in generations to come will turn to Terry's work for the central story, for the rich and informative account of what happened, for the real history of business.

But Terry will not only be remembered for his scholarship, peerless though it is. He took over as Director of the Business History Unit (BHU) at the London School of Economics in the mid-1980s and has remained in this post ever since. The Unit, established by Les Hannah, some years earlier, was intended to be the leading business history centre in the UK. Under Terry's leadership the BHU has carried on this central role, providing a welcome working environment for a legion of business historians from Britain, and around the world. Many lasting friendships have been formed among those whom Terry has welcomed through the doors of the Unit. The weekly seminar series has seen papers from every leading business historian of a generation. Research projects undertaken at the Unit have formed the basis of many careers and many fields of new research. But for many the BHU *is* Terry Gourvish. In running the BHU, Terry has not merely provided a home for research, he has provided support, guidance, and above all friendship. Countless numbers of scholars new to London, or new to Britain have found a mentor, a guide, and a genial host in Terry Gourvish. True, many have had to endure lengthy hikes, through all kinds of urban (and some not so urban) terrains in search of some fabled pint of beer or micro-brewery, or learned to live with the downside – the sense of martyrdom – which comes with being a Leicester City supporter. And some have experienced the occasional Fawlty moments. But it is all part of the Gourvish persona, always self-effacing, unstintingly generous in both time and effort whether for academic or social purposes.

When we first began to compile the list of scholars we might invite to contribute to this volume we very soon ran into problems. Those who know and respect Terry comprise a very large community of business historians throughout the world. By narrowing the field to British business history we were hardly any better off. Terry can count so many historians of British history among his friends that it would take many volumes to include essays from them all. In some ways this made our task a little easier, in that though this is a festschrift for Terry, it is also intended to be a book with a cohesive structure and a clear focus. So we had the luxury of a very wide field from which to invite contributions. And we take this opportunity to apologize to those many scholars we left out, as we know many more of Terry's colleagues would have liked to contribute. It is a testament to everyone's fondness and respect for Terry that all those who were asked to contribute to this volume agreed without hesitation. We hope this book conveys an indication of the way, amongst a very broad constituency of business and economic historians, Terry Gourvish will always be respected and loved.

Richard Coopey
Worcester

Peter Lyth
Nottingham   September 2008

Introduction

British Business in the Twentieth Century:
Decline and Renaissance?

Richard Coopey and Peter Lyth

Broadly speaking, the story of the British economy after the mid-1980s was one of renaissance. From being 'the sick man of Europe' in the troubled years of the 1970s, Britain's economy recovered to become one of the strongest in Europe by the turn of the twenty-first century. British business regained a level of confidence and prestige which few would have predicted when peering through the gloom of the so-called 'winter of discontent'.[1] But the idea of a troubled British economy stretches back much further than the 1970s. For many years the debate about the British economy was dominated by the idea of a decline which began at least a century earlier. From its high point in the mid-nineteenth century, Britain's multiple roles as the 'workshop of the world', and perhaps more importantly, the financier, merchant, and general service provider of the world, were variously held to be subject to readjustment, with manufacturing industry weakening comparatively as the century wore on. From around 1870, Britain's industrial economy appeared to be vulnerable, losing its pre-eminence to Germany and the United States in particular. While the City and Hobson's rentier economy in South East England continued to prosper, the industrial heartlands experienced a series of difficult periods as markets were challenged and competitors sprang up with their own comparative advantages. One by one Britain's great staple industries – cotton textiles, shipbuilding, coal, iron and steel – together with a wide range of manufacturing industries, seemed to be losing their lead to other countries with younger, more dynamic economies.

But were they all in trouble? Britain's economy was not simply divided into north and south. Regionalization and clustering, linked by a complex transport and communications infrastructure was a key feature – the great textile towns of the 'north'; the potteries in the north Midlands; the coalfields, iron and steel in south Wales and the north-east; the shipbuilding of the south west of Scotland and north east of England; the great international ports and trading houses of Bristol, Glasgow, Liverpool, and London; Birmingham the 'city of 1,000 trades' – all were part of an uncompromisingly baroque economic landscape. Smaller, less 'significant' industries were also clustered around centres, where they dominated the local economy – carpets in Kidderminster, gloves in Worcester, hats in Luton and so on. Did all these sectors experience the same decline? Did they all suffer from the same symptoms or causes? Clearly, the answer is no. Yet the literature of decline for a long time was obsessed with finding answers in a specific, all embracing causality.[2]

Historians pointed the finger at the failure of owners and managers to invest in new technological processes, or the failure to provide systematic engineering and scientific education geared to industry; they flagged up the duality of the British economy – the gentlemanly capitalists and City bankers with no interest in the grimy industry of the 'north'; they pointed to the institutional inertias ranging from entrenched management practice to recalcitrant trade unionism; they flagged up a damaging prioritization of military over civil R&D. They highlighted an enduring hostility towards industry on the part of a bloody-minded Treasury, and finally and most controversially, they looked for cultural explanations, leading many of their opponents to slip the safety catch on the Browning and instigating perhaps the most heated of all the 'decline debates'.[3] This cultural debate stretched across the territory of the other causalities – the educational cultures of the elites; the vestigial power, influence or appeal of a rural-minded aristocracy; the anti-industrialism of cultural-political movements from arts and crafts onwards; the distractions and indulgencies enjoyed by decaying industrial dynasties; the twisted political economy of welfarism in its various guises and so on.

From the beginning, one key feature of the 'decline debate' has been an almost obsessive emphasis on international comparison and contrast; indeed comparison with other countries and economies has been central to nearly every approach to the debate. Thus, the British economy declined *relative* to that of Germany, the United States, France, or Japan. And the corollary of this focus on comparison has been the portrayal of decline in terms of a *race* which Britain lost, and is perhaps still losing. Of course, the debate has also been subject to much revisionism and some historians have even denied that there is any 'case' to answer at all, arguing that the waning of British economic power was an inevitable result of the capitalist process and that her businessmen did the best they could under the immutable laws of the marketplace.[4]

What can we take with us from these reflections on the methodology of 'declinism'? How do we reconcile the changing fashions for different causes, critical time frames, explanatory models and ideological preferences which have characterized the debate over British economic decline for over a century? The short answer is, of course, we can't. The more considered response is that we should not try; despite the eagerness of historians to come up with a single new truth, the picture remains immensely complex, with sectors rising and falling and individual firms experiencing prosperity and bankruptcy, but seldom in unison. And, meanwhile whole new industries and markets emerge, if not to entirely replace the old, then to form part of a process of constant reconfiguration. Which brings us to the other major problem with the literature of decline – periodization. New sectors and leading firms emerged even in the depths of the interwar depression. The British car industry, consumer electronics, aero engines, retail chains, the leisure industry producers and retailers in the age of cinema, and the music industries all emerged at this time, not from any Schumpeterian shake out, but from the birth of new markets. New regions emerged – from the ribbon developments and trading estates of the South East to the expanding industrial regions of the Midlands. In the post-war period we can see, after the difficult readjustment of the late 1940s, not a return to depression, as many expected, but rather a flourishing revival. The car industry of the later 1950s and early 1960s, for example, did not look like a basket case at the time, meeting unprecedented demand with popular mass production models as well as iconic and revolutionary car designs such as the Mini or the Jaguar E-type. These models are easy to criticize with the benefit of hindsight, in terms of durability and performance, but were unquestionably world leaders of their time. It shouldn't be forgotten that British marques dominated the American sports car market during the 1950s, British aircraft producers competed head to head with those of the United States, the world's first business computers were produced here, ahead of IBM, and the first public access to civil nuclear power took place in Britain during this decade. From this perspective, the audit of war, or at least its medium-term legacy, seems to suggest a positive balance sheet in terms of modernization and industrial health. And a similar story can be told of the 1960s: while *angst* circulated about the great 'American Challenge', and growing British dependency on US technology and penetration by US multinationals, British capital was crossing the Atlantic in the other direction and British cultural leadership was manifesting itself in healthy profit margins for firms like EMI.

To list these signs of vivacity is not, of course, to deny that at various moments in the modern period whole sections of the British economy fell on hard times. What it does show however is that the picture is a remarkably complex one, with the ebb and flow of the British economy being characterized by cross-currents and undertows, pools and rapids. It also follows that any concept of 'renaissance' must be rooted in the same complexity. At the time of publication (the autumn of 2008) it is tempting to call for a rather positivist history of British renaissance, the seemingly catastrophic problems of the financial sector notwithstanding. But to posit some kind of post-1980s market-led triumphalism would be mistaken, indeed it would be to slip into a trap into which other histories have already fallen.

The explanation for change based on a simple version of post-1980 reform is indeed a seductive one. In this scenario the Blair–Brown years are seen as a continuum of the tough but necessary interventions of the Thatcher Governments. These interventions are in turn based on a mix of Friedmanite monetarism (failed) and Schumpeterian enterprise liberation, through a successive, if somewhat opportunistic, programme of fiscal reform, privatization, hard-headed industrial policy and so on. Interestingly for historians, the belief that economic decline is inevitable, and the accompanying idea that the state should seek to *manage* rather than *reverse* it, seems to fit the actual running of the British economy in the years between the end of the Second World War and the assumption of power by Margaret Thatcher's Conservative government in 1979. Viewed from this historical vantage point, the Thatcher government's attempt to reverse decline, rather than simply accommodate a historical process, can be characterized as revolutionary – in the Schumpeterian rather than the Marxist sense. For business historians Joseph Schumpeter makes an interesting contrast with Alfred Chandler. Both were Harvard men, essentially trying to explain the power of American free market capitalism, yet it is becoming increasingly clear that it is Schumpeter whose work will endure. If we accept Schumpeter's premise that capitalism is a continuously revolutionary process, the revolutions being driven by historical cycles of technological innovation (steam-power, electrification, motorization, computerization, etc.), then national decline is inevitable because success in each revolution is dependent on a precise set of relationships existing between several variables (e.g. technological innovation, social structure, economic development, institutional framework, cultural standards) and the likelihood of getting the relationships between all these variables right, indefinitely, and in the face of exogenous historical developments, is practically nil. National economies must decline, because the innovatory impulse is bound to run aground somewhere on the topography of variables which are critical to success.[5] Schumpeter saw the development of capitalist organizations, from the craft shop to the multinational corporation, as a process of continuous revolution from within, which he famously characterized as 'creative destruction': the old being continually destroyed by the process of creating the new. For Schumpeter, continuous innovation was 'endogenous' to capitalism.[6] But that process of innovation runs out of steam without 'the propelling force' of entrepreneurship.[7] Whether or not Thatcher and her neo-Thatcherite successors, Tony Blair and Gordon Brown, were Schumpeterian, she, and they, clearly sought to encourage entrepreneurship, led by the guiding light of the liberalized market. For them British decline was to be reversed by a new generation of entrepreneurs, who would ride a wave of 'creative destruction' sweeping away the bad old ways of decline *management*.[8] To a degree she (and they) was successful, although it is fair to say that more was achieved by way of 'destruction' than 'creation'. Where the greatest difficulties have arisen in the crusade to reverse decline, however, is in the relationship with the Schumpeterian 'variables', in particular between institutional framework, and social and political culture.

Perhaps the clearest expression of this difficulty lies in Britain's short-lived flirtation with industrial planning. By 1980 and the onset of Thatcherism, without ever being given what most scholars of the subject would call a serious trial, industrial policy and planning had been banished to the realm of economic and political heresy. Before that, Britain experienced the rather timid planning initiatives of the 1940s, which were abandoned in the 1950s, a move which was then regretted in the 1960s, as British leaders became aware that other countries (notably France) had managed post-war economic recovery rather better than itself and done so largely through the use of creative state intervention in the economy. The new planning apparatus of the 1960s, the Department of

Economic Affairs, did for a short while offer the hope of a new dawn in industrial policy, but fell victim to a mixture Sterling crises and Treasury intransigence, combined with a growing ideological hostility towards planning in the early 1970s.[9] It is one of the curiosities of British economic history in the twentieth century that industrial planning – indeed any intervention by the state in workings of the economy – has been routinely condemned as 'ideological', while deregulation and the untrammelled operation of the market is seen as somehow 'ideology-free'. For historians, however, as Schumpeter himself pointed out with reference to the usefulness of perfect competition as a starting point for economic analysis, what might be deduced from ideological conviction does not necessarily tally with historical fact. The British company Rolls-Royce, bankrupted by the high cost of developing jet engines in the late 1960s, was rescued by a Conservative government in the early 1970s. Its rescue was done with great reluctance but nonetheless has proved to have been a piece of interference in the 'natural' workings of the economy which led not only to the company's survival but also to its twenty-first century status as Britain's sole remaining 'national champion' in high technology manufacturing.[10]

Histories are usually a reflection of their times. Elbaum and Lazonick's British decline book, for example, served two currencies: the problems of the British economy, and the concern that the United States might be following the same pre-determined path.[11] The 1970s, with its 'winter of discontent' in Britain, was the backdrop to this pessimism. Is this book guilty of the same, narrowly conceived motivation? We hope not. Clearly the revival of the British economy since the 1980s is an issue which needs to be addressed; indeed the manifest revival of some sectors often brings into question the basic precepts of the declinist literature, exposing it as simplistic and one dimensional. In addressing the issue of renaissance, this book provides no prescriptive solution – indeed this should probably never be the purpose of historians – rather it points to the extreme complexity of the issues involved. And in doing so, it reveals the shallowness of the notion that merely chanting the mantra of 'market forces' loud enough, down the years since the 1980s, was enough to spark a British renaissance. There is more to it than that.

So, what can business history contribute to the debate about the nature of the post-war British economy? Thankfully the days are gone when this branch of the discipline could be pejoratively (and tautologously) referred to as 'the deadest of dead ends'. Uncritical commissioned histories and sycophantic hagiographies of great men of enterprise are now rare. Over recent years the discipline has broadened its outlook, engaging with theoretical issues and enlarging its boundaries. The nature of entrepreneurship, networks, gender, business cultures and the relationship between culture and business are among the new interests which business historians have brought to the fore. For many years the Alfred Chandler paradigm of business history held sway. In Chandler's model Britain generally came off rather badly, seen as dominated by outdated family capitalism while the juggernaut of the American large-scale, managerially run, multidivisional firm carried all before it. Historians of British business have done much to counter this rather limited view. Not the least among them is *Leslie Hannah* whose opening chapter in this volume brings the debate over Chandler and his contribution to business history up to date with an invigorating and upbeat critique of the Chandlerian paradigm. In his treatment of non-ferrous metal producers in the early twentieth century and the US firm American Tobacco in the same period, *Hannah* reveals the threads of underlying weakness in Chandler's method, dismissing as 'a fable' Chandler's view of American Tobacco's president, James Duke, as a 'modern managerial titan of American mass production'. For *Hannah*, while Chandler's early work (*The Visible Hand, Strategy and Structure*) 'really did contribute models for a universal social science', the international comparative perspectives and the 'set of central hypotheses in US–European comparative business history' put forward in the later *Scale and Scope* have been 'substantially falsified'. And so far as British business is concerned, Chandler's errors 'are highly skewed to under-valuing British performance'. In fact, business history is now moving beyond Chandler and business historians are more likely to engage with Schumpeter or even Foucault, than reprise old feuds with the apostle of American corporate power when trying to explain the trajectory of British enterprise or business methods. *Hannah*'s contribution, through his pointed dissection of Chandler's later work, helps us to understand why.

If we look at specific components and sectors of the British economy in terms of decline or renaissance, major issues of complexity and periodization arise. The British banking sector is a good place to begin, especially in view of the recent spotlight thrown onto its activities. The year of 2008 is not the first time that this sector has come under public, government, or indeed historical scrutiny. The banking system has been implicated in the decline of British industry on numerous occasions from the alleged banker's ramp of the 1930s to the launching of lifeboats in the 1970s. Whatever the culpability of the banks in Britain's industrial decline, there is also another, often neglected, story to be told and that is of the banks themselves, as businesses, on both the domestic and international scene. In the chapters by *Lucy Newton* and *Geoffrey Jones* the performance of the British banking sector is analysed to show how, as enterprises, British banks perform against a complex contextual background. Phases of competition, cartelization, concentration in London, revived local autonomy, formal and informal regulation, global restructuring, strategic blunders and steep learning curves, all feature. And if there is a general pattern, it is towards a 'renaissance' in the 1970s, as liberalization of controls and heightened competition forced new approaches; one of many indications of renaissance, at least on the domestic front, out of phase with the pattern of declinist literature, in general, and the chronology of Thatcherite reform, in particular. On the international front, there are failures and successes, new entrepreneurial phases and periods of stasis, but again with no obvious connection to the accepted chronology of decline in Britain. If there is a story of 'renaissance' here it is a later story, set in the 1990s.

While *Newton*'s account of domestic banking provides something of a counterfactual in terms of decline in the 1970s, this was undoubtedly the 'troubled decade' as far as manufacturing industry was concerned. In his chapter on British industrial policy since the Second World War, *Geoffrey Owen* adopts the familiar periodization of three decades after 1945, followed by 'the reforms that were introduced in the 1980s', in his analysis of how and why British industry evolved in a different way to France (where overt state intervention and 'economic patriotism' characterized governments of both the Left and the Right), or Germany (where 'long-established institutions and attitudes' achieved the same objectives). *Owen* confirms that the 1970s was the decade in which large sections of British manufacturing industry (cars, aircraft, machine tools, electronics) started to fall apart, despite the efforts of Labour's planning instrument, the National Enterprise Board, to save them after 1974. Yet, is it correct to highlight the decade as the culmination of long-term structural problems in the British manufacturing economy, the decade when the Keynesian chickens, so to speak, came home to roost in a stagflationary henhouse? *Jim Tomlinson's* chapter offers compelling evidence to the contrary. In taking to task the empirical basis of the many studies on productivity, he asserts – in contrast to *Owen* – that the problems of the 1970s were just that – 'largely the consequences of short-run forces'. Whether or not *Tomlinson* is right, his work does offer further reasons why we might want to reconsider the conventional view of the 1970s as a deeply troubled period in British business history, the nadir in a long-term trend of decline stretching back to 1945, if not 1875. And if we reconsider the 1970s, then, of course, we must also reconsider the 1980s and the years since then. For *Owen,* while recognizing the legitimate worries that exist in some quarters that Britain has allowed too much of its manufacturing industry to wither away, or that it has allowed too many foreigners to buy what's left, business historians can, nonetheless, be sanguine about Britain's record since the 1980s and reassured that it has 'gained far more than it lost through its openness to inwards investment'. Moreover, he reassures us that while industrial policy of the old school has gone, governments will continue with 'policies aimed at institutional weaknesses that impede the growth of productivity'.

While *Owen* points to education as an example of such a weakness, another possible fault line is Britain's ill-coordinated and under-funded transport system, the subject of the chapter by *Mike Anson* and *Gerald Crompton*. For them, government has continually underestimated the reciprocal relationship between transport and economic growth, and they point to the fact that, in comparison with all other Western European countries, transport infrastructure in Britain has suffered long-term neglect. Their explanation for this lies in a combination of Treasury hostility to proper investment in the railways – a stance that 'encouraged persistence with network reduction' rather than modernization of the system – combined with the extraordinary triumph of the road lobby in the 1960s when the idea of a car-owning democracy established deep roots in the political psyche of successive British governments. For *Anson* and *Crompton* the verdict on the Thatcher revolution is more damning and they see rail privatization in particular as a disaster – delivering 'none of the benefits claimed for it'. Today the trials and tribulations associated with transport are never far from the news and tend to be debated within the confines of transitory economic and political worries – the

price of petrol, the spread of congestion charges, taxes on travel by car or plane –
but there are more fundamental issues at stake, and *Anson* and *Crompton*
highlight an important one when they quote the former head of British Airways,
Sir Rod Eddington, who warned recently that the UK had 'nearly reached
the point of no return at which its transport infrastructure became so bad that
it deterred foreign investment'.

In his concern for foreign investment, Eddington touched on a seminal issue in
the debate on the reality of British economic 'renaissance'. If the path towards
renaissance does lie partly in the increasing attraction of foreign direct investment
(FDI), then it would represent a strategy with a very long pedigree: the Japanese
and Russian economies tried it in the closing decades of the nineteenth century
and more recently it has formed part of the debate around the growth of
globalization and multinational enterprise. Is FDI a route to modernization?
Do multinationals bring spin-offs in terms of technology, labour processes and
management best practice? Or do they only bring employment, reserving control
and innovation functions to the headquarters and home economy? In his chapter,
Peter Scott tracks the long term history of foreign firms in Britain. They found a
particularly receptive home, if occasionally manipulated by governments trying
to engineer new sectoral profiles. They often displayed 'demonstration effects'
and best practices – and imposed these on supplier firms. The positives should
not be taken too far, however, and much FDI attracted during the 1980s has
proved to have little long-term loyalty to the development areas in which they set
up, leaving British industry more vulnerable to fluctuations in the world trade
cycle. As *Scott* shows, opinion remains divided on the long-term benefits of much
of the FDI which appeared as part of the British 'renaissance' of recent years.

One component of a modern economy which has drawn increasing interest
from business and economic historians in recent years has been that of regionalization. Initially questioned as an alternative to the teleological, Chandlerite
multidivisional Fordized firm, regional clusters have been part of renaissance
or new sectors from the textile sectors of Northern Italy to the new silicone
topographies found everywhere from Southern California to Bangalore. Is there a
British regional renaissance to be found? *Andrew Popp* and *John Wilson* examine
the question of British regional economies and clusters in their chapter. Pointing
out that the British economy was based in strong regionalization they produce a
complex account of the life cycle of such developments, going through phases
of critical mass, take off, cooperative competitiveness, saturation, maturity, and
renaissance. But they argue persuasively that regions can also suffer from 'lock-in'
– a cognitive, functional, political, and structural inertia, which may impair
the ability of 'old' industrial districts to change or modernize. They provide
important distinctions between the old industrial regions and the newer forms
of clustering, which are a feature of many emergent economic areas.

One of the central questions in the debate over the nature of the British
economy is that of leadership – the pattern of ownership and management, and
of entrepreneurial profiles. From Chandler's assertion of the debilitating effect
of family ownership of the earlier twentieth century, to the Schumpeterian

privileging of the entrepreneur in the 1980s, the emphasis has been on the role of management and ownership, and it has generally been critical. Many of the chapters in this collection deal with this issue either directly or indirectly. *Youssef Cassis* provides a salutary demonstration of the complexity of these issues, identifying many different concepts of elites in business. Did the 1980s unleash a cadre of new entrepreneurs, a new élite to lead the renaissance? The picture is not clear. Certainly the notorious old networks of public school and Oxbridge elites featured throughout the twentieth century, but there was perhaps a new permeability in recent decades. *Cassis* asserts that the existing scholarship on this issue is still surprisingly lacking and understanding is poor. Rival economies exhibited the same elitism as Britain for example, yet it seems to have done them far less harm. In addition, the division between industry and City in Britain, may not be so evident in terms of elites and networks. Continuing the theme of leadership, *Nick Tiratsoo* looks specifically at the quality of British managers. Did the 1980s simply empower a new vanguard of leaders with new powers to manage? Was there a new cadre of managers, inspired by the Branson effect, with MBA certificate proudly displayed behind the desk? Once again, no simple prescription comes to hand. And again the lack of good research available on this topic is evident. How does education relate to performance, for example? In an impressive critique of the histories and a marshalling of the available authoritative surveys, *Tiratsoo* sees continuity rather than change with 'the same flaws and difficulties . . . identified again and again'.

If entrepreneurship, management, and ownership of business are freed from restraint in the 1980s, are they subsequently hedged around with obligations from other directions? The expectation placed upon the modern corporation, or the executives within it, is that they will be sensitive to a sea change in broader societal values. Two major issues stand out. Firstly changes in attitude to the role of women in British society. This topic needs to be understood both from the perspective of society and from the perspective of historians, and these two views are not always in accord. *Katrina Honeyman's* chapter addresses both, taking business historians to task for their 'longstanding and institutional gender blindness' while pointing out that women have been actively involved in business for a long time – although usually not the sort of business about which business historians are fond of writing. She demonstrates that despite a few high profile examples of women entrepreneurs in large corporations, they are more likely to be found in the self-employed or SME sectors. This may be due to a range of factors from the limiting effects of patriarchal systems, to the natural affinity of women for networks rather than hierarchies, but it remains a growing and important factor in changes in the British economy. A similar broad change in values has placed a range of ethical expectations upon the firm. Again, the spectrum is a wide one, stretching from stakeholder responsibility to concern for the environment. The paradox is that the very market forces which brought the idea of 'freedom' to the 1980s also set up a charter for ignoring these new issues of concern. *David Jeremy* takes the long view of corporate ethics, asking a series of probing and intriguing questions about the social responsibilities and expectations placed upon British business, and whether or not it measures up. Interestingly, he points to the 1890s and the final two decades of the twentieth century as low points in this respect.

Understanding the emergence of new sectors is a major factor in anatomizing change or economic renaissance in Britain in the twentieth century. Several chapters in this volume demonstrate the ways in which business history is exploring these new sectors of the economy. *Peter Miskell* and *Dil Porter* investigate the quintessentially late-twentieth century, post-modern industries of film production and sport. Film, while not a new industry in itself – at over 80 years old it is of the same vintage as aircraft manufacturing – is certainly new to business history. Interest in this part of the 'creative economy' is growing, not least because leisure-based industries – from tourism to professional football – are increasingly recognized as important growth areas of future economies. Definitional debates proliferate about quite where the boundaries of the 'creative economy' might lie, but the film industry is certainly a central part of the story. *Miskell's* study of the British film industry charts the complex relationship between enterprises involved in production and distribution, against the backdrop of a turbulent market which was periodically shaken by new forms of competition, rapid technological development and market reconfigurations. It is a story of episodic success and a fair measure of renaissance. And, in common with many other chapters in this book, it is a story of engagement with, or attempted resistance to, US economic predations. Meanwhile *Dil Porter's* chapter opens with the telling words 'Sport is not a game. It is a business' and shows how British sports like rugby, cricket, football, golf, tennis, and motor racing, all abandoned a long-held and cherished belief in the amateur ethic, in order to embrace professionalism and commerce. One is tempted to ask whether this is another example of the inexorable spread of Thatcherism, but *Porter* shows that the conversion of sport from 'a game' into a serious business started earlier, in the 1960s. With the growth of the consumer society and the extraordinary expansion in the power and diversity of television, an increasing proportion of people's income was spent on 'experiential commodities' such as holidays and leisure activities. This led to a change in attitude to sport: with all the paraphernalia of sports clothing and equipment, it became a business to be managed like any other. Lucrative commercial sponsorships paid the (occasionally mind-boggling) wages of sportsmen and women, and the markets ruled on the football field, the golf course, the cricket pitch and the tennis court, just as they did on the floor of the Stock Exchange.

Not surprisingly, the advance of the consumer society in Britain also looms large in the chapters on marketing and retailing by *Robert Fitzgerald* and *Carlo Morelli*. The history of marketing has in recent years become an increasing focus for business historians and *Fitzgerald* has led the way in this new sector of business history with his path-breaking study of the confectionary manufacturer Rowntree. In this volume he shows that the assumption of the marketing-orientation in businesses was a response by many leading enterprises to the greater individual spending power of the consumer, becoming a managerial 'philosophy' by the time of the consumer boom of the 1950s and 1960s. It was this boom, noted also by *Miskell* and *Porter*, which suggests that there was a 'renaissance', at least in consumption, well before the Thatcher revolution of the 1980s. As *Fitzgerald* puts it, while the British may have 'lost an Empire, or looked enviously at US or German growth rates; in truth, the average Briton had never lived better.' Heralds of the consumer society like TV advertising and the appearance of supermarket grocery stores were all novelties of the fifties and sixties. For *Fitzgerald,* the 'corporate case evidence from the post-war consumer boom reveals significant progress in British marketing management, not failure'. It was perhaps the growing marketing and advertising expertise of British business, just as much as the more usually cited factors of rising real wages and falling prices, which drove the 'good times' or, to adopt the recent language of the governor of the Bank of England, 'the nice decades'. *Carlo Morelli's* chapter on retailing fits seamlessly into *Fitzgerald's* interpretive view. Charting the rise of large-scale stores, *Morelli* shows that the sector represents one of the true success stories of British business in the second half of the twentieth century. Key to this success were radical innovations in store design and size, supply chain management and the introduction, and creative use of information technology from the mid-1970s onwards. Taking the example of the supermarket giant, Tesco, he focuses on the value-chain as the mechanism by which large retailers developed competitive advantage. By disengaging from warehousing and distribution functions, and 'retreating into their core competences', stores like Tesco were able to add value to the goods they sold by deep discounting – the so-called 'pile 'em high, sell 'em cheap' strategy – and shrewd marketing made possible by the constant flow of intelligence from customer information databases built into electronic point of sale technology.

Technological competence formed one of the central issues around ideas of decline in the late nineteenth century, with the alleged failure of British industry to grasp new textile machinery or chemical processes, for example. If we look for new science or technology-based industries as a component of the modern British renaissance the picture is a complex one. Whole areas of industry seem to have effectively disappeared, such as the consumer electronics sector, replaced firstly by the Japanese, then Asian Tiger economies, and more recently China. The relationship between these economies is not of serial replacement, but rather a complex of multinational activity, outsourcing, R&D, production networks and agreements and FDI. Within this broad picture and with the benefit of hindsight from the early twenty-first century, the place of British industry is certainly diminished. Yet it should be remembered that in the 1950s and 1960s science and technology-based industries were held up as shining examples of Britain's future. In their chapter *Richard Coopey* and *Peter Lyth* follow the fate of two of these 'hopefuls' – IT and aircraft. The story in both sectors follows a similar path – civil–military duality and government influence, intensive US competition, mistaken strategies related to the legacies great power status and world leadership.

But the outcomes are markedly different, again pointing up the complexity of the sectors' history and the pitfalls in any unicausal account of decline or renaissance. The general notion of British industry continually failing to place sufficient emphasis on science or technology – particularly in terms of research and development – is challenged by *Sally Horrocks* in her chapter. She argues persuasively that much of the data on Britain's R&D effort has been misunderstood and misinterpreted. Key sectors of British industry in fact invested in science-based activities at increasing levels throughout the twentieth century. In contrast to *Corelli Barnett's* bleak notions of post-war misdirection,[12] *Horrocks* demonstrates firstly that there were considerable positive spin-offs from increased government sponsorship of R&D into the 1950s, and secondly that even if levels of expenditure on R&D levelled off into the 1960s and 1970s, there was nonetheless an accompanying compensatory emphasis on better management of this component of modernization.

One of the fundamental weaknesses with many of the earlier explanations of British decline has been their dogmatic adherence to a general idea; it was the enervating role of the City, failures of technology, institutional sclerosis, etc. Another problem has been rigid periodization. In reality some sectors, and some firms within sectors, were on the rise while others were falling. Explanations of decline had greater validity in one period than in another. As this volume repeatedly demonstrates, the renaissance of the British economy is a partial and shifting thing. We need both long and short term history to understand the inertias involved, and the impact of the legacies. While we accept that some sectors of the economy have 'recovered', or emerged afresh, others have been lost, and are not a component of any renaissance. We must also remember that the constituency of the business historian is a broad one – and getting broader. Readers will find no great uniformity of either theory or perspectives in this book and, perhaps oddly, we believe this to be one of its key strengths. The contributors were asked to consider the question of decline and renaissance, and to offer their interpretation of how this question might be addressed; in other words, to what extent either term might be usefully applied to British business, from a range of industries, sectors, and perspectives. And while we are talking of caveats, it should be noted, of course, that this book is not meant to be fully inclusive. There are clearly sectors, firms, or perspectives which we might have included – the pharmaceutical and energy industries, SMEs, and entrepreneurs, for example. Instead, the purpose has been to point the way for further analysis and research. Some chapters are explicit in this sense: *Honeyman's* call for more gender analysis, *Cassis* for more work on elites, *Popp and Wilson* for an improved understanding of the nature of industrial clusters, *Tiratsoo* for a more considered understanding of management, and *Fitzgerald* for a deeper investigation of marketing's role. Other contributions, by implication, call for further consideration and debate about the issues which they raise. This book could not possibly be the last word on the topic of British economic renaissance, nor is it intended to be – quite the opposite, it points to the need for a debate about the nature, timing, extent, and durability of renaissance, indeed, the validity of the term itself. What this book can claim to be is a call for a greater acknowledgement of the *complexity* of the British business environment and, in so doing, a call for an end to the simplistic mantra of rejuvenating market forces.

NOTES

1. Richard Coopey and Nick Woodward, *The Troubled Economy: Britain in the 1970s*, Routledge, 1996.
2. This is not an unusual practice in academic history. Historians, by their nature tend to look for the new element to flag up – the neglected single factor which will bring notice to their work. It is in the nature of the game. And not, of course limited to decline. The literature on the Japanese 'economic miracle' for example, is a mirror image of British decline literature. Started by Chalmers Johnson and his assertion that MITI masterminded the success, he was followed by a series of single issue challenges – work culture, geo-political support, enterprise structure, networks, Keiretsu groups and so on.
3. Britain's insistence on maintaining a military posture out of keeping with its dwindling economic power, and the allegedly malign influence that it had on her R&D effort has been widely cited as a contributory factor in British decline, see for example David Coates, 'The Character and Origin of Britain's Economic Decline', or Nigel Harris, 'The role of Defence Expenditure in Industrial Decline', both in David Coates and John Hillard, eds., *The Economic Decline of Modern Britain: The Debate between Left and Right*, Wheatsheaf Books, Brighton, 1986. Also useful is Maggie Mort and Graham Spinardi, 'Defence and Decline of UK Mechanical Engineering: The Case of Vickers at Barrow', *Business History*, 46, 1, 2004: 1–22. Terry Gourvish pointed out the Treasury's 'growing emphasis on the need for state-owned enterprises to behave more commercially', in his 'The Rise (and Fall?) of State-Owned Enterprise', in Terry Gourvish and Alan O'Day, eds., *Britain Since 1945*, Macmillan, Basingstoke, 1991: 122. See also Bernard Elbaum and William Lazonick, "An Institutional Perspective on British Decline", in Elbaum and Lazonick, eds., *The Decline of the British Economy*, Oxford and New York, 1986; and M.J. Weiner, *English Culture and the Decline of the Industrial Spirit, 1850–1980*, Cambridge University Press, 1981. The nature and historiographical range of British economic 'decline' is laid out in David Coates, *The Question of UK Decline: State, Society and Economy*, Harvester/Wheatsheaf, 1994: 3–23. For a more light-hearted look at the question, see Deirdre McCloskey's 'The Politics of Stories in Historical Economics', in her, *If You're So Smart: The Narrative of Economic Expertise*, University of Chicago Press, Chicago and London, 1990: 40–55.
4. See for example David Edgerton, *Science, Technology and the British Industrial 'Decline', 1870–1970*, Cambridge University Press, Cambridge, 1996: 4.
5. Chris Freeman and Francisco Louçã, *As Time Goes By: From the Industrial Revolutions to the Information Revolution*, Oxford University Press, Oxford, 2001: 5.
6. Joseph Schumpeter, *Capitalism, Socialism and Democracy*, Harper Perennial edition, New York, 1975: 83–4.
7. Schumpeter, *Capitalism, Socialism and Democracy*: 101–2, 110.

8. Since the 1980s Schumpeter's views on entrepreneurship, first expressed in *Theorie der wirtschaftlichen Entwicklung*, Duncker and Humbolt, Leipzig, 1912, have enjoyed something of a renaissance; see recent publications from economic and business historians such as Youssef Cassis and Ioanna Pepelasis Minoglou, eds., *Entrepreneurship in Theory and History*, Palgrave/Macmillan, Basingstoke, 2005; Ioanna Pepelasis Minoglou and Youssef Cassis, eds., *Country Studies in Entrepreneurship: A Historical Perspective*, Palgrave/Macmillan, Basingstoke, 2006; Geoffrey Jones and R. Daniel Wadhwani, eds., *Entrepreneurship and Global Capitalism*, Edward Elgar, Cheltenham, 2007.

9. The Department of Economic Affairs was launched by the new Labour government in 1964 and sank in the fall-out from the Sterling crisis of 1966. According to one commentator, 'indicative planning has never recovered from this setback,' Aubrey Silberston, 'Industrial Policies in Britain, 1960–80', in Charles Carter, ed., *Industrial Policy and Innovation*, Heinemann/National Institute of Social and Economic Research, London, 1981: 46. According to David Edgerton, Britain did have a highly developed set of industrial planning arrangements, but they were part of a *military* industrial rather than a *civil* industrial policy, see his *Warfare State: Britain, 1920–1970*, Cambridge University Press, Cambridge, 2006. Edgerton's rebuttal of the thesis that Britain devoted too much of its energies to military research and his alternative proposal that this was a deliberate albeit rather ill-directed policy which amounts to industrial planning, is developed in D.E.H. Edgerton and S.M. Horrocks, 'British Industrial Research and Development Before 1945', *Economic History Review*, xlvii, 1994: 213–38; David Edgerton, 'Science and the Nation: Towards New Histories of Twentieth Century Britain', *Historical Research*, 78, 199, Feb. 2005: 106; and David Edgerton, *England and the Aeroplane: An Essay on a Militant and Technological Nation*, Macmillan, 1991: 141.

10. As will be seen further in Chapter 12, the Rolls-Royce case supports the argument that governments are often needed to support the early steps on the road to establishing a market position in high technology manufacturing, where there is often the promise of future growth but no immediate prospect of commercial profit. See Keith Pavitt, 'Technology in British Industry: A Suitable Case for Improvement', in Charles Carter, ed., *Industrial Policy and Innovation*, Heinemann/National Institute of Social and Economic Research, London, 1981: 106.

11. Bernard Elbaum and William Lazonick, *The Decline of the British Economy*, Clarendon 1987. Hence, also, the similarly enthusiastic reception for Paul Kennedy's *Rise and Fall of Great Powers*, Fontana, 1989.

12. Correlli Barnett, *The Audit of War: The Illusion and Reality of Britain as a Great Nation*, Macmillan, London, 1986.

1

Strategic Games, Scale, and Efficiency, or *Chandler goes to Hollywood*[1]

Leslie Hannah

The business history literature on Britain in the twentieth century has a distinct whiff of failure about it and, in that sense, the jaded perspectives of Alfred D. Chandler on British management quality follow a well-established native tradition.[2] The reasons for such perspectives are not difficult to grasp. According to the most widely used metric of GDP per head in purchasing power parity terms, Britain started the century off – with a few other countries like Australia and the US – as one of the richest in the world.[3] Yet, at the end of the century, its GDP per head was slightly below France, Canada, and Japan and only a little ahead of Germany and Italy. Kindly American economic historians like Deirdre McCloskey have suggested that pessimism about this performance is overdone and that Britain's growth rate in GDP per head was only modestly below the advanced country norm.[4] Yet even small differences – such as Britain's century-long average of 1.5 per cent per annum against Germany's 1.8 per cent or France's 1.9 per cent – when cumulated over four generations led to catch-up and, in the case of France, leapfrogging. Britain's growth rate in GDP per head between 1900 and 2000 was only 77 per cent of that of the US, while Australia, beginning the century on a par with these two, was able to achieve 87 per cent of the US growth rate. Naturally countries that began the century poor, like Italy or Japan, achieved much higher growth rates than these leaders: the drive to catch-up from such considerable backwardness can be painful and faltering (as the, initially similar, Russian case, and many others show), but can be very rapid and (at least until recently) sustained for the few who get it right.

Countries like Argentina, France, Germany, and Canada – closer followers of the leaders in 1900 – can more reasonably be compared with them. They all began the twentieth century with living standards about a third less than the US/UK/ Australia and could have been expected to do a little better than these leaders, given some catch-up emulation. The best performing of these countries was Canada, whose GDP per head indeed grew 5 per cent faster in 1900–2000 than that of the US.[5] If we benchmark the other 'close followers' against this higher Canadian standard, France comes out best with 97 per cent of the Canadian level and Germany with 90 per cent; only Argentina was so unlucky or mismanaged as to achieve only 55 per cent of the benchmark, propelling its spectacular relative decline. In terms of the shortfall in growth performance (defined as the number of percentage points below the relevant North American benchmark), then, the UK's twentieth century under-performance can be placed in comparative context. It was substantially worse than France, Germany, and Australia, and only twice as good as Argentina. The accuracy of such estimates should not be exaggerated: some of these differentials are well within the margins of error in the data.[6] Indeed, by some measures, American living standards were already above Britain's in 1900, implying – given modern purchasing power parity comparisons – that the twentieth century per capita growth rates of the two countries hardly differed.[7] Yet the European differentials cannot seriously be disputed: observers of the two largest west European economies at the start of the century were in no doubt that Britain was then the more prosperous, whereas few today would deny that Germany and Britain are about equal in living standards.[8]

I. THE SEARCH FOR CAUSES

The roots of Britain's disappointing growth performance have been avidly sought in its business culture, firm and industry structures, finance and governance. Those who seek often find. Among the multiple causes that have been diagnosed, one of the most comprehensively ambitious and initially widely accepted was Chandler's view that the British created fewer of the large managerial corporations that came to dominate global industrial oligopolies in the early twentieth century, thus condemning her manufacturing sector to sharp relative decline. Chandler also offered a clear explanation of what would, otherwise, have been a puzzling behavioural anomaly: the unusually deeply rooted British devotion to their archaic management culture of personal and family ownership. By contrast, in the US and Germany, he believed, entrepreneurs more quickly understood the importance of assembling productive resources of critical scale and scope by ceding ownership to outside shareholders, while recruiting professional managers to build modern organizational hierarchies and production and marketing capabilities. There have been many, reinforcing explanations, also emanating from America, following Chandler's influential lead. De Long argued that Britain's securities markets lacked the quality certification mechanisms that Deutsche Bank provided in Germany or J. P. Morgan in the US and that this meant that family owners were reluctant to list in London, while British investors were forced to seek alternative, more professionally-intermediated investments overseas.[9] David Mowery identified a weak corporate commitment to science and technology as a crippling source of British backwardness, relative to Germany and America.[10]

Many other flaws in British business institutions have been vigorously exposed. The London Stock Exchange was populated by rogue promoters, gamblers, and bankers privileging overseas loans over domestic needs. Hence, builders of British businesses with real potential could not raise the funds there: in particular, it was extremely expensive for small, rapidly-growing firms who most needed it.[11] British businessmen regarded progress as something rather vulgar and regrettable: effortless superiority was the gentlemanly objective, while clever and regimented Germans, design-crazy Frenchmen, and thrusting, upstart Yankees would see to other needs. Accounting information was woefully inadequate and mergers tended to occur only in old industries for defensive reasons. New methods were neglected by hidebound, traditional managers, whom family owners complacently tolerated or outside shareholders were powerless to discipline. The consequence was that British firms, especially in new industries, were not only decisively driven out of foreign markets by better managed German and American enterprises that had wisely made the 'three-pronged' investment in marketing, production, and management; they were even forced to yield the domestic British market to triumphant German and American multinationals.[12] Amateurish management and relative industrial decline were tolerated because the British never really developed a modern, pro-business, science-driven, pro-manufacturing culture with the professional, egalitarian dynamism on which modern capitalism thrives. Deep down, they really wanted to be traditional country squires cocooned in a comfortably reassuring class consciousness as they complacently and uncomprehendingly contemplated their fading imperial grandeur from their gentlemanly capitalist nirvana.[13]

Such descriptions of the shortcomings of British (and many other countries') businesses are, of course, entirely accurate in *some* cases: conservatism, the Buddenbrooks effect, self-satisfaction, tiredness, misplaced over-confidence, and self-indulgent hedonism are human universals. It is perfectly plausible that Britain experienced the syndrome more than societies which were poorer (one thinks of Germany) or newer (one thinks of the US). Before the First World War, the proportion of the population aged over 60 was 26 per cent higher in the UK than the US, and 8 per cent higher than in Germany.[14] Moneymaking can be addictive, but at some stage the old and the wealthy like to enjoy their wealth and in 1900 more of those – and not only from Britain – who had both the fortune and the imagination to choose their venue preferred London (or Paris) to New York or Berlin. Yet, is it plausible that such a syndrome permeated an entire economy or a significant part of it? As one wades through 'declinist' dirges on British business, one begins to wonder whether the laziness of Hollywood History stereotypes has taken over from critical scholarly discourse.[15] Is this stagnant backwater the same as the country that still had the self-confidence to allow tariff-free imports domestically and in its Empire, while politicians in Austria-Hungary, France, Germany, Russia, and the US zealously coddled their businessmen with tariffs and other barriers? Is this the nation whose citizens were eight times as likely as Americans to win Nobel prizes in science, more likely than any non-Americans to register a US patent and had incorporated more limited companies than the rest of Europe put together? Is this the country that in 1913 managed to export 24 per cent more manufactures than Germany and 165 per cent more than the US (with a significantly smaller national labour force than either)? Did it really achieve this, not only with all its allegedly crippling social, cultural, political, and economic disadvantages, but also with one hand apparently tied behind its back, that is, while in some years sending half its savings and large numbers of its managers to found, finance, manage, and develop businesses overseas? The UK was, after all, the world's dominant overseas investor in the decade before 1914; and Britons were directors, chief executives, or managers of, among other significant enterprises, one of France's largest banks (Société Générale) and one of its largest railways (Compagnie du Nord); one of Germany's largest chemical producers (Dynamit-Trust); Italy's largest manufacturer (Ansaldo); Spain's largest industrial (Rio Tinto); Russia's largest hydro-powered cotton mill complex (Krenholm); continental Europe's largest international passenger train operator (Wagons-Lits et Grands Express Européens) and largest oil company (Royal Dutch Shell); India's, Africa's, and Latin America's largest companies (Great Indian Peninsula, Suez, and Buenos Ayres Great Southern); the world's largest gold producer (Wernher Beit); Australia's largest manufacturer (British Tobacco); Canada's largest miner (International Nickel); Mexico's largest contractor and oil company (Pearson-El Aguila); Japan's largest brewery (Kirin); China's largest bank (Hongkong & Shanghai); and America's three largest manufacturers of consumer durables (Kodak, Singer, and Ford).[16] Chandler's curiously implausible notion that Britons proved serially incapable of developing or running professional management hierarchies – if it is to be sustained – demands some explanation, not only of why they had so many large and growing enterprises at home, but of why they appear to have initiated (or been recruited by) more large and successful enterprises abroad. The urge to explain the decline is so firmly ingrained, however, that it will perhaps not be long before someone reading this generates a new hypothesis: British managers were so busy successfully using their exceptionally well-honed skills in managing such giant enterprises overseas that the performance of home equivalents – deprived of this talent – necessarily suffered!

That hypothesis – giving a managerial twist to the pessimistic Hobsonian view of capital export, or an economic twist to Kennedy's critique of 'imperial' overstretch (though, actually, more than three-quarters of the cited cases were *not* in the Empire) – may be correct, but it is wise to pause before adding yet another chapter to the archive of 'declinism.' At the very least, one might first reflect on whether the later (roughly parallel) ubiquity of US expatriate managers worldwide from around 1950 onwards would be similarly interpreted as an indicator/cause of American business failure.[17] We surely already have a vastly over-determined model in which the many diagnosed causes of long-run British relative decline would not merely have reduced the country to the level of Argentina, but ensured its regression to the Dark Ages? If the hallmark of quality or significance of any comparative article or book in the field is that it must (whatever the subject) explain why Britain declined, while Germany and America succeeded, the result can be predicted. Historians diligently search for – and not surprisingly find – what they are looking for: success in America and Germany and failure by Britain's managers. A more appropriate way of proceeding is to formulate a hypothesis and then apply the same standards to all cases studied, rigorously excluding any bias from hindsight and looking for similarities as much as differences to avoid diagnosing 'false positives'.[18]

II. COPPER: A CLASSIC HALLUCINATION

The contrasting results of the two methods can be illustrated in the global nonferrous metals industries, notably in copper mining and manufacturing. This was a growth industry that was critical to twentieth century development, with burgeoning demand from the electrical industry and considerable scale economies in new refining processes. As many as a dozen electrolytic copper refining plants were built in the US before the First World War and Chandler correctly recognizes American primacy in this natural resource industry, pointing to the development of five giant firms: Anaconda, Phelps Dodge, American Smelting, Kennecott, and American Metal, the latter a subsidiary of Germany's Metallgesellschaft (a company he describes as 'the European market leader'). Remaining copper deposits in Europe, he acknowledges, were too meagre to justify similarly numerous or massive investments: the fewer plants that were built in Europe were of smaller scale. However, with its American and Belgian Congo production and a global trading network, Metallgesellschaft 'had become the one major European contender in the global copper oligopoly'.[19] He notes that Britain headquartered a weak competitor – Rio Tinto – but cannot seem to find a family on whom to pin that company's failure. (He was not sufficiently assiduous: the chairman was from the gentlemanly and imperial Keswick family, supported by the aristocrats of European finance, the Rothschilds: surely both perfect 'declinist' targets? But Rio Tinto was a quite widely held public company and the German and American copper firms were substantially family-owned by Mertons, Rockefellers, Guggenheims, Dodges, and their like, so this perhaps looked an unpromising line of comparative enquiry).

Chandler does, however, manage to find one *strategic* explanation for British failure. The British managers of Rio Tinto located their mine in Spain (a wise decision: after centuries of mining elsewhere, Spain had Europe's largest remaining copper deposits). Having got that right, however, the company failed to grasp the obvious investment opportunity: 'there was no reason why a smelting and refining complex comparable to, though somewhat smaller than, the one that arose in New York harbor area could not have been built in South Wales'.[20] It is difficult to know quite how to assess this strategic criticism: one is reminded of the indignant diner's complaint to the waiter that the minestrone betrays a distinct taste of tomato. Rio Tinto's British managers and financiers located their large-scale copper pyrites processing plant near their mine in the south of Spain, as well as shipping some ore and by-products, via the railway and port they had built, to processors throughout Europe (including Wales) and America. No explanation is given of how this 'failure' (vertically integrating logistics, mining and manufacturing in one region, whose location was determined by geology, while flexibly serving global distribution and processing networks) differs from Anaconda's location of its main processing plants in Montana rather than Massachusetts, or Metallgesellschaft's decision to own smaller plants both near American mines *and* closer to European demand. Yet, Rio Tinto's 'failure' is presented as a paradigmatic illustration of the dire consequences for firms that omit to make the 'three-pronged' investment in production, management, and marketing and are thereby locked out. With dramatic finality, Chandler concludes his assessment of the merciless dictates of global competition in this industry: 'By 1900 the opportunity for a British firm to become a major player in the global copper oligopoly was gone, never to return'.[21] This is a classic case of what I have called Hollywood History. The British live up to their doomed stereotype: unsurprisingly, given that the underlying research paradigm appears to be: 'Find out what British managers were doing and analyse why it was wrong'.

The alternative approach is to examine a population of firms defined *ex ante* to see how those of different nations (or different governance structures or different strategies) progress over time. A list of global nonferrous metal producers in 1900 – the date Chandler insists the British were decisively and permanently locked out – can easily be assembled. The two measures of corporate size that Chandler favoured in *Scale and Scope* were market capitalization and balance sheet assets. At the beginning of the twentieth century, none of the ten global nonferrous metal firms that exceeded $40 million by either measure were German, three were American and as many as seven were British. All *three* of the American-based nonferrous firms, including the largest, Anaconda (capitalized at $80 million, which had definitively passed from Anglo-French [Rothschild] to American [Rockefeller] control only in 1899), were in copper, as was the *fourth* largest of the seven British firms, Rio Tinto (capitalized at $95 million).[22] Metallgesellschaft simply does not figure, because the diverse nonferrous manufacturing and trading activities of what Chandler calls the 'German giant' were not yet big enough, though its (unquoted) capital had increased from $0.5 million on foundation in 1881 to nearly $3 million by 1900.[23] The largest German copper producer was the Mansfeld'sche Kupferschieferbauende Gewerkschaft – possibly Europe's oldest bourse-listed enterprise – which had a market capitalization of $25 million on the Leipzig exchange, though, after 700 years of operation (and a little later than many English nonferrous mines), its ores would soon approach exhaustion. Chandler's British 'failure' – Rio Tinto – was, in fact, the largest copper producer in the world by market capitalization and nearly four times the size of its closest (and soon to disappear) German rival.[24] Chandler's characterization of the global copper oligopoly of 1900, and especially of European capabilities within it, is simply a work of imaginative fiction.

His core notion that new entrants were at this time locked out of global oligopolies by first mover entrenchment is equally absurd. It is unclear which barriers to entry Chandler thought were insurmountable in copper around 1900, since he treats the matter as self-evident. However, copper was plainly a commodity product whose global price (then as now) was set by trading on the London Metal Exchange: there were contemporary attempts to corner this competitive market by both European and American speculators, but they were notoriously ineffective. Copper quality was important for expanding uses like electrical wiring (if not for traditional ones like casting bronze), but long-term contracts specifying purity levels were offered by a wide range of competitive suppliers. Discovering, mining, refining, and trading copper, it is true, required a complex range of both explicit and tacit knowledge, slowly accumulated and effectively organized, but trained, experienced people could be recruited from an increasing number of consultancies and corporations (not only in copper, but in related mining/processing industries) and they were being topped up by the usual, responsive, intellectual supply chains (even newly self-governing, frontier regions – like the US state of Montana or Britain's Cape Colony – had their Schools of Mines: Kimberley from 1896, Montana from 1900). This market in talent may not always have worked perfectly (Herbert Hoover, a Stanford graduate, could not get the US job he aspired to, and worked for most of his early career in British mining firms operating overseas), but that it worked passably is suggested by such international mobility of managers and engineers, by shifting shares in global production of established companies and by new entry. One good example is the nimble, skilled, and efficient Metallgesellschaft, which quickly expanded its initially modest copper operations and soon deserved Chandlers' epithet 'giant', definitively leaving behind its 1900 lag.[25] Australian, Belgian, Canadian, Chilean, Congolese, Japanese, Rhodesian, and Russian (not to speak of Arizonan and Utahn) contenders also all later entered the copper oligopoly, or successfully expanded smaller operations to larger scale. Any barriers to entry or growth that may have existed in this industry in 1900 were hardly insurmountable by those with access to efficient international capital markets or high operating profits in related industries, enabling them to match the efficiency of existing large scale producers (though, in some of these cases, only with foreign help).

Such new challengers did not, of course, prevent any pioneer giant, with persisting and shrewdly developed organizational capabilities, remaining as a leader of the global copper oligopoly, even for as long as a century, as Chandler repeatedly insists was the norm. A compelling example of the staying power of an entrenched oligopolist lies readily to hand. The *Fortune* and *Business Week* listings of recent decades show that Rio Tinto (despite ups and downs of the kind most giants experienced over the century, including Franco's 1950s effective nationalization of its core Spanish assets) is still today (and was at multiple earlier date points), a global leader, by market capitalization or sales turnover.[26] By contrast, Chandler's allegedly entrenched leaders have disappeared, leaving only modest traces: Metallgesellschaft (bankrupted by its oil speculations in 1993, only its engineering rump surviving the crash) and Anaconda (whose organizational capabilities proved insufficient to survive Allende's 1970s nationalization of what since 1923 had become its most important (Chilean) asset, Anaconda's Montana rump eventually passing to the control of British Petroleum). Rio Tinto's main rival today, as a diversified mineral miner and processor, is BHP Billiton, an Australian company founded more than a century earlier as a silver, lead, and zinc miner, Broken Hill Proprietary. If such initial rankings and long-run outcomes are to be described as a 'British failure' to establish a foothold in the global oligopoly, it would be interesting to know precisely how Chandler would identify a twentieth century success!

III. TOBACCO: A MORE SUBTLE MISJUDGEMENT

Chandler's judgements about initial size or long-run oligopolistic entrenchment are flawed not only in copper, but in other industries.[27] Yet Chandler is not always wrong on matters of relative corporate size: for example, he correctly identifies American Tobacco as the largest private tobacco group in the world in the early twentieth century (as would be expected, given that the US economy was the world's largest, with tobacco taxes among the lowest). Yet his triumphalist account of American Tobacco in the pre-1914 period falters on other dimensions. US tobacco productivity was below that of France's, impressively professionally-managed, state monopoly and of the UK's private firms. In particular, the British firm, WD & HO Wills, used and developed more of the key cigarette-making machine technologies more effectively, while American Tobacco was among the slowest in the world to convert tobacco consumers from older products like cigars, plug, snuff, and smoking tobacco to 'modern' cigarettes (only China among the major tobacco markets was slower). This suggests some scepticism about Chandler's confidently celebratory interpretation of the firm as the pre-eminent global first mover in standardization, mechanization, and mass market-ing of cigarettes.[28] However, other indicators – American Tobacco's initial success in exporting to China and Japan and its dominant share in the leading multina-tional British-American Tobacco – are compatible with Chandler's favourable assessment of the company relative to Britain's Imperial Tobacco. Of course, business performance has many dimensions and neither overseas success, nor size of output, nor total profits (of American Tobacco), nor the profit rate, productivity, and more effective deployment of innovative machines to make modern products (on the part of Wills and its successor, Imperial Tobacco) tell the whole story.

Whatever merits James B. Duke, President of American Tobacco, had as a manager, tact was not the most evident. The most elementary strategic objective of any business is to maintain the right to continue doing business. The 'license to operate' is for some businesses like airlines or TV stations explicit, but for most it simply means not transgressing the law or social norms in such a way that the state (or civil society) effectively makes it impossible to operate, or no longer possible to operate in the favoured mode. Many businesses most of the time meet this minimal objective, and indeed many would not even consider it worth listing as a strategic objective. Yet a very few businesses are broken up, nationalized, forced to change ownership, or forbidden to produce, advertise, or sell major products. It is hard to think of any businessman conducting legitimate business in civilized societies who lost his licence to operate or came close to it more frequently or in more countries than Duke. Not only was what Chandler sees as his principal product – cigarettes – banned in fifteen American states and his main holding company broken up into fourteen separate businesses by US antitrust decree in November 1911, but cigarettes were also, in principle, outlawed by the Canadian parliament (though the resolution was never implemented), his subsidiary in Japan (one of the largest foreign investments ever made there) was nationalized in 1904, and his Australian subsidiary was lucky to avoid the same fate. In Germany, Britain, and China his subsidiaries produced strong anti-American press campaigns and boycotts by, variously, consumers, workers, and government agencies. It is hard to resist the conclusion that, at the very least, he may be accused of lacking political and diplomatic skills: to some contemporaries, he seemed to be the international 'robber baron' *par excellence.*

Yet the financial results of Duke's international efforts were impressive. Assessing the international score appears simple because it was done for us by the formation in 1902 of the British-American Tobacco Company, which accounted for almost all multinational investment in tobacco manufacturing at the time. American Tobacco received two-thirds of its shares and Imperial one-third, suggesting a US 'win', on points, of two to one. Each company retained its domestic businesses, transferring international businesses, brand rights, and export factories to British American Tobacco (BAT). British industrial firms generally were no slouches at multinational investment – they accounted for four times as much international direct investment as American firms about this time – though this could have had more to do with capital market advantages than with relative technical or managerial prowess. Yet, in tobacco, the Wills family and their colleagues at Imperial were willing to concede to Duke two-thirds voting control, even though BAT took over all their export business and overseas subsidiaries. That was not all: Duke also obtained a 14 per cent holding in Imperial. Moreover, while all Imperial's overseas interests were ceded to BAT's control, all American Tobacco assets in the new US possessions of Cuba, Puerto Rico, and the Philippines were retained by Duke, influenced perhaps by residual uncertainty as to whether America's national boundaries or tariffs would be extended there (as with Hawaii and Alaska) or possibly by a desire to exclude products that he thought were most strategically important for the American trust. Interestingly, BAT was, like the British domestically, focused on cigarettes, while the excluded assets were heavily involved in cigars, the product that, by 1902, had superseded cigarettes as Duke's central strategic concern in the Americas. He employed ten times as many people in the US on cigars than on cigarettes and had just purchased Henry Clay & Bock, the dominant exporter of Havanas, from a separate group of British capitalists, who had reorganized the Cuban cigar industry on large-scale, integrated lines ten years earlier.

In order to understand the 1902 BAT agreement, we have to understand the drivers of international competition in trade and multinational investment in manufactured tobacco around the turn of the century. Trade in tobacco products between industrial countries was relatively modest. State tobacco monopolies – which controlled France, Austria-Hungary, Italy, and several smaller European countries – mainly confined their sales to their own national territories and permitted imports only at high prices and largely to cater for expatriate or other niche tastes.[29] The US industry was also sheltered behind tariffs so high that there was limited prospect of import competition, except in high quality cigars, almost irrespective of the inefficiency of the trust. Even the British, who, as the leading champions of open trade, could normally be relied on to provide tariff-free access, made an exception of manufactured tobacco: they compensated for the revenue tariff on leaf tobacco imports, by imposing a, more-than-proportionate, tariff on manufactured tobacco imports. This provided a modest degree of protection for domestic manufacturers, so that when they were inefficient (as in their initially slow implementation of the Bonsack), American imports could just compete. Nonetheless, the British had quickly recovered and had overtaken aggregate sales of cigarettes in the US by 1898. By then Duke's London depot was making losses and his exports to Canada and Australia were also increasingly compromised by these self-governing colonies' protectionism (in tariff policy, the self-governing dominions were generally more American than British).

Effectively, then, the export of manufactured tobacco seemed likely after 1900 to be confined to niche products or exports to those parts of the underdeveloped world that lacked tariff autonomy. America's largest tobacco export was plug (chewing tobacco): a core domestic product in which it had built up a strong productivity advantage. America was – as disgusted foreign visitors painfully noted[30] – the land of the spittoon (chewing tobacco sales exceeded smoking sales until around 1908), but in major export markets, like the UK and Australia, plug was a niche product that was not worth producing locally: it was largely used by miners who could not ignite cigarettes or other smokes at work. For both Britain and America, the three main export markets for cigarettes and other *smoking* products were China (subject to the unequal treaties imposed by western powers), India (whose colonial authorities were still guided by London's free trade policy), and the Straits Settlements (including colonial Singapore, already carving out its role as free-trading *entrepot* for South East Asia). A fourth market, Japan, had recovered tariff autonomy in 1899 and imposed a 100 per cent tariff, which kept most foreign tobacco products out. British Empire markets still under London's control were, by contrast, in the early twentieth century as open to imports from the US as from Britain, given the latter's unilateral commitment to free trade.

In general, Asia's underdeveloped consumer markets were not ideal prospects for western exports because of their low income levels, but in the case of cheap, addictive goods like tobacco, they offered more potential. There is no doubt that, in China and South-East Asia, especially, the marketing methods of Duke and his US colleagues were highly effective. By what was termed 'sampling' – that is handing out free cigarettes to establish addiction – and then providing the logistic and advertising support for repeat sales of its brands, the American Tobacco Company had, by 1901, established total export sales of 1.2 billion, probably more than their British rivals.[31] An important motive in exporting at this time was to absorb the surplus production from the US factories created by the fiscal assault, monopolistic pricing, and product differentiation policies that had greatly reduced Duke's sales of cigarettes in America. By 1901 – judging by the decline in domestic sales – the trust had surplus capacity of at least 1 billion cigarettes and, since it also bought some competitors around that time, its actual surplus capacity was probably greater. The company therefore *had* to export more, at any price in excess of short-run marginal cost, as part of its domestic monopolization and high-price strategy. This imperative caused downward price pressure in overseas markets and had a severe impact on Wills' exports: from 1897, their exports were less profitable than domestic sales. At home, however, Wills confidently espoused a low-price, high-volume strategy for cigarettes (the policy that, paradoxically, Chandler mistakenly attributed to Duke in America). American Tobacco was not technically dumping (in that the much lower pre-tax prices it charged in China than in America covered marginal costs), but it meant that Duke was getting a much lower return on capital abroad than he did on domestic sales. A partial solution was to export from lower-cost Japan, and Duke had made a major investment there by merging with a local company, Murai Brothers, taking a 60 per cent interest in the merged firm, which had a quarter of Japanese cigarette sales. He had also made direct investments in Australian and Canadian producers in response to increasing protectionism there. At the turn of the century, Duke was also considering doing the same in the major European countries that did not have state monopolies. The leading British firms also realized that direct investments would be necessary to maintain a presence in some markets. They were slower than Duke in making direct investments in Asia-Pacific, but it is not clear whether this was because their (probably more efficiently produced) export cigarettes remained competitive for longer or because of a greater reluctance (unusual for Britain) to commit capital abroad.

The method that would naturally have occurred to Duke to meet Wills' export competition in Asia-Pacific was the threat of predatory pricing that he was using in the American domestic market in his attempts to monopolize plug, snuff, and cigars. Antitrust economists are now sceptical about the use of predatory pricing as a weapon to establish market control, seeing voluntary merger as a cheaper alternative. However, there is plenty of incriminating evidence that Duke preferred to get on as fast as possible by using both. The critical resource in a predatory pricing war was a 'long purse', that is the capital resources to back credible threats to beat competitors into submission by sustaining below-cost prices for a long enough period to bankrupt them. The ideal was not actually to do that, but rather firmly to convince rivals that you were going to do so: this was essentially a poker game or, in the language of modern game-theory based strategy texts, a game of 'chicken'. Yet Duke had been badly caught out in the US plug wars by precisely the high costs that have convinced modern antitrust economists that predatory pricing is an unattractive policy. Wall Street financiers, realizing his vulnerability, had called his bluff and created the rival Union Tobacco Company in the late 1890s. Because they clearly had the longer purse, they effectively pressured him into giving them a substantial payoff in cash and board positions. This also consolidated his privileged access to Wall Street capital, and in his later initiatives he made very sure that his opponents knew of the extent of surplus capital to which the trust had access. It is very difficult to make any sense of the amount of cash held in banks and short-term investments by the trust, except in terms of the need to demonstrate a 'long purse' in predatory pricing wars: the large amount of capital issued in the early twentieth century was certainly not used exclusively for productive investments (indeed, cigarette production remained flat in this period).

Duke was by no means wedded to predatory pricing as the only method of taking control: he also had considerable success in buying out rival businesses at home and abroad. Almost all enterprises in the global manufactured tobacco industry that were not state-owned were family firms, with no stock exchange quotation. This meant that they were rarely sold, but when they were, as, for example, partnership interests in Duke's family firm had been in the 1880s, they normally sold on price-earnings ratios of around six, or, in contemporary parlance, at six years' purchase. Stock exchange securities, by contrast could be floated with a p/e (price–earnings ratio) of ten or even twenty, and this had recently tempted a few firms like Lorillard in the US or Ogden in Britain to make a public flotation, though the majority of tobacco firms globally continued to finance their expansion internally from high profits, with, sometimes, bank loans to finance stocks and work-in-progress, which in this industry were the bulk of capital requirements. Duke's ambitious American acquisitions programme required a much higher rate of investment (in the few years around the turn of the century his balance sheet assets increased sevenfold). The stick of the predatory pricing threat was one means of getting family firms to cede control to the trust, but the carrot of those high p/es was also available after Duke floated his company's ordinary capital on the New York Stock Exchange in 1895. Many family-owned tobacco firms, from the Lorillards, Drummonds, and Alvarezes in America to the Murais in Japan, accepted it. The stability of addictive goods and high profits of tobacco made the trust's securities highly attractive, but increasingly Duke's Wall Street partners realized there was no need to share the benefits so widely with the investing public, since they could be induced to accept fixed interest securities at relatively low yields, leaving the prospects of high capital gains to their insider group that owned most common stock. The retrospective analysis by the Commissioner of Corporations essentially suggests that they engineered this by losing money on several initiatives in the early 1900s to lower shareholder expectations, persuading public investors to accept fixed interest securities with prior rights, while concentrating their own investments on the common (whose dividends they knew would rise sharply when the benefits of post-predation monopoly and tax reductions were realized).

Whether that allegation is true or not, Duke concluded by 1901 that his international strategy had to focus on bringing the British – his only serious international competitors – to heel. That required invading their home ground. Duke's first foray, to buy Players, the second ranking British firm, either betrayed his usual lack of diplomacy ('Hello, Boys, I'm Duke from New York and I'm here to buy your business') or was a brilliantly theatrical opening salvo in a predatory price war. Either way, it was rebuffed. He therefore went for the only quoted firm, Ogdens, which had been the most effective domestic challenger of Wills' dominance recently. Yet, as the only stock exchange play in cigarettes available to the British investor, it was fully valued, so he had to pay handsomely for it: twice its flotation value of a few years' earlier. In answering their British critics, the Ogden directors justified taking Duke's shilling because of the generous price and Duke's explicit threat of a predatory price war backed by his long purse ('war chest' was the phrase they quoted). This was more than an idle threat: after buying Ogden's, Duke backed expansion with a massive advertising assault on the British market to challenge the dominance of Wills, and authorized much lower Ogden's retail cigarette prices than, as a near-monopolist, he was able to charge Americans, despite British taxes being higher. He also assuaged patriotic small business and consumer fears in Britain by publicly guaranteeing that he would make *no* profits, offering to distribute all local profits to British retailers, whose support was vital (though, for obvious reasons, many disbelieved this could be anything more than a short-term ploy).

It is important, in assessing the outcome of this tobacco war in the British market, to know precisely what Duke and his opponents knew about each other, at this critical conjuncture of strategic decision-making. Much information on relative efficiency and profitability that we now know was, of course, not then known to either side in the tobacco war. Ogdens apart, all major British cigarette firms were private and issued no public accounts, until the Imperial initial public offering required the disclosure of their aggregate profits record (but not the exceptionally high profits of cigarette specialists like Wills). Ogden's accounts after the Duke takeover were not published in time for the British to know whether the firm was still making good profits, as it had been when Duke took over. However, we do now know that Duke lost around one-quarter of the cost of every packet of cigarettes he sold in the UK. His annual UK losses in 1901–2 were the same as his average annual losses from his disastrously ineffective predatory pricing in US cigars in 1902–3, and proportionately to sales revenue, higher. By contrast, even the British tobacco firms that had been competing with the Wills for so long had no idea of how highly profitable that firm's focus on low-margin, high-volume, mass marketing of cigarettes had been: they were shocked when the merger accountants revealed that Wills made more than twice as much as all the other firms that amalgamated in the 1901 Imperial Tobacco merger put together. Wills remained profitable in 1901–2 (and had greater scale than Duke in its modern all-electric cigarette factories), even as Duke made massive losses. Yet the Imperial directors could not fully know how unprofitable cigarette manufacture had become for Duke, nor the level of losses he was currently taking in other sectors, because the US published accounts of the inter-related trust holding companies were opaque.

They therefore had to assess the threat not on the basis of knowing Duke's actually weak competitive position, but on his revealed apparent advantage in the product marketplace. They simply observed Duke's overall profits in the much larger US market (higher, absolutely but not proportionately, than theirs in the smaller British market), the reality of strong price competition in overseas markets, and the apparent willingness of Duke to finance a predatory price war with no limit in Britain. Duke at first thought little of the British and he may – if he based his calculations on US costs – not have even understood that the main

British producers' costs were too low for him to sustain his policy against determined opposition. Despite their public anti-American stance, some Wills directors were also uncertain they had a competitive advantage and so were willing to consider selling to Duke. They were perhaps influenced by the contemporary press stories from other, particularly light engineering industries, of the successful American invasion of the British market, that British firms had proved unable to resist in the product market. On the other hand, the Wills' knowledge of their own profitability, and the ease with which they quickly raised the debenture and preference capital on the London market to form Imperial, meant that Duke's 'long purse' really held few terrors for them in the longer term, unless he had some sustainable advantage. They, therefore, made known their own willingness to out-Duke Duke by opening a factory in the US, taking the war to his home ground.

Neither party could benefit from such an extension of the war to America or from a prolongation of the British price war, but each had a strong incentive to bluff about true resources and intentions in order to get the best deal. The strategy text book says that companies should avoid playing such strategic games, since they generate large losses and few winners.[32] The textbooks are silent on what you should do if someone who has not read the book starts challenging you to play 'chicken' in your own back yard. There seems little doubt that Duke played this foolish game skilfully, down to threatening to withdraw just before the final settlement creating BAT was signed. The actual division of BAT shares appears to have been largely determined on the basis of the amounts invested by the two companies in overseas subsidiaries and their domestic export factories, rather than an analysis of competitive potential of each in overseas markets. The actual assets handed over to BAT under the 1902 agreement appear to have determined the division of shares, and one, very large foreign investment, Duke's investment in Japan, was clearly thereby overvalued. When the Meiji government nationalized it two years later – with compensation initially based on revenues rather than profits or brand values, though later somewhat improved by Anglo-American diplomatic pressure – some of that anticipated value disappeared. We can only speculate about the BAT negotiation process, but the information about Duke's massive losses in Britain and precarious position in Japan that came out after the settlement suggest that the true relative strengths of the parties may not have been accurately reflected in the division of BAT spoils. The BAT ratio was plausibly as much the outcome of a brilliant strategic bluff, as of informed assessment of sustainable profits or overall advantage in production and marketing skills.

Events after the merger are also compatible with that view. Imperial was outwitted in the 1902 negotiations, but the Wills' empire, subtly but surely, fought back with profitability, efficiency, and (eventually) greater financial and managerial control. The establishment of a near-monopoly by combining British and US forces in BAT in markets such as Australia, Canada, China, India, and the Straits Settlements did, of course, confer tremendous monopolistic advantages on both Imperial and American, as the sole owners of BAT. The agreement not to compete in the US and UK domestic markets and to combine resources overseas probably significantly raised monopoly profits at home and abroad for both parties. Majority-owned BAT subsidiaries like Imperial Tobacco of Canada and British Tobacco (Australia) soon became the largest manufacturing firms (by market capitalization) in their host economies, giving the large private benefits of tariff protection to the Anglo-American monopoly of BAT. This new company's British and American managers cooperated well and came to like and respect each others' differing strengths, though the British were sometimes upset by Duke's willingness to undermine implicit contracts with their workforce (whose trust had enabled them rapidly to introduce new technology and achieve high productivity). The marketing skills of North Carolina farm boys in China remained a powerful asset, and massively increased demand there was supplied by a new factory in Shanghai as well as exports from the UK and US. However, the increment in cigarette supply required globally was mainly sourced from the British bonded export factories acquired by BAT as part of the 1902 agreement, rather than from its American factories. Production for export had originally been about equally divided, but by 1913, exports from Britain were 8.6 billion cigarettes, against only 1.9 billion from the US. It is hard to see – given the initial predominance of American Tobacco men on the BAT board – why the weight of export production was so decisively shifted, unless it was because the inherited, new British all-electric factories (mainly built around 1900 near global shipping links and on a larger scale than Duke's American factories) were more efficient, as other indicators (such as tobacco manufacturing productivity levels and US/UK comparisons of brand cost accounts) also suggest.

When the American Tobacco trust was dismantled under the antitrust order of 1911, Duke – in a huff about the federal government's perfidy – opted to take the helm at BAT himself, moving to Britain as its chairman and offering American shareholders a way out via an IPO to investors on the London Stock Exchange. However, after the outbreak of the First World War he resettled in the US, developing his old favourite, the niche product of Turkish cigarettes, by acquiring (through a new American consortium) firms like Philip Morris (a small, then British, producer of Turkish cigarettes which had opened a New York factory). When he finally handed over the chairmanship of BAT to a son-in-law of the Wills family and long-term heir apparent in 1923, the majority shareholding had long passed to British managers and shareholders. By 1927 – a quarter century after Duke blocked British entry – BAT began competing in the American domestic market (in which it eventually became the second largest producer); and also in many other new markets (though it left the UK to Imperial, since 1912 its largest shareholder). By the 1930s, cigarette manufacturers in the US had achieved the same dominance domestically over other tobacco products that Wills and their colleagues had achieved in Britain before the First World War, though the British had, of course, not stood still. The two largest cigarette firms in the world by 1937 were both British: BAT and Imperial. What American Tobacco and the Philip Morris consortium had in common was that they both increased their cigarette sales much faster after Duke – with his belief in product multiplication – ceased to manage them, but they still had some way to go to catch up.

Meanwhile, the subsidiary that Duke forbade to make cigarettes, R.J. Reynolds, after regaining independence under its original family owners in 1911, had become the largest American cigarette producer. It is not easy to see how this sorry tale – of Duke's persistent post-1895 failure fully to develop cigarettes as a low-price, high-volume, mass-market product – was transmuted, in *Scale and Scope*, into the fable of Duke, the modern managerial titan of American mass production, trouncing dozy family businesses. Chandler (generally correctly) viewed German firms as developing branded packaged products only weakly, but even they had converted a higher proportion of German consumers to cigarettes before the First World War than Duke in the US! Nor is it easy to accept Chandler's picture of the lacklustre performance of the Wills and Imperial, which, he felt, just could not hack it with the professional managerial organization that this quintessentially modern industry required. Yet, even under the crippling weight of these weak organizational capabilities, imaginatively diagnosed by Chandler, its amateurish family leaders pluckily struggled to look the serious American business professionals in the face. Christopher Schmitz shows that it was the second largest industrial firm in the world – after General Motors, but ahead of Du Pont, Standard Oil, and General Electric – by market capitalization in 1937, and three times the size of R.J. Reynolds or American Tobacco (ranked 23rd and 26th globally)![33]

IV. WHENCE THE ERRORS?

While Chandler did not go far wrong when he stuck to conventional wisdoms (such as the impressive performance of Germany in fine chemicals and heavy current electricity, of America in light machinery and mass produced automobiles), much of the Chandlerian narrative of German/American/British business performance contrasts in other industries is of dubious value.[34] Two explanations of the failure of *Scale and Scope* to survive in the court of post-publication critical testing can clearly be rejected. General authorial incompetence is hardly worth considering. Alfred D. Chandler, when he died in 2007, was commonly rated by his obituarists as the world's most distinguished business historian.[35] The editors of Britain's foremost business history periodical in 1992 rated Chandler, with Michael Porter, as 'two of the greatest living thinkers on capitalism and the processes of global competition'.[36] Two of Chandler's earlier books: *Strategy and Structure* and *The Visible Hand*, like all thought-provoking and broad-brush interpretations, have, it is true, been mildly criticized for their *emphasis* (more attention should have been paid to politics or labour, successful mergers were more monopolistic than he allowed, etc.). However, their central *ideas* (strategy follows structure; multidivisional organization facilitates corporate diversification; managerial hierarchies are sometimes more efficient than markets in co-ordinating business activities) found general support. He rightly attracted approbation for these books, which overcame the inconsequential narrative and theory-less density of much earlier business history writing. Moreover many international comparisons derived from his early work have been validated by further research: Chandler really did contribute models for a universal social science.[37] It is only the explicit and adventurous internationally comparative perspectives in *Scale and Scope* from Chandler's own hand that, after nearly two decades of further research, now stand as a set of central hypotheses in US–European comparative business history that have been substantially falsified.[38]

If serial incompetence were involved, the errors in *Scale and Scope* would be randomly distributed, while in fact they are highly skewed to under-valuing *British* performance. Is nationalistic prejudice, then, the significant driver? Anglo-American mutual perceptions are a complex mix: Chandler was proudly American, but he also admired and respected many aspects of British life from close personal, and family, acquaintance. British visitors invited to join his duck-shooting expeditions on the Massachusetts coast recalled only with difficulty that they were with a Boston Brahmin, not an English country gentleman. He was perfectly capable of damning American (and praising British) management. For example, he took a dim view of much teaching by US business schools and was distinctly uncomplimentary about US Steel management generally, Ford management between the wars, or General Motors management from the 1960s. By the same token, if one ignores headline statements, *Scale and Scope* is full of positive ratings of particular British managers, as at Dunlop, Courtaulds, or ICI.[39] This was plainly a highly skilled, original, and cosmopolitan scholar genuinely attempting to achieve critical balance, while making significant and penetrating new judgements.

His noble quest went badly wrong, partly because seriously comparative history is *very* difficult, but his core failures were driven principally by his ambitious ideological stance. Time and again, his errors of fact, classification, and interpretation derive from his 'big idea' of interpreting modern, global, corporate history as an inexorably unfolding story of rising and declining nations in which 'professional' American and German managers develop their firms more numerously and more lastingly than their failing British 'personal and family' counterparts.[40] Why, then, did he feel he had to develop his earlier work in this direction? Richard John is surely right to identify him as an heir of the Progressive[41] historical tradition of Frederick Jackson Turner and Charles Beard.[42] As with British Whigs, with whom others have compared him, that tradition exposes its adherents to appalling temptations when generalizing and Chandler was, unfortunately, besotted.[43] In the Harvard of his time, this perspective had a long and distinguished genesis, traceable to Joseph Schumpeter's Anglo-German-American comparisons in his (misnamed) 1939 book *Business Cycles*, chewed over repeatedly in the Harvard Center for Research in Entrepreneurial History (of which Schumpeter was the inspiration and Chandler a junior member) in 1948–58 and most memorably recycled in David Landes' lasting 1969 masterpiece, *The Unbound Prometheus*.[44] All these interpretations had a Whiggish technological and entrepreneurial tinge, but Chandler went much further in privileging the role of professional managers as the drivers of change. All the

Harvard group shared a compelling desire to explain how the (right and proper) triumph of many aspects of modernity could be traced to successful, progressive historical actors, while other, more archaic, groups floundered, or even set their face against the clearly discernible and relentlessly advancing historical tide of large-scale and high-tech business development. In *Scale and Scope*, more egregiously than in his earlier works (or than those of his Harvard colleagues), Chandler used historical evidence selectively to confirm stereotypes of contrasting styles leading to stylized outcomes, not impartially to investigate the performance of alternative corporate strategies and structures in the long run. Fatally, he also abandoned his earlier practice of testing generalizations against representative samples of leading firms and resorted more exclusively to highly selective and subjective thick descriptions rather than the quantitative indicators (such as trade and production statistics), which had more largely (though still imperfectly) disciplined the generalizations of Landes and Schumpeter.[45]

This not only seriously distorted his treatment of particular industries and countries but led to grotesque misclassifications of the supposed causal determinants. He is prone to describe meritocratically promoted, British managers unrelated to the owning families as 'family', while American heirs of the fourth generation, born with a very silver spoon in their mouths, are easily admitted to the accolade 'professional'.[46] He recognizes that both Cadburys and its German equivalent, Stollwerck, were substantially family-owned, but insists that the German firm recruited a larger management hierarchy. Yet the sources he quotes – centenary histories that both firms commissioned in the 1930s – in fact show that the number of managers, clerks, and salesmen in the two firms paralleled each other very closely! This is not serious historical analysis. Such misjudgements are not driven by incompetence or by national prejudice, but simply by his, tragically misplaced, Progressive/Whig conviction that he has identified the magic ingredient that determines the true path to modernity and hence the changing wealth of nations. This easily descends into Hollywood History. It is his need to compress the unwilling evidence into that straitjacket that is repeatedly the source of error and misinterpretation.

This naive oversimplification of the complex and messy process of industrial evolution took him down a fatal pathway in which even a large part of his *explicandum* is wrong.[47] Germany's success in creating more giant managerial enterprises than Britain – the identified proximate cause of differential growth that Chandler's statistically undisciplined thick description so assiduously explains – *in fact never happened*. Whichever twentieth century date is chosen, and despite Germany's GDP being larger for almost the whole century, Britain had *as many* giant industrial firms as Germany (indeed, surprisingly, usually substantially *more*, with the British lead *increasing* as the century advanced[48]), though Britain *did* always have fewer than the US (as would be expected in an economy only a fraction of the US's size throughout).[49] Even on Chandler's own *Scale and Scope* data (he lists values of each country's top 200 in the appendices to his book, but neglected to add them up and divide by 200), the British had firms as large or larger than Germany's at all three of his chosen twentieth century benchmarks.[50]

If one extends the study of giant enterprise beyond industrials – and in the early twentieth century three-quarters of the equities on leading stock exchanges were issued by companies in services (notably transport and finance) not manufacturing – then Britain headquartered about as many giants proportionately to its economic size as the US, Germany far less.[51] It is highly implausible that British entrepreneurs (closely followed and soon outpaced by Americans) could have led the global movement to large scale business enterprise, in services or manufacturing, if those on one side of the water were constitutionally incapable of financing and organizing a professional management hierarchy. Open, competitive markets in advanced, fully functioning, peaceful societies only rarely allow such alleged follies to prosper for long.[52]

These data would still be compatible with Chandler's model if British firms could be shown to be more inadequately structured or managed, yet, for some reason, still impervious to the 'very democratic and effective selection of brains' that Schumpeter diagnosed as resulting from market competition among factory owners and tycoons.[53] No economy was more open, contestable and competitive around 1900 than the UK's, because it had fewer and lower tariffs, cheaper freight transport, higher urbanization, smaller government, and weaker cartels than most near rivals. Chandler's own evidence on incompetence in building managerial hierarchies is speculative and unreliable: there is reason to believe that both bad managers and more organizationally creative ones were more evenly distributed among countries than his treatment suggests. For example, Chandler quietly dismisses enormous, inefficient, multiplant holding companies in America, such as US Leather, with six others in one sentence, while a smaller British equivalent, Calico Printers' Association (CPA), is berated in three separate paragraphs for its loose and inefficient managerial organization, which was actually put right within two years of its formation.[54] Even when Chandler's own research students produced quantified evidence from representative samples that Britain adopted the multidivisional organization faster than Germany, he simply ignored it.[55] Many of his *ex cathedra* statements – such as that a 1920s manager was 'one of the few experienced industrial administrators in Britain' – are so patently ludicrous that they cast serious doubt on all his pronouncements on management quality.[56]

Aggregate data on outcomes are no more supportive: British giants were at least as likely to survive and grow in the twentieth century as German and American ones. 47 per cent of the British firms among the global top 100 of 1912 (firms like Rio Tinto, including several others ignored or misdescribed by Chandler) were still in the top 100 in the final decade of the twentieth century, and 29 per cent of large German ones, but only 17 per cent of large American ones.[57] These average outcomes for precisely defined comparable populations are based on inadequately small samples but are the opposite of those that Chandler's model would predict and not easily reconciled with his hypotheses on relative organizational capabilities.[58]

One of the reasons for the greater sustainability of British firms may be that stock market finance, the divorce of shareholder ownership from management control, and the attendant corporate governance techniques were further developed in the early decades of the century in Britain than in America.[59] Personal ownership – perhaps less inherently stable than professional management bureaucracies, because of possible succession or financing problems – was initially more the norm in America and Germany than in Britain (again, precisely the opposite of Chandler's assertions); and in Germany it remains so.[60]

However such factors may not be the main driver of differential national large firm survival rates. An alternative explanation is simply that the leading edge of twentieth century business development, particularly in the US as it consolidated its industrial leadership, rapidly became more Schumpeterian than Chandlerian.[61] Creative destruction of market leaders and their replacement by dynamic new firms and industries was, arguably, more important to outcomes than the long-run entrenchment of early twentieth century global oligopolists. Chandler chose to put Du Pont, General Electric, and Exxon at the centre of his analysis and they really were, as he insisted, both important and entrenched, but *more* important for America's rising industrial superiority was its higher rate of replacement of once-entrenched giants like American Agricultural Chemical, Westinghouse, Swift, and International Harvester by firms like Boeing, Hewlett Packard, ConAgra, and Merck. Critically, it appears to have been this Schumpeterian impulse, rather than the Chandlerian one, that confirmed America's distinctive lead in large scale enterprises over Europe (both Germany *and* Britain) as the twentieth century advanced.[62]

As critics of 'declinism' have alleged, historians of British business have a penchant for exploring what was irredeemably wrong with British managers, bankers, shareholders, stock exchanges, and governments. In fact, what we have to explain about the global business world around 1900 is why the British successfully pioneered many aspects of the large managerial enterprise, why they had the largest stock market in the world until the 1920s and why giant quoted British industrial enterprises were probably more resilient than giants in other countries in the twentieth century; all of this *despite* the somewhat below-par performance of their headquarters economy. If large British corporations did exceptionally well, despite their – in the event unlucky – choice of headquarters location, we need to enquire into the reason they were able to overcome their misfortune of nationality. This does not *necessarily* lie in superior British corporate finance, governance, technology, marketing, or managers, but it is certainly not obvious that the *standard* agenda of business history research should be why all of these were *inferior* in large British corporations.

Chandler's characterization of American/British relative performance is more plausible at the end of the period on which his book focuses (the early 1950s) than in 1900, though his characterization of Germany remains problematic. The tendency of British firms to be more sustainable had disappeared towards mid-century, though neither US nor German ones had become more sustainable.[63] The divorce of ownership from control in the US had more closely approached that of the UK in the 1920s, though again Germany remained far 'behind' on this dimension.[64] Some managerial techniques by around mid-century were more widely adopted by US firms than by European firms and the US productivity lead had increased; it took some time for Britain (and, more slowly, Germany) to reduce this gap and, even now, full catch-up remains elusive.[65] Chandler is a slightly more reliable guide to the mid-century decades than the earlier ones on Anglo-American comparisons, but, because of his flawed adherence to his 'big idea' still hopelessly unreliable on Anglo-German comparisons. The problems of centralized inefficiency and distorted objectives imposed on German capitalism in 1933–45 are understandably minimized in Chandler's book, so much so that the French translation's subtitle (arguably, not inaccurately) describes it as covering Germany only to 1933.[66] Britain's strong growth performance in the 1930s hardly surfaces.[67] Some of Chandler's earlier mistakes of assessing strategy, scale, and productivity are perpetuated.[68] New misjudgements are introduced, such as overvaluing some and undervaluing others among the (temporary) gains that Britain derived from its decisive abandonment of its long-standing policy of tariff-free imports into the home market from 1932 and its related imperial retaliation against decades of rivals' protectionism by locking American and German firms out of the Empire by tariff preference.[69] It is his flawed methodology – the Whig imperative supporting his underlying theme of the sources of nationally differential business progress – that ensures continuing problems. It is only the stark fact of America's (then massive) industrial supremacy that make more of his mid-century characterizations plausible: at some stage in a rapidly changing situation *some* of what he perceived in the more distant past became truer (though, since much of this came *after* what he purported to be explaining, that can hardly be considered supportive of his causal analysis). If British firms were sclerotic after 1945, it is more likely to be because of tariffs, imperial preference, war-weariness, and cartels, than something they inherited from their open, cosmopolitan, and competitive earlier twentieth century business culture.

It is, of course, also arguable that Chandler's Hollywood History paradigm should be inverted: that Britain's mild relative decline occurred *because* it developed securities markets and managerial enterprises earlier and faster than Germany and America, at a time when there were inadequate governance procedures to limit the agency problems of the divorce of ownership from control. That is essentially the argument of another American scholar, William Kennedy, though his views, like Chandler's, have been vigorously contested.[70] Other sources of British pre-war failures, like those suggested by Gourvish, Crafts, Leunig, and Mulatu on the railways – the major quoted companies of the day, which absorbed a large proportion of national capital stock in all advanced nations and which were quasi-monopolized and very differently managed and financed in America, Germany, and Britain – surely also deserve some attention, as we pursue the quest for understanding the institutional underpinnings of growth that so rightly – and usually more productively – animated Chandler.[71]

NOTES

1. This chapter has benefited from criticism at Sir Geoffrey Owen's LSE Management seminar and Mary O'Sullivan's Wharton Management seminar.

2. Alfred D. Chandler, *Scale and Scope: The Dynamics of Industrial Capitalism*, Cambridge MA, Harvard University Press, 1990, is the *locus classicus* of his views on Britain.

3. The statistics in the following paragraphs are calculated from data in Angus Maddison, *The World Economy: Historical Statistics*, OECD, Paris, 2003.

4. Deirdre McCloskey, '1066 and a wave of gadgets: the achievements of British growth', in Jean-Pierre Dormois and Michael Dintenfass, eds., *The British Industrial Decline*, Routledge, London 1999: 27–44.

5. It is a puzzle that there are no celebrations of the 'Canadian miracle,' though all other G8 countries have generated such supernatural claims at some stage in their chequered histories, often with less justification. Canadian history is a story of doing the right thing quickly, willingly, and decisively in both twentieth-century-defining (if stupidly unnecessary) world wars (rather than, as the, half-American, Winston Churchill noted of his mother's country, only when 'all other alternatives have been exhausted'). Yet, despite this moral superiority (continued in its post-war humanitarian peacekeeping roles), it still overcame its mild initial developmental disadvantages to beat US long-run productivity growth (though never greedily exceeded US *levels*), while rewarding its citizens with some of the best aspects of European and American lifestyles. This is perhaps too complex and sensible an achievement for simple-minded foreign ideologues (or even quietly self-satisfied Canadians) to celebrate.

6. Volker Hentschel, 'Production, Growth and Productivity in Britain, France and Germany from the Middle of the Nineteenth Century to the First World War', in *German Yearbook on Business History, 1982*, Berlin, Springer, 1982.

7. Marianne Ward and John Devereux, 'Relative U.K/U.S. Output Reconsidered: A Reply to Professor Broadberry', *Journal of Economic History*, 64, 3, Sept. 2004: 879–91. The question of exactly *when* the UK economic slowdown occurred remains an even more contested issue, sensitive to the GDP series and the statistical methodology adopted to deal with the problems of business cycles and wartime structural breaks, see, for example, the contributions in Dormois and Dintenfass, eds., *British Industrial Decline*.

8. Recall that we are discussing GDP per head of population. Of course, Germany's population was, and is, much bigger than Britain's and, with catch-up growth, Germany was bound to become the leading European economy, if it did not make massive mistakes. Unfortunately the latter condition was not fulfilled: by invading Belgium in 1914 and Poland in 1939, Germany induced its own regression to the mean (not helped by its twice-defeated population being eventually squeezed into a modern area only two-thirds of that of 1913) and – in addition – ensured America's dominance over an enfeebled Europe. What is, otherwise, most astonishing about the twentieth century is that in 1900 Britain was the largest exporter of manufactured goods and the dominant global power, *despite* then having a *smaller* national workforce not only than the US (which already had a much larger GDP), but also than Germany, Austria-Hungary, Japan, France, or Italy. The key differentiation in policy choice was the US's somewhat wiser response to that (inevitably temporary) power situation than Germany's fatal neuroses, whether viewed in political, military or business terms, or from the point of view of employees' and consumers' welfare in *any* of the main protagonists. Sadly, the depiction of international business competition in warlike terms as a zero-sum game in much of the literature is precisely the sort of mistaken thinking that stoked the tragic German neurosis in the first place.

9. Bradford J. De Long, 'Did JP Morgan's Men add value?' in Peter Temin, ed., *Inside the Business Corporation*, University of Chicago Press, Chicago, 1991. For true believers, the fact that the London Stock Exchange (LSE) was larger than the Berlin Bourse and NYSE combined, or that the divorce of ownership from control was more fully developed in London than elsewhere, was no barrier to the formulation of hypotheses explaining why the opposite must be true! It should be noted that Chandler himself tended to downplay the role of US bankers and execrated some of Morgan's works, such as US Steel.

10. David Mowery, 'Industrial Research in Britain, 1900–1950', in Bernard Elbaum and William Lazonick, eds., *The Decline of the British Economy*, OUP, Oxford, 1986. David Edgerton (*Science, Technology and the British Industrial 'Decline'*, CUP, Cambridge, 1996) has, however, shown such Whiggish perspectives to be largely baseless.

11. Such views persist, despite the fact that venture capital for some new firms was then available from the LSE, while the minimum issue size on the NYSE was much higher and only for seasoned firms.

12. Such judgements can only survive with highly selective storytelling, given that Britain before 1914 had a large and increasing net trade surplus in machinery, transportation equipment, electricals, and chemicals (though it ran a deficit in automobiles and clocks) and accounted for more multinational investment than America and Germany combined (James Foreman-Peck, 'The Balance of Technological Transfers, 1870–1914', in Dormois and Dintenfass, eds., *The British Industrial Decline*: 114–38.).

13. The 'declinist' literature is too voluminous and mutually contradictory to describe or cite exhaustively, but other representative contributions, ranging from the ridiculous to the sublime, include Martin J. Wiener, *English Culture and the Decline of the Industrial Spirit, 1850–1980* Penguin, Harmondsworth, 1992; P. J. Cain and A. G. Hopkins, *British Imperialism: Crisis and Destruction, 1914–1990*, Longman, London, 1993. Among the more efficacious antidotes are Peter Clarke and Clive Trebilcock, eds., *Understanding Decline: Perceptions and Realities of British Economic Performance*, Cambridge University Press, Cambridge, 1997; Richard English and Michael Kenny, eds., *Rethinking British Decline*, Macmillan, Houndsmills, 2000.

14. W. L.Woytinsky, *Die Welt in Zahlen*, Volume 4, Mosse, Berlin, 1926: 46.

15. I use the term 'Hollywood History' because, as the *Tinseltown* caption frankly admits, it is only 'based on a true story.' This mode of business history writing is not a scandal of total falsification, rather a creative rearrangement and selective omission of known facts to conform to popular American intuitions and stereotypes. In 'Hollywood History' the Alamo had no Hispanic defenders, Muslims and Christians delighted in killing each other rather than heretics of their own kind, the Russians did not account for 80 per cent of all combatant German casualties in the Second World War, the *Titanic* was not an American-owned ship and the Battle of Britain was won by an American volunteer pilot (rather than by the Poles, Canadians, and British who actually downed all the stricken German planes). Apparently historical truth does not play well to middle America. However, it is, of course, equally silly to stereotype business historians, middle America or even Hollywood, which does sometimes license fantastical complexity (James Bond is sexy, fearless, pro-active, high-tech, intelligent, effective, and only when he wants to be a gentleman; US agents merely his pliant tools).

16. The degrees of – and reasons for – these firms' 'Britishness' were very diverse: Wernher and Beit were German-born entrepreneurs who chose to become British

subjects and headquarter the international financing and trading part of their business in London (and jointly became as rich as Krupp in Germany); Singer was one of the earliest genuinely transnational corporations drawing managerial talent and ideas from many countries (including, from 1905, its Scottish president, Sir Douglas Alexander); raising capital in London induced Kodak's recruitment of British directors in 1898 (and some were retained even when the company's headquarters moved from London to Rochester, NY, in 1902); Ford was a more conventional US multinational, mainly using English managers in England, but in 1905 it recruited an English expert to produce for Detroit the light and strong vanadium steel that US Steel could not supply; at Société Générale an émigré, Francophile, catholic Englishman was PDG of an otherwise very French bank; the Swedish inventor, Alfred Nobel, impressed by British finance and management, had decided to consolidate his German dynamite interests under the control of his London-headquartered company; British directors in Royal Dutch Shell represented only a minority of shareholders (most of whom were Dutch and French), Ansaldo needed English shipbuilding expertise to build the Italian navy; the Britons in (Paris-headquartered, Egyptian-registered) Suez partly represented the British government's 40 per cent shareholding, partly the canal's main users; and Krenholm (a German-owned factory in Russian Estonia) recruited 30 Lancashire men to manage and supervise 8,000 local workers using complex imported machinery. British initiatives overseas account for many more of the above cases – such as Pearson, Rio Tinto, and Kirin – and many others unmentioned.

17. Although some US business controllers abroad in 1950 were there by virtue of recent military conquest, the major reason was surely that US finance was then globally more dominant and its business management practices clearly superior on several dimensions. As with Britain earlier, the following two decades also saw US growth rates at a low point relative to other OECD countries (including Britain and Germany, in both of which US capital and managers were active in facilitating, their, then badly needed, catch-up after three decades of the intermittent and economically devastating 'European civil war'). And, just like the mid-century US, early twentieth century Britain was not only a large exporter of managers, but (as is not unusual in vigorously global and competitive economies) a large importer too (though Chandler alluded only to the latter in Britain, and as evidence of failure).

18. Models of this approach, which still find some plausibility in carefully specified and testable (and therefore highly untypical) versions of the 'declinist' view, are Andrew Godley, *Jewish Immigrant Entrepreneurship in New York and London, 1880–1914,* Palgrave, London; and Francesca Carnevali *Europe's Advantage: Banks and Small Firms in Britain, France, Germany, and Italy since 1918,* OUP, Oxford. Revealingly, both would imply British performance shortfalls focused more on small than large enterprises, an emphasis more in accord with the macro-data than Chandler's (Leslie Hannah, 'Marshall's "Trees" and the Global "Forest": Were "Giant Redwoods" Different?' in Naomi Lamoreaux, Daniel M.G. Raff and Peter Temin, eds., *Learning by Doing in Markets, Firms and Countries,* University of Chicago Press, Chicago, 1999: 274).

19. Chandler, *Scale and Scope*: 488.

20. Chandler, *Scale and Scope*: 280. Although Britain mined virtually no copper, while Germany mined a little, the output of copper smelters in Britain (using imported ores) in 1901 was double that of German ones (using home and imported ores), though these outputs were trivial compared with the US (see Woytinsky, *Die*

Welt in Zahlen, 4: 176). As Europe's leading copper users, with inadequate domestic ores, both Britain and Germany increasingly imported American copper or integrated mining and smelting on sites they developed abroad.

21. Chandler, *Scale and Scope*: 281. For a fuller treatment of the leading UK and US firms, see Charles Harvey, *The Rio Tinto Company: An Economic History of a Leading International Mining Concern, 1873–1954*, Penzance, 1981; and Michael P. Malone, *The Battle for Butte: Mining and Politics on the Northern Frontier, 1864–1906*, University of Washington Press, Seattle, 1981.

22. Author's calculations at opening market prices on the first trading day of 1900, with the addition to the Anaconda valuation of the interests of Amalgamated Copper, William Rockefeller's acquisition vehicle. The other six were in gold mining, a major global industry dominated by British, French, and German capital, but in which American enterprises were relatively small (Homestake, the largest US gold mining firm, had just $10 million market capitalization). Chandler simply ignores the nonferrous sector in which there were no giant US enterprises, emphasizing instead smaller nonferrous industries, like aluminium, which American and Swiss producers dominated in 1900. Chandler's first appendix list of large firms deals with the Rio Tinto problem very simply: by omitting it, and other large British nonferrous firms, and treating Mond Nickel – the twelfth largest – as Britain's largest. The reason for the omission is unclear. It cannot be because Rio Tinto mainly operated abroad, since this did not disqualify Metallgesellschaft, Mond Nickel, Shell, Burmah, and others from his lists. One clue is that Chandler explicitly says that he is excluding firms with no British manufacturing, but since he obviously failed in this endeavour (that rule would exclude some firms just named, while he instances British-American Tobacco as 'excluded because the company did not have manufacturing facilities in Britain until well after World War II' (p. 631), despite BAT's main manufacturing base actually being in Britain from shortly after its formation in 1902, see p. 29, above), so he may have overlooked the, more modest, British manufacturing of Rio Tinto (though it is clearly stated in Harvey, the source he cites). A year before *Scale and Scope*, Mira Wilkins – in a volume edited and prefaced by Chandler – treated European enterprise in this sector more satisfactorily (Mira Wilkins, *The History of Foreign Investment in the United States to 1914*, Cambridge MA, Harvard University Press: 264–75).

23. Susan Becker, *Multinationalität hat verschiedene Gesichter*, Stuttgart, Steiner, 2002: 70. In 1900 its German factory, Metallurgische Gesellschaft, is also noted in *Saling's Börsenjahrbuch*, with balance sheet assets of $2 million, while Wilkins notes its subsidiary American Metal's capitalization as $1 million in 1899 (Wilkins, *History*: 271). Even adding these and allowing for other assets, it is difficult to see these being worth more in 1900 than Mansfeld; in copper output it also appears smaller, see n. 24, below.

24. Rio Tinto was more diversified (into pyrites by-products), partly accounting for its large *capitalization*. In 1899, in copper alone, Rio Tinto produced 33,705 tons, so its *production* was smaller than Anaconda in Montana (47,830 tons) and than the Michigan mining firm, Calumet and Hecla (41,101 tons), but larger than Mansfeld (18,045 tons). By this alternative mine output measure, Britain headquartered two, Germany one, and America five of the top eight copper producers, which together accounted for half world output (Raphaël-Georges Levy, 'La Production de L'Or, de L'Argent et du Cuivre dans le Monde', in Congrès International des Valeurs Mobilières, *Documents, Memoires et Notes Monographies*, 3e fascicule, Du Pont, Paris, 1900: 14).

25. Chandler's appendixes (*Scale and Scope*: 700) show Metallgesellschaft's balance sheet assets as $20 million in 1913. Rio Tinto is omitted from Chandler's lists but its annual report shows its 1913 assets as $27 million, a considerable undervaluation judging by its market capitalization of many times that.

26. Chandler continues to shed copiously understanding tears over Rio Tinto's ineffectiveness in global competition in later decades, again dealing with the embarrassing fact of its giant size idiosyncratically: by omitting it from his 1930 and 1948 lists! He *does* allude to its partly owned, 'bankrupt', and 'almost worthless' Amalgamated Metal subsidiary (*Scale and Scope*: 320–1, 781), without reflecting on his own appendix data (pp. 677, 684), which show Amalgamated Metal's market capitalization *alone* as $21 million in 1930 and $24 million in 1948.

27. In addition to omitting the other large British nonferrous metals producers mentioned in note 21, above, and De Beers (the giant, vertically integrated, initially British-owned, London-quoted, Cape-registered firm that controlled the world diamond industry for the whole century), Chandler also includes remarkably little on the building of warships and ocean liners, the most expensive capital goods of the time, assembled by large, vertically integrated plants which were more concentrated than any other major industry except steel. In the high-tech end of this industry, large German, French, and UK corporations had almost completely driven once-strong American rivals from global markets by the early twentieth century. He also contrives to suggest that, around 1900, in brewing Guinness was smaller than Pabst or Schultheiss and that in alkali production Brunner Mond was smaller than Solvay Process Company or Deutsche Solvay. In each case the opposite is true and by a wider margin than Anaconda/Rio Tinto. The reader also has to work very hard in Chandler's dense narrative of chemical developments, larded with imaginatively pessimistic comments on restrictions on Britain's markets overseas, to discern either that America had substantially fewer large (but more small) chemical plants than Germany *or* Britain or what were the main global firms' relative sizes. In 1900 Du Pont was a small, family partnership, heading a series of loose explosives cartels within the US, while the British industry had long been consolidated into the larger, quoted, managerial, multinational, London-headquartered Nobel Dynamite Trust, which, with its associated Nobel Latin group, dominated explosives production and sales, not only in Britain, but in most other world markets (including Germany)! The exception was the US, where Nobel technology was licensed to Du Pont and two other firms, whose exports really *were* restricted! What is especially damning is that the transforming technical impetus in both alkalis and explosives came, respectively, from Belgium and Sweden, so giant British firms' initial 'superiority' over the US and Germany in these fields clearly derived from public stock issuing capability/professional management advantages (that Chandler emphasizes), more than technical/patenting advantages (emphasized by other writers on chemicals). Where the latter was most important, in dyestuffs, Chandler's exposition of the devastating elimination of unprotected British producers, by three superior German firms, is correct, but leaves the reader under-informed about the, even greater, German export success in the American market (the US exempted dyes from the tariff to benefit domestic textile producers, and its own dyestuffs production was even smaller than Britain's!) Despite America's delayed penetration of these global oligopolies, Chandlerian lockout was difficult for European first movers to achieve here, too. After 1900, except in diamonds and gold, America developed more serious players in all these fields, with varying success (swiftly and permanently in explosives, more slowly and only temporarily in shipbuilding).

28. Leslie Hannah, 'The Whig Fable of American Tobacco, 1895–1913', in *Journal of Economic History*, Mar. 2006. The fuller treatment of international aspects that follows also draws on: B.W.E. Alford, *W.D. & H.O. Wills and the Development of the UK Tobacco Industry, 1785–1965*, Methuen, London, 1973; Commissioner of Corporations, *The Tobacco Industry*, 3 Vols, GPO, Washington, 1909, 1911, 1915; Howard Cox, *The Global Cigarette: Origin and Evolution of British American Tobacco, 1880–1945*, OUP, Oxford, 2000; Richard F. Durden, *The Dukes of Durham, 1865–1929*, Duke UP, Durham, NC, 1975; Richard F. Durden, 'Tar Heel Tobacconist in Tokyo, 1899–1904', *The North Carolina Historical Review*, 53, 1976; and R. Kluger, *Ashes to Ashes*, Knopf, New York, 1996; and Nannie May Tilley, *The R. J. Reynolds Tobacco Company*, UNC Press, Chapel Hill, NC, 1985.

29. Exceptions included the Austrian state monopoly, which had significant exports to southern Germany, and Toa Tabako Kabushiki Kaisha, a private Tokyo-based company, associated with the Japanese monopoly, which handled exports and direct investments in Korea and, later, China.

30. Judging by the frequency of European and Japanese tourist complaints before 1914, the sight of expectorated brownish liquids streaming towards the spittoon in Eastern hotels and restaurants vied with body odour on trains out West.

31. Cox, *Global Cigarette*: 34, 52.

32. John Kay, *Foundations of Corporate Success*, OUP, Oxford, 1993: 46–8.

33. Christopher J. Schmitz, *The Growth of Big Business in the United States and Western Europe, 1850–1939*, CUP, Cambridge, 1993: 24. Whether this was good for the British economy is a quite different issue: Imperial's monopoly was bad for the British consumer and the US and Germany arguably became the more efficient cigarette producers after 1945, having moved more rapidly to a (state-imposed) competitive structure.

34. Any reader considering re-shelving *Scale and Scope* with historical novels in their libraries should nonetheless hesitate. Much of the book is indeed fiction and Chandler's own summaries of his international contributions – 'The Enduring Logic of Industrial Success', *Harvard Business Review*, 90, 1990; 130–40 and 'Managerial Enterprise and Competitive Capabilities', *Business History*, 34, 1, Jan. 1992: 11–41 – even more seriously descend into banal self-caricature, but something useful survives. Generalizations such as the tendency of large managerial firms everywhere to cluster in some industries, originally developed in *Strategy and Structure* are usefully extended to Germany and Britain in *Scale*. It is the original and central interpretative themes and comparative, implicit quantifications that are comprehensively falsifiable.

35. Including the obituary by the present author in *Financial Times*, 17 May 2007.

36. Charles Harvey and Geoffrey Jones, 'Introduction: Organisational Capability and Competitive Advantage', *Business History*, 34, 1, Jan. 1992: 9.

37. Richard Whittington and Michael Mayer, *The European Corporation: Strategy, Structure and Social Science*, OUP, Oxford, 2000, is a triumphant reaffirmation of the earlier Chandlerian propositions, but compare n. 55, below, for its less supportive findings in relation to *Scale and Scope*.

38. Some reviewers of *Scale and Scope* (B.W.E. Alford, 'Chandlerism. The New Orthodoxy of US and European Corporate Development?' *Journal of European Economic History*, 23, 1994: 631–43; Roy Church, 'The Family Firm in Industrial Capitalism: International Perspectives on Hypotheses and History', *Business History*, 35, 1993: 17–43; Leslie Hannah, 'Scale and Scope: Towards a European Visible Hand?' *Business History*, 33, 1991: 297–309; Barry Supple, 'Scale;' Christian Kleinschmidt and Thomas

Welskopp, 'Zu viel "Scale", zu wenig "Scope": ein Auseinandersetzuing mit Alfred D. Chandlers Analysen der deutschen Eisen und Stahlindustrie in der Zwischenkriegzeit', in *Jahrbuch für Wirtschaftsgeschichte*, 2, 1993: 251–97) early suggested that some its findings were potentially unsafe, but I only realized later what strikingly incompatible standards Chandler had applied to his American, German, and British cases (Leslie Hannah, 'The American Miracle, 1875–1950 and After: A View in the European Mirror', *Business and Economic History*, 24, 2, 1995: 197–262; Leslie Hannah and Kazuo Wada, *Miezaru te no Hangyaku*, Yuhikaku, Tokyo, 1999). Nonetheless, it is by hypothesis generation and falsification that knowledge advances and the initiator of dialogue in an admirably ambitious work – however ultimately unfruitful – does not deserve carping condemnation, rather research-driven, informed, and balanced correction, enabling us to move on to more plausible models.

39. As a matter of fact, *Scale and Scope* often appears fulsomely complimentary in more British than German cases. It is merely Chandler's grand summary passages that imply the opposite. Moreover, American 'new economic historians,' whose work Chandler knew (without enthusiastically endorsing), far from 'Britain-bashing,' had actually led the intellectual assault against the, mainly British, exponents of 'declinism.' Historians are not, generally, slaves to national pride.

40. Moreover, when errors relate to America, as in Chandler's statement that American Tobacco (a corporate giant) rather than R. J. Reynolds (a medium-sized family firm) introduced Camels, the largest ever mass market American cigarette brand of 1913, a similar ideological (not national) bias is evident. The originally planned 'fourth leg' of his work – Japan – also obviously struggled to fit this paradigm, see Mark Fruin, *The Japanese Enterprise System*, Clarendon Press, Oxford, 1994; Hannah and Wada, *Miezaru*.

41. The term is used in the restricted early twentieth century American, rather than modern European, sense (political labels – another example is 'liberal' – do not travel well).

42. Forthcoming article in *Business History Review*.

43. Naomi R. Lamoreaux, Daniel M. G. Raff, and Peter Temin, 'Against Whig History', *Entreprise and Society*, 5, 3, 2004: 376–87. British Whigs maintained their Panglossian optimism best in their Victorian heyday, though 'declinism' can be interpreted as a disappointed Whig's psychotic reaction to changed twentieth century circumstances: the grotesque distortions are simply reversed and everything the goodies do becomes bad and vice-versa. Much of the rhetorical power of Chandler's version of American progressivism also came from that (now curiously outdated) 1980s American conviction that America would soon go the way of Britain under a business onslaught from Japan (see, for example, Thomas K. McCraw, ed., *America versus Japan*, HBS Press, Boston, MA, 1986)!

44. Thomas K. McCraw, *Prophet of Innovation: Joseph Schumpeter and Creative Destruction*, Harvard University Press, Cambridge, MA, 2007: 251–78, 471–4; David Landes, *The Unbound Prometheus*. Not all members of the Center succumbed to the same temptation: both Lance Davis and Barry Supple later developed more nuanced tales of international comparison (though their views were less popular: the market rewards Whiggish simple-mindedness!).

45. Compare Chapter 7 of *Strategy and Structure*, with the more discursively descriptive approach of *Scale and Scope*. Whereas in the former four detailed case studies are validated by testing against a larger population, the 200 firms in the appendixes of *Scale* are, basically, unused ornamentation, mere triggers for selectively biased Whig search. Landes and Schumpeter succumbed to similar methodological flaws, but their

books contain fewer and less egregious errors of international comparison than Chandler's.

46. The cases of (British) Distillers and (American) Du Pont in *Scale and Scope* are extreme examples of such routine misclassification. Chandler's implied critique of Pilkington's recruitment of the Cambridge-educated engineer, Alastair Pilkington, as a graduate trainee with accelerated promotion, is puzzling, given that he was – despite the common surname – in no way related to the owning family, that he invented float glass (the technical transformation that propelled Pilkington to leadership of the global glass oligopoly), and that he deservedly made it to the chairmanship! More generally, personal capitalism was substantially less common in early twentieth century Britain than in the US or Germany, though America, if not Germany, had more or less caught up in the 1930s (Lance Davis, 'The Capital Markets and Industrial Concentration: The US and UK, A Comparative Study', *Economic History Review*, 19, May 1966: 255–72; Leslie Hannah, 'The Divorce of Ownership from Control from 1900 Onwards: Re-calibrating Imagined Global Trends', *Business History*, 49, 4, Jul. 2007: 404–39).

47. See also Colleen A. Dunlavy and Thomas Welskopp, 'Myths and Peculiarities: Comparing US and German Capitalism', *GHI Bulletin*, 41, Fall 2007: 34–64, who broaden this problematic in German–American comparisons.

48. By 1995 (Leslie Hannah, 'Survival and Size Mobility among the World's Largest 100 Industrial Corporations, 1912–95', *American Economic Review, Papers and Proceedings*, 88, 2, May 1998: 63) under severe competition from large corporations in resurgent Japan and EU-empowered small European countries, Britain's share of the world's top 100 industrial firms by equity capitalization declined slightly (from 15 in 1912 to 13 in 1995), as did the United States' (from 52 to 40), but Germany's share was halved (from 14 to 7). What is remarkable is that this happened while Germany was proportionately more successful than either the US or the UK in maintaining its manufacturing base and export share. As in the case of the UK (see n. 18, above), the macro-evidence supports a search for a source of German manufacturing prowess elsewhere than the Chandlerian corporation (an argument powerfully developed in Gary Herrigel, *Industrial Constructions: the Sources of German Industrial Power*, CUP, New York, 1996).

49. Only in the last decade (a period when its growth performance has lagged Britain's) has Germany again begun to reverse the twentieth century trend, see the annual *Business Week* listings.

50. In 1913/19, for example, the mean size of his top 200 US firms was $85 million, of his top 200 British firms $21 million and of his top 200 German firms $10 million (calculated from the appendix data of Chandler, *Scale*). The medians are in similar ratios at about half the level of the means. However, such figures also suggest Chandler's lists cannot sensibly be compared. Apart from the problems of omissions and of comparability of 200-strong lists (irrespective of the size of the host economy), the American and British lists are probably pitched with numbers that are too high, relative to Germany, because of the differentially changing impact of watered capital and inflation on American and German balance sheets and the use of market values only for Britain. Most other studies (some of which have avoided these pitfalls) imply more than twice as many large industrial firms in the US than in any European country, with giant firms in roughly equal numbers in Germany and Britain around 1912, or Britain leading, see e.g. Youssef Cassis, *Big Business: The European Experience in the Twentieth Century*, OUP, Oxford, 1997; Hannah, 'Marshall's Trees'; Renato

Gianetti and Michelangelo Vasta, *Evolution of Italian Enterprises in the 20th Century*, Physica, Heidelberg, 2006: 99; or Hannah and Wada, *Miezaru*. The main sources usually quoted for Britain having fewer large firms than Germany or the US before 1914 are the, somewhat outdated, works by Payne, ('Large-Scale Enterprise,') and Leslie Hannah (*The Rise of the Corporate Economy*, Methuen, London, 1983: chapter 2) It should be noted that both explicitly excluded British firms such as Rio Tinto and Shell, which operated principally abroad and were fully covered in multiple works by Geoffrey Jones. Chandler wished to remedy that deficiency in his lists, as was appropriate given his wider interest in the competence of British management on the global stage, rather than purely on domestic production within the UK.

51. Hannah, 'Divorce': 406; Peter Wardley, 'The Top 100 Global Firms of 1912', Paper delivered at Tokyo University Conference, 2007. In 1912, 50 of the global top 100 quoted companies *in all sectors* by equity capitalization were US-headquartered, 27 British-headquartered, 12 French-headquartered, and 4 German-headquartered. If railways are excluded (Germany's were nationalized and therefore could not figure), the numbers are US 29, UK 11, France 8, and Germany 4. Only using a measure that de-emphasizes modern, brand-, technology- and capital-intensive industries, like workforce size, does Germany modestly exceed Britain's total (17 against 13 in the global top 100 by employment). If Maddison's shares in real global GDP in 1912 are used as a yardstick of expected share, the US should have had 130 per cent and Germany 5 per cent more giant firms than Britain, France 33 per cent fewer. By this relative measure, the French, American, and British propensity to develop large quoted firms is greater than the German. The problem that particularly requires explanation is not that defined by Chandler but, rather, Germany's *absence* of giant firms, except in sectors like banks, shipping, coal/steel, armaments, chemicals, and electricals, in all of which (except electricals) the British had at least one, and usually more, large (often larger) contenders before 1914. The picture is much the same for plants as for firms, see Leslie Hannah, 'Logistics, Market scale and Giant Plants in the Early Twentieth Century: A Global View', *Journal of Economic History*, Mar. 2008: 46–79.

52. There is, however, in all societies a wide spread of efficiency among surviving firms (especially when new generic technologies such as electric power are spreading or tariffs inhibit foreign import competition), so it is not difficult, anywhere, to identify *some* firms using inferior technology or management techniques. What is harder to establish with the available pre-1914 data is whether this was more prevalent in one country than another.

53. Translation from Schumpeter's *Die Tendenzen unserer sozialen Struktur* in McCraw, *Prophet*: 159. Chandler sometimes shows awareness that Britain had an unusually large number of large companies, but he responded to critics by saying that the key point was that they were not managed by an extensive management hierarchy, but by families. He did not feel the need to explain why, if this amounted to not being well-managed, these large British firms survived and grew. This line of argument is particularly clear in *Scale*: 240, though in other places (e.g. 'Enduring Logic') he asserts that Britain did not create as many first movers in global oligopolies as Germany.

54. Chandler, *The Visible Hand*: 334 for US Leather (not mentioned at all in the text of *Scale*, but compare the latter, pp. 288–9, 332, 358, for CPA). US Leather was one of the first industrials to be traded on the NYSE and was the seventh largest US industrial in 1900; Calico Printers was the only the 13th largest British industrial on its formation in

the same year. On its (soon centralized) structure, see Simon Pitt, 'Strategic and Structural Change in the Calico Printers Association, 1899–1973', London Business School, Ph.D., 1990: 39–64. Chandler (*Scale*: 443–8) takes a positive view of the similar reorganization of another loose US holding company, US Rubber. The notion that Britain had more multi-plant holding companies is not easily reconciled with the statistical likelihood that America actually had more such firms, which Chandler chose to de-emphasize, see Hannah, 'Logistics': 73.

55. Whittington and Mayer (*European Corporation*: 164, 168, 174) suggested that, in 1950, 6 per cent of Britain's large firms, but none in Germany or France, had adopted the multidivisional organization and that the British lead persisted into the 1990s. Using a more encompassing definition, I calculated ('Marshall's Trees': 273), also for 1950, that 17 per cent of American, 13 per cent of British, 8 per cent of French, 7 per cent of Italian, but only 5 per cent of German large firms had adopted the M-form. Since Chandler supervised the Harvard Business School theses by Channon, Thanheiser, Dyas, and Pavan from which these estimates are ultimately derived, he obviously, at least subliminally, knew that Britain was likely ahead of Germany on this dimension, though both were behind the US. This partially negative evidence relating to a central theme of *Scale and Scope* was dealt with in that book simply by omitting to mention it. This is a striking testimony to Whiggery's banal power to subvert the fundamental honesty and assiduity of a dedicated scholar like Chandler.

56. Chandler, *Scale*: 329.

57. Hannah, 'Marshall's Trees': 263. The average equity capitalization of the British companies was slightly higher than American corporations and 60 per cent higher than German ones in 1912. The correct reading of this is that *both* British and German firms were significantly more Chandlerian and less Schumpeterian than American ones (the lower German figure for stability than Britain's is because initially smaller German giants could more easily drop out than British or American ones, even with the same growth rates). Chandler's own appendix data also fails to support his model's prediction that German and American oligopolists were the more securely entrenched.

58. It is *possible* that German and American firms did better among the many more firms in, say, the $10–25 million size range below the $26–741 million range of the top 100, but not easy to think of reasons why.

59. Leslie Hannah, 'Pioneering Modern Corporate Governance: The View from London in 1900', *Enterprise and Society*, 8, 3, Sept. 2007: 642–86. Another possible explanation is that the British 1912 giants, being headquartered in a largely tariff-free country and having a wider multinational spread, were more likely to be large because they were efficient, rather than merely monopolistic (Hannah, 'Marshall's Trees': 264).

60. Hannah, 'Divorce'; Jeffrey Fear, *Organizing Control: August Thyssen and the Construction of German Corporate Management*, Harvard University Press, Cambridge, MA, 2005; and Whittington and Mayer, *European Corporation*: 108.

61. Hannah, 'Survival'. I treat these as alternatives, though Schumpeter, like Chandler, subscribed to the theory of the bureaucratization of invention (for a robust justification of the contrary view, see McCloskey, '1066': 31). Chandler also sometimes described himself as a Schumpeterian, though he was more influenced by the equilibrium concepts of Parsonian/Weberian sociology. It is difficult to imagine Chandler saying, with Schumpeter, that 'the problem that is usually being visualized is how capitalism *administers* existing structures, whereas the relevant problem is how it creates and *destroys* them' (quoted in McCraw, *Prophet*: 352; my emphases). Chandler's later

works, for example on the electronics and pharmaceutical industries, can be seen as an attempt to rescue, by thick description, the reputation of the Chandlerian corporation in what others have seen – in marketing, managerial, and technological terms – as a post-Chandlerian age of vertical disintegration, strategic focus, and distributed information (compare Michael J. Piore and Charles Sabel, *The Second Industrial Divide: Possibilites for Prosperity,* Basic Books, New York, 1984; Hannah and Wada, *Miezaru*). Others see much earlier signs of non-Chandlerian developments, especially in Europe (Herrigel, *Industrial constructions;* Charles Sabel and Jonathan Zeitlin, 'Historical Alternatives to Mass Production', *Past and* Present, 108, August 1985: 133–76; and see n. 18, above).

62. And, within Europe, Britain not only exceeded Germany's total of Chandlerian firms (1912 giants still surviving in the global top 100 in 1995), but also had more Schumpeterian ones (firms in the top 100 in 1995 that had not been there in 1912) (Hannah, 'Marshall's Trees': 263).

63. An unpublished study by the author suggests that large British firms' superior sustainability to German and American ones disappeared by a 1937 benchmark and in the post-1945 decades other British (and German) performance indices were at their lowest twentieth century ebb relative to the US.

64. See n. 55, above.

65. See n. 56, above.

66. Compare Adam Tooze, *The Wages of Destruction: The Making and Breaking of the Nazi Economy,* Penguin, London, 2006; Kleinschmidt and Welskopp, *'Zu viel "Scale".'*

67. H. W. Richardson, *Economic Recovery in Britain, 1932–9;* Weidenfeld and Nicolson, London, 2006. Maddison's data even suggest that the UK's real GDP per head exceeded the US's in several years of the 1930s, for the first time since 1904, though that obviously owes more to superior macro-policy and the benefits of having little agriculture and earlier rearmament, than to the underlying productive potential of the two economies' manufacturing sectors.

68. Not only those already noted in copper and tobacco, but see also Stephen Broadberry and N. F. R. Crafts, 'Britain's Productivity Gap in the 1930s: Some Neglected Factors', *Journal of Economic History,* 52, 3, 1993: 534–5, 548–9, 553–5.

69. Chandler's praise of the, suitably named, national champion, Imperial Chemical Industries, for its management and research organization after its formation in 1926, is justified, but he exaggerates the degree of change and ludicrously describes it as the only, successful British industrial comeback (whereas, as we have seen, its two major components, Nobel and Brunner Mond, were already in 1900 impressive by comparison with German and American equivalents). Where Britain was clearly behind before 1914, he underplays the success of new or expanded inter-war British competitors in his generalizations in 'Enduring Logic', which are themselves contradicted by case studies in *Scale and Scope.* In electrical machinery, for example, English Electric, AEI, and GEC for the first time approached Westinghouse and AEG in scale and research capabilities and the British industry improved its share of world exports slightly (from 28% to 30%) in 1913–37, whereas Germany's once dominant share was squeezed (from 53% to 39%) by US competition. It is true that the British electrical firms – merged in the 1960s into GEC – in the late twentieth century succumbed to mismanagement and superior competition from Siemens, GE, and French and Japanese newcomers, but so did AEG and Westinghouse (and, in chemicals, ICI)! Britain, in the long run, arguably gained only limited sustainable capabilities from its temporary flirtation with imperial protectionism and Chandlerian national champions.

70. William P. Kennedy, *Industrial Structure, Capital Markets and the Origins of the British Economic Decline*, Cambridge University Press, Cambridge, 1987.

71. Terence Gourvish, *Railways and the British Economy, 1830–1914*, Macmillan, London, 1980; Nicholas Crafts, Tim Leunig and Abay Mulatu, 'Were British Railway Companies Well-Managed in the Early Twentieth Century?' *LSE Working Paper*, 2005. See, more generally Stephen Broadberry, *Market Services and the Productivity Race, 1850–2000*, Cambridge University Press, Cambridge, 2006, for a very different perspective on the source of British/German/American performance differentials to Chandler's, which is nonetheless sympathetic to applying Chandlerian perspectives to service sector companies. Terry Gourvish (like many in the 1980s) was respectful of Chandler's perspectives, but, even before the tragedy of *Scale and Scope* (*Business History*, Oct., 1987: 34), also expressed fears that the notion of British 'corporate lag' might be overplayed.

2

Industrial Policy in Twentieth Century Britain

Geoffrey Owen

Having once been the leading industrial nation, Britain is now a second-ranking power in an increasingly crowded world market. How that transition was handled is one of the central themes in British business history. Relative decline was unavoidable as other countries caught up, but did it have to be as steep as it was? Would British industry be stronger today if governments had played their cards differently, especially in the period after the Second World War?

This chapter looks at one aspect of the government's record – the use of industrial policy to influence the structure and performance of industries and firms. Industrial policy is sometimes defined broadly to encompass all government actions that affect the competitiveness of firms, including trade policy, competition policy, and even training and education policy. This chapter, following a recent authoritative analysis of the topic, defines industrial policy as 'any type of selective intervention or government policy that attempts to alter the sectoral structure of production towards sectors that are expected to offer better prospects for economic growth than would occur in the absence of such intervention'.[1] The emphasis is on selective policies, as opposed to broad, non-discriminatory policies which affect all industries.

In this area, as in the management of the British economy more generally, the 1980s marked a sharp break with the past. Whereas previous Labour administrations (and some Conservative ones) had intervened in industry on a substantial scale, the government led by Margaret Thatcher was determined to let business fend for itself. There were to be no more rescues of 'lame ducks', and no more state-supported national champions; the ones that had been created in the 1960s and 1970s should be returned to the private sector as soon as possible.

The new approach was justified on the grounds that excessive intervention in industry had contributed to Britain's relatively poor economic performance in the earlier post-war decades. That view came to be accepted across the political spectrum, so that Tony Blair's 'New Labour', when it came into office in 1997, followed the Thatcherite line that government should neither pick winners nor bail out losers; it also acquiesced, as the preceding Conservative administrations had done, in the increasing trend for major British industrial companies to be taken over by foreigners. Yet, while there was a broad consensus that the structure and ownership of industry (and the balance between manufacturing and services) should be determined by the market, not by government, there remained some anxiety in the first years of the twenty-first century that Britain's position as a major industrial power might have been weakened by the hands-off policies followed since 1980. If there had been too much intervention before, had the shift to non-intervention gone too far? An obvious contrast was with France, where successive governments of the Right and Left had continued to support major French-owned companies in important industries, and to prevent them from falling into foreign hands. Whether 'economic patriotism' had been good for the French economy was questionable, but France did retain an array of powerful companies in industries which in Britain had greatly diminished in size or were largely controlled by non-British groups. Germany, too, had an impressive number of nationally owned industrial giants, although the survival of these firms had less to do with industrial policy than with a set of long-established institutions and attitudes which underpinned the strength of the German manufacturing sector.

Why did British industry evolve in a different way? To what extent was the outcome due to industrial policy, or the lack of it? To answer these questions, this chapter looks first at the policies pursued in the first three decades after the Second World War. It then considers the reforms that were introduced in the 1980s and the evolution of industrial policy during the 1990s and 2000s. The concluding section assesses the state of British industry in the light of the changes that have been taking place, as a result of globalization, in the structure and location of major industries.

POST-WAR INDUSTRIAL POLICY

Before the Second World War, industrial policy – in the sense of direct intervention in the affairs of particular industries and companies – did not figure prominently in the armoury of British governments. The principal exponents of such policies had been the late-industrializing countries, especially Germany. Frederick List, the German economist, had argued in the 1850s that, while free trade and laissez-faire might suit Britain, which was then overwhelmingly the world's strongest industrial nation, such policies were not appropriate for countries trying to catch up. Infant industries in these countries needed to be shielded from foreign competition, and given time to master the techniques perfected by their more advanced overseas rivals; when the gap was closed, tariffs and other barriers to competition would come down.[2]

Up to 1914 Britain did not need, or did not appear to need, infant industry protection. Yet as industrialization gathered pace in the US and Germany, and British manufacturers came under greater competitive pressure, the laissez-faire doctrine began to be modified. An early response to Germany's technological superiority was the creation of the National Physical Laboratory in 1900, a state-supported central research organization designed to encourage the application of science in industry; this was later incorporated into a new government agency, the Department of Scientific and Industrial Research.

British weakness in science-based industries was highlighted during the First World War by the cut off in supplies of synthetic dyestuffs and pharmaceuticals from Germany. This led indirectly to the four-company merger that created Imperial Chemical Industries in 1926; encouraged though not actively sponsored by government, the amalgamation was an attempt to create a British counter-weight to the all-powerful German chemical industry.

These moves implied a greater concern on the part of government with the structure and organization of industry, a concern that became more acute during the depressed trading conditions of the 1930s. Among the worst hit sectors were steel and shipbuilding, which became the subject of largely abortive efforts by the Bank of England to promote consolidation and rationalization. But these were old industries whose structural problems stemmed in part from Britain's early start in industrialization. The primary focus of industrial policy, as it came to be developed after the Second World War, was on the newer industries.

The successful prosecution of the war, one historian has written, 'was seen to vindicate an expanded and more interventionist state'.[3] The most extreme form of intervention was nationalization, and this was a central part of the Labour government's programme when it entered office in 1945. But the industries that were taken into public ownership were either public utilities or basic industries such as coal, and the motivation was as much political as economic. Apart from steel, which was nationalized towards the end of its term of office and sold back to the private sector by the Conservatives in 1953, the post-war Labour government largely eschewed direct intervention in manufacturing; there was no industrial policy as the term came to be used in the 1960s and 1970s.

The exceptions were those industries that were seen as vital to national security and national prestige. The aircraft industry had expanded its output enormously during the war, and it was recognized that capacity would have to be reduced. But both the war-time coalition and the incoming Labour government believed that the industry was a national asset that must be supported as it made the transition to peacetime conditions. The aim, as a Cabinet minute put it, was 'to secure the production after the war of British transport aircraft, civil and military, of a scale and quality in keeping with our world position'.[4] This involved both protection – the state-owned airlines were obliged to buy their equipment exclusively from British manufacturers, as was the Ministry of Defence – and financial support for new aircraft and aeroengine projects.

The aircraft manufacturers had performed outstandingly well during the war. Yet it was in this industry that the gap between Britain's post-war aspirations and its technical and financial resources first became evident. Even though the de Havilland Comet was the first jet airliner to enter commercial service, the British industry was soon outgunned by the big American aircraft manufacturers, led by Boeing and Douglas. While avoidable mistakes on the British side contributed to this outcome – the Comet was almost certainly put into service too early – the fundamental problem was that the US market for both civil and military aircraft was far larger than in Britain; American manufacturers enjoyed economies of scale that their British counterparts could not match. The Conservative government tried to alleviate this problem at the end of the 1950s by enforcing a series of mergers in what was then a fragmented industry, but the two principal airframe makers which emerged from this process, British Aircraft Corporation and Hawker Siddeley, continued to lose ground to their US competitors, although Rolls-Royce, the principal aero-engine manufacturer, was able to build on its first-mover advantage in jet engines.

The other high-technology industry which became the target of government intervention after the war was computers. The quality of British research in this field had been on a par with that of the US during the war, and in the late 1940s it was not unreasonable to hope that British computer manufacturers could hold their own against American competition. Yet by the end of the 1950s, when IBM of the US was establishing a dominant position in the world market, it was clear that any hope of keeping pace with the Americans had been lost. One historian has suggested that part of the fault lay with the two government agencies most closely concerned with the industry – the National Research Development Corporation, which supported the manufacturers with research funding, and the Ministry of Defence, which at that time was the principal purchaser of computers; if they had worked together more effectively, a more viable industry might have emerged. But the biggest problem, as the writer points out, was the small scale of the British market. 'By no stretch of the imagination could the British armed forces have ordered first-generation computers in production-run quantities, as happened in America for the IBM 701 and ERA 1103. Nor could they have mounted a defence project a mere fraction of the scale of the SAGE air defence system'.[5]

Thus it is misleading to suggest that Britain threw away opportunities for leadership in high-technology industries in the first few years after the war. It would be more correct to argue that Britain took too long to recognize that, as a medium-sized power, it could not hope to match the Americans in every major industry, but should look for opportunities in areas where American firms did not have an overwhelming advantage. One of the outstanding British successes in the aircraft industry was the Vickers Viscount, a short-range turboprop airliner which did not have a direct competitor in the US. A potentially more promising way of keeping up with the Americans in these sectors was to collaborate with other countries, and this was the rationale behind the Anglo-French Concorde supersonic airliner project, initiated by the Conservative government in the early 1960s. The hope was that, having lost the subsonic jet race to the US, the Europeans could leap ahead in the next generation. But Concorde was a commercial and financial disaster.[6]

Outside the aircraft industry, industrial policy was not a major preoccupation for the Conservative governments which held office between 1951 and 1964. There was some awareness of the need to strengthen Britain's technological capacity – hence the creation of a Ministry of Science in 1959 – and some response to particular crises, as in the abortive attempt to reorganize the Lanca- shire textile industry through the 1959 Cotton Industry Act.[7] But the main concern was that Britain was falling behind the leading Continental countries in overall economic performance. The solution was sought in better macroeco- nomic management rather than industrial policy.

The election of Harold Wilson's Labour government in 1964 marked the start of a much more interventionist approach. The plan was for the government to identify industries and companies which needed support, and to use the power of the state to bring about whatever changes were necessary. A new department was established – the Ministry of Technology – charged with guiding and stimulating a major national effort to bring advanced technology into British industry. The government also believed that too many British companies were too small to compete effectively in the world markets; a new agency, the Industrial Reorgani- sation Corporation (IRC), was charged with the task of identifying industries which would benefit from being reorganized into larger groups. Two of the most spectacular results of the IRC's activities were the restructuring of the electrical industry under the leadership of the General Electric Company (GEC) and the integration of virtually all the British-owned car and truck manufacturers into a single giant company, British Leyland Motor Corporation. A third important deal was the creation – again through government-induced mergers – of a national champion in computers, in the form of International Computers Limit- ed (ICL). Of these three transactions, only the first was successful, and this was because the enlarged GEC had an exceptionally able leader in Arnold (later Lord) Weinstock, who was able to drive through the necessary rationalization and achieve impressive gains in productivity. British Leyland, by contrast, remained a hotch-potch of semi-autonomous companies which were never integrated into a coherent whole. As for ICL, this company was encouraged by the government to compete head-on against IBM, but neither subsidies nor protection (in the form of a requirement for government departments to buy ICL machines) were of much help in achieving what with hindsight was an unrealistic objective.[8]

There was a strong element of wishful thinking in Labour's industrial policy during those years, and a reluctance to accept that in some industries Britain would need to rely on non-British suppliers. A curious but revealing episode was the decision by the IRC to oppose the take-over of the leading British ball bearings company, Ransome & Marles, by the Swedish company, SKF. The IRC and the government took the view that the production of ball bearings – precision components used in a wide variety of industrial products – needed to be kept within the UK; a 'British solution' was engineered, involving the merger of Ransome & Marles with two other British ball bearings producers.[9]

The change of government in 1970, bringing the Conservatives under Edward Heath back to power, seemed to presage a sharp change in industrial policy. The new government was supposedly committed to disengagement from industry. It closed down the IRC and broke up the Ministry of Technology; most of its functions were transferred to the Department of Trade and Industry (DTI).

In practice, however, its approach to industrial policy was not radically different from that of its predecessor. It continued to support ICL, the computer maker, and to provide launch aid for civil aircraft projects. When Rolls-Royce, the aero-engine manufacturer, came near to bankruptcy, the government stepped in to save the company, making it effectively a ward of the state. As unemployment rose, the government felt the need for wider powers to intervene in industry – hence the 1972 Industry Act, which gave 'more or less carte blanche for crisis-driven intervention, although it lacked much in the way of strategic orientation'.[10]

Strategic direction was what the next Labour government, taking office in 1974, was determined to provide. The government set up the National Enterprise Board (NEB), which was given wider powers than the IRC; it had the authority and the funds to acquire majority control of industrial companies and to start new ventures of its own. This was part of a comprehensive programme aimed at modernizing and strengthening British industry under government direction. In the event, Labour's six years of office were dominated by macroeconomic problems, which constrained the government's room for manoeuvre in industrial policy. British Leyland, which was made the responsibility of the NEB, plunged into a financial crisis, caused partly by mismanagement, partly by a collapse in sales following the 1974 oil crisis. The government's response was to take the company into public ownership and to set in train a rescue plan based on the assumption that, with more money, better management, and more harmonious labour relations, British Leyland could be a viable competitor in all segments of the automotive market. That assumption proved unrealistic, and by 1979, when Labour fell from office, the company was losing money at an alarming rate.

Thus, instead of spearheading the modernization of British industry, the NEB found itself mostly dealing with companies in varying degrees of financial trouble. Apart from British Leyland, other casualties which formed part of the NEB's portfolio included Alfred Herbert, the largest British machine tool manufacturer, and Ferranti, the electronics company. Yet the NEB had another role, as a provider of venture capital to start-up and early-stage businesses, and towards the end of Labour's term of office this side of its activities assumed greater importance.[11]

Past experience had shown that size per se was not necessarily a source of competitive advantage, especially if it was brought about by artificial means, and that a better approach might be to foster the growth of new firms comparable to the ones that had been so successful in the US. One such venture launched by the NEB was an innovative semiconductor company called Inmos. The NEB believed that the UK should not rely for the supply of its semiconductors on foreign companies, even if those foreign companies set up factories in the UK. Since the established British semiconductor producers, principally GEC and Plessey, were unwilling to compete directly against the big American suppliers, the NEB decided to back a new venture, conceived by a group of British and American entrepreneurs.[12] Although the Inmos project did not survive long after Labour lost office in 1979, it was a harbinger of a different approach to industrial policy that was to become more important in the 1980s and 1990s.

Meanwhile, the future of the aircraft industry continued to be a source of concern. The failure of Concorde appeared to weaken the case for European collaboration, and the previous Labour government had decided in 1969 not to join the Franco-German Airbus project, although Hawker Siddeley made a private contract to supply the wings for the new aircraft. However, by the mid-1970s the two main British airframe manufacturers were short of civil work, and it was not clear how they could compete in a US-dominated market. Labour decided to nationalize the industry, apparently on the grounds that its dependence on public funds made private ownership anomalous, but this did nothing to solve its strategic problems. By the late 1970s the government was faced with a choice: should the new state-owned company, British Aerospace, join the Airbus consortium, or should it accept Boeing's offer of partnership on its new 757 airliner?[13] The Labour government, now led by James Callaghan, plumped for a European partnership.

While this decision marked a recognition that the UK could not always go it alone in high-technology industries, there were still reservations about allowing whole industries to fall under foreign control. In the manufacture of TV sets, for example, Japanese companies had established an edge in quality and productivity over the British companies. Sony and Matsushita were encouraged to set up assembly plants in the UK, on condition that at least half their components were British-made. But when Hitachi announced plans to build a TV plant in the north-east, it was fiercely opposed by the industry, and the Japanese companies then came under pressure to form partnerships with British companies (as Hitachi did with GEC) or to take over existing capacity.[14] Thorn, the largest and most successful of the British TV set makers, remained independent.

Here, as in other sectors, there was not much sign of the strategic approach to industrial policy that Labour had promised when it came into office in 1974, nor was there any evidence that lessons had been learned from the failed interventions of the 1960s. It is hard to disagree with the assessment of Labour's industrial policy made by one commentator in the mid-1970s: 'The basic objectives have not been clear, trade-offs between competing objectives have not been calculated in advance, the relevance of intermediate to final objectives has been obscure, and the efficiency of the methods employed have been uncertain'.[15]

Did other countries do better? Japan has often been seen as the prime exemplar of successful industrial policy. It is certainly true that the Japanese government, through the Ministry of International Trade and Industry, did intervene in several industries during the 1960s and 1970s, and did so more intelligently than its UK counterpart; there was no attempt to create single national champions like British Leyland or ICL, but rather a policy of controlled competition among selected companies.[16] But in several of the industries which performed outstandingly well in the 1960s and 1970s, notably cars and consumer electronics, government intervention was not significant. The impact of industrial policy on the performance of the Japanese economy was probably less than its would-be imitators in Europe believed.[17]

Among European countries, France has been the most determined exponent of selective intervention in industry, and, despite the general shift towards more liberal economic policies in the 1990s and 2000s, there has been no Thatcher-type abandonment of industrial policy, even under governments of the right. Indeed, there is a high degree of consensus across the political spectrum that governments can and should intervene to support particular industries and companies. The motivation has been partly political – to ensure that 'strategic industries' (a term that is capable of wide definition) do not fall under foreign control – and partly economic, to preserve and support industries that are important because of their contribution to exports or employment.

Whether these policies have been good or bad for the French economy is a much disputed question, but there is not much doubt that, taking the post-war period as a whole, the French have been better at industrial policy than the British. Although there have been some egregious failures, notably in computers, there have been enough successes to suggest that, in some circumstances, governments can help to create successful industries which would not exist, or at least would be very much smaller, if the initiative is left entirely to the private sector. The outstanding case is the Airbus, which, though a joint project with other European countries, has been driven from the start by France. Another example is nuclear power, where co-operation between the government, the state-owned utility and the manufacturers of electrical equipment was the foundation, not only for a successful programme of nuclear power station construction, but also for the emergence of a French nuclear industry which looks well set to profit from the expected revival of nuclear power in coming years.

There is a long tradition of dirigisme in France, which has no counterpart in Britain, and a much closer rapport between government officials and managers of large companies, but the important difference, as far as the post-war period is concerned, is that selective intervention in France has been associated with success, not, as in Britain, with failure. There is a perception, probably somewhat exaggerated, that industrial policy contributed to the resurgence of the French economy after the war and helped to preserve powerful, nationally owned companies such as Renault and Alcatel, whose continued existence is a source of strength for the economy. In Britain, industrial policy as practised in the 1960s came to be associated with propping up large industrial companies like British Leyland which had been run into the ground by incompetent managers and were then kept alive by government intervention that did nothing to ensure their long-term viability. As seen by Margaret Thatcher's Conservative Party in the second half of the 1970s, ill-planned rescues of this kind were symptomatic of a thoroughly misconceived approach to economic management, which should be consigned to history.

THE THATCHER SHOCK

The change of government in 1979 came at a time when external competitive pressures on British industry were intensifying. The pressures came partly from Continental Europe – Britain had joined the Common Market in 1973 – but increasingly also from Japan and other East Asian countries. The process that came to be known as globalization was gathering pace, and it involved, not just trade in goods, but also increasing freedom for capital to move across borders. One of the earliest and most important changes made by the Thatcher government was the removal of exchange controls. As Nigel Lawson, later Chancellor, has written, this was the first significant act of market liberalization. 'Industrially, by enabling British firms to invest where they liked, it ensured that investment in the UK would yield a worthwhile return – the economy had to compete'.[18]

The dominant theme in the Thatcher government's economic management was to allow markets to work freely and to rely on competition as the principal instrument for improving industrial performance. Given the legacy of intervention under previous governments and the dire state of several state-owned companies, the speed of the transition was slower than the Prime Minister would have liked. The NEB was soon disbanded; it was merged with the National Research Development Corporation to form the British Technology Group, which was later privatized. Most of the smaller NEB investments, including Inmos, were sold to the private sector. But the larger 'lame ducks' posed more difficult problems.

In the case of British Leyland, there was no early prospect of selling the company as a whole to the private sector. The first step was to sell off those parts which were profitable – hence the privatization of Jaguar in 1983. Then came an ambitious proposal to sell the car side to Ford and the truck business (including Land Rover) to General Motors, but this had to be withdrawn in the face of protests from Conservative members of Parliament; they objected to the loss of national control of what was still thought to be a strategically important company. Mrs Thatcher reluctantly conceded to this pressure, and later presided over a 'British solution' – the sale of British Leyland to British Aerospace.[19] However, by that time the truck side of the company had already been sold to a foreign acquirer, and the British Aerospace deal provided only a short-term solution to the company's problems. In 1994, British Aerospace sold what was left of the company – now called Rover – to BMW of Germany, and this time there was no serious political objection. Indeed, the withdrawal of the Ford/General Motors proposals was something of an aberration in a period which saw several once-favoured companies pass into foreign control. Thus ICL, the computer company, was sold to Fujitsu of Japan. Ransome Hoffman Pollard, the ball bearings group which had been constructed by the IRC to fend off a Swedish take-over, was also sold to a Japanese company. The principal British TV set maker, Thorn, was sold to Thomson of France.

All this was part of a deliberate policy on the part of the Conservative government to encourage the integration of British industry into the world market, and to promote inward investment, especially in sectors where indigenous companies were weak. The most striking example was in cars. The decision by Nissan to build an assembly plant in Sunderland (opened in 1986) was regarded as a triumph, a striking contrast to the row over the Hitachi TV set factory in the 1970s. Nissan was followed into the UK by Toyota and Honda, and by the mid-1990s, these three companies accounted for nearly half the motor industry's exports.

To the extent that the Thatcher government had an industrial policy, it was geared mainly to the promotion of small firms. Several schemes were introduced during the 1980s to support start-up firms, and tax incentives were introduced to stimulate the growth of the venture capital industry. As for direct financial assistance, the DTI continued to run some support schemes – for example the Small Firms Merit Award for research and technology – but the amount of money involved was small. Expenditure on industrial subsidies fell from about £5 billion in 1979 to a little over £300 million in 1990 (at 1980 prices).[20] The one industry that continued to receive favourable treatment was aircraft. Although both British Aerospace and Rolls-Royce were privatized, they continued to receive launch aid for new projects. Despite Mrs Thatcher's well-known scepticism about Europe, she approved several tranches of aid for new models of the increasingly successful Airbus family.

After Mrs Thatcher's resignation in 1990, the government led by John Major pursued similar policies, although there was a change of tone when Michael Heseltine was appointed Secretary of State for Trade and Industry in 1992. In his speech to the party conference in that year Heseltine had famously declared:

'If I have to intervene to help British companies, I'll intervene before breakfast, before lunch, before tea and before dinner. And I'll get up the next morning and I'll start all over again'.

He wanted to strengthen the DTI and place it 'at the hub of a national effort to make Britain fully competitive in a cut-throat world'.[21] Yet the DTI's ability to engage directly with companies was limited by the small amount of funds at its disposal; even under Heseltine's enthusiastic leadership, its impact on the structure and performance of British industry was minimal.

More remarkable, in the light of what had happened under previous Labour governments, was the continuity in British industrial policy after 'New Labour' gained power in 1997. This did not imply any lack of concern with competitiveness. On the contrary, Gordon Brown, the Chancellor, took a much greater interest in supply-side policies than any previous holder of that office; he was the principal driver of the government's productivity agenda, aiming at closing the gap in output per man which separated the UK from the US, Germany, and France. But the instruments on which Brown relied were very different from those used by Labour in the past. This was spelt out clearly in the government's first competitiveness White Paper, published in 1998.

'The present government will not resort to the industrial policies of the past. In the industrial policy making of the 1960s and 1970s, to be modern meant believing in planning. Now, meeting the requirements of the knowledge-driven economy means making markets work better'.[22]

An early test of the government's commitment to a non-interventionist policy came in 2000, when BMW announced its intention to withdraw from its investment in Rover. While the German company retained the Cowley plant for the production of a re-designed Mini, it had no use for the Longbridge factory outside Birmingham. BMW's initial plan was to sell Longbridge to a venture capital firm, which planned to use it to make sports cars, and eliminate some 4,000 jobs. The government made clear its preference for a rival offer from the Phoenix consortium, which promised to maintain production of saloon cars and to keep employment at a much higher level. As later events were to prove, this was a mistake on the government's part, but it did not involve any direct financial assistance (which would in any case have been difficult to justify under EU rules), and the subsequent travails of the Phoenix-owned business did not elicit any further government intervention, even of a rhetorical kind. The Secretary of State for Trade and Industry, Stephen Byers, accepted later that the Longbridge affair had put the government in a difficult position, and that the main conclusion that he drew was that the job of his department was to 'help business cope with change rather than pay to insulate them from it'.[23]

The crisis at Rover had a special political resonance because of the involvement of earlier governments, but several other large industrial companies went through difficult times as global competition became more intense. A striking example was the decline of GEC. Following the mergers promoted by the IRC in the late 1960s, this company became one of the country's strongest industrial groups, operating mainly in defence electronics, power engineering, and telecommunications equipment. The long-serving managing director, Lord Weinstock, retired from the company in 1996, and the new management team took the view, in line with the management fashion of the day, that the company should focus on fewer businesses. The most promising sector, in the new team's view, was telecommunications equipment, and the company set about expanding this side of the business (principally through acquisitions in the US) and disposing of the rest; the company was re-named Marconi to signal its new vocation. The change of strategy turned out to be a disastrous error. Marconi nearly went under when the worldwide telecommunications boom came to an end in 2000, and its problems were compounded by the loss of business within the UK. Traditionally GEC had been a major supplier to the Post Office, but by the end of the 1980s the telecommunications side of the Post Office had become the investor-owned British Telecom (BT), and its relationship with suppliers was looser than in the days of state control; it was more willing to buy from non-British companies. However, BT was still an important customer, and this business became even more crucial as Marconi's financial troubles deepened in the early 2000s. Whether by then Marconi could have survived as an independent company is doubtful, but the final blow came in 2005, when Marconi failed to win any part of the £10 billion contract for BT's 'twenty-first century network'; the orders were spread among ten non-British firms, including one from China.[24] Shortly afterwards Marconi was bought by Ericsson of Sweden.

There are some similarities with what happened to GEC's power engineering business. In 1989, GEC put this business into a joint venture with its French counterpart, Alcatel-Alsthom. For most of the 1990s GEC–Alsthom did well. At the end of the decade it was detached from its parents and floated on the stock exchange, under the name of Alstom. It then ran into a financial crisis, caused partly by an ill-judged acquisition, and in 2002 it came close to bankruptcy. Only intervention by the French state kept it afloat; the French government was not prepared to see Alstom go under, or be sold to a foreign company. Today Alstom is a French company employing some 70,000 people, while the part of GEC that went into the joint venture – what used to be known as GEC Power Systems – has virtually disappeared. Although some parts of the old GEC business survive under different ownership, the UK no longer has a large, nationally owned manufacturer of power engineering equipment.

The Labour government played no role in these events, nor did it stand in the way of moves by other large British companies to restructure their operations, often involving disposals to non-British firms. ICI, for example, sold off most of its heavy chemical businesses during the 1990s in order to focus on what it believed to be the more profitable sector of speciality chemicals. Much of the traditional heartland of the British chemical industry – the network of inter-connected ICI plants in the north east of England – is now in the hands of non-British companies. No objection was raised when Corus, the Anglo-Dutch steel company that had been created out of the state-owned British Steel Corporation, was bought by Tata of India, or when Pilkington, the glass maker, was bought by Nippon Sheet Glass of Japan. By 2006 foreign ownership of the UK corporate sector (excluding domestic unquoted companies) had reached around 50 per cent, compared with just under 30 per cent in 1990.[25] None of these transactions aroused significant political or popular concern. The welcome for inward investment was shared across the political spectrum, though there were a few dissenting voices in industry. Sir John Rose, chairman of Rolls-Royce, expressed some concern that the UK was becoming an 'aircraft carrier' for foreign companies and warned that those owners might take decisions in their own national interest rather than Britain's.[26]

In its approach to industrial policy, the Labour government was less interested in preserving old companies than in fostering new ones, especially in the knowledge-based sectors which were thought to offer the best opportunities for high-wage countries like the UK. Gordon Brown, the Chancellor, sought to encourage high-technology entrepreneurs through changes in the capital gains tax regime and more generous tax treatment of stock options. Biotechnology was a particular priority, although even here direct financial support from the state was small. The main focus was on creating the conditions under which a strong biotechnology industry could flourish. This included an attempt to emulate what was widely seen an important contributor to American success in this field – the development of clusters. The importance of clusters as a source of competitive strength had been strongly emphasized by Michael Porter, the Harvard economist, and his work influenced the Labour government's thinking.[27] In 1999, a government–industry team led by Lord Sainsbury, the Science Minister, examined biotechnology clusters in Britain and the US and made a number of recommendations, including changes in the planning system.[28]

Although the biotechnology sector did not grow as quickly as the government had hoped, the effect of Labour's policies, building on what earlier Conservative governments had done, was to make the UK a more conducive environment for entrepreneurial activity. The flow of start-up firms in high-technology sectors was impressive. In semiconductors, for example, firms such as ARM, Cambridge Silicon Radio, and Wolfson Microelectronics did well. In terms of employment, none of these firms were in the same league as the giants of the US electronics industry. Apart from Vodafone, there was a dearth in the UK of what are sometimes called 'big gorillas' in high technology, comparable to Amgen or Cisco in the US.[29] But this largely reflected the specialized nature of the technologies from which firms like ARM and Autonomy developed, and of the markets they served.[30]

BRITISH INDUSTRY AT THE BEGINNING OF THE TWENTY-FIRST CENTURY

The two most powerful forces affecting British industry over the last two decades have been globalization and the continuing shift from manufacturing to services. Neither the Conservatives, who held office from 1979 to 1997, nor the Labour governments that followed, sought to obstruct these forces. To a much greater extent than their French and German counterparts, they embraced globalization, including the globalization of financial markets. In contrast to the Labour governments of the 1960s and 1970s, Tony Blair and his colleagues did not attempt to substitute the judgements of politicians and civil servants for those of entrepreneurs and managers. As the Prime Minister remarked, 'Government should have a role that is enabling: supporting small businesses, encouraging technological advance, investing in science – above all, promoting competition and removing the barriers to business growth'.[31]

The focus on competition and deregulation which began in the 1980s produced a flexible economy which, two US commentators have argued, brought to an end 'the nearly century-long trend in relative economic decline of the United Kingdom relative to its historic competitors, Germany and France'.[32] Most of the key reforms – notably in the labour market – were not directly related to industrial policy; indeed, the absence of industrial policy almost certainly helped to make the economy perform better.

Some commentators have suggested that this positive verdict on what has been achieved since the 1980s failed to take account of three less favourable developments: the manufacturing sector had been allowed to decline too far; there was too little investment by business in research and development; and too much of British industry was controlled from outside the UK. On the first issue, two economists, Michael Kitson and Jonathan Michie, have argued that the UK economy cannot hope to flourish internationally in the absence of a strong manufacturing sector. According to this view, errors in UK macroeconomic policy since 1945, leading to an over-valued exchange rate and high interest rates, have seriously damaged the manufacturing sector, while 'industrial policy has been ineffectual, with little attempt to use the public sector as a modernising force'.[33] The Trades Union Congress, arguing along similar lines, published a report that called for a sector-based industrial policy and a partial return to 'picking winners'. The British government should be willing to identify national champions and to support them when they run into financial crises. France, the authors pointed out, 'has a much better record than Britain at retaining its industrial technological base'.[34] Another plea, if not for an active industrial policy at least for a greater commitment to manufacturing, came from one of Britain's leading industrialists. Sir John Rose, chief executive of Rolls-Royce, deplored the loss of expertise in such industries as railways, power generation, and nuclear power, comparing the continued success of French and German companies like Siemens and Areva with the virtual disappearance of their British counterparts. Rose urged the government to develop a much clear sense of direction for industry. 'We need', he said, 'a framework, or a business route map, to create context, drive focus and help prioritise public and private sector investment. Unfortunately the fear of returning to anything that remotely resembles centralised industrial planning has resulted in even the discussion of such a framework being off limits'.[35]

Much of the concern about manufacturing focuses on the balance of payments. The UK has been running a trade deficit in manufactured goods which is partially offset by the growing surplus on trade in services and by income from overseas investments. The resulting current account deficit, amounting to about 2 per cent of GDP, has been fairly stable for the last few years, and has been financed without difficulty. Manufactured exports have held up quite well, suggesting that the manufacturing sector, though smaller than it used to be, has increased the proportion of its output that goes into exports; British companies, whether owned within the UK or from overseas, are adapting well to the new international division of labour.

The UK will certainly need an efficient manufacturing sector for the foreseeable future, but it is wrong to overstate the extent of the decline that has taken place. It is an exaggeration to suggest, as did *The Economist*, that 'just as Britain led the world into industrialisation, so now Britain is leading it out'.[36] The proportion of value added that comes from manufacturing is actually slightly lower in France than in Britain, despite the British neglect of industrial policy; it is Germany, with a much larger commitment to manufacturer, which is the outlier in this

Table 2.1. Value added as % of total value added in 2006

	UK	France	Germany
Industry	17.5	14.4	25.4
Agriculture	0.9	2.0	0.9
Services and other non-manufacturing	81.6	83.6	73.7

Source: OECD.

dimension (Table 2.1). Moreover, the distinction between manufacturing and services is no longer as sharp as it used to be; as industrial companies outsource much of their manufacturing to low-cost locations, they increasingly rely on selling 'solutions' to their customer's problems, involving consulting advice and other service-type activities, rather than the provision of hardware.

As for innovation, it is true that, compared to other industrial countries, the UK scores poorly in the amount of business-funded research and development, despite the continuing strength of the science base (as measured by the number of scientific publications per head). To some extent this reflects an industry mix which is different from that of other countries. The UK is strong in pharmaceuticals – this sector accounts for a quarter of all business-funded research – but it is less strong in the medium–high technology industries such as motor vehicles and engineering, and this is where the gap with Germany in business-funded research is greatest.[37] Even though foreign companies such as Toyota and Nissan have invested in the UK, they perform little research here.[38]

On the other hand, the UK has an innovative services sector that contains some branches, such as producers of software and information technology services, which are research-intensive. It also includes contract research organizations which are growing in importance as more companies scale down their in-house R&D. But the kind of innovation that providers of most business services undertake is different from what is done in manufacturing, and harder to measure, but not necessarily less valuable.[39] Most services firms, even large ones, do not have laboratories of their own, and apply for few patents.[40] Whereas manufacturers source advanced technologies largely through in-house R&D, providers of services do so through collaboration with customers and suppliers, often finding specific solutions to specific problems. Much of their focus is on innovation in organization and management, rather than on product and process innovation.[41]

Is this enough to allow the UK to prosper in the knowledge-based sectors? There is a link here with the question of ownership. Some commentators have argued that countries benefit from having within their borders the head offices of large, nationally owned companies which are at the hub of global networks of research, development, and production. These are the systems integrators, or network flagships, which may outsource much of their manufacturing and even their product development, but keep the intellectual core of the business, where the most advanced research take place, in their home country.[42] Rolls-Royce, the aero-engine manufacturer, falls into this category, as do the two British pharmaceutical companies, GlaxoSmithKline and AstraZeneca.

The existence of such companies is undoubtedly a source of strength, but there is no magic wand available to government that will create them, nor is there any evidence that protecting the ones that already exist from being taken over by foreigners would be good for the economy. The UK has gained far more than it has lost through its openness to inwards investment; it is part of what has been a generally successful adaptation to globalization over the past twenty-five years. The structure of the economy will continue to evolve in a way that cannot easily be predicted, still less steered, by governments. Industrial policy in the old sense has been discarded in favour of horizontal, non-selective policies aimed at correcting institutional weaknesses that impede the growth of productivity. That there are such weaknesses – for example, in the education system – is not in dispute. But as far as microeconomic or supply-side policies are concerned, the UK is likely to stick to the market-based approach, and to promote the flexibility that facilitates the transfer of resources out of activities that cannot compete in the world market into those that can.

NOTES

1. Howard Pack and Kamal Saggi, 'The Case for Industrial Policy: A Critical Survey', World Bank Policy Research Working Paper, No. 3839, Jan. 2006.
2. F. List, *The National System of Political Economy*, Philadelphia, 1856.
3. Peter Howlett, 'The War-time Economy 1939–1945', in Roderick Floud and Paul Johnson eds, *The Cambridge Economic History of Britain, Vol III*, Cambridge 2004.
4. Keith Hayward, *The British Aircraft Industry*, Manchester 1989: 40.
5. John Hendry, *Innovating for Failure: Government Policy and the Early British Computer Industry*, MIT Press, Cambridge, MA, 1984: 163.
6. P.D. Henderson, *Two British Errors: Their Probable Size and Some Possible Lessons*, Oxford Economic Papers, 29, 1977.
7. Caroline Miles, *Lancashire Textiles: A Case Study of Industrial Change*, Cambridge, 1968.
8. Martin Campbell-Kelly, *ICL: A Business and Technical History*, Oxford, 1989: 264.
9. Douglas Hague and Geoffrey Wilkinson, *The IRC: A Study in Industrial Intervention*, George Allen & Unwin, 1983: chapter 6.
10. Jim Tomlinson *Government and Enterprise since 1900*, Oxford, 1994: 301.
11. Daniel C. Kramer, *State Capital and Private Enterprise*, Routledge, 1988.
12. W. B. Willott, 'The NEB's Involvement in Electronics and Information Technology', in Charles Carter (ed.), *Industrial Policy and Innovation*, Heinemann, 1981.
13. For a description of this episode, see John Newhouse, *The Sporty Game*, Knopf, 1982: 201.
14. Keith Geddes, *Setmakers: A History of the Radio and Television Industry*, BREMA, 1991: 397–8.
15. G. Denton, 'Financial Assistance to British Industry', in W. M. Corden and G. Fels (eds.), *Public Assistance to Industry*, Westview Press, 1976: 150.
16. Martin Fransman, *The Market and Beyond*, Cambridge, 1990.

17. Marcus Noland and Howard Pack, *Industrial Policy in an Era of Globalisation: Lessons from Asia*, Institute for International Economics, Washington, 2003.
18. Nigel Lawson, *The View from No 11*, Corgi edition, 1993: 41.
19. Margaret Thatcher, *The Downing Street Years*, HarperCollins, 1993: 118.
20. Colin Wren, *Industrial Subsidies: The UK Experience*, Macmillan, 1996: 197.
21. 'Heseltine's Plan to Help Britain Win', *Financial Times*, 26, Apr. 1993.
22. 'Our Competitive Future: Building the Knowledge-driven Economy', The Government's Competitiveness White Paper, Cmd 4176, Dec. 1998.
23. *Financial Times*, Aug. 4, 2000.
24. *Financial Times*, Apr. 29, 2005.
25. HM Treasury and HM Revenue and Customs, 'Taxation of Companies' Foreign Profits', discussion document, Jun. 2007.
26. *Financial Times*, 10, Feb. 2007.
27. Michael Porter, 'Clusters and the New Economics of Competition', *Harvard Business Review*, Nov./Dec. 1998.
28. 'Biotechnology Clusters', Report of a team led by Lord Sainsbury, Minister of Science, Department of Trade and Industry, HMSO, Aug. 1999.
29. For a discussion of British and American high-technology policy, see Geoffrey Owen, *Where Are the Big Gorillas? High-technology Policy in the UK and the Role of Public Policy*, Diebold Institute for Public Policy, Dec. 2004.
30. Neil Golborne, 'R&D Intensive Businesses in the UK, DTI Economics', Paper No 11, Mar. 2005.
31. Tony Blair, speech to the World Economic Forum in Davos, 18 Jan. 2000.
32. David Card and Richard Freeman, 'What Have Two Decades of British Economic Reform Delivered?' in David Card, David Blundell and Richard Freeman eds., *Seeking a Premier Economy*, National Bureau of Economic Research, 2004.
33. Michael Kitson and Jonathan Michie, 'Does Manufacturing Matter?' *International Journal of the Economics of Business*, 4, 1, 1997.
34. An industrial strategy for the United Kingdom, TUC Discussion Paper, Trades Union Congress, Dec. 2005.
35. Sir John Rose, Gabor lecture at Imperial College, 15 Nov. 2007.
36. *The Economist*, 23 Jun. 2007.
37. OECD Economic Surveys: United Kingdom, 2005; chapter 7.
38. Neil Golborne, 'R&D Intensive Businesses in the UK', DTI Economics, Paper No 11, Mar. 2005.
39. For an overview, see Dirk Pilat, 'Innovation in Productivity and Services: The State of the Art', in *Innovation and Productivity in Services*, OECD, 2001.
40. Bruce Tether, 'Do Services Innovate (Differently)?' CRIC Discussion Paper No 66, Nov. 2004, Centre for Research on Innovation and Competition, University of Manchester.
41. 'Promoting Innovation in Services', OECD 2005.
42. Keith Pavitt, 'Specialisation and Systems Integration: Where Manufacturing and Services Still Meet', in Andrea Prencipe, Andrew Davies, and Michael Hobday eds., *The Business of Systems Integration*, Oxford, 2003.

3

Business in the Regions: From 'Old' Districts to 'New' Clusters?

Andrew Popp and John Wilson

Surveyed from the heights of mid- to late twentieth-century corporatist England the regions appeared, at best, peripheral. At worst, those of an industrial nature were highly problematic sites of seemingly inevitable and terminal decline, particularly as de-industrialization, echoing earlier periods of trauma afflicting the staple industries in the 1920s and 1930s, began to bite hard from the early 1970s. In terms of wider narratives in British economic and business history, the regions were significant largely in relation to the question of decline, with spatial concentration exacerbating the effects of national economic over-dependence on a few core staple industries, notably cotton, heavy engineering, steel, and coal. But even from this perspective, spatial factors were rarely at the core of analyses. For most economic and business historians, the geographical structure of English industry was, at most, symptomatic rather than causal and played little part in explaining either growth or decline, whether at the level of firms, sectors, or the nation.

Today, however, the picture appears somewhat different, for two reasons. First, a new wave of scholarship emanating from a range of cognate disciplines has, through a reassessment of the place of regions in English business and economic history, emphasized just how deeply regionally differentiated was the country's experience of both industrialization and economic growth and development.[1] Moreover, these studies have increasingly taken this spatial differentiation as a serious causal or explanatory factor. Second, the last two or three decades have seen a resurgence of the 'local', particularly in the form of new industrial clusters in leading sectors of the 'third industrial revolution', such as information and communication technology, biotechnology, and pharmaceuticals. Similarly, larger, often multinational corporations have been moving towards more heterarchic organizational structures that mimic or recall older, apparently obsolete, networked structures, a development associated with the construction of global supply chains, joint ventures, and off-shoring – strategies that led to a greater emphasis on regional clusters. Still, the threads linking these phenomena seem somewhat disparate and unrelated. First, many highly concentrated and specialized regional economies can appear so unique or specific as to hold little relevance to the analysis of other locations. Second, it is certainly the case that in many aspects the new clusters and the old districts appear to share little, for they are found in different sectors and seem to have been structured and to have operated in quite different ways. Further, they inhabit very different contexts in terms of their relationship to wider forces and national economic fortunes and performance. Thus, where 'old' districts are indelibly associated with decline, the 'new' clusters are seen as at the vanguard of English economic vitality and resurgence.

Is there an arc that links these two eras? Can one detect a renaissance at work in the older regions, indicating a vibrant new phase in their life cycle? What might attempting to follow these stages teach us? This chapter will seek to reintegrate these varied threads and to ask how a regionally oriented perspective can add to or alter dominant narratives in English economic and business history. Through a structured, dynamic analysis of these two apparently distinct eras, during which the local came to the fore, the chapter will argue that spatial factors are not incidental to long-run processes in English economic history; that powerful spatial factors have not simply been path-dependent but also path-forming; and that these factors can play a significant role in explaining long-run processes of restructuring, at organizational and strategic as well as at spatial levels, and thus bear an important relation to questions of national economic performance. Consideration of these issues requires an appreciation of the strategic and organizational characteristics and competitive advantages associated with clustering and of their dynamic properties. Two concepts are key to the latter issue: life cycle and lock-in. Throughout, we will attempt to deploy these concepts whilst combining them with the historians' appreciation of narrative, agency and contingency.

THE PROPERTIES AND DYNAMICS OF DISTRICTS AND CLUSTERS

We do not intend to rehearse in detail the special properties commonly claimed for industrial districts and clusters, for these are well known and are derived principally from Marshall's concept of external economies of scale.[2] These external economies, generated amongst constellations of geographically concentrated firms that are typically small or medium in size, may be divided into two categories: static agglomeration economies and dynamic external economies. The presence of external economies of scale is associated with particular patterns of organizational structure at the level of firm and cluster, as well as particular strategic orientations and sources of competitive advantage, again at the level of the firm and the cluster. As already suggested, external economies of scale and scope are most likely to be generated by concentrations of numerous, relatively small or medium-sized firms, often performing only partial processes as part of a decomposed chain of production and distribution operations. It is worth noting, however, that the structures of industrial districts in fact show considerable variation, while with that variation comes also differences in the precise array of economies and competitive advantages available to firms in a district. Thus, some clusters will be driven much more by large-scale economies in the production of relatively undifferentiated commodities, such as heavy chemicals or some textiles; others may emphasize extreme flexibility, as in many fashion-driven consumer products; whilst yet others will pursue learning and innovation, whether in products or processes. In detail, external economies are driven by pooling effects across a range of tangible and intangible resources and inputs, as well as by learning effects and spillovers fostered by spatial proximity. In addition, the conditions created by spatial proximity are often held to reduce costs, such as transaction and information costs, by privileging co-operation over competition. This raises two important and interdependent dimensions of districts and clusters: their socio-economic characteristics and what might be referred to as their governance systems. They are interdependent because the particular socio-economic characteristics of districts are held to shape governance of the district as a system through relatively smooth and natural means, most commonly in the form of networks, an issue to which we shall return.

Work on the dynamics experienced in districts and clusters is less well-known; indeed, there have been laments about the lack of historical perspective in most work in this area, but one promising avenue is provided by the life-cycle concept.[3] A range of studies have detected patterns and regularities in the cycle of growth, maturity, and decline experienced by districts and clusters.[4] Building on this work, we would like to propose a framework on which our long-term analysis can be based. The basic stages in this model are:

- *Critical Mass* – the initial clustering of expertise and factors of production.
- *Take-Off* – often associated with key inventions or innovations, which alongside the clustering of expertise and factors of production give the district a significant competitive advantage.
- *Cooperative Competitiveness* – balancing the hierarchical and heterarchical advantages of clustering and networking and achieving competitive advantage over rival clusters.
- *Saturation* – the costs of clustering start to outweigh benefits, with rate of growth falling away, innovation rare, and competition increasing from lower-cost producers.
- *Maturity* – rival clusters offer superior advantages for new firms and decline sets in across the older district.
- *Renaissance* – new industries locate in the cluster, attracted by either cheap factors of production, demand for their products or the activities of regional planners.

Drivers of this life cycle (which should not be interpreted as in any sense deterministic or inevitable) include, of course, technological and product life cycles, but also life cycles in industry structures and changes and adaptations in governance systems responding both to the emerging life cycle of the cluster and to environmental change, for example, in markets. These last elements thus necessarily introduce elements of both contingency and agency into the historical analysis of districts and clusters.

One of the factors most critical in determining how a specific district will experience the life cycle is the extent to which it develops 'lock-in'. The lock-in concept refers to the inability of a district or region to reorder itself in the face of pressures for change. There are four principle sources of lock-in: functional, political, cognitive, and structural.[5] Lock-in may be thought of as a position of constrained choice or agency – or as a failure of governance systems. Because lock-in reflects constrained agency resulting in an inability to reorder, it may be illuminated by reference to resource issues and, in particular, resource bases and resource dependency.[6] Resource bases refer to the distribution of resources across firms and the cluster as a whole and are arranged on a continuum from internalized to externalized. To a large degree, resource distribution both reflects and further shapes the economies, strategies, and competitive advantages available to a district. Resource dependency may be thought of as a governance issue and refers to the extent to which firms, and districts, are dependent on outside resource providers. Resource dependency is ranged on a continuum from high to low. Concurrent analysis of resource bases and resource dependency gives us a way of thinking about issues of structure, strategy, and governance in combination. Tracking the evolution of resource bases and dependencies across the life cycle injects dynamics into district studies, helping us to illuminate changing competitive advantages and fortunes over time. Thus, for example, in many empirical cases we have found that the maturity phase in the life cycle is associated with a rigidity in resource bases operating in combination with low levels of external resource dependency, which reduces external pressure for change. In other words, lock-in accumulates and decline becomes entrenched unless or until events conspire to disrupt the pattern.

In the empirical sections that follow, we will trace the intersection of firm and cluster structures, strategic orientations, and fluctuating competitive advantage as life cycles unfolded, contexts changed, and lock-ins developed.

BUSINESS IN THE REGIONS: THE 'MARSHALLIAN' DISTRICTS

England's classic 'Marshallian' industrial districts were both parents to and children of industrialization and the industrial revolution.[7] Significant districts that were to enjoy long-lasting international competitive advantage rapidly developed across a range of regions and sectors, including the very well-known, such as cotton textiles in Lancashire, woollen textiles in West Yorkshire, ceramics in North Staffordshire, metal-using trades in the West Midlands, jewellery in Birmingham, cutlery and steel in Sheffield, shoes and other leather products in Northampton, lace in Nottinghamshire and Leicester, watches and other precision instruments in Coventry and on Merseyside, and the less well-known or less studied, such as gloving in Worcester, furniture in High Wycombe, fancy glass in Stourport, and carpets in Kidderminster. Oft-forgotten but no less important was an array of districts clustered in London, many focused on consumer products such as furniture and clothing.[8]

All of these districts, no matter what other differences they displayed, emerged somewhat spontaneously in the particular context of early industrialization.[9] The context of early industrialization, because of the resource implications that it held, profoundly affected the character and subsequent development of England's classic industrial districts. Clustering was a response to underdevelopment and a way of substituting for resources that could not be acquired from elsewhere. Extensive externalization of resource bases was a logical and highly effective answer to shortages of, in particular, financial capital. Highly localized markets for capital, often in the form of credit as a means of providing working capital, quickly emerged. In a context of relatively weak institutional safeguards, it frequently made sense to seek financial and other resources from those that were already known, reducing the dangers of adverse selection and the need for monitoring, at least in theory. Obvious candidates included family and, in some cases, co-religionists, leading to the creation of some quite long-distance networks, for example, amongst Quakers. Also, those rooted in spatial proximity, where participants could be closely and constantly observed, were probably at least as important.

Extensive externalization of resource bases quickly came to be matched with high levels of resource dependency at the level of the individual enterprise, but relatively low-resource dependency at the level of the district or wider region. Districts became self-sustaining and characterized by strongly centrifugal forces. Self-reliance was further promoted by very low levels of government intervention, a classic feature of early industrialization. Local industrial and political elites were closely identified, and often very heavily overlapped, reinforcing patterns of spatial concentration in industrialization by overlaying it with high levels of local-political autonomy and an often powerful sense of local identity and pride inextricably bound up with regional industrial specialisms. We need look no further than the appellations 'Cottonopolis', 'Steel City', or 'the Potteries' to gain some sense of this. Autonomy was not an unalloyed boon and one potentially problematic consequence was relative underdevelopment of links between the industrial regions and resource providers in the capital.

At the same time, the 'Chandlerian' concept of personal capitalism, which privileges an interpretation of British governance arrangements in the nineteenth century as highly individualistic, does not adequately capture the very dense, localized mesh of resource dependencies typical of most industrial districts.[10] No more satisfactory is the unproblematized view of community-rooted networks dominant in much of the literature on industrial districts, which pays little attention to how resource issues might introduce power and hierarchy into the governance of local systems, and instead chooses to emphasize equality and co-operation in both behaviours and outcomes. The distribution of resources in many districts instead created dependencies that could equally bind and constrain, a problem that was to become more apparent as life cycles progressed.

Extensive externalization of resource bases also had structural and strategic implications. Externalization of resources encouraged the proliferation of firms, entrenching nascent patterns of resource distribution by consistently lowering barriers to entry. Though specific configurations and patterns of vertical and horizontal integration necessarily also reflected technological realities and imperatives, as in the relatively highly integrated pottery industry, districts primarily expanded on the basis of a growth in the number of firms, rather than through the growth of individual firms. A necessary corollary in most cases was a dedication to specialization and partial process operations, taken to extremes in locales such as the Birmingham Jewellery Quarter.[11] Another exemplar of this process was the Lancashire cotton textile complex (in reality a whole series of interlinked industrial districts orbiting around the commercial hub provided by Manchester), where whole towns became dedicated to both particular stages in the production process and particular grades or qualities of yarn or cloth.[12] In turn, the concentrated, critical mass of potential customers generated by clustering allowed, or even demanded, the emergence of supporting auxiliary sectors that thrived on delivering highly specialized inputs and services to primary producers.

In strategic terms, industrial districts are typically associated with an orientation towards specialty production, flexibility, customization, and fashion. Certainly, such strategies were central to the success of many English districts, where the combination of a decomposed production process supported by specialist auxiliaries allowed for a dizzying array of goods to be produced and its mix constantly altered, delivering powerful external economies of scope. But it is also the case that clustering delivered across many sectors vast external economies of scope, lowered costs, and dynamic competitive advantage in international markets. In effect, many English districts offered a model of mass production without mass producers.

These vast streams of goods demanded an outlet and the one significant exception to the general position of low external resource dependency typical of English districts was in the area of markets and demand. All of England's classic and most important industrial districts were deeply embedded in highly internationalized trade networks and global markets, demanding an interaction with agents far beyond local boundaries. As befitted the decomposed production processes and structures of districts, these interactions were largely handled without extensive forward integration into marketing and distribution. The highly developed and sophisticated merchanting sectors associated with the largest and most successful districts and regions, most notably Lancashire cotton textiles, proved adept at handling this challenge and, it has been argued, for many decades delivered the region a powerful competitive advantage in accessing and parcelling out amongst manufacturers a truly global demand for English goods.[13]

These forces rapidly propelled many districts through the initial take-off, critical mass, and, during their heyday across the mid-decades of the nineteenth century, cooperative competitiveness phases of the life cycle. These districts presented a multitude of vibrant prospects. Crucially, these prospects were highly specific to particular sites, English industrial districts acquiring deep reserves of that *genus loci* or 'industrial atmosphere' that has so animated district studies and models since Marshall coined the term. The fact of English industrial competitive advantage cannot be divorced from the fact of intense regional and sub-regional specialization or clustering.

At the same time, patterns of resource distribution and resource dependency that emerged during industrialization and that allowed English districts to meet the challenges inherent in early industrialization, propelling both individual districts and the nation as a whole to a position of international dominance, proved a fertile breeding ground for future lock-in as life cycles developed and as the outside world changed and threw up new challenges – particularly new sources of competition. As already suggested, the saturation and maturity phases of the district life cycle are often marked, or even hastened, by the emergence of rival clusters overseas offering superior competitive advantage. Given England's position in the world markets by the late nineteenth century, it was natural that many of these challenges would emerge from locations in late-industrializing countries, such as Germany. The saturation and maturity phases are not marked simply by heightened inter- and intra-district competition, but also by declining levels of innovation. Existing patterns of resource distribution within and, especially, between firms proved increasingly hard to alter as they became evermore entrenched. It is important to emphasize that such lock-ins are not given or inherent, but instead are created over time.

In part, this could be due to a failure to recognize the need for a reconfiguration of resources. Many actors displayed an intense cognitive commitment or lock-in to existing practices, processes, and technologies. Cognitive lock-in ensures that key actors and change agents failed to recognize, or to accept, signals that change was urgent. This was true of entrepreneurs, managers, and technologists across a range of industries, from Lancashire cotton textiles, through the Leblanc-based alkali industry to the North Staffordshire Potteries.[14] However, owners and managers were not the only ones to exhibit these traits, workers and unions were equally committed to past practices. Such commitments were not simply cognitive – that is rooted in understandings of the world – but also, to some extent, emotional or psychological, with local industrial specialisms, craft, and pride being keystones of self-identification amongst both bosses and workers.[15]

The fact that both capital and labour showed high levels of cognitive lock-in is a reminder of the extent to which many English districts came, by the late nineteenth century, to suffer from high levels of functional lock-in. Functional lock-in occurs where change requires coordinated action amongst interdependent but independent parties, such as amongst contracting partial process firms, as seen to very widespread effect between the spinning and weaving branches of the cotton textile industry, or between organized labour and capital, as seen in the case of the Potteries.[16] The necessary ability to overcome cognitive and functional lock-in was in many cases further weakened by powerful instances of political lock-in. Political lock-in in English districts took two forms. In the first, powerful vested interests were able to defend the status quo and their own positions. The role of Manchester as the hub of the Lancashire cotton textile industry is a good example of how local industrial elites can frustrate pressures for change.[17] In the second, conversely, local norms of both co-operation and competition break down and intra-district political infighting erupts. In the Potteries, such infighting had the effect of eroding the competitive advantages long enjoyed by both the district and its constituent firms as rivals bid each other down in spiralling price wars that did little more than erode reputations for quality.[18] Districts able to find a way through this morass, such as the Birmingham Jewellery Quarter, were rare indeed.[19]

The traditionally identified forms of lock-in in old industrial regions – cognitive, functional, and political – should, we believe, be joined by a fourth, the structural.[20] Structural lock-in may be thought of as a congestion effect and is intimately related to some of the most basic characteristics of districts and clusters. We have seen how early in the life cycle of a district, spatial clustering allows firms to overcome resource deficiencies through strategies such as the decomposition of the production (and distribution) process. These same effects, however, have over time the consequence of creating and maintaining very low barriers of entry to the industry (and of making exit less painful, further encouraging entry). One outcome in mature districts is the constant recycling between exits and entrants of increasingly obsolete resources, such as plant. Waves of entrants constantly crowded out more innovative responses to challenges and exacerbated all three other forms of lock-in. Here we see that lock-in is directly related to the patterns of resource distribution established during, and vital to, the vigorous phases of growth seen during the earlier stages of the life cycle. To some extent, then, the potential for decline was generated through the conditions that had created growth; that is unless existing patterns of development could be disrupted.

In part, the ability to disrupt the dynamics inherent in the life cycle depended on access to resources, or resource dependency. But again we find that conditions associated with the growth stages in districts had, to varying degrees, encouraged many English districts to adopt positions of relatively low dependency on external resource providers. When the time came to restructure through accessing new resources, the links to external sources that would have made this easier were relatively underdeveloped. Indeed, somewhat as with the dynamic associated with structural congestion and lock-in, links to external resource providers actually became weaker over time in many locations. Districts and the actors in them became inward-looking, clique-ridden, and proud of their self-sufficiency. Again, the single most important English district or complex, the Lancashire cotton textile industry, provided a powerful illustration of this effect, but other examples can also be found.[21] In particular, with their headquarters inevitably located in the provinces, many district firms remained remote from vital sources of political and financial resources to be found in the capital, significantly undermining their competitiveness at a time when other clusters were beginning to erode, even eliminate, Britain's earlier advantages.[22]

The result was that as lock-ins emerged and tightened, just at the moment when many districts founded during industrialization in the eighteenth century entered the maturity phase of the life cycle, competitiveness across a wide swathe of industries was undermined or collapsed. The depth of these problems first became apparent during the years of depression that stretched across much of the last three decades of the nineteenth century and were confirmed by the two deep recessions of the inter-war years.[23] Many of England's proudest industrial districts never fully recovered from these shocks. Certainly, new and more dynamic areas of industrial activity did emerge during those same inter-war years, particularly in the West Midlands and the south-east, concentrating in light consumer industries, but until the rediscovery of the local in the 1980s it appeared that England's economy was to be dominated by corporate and metropolitan interests. The districts had had their day, at least for the time being.

FROM 'MATURITY' TO 'RENAISSANCE'?

If by the 1930s almost all of Britain's significant industrial districts were displaying sure signs of 'Maturity', little relief was administered by either government or private enterprise in the following four decades. In spite of a general commitment to 'Full Employment' macroeconomic policies from the mid-1940s, and some clumsy attempts at forging regional policies from the late-1950s, up to the 1980s the nexus of economic power gravitated much more to the growth areas, especially the Home Counties. Of course, nationalization of the coal and steel industries significantly assisted those regions (South Wales; central Scotland; South Yorkshire) that would otherwise have been blighted by a lack of diversification, even if this only delayed inevitable rationalization for a later generation of politicians. Indeed, robust post-war economic growth shrouded the regional problems with the general belief that Britain 'had never had it so good', even though the industrial districts of the Industrial Revolution era were dwindling significantly in strength and prospects. In this section, we want to survey the forces that apparently fed into a renaissance of clustering in the late twentieth century, most obviously at sites such as 'Silicon Fen' around Cambridge or the M4 corridor west of London.

The mid-twentieth century was, indeed, a difficult period for those industrial districts that had provided the bedrock of Britain's industrialization. Apart from changing market dynamics that moved decisively against the old staple industries, undoubtedly one of the key reasons behind their diminution in power was a significant transfer of power from the regions to London. For example, as Jeremy, Abe, and Saseki have noted, while in the period 1902–7, 82 per cent of the North West's Top 50 firms had their headquarters in that region, by 1992–3 this had fallen to 42 per cent.[24] This process was also overlaid by intense merger waves that were driven by the desire of senior management both to eliminate competition and internalize activities that in the past were performed across specialized industrial districts. Indeed, the mid-twentieth century was the high-point of British industry's association with mass-production techniques and the internalization of value chains, leading to intense industrial relations problems and declining competitiveness. So entrenched, or locked-in, were decades old structures and practices, within and between firms, that any confrontation with them was almost inevitably partial and ineffective amid the multiple compromises that took place. Much British manufacturing industry remained located in the regions, but clustering had ceased to be a source of growth and prosperity. Tellingly, some of the most dynamic industrial concentrations in Britain in the mid-twentieth century were entirely new ones to be found in the south-east, where they were free to develop unfettered by the dead hand of past conditions.[25]

Having noted earlier that English industrial competitive advantage in the nineteenth century was linked inextricably with intense regional and sub-regional specialization, or clustering, as the latter declined in strength during the mid-twentieth century, it is apparent that core industries lost competitiveness. While the causative relationship between these trends needs much more intense quantitative analysis, it is clear that the major industrial districts suffered badly when compared to the newer centres of economic power in the Home Counties. Moreover, because during the saturation phase of their life cycle the older districts had failed to diversify their industrial base and their lock-in (cognitive, functional, political, and structural) became even more intense, decline became the hallmark of their fortunes up to the 1980s. Renaissance was stymied.

By the 1980s, however, a combination of trends and revelations was beginning to alter attitudes at both national government levels and on the ground. Although since the 1940s limited regional policies had been pursued by successive governments, these had been hampered by a preference for Keynesian macro-management and micro-policies aimed at growth sectors such as automobiles and domestic electrical appliances, as well as high technology industries. It was increasingly obvious by the 1980s, though, that clustering had been at the root of international success stories such as Silicon Valley in the USA, Northern Italy, and some regions in West Germany. An increasingly influential literature also emerged at that time, highlighting what Granovetter has termed the 'strong embeddedness' perspective on regional business networks.[26] This literature included the work of Piore and Sabel, Sabel and Zeitlin, and Staber et al., each of which espoused the virtues of powerful, cohesive district-wide governance derived from deep implantation of actors in robust regional and sub-regional socio-cultural structures.[27] From this perspective, the principal outcome of the distinctive-embedded governance systems of the 'ideal–typical industrial district' is regarded as a creative balance between co-operation and competition, maintained by the sway of widely held, consensual, normative value systems.

Another vital influence on this trend was the introduction of electronic technologies that radically transformed production possibilities, in effect providing the basis for flexible production processes that were effectively overlaid on to the mass-production facilities of major manufacturers. Flexible production provided an impetus to the resurgence in interest in capturing external economies of scale, given the enormous success Japanese automobile and electronics manufacturers had achieved in developing such techniques as *kanban* and just-in-time production systems. While the mass-production technologies that had come to dominate British industry since the 1930s were based on extensive internalization of processes, the new electronic technologies – computer-aided design and computer-aided production – stimulated much wider interest in external economies of scale, providing a much stronger rationale for industrial clustering. However, with both the older industries having virtually disappeared by the 1970s, and many other industries suffering from their widely acknowledged lack of international competitiveness, it remained unclear who would be responsible for the renaissance of industrial clusters that had for decades been in decline.

Even though these trends resonated strongly with those who were well aware of the Marshallian industrial district concept, national government was still slow to respond to widely publicized examples of successful clustering. Indeed, it was not until 1997 that legislation was enacted to establish regional development agencies (RDAs), while in 2002 the government commissioned a report from Michael Porter on how clustering might be revitalized in the UK. The principal purpose of the latter was to provide government ministers with advice from a prominent American social scientist, leading to the production of a report that extolled the virtues of clustering.[28] As Porter had already gone on record as an enthusiastic advocate of clustering, not surprisingly he was keen to stress that these are vitally important in a modern economy, capable of simultaneously increasing productivity, innovation, and new business formation. While Porter and Ketels would appear to have ignored much of the country's industrial history, claiming that 'Overall, the UK does not rank high on measures of cluster development', they felt that future strategies ought to be directed to resolving this apparent problem.[29]

Tiratsoo and Tomlinson have conducted a forensic assessment of the Porter and Ketels report, concluding that on matters of history, analytical content, and policy application it lacks credibility.[30] This leads to a series of questions concerning recent cluster development policy, because in spite of its inadequacies the Porter and Ketels report has been used as the basis for a policy aimed at encouraging all RDAs to focus their attention on clustering. As Tiratsoo and Tomlinson conclude, 'there must be at least some suspicion that Porter has simply taken a trademark "off the shelf" medicine and applied it to the UK, regardless of whether this is appropriate or not'.[31] They have also added that the

Labour government's behaviour can be linked to deeper and more established ideological currents, in that since the 1940s when in power its leaders have always sought American solutions to Britain's relatively poor productivity record.[32] With specific reference to Porter's advocacy of clustering, this reflects a rather curious twist to policy formulation, given the inherent inadequacies of his report and the way in which the RDAs had gone about implementing these ideas.

As we have already noted, since their creation in 1997, the RDAs had been working feverishly on cluster formation policies, actively engaging local firms and entrepreneurs in the process of collaborating and cooperating. As Hedlund had noted much earlier, multinationals had already been developing collaborative, heterarchic approaches towards organizational evolution, in contrast to the older hierarchical styles of management that had prevailed for decades.[33] Indeed, the most striking developments in recent international business have been the emergence of radical new strategies and structures associated with a much more heterarchic approach to markets. Of course, collaboration is far from being unique to the last generation of business managers, given the extensive exploitation of external economies of scale by British firms operating out of intricately connected industrial districts and the way in which they worked closely with intermediaries, suppliers, and subcontractors.[34] Whilst it is true these advantages had melted away as many of the older districts experienced rapid decline from the 1920s, more recently, as Phelps notes with specific regard to technology transfer, there has been a 'renaissance of inter-firm linkages'.[35] It is also apparent that multinational firms have played a major role in reviving this system, highlighting their importance in the emergence of what Cooke and Morgan describe as an 'associational economy', albeit in a very different framework of resource distribution and resource dependency that had prevailed in earlier industrial districts.[36]

Hedlund's work was consequently extremely timely, in stressing the enormous advantages associated with heterarchical forms of organization, arguing that the dissemination of knowledge can be significantly enhanced when firms share information and collaborate. He went on to claim that a network-form (N-form) of organization was beginning to replace the hierarchical multidivisional-form (M-form) of organization, a point apparently substantiated by the research of leading authorities like Bartlett and Ghoshal, Dunning, and Ferlie and Pettigrew.[37] At the heart of this hierarchy-substituting innovation is a high level of trust between firms operating in extensive supply-chain relationships. Given this high-trust relationship, it is clear that partners can gain significant economic, technological, and political benefits from working heterarchically.[38] While Pettigrew and Fenton have highlighted the dangers of exaggerating the impact of the N-form, especially in Europe, there remains considerable evidence that many firms, large and small, have realized the advantages associated with a heterarchic approach to both strategy and structure.[39]

The multinational enterprise (MNE) and its supply chain are clearly central to understanding how and why heterarchy has replaced hierarchy over the last twenty years – a development that has fed into the renaissance of clustering. In essence, MNEs are attempting to reduce the uncertainty levels associated with establishing expensive facilities in new markets, thereby improving the chances of success. It is also clear that many local firms have gained significantly from this relationship, because as further NIERC research by Roper and Hewitt-Dundas has demonstrated, there is a positive relationship between heterarchical relationships and innovation within regional business communities, such as that in Northern Ireland.[40] In particular, high-technology sectors like aerospace, electronics, and electrical and optical equipment reveal the greatest benefits. These linkages have been particularly beneficial 'in speeding-up product and process developments . . . accessing specialist expertise and making development activity more cost-effective'.[41] Admittedly, large firms were three times more likely to engage in this kind of relationship than smaller enterprises, posing a challenge for policy-makers in ensuring that the benefits percolated down to those ventures lacking the resources to invest in innovative activity. On the other hand, it is clear that by the mid-1990s the heterarchic model had been extensively developed as a benchmark against which others might measure their own progress.

Having highlighted these issues, however, it is important to end this section by linking the work on heterarchy with the recent research undertaken by INN-FORM. Coordinated by Pettigrew and Fenton, this project has firstly emphasized how, over the last fifty years at least, organizational innovation has been a consistent feature of the business world.[42] Moreover, they note that organizing is not only a dynamic process, but also part of a firm's strategic evolution. Surveying a cross-section of 460 European firms, they discovered that two-thirds of the sample had increased the amount of outsourcing they undertook, while a similar proportion had also negotiated long-term strategic alliances. On the other hand, although their evidence supported the claim that the N-form of organization was increasing in popularity, it was clearly regarded as a risky activity, given the enormous managerial challenges associated with maintaining the increasing number of links. In this context, firms were also seeking to strengthen their hierarchical attributes, as a means of creating appropriate internal control mechanisms. There were consequently dual, or complementary, organisational trends at play, because 'firms are simultaneously building hierarchies *and* networks; seeking greater performance accountability upward *and* greater horizontal integration sideways; and attempting to centralize strategy *and* decentralise operations'.[43]

The INNFORM project has provided an improved sense of balance to our understanding of why and how European firms have been indulging in networks, alliances, and syndicates. It is also vital, finally, to link this with the work of the RDAs, because potentially this could work against the tendency of MNEs to operate heterarchically. There is, indeed, a natural tension between governmental strategies and those pursued by private business, in that while the latter prefer to operate in an unfettered marketplace, working closely with government inevitably implies some degree of compromise, maybe even control. This highlights the potentially false nature of more recent clustering, in that not only have firms and entrepreneurs been cajoled into joining these groupings, they also lack many of the path-dependent characteristics of the historical predecessors. Furthermore, it is also possible that where the first generation of districts and clusters over time lacked the external resource dependencies that might have helped negotiate the challenge of change, this second generation is almost entirely dependent on resources provided from outside the cluster itself. The basic foundation in externalized resources bases and in external economies of scale and scope remain central, but they now operate in a context of largely delocalized governance. This may promote adaptability but not necessarily rootedness and longevity. Of course, it is largely irrelevant that the recent clusters are focused on different industries – for example, aerospace in the north-west, as opposed to cotton textiles – in that it would have been folly to have attempted to revive the old industries. On the other hand, it is apparent that most of the recent clusters struggle with the concept itself, and many constituents question the rationale behind the policies. This lack of cognitive commitment consequently undermines the inherent dynamism of these groupings, especially when significant numbers of transient MNEs are involved in the clusters.

CONCLUSIONS: CONTINUITIES AND CONTRASTS

In surveying the long-term evolution of Britain's industrial districts, it is clear that in its early stages clustering delivered significant economies of scale and scope that were the foundation of many industries' international competitiveness. These strengths were reinforced by a commitment to indigenous characteristics, providing a social dynamic that proved to be enduring, at least until the mid-twentieth century – when commitment slowly came to resemble 'lock-in' and inertia instead. As the older industrial districts declined in both competitiveness and international impact, especially from the inter-war era, most entered a 'mature' phase, ushering in decline that neither governments nor private enterprise proved capable of halting. Only since the 1980s, and in high-growth sectors such as aerospace and service industries such as leisure and tourism, has there been a 'renaissance' in many of the older industrial districts, partly born of government prompting, but principally arising from the heterarchic activities of multinational corporations seeking external economies of scale and scope in expanding their supply chains. It is increasingly clear, however, that more recent clustering activity has failed to develop the kind of path dependency and dynamic growth potential of their nineteenth-century predecessors, given that the lead firms rarely identify themselves long-term with these regions, while more local business attitudes towards the role of RDAs and government intervention remain cautious.

Although clustering remains a major dynamic in both public and corporate strategies, it remains questionable whether the 'Renaissance' of older industrial districts – or the clustering concept – possesses the permanency of the processes at play in the eighteenth and nineteenth centuries. In particular, the way in which recent clustering has become contingent upon international linkages, whether commercial or political, creates a degree of fragility that differs strikingly from the characteristics of older industrial districts.

NOTES

1. See in particular, J. F. Wilson and A. Popp, eds., *Industrial Clusters and Regional Business Networks in England, 1750–1970*, Ashgate, Aldershot, 2003.
2. A. Marshall, *Industry and Trade*, Macmillan, Basingstoke, 1919.
3. R. Chapman, 'From "Growth Centre" to "Cluster": Restructuring, Regional Development and the Teeside Chemical Industry', *Environment and Planning A*, 37, 2005: 597–615.
4. G. M. P. Swann, M. Prevezer, and D. Stout, *The Dynamics of Industrial Clustering: International Comparisons in Computing and Biotechnology*, Oxford University Press, Oxford, 1998; Wilson and Popp, *Industrial Clusters and Regional Business* Networks; J.F. Wilson, P. Bracken, and E. Kostova, *Creative Cluster Formation: Longitudinal and Contemporary Perspectives in the East Midlands: Final Report*, HEROBC Innovation and Regional Fellowships, Nottingham University Business School, University of Nottingham, 2005; A. Popp and J. F. Wilson, 'Life-cycles, Contingency, and Agency: Growth, Development and Change in English Industrial Districts and Clusters', *Environment and Planning A*, 39, 2007: 2975–92.
5. Popp and Wilson, 'Life-cycles, Contingency, and Agency'.
6. A. Popp, J. S. Toms, and J. F. Wilson, 'Industrial Districts as Organizational Environments: Resources, Networks and Structures', *Management and Organizational History*, 1, 2006: 349–70.
7. The term 'Marshallian' acknowledges the founding role played by Alfred Marshall in the development of the industrial district concept, which emerged from empirical observations of England's industrial regions conducted by Marshall in the late nineteenth-century. Thus the industrial district concept is rooted in those English clusters created during the industrial revolution.
8. Wilson and Popp, *Industrial Clusters and Regional Business Networks in England*; P. Scott, *Triumph of the South: A Regional Economic History of Early Twentieth Century Britain*, Ashgate, Aldershot, 2007. We do not intend in this chapter to deal with those regions, often geographically peripheral, dedicated to the nexus of coal mining, iron, and, in some cases, shipbuilding, for these displayed important differences to the 'Marshallian' districts and were later to present different, though no less important, problems.
9. A. Gershenkron, *Economic Backwardness in Historical Perspective: A Book of Essays*, Belknap Press, Cambridge, MA, 1962.
10. J. F. Wilson and A. Popp, 'Business Networking in the Industrial Revolution: Some Comments', *Economic History Review*, LVI, 2003: 355–61.
11. F. Carnevali, '"Malefactors and Honourable Men": The Making of Commercial Honesty in Nineteenth-century Industrial Birmingham', in Wilson and Popp, eds., *Industrial Clusters and Regional Business Networks in England*: 192–207.
12. J. F. Wilson and J. Singleton, 'The Manchester Industrial District, 1750–1939: Clustering, Networking and Performance', in Wilson and Popp, *Industrial Clusters and Regional Business Networks in England*.

13. S. Broadberry and A. Marrison, 'External Economies of Scale in the Lancashire Cotton Industry, 1900–1950', *Economic History Review*, LV, 2002: 51–77.
14. Wilson and Singleton, 'The Manchester Industrial District'; A. Popp, 'Governance at Points of Corporate Transition: Networks and the Formation of the United Alkali Company, 1890', *Enterprise and Society*, 7, 2006: 315–52; A. Popp, *Business Structure, Business Culture and the Industrial District: The Potteries, c.1850–1914*, Ashgate, Aldershot, 2001.
15. A. Popp, '"The True Potter": Identity and Entrepreneurship in the North Staffordshire Potteries in the later Nineteenth-century', *Journal of Historical Geography*, 29, 2003: 317–35.
16. Popp, *Business Structure, Business Culture and the Industrial District*.
17. Wilson and Singleton, 'The Manchester Industrial District'.
18. A. Popp, '"An Indissoluble Mutual Destiny": The North Staffordshire Potteries and the Limits of Regional Trade Associationalism', *Organization Studies*, 26, 2005: 1831–50.
19. Carnevali, 'Malefactors and Honourable Men'.
20. R. Hassink and D-H. Shin, 'The Restructuring of Old Industrial Areas in Europe and Asia', *Environment and Planning A*, 37, 2005: 571–80; Popp and Wilson, 'Life-cycles, Contingency and Agency'.
21. J. S. Toms and I. Filatotchev, 'Networks, Corporate Governance and the Decline of the Lancashire Textile Industry', in Wilson and Popp, eds., *Industrial Clusters and Regional Business Networks in England*, 68–89; G. Cookson, 'Quaker Networks and the Industrial Development of Darlington, 1780–1870', in Wilson and Popp, eds., *Industrial Clusters and Regional Business Networks in England*: 155–73; Lloyd-Jones, R. and M. J. Lewis, 'Business Networks, Social Habits and the Evolution of a Regional Industrial Cluster: Coventry, 1880s–1930s', in Wilson and Popp, eds., *Industrial Clusters and Regional Business Networks in England*.
22. M. C. Casson, 'An Economic Approach to Regional Business Networks', in Wilson and Popp, eds., *Industrial Clusters and Regional Business Networks*: 19–43.
23. Scott, *Triumph of the South*.
24. D. J. Jeremy, T. Abe, and J. Saseki, 'Comparisons between the Development of Big Business in the North West of England and in Osaka, 1900–1990s', in D. A. Farnie, T. Nakaoka, D. J. Jeremy, J. F. Wilson, and T. Abe, eds., *Region and Strategy in Britain and Japan: Business in Lancashire and Kansai, 1890–1990*, Routledge, London, 2000: 78–114.
25. Scott, *Triumph of the South*.
26. M. Granovetter, 'Problems of Explanation in Economic Sociology', in N. Nohria and R. Eccles, eds., *Networks and Organizations: Structure, Form and Action*, Harvard University Press, Cambridge, MA, 1992: 5.
27. M. Piore and C. Sabel, *The Second Industrial Divide: Possibilities for Prosperity*, Basic Books, New York 1984; C. Sabel and J. Zeitlin, 'Historical Alternatives to Mass Production: Politics, Markets and Technology in Nineteenth-century Industrialization', *Past and Present*, 108, 1985: 133–76; U. Staber, N. Schaefer, and B. Sharma, eds., *Business Networks: Prospects for Regional Development*, de Gruyter, Berlin 1996.
28. M. E. Porter and C. H. M. Ketels, *UK Competitiveness: Moving to the Next Stage*, Department of Trade and Industry, London, 2003.
29. Porter and Ketels, *UK Competitiveness*: 27.
30. N. Tiratsoo and J. Tomlinson, *The Porter Report on British Productivity*, EBK Working Paper, 2004/1, 2004.

31. Tiratsoo and Tomlinson, *The Porter Report*, 8.
32. Tiratsoo and Tomlinson, *The Porter Report*. J. Tomlinson, 'The Labour Party and the Capitalist Firm, c.1950–1970', *Historical Journal*, 47, 2004: 685–708.
33. G. Hedlund, 'The Hyper Modern MNC – A Heterarchy?', *Human Resource Management*, 25, 1986: 9–35.
34. Wilson and Popp, *Industrial Clusters and Regional Business Networks in England*.
35. N. A. Phelps, 'Collaborative Buyer-Supplier Relations and the Formation of Centralised Networks', *Geoform*, 27, 1996: 395.
36. P. Cooke and K. Morgan, *The Associational Economy: Firms, Regions and Innovation*, Oxford University Press, Oxford, 1998.
37. C. Bartlett and S. Ghoshal, *Managing Across Borders: The Transnational Solution*, Cambrdige, MA: Harvard University Press, 1989; J. H. Dunning, *The Globalization of Business: The Challenge of the 1990s*, Routledge, London, 1993; E. Ferlie and A. M. Pettigrew, 'Managing through Networks: Some Issues and Implications for the NHS', *British Journal of Management*, 7, 1996: s81–s99.
38. Cooke and Morgan, *The Associational Economy*, 53–5.
39. A. M. Pettigrew and E. Fenton eds., *The Innovating Organization*, Sage, London, 2000.
40. S. Roper and N. Hewitt-Dundas, *Business Innovation in Ireland – Lessons for Managers*, Oak Tree Press, Dublin 1998: 21.
41. Roper and Hewitt-Dundas, *Business Innovation in Ireland*: 27–8.
42. Pettigrew and Fenton, *The Innovating Organization*.
43. Pettigrew and Fenton, *The Innovating Organization*: 295–6.

4

Elites, Entrepreneurs, and British Business in the Twentieth Century

Youssef Cassis

Terry Gourvish's writing on business elites and entrepreneurs is a good starting point for reflecting on this vexed issue of British economic and business history. In 1973, Terry Gourvish published 'A British Business Elite: The Chief Executive Managers of the Railway Industry, 1850–1922' in *Business History Review*.[1] It was an important contribution, especially as few collective biographies of business leaders had been published in Britain.[2] Moreover, in connection with the 'relative decline' debate, two aspects of this article stand out as new and breaking with the then dominant view in British business history: first, it did not deal with industrialists; and second, its assessment was rather positive.[3] Gourvish's later contributions to the subject have dealt mainly with entrepreneurs – a topic returning to the fore – and proved equally innovative, not least by taking into account a neglected and often dismissed group, the leaders of state enterprises in post-war Britain.[4]

In a nutshell, we have here the four main issues raised by any discussion of elites and entrepreneurs in British business in the twentieth century.[5] The first is the 'collective biography' (also termed sociological or prosopographical) approach – how much can we learn from it? The second has to do with industry, finance, and services and their respective share in the composition and performance of the British business elite. The third concerns entrepreneurs, understood in the narrow, Schumpeterian sense of creators and innovators. And the fourth is the long standing debate over business and entrepreneurial success or failure in Britain since the late nineteenth century.

This chapter seeks to address these four issues and is accordingly divided into four parts. The first part will provide some definitions of business elites and entrepreneurs and discuss the relationships existing between the two. The second part will assess the composition of the British business elite and its change in the course of the 20th century. The third part will consider the socio-professional characteristics of the British business elite. And the fourth part will revisit the debate about the success and failure of British entrepreneurs in the view of the changing fortunes of the British economy in the last twenty years.

ELITES AND ENTREPRENEURS

A simple and operational way of defining the business elite is to consider that it includes those who have reached a top position within the business world – individuals who, in Anthony Giddens's definition, 'occupy formally defined positions of authority'.[6] This in turn raises the question of what is a top position within the business world. The answer seems fairly straightforward for most of the twentieth century, as business has become dominated by large registered companies whose leaders can be easily identified.[7] The question of who are the individuals occupying a position of authority within a business enterprise could pose more problems. The obvious answer is that board members are in such a position. However, should non-executive directors be included? The answer is probably yes, though, depending on the type of study undertaken, a distinction could be made between the two categories – a distinction which, however, was not clearly established in earlier periods. New questions have arisen as business structures have become more complex. For example, should only main board members be considered as belonging to the business elite or should the definition be extended to directors of subsidiary companies? And what about senior managers outside the board of directors – a situation which was quite common in the first part of the twentieth century? At the opposite end of the scale, should a hierarchical division be introduced within the business elite, for example between chairman, vice chairman, director, and manager?

There are no obvious answers to these questions, which show that any definition of the business elite must contain an element of arbitrary choice. My own studies, for example, have included senior managers outside the board.[8] The focus on chairmen as an 'elite within the elite' can also be justified.[9] The same degree of arbitrariness applies to the selection of the companies whose leaders are considered to constitute the business elite: the top 50, 100, 200, 500, or 1,000? A few objective criteria can be applied, such as a minimum size, though only to a limited extent. What to do, for example, with highly influential but comparatively small companies, such as the merchant banks in the City of London during most of the twentieth century? Scholars have dealt with the matter in a pragmatic way, depending on the type of analysis undertaken.

In fact, there is to this day no comprehensive analysis of the British business elite in the twentieth century – in other words a study taking into account all senior executives of, say, the 100 largest companies at six or seven benchmark years spanning the entire period. This would prove a formidable task, with a database amounting to possibly 7,000 or 8,000 individuals on whom information would not always be easy to gather. As is common in social analysis, sampling has been the rule, though not, as would be expected, on a random basis. While primarily relying on size, companies have been selected according to varying criteria, for example, in order to facilitate comparisons between the City and industry,[10] or to capture big business in a comparative perspective.[11] Executives have usually been selected on the basis of their position within the company.[12] Other selections have been made on the basis of industries,[13] wealth,[14] or have been comprehensive but limited to a single benchmark year.[15]

A special mention must be made here of the *Dictionary of Business Biography* (DBB), the broadest inquiry undertaken so far in Britain.[16] The DBB contains 1,181 biographical notices of business people active from 1860 to 1980 drawn from all sectors of the British economy. Entries to the DBB have been selected on the basis of business achievement, a criterion which necessarily entails in part arbitrary choice. For example, the DBB clearly favours manufacturing industry at the expense of trade, banking, and finance.[17] As in any work of this type, questions can be raised about both inclusions and omissions. Nevertheless, despite inevitable shortcomings, the DBB has proved an invaluable research tool in business, economic, social, and political history. It also provides a unique sample for the long-term analysis of British business leaders, though only a limited number of studies have made a systematic use of the available data.[18] Another issue is raised by the very conception of the DBB. Does business achievement automatically lead to an elite position? The answer is no – not automatically, and this highlights the difference between business elites and entrepreneurs. The difference is mainly one of emphasis – an emphasis on the social context for the former, on the economic one for the latter. Social scientists have been primarily interested in issues related to wealth, status, and power when discussing elites in general and business elites in particular, in business achievement when discussing entrepreneurs.

While the notion of business elites accurately describes all individuals occupying a top position within the business world, whatever their ability, the same cannot be said of the far more elusive concept of entrepreneur. The entrepreneur is usually, and rightly, considered as the driving force of capitalism. But who exactly is he or she? Are there several entrepreneurs within a company or a single one? Can salaried managers be considered as entrepreneurs insofar as they are responsible for the allocation of resources, or should the label be reserved for the owners of capital who, in the last analysis run the risks involved by investment and expansion? Economic theories of the entrepreneur, whether Schumpeter's destructive creativity, Kirzner's arbitrage, or Casson's judgemental decision-making,[19] however useful in explaining the role of entrepreneurs, do not really help to answer these questions. There is no escaping the choice between two extremes: at one end an improbable hero, at the other a fairly ordinary executive entrusted with a certain degree of responsibility, in other words an impersonal member of the Chandlerian managerial hierarchy. The latter trend was undoubtedly dominant from the 1960s to the 1990s, when the Chandlerian synthesis was the dominant paradigm in business history. However, there has been a renewed interest in entrepreneurship and the individual entrepreneur in the last fifteen years, from both economists and historians.[20] As a result, entrepreneurs – somewhere in-between the two extremes – will hopefully come to be better identified within the broader business elite.

CONTINUITY AND CHANGE

How much has the socio-economic structure of the British business elite changed in the course of the twentieth century? Three points deserve some attention: sectoral distribution, ownership and control, and network of relationships.

At first sight, the change in the sectoral distribution of the British business elite seems quite clear and should reflect the decline of manufacturing industry and mineral extraction and the rise of finance and services which took place in the last quarter of the twentieth century.[21] Things were a little more complex at the level of big business. Broadly described, the trend shows that in the early twentieth century, manufacturing industry only formed a small part of big business, which was then dominated by transport and financial services. The share of manufacturing industry grew from the end of the First World War to the 1970s, before declining again, with utilities, distribution, and financial services coming to the fore in the closing decades of the century.

In 1905, 22 of the 50 (and the top ten) largest British companies, measured by market capitalization, were railway companies and another ten were banks. Altogether, transport, financial services, communications, and utilities companies made up 80 per cent of the country's largest companies.[22] Put another way, at the beginning of 1900, railways made up 49 per cent of the market capitalization of the London Stock Exchange, financials 17 per cent, and industrials 34 per cent.[23] The sectoral distribution was of course different in a group of top companies measured by employment rather than market capitalization. Thus, 91 of the 125 largest British employers in 1907 were 'goods-producing firms', as against 34 'services-producing firms'. However, services together employed 871,094 people as against 802,093 for industrials[24] – another indication of the weight of services, even when choosing a criterion clearly favouring labour intensive industries. In 1998, 38 of the top 100 UK companies were engaged in industry (including two in mining), as against 19 in finance, 17 in utilities, 11 in distribution, and 15 in other services (communication, media, transport, and others).[25] The overall distribution was thus not very different from that of the early twentieth century (taking into account 100 instead of 50 companies in 1905 would have increased the share of industrials close to the 1998 level). It is as if the privatized utilities had taken the place of railways and the demutualization of building societies had made up for banking concentration, in addition to the growth of distribution and other services.

Such parallels between two eras of globalization, however, should not conceal significant differences, which have implications for business elites. There have been changes in terms of size (from about 30,000 to more than 200,000 for the largest industrial employer) and ownership (which we will discuss below), but also in terms of location, with large companies increasingly based in London (the trend started in the 1920s, when several large companies moved their head office to the capital or, especially in the 'new' industries, settled from the start there. This process has not ceased since). And if the overall sectoral distribution displays some similarities, important changes took place within sectors, especially in manufacturing industry. Again, the turning point dates back to the middle decades of the twentieth century, from the 1930s to the 1950s, when the 'new' industries (electrical engineering, chemicals, motor cars, oil, rubber, aerospace) became the dominant force within big business. The industries of the 'third' industrial revolution (information technology, biotechnology), on the other hand, have not had the same impact, in the UK at any rate, and more generally in Europe, as opposed to the US.

Should prosopographical studies of business elites take greater account of the weight of finance and services in the early twentieth century?[26] The answer is not obvious. One problem comes from the railway companies which, in a small sample (50 or even 100 companies), are clearly over-represented, especially as, by the turn of the twentieth century, they had become increasingly regulated and assimilated into public services, and had thus drifted to the fringes of big business. Another problem comes from the criterion chosen to rank companies. Workforce favours manufacturing industry, in earlier periods far more than in later ones, but the measure is meaningful: large employers formed a significant part of big business in the early twentieth century. So corrections might be needed and the contours of the business elite redrawn, but only to a limited extent.

The same applies to the issue of ownership and control with, as a general trend, private firms increasingly giving way to public companies in the course of the twentieth century. There is no systematic study of the ownership of largest companies, but there are some clear pointers, for example the proportion of founders and inheritors amongst the chairmen and managing directors: the former decreased from 21 per cent for the generation active in 1907 to 4 per cent in 1989, the latter from 34 to 2 per cent.[27] Data is more precise for the late twentieth century and shows that less than 10 per cent of the top 100 industrial companies (8% in 1983, 4% in 1993) were under personal ownership.[28] An analysis of ownership based on a sample including a higher proportion of services would probably weaken the contrast between the beginning and the end of the century, as railway and finance companies were the first to experience a separation between ownership and control and, with very few exceptions, had become managerial companies before 1914.[29] Here again, more subtle differences should not be overlooked – *notables* (in other words individuals enjoying a fair amount of prestige in the world of business, society, or politics), who were the dominant figure amongst company directors, have been increasingly replaced by full time professionals since the 1960s.

Did *notables* hold more directorships than professionals? The issue of over-lapping directorships has never really caught the attention of British business historians. The field has mainly been developed by sociologists and political scientists, who have given it various labels, such as 'social network analysis' or the 'structural analysis of business'.[30] The analysis of interpersonal and inter-corporate relationships, whether in popular, political or academic form, really took off in the mid-1950s[31] and gained momentum in the following decades, with particular interest in the relationships between the City and industry on one hand,[32] and business and politics on the other.[33] Without ignoring these studies, historians have approached these issues from a different perspective. The main reason has probably to do with the nature of the relationships between finance and industry in Britain: interlock analysis appears better suited to comprehending universal banks, in principle closely linked to industrial companies, than deposit banks, usually seen as more distant from their industrial customers. Interlock analysis also has its limits, not least a risk of oversimplifying complex relationships. As a result, historians have used qualitative or other types of quantitative methods to understand the role of the banks in the British economy, the position of bankers and financiers within the business elites, and the interactions between business and politics.[34]

ECONOMY AND SOCIETY

One of the objects of the social history of business elites is to help to understand the economic achievements of entrepreneurs. It is not the only one: issues related to social mobility or political democracy might first spring to mind when considering the social origins, education, and social status of business leaders. But it is one of them and it provides an interesting link between the economic and the socio-political sides of the entrepreneur. We will examine the social side in this section and discuss its relationships with economic achievement in the following one.

The question of opportunities for upward mobility offered by business activities has long been answered, especially as far as the upper echelons of the business hierarchy – the business elite – are concerned. National as well as comparative studies have consistently shown that business leaders, in the nineteenth and even more in the twentieth century, were in their overwhelming majority (around 80%) recruited from the upper and upper middle classes – landowners, businessmen, senior civil servants, and professionals. Moreover, up to the generations active in the 1960s, more than half were themselves sons of businessmen – without, however, necessarily being inheritors in a family firm. The rise from bottom to top in one generation remained an exceptional phenomenon, while the 'new' industries offered a small window of opportunity for individuals from a middle and lower middle class background. Most inquiries undertaken since the 1960s have produced broadly similar results.[35]

Understandably, there has hardly been any new evidence or interpretation on the matter in the last ten to fifteen years – with one exception, the recruitment of British business leaders at end of the twentieth century. Studies published in the 1990s revealed a sharp increase in the proportion of business leaders originating from a working class and lower middle class background: 39 per cent for the generation active in 1989.[36] Given that the percentage remained far lower for France and Germany (respectively 9 and 6%) the question could be asked whether this reflected a profound transformation of British society – the results of the education reforms of the post-war Labour governments for the early part, and of the cultural transformation brought about by Thatcherism for the later part, of their careers – or should be attributed to erratic statistical results. Interestingly, an inquiry based on a generation of business leaders active a decade later has confirmed these results, with 25 per cent of the top 100 directors in 1998 coming from a lower middle and 11 per cent from a lower class background, a higher proportion than in France (respectively 19 and 4%).[37] What can be observed at this stage is that, on one hand business leaders have continued to be mainly recruited from the upper reaches of society, and on the other hand the possibility of reaching the top appears to have increased by about 10 to 15 per cent for individuals coming from a less privileged background.

With membership of the business elite being to such a large extent determined by social origins, the role of education must be put in perspective and discussed in terms of quality and adequacy of training rather than as a factor of social mobility. There has been a long standing debate about the education of the British business elites, centring around two main issues. One is the level of formal qualification attained by business leaders: has it been sufficiently high, especially in comparison with the country's main competitors? The other is the nature of the educational system, in particular the impact of the public schools and the two ancient universities, Oxford and Cambridge.

On the first count, there is clear evidence that throughout the twentieth century, British business leaders had a lower level of education than their German and French counterparts. However, the percentage of those with a university or other type of higher education grew consistently in the course of the century, from 35 per cent for the generation active in 1907 to 45 per cent in 1953, 59 per cent in 1972 and 64 per cent in 1989. By contrast, 72 per cent of the French business leaders active in 1907 had a higher education, with the percentage soon reaching 90 per cent and more; while Germany was in between, rising from over 50 per cent in the first part of the twentieth century to 75 per cent by the mid-1950s and nearly 90 per cent by the late 1980s.[38] Such differences have often been attributed to a persistent suspicion of higher education within British business circles. A more revealing explanation probably lies in the conditions of access to university education which, for all social classes, was more restricted in Britain than in France and Germany.[39] For a long time, education at a major public school mattered more, in terms of socio-professional status, than studying at a university. In addition, from the 1950s onwards, this low university intake was somewhat compensated by professional training, provided partly by the self-regulated professions, such as chartered accountants, which combined theoretical studies with practical experience and delivered their own diploma; and partly by technical colleges and engineering schools.[40]

As far as elite institutions are concerned, evidence shows that attendance at a major public school has been very uneven amongst members of the business elite, with a higher percentage for the leaders of the country's largest companies than for provincial *notables*, especially before 1914,[41] and with even bigger differences between the financial and the industrial elites.[42] However, percentages have increased overall and differences narrowed in the course of the century. As far as higher education is concerned, a majority of British business leaders who went on to university attended an elite establishment, namely Oxford or Cambridge: 43 per cent before 1914, 65 to 70 per cent from the 1920s to the 1970s,[43] though the percentage seems to have decreased in recent years.[44] Beyond these variations, a regular swing of the pendulum can be observed in the perspective from which elite institutions have been assessed, that is, their impact on British economic performance on one hand, and their role in the production and re-production of elites on the other.

One of the social aspects of education relates to the integration of business elites into the upper classes, an issue which has itself been linked to entrepreneurship – to what extent can the attributes, or the pursuit, of an upper class status be considered as detrimental to the 'entrepreneurial spirit'? If education at a major public school and one of the ancient universities is taken as a criterion of absorption into the upper classes, then, as we have just seen, a dividing line separated the City elite from the industrial elite before the First World War. Other indicators, especially social life and marriages, point to the merger of the City aristocracy with the landed aristocracy in the late nineteenth and early twentieth century, leading to the formation of a renewed elite – the embryo of what would become known as the Establishment.[45] The concept of 'gentlemanly capitalism' coined by Peter Cain and Tony Hopkins, while encapsulating, at an economic, social, and political level, most of the characteristics of this group, describes a wider section of British society, namely the financial sector and more generally the services industries based in the south-east.[46]

A major change started to take place in the 1920s, with the gradual integration of top industrialists into the social elite. Significantly, the proportion of public school educated heads of industrial companies rose from 18 per cent in 1907 to 37 per cent in 1929, and stabilized thereafter.[47] The financial world no doubt remained more solidly entrenched in the Establishment, but the demarcation was no longer between two monolithic blocks, finance and industry. It was rather between the 'business elite', in other words high finance (the 'big five' commercial banks and the leading merchant banks) and the leading London-based industrial companies on the one hand; and the lower echelons of the business world (provincial industry and lesser financial and commercial firms) on the other. The business elite became the core of the country's upper classes after 1945, and the pre-eminence enjoyed, as a group, by the leaders of the largest corporations – the dominant fraction of the dominant class, to use Bourdieu's terminology – has prevailed to this day over other possible internal cleavages.

SUCCESS AND FAILURE

In the end, and from a business history perspective, business elites are assessed in terms of success and failure – in other words, in terms of entrepreneurial achievement. In the case of the British business elite in the twentieth century, failure has been much more debated than success, especially during the periods of perceived 'relative decline' of the British economy, the pre-1914 years and the three or four decades following the Second World War.

Family origins, education, and social status have all been linked with entrepreneurial failure during the first period. The arguments are well known. As far as family origins are concerned, the persistence of the family firm has been considered as a cause of British industrial decline in the late Victorian and Edwardian ages. David Landes has accused third generation businessmen of amateurism, of having lost not only the founder's innovative and combative spirit, but also the will to enlarge and consolidate the firm, often found in the second generation.[48] Alfred Chandler couched the same arguments in slightly different terms, considering that 'personal capitalism' was the main cause for the late emergence of the 'new industries', the failure of the family firms being rooted in their inability to create the organizational capabilities required by the modern industrial enterprise.[49] Such arguments have today lost all currency. For one thing, the performance of family-run large firms does not appear to have been inferior to that of joint stock companies, whether in terms of size or innovative capacity, in Britain or elsewhere.[50] In Britain, they were actually dominant in industries where the country enjoyed a strong competitive advantage, such as consumer packaged goods, or finance.[51] And for another, 'family capitalism' was far from being a British peculiarity: on the contrary, in 1900 the divorce between ownership and control appear to have been more advanced in Britain than in the United States, the country traditionally seen as the seedbed of managerial capitalism.[52]

Similar comparative observations can be made about education. According to a deeply rooted tradition in the British historiography, public schools, with their primary objective of shaping a gentleman, caused devastating damage to British industry, while the two ancient universities reinforced prejudices against applied science and industry and thus left a gap in the training of future business leaders.[53] This interpretation has been rejected by historical research.[54] One of its major weaknesses is that it does not stand up to international comparisons. The study of classics, for example, was as dominant in French *lycées* and German *Gymnasien* as in English public schools; and the theoretical nature of university education was probably at its highest level in the French *grandes écoles* and not much lower in the German universities, including the *technische Hochschulen*, once they had been granted university status at the turn of the twentieth century.[55] But the public schools and Oxbridge have also been praised, and sometimes imitated abroad, for their unique capacity to train an elite, instil in their students an *esprit de corps* and prepare them to assume the role of leaders, whether in business, politics, and society.

Two aspects of the social status of the business elite have been seen as possible causes of entrepreneurial failure. The first is the divide between finance and industry. Bankers have been long criticized for neglecting British industry, but historical research has by now clearly established that manufacturing industry was provided with adequate funding.[56] At the same time, the enduring success of the City of London has been properly integrated, over the last twenty years or so, into British business history. The second is integration into the upper classes: buying an estate, marrying into the aristocracy, and moving into high society have all been seen as diversions from business purposes. Yet there is no evidence that these choices dampened energies and led to complacency in the business elite, where a sufficient pool of talent was available to replace individual defections. Social status should rather be viewed as an undeniable mark of business success and of a recognition of business values by society as a whole – and Britain scored very highly in this respect.

The emphasis has shifted from entrepreneurs to business organizations in discussions of the post-1945 period – in line with the Chandlerian approach to business history. Attention has been paid to the ownership, strategy and structure of the firm. In the 1960s and 1970s, Britain was found to be closer to the American model than any other European economy, in terms of company size, separation between ownership and control, or adoption of a multidivisional structure of organization.[57] This time, however, it seemed to play to Britain's disadvantage: there might have been plenty of Chandlerian large firms, but they were apparently poorly managed,[58] while a lack of high-performing small and medium-sized enterprises, comparable to the German *Mittelstand*, was now judged to be a weakness.[59]

With a higher proportion of business leaders attending university, greater attention has been paid to the disciplines in which business leaders were trained, in particular management.[60] In fact, management and business hardly played any role in the education of the European business elites for most of the twentieth century. A slight increase is noticeable for the generation active in the 1980s, not least in Britain, mainly as a result of a growing proportion of accountants who reached the top of large corporation.[61] However, this type of commercial and financial training has also been judged as potentially damaging to British industry, especially in the context of firms becoming increasingly governed by financial rather than industrial objectives. As for social status, the glamour of the financial world has revived the belief in a persistent anti-industrial spirit driving the country's best talents towards the City, politics, or the professions – a contributing factor to industrial and economic decline.

Post-war British entrepreneurs have not yet gone from 'damnation to redemption', unlike, in the judgement of an increasing proportion of scholars, their late Victorian and Edwardian predecessors. It is difficult to predict how long they will remain in purgatory. But with the revival of the British economy since the mid-1990s, a more positive view of British business, past and present, has been prevailing, though not always explicitly formulated. Slower economic growth in the pre-1914 and post-1945 years has tended to be explained by catch-up and convergence theories rather than entrepreneurial failure. The advent of the post-Chandler era in business history has heralded a new interest, on one hand, in the entrepreneur as an innovator and decision maker, and on the other in corporate governance and the legal and institutional framework of business activity, two areas in which Britain appears in a favourable light at the dawn of the twenty-first century, at least within a European context. However, this latest trend will not dispense with the need for a proper assessment of the entrepreneurial achievements of the British business elite in the twentieth century, an assessment which remains to be done.[62] Achievement rather than failure should be the starting point of a research which can only bear fruit if undertaken from a European comparative perspective and using a methodology linking quantitative measures of business performance with an institutional history of the firm and a social history of its leaders. Terry Gourvish has been involved, with myself and a group of European scholars, in a research project on the performance of European business in the twentieth century, aiming specifically at this. Its impending completion will hopefully further advance the debate on business elites, entrepreneurs, and British business in the twentieth century.[63]

NOTES

1. T. Gourvish, 'A British Business Elite: The Chief Executive Managers of the Railway Industry, 1850–1922' *Business History Review*, 47, 3, Autumn 1973: 289–316. A revised version of this article was published in French a few years later in M. Levy-Leboyer, ed., *Le patronat de la seconde industrialisation*, Paris, 1979.
2. Charlotte Erickson pioneered this field with *British Industrialists: Steel and Hosiery, 1850–1950*, Cambridge, 1959.
3. The article, in particular, found no evidence on what was then seen as two major weaknesses in British business in the late nineteenth and early twentieth century: the group was able to bridge the gap separating the salaried employee from the great capitalist, and railway companies were efficient and progressive in their choice of senior managers.
4. T. Gourvish, 'The Rise (and Fall?) of State Owned Enterprises', in T. Gourvish and A. O'Day, eds., *Britain Since 1945*, Basingstoke, 1991; *British Railways 1948–73: A Business History*, Cambridge, 1986; and *British Rail 1974–97: From Integration to Privatisation*, Oxford, 2002.
5. See Y. Cassis, ed., *Business Elites*, Aldershot, 1999.
6. A. Giddens, 'Elites in the British Class Structure', in P. Stanworth and A. Giddens, eds., *Elites and Power in British Society*, Cambridge, 1974: 4.
7. For earlier periods, business leaders – another way of calling business elites – had to be identified through indicators, such as wealth and status, which are easier to apply at regional than at national level. A good example related to Germany is provided by W.E. Mosse, *Jews in the German Economy: The German-Jewish Economic Elite, 1820–1935*, Oxford, 1987.

8. Y. Cassis, *City Bankers, 1890–1914*, Cambridge, 1994; and *Big Business. The European Experience in the Twentieth Century*, Oxford, 1994.

9. P. Stanworth and A. Giddens, 'An economic Elite: A Demographic Profile of Company Chairmen', in Stanworth and Giddens, eds., *Elites and Power*: 81–101; Cassis, *Big Business*.

10. Stanworth and Giddens, 'An Economic Elite'.

11. Cassis, *Big Business*.

12. Chairmen in Stanworth and Giddens, 'An Economic Elite', chairmen and managing directors in Cassis, *Big Business*. Note, however, that Maurice Lévy-Leboyer picked the first, sixth, eleventh, and so on, in the alphabetically ordered list of all company directors included in his study 'Le patronat français, 1912–73' in M. Lévy-Leboyer, dir., *Le patronat de la seconde industrialisation*, Paris, 1979: 137–88.

13. Erickson, *British Industrialists*; Gourvish, 'A British Business Elite'; Cassis, *City Bankers*.

14. W.D. Rubinstein, *Men of Property: The Very Wealthy in Britain Since the Industrial Revolution*, London, 1981.

15. M. Maclean, C. Harvey and J. Press, *Business Elites and Corporate Governance in France and the UK*, Houdmills, Basingstoke, 2006.

16. D.J. Jeremy, ed., *Dictionary of Business Biography*, 5 vols., London, 1984–6.

17. See, for example, W.D. Rubinstein, 'Wealth Making in the Late Nineteenth and Early Twentieth Centuries: A Response', *Business History*, 42, 2, 2000: 141–54; and T. Nicholas, 'Wealth Making in Nineteenth- and Early Twentieth-Century Britain: The Rubinstein Hypothesis Revisited' *Business History*, 42, 2, 2000: 155–68.

18. See in particular the first overview by D.J. Jeremy, 'Anatomy of the British Business Elite, 1860–1980', *Business History*, 26, 1, 1984: 3–23; and the more recent analyses of T. Nicholas, 'Businessmen and Land Ownership in the Late Nineteenth Century', *Economic History Review*, 52, 1, 1999: 27–44, 'Wealth Making in Nineteenth- and Early Twentieth-Century Britain: Industry v. Commerce and Finance', *Business History*, 41, 1, 1999: 16–36, 'Clogs to Clogs in Three Generations? Explaining Entrepreneurial Performance in Britain since 1850', *Journal of Economic History*, 59, 3, 1999: 688–713.

19. J. Schumpeter, *The Theory of Economic Development*, Cambridge, MA, 1911; M. Kirzner, *Competition and Entrepreneurship*, Chicago, 1973; M. Casson, *The Entrepreneur: An Economic Theory*, Oxford, 1991.

20. See Y. Cassis and I. P. Minoglou ed., *Entrepreneurship in Theory and History*, Houdmills, Basingstoke, 2005.

21. Employment dropped from 32.1 per cent in 1911 (and 34.9 per cent in 1950) to 20.1 per cent in 1990 in manufacturing, and rose from 20.2 per cent in 1911 (and 19.5 per cent in 1950) to 37.5 per cent in 1990 in finance and services. See S. Broadberry, 'How Did the United States and Germany Overtake Britain? A Sectoral Analysis of Comparative Productivity Levels, 1870–1990', *Journal of Economic History*, 58, 2, 1998: 385.

22. P. Wardley, 'The Anatomy of Big Business: Aspects of Corporate Development in the Twentieth Century', *Business History*, 33, 2, 1991: 268–96.

23. L. Hannah, 'The "Divorce" of Ownership from Control from 1900 Onwards: Re-Calibrating Imagined Global Trends', *Business History*, 49, 4, 2007: 404–38.

24. P. Wardley, 'The Emergence of Big Business: The Largest Corporate Employers of Labour in the United Kingdom, Germany and the United States c. 1907', *Business History*, 41, 4, 1999: 88–116.

25. Percentage calculated from the Appendix A.2.2 in Maclean, Harvey and Press, *Business Elites and Corporate Governance*: 272–4. The list of the top 100 UK companies was

established by a using a composite measure developed by the authors and including capital employed, turnover, profit before tax, and number of employees, as each taken separately would have favoured a specific sector.

26. Manufacturing industry, for example, accounted for 54 per cent of entries (A-C subjects) in the DBB, as against 10 per cent for finance and 36 per cent for 'other', with little variation between generational cohorts; see Jeremy, 'Anatomy': 4. In my own sample for 1907, which excluded railway companies, manufacturing industry made up 63 per cent of the total, finance and services 31 per cent, and colonial companies 6 per cent (Cassis, *Big Business*), and yet several reviewers pointed out that, unlike previous studies, my analysis offered a new perspective on big business by adding the tertiary sector to manufacturing industry.

27. Cassis, *Big Business*: 126, 146. The DBB shows a stronger resilience of the family firm, with the percentage of founders decreasing from 49 per cent for the generation born before 1839 to 15 per cent for that born between 1900 and 1920, and that of inheritors actually increasing from 38 to 39 per cent; see Jeremy, 'Anatomy': 6. The difference is most probably due to the longer time span covered by the DBB, which includes the second half of the nineteenth century, and to the selection criteria.

28. R. Whittington and M. Mayer, *The European Corporation: Strategy, Structure and Social Science*, Oxford, 2000: 94.

29. Gourvish, 'A British Business Elite': Cassis, *City Bankers*.

30. See for example, M.S. Mizruchi and M. Schwartz, eds., *Intercorporate Relations: The Structural Analysis of Business*, Cambridge, 1987.

31. See in particular S. Aaronovitch, *Monopoly. A Study of British Monopoly Capitalism*, London, 1955, and *The Ruling Class: A Study of British Finance Capital*, London, 1961, which analyse British big business from a Marxist-Leninist point of view relying partly on interlocking directorships. See also T. Lupton and C. Shirley Wilson, 'The Social Background and Connections of "Top Decision Makers"', *The Manchester School*, 1959, the first socio-political analysis of the City of London. It was related to the Bank Rate Tribunal of 1957, which investigated whether there was any truth in the allegations that information about the raising of Bank Rate was improperly disclosed.

32. See for example R. Whitley, 'The City and Industry: The Directors of Large Companies, their Characteristics and Connections', in Stanworth and Giddens, eds., *Elites and Power*: 65–80. Whitley concluded that the City and Industry were in fact very close, a view prevailing in the 1960s and 1970s.

33. See especially M. Useem, *The Inner Circle. Large Corporations and the Rise of Business Political Activity in the US and the UK*, Oxford, 1984; and J. Scott, *Corporations, Classes and Capitalism*, London, 1979; and *Corporate Business and Capitalist Classes*, Oxford, 1997.

34. There is a vast literature on all these subjects. The most recent titles include M. Collins and M. Baker, *Commercial Banks and Industrial Finance in England and Wales, 1860–1913*, Oxford, 2003; F. Carnevali, *Europe's Advantage. Banks and Small Firms in Britain, France, Germany and Italy since 1918*, Oxford, 2005; R. Michie and P. Williamson (eds.), *The British Government and the City of London in the Twentieth Century*, Cambridge, 2004.

35. See Stanworth and Giddens, 'An Economic Elite'; Jeremy, 'Anatomy'; Cassis, *Big Business* for national studies covering all sectors. For comparative data see H. Kaelble, 'Long-Term Changes in the Recruitment of Business Elites: Germany compared to the U.S., Great Britain and France since the Industrial Revolution', *Journal of Social*

History, 13, 3, 1980. The most important articles in English are gathered in Cassis (ed.), *Business Elites*.

36. Cassis, *Big Business*; 124. The result might have been distorted by a particularly high number of cases without information, but 24 per cent of all cases remain a very high percentage. See also L. Hannah, 'Human Capital Flows and Business Efficiency', in K. Bradley (ed.), *Human Resource Management: People and Performance*, Aldershot, 1992.

37. Maclean, Harvey and Press, *Business Elites*: p. 91. Lower middle class has been defined as 'a middling income and comfortable lifestyle. Some evidence of advantages resulting from economic and cultural capital', and lower class as 'a family with a modest or low income. Little evidence of advantages resulting from family possession of significant amounts of capital of any kind' (p. 266).

38. Cassis, *Big Business*: 133.

39. F. Ringer, *Education and Society in Modern Europe*, Bloomington, Ind., 1979: 230.

40. See M. Sanderson, *The Universities and British Industry 1850–1970*, London, 1972.

41. 27.3 per cent for the chairmen and managing directors of the largest companies active in 1907 (Cassis, *Big Business*: 199), as against 19.6 per cent of provincial businessmen from Birmingham, Bristol and Manchester (H. Berghoff, 'Public Schools and the Decline of the British Economy, 1870–1914', *Past and Present*: 129, 1990).

42. 74 per cent of the members of the banking community between 1890 and 1914 attended a public school (Cassis, *City Bankers*) compared with 31 per cent of the steel industrialists active between 1905 and 1925 (Erickson, *British Industrialists*).

43. Cassis, *Big Business*: 137. See also Stanworth and Giddens, 'An Economic Elite'.

44. Maclean, Harvey and Press, *Business Elites*: 117–18.

45. See Cassis, *City Bankers*.

46. P. J. Cain and A. G. Hopkins, *British Imperialism: Innovation and Expansion 1688–1914*, London, 1993; and *British Imperialism: Crisis and Deconstruction 1914–1990*, London, 1993.

47. Cassis, *Big Business*: 217.

48. D. Landes, *The Unbound Prometheus*, Cambridge, 1969.

49. A. D. Chandler, *Scale and Scope*, Cambridge, MA, 1991.

50. See A. Colli, *The History of Family Business 1850–2000*, Cambridge, 2003.

51. See Cassis, *Big Business*: 128–32.

52. See Hannah, 'The "Divorce" of Ownership from Control'.

53. The best-known exponent of this thesis is M. Wiener, *English Culture and the Decline of the Industrial Spirit*, Cambridge, 1981.

54. See in particular Berghoff, 'Public schools'; and W. D. Rubinstein, *Capitalism, Culture and Decline in Britain, 1750–1990*, London, 1993.

55. Penetrating comparisons between Britain and Germany can be found in S. Pollard, *Britain's Prime and Britain's Decline: The British Economy 1870–1914*, London, 1989. See also Ringer, *Education and Society*.

56. There is a vast literature on the relationships between banks and industry. See Collins and Baker, *Commercial Banks and Industrial Finance* for the most recent discussion of the issue.

57. See D. F. Channon, *The Strategy and Structure of British Enterprise*, London, 1973; L. Hannah, *The Rise of the Corporate Economy*, London, 1976.

58. G. Jones, 'Great Britain: Big Business, Management, and Competitiveness in Twentieth Century Britain', in A. D. Chandler, F. Amatori and T. Hikino, eds. *Big Business and the Wealth of Nations*, Cambridge, 1997; S. Toms and M. Wright, 'Corporate

Governance, Strategy and Structure in British Business History, 1950–2000', *Business History*, 44, 3.

59. P. Hirst and J. Zeitlin, eds., *Reversing Industrial Decline*, Oxford, 1988.
60. T. Gourvish and N. Tiratsoo, eds., *Missionaries and Managers: American Influences on European Management Education, 1945–1960*, Manchester, 1998.
61. Cassis, *Bug Business*: 138–9.
62. Tom Nicholas, 'Clogs to Clogs in Three Generations?', has recently proposed a new method to test cultural explanations of entrepreneurial performance, measuring the latter by lifetime wealth accumulation. However, the poor reliability of the data casts doubts on the results.
63. For a presentation and some preliminary results of the project, see C. Brautaset, ed., 'Essays in European Business Performance in the 20th Century', Business History Unit Occasional Paper 2005, No 1, Business History Unit, London School of Economics and Political Science.

5

Invisible Entrepreneurs?

Women and Business in Twentieth Century Britain

Katrina Honeyman

Men and women have interacted in business for centuries: within and outside markets and firms; as producers and consumers; as partners and competitors. Yet, business is seen as a male activity: it is driven by male determinants of what constitutes success; and this male perspective is confirmed by a male-dominated business history. There is no doubt that women have been more important to British business than is suggested by the historical record. This chapter will both identify the deficiencies of existing business history in dealing with the gender dimension of enterprise and suggest ways to remedy the situation. Its focus will be on women's business in the second half of the twentieth century for two reasons: because of the higher levels of measured female entrepreneurial activity reached during that time; and because of growing research interest in that field, less from business historians than from sociologists and from students of management. The following sections will explore several assumptions: first that women's role in business has reflected their role in the wider labour market; second that women's participation in business, either as entrepreneur or manager, was different to men's; and thirdly that given the traditionally high representation of women in the service sector, opportunities for women in business have risen as the size and proportion of the service sector in the British economy increased in the twentieth century. It will provide quantitative evidence for women's entrepreneurial and management activity in the service industries; it will explore examples of female-specific businesses and reveal alternatives to the prioritizing of profit maximization. Finally, it will argue that by moving women out of the shadows and exploring their vital role in the culture of enterprise, business history will more accurately reflect the gendered reality of business.

THE BUSINESS OF WOMEN AND THE HISTORIAN
OF BUSINESS

The lens through which the history of business enterprise is viewed is a male one.[1] This, compounded by the longstanding barriers to women's entrepreneurial and managerial activities, creates the sense of a male-dominated business world.[2] The approach of British business historians, the majority of whom are male, is to consider what is most visible, namely large businesses run by men, rather than to question why a potentially important driver of business activity is either absent or under-represented.[3] Historians of women are more accustomed than male or mainstream historians to digging deep and imaginatively to retrieve their less-obvious history. It is possible that business historians' neglect of women's enterprise, or their failure to consider fully the significance of gender distinctions in business activity is the result of women's relative ineffectiveness in that sphere. Yet, while women may have been less visible than men in the world of business, and may have occupied different places, developed different styles of business, pursued different objectives, and generally failed to measure up to the male indicators of success, there is no doubt that businesswomen existed. The sluggish progress of gendered business history in Britain is not only the outcome of the failure of male business historians to contemplate gender issues, but is also the result of gender historians – be they male or female – failing to pursue their concerns within business history. It is inconceivable that business historians will continue to justify their neglect of women's businesses or female entre-preneurship, as these become increasingly visible in the economic and commer-cial landscape.

Despite the longstanding and institutional gender blindness of the discipline, it is nevertheless surprising that business historians have neglected the contribu-tion made by women to British enterprise and economic expansion during the twentieth century. Not only were large and small female-run businesses and women's participation in family businesses of growing significance during this time, but the discipline of business history was, at least for the past two or three decades of the century, deemed to be departing from its narrow focus on the masculine world of big business and embracing a range of methodological approaches. Recent explorations of the business history literature, for example, suggest that the discipline and its practitioners are becoming more theoretically open and eclectic in approach. Business history's 'strength in depth';[4] and the 'endless novelty' of its research 'suggests an optimistic future for the discipline'.[5] Despite such alleged liveliness and promise, British business historians have been unenthusiastic in their exploration of the contribution of women to busi-ness activity; a weakness identified by scholars in the more gender-inclusive field of American business history.[6] There should be, as Mansel Blackford, for example, had argued, 'more of an effort to move in new directions ... [espe-cially] ... the role of gender and race ... in business development'.[7]

WOMEN'S EMPLOYMENT AND SELF-EMPLOYMENT IN THE TWENTIETH CENTURY

Female entrepreneurship was by no means new to this period, but business historians have written disappointingly little on the early history of the subject. Nevertheless, scholars of other disciplines, mainly women's history, have produced valuable research which demonstrates the capacity of women to sustain independent enterprises, to develop managerial skills, to contribute to family businesses, and to invest in commercial ventures throughout the period from the late seventeenth to the early twentieth centuries.[8] Much of this work emphasizes the particular business sectors in which women were concentrated and the distinctiveness of their business style. To some extent this theme has permeated more recent work on women's entrepreneurial activity. There is no doubt that after the Second World War, women gained a stronger place for themselves within the labour market and, in due course, in the area of self-employment and small business.

The twentieth century witnessed significant changes in the socio-economic position of women, who also benefited from progress towards greater legal and political equality. The gendering of employment and the labour market which had restricted women's access to paid work, and disadvantaged their position in the workplace from the early nineteenth century, showed some sign of abating.[9] During the two World Wars women had demonstrated a capacity to perform a range of tasks, including those previously identified as skilled male work, and shown a desire to gain more equal access to work. Although many such changes were temporary, women's wider engagement in the labour market encouraged more open perceptions of women's position in society. Despite the introduction of the welfare state which privileged traditional gender roles and family structure, female participation rates began to rise substantially from the 1950s. Employment opportunities for women were enhanced during the second half of the twentieth century by periods of economic expansion and 'full' employment and by structural changes in the economy, which together improved the employment prospects of both men and women. Most importantly, the growth of service-sector activity as the British economy matured, created a demand for labour which drew unprecedented numbers of women into work. A large proportion of these were married women entering part-time employment.[10]

The association of women with the service sector in the twentieth century continued a trend established many decades earlier. Occupational censuses indicate that women accounted for about 70 per cent of service-sector workers – mainly as domestic servants – between 1841 and 1911. During the inter-war period, both the scale and diversity of service-sector employment increased. Women rejected domestic service choosing instead jobs in retailing, clerical and financial work, and 'entertainment'.[11] The most dramatic change in women's labour market position, as in their self-employment and other business activity,

Table 5.1. Service employment by gender, UK, 1956–97 (percentages)

Date	Female	Male	Total*
1956	60.0	39.3	46.3
1959	62.0	39.9	47.4
1962	62.9	40.4	48.2
1965	64.2	40.5	48.9
1968	67.0	42.6	51.3
1971	69.1	43.9	53.1
1974	71.0	45.0	55.0
1977	74.1	47.0	57.7
1980	76.5	48.7	59.9
1983	79.9	52.8	64.0
1986	80.0	51.5	63.7
1989	81.4	52.7	65.1
1992	82.8	55.6	67.8
1995	84.8	58.9	70.5
1997	85.8	59.4	71.3

*Service employment as a proportion of all employment.

Source: OECD, *Labour Force Statistics*, 1998.

occurred after the Second World War. The expansion of the service sector from the 1950s included further growth in clerical and retail activity as well as significant expansion in the areas of leisure and tourism; finance and legal; and personal care. The most rapidly growing areas of the economy were located in services; and the work of women played a key role in this. By the end of the twentieth century, as Table 5.1 indicates, 86 per cent of employed women and 60 per cent of employed men worked in the service sector.[12] Table 5.2 indicates the gender distribution of service-sector employees according to employment group.

Women had accounted for about 30 per cent of all workers through most of the nineteenth and early twentieth centuries. Between 1950 and 2000, this proportion rose steadily to 50 per cent, the largest absolute rise in the female activity rate taking place among married women.[13] But most of the increase in female employment especially in the service sector was in part-time rather than full-time work, and the most recent figures suggest that 45 per cent of all female workers are part-timers.[14] Generally, women also tend to be less valued than men in both pay and status of their employment, being particularly disadvantaged at the higher managerial levels. But although labour market segmentation persists, structural changes within the British economy, especially the expansion of service-sector employment, and its more recent diversification, can be seen to have offered women greater opportunities for work and for self-employment.

It can be argued that the growth of women's labour force participation generated new possibilities for women beyond the workforce.[15] Thus, as more women engaged in business as workers, and therefore acquired relevant experience, so more women found opportunities for self-employment. As will be discussed below self-employment was an option some women took when they

Table 5.2. Employees in service industry group by gender, UK, 1984–98, thousands (percentages)

Date	D. H. R women	Men	B. F. I women	Men	PA. E. H women	Men	Other services women	Men	Total services women	Men
1984	2,303	1,718	1,057	1,117	3,086	1,751	590	498	7,299	6,116
	(57)	(43)	(49)	(51)	(64)	(36)	(54)	(46)	(54)	(46)
1998	2,520	2,131	1,611	1,735	4,313	1,917	670	560	9,520	7,476
	(54)	(46)	(48)	(52)	(69)	(31)	(54)	(46)	(56)	(44)

Notes: D, H, R: Distribution, Hotels, and Restaurants; B, F, I: Banking, Finance, and Insurance; PA, E, H: Public administration, Education, and Health.

Source: Office of National Statistics, *Labour Force Survey, Historical Supplement*, Spring Quarters, 1984–98.

felt constrained by their opportunities at work. It has also been argued that there was something specific about women's association with service-sector activity; and the expansion of the sector was associated both with more employment opportunities and more business opportunities, particularly for women.

In the latter part of the twentieth century, the correlation between women's employment and self-employment was particularly pronounced mainly because women were more likely to choose the area of their business on the basis of their employment or other experience. Research has also suggested that female entrepreneurs may seek out business areas with low technical and financial barriers to entry, and in which managerial requirements are not central to success or failure; 'thus the choice of business can be seen in terms of high motivation to immediate independence tempered by economic rationality, rather than a conscious desire to operate "female-type" businesses'.[16] Nevertheless, although women's enterprise continues to be distributed through the economy, the overwhelming majority of it, as measured either by female self-employment or by the well-known, large, and successful businesses, is increasingly located in the service sector.[17] Today as a century ago, successful women's businesses are mainly in publishing, public relations, entertainment, and retailing.[18]

In much of the discussion below, it is argued that for both men and women, self-employment serves as a proxy for small business ownership. A large proportion of business enterprise of both men and women consists of 'self-employment', a trend that is likely to continue in the context of the 'new economy', and the expansion of internet opportunities. Data on self-employment are more accessible than those on other forms of business. Such a category of activity has accounted for the bulk of the expansion in female enterprise over the past thirty years. It has been suggested that the growth of women's business has created a need for new definitions of self-employment and a more prominent inclusion of this category in business histories.[19] In the meantime, however, it is necessary to decide how representative 'self-employment' is of business activity generally. According to David Blanchflower, 'self-employment is the simplest kind of entrepreneurship';[20] and for Ferry de Goey, small and medium enterprises (SMEs) and self-employment are closely related, as most owners of small enterprises are self-employed.[21] De Goey also argues that in the wake of the expansion of self-employment especially from 1970 onwards, 'the self-employed became the new hero'; and especially notable were 'new groups of self-employed . . . such as women entrepreneurs and ethnic entrepreneurs'.[22]

Existing data confirm the growing extent of small enterprise in the last decades of the twentieth century. The number of small businesses in the UK rose from 1.3 million in 1980[23] to 3.7 million in 1999.[24] Yet, specific information on the gender of business ownership is rarely provided not least because 'the difficulties inherent in separating ownership from managerial contributions and control coupled with the prevalence of jointly owned family firms ensure that the complexities of business ownership are not easily reduced to reveal the gender of a single or multiple owners'.[25] The *Labour Force Survey* (*LFS*), which provides information on self-employment – but not other forms of small business – is one of the few data sets which are broken down by sex. By applying the gender ratio (roughly 75:25) found in the LFS, to the small- and medium-sized business enterprise figures provided by the Department of Trade and Industry (DTI), it is possible to estimate the number and proportion of small-business owners by gender. Such a calculation suggests that the number of women-owned businesses in the UK approached 1 million by the end of the twentieth century. Even so, it still underestimates women's full business contribution, omitting as it does the 'entrepreneurial efforts dedicated to family businesses and masked by co-ownership'.[26]

Since the mid-1950s, there has been a doubling in the rate of self-employment, much of the expansion taking place during the early 1980s, when the number of self-employed women grew more rapidly than the male equivalent.[27] Through the 1980s, as Table 5.3 shows, there was a rise in the proportion of female self-employed in the female-active population from 4.3 to 8.7 per cent, and in the percentage of female self-employed in the total self-employed population from 20 to 25. In the early 1990s, the number of self-employed women increased slightly as that of male self-employed fell. By 1993, there were 3.2 million self-employed people – 13 per cent of the total population – and in the previous decade, female self-employment increased 2.5 times while the male equivalent increased by 82 per cent.[28] Such a rise can be attributed both to structural shifts in the economy which favoured female employment but also to limited chances for promotion or mobility offered by such work. Frustrations emanating from constraints on career development may have encouraged women to seek gains through self-employment.

Women's enterprise has been narrowly based. In 1984, for example, 84 per cent of self-employed women were located in the service sector, of which almost half were active in the Distribution, Hotels, and Restaurant group. By 1998, 90 per cent of self-employed women were active in the service sector, and the distribution of these among the component groups was more even. As Table 5.4 shows, much of the growth over the period was located in the public

Table 5.3. Female self-employed, UK, 1956–2001

Date	Self-employed as % of total active	Female self-employed as % of female active	Female self-employed as % of self-employed
1956	7.5	4.1	19
1961	7.2	3.9	19
1966	6.6	4.0	22
1971	8.4	4.6	20
1976	8.0	4.0	20
1981	8.9	4.3	20
1986	13.2	8.0	25
1991	14.7	8.7	24
1996	14.6	8.5	25
2001	12.2		25

Sources: Derived from OECD, *Labour Force Statistics*; ONS, *Labour Force Survey*.

Table 5.4. Self-employed in service industry group by gender, 1984–98, thousands (percentages)

Date	D, H, R women	Men	B, F, I women	Men	PA, E, H women	Men	Other services women	Men	Total services women	Men
1984	266	533	72	222	73	76	117	119	541	1,071
	(33)	(67)	(24)	(76)	(49)	(51)	(50)	(50)	(34)	(66)
1998	198	441	147	441	193	113	182	182	741	1,362
	(31)	(69)	(25)	(75)	(63)	(37)	(50)	(50)	(35)	(65)

Notes: D, H, R: Distribution, Hotels, and Restaurants; B, F, I: Banking, Finance, and Insurance; PA, E, H: Public administration, Education, and Health.

Source: Office of National Statistics, Labour Force Survey, Historical Supplement, Spring Quarters, 1984–98.

administration, education, and health group. Over the same period, the proportion of self-employed men in the service sector rose from 54 per cent in 1986 to 56 per cent in 1998.[29]

In any event, women have accounted for a substantial proportion of the rise in self-employment since 1981. At least in terms of self-employment, British women's contribution to the business sector has grown both absolutely, and relative to men. Their relative position is probably among the best in Europe, but still way behind the US where 38 per cent of small businesses are owned and run by women. According to Alan Johnson, Speaking Trade and Industry Secretary in November 2006, if British women were as entrepreneurial as in the US, the UK would have '750,000 more businesses'.[30]

WOMEN AND BUSINESS: AN UNEVEN PLAYING FIELD?

Women gained greater visibility in business through the twentieth century and especially after the Second World War, yet the business environment remained unfavourable to women. Their contribution was inadequately recognized by both their male contemporaries and by scholars, possibly because despite the gains achieved, women are still a minority among business owners, and also because their style is sometimes different from the male approach. As Lina Gálvez Muñoz has argued, 'female entrepreneurship is seldom a Schumpeterian one'.[31] Measured against the male yardstick of success, women may be seen as deficient.

This section considers the reasons why, despite gender convergence in many aspects of socio-economic existence, and despite their greater involvement in business, women are still less likely than men to choose entrepreneurship as a career; more likely to operate in a smaller way than men; and more likely to fail. It is argued that women were sometimes motivated to enter self-employment or begin their own business as an escape from inadequate opportunities in the workplace. Although women have become numerically equal in the labour market, they have yet to achieve equality of opportunity at the managerial level. Men outnumber women as managers, executives, and company directors. It is such inequity as well as unequal pay and working conditions which has led to the complaint of a glass ceiling.[32]

Women account for 50 per cent of employees but only 25 per cent of self-employed, and an even lower proportion of all business proprietors. Thus, despite gains made in closing the gender gap and in reducing inequalities in social relations of gender, differential access to business success remains. So rather than being surprised that women exist at all within the business sector, we should be asking why there are so few of them. Especially as in current context, British government agencies are urging 'all sectors of the population . . . to consider self-employment'.[33]

Much of the recent research – conducted by sociologists and management theorists (rather than business historians) has explored the motivations for women's entry into self-employment. The work of Epstein uses the concept of 'push and pull' to explain this movement, describing how women may be pulled into self-employment 'by the potential profit or pushed because of lack of alternative choice'.[34] Employment constraints range from unemployment or underemployment, through occupational segregation and restricted job choice, to the glass ceiling. Catherine Hakim attributes part of the growth in female self-employment to an expansion of flexible (i.e. part-time and temporary) working.[35] Sheila Allen and Carole Truman consider future progress and suggest that a breakdown in occupational segregation is necessary so that women's business is not just a product of the expansion of the service sector.[36] David Clutterbuck and Marion Devine implicitly refer to the glass ceiling question when they argue that women have increasingly high expectations but are often frustrated and therefore seek such alternative routes to success as entrepreneurship and self-employment.[37]

Carter et al. suggest that the recent research on the subject has identified differences between men and women in motivation, and that for many women – but few men – starting a business was seen as a means of breaking through the glass ceiling.[38] Marlow adds this to other constraints, interpreting the glass ceiling as a reflection of broader patriarchal forces: 'if women begin new, small firms because they feel thwarted as women in their careers', she suggests, 'if a woman's notion of business success differs from male counterparts because her ambitions are moulded by gender experience, and if women are utilizing self-employment as a solution to dual demands of domestic and waged labour, then the experience of self-employment is tainted by patriarchal expectations'. She concludes that it is necessary to understand the way in which gender affects the experience of self-employment in order to evaluate the 'experiences of self-employed women and the contribution made by their businesses'.[39]

Because women continue to be subordinated by patriarchal pressures in society, it could be argued, these will affect their experience of self-employment from initiation of the firm, to development of the enterprise, through to the manner of daily management challenges.[40] The influential work of Goffee and Scase, for example, took as its theme 'the assumption of women's subordination' and identified a range of difficulties, including sexism, lack of credibility, and tensions with other responsibilities.[41] Birley, however, is sceptical of this position and further anticipates that 'the profile of women entrepreneurs in the future will continue to match their changing situation, and move ever closer to that of their male colleagues'.[42] She argues that the differences between men and women in business are not marked except with respect to self-confidence.[43]

There are, however, a number of areas in which experience reflects gender differences. For example, women may be disadvantaged by differential access to capital, though scholars are not yet agreed whether it is more difficult for women to raise finance for initial and for longer-term requirements. It can be argued that, historically, women both owned less capital than men and enjoyed less freedom in their use of it. Although gender-specific legal constraints have long since disappeared, women remain less wealthy, on average, than men, mainly because of their lower lifetime earning potential. Women's borrowing capacity may thus be commensurately less, but not so little as to preclude business start-up. Nevertheless, research has tended to indicate gender differences in the way in which capital is accessed and employed in late twentieth century business. Birley's assessment that the female entrepreneur's access to capital does not differ from that of men[44] is not borne out by most recent scholarship including that of Susan Marlow who finds that women have more difficulty obtaining loans, a disadvantage compounded by not having access 'to the same levels of business advice as men'.[45] Schwarz found financial discrimination to be one of the 'greatest barriers to female success'.[46]

The real or perceived absence of full institutional support has driven a greater proportion of women than men to draw upon personal or familial sources of capital, and to seek areas where initial capital costs are low.[47] Whether or not women have 'credibility problems' when dealing with bankers, such quantitative evidence as exists demonstrates that 'women start in business with only one-third the amount of capital used by men'; and further, that men 'are more likely to use external financing for the on-going business' than are women.[48] Specifically, therefore, a number of factors converge to undermine businesswomen's financial position. Women may be 'disadvantaged in their ability to raise start up finance; guarantees required for external financing may be difficult given women's personal assets and credit track record; ongoing finance may be difficult for women to get because of difficulty in penetrating informal networks; relationships with bankers may be disadvantaged because of sexual stereotyping and discrimination'.[49]

It is possible that the part-time nature of some women's business is interpreted as lack of commitment by financial institutions, resulting in a greater chance of failure. Although for a combination of reasons women's businesses were more likely to be small, founded on their own capital, and expanding only gradually; research has found high failure rates among them. 'While since the mid 1980s women have continued to choose self-employment in increasing numbers, there has been a substantial increase in the failure rate of these firms to maintain a fairly constant percentage of self-employed women in the sector.'[50]

Aside from possible capital constraints, there may be other ways in which women were less well-equipped to enter the business world. It is argued, for example, that compared with men, 'when women enter self-employment they do so with fewer financial assets, less experience in management and under-resourced in terms of their human and social capital'[51] Women have less access to training and are less likely than men to invest in their human capital through seeking qualifications.

Traditionally, women were allocated primary responsibility for family and childcare, which limited their career options both in employment and in business. Although women are confined less by their domestic responsibilities than was once the case, these continue to shape women's participation in the public sphere. Paradoxically, perhaps, home and family can be seen to provide both constraint and impetus for female self-employment. For example, self-employment can offer flexibility for women with 'other responsibilities'.[52] Women-owned businesses are often constructed as a system of cooperative relationships, not least between work and family.[53] But while business may offer the means by which women with dependants can earn a living, such responsibilities may also limit the success. Women are less likely to sustain a focus on their business, and/or to operate on a part-time basis. Research on the part-time nature of women's business activity is limited, but activity of this type is almost certainly more common among women than men.

It is possible that women have been deterred from business activity by the shortage of role models. A number of high-profile successes are probably as well known as any individual businessman; but they are famous because they are exceptions. Among the long-standing successes are Anita Roddick (Body shop), Laura Ashley (Laura Ashley Home Furnishings), Ann Gloag (Stagecoach), Nicola Foulston (Brands Hatch Leisure); Sophie Mirman (Sock Shop), and Debbie Moore (Pineapple).[54] More recently, in the context of dot.com businesses and other knowledge-economy activity, high achieving women are among the new breed of business leader. They include Lopa Patel, voted Asian woman of the year in 2005, who founded redhotcurry.com, 'the only female-owned Asian website, entirely self-financed'; and Shaa Wasmund, the online entrepreneur, owner of Bright Station venture, who also helped to establish a venture-capital business designed to invest in social networking sites.[55]

NEW ECONOMY – NEW OPPORTUNITIES?

Just as the expansion of the service sector during the twentieth century, and especially since the Second World War, provided jobs and business opportunities taken up disproportionately by women, so the recent diversification of this sector into 'knowledge work' or the 'knowledge economy' offers both new forms of employment and potential areas for female entrepreneurial expansion.

It is possible that women face fewer barriers to entry to the current knowledge-based business opportunities, as these, so far, appear to be less gendered than previous openings. Sylvia Walby has argued that the new economy has implications for self-employment because of its association with flexible working in both time and place, and specifically because it introduces 'new contractualities', especially the freedom to be one's own boss. To support her argument, Walby has shown that much self-employment growth in the 1990s has been in groups that are consistent with the knowledge economy thesis, namely finance, real estate, community, social and personal services, and new media and cultural industries.[56]

That some activities in the knowledge economy might provide proportionately more opportunities for women than for men is indicated by the recent research of

Forson and Ozbilgin into 'dot.com' women entrepreneurs, which suggests that the internet, a subdivision of the hitherto male-dominated technology sector, appears to have attracted women. Technological developments permit new forms of flexible employment including home working, as well as home-based business. Both men and women can benefit from such possibilities, but the gains may be especially great for those women whose domestic responsibilities preclude operating in a rigid business structure. Furthermore, female entrepreneurs are likely to be particularly sensitive to the new and growing market for women's internet needs.[57] In this sector, women can be rewarded for creating networks and relationships (rather than the hierarchical structures to which men are instinctively drawn) which enhances e-commerce or online business. The conclusion of Forson and Ozbilgin's study, however, is that self-employment – even when successful – does not always provide the anticipated escape from patriarchal relations in paid work which, it is believed, drives many women into business.[58]

Indeed, despite the general convergence of gender roles and expectations reflected in the labour market – by no means all components of the new economy are gender neutral. As Susan Durbin has argued, 'the knowledge economy is ... divisive, producing "winners" and "losers" as it becomes the main source of wealth and inequalities'.[59] Knowledge-based economies are characterized by substantial reliance on new information technologies, not only for communication but also for the creation of new knowledge.[60] Karen Shire's research suggests that there is a greater concentration of women in the knowledge-intensive industries in Britain, correlating with part-time female labour. This indicates that the knowledge economy, while applying new techniques and offering profitable opportunities to some, also reaffirms elements of women's disadvantage.[61] Durbin's work on call centres, for instance, demonstrates that women have restricted access to embedded knowledge which 'is a function of the distribution of power and is gendered because women are poorly represented at the levels of the organisation at which this knowledge type is created'.[62] She concludes that

the higher orders of knowledge continue to be gendered and perpetuate the gendering of knowledge. Knowledge, the core product of the knowledge economy, is being combined and applied in organisations to create new gendered knowledge. ... women are 'losing out' because yet again, men have consolidated their positions of power where they control knowledge and management structures.[63]

So although women in the early twenty-first century as in the eighteenth and nineteenth centuries can be found in the dynamic sector of business, they continue to suffer from external constraints and prejudices; and their talents and abilities ignored or underplayed. Thus it appears that gender relations of society remain powerful irrespective of the form of economic activity.[64] Women's business activity may be more likely than men's to be small scale but this is surely no justification for ignoring what was clearly a sizeable proportion of total British business activity.[65] On the contrary, greater attention to such activity would clarify the heterogeneous nature of British business.

CONCLUSION

Where can business history go from here? First the discipline needs to overcome its antipathy to gender concerns. This may happen indirectly, for example, as interest in the SME and self-employment sectors becomes more prominent; or as concern with the family firm begins to recognize the gender of its participants; or an interest in the culture of business takes hold; or as the gendered nature of the external business context becomes recognized.[66] It is also possible that the gendering of business objectives and performance measures might offer insights in a relatively painless way. It has been suggested above that women may be less driven by profit, and that their desire for personal fulfilment and achievement, or their concern for social justice and ethical and environmental issues might also be important.[67] It would be interesting to discover if, as it appears, women have been and continue to be more active than men in businesses that are environmentally friendly, designed to promote global equality and development, and generally serve purposes other than simply profit maximizing.[68] Women in business and women's businesses have, in the past, been judged as exceptions to male indicators of success, rather than as 'part of the gendered history of economic life'.[69] Such issues relate to the culture of business; and each business may have a different 'culture' determined at least partly by the gender of its participants.[70] It is time to take greater account of these aspects.

There is clearly a gap between women's contribution to British business enterprise in the twentieth century and recognition of this, not only by business historians but by society more generally. Such research as has been conducted has tended to focus on the distinctive attributes of women's and men's entrepreneurial endeavours and their different motivations. Such adding of women to the historical investigation of British business activity constitutes an inevitable first stage in filling the gap, but it is not ultimately satisfactory. For example, the emphasis placed on women's participation in the service sector – as employees, as self-employed, and more specifically as business proprietors – has encouraged its analysis as a separate female sphere and implicitly as less important. It is true that some women are less driven by a single focus on profit maximization, but concern with the wider implications of their business does not weaken their entrepreneurial expertise nor does it undermine the success of the business. Business history, with its growing interest in a broad range of methodologies and theories, will benefit from incorporating a gender analysis into its approach. The neglect of women and lessons learned from recognizing this may also apply to the question of race and ethnicity. Paying greater attention to gender and ethnicity may be important in reshaping notions of business culture and entrepreneurship. Profit seeking is not the only driver of business activity nor the only measure of business success. Distinct social and economic groups who may be distinguished by gender or by race/ethnicity, but in many other ways too, may also be distinguished by motivations and aims. It has been suggested, for example, that women may be driven more than men by issues of community, of social justice, of ethics, and of environment, but even if this is the case it does not mean that no men are motivated by such concerns, nor that all women are. Women and indeed men are not homogeneous, yet gendered experiences are nonetheless real.

Bringing women further into the worlds of both business and business history would enhance them both. Business endeavour, and the economy more generally, would benefit from the entrepreneurial expertise and the capital of women; resources hitherto untapped. By the end of the twentieth century, one quarter of the self-employed population was female. In terms of both number and proportion, this is a historically unprecedented level; and is to be welcomed. Yet, it implies that the business community is missing out on much skill – assuming an even distribution of entrepreneurial talent across the gender divide – and finance – even though men and women have different borrowing capacities and quantities of capital available for investment. The discipline of business history would also benefit. Recent – indeed current – historical research on women and investment has begun to unearth the extent of women's investment practice and potential from the mid-nineteenth century into the early twentieth century.[71] This demonstrates both that more women owned capital and more women took risks with that capital in the form of investment in business enterprise than is hitherto realized.

The British business landscape of the later twentieth century was undoubtedly re-energized by the entrepreneurial pool of women, yet there is much more potential still to be realized. Nevertheless progress over the past 200 years has been great. Contrast the present situation with that of the eighteenth century described by Peter Mathias:

If a business man had only a daughter and no son to succeed him, the wisest investment which could be made was for the daughter to marry the chief clerk (if socially eligible) or the person chosen to carry on the business in the next generation . . . the typical eighteenth century tragedy of a family business without a male heir to carry on the trade in the next generation.[72]

NOTES

1. Margaret Walsh, 'Gendered Endeavours: Women and the Reshaping of Business Culture', *Women's History Review*, 14, 2, 2005: 181.
2. For example, participants at the past two conferences of the Association of Business Historians were not only overwhelmingly male, but the majority of those women attending were either graduate students – clearly a good thing in terms of future development – or visiting scholars from the US or the continent of Europe.
3. Here, race and class are relevant as well as gender.
4. Michael French, 'British Business History: A Review of the Periodical Literature for 1997', *Business History*, 1999: 11.
5. Steven Toms, 'British Business History: A Review of the Periodical Literature for 2000', *Business History*, 2002: 13.

6. There is also a difference between the US and UK in terms of women's entrepreneurial activity. In the US, women comprise 38 per cent of small-business owners in 1999 compared with a quarter of the self-employed in Britain. Sara Carter, Susan Anderson, and Eleanor Shaw, 'Women's Business Ownership: A Review of the Academic, Popular and Internet Literature', Report to the Small Business Service, DTI, August 2001: 18.

7. Mansel G. Blackford, 'British Business History: A Review of the Periodical Literature for 2001', *Business History*, 2003.

8. For more discussion of the period before 1900, see Katrina Honeyman, 'Doing Business with Gender? Service Industries and the Gendering of British Business History', *Business History Review*, 81, 3, 2007. See also such key recent works as Josephine Maltby and Janette Rutterford, 'She Possessed Her Own Fortune: Women Investors from the Late Nineteenth Century to the Early Twentieth Century', *Business History*, 48, 2, 2006: 220–53. Research published in a special issue of *Accounting, Business and Financial History*, 'Women, Accounting and Investment', 16, 2, 2006, edited by Maltby and Rutterford, indicates recent progress in investigating women's roles as accountants and investors during the eighteenth as well as nineteenth century; Christine Wiskin, 'Urban Businesswomen in Eighteenth Century England', in Rosemary Sweet and Penelope Lane, eds., *Women and Urban Life in Eighteenth Century England: On the Town*, 2003; Robert Beachy, Beatrice Craig, and Alastair Owens, 'Introduction', *Women, Business and Finance in Nineteenth Century Europe: Rethinking Separate Spheres*, 2006; Janette Rutterford and Josephine Maltby, "The Widow, the Clergyman and the Reckless". Women investors in England 1830–1914', *Feminist Economics*, 12, 1, 2006; Sarah Hudson 'Attitudes to Investment Risk Among West Midland Canal and Railway Company Investors, 1760–1850', PhD thesis, University of Warwick, 2002; Nicola Phillips, *Women in Business, 1700–1850*, 2006; Stana Nenadic, 'The Social Shaping of Business Behaviour in the Nineteenth-century Women's Garment Trades', *Journal of Social History*, 31, 3, 1998; Leonore Davidoff and Catherine Hall, *Family Fortunes: Men and Women of the English Middle Class, 1780–1850*, 1987; Hannah Barker, *The Business of Women: Female Enterprise and Urban Development in Northern England 1760–1830*, 2006.

9. Katrina Honeyman, *Women, Gender and Industrialisation in England 1700–1870*, 2000.

10. See Sylvia Walby, *Gender Transformations*, 1997: especially chapter 2.

11. UK Census 1921 and 1931.

12. 'Trends in Female Employment', *Equal Opportunities Review*, 112, 2002: 22.

13. Walby, *Gender Transformations*: 27.

14. 'Gender and the Labour Market in the European Union', *Equal Opportunities Review*, 129, May 2004: 20. Catherine Hakim, 'The Myth of Rising Female Employment', *Work, Employment and Society*, 7, 1, 1993: 114.

15. Self-employment and small- and medium-sized business are closely related as most owners of small enterprises are self-employed. Ferry de Goey, 'Economic Structure and Self-employment During the Twentieth Century', paper delivered to the EBHA conference, Barcelona, 16–18 Sept. 2004; 2. De Goey argues that business historians have so far neglected small- and medium-sized business; but despite the importance of women in this sector, he proceeds to refer to the entrepreneur as male.

16. Jean M. Watkins and David S. Watkins, 'The Female Entrepreneur: Her Background and Determinant of Business Choice – Some British Data', in James Curran, John Stanworth, and David Watkins, eds., *The Survival of the Small Firm, Volume 1, The Economics of Survival and Entrepreneurship*, 1986: 225 and 230. They studied 58

women running 49 businesses, 61 per cent of which were in services. Clutterbuck and Devine, 'Is Entrepreneurship the Way Ahead?': 136, however suggest that women tend to enter business with less experience or knowledge than men because of their strong motivation to autonomy and achievement.

17. Cynthia Forson and Mustafa Ozbilgin, '"Dotcom" Women Entrepreneurs in the UK', University of Hertfordshire Business School, Employment Studies Paper 40, 2002: 1. Clutterbuck and Devine, 'Is Entrepreneurship the Way Ahead?': 136, however suggest that women tend to enter business with less experience or knowledge than men because of their strong motivation to autonomy and achievement.

18. *The Lady's Who's Who*, published for the first, and seemingly only time in 1938, devoted a small section to 'Women in Business'. A significant proportion of women were also breeders of dogs and rare cattle.

19. Angel Kwollek-Folland and Margaret Walsh, 'Women and the Service Industries: National Approaches', Special Issue of *Business History Review*, 81, 3, 2007: 2–3.

20. Cited in de Goey, 'Economic Structure and Self-employment': 6.

21. De Goey, 'Economic Structure and Self-employment': 2.

22. De Goey, 'Economic Structure and Self-employment': 5.

23. Carter et al., 'Women's Business Ownership': 16.

24. DTI, 1999. A large proportion of these were in London and the south-east of England.

25. Carter et al., 'Women's business ownership'; 16.

26. Carter et al., 'Women's business ownership'; 17–18.

27. There was a doubling in the number of self-employed women, while the total self-employed rose by only 60 per cent. Such gains were sometimes perceived at the time as the result of high levels of unemployment and the search for alternative means of support. Sara Carter and Tom Cannon also emphasized the particular problems faced by female entrepreneurs when setting up and sustaining business. 'Women in business', *Employment Gazette*, October 1988; 570.

28. Susan Marlow, 'Self-employed women – new opportunities, old challenges?', *Entrepreneurship and Regional Development*, 9, 1997; 199.

29. In 1986, when approximately half of women self-employed in services were located in the D, H, R group, only 30 per cent of employed women could be found there, whereas 45 per cent of women employed in services worked in the PA, E, H group, where only 16 per cent of self-employed women were occupied. The 1998 figures indicate more correspondence, especially in D, H, R where the percentages were around 25 per cent for each. 45 per cent of employees worked in PA, E, H, and the proportion of self-employed women in that group had risen to 25 per cent. Data from *Labour Force Survey*, Office of National Statistics.

30. *BBC News* web site, 14 November 2006.

31. Lina Gálvez Muñoz, 'Gender in Business History', 2006, cited in Franco Amatori, 'Entrepreneurship', in *Imprese e storia*, 34, 2006: 256.

32. *Equal Opportunities Review*, 103, Mar. 2002: 14–7. Sheila Allen and Carole Truman, 'Prospects for Women's Businesses and Self-employment in the Year 2000', in James Curran and Robert A Blackburn, eds., *Paths of Enterprise: The Future of Small Business*, 1991: 114–27.

33. Sue Birley, 'Female Entrepreneurs: Are They Really Any Different?' *Journal of Small Business Management*, 27, 1, 1989: 32.

34. T. Epstein, 'Female Entrepreneurs and Their Multiple Roles', unpublished paper, 1989, cited in Allen and Truman, 'Prospects for women's businesses': 117.

35. Allen and Truman, 'Prospects for Women's Businesses': 118.

36. *Ibid.*: 125.
37. David Clutterbuck and Marion Devine, 'Is Entrepreneurship the Way Ahead for Women?', in Clutterbuck and Devine, eds., *Businesswoman: Present and Future*, 1987: 130.
38. Carter et al., 'Women's Business Ownership': 4.
39. Marlow, 'Self-employed Women': 208.
40. Ibid.: 199.
41. Robert Goffee and Richard Scase, *Women in Charge: The Experiences of Female Entrepreneurs*, 1985: passim.
42. Birley, 'Female Entrepreneurs': 37.
43. Ibid.: 33.
44. Though Birley acknowledges that women appear to depend more on personal savings.
45. Marlow, 'Self-employed Women': 202.
46. E. B. Schwarz, 'Entrepreneurship: A New Female Frontier', *Journal of Contemporary Business*, Winter 1976; 47–76: cited in Carter et al., 'Women's Business Ownership': 24.
47. Marlow, 'Self-employed Women': 202.
48. Carter et al., 'Women's Business Ownership': 6–7.
49. Ibid.: 33–4.
50. Marlow, 'Self-employed Women': 202.
51. Carter et al., 'Women's Business Ownership': 30.
52. Marlow, 'Self-employed Women': 200.
53. Candida G. Brush, 'Research on Women Business Owners: Past Trends, a New Perspective and Future Directions', *Entrepreneurship: Theory and Practice*, Summer 1992: 24.
54. Several of these had a monied male partner. Marlow, 'Self-employed Women': 200; David J. Jeremy, *A Business History of Britain 1900–1990s*, 1998: 408.
55. *Times* online, 24 Jun. 2007.
56. Though in these cases, self-employment may reflect a particular form of employment contract rather than a type of small business. Sylvia Walby, 'Mainstreaming Gender Into the Analysis of the New Economy and New Employment Forms', paper presented to the ESRC seminar on 'Gender Mainstreaming, the New Economy and New Employment Forms', University of Leeds, 3 Sept. 2004: 24.
57. Forson and Ozbilgin, '"Dotcom" Women': 3–4.
58. Robert Goffee and Richard Scase, *Women in Charge. The Experiences of Female Entrepreneurs*, 1985: 19–21 and 143. Forson and Ozbilgin, '"Dotcom" Women': 7.
59. Susan Durbin, 'The Gendering of Knowledge Work in Call Centres', paper presented to the ESRC seminar on 'Gender Mainstreaming, the New Economy and New Employment forms' University of Leeds, 3 Sept. 2004: 15–6.
60. D. Foray, 'Introduction and General Perspectives', *International Social Science Journal*, 171, 2002: 5.
61. Shire's research is cited in Durbin, 'The Gendering of Knowledge Work': 2.
62. Durbin, 'The Gendering of Knowledge Work': 16.
63. Durbin, p. 16. Walby, 'Mainstreaming Gender', makes a similar point.
64. Forson and Ozbilgin, '"Dotcom" Women': 23–4.
65. Stana Nenadic argued, in 'The Social Shaping of Business Behaviour in the Nineteenth-Century Women's Garment Trades', *Journal of Social History*, 1998, that the vast majority of businesses in nineteenth-century Britain were small in scale, and unmodernized in their structure and strategy.

66. Mary B. Rose in particular has contributed to research on this subject. See, for example, Mary B. Rose, 'Networks, Values and Business: The Evolution of British Family Firms from the Eighteenth to the Twentieth Century', *Enterprises et histoire*, 22, 2, 1999: 30; Jonathan Brown and Mary B. Rose, 'Introduction', in Jonathan Brown and Mary B. Rose, eds., *Entrepreneurship, Networks and Modern Business*, 1993: 1–8; Mary B. Rose, 'Beyond Buddenbrooks: The Family Firm and the Management of Succession in Nineteenth-century Britain', in Brown and Rose, eds., *Entrepreneurship, Networks and Modern Business*; 127–43.

67. Angel Kwolek-Folland makes the suggestion that women's participation in business may be influenced by domestic experience and internalize values other than pure profit and individual success, in 'Gender and Business History', her introduction to *Enterprise and Society*, special issue, 2001.

68. Anita Roddick of the Body Shop is a good example; others include Safia Minney who, in 1990, began Global Village, which campaigned on environmental and social justice issues. She then launched Fair Trade company; and in 1997 founded People Tree, a fashion collection using ecotextiles. In a recent *Guardian* interview, she said she would like to be remembered as 'having helped to tip the balance towards sustainability'. *Guardian Weekend* 7 Aug. 2004. Stana Nenadic's study of the Edinburgh women's garment trades, demonstrates that such activity was not solely concerned with profit maximization, but rather emphasized 'non-utilitarian satisfactions'. See 'The Social Shaping'.

69. Wendy Gamber, 'Gender and Business History', *Business History Review*, 1998: 191.

70. As Alice Kessler Harris suggests, if 'we want to approach a multi-dimensional perspective, we need to be aware of the full range of cultural signals that guided decision making at all levels'. 'Ideologies and Innovation: Gender Dimensions of Business History', *Business and Economic History*, 1991: 51.

71. See especially, Maltby and Rutterford, 'She Possessed Her Own Fortune'.

72. Peter Mathias, 'Entrepreneurs, Managers and Business Men in Eighteenth-century Britain', in Peter Mathias and John A. Davis, eds., *The Nature of Industrialisation, Volume 3, Enterprise and Labour from the Eighteenth Century to the Present.* 1996: 20.

6

From a Solution to a Problem?

Overseas Multinationals in Britain during Economic Decline and Renaissance

Peter Scott

> The British economy is remarkable. Despite all the well-known problems of slow growth, de-industrialization, and high unemployment, it remains an extremely popular base for multinational companies... Some observers consider that the chronic weakness of the British economy has been exacerbated by this very dependence on multinational companies. To others, the strength of the multinational involvement points to hidden virtues in the British scene.[1]

One of the long-term characteristics of British industry, and particularly British manufacturing, has been the peculiarly important role played by foreign-owned enterprises. These have come to dominate production in a number of key industries, including motor vehicles and civil electronics, and have played an important role in most high-growth sectors. They are often viewed as having superior attributes to domestic incumbents regarding a broad range of managerial competencies, and acting as a channel for the diffusion of these competencies to British firms. This chapter will review the role and impact of overseas multinationals in Britain over the twentieth century.

As the above reference to Stopford and Turner's 1985 study (see n. 1) illustrates, the success of overseas multinationals during Britain's period of relative economic decline raised some awkward questions regarding the nature of the British malaise. Simplistic neoclassical prognoses in terms of unsuitable factor costs or market conditions for mass production fail to explain why overseas entrants found Britain a much more productive base than incumbent manufacturers. While multinationals generally failed to achieve the productivity performance of their parent plants, they nevertheless performed markedly better than British firms which – according to such arguments – had production techniques more suited to British conditions.

Yet as the British economy has improved its relative performance over the past twenty-five years, analyses of the net impacts of overseas firms on the domestic economy have become much more pessimistic than those for earlier decades. This chapter seeks to explain this apparent decline in the magnitude of positive 'spin-offs' from inward investment, during a period when the British economy has enjoyed renewed vitality and the technological (and, perhaps, managerial) gap between UK industries and international best practice has narrowed.

EARLY INWARD INVESTORS

Foreign direct investment into the UK can be traced back to the 1850s. However, despite some important earlier entrants (such as Singer, British Westinghouse, and Ford) it is only during the inter-war years that the annual number of new entrants became substantial. It has been estimated that 167 new manufacturing subsidiaries of overseas firms were established in Britain during the 1920s, compared to 76 from 1900–9 and 58 from 1910–19.[2] An important (arguably key) stimulus to the growth in inward foreign direct investment (FDI) over the inter-war years was access to the British market, as Britain progressively moved from free trade to protectionism.

Britain was one of the most reluctant and slowest countries to raise tariffs. Nevertheless, from the First World War it began to introduce protectionist measures. The first major move was the McKenna duties, imposed in 1915 to raise revenue and save shipping space: 33.3 per cent *ad valorem* tariffs were levied on gramophones, clocks, watches, cinematograph film, and certain motor vehicles and components. Although ostensibly emergency war-time measures, they were subsequently renewed until absorbed into the general tariff in 1938.[3] More obviously protectionist were two pieces of legislation enacted in 1921 – the Dyestuffs Act, which prohibited dyestuffs imports except under licence and, of wider application, the Safeguarding of Industries Act. The coverage of 'safeguarding' was extended at various times during the 1920s, and in 1925 silk duties, which included artificial silk, further extended Britain's tariff wall. By the end of the decade protection was still modest, almost 85 per cent of imports entering duty free.[4] Yet its sectoral incidence proved a powerful inducement for FDI.

The McKenna Duties were an important factor behind US direct investment in the British motor vehicle industry, stimulating General Motors' acquisition of Vauxhall; the decision by Ford to move to 100 per cent UK production; and Citroen's decision to commence manufacture at Slough.[5] In 1927, rubber tyres were added to the McKenna list, inducing major manufacturers such as Firestone (which was paying £15,000 per week in import duties), Goodyear, Michelin, and Pirelli, to leap the tariff wall by establishing UK factories.[6] Similarly, the 1925 silk duties attracted a number of foreign companies, including Dutch-based Enka (1925) and German-owned British Bemberg (1926).[7] The need to rapidly develop an oligopolistic position in these newly protected industries may also partially explain the relatively high proportion of entrants via acquisition rather than green field investment during the 1920s. Jones and Bostock found that acquisitions accounted for 41 per cent of US entrants (for which the entry mode was known) during the 1920s, compared to only 27 per cent during 1908–19 and 24 per cent during the 1930s.[8]

The introduction of comprehensive tariff protection in November 1931, together with the depreciation of Sterling following Britain's departure from the gold standard, resulted in a further increase in the flow of overseas-based firms to Britain. According to government figures 275 firms of overseas origin commenced manufacturing in Britain during the eighteen months from November 1931.[9] These were overwhelmingly from western European countries severely effected by the new tariffs and were concentrated either in sectors which had now become highly protected: such as the clothing and footwear, textile, and leather industries – plus three more capital-intensive sectors that had witnessed heavy FDI during the 1920s – electrical equipment and chemicals (both partly covered by earlier tariffs) and other metal goods.[10] This upsurge in inward investment led the UK to initiate a formal admissions policy for overseas firms. The government used its very limited powers over overseas entrants (stemming from the Aliens Order of 1920, which required licences for foreign key workers) to deter any projects deemed detrimental to Britain's industrial position. In practice, very few proposals were rejected, though a number of potential entrants were asked to modify projects to make them more consistent with the government's goals of promoting competition, technology transfer, and employment creation (especially in high unemployment areas).[11]

In addition to tariffs, Britain's continued openness to overseas enterprises provided a further attraction for foreign multinationals. It was seen as a country with relatively red-tape-free attitudes to overseas firms, cultural proximity to America (which dominated inward FDI during this decade), a large internal market, and export links to the Empire and continental Europe.[12] Meanwhile an intensification of nationalistic sentiment, expressed in an invigorated 'Buy British' movement – which encompassed local and central government, many corporations, and individual consumers – placed further pressure on overseas manufacturers to service the UK market via British production.[13]

Theory suggests that successful inward investors must have 'ownership advantages' over host-nation firms – a range of competitive strengths they can transfer abroad. In the absence of such firm-specific competitive advantages, domestic producers would be better able to capture the benefits of local production.[14] The literature highlights two types of ownership advantages. The first type, widely considered the most important, concern asset or production-cost advantages: a firm's possession of proprietary intangible assets created by investments in, and experience of, technological and marketing activities, together labelled 'product differentiation'. Such assets may also include special managerial skills and surplus entrepreneurial labour. The second type involves the large size of multinationals, which partly captures product differentiation advantages, but also provides additional benefits such as access to capital markets, diversification of risk, superior information, and greater political influence.[15]

Jones and Bostock found that early US entrants had substantial ownership advantages because of America's superiority in mass-production and science-based industries derived from Chandlerian three-pronged investment in manufacturing, marketing, and management.[16] US investment was concentrated in capital-intensive industries such as machinery, chemicals, branded foodstuffs, and vehicles, in which America had a substantial technological lead and in which extensive managerial hierarchies were particularly important. The ownership advantages of American corporations, which dominated FDI during the 1920s, therefore appear to have been of both types. Conversely, firms attracted to Britain in the aftermath of the general tariff were typically much smaller European companies producing branded consumer goods, in sectors where quality and design were of considerable importance. The first type of advantage, superiority in product differentiation, entrepreneurship, and so on, thus appears to have dominated: firms gaining advantages via knowledge of specialist processes or products, or superiority in areas such as design.[17]

Overall verdicts on the impact of overseas entrants during this period are extremely positive. Jones found that inter-war multinationals transmitted a range of benefits to British industry, diffusing both superior technology and managerial and entrepreneurial skills (though he argues that these were not always appropriate for British conditions).[18] When Ford opened its new assembly plant at Trafford Park, Manchester, in 1911, it introduced a powered assembly line, only months after the completion to the world's first moving chassis assembly line in Detroit.[19] Similarly, Smithies' study of inter-war Luton emphasized the demonstration effect to local businessmen of Vauxhall's plant layout and production line techniques, as well as the plant organization and personnel management systems of Electrolux and Skefco.[20] According to Law, such diffusion had a significant influence on the long-term industrial development of the south-east (where inter-war multinationals were strongly concentrated), which reinforced the region's capacity for innovation, stimulated the development of local suppliers and supporting industries, and introduced new production and management processes which diffused to other firms in the region.[21]

Around 50 per cent of multinational plants established in Britain by 1939 were located within Greater London and over two-thirds were in the south-east. FDI during this period was generally market-seeking and London's role as a trading, distribution, and administration hub proved a powerful attraction. Many plants were established in new 'green field' areas to the north and west of London, such as the Slough and Park Royal industrial estates, the Great West Road, Letchworth, Welwyn, and Luton. Their presence contributed to the long-term growth of these areas as clusters of relatively high-tech manufacture in expanding sectors. In the context of a world rapidly moving towards protected trading blocs, Britain's combination of protectionism with liberal access to incoming overseas enterprises had allowed it to capture some of the economic gains offered by overseas production techniques that would otherwise have been lost as tariff walls priced foreign suppliers out of British markets.

INWARD FDI DURING THE POST-WAR 'LONG BOOM'

Britain emerged from the Second World War facing an acute shortage of dollars – which was to colour its approach to US inward investment for more than a decade. Meanwhile North American firms came to see FDI more as a substitute for exports in a world of dollar scarcity and trade barriers, than part of an international marketing strategy. This led smaller US firms to consider investment in Britain, tilting the balance between product differentiation and economy-of-scale advantages in favour of the former.[22] Britain's foreign exchange control system provided both the key incentive for inward investment and the mechanism for regulating the FDI inflow. Imports from the dollar area were closely regulated, particularly during the early post-war years. As late as 1950, some 98 per cent were subject to government purchase or licensing.[23] Meanwhile potential British demand for US goods was high, boosted (for capital goods) by America's technological and productivity lead and (for consumer goods) by rising consumer affluence during the 1950s.[24] The wider currency restrictions of the Sterling Area provided further markets more easily served from Britain than from dollar sources.[25]

British governments appreciated both the advantages that US FDI offered Britain and the strong discretionary powers that exchange controls gave them regarding investment propositions. There was widespread concern about the extent of the Anglo-American 'productivity gap'.[26] For example, a 1954 Organisation for European Economic Co-operation (OEEC) report noted that American corporations brought substantial benefits to western European hosts in the form of intangible assets such as superior technology, production, and sales methods, management systems, and skilled personnel.[27] American firms were perceived to have 'system-wide' advantages that encompassed the broad range of their activities. Their ownership advantages were thus 'tacit' (not amenable to articulation and codification), being embedded in their 'organizational routines.'[28] This made it very difficult to transfer them through other avenues, such as licensing or government-sponsored technical assistance. Yet productivity considerations represented only one of the factors shaping government policy. Hodges has identified four factors determining the salience of inward FDI as a policy issue for host governments, its importance rising with increases in:

1. government intervention in the host economy,
2. the level and industrial distribution of the FDI,
3. the degree of control over the subsidiary exerted by the parent, and
4. policymakers' perceptions that foreign-owned subsidiaries behave differently from domestic firms.[29]

The first two factors proved central. Particularly during the early post-war years, government exercised tight control over not only foreign exchange and imports but also the domestic allocation of physical resources and production. Meanwhile, the volume of potential FDI was sufficiently large to have a substantial impact on exchange and resource allocation policy, making detailed scrutiny and regulation of applications unavoidable. Political factors also played a role – government being keen to avoid the appearance of discrimination against North American firms, given Britain's reliance on American and Canadian loan finance and the strategic importance of good Anglo-American relations.

During the immediate post-war period Britain took the lion's share of North American investment, receiving well over 40 per cent of U.S. FDI into OEEC countries from 1947 to 1952.[30] However, the volume was low relative to the boom of the 1950s. Between 1950 and 1960 the estimated book value of US direct manufacturing investments rose from £194 million to £774 million, oil sector investments from £44 million to £277 million, and total American direct investments in the UK from £303 million to £1,155 million.[31] Estimated Canadian FDI into Britain also rose sharply, from £19 million at the end of 1949 to £95 million by 1960.[32] American firms accounted for 58.9 per cent of the UK's inward FDI stock in 1960, Canadian concerns contributed a further 13.7 per cent, while western Europe made up only 22.8 per cent, with Switzerland (8.7%) and the Netherlands (6.4%) the most important countries.[33]

Britain developed a strong but flexible framework of FDI controls, arising in part from the 1947 Exchange Control Act. Discretionary powers permitted substantial flexibility, as the Treasury could alter policy by directives without recourse to Parliament.[34] Firms seeking to establish plants in Britain had to apply to the Bank of England for exchange approval. They were also subject to a variety of other controls over the allocation of scarce capital and materials, together with planning and factory development restrictions. However, such restrictions applied equally to British firms.[35] From the second half of 1949, policy and events, centred on the second post-war sterling crisis, conspired to make the British government keener on inward investment, marking the start of a gradual relaxation of controls which was to continue for the next decade.[36]

Meanwhile the flexibility of the exchange control system facilitated wide-ranging negotiation with individual companies. For example, concern regarding the dollar cost of oil imports led the British government to inform US officials in September 1949 that it was introducing discrimination against American oil companies. A series of agreements with individual oil companies subsequently resolved the problem by reducing their exchange burden through an expansion of UK production, refining capacity, and equipment purchases – producing dollar-savings well in excess of that stipulated. Schenk argues that while these controls were first necessitated by urgent exchange problems, their persistence is best explained by the government's desire to increase inward FDI, support British supply companies, and facilitate the access of British oil companies to the marketing services of their American counterparts.[37]

Negotiations with manufacturers were often protracted, causing delays and frustrations that may have deterred other potential investors. Subsequent delays in gaining approval for factory development – partly necessitated by raw-materials shortages – exacerbated such frustrations.[38] Yet the controls were successful in shifting the sectoral composition of inward investment to areas prioritized by government. Of the sixty US firms that commenced manufacture in Britain between 1945 and 1953, forty-two were capital equipment producers, most of which satisfied the criterion that projects should significantly contribute to British industrial efficiency by introducing superior foreign techniques. Meanwhile, in keeping with the criterion that projects should make a major contribution to exports, their ratio of exports to output, estimated at 52 per cent, compared with 35 per cent for subsidiaries established before 1939.[39] Controls also proved successful in steering a substantial proportion of US firms to the regionally assisted 'Development areas', particularly the Scottish Development Area promotion of which capitalized on the strong cultural ties many Americans and Canadians felt with Scotland.[40]

American corporations often proved skilled negotiators. For example, the siting of Ford's major new car plant at Halewood on Merseyside in 1960 has been widely viewed as an example of government intervention leading to a sub-optimal location choice. In fact, Ford planners had already concluded that internal congestion and limited access made expansion at their main Dagenham site impractical. Given labour shortages and higher wages in the south, they had identified Halewood as the best available location. Yet, in order to get the maximum financial benefit from government regional policy inducements Ford asserted that it would have preferred Dagenham, and put forward the London new town of Basildon as its proposed site – in the knowledge that it would be rejected.[41]

The election of a Conservative government in October 1951 had brought little initial change in policy towards inward investment, apart from reducing the emphasis on location in high unemployment areas. During the early- to mid-1950s, inward FDI continued to be judged according to three main criteria: whether or not the project would (1) save imports, particularly dollar imports; (2) lead to a net increase in British exports, particularly to the dollar area; and (3) make a contribution to British industrial efficiency of sufficient value to compensate for any dollar loss. Projects meeting any of these conditions were likely to be accepted.[42] Where the advantages appeared evenly balanced, government tended to give the benefit of the doubt to the investor. Projects involving 'inessential consumer goods for home consumption' were normally refused, as were British proposals of this type (under domestic capital-issues controls).[43]

Britain still faced severe capacity constraints: instead of creating welcome employment, inward investment might compete for scarce labour, materials, and capital.[44] Yet as capacity expanded and the dollar gap narrowed, the case for controls (which ran contrary to the government's neo-liberal economic philosophy) increasingly came under question. Britain faced rising competition for North American FDI from a recovering western Europe, particularly following the formation of the European Economic Community (EEC). Government reacted by progressively liberalizing controls; the proportion of rejected applications falling from 10.2 per cent by value over the two years to 31 March 1954 (excluding oil, film, shipping, and insurance) to only 2.0 per cent over the fifteen months to 30 September 1957.[45] Rejections became restricted to sectors such as US advertising firms seeking to cash in on commercial television and 'luxury items' such as white goods, demand for which was being suppressed by government as an instrument of monetary policy.[46]

In July 1958 it was announced that future exchange control permission would be freely given.[47] The Board of Trade had found it difficult to monitor agreements with firms, or enforce their compliance. However, multinationals had generally proved reasonably willing to go at least some way towards meeting government requirements. Though exchange considerations dominated negotiations, modifications to improve the dollar impact of projects generally led to an increase in domestic content and employment, with the establishment of manufacturing branches rather than mere assembly operations (which would entail greater imports). Thus negotiations often increased the scale and scope of inward investment projects, with a greater proportion of value added and an increased likelihood of continued production after the controls ceased. The restrictions had enhanced the quality of inward investment during the initial period of severe capacity and dollar-balance constraints, which necessitated rationing and the selection of projects offering the highest social return. Yet a recovering Europe and liberalizing world economy had undermined Britain's bargaining power. By 1960, the relaxation of the Sterling Area's exchange controls, together with the successful launch of the EEC, had shifted the balance of British FDI policy from rationing to promotion.

Monitoring of FDI via takeovers remained; officials being wary of cases that might give rise to 'public political interest.'[48] Government intervention proved rare, despite the fact that such takeovers were becoming politically controversial. As Figure 6.1 shows, an average of 10.5 British firms were acquired by new US entrants to Britain each year over the period 1950–62, more than twice the number during the previous peak in the 1920s. There were also many takeovers of British companies by overseas multinationals already established in the UK, which this data does not include. The growth of acquisitions accelerated during the decade and by 1959 the Labour opposition was raising objections regarding high-profile takeovers of firms such as British Aluminium, British Timber, and Massey-Ferguson.[49] Even the *Economist* questioned the wisdom of allowing takeovers of major firms such as the British Motor Corporation, with regard to both national prestige and potential impacts on British exports and R&D capacity.[50]

Empirical studies for this period support the official view that overseas entrants offered important productivity-enhancing advantages, in addition to short-term foreign exchange and balance of payments gains. Foreign multinationals had strong qualitative differences to domestic industry and substantially outperformed British firms in growth, profitability, and productivity.[51] The period from 1945 to 1960 marked the high point of the Anglo-American productivity gap and American inward investment was partly motivated by the desire to capitalize on this superiority. US multinationals were highly concentrated in science-based and capital-intensive sectors, such as chemicals, office machinery, engineering, and motor vehicles, in which US firms had a particularly strong international position.[52] This was reflected in their contribution to British capital formation: between 1950 and 1957 American subsidiaries accounted for 12.5 per cent of fixed capital formation in British manufacturing, despite employing only 5 per cent of its workforce.[53]

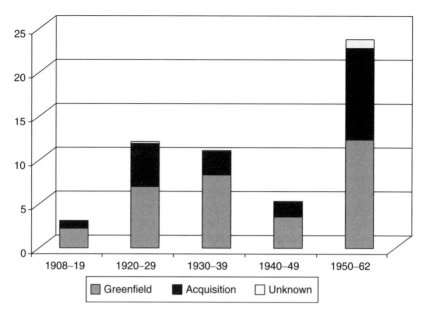

Figure 6.1. New US entrants to the UK, by mode of entry, 1908–62 (average per year)

Source: Jones and Bostock, 2006.

Dunning's seminal 1958 study indicated that American firms offered a number of major productivity and technology-related benefits, including access to American research, manufacturing, and managerial expertise. An American corporation tended to 'treat its supplier as an integral part of its organization,' supplying detailed specifications or prototypes and often sending specialists to assist with the introduction of new production methods.[54] This was sometimes necessitated by severe dissatisfaction with British suppliers: a 1954 survey of American plants in the Glasgow area revealed complaints about local suppliers' 'endemic' failure to meet delivery dates and supply of substandard materials and parts. Despite observations that, 'in some cases British management apparently considers inspection and quality control an unwarranted overhead,' many initial problems had been resolved through working closely with their suppliers' technical and production staffs.[55] There were also strong demonstration effects: for example, overseas-based pharmaceutical corporations' high research expenditure encouraged similar action by UK firms, paving the way for their subsequent research-led growth.[56] Meanwhile there is little evidence of substantial negative impacts from inward FDI during this period.

The 1964–70 Labour governments were less sanguine than their Conservative predecessors regarding the growing US stake in Britain's domestic manufacturing base, particularly in key industries. By the mid-1960s American affiliates accounted for over 50 per cent of the British market for a considerable range of products, including cars, vacuum cleaners, typewriters, and breakfast cereals, while holding over 30 per cent of the market for computers, tyres, soap and detergents, refrigerators, and washing machines, and a variety of other high-tech or marketing-intensive products.[57] Labour sought assurances from inward investors such as Ford, Chrysler, and Philips regarding their contributions to employment, capital investment, and UK exports, but – like their Conservative predecessors – were unable to find effective ways of policing these arrangements.[58]

Safarian argued that the 1964–70 Labour governments' positive approach to mergers and industrial reorganization, embodied in legislation such as the 1965 Monopolies and Mergers Act and 1966 Industrial Reorganization Act, can be regarded as being in part designed to reduce the vulnerability of UK firms to foreign takeovers.[59] For example, the Industrial Reorganisation Corporation (IRC), established under the Industrial Reorganisation Act, was successful in preventing a further loss of control over the ball-bearing sector (dominated by six major UK manufacturers, three of which were wholly foreign-owned). An investigation launched in May 1968 – in the face of a threatened takeover of the leading British-owned producer, Ransome & Marles, by the UK subsidiary of Swedish multinational Skefko – found that, given the size and scope of SKF's European operations, it might rationalize its international production, R&D, and sourcing in ways detrimental to the British economy. It therefore blocked the threatened takeover, consolidation of the UK industry being achieved instead via an IRC-backed merger of the three British companies.[60] Yet Labour's attempts to promote 'national champions' in sectors such as ball-bearings, motor vehicles, and computers generally gave rise to firms with disappointing long-term performance, usually culminating in their acquisition by foreign competitors.[61]

POLICY AND IMPACTS SINCE 1970

The activities of overseas multinationals remained subject to little significant political controversy throughout the period 1945–70.[62] Academic and official analyses were generally favourable; for example, a major investigation for the Department of Trade and Industry, published in 1973, found concerns regarding negative impacts to be generally unfounded.[63] However, the situation was to change during the 1970s, in the face of an unstable world economy, slower growth, and rising unemployment. There were also changes in the character of inward investment projects. During the early post-war years many US MNEs took a market by market approach to Europe, establishing miniature replicas of their US manufacturing plants both in the UK and other European countries. The enlargement of the EEC in 1973, together with a move to less buoyant and more unstable economic conditions, led to a rationalization of this capacity – with a reallocation of production between these European plants to foster horizontal or vertical integration.[64]

The strength of exchange controls, which had acted as an early warning system regarding inward investment, was much reduced during the 1970s and controls were finally abolished following the election of the Thatcher government in 1979. With the exception of a few sectors, such as oil and banking, the only significant remaining channel for blocking proposals considered unfavourable to Britain's interests was a provision of the 1975 Industry Act (in practice never used), which enabled the Minister to prevent attempts by foreign companies to acquire UK manufacturers.[65] Most other European countries had stronger restrictions on overseas-based takeovers. This contributed to a particularly high rate of such acquisitions in Britain; in some cases (such as the takeover of Rowntrees by Nestle in 1987) it was argued that in the absence of protective legislation in the acquirer's country, the takeover might have been in the opposite direction.

Despite a more sceptical stance towards inward investment by the 1974–9 Labour governments than their 1970–4 Conservative predecessor, in practice both parties pursued a liberal policy when in office, during an era when rising unemployment forced governments to place increased emphasis on job creation. The aftermath of the 1970s oil shocks led to a further intensification of international competition for inward FDI, in the face of a new international climate of slower growth and high unemployment. EU and other European countries sought to outbid each other regarding incentives. Britain's growing efforts were reflected in the establishment of the Invest in Britain Bureau by the DTI in 1977, to coordinate the activities of the various regional development agencies. Canada and the US (often at state rather than federal level) offered their own incentives to potential investors and by the 1990s even the Japanese, which had traditionally been the most anti-inward investment of the major capitalist nations, had entered the fray.[66]

Rising British unemployment was matched by a return of markedly higher (and, during the 1980s, mass) unemployment in the regionally assisted areas. Governments increasingly turned to multinationals – which were regarded as being substantially more 'footloose' than British companies, as an instrument of regional policy. Large projects concerning, say, Japanese motor vehicle manufacturers, offered the potential to create several thousand jobs at a stroke. There was also substantial international competition among governments to attract such projects; assistance could therefore be justified on the grounds that in its absence the corporation might locate overseas. By the early 1990s over 40 per cent of Regional Selective Assistance was being paid to foreign-owned companies.[67] Discretionary incentives enabled government and its national and regional agencies to resume the type of detailed negotiations regarding the character of inward investment proposals which typified policy during the early post-war years. Considerations included location in a high unemployment region, technological impacts, and (of particular importance during the 1980s) agreements as to minimum local content – a minimum of 60 per cent was often taken as the standard, though this varied according to the particular circumstances of the proposition.[68]

UK assisted areas accounted for 52.3 per cent of all foreign-owned plants established over 1966–83, multinationals being steered to these regions by generous financial incentives. Meanwhile over 1971–83 inward manufacturing investors increased their share of net capital expenditure for all manufacturing enterprises in UK assisted areas from 17.0 to 27.9 per cent – suggesting that they continued to offer important benefits in addition to employment creation.[69] The emphasis on attracting multinationals led to increased concentrations of multinational plants in Britain's peripheral regions – as shown in Table 6.1, which gives location quotients for each main assisted region's share of foreign-owned manufacturing employment relative to its share of UK manufacturing employment in 1979, 1983, and 1993. By 1993 all the main assisted regions had markedly higher shares of foreign-owned manufacturing employment than the UK average, while (with the exception of Northern Ireland) all had become more reliant on overseas manufacturers since 1979 (relative to the UK average).

However, tackling regional policy via subsidies to inward investment proved a double-edged sword, as these plants proved particularly vulnerable to closure during recessions. Studies during the late 1970s and early 1980s indicated that inward investment assisted the British economy in restructuring towards higher growth sectors, yet increased its exposure to the international business cycle, which impacted disproportionately on Britain's peripheral regions. Multinationals accounted for 30.0 per cent of closures for large plants (employing more than 500 people in 1978) in Wales over the period 1978–82, 33.3 per cent in Scotland, and 55.5 per cent in Northern Ireland, compared to only 13.2 per cent in England. Meanwhile evidence suggests that the shedding of jobs during this period by multinationals based in the south-east was substantially lower than that for MNEs in assisted areas. Multinationals in peripheral regions did appear to perform better (or at least no worse) than indigenous firms in terms of job losses.[70] Yet, given that these regions were typically dominated by indigenous firms in rapidly declining sectors such as steel and textiles, little comfort can be drawn from this conclusion. The problem was exacerbated by the large size of many overseas-owned plants, closure of which could have devastating impacts on local communities. In 1981, the 100 largest inward investors accounted for about 60 per cent of Britain's FDI stock, while no fewer than 402 of the largest 1,000

Table 6.1. Location quotients for each main assisted region's share of foreign-owned manufacturing employment relative to their share of UK manufacturing employment

Region	1979	1989	1993
Northern Ireland	1.60*	1.10	1.56
Scotland	1.34	1.49	1.37**
Northern England	0.85*	1.34	1.26
Wales	1.38	1.78	1.87
UK	1.00	1.00	1.00***

Notes: *Based on 1978. **Based on 1992 figures for foreign employment. ***Relates to 1991.

Source: Stone and Peck, 1996.

firms in Britain were foreign-owned (around four times the proportion in the late 1960s).[71]

There were also increasing doubts regarding the long-term, developmental benefits multinationals brought to assisted regions. Young, Hood, and Hamill found that the benefits of MNEs (particularly in assisted areas) were strong in employment and investment terms but much more questionable in terms of dynamic, developmental impacts. Headquarters functions were commonly located outside the assisted areas, local linkages were weak, and there were only fairly isolated examples of spin-off enterprises emerging from the multinational sector, with no indications of improvements over time. They argued that the assisted regions were becoming classic dual economies, 'with the high-tech MNE subsidiaries somehow cocooned, like the antiseptic work environs of their electronics factories, from the real problems of the regions'.[72]

Meanwhile the geographical composition of FDI hosts was undergoing substantial long-term changes, including a sharp decline in the relative importance of the US. In 1962 America had accounted for 64 per cent of Britain's inward FDI stock, while the EEC represented only 10 per cent. Twenty years later the EEC's share had doubled to 20 per cent, while the US's share had fallen to 49 per cent. Japan's contribution to Britain's FDI stock remained at below 1 per cent as late as 1978, but rose sharply during the early 1980s, reaching 4 per cent in 1982–3.[73] Japanese entrants found Britain more linguistically and culturally accessible than the other EU nations and it rapidly became their preferred base for European subsidiaries. Henceforth Britain was to look increasingly towards East and Southeast Asia for new inward direct investment.

Japanese manufacturers pioneered single-union, no-strike agreements, involving binding arbitration in the event of disputes. They were fortunate to find a partner in the Electrical and Plumbing Trades Union which, unlike most of its counterparts, was willing to enter into such agreements. British firms had been fond of attributing Japanese success in electronics and motor vehicles to special factors such as an obedient workforce and government assistance. The success of Japanese plants in Britain put an end to claims that Japanese methods were impractical for the British environment. In particular their quality control and industrial relations practices exerted a strong demonstration effect regarding what could be achieved with British labour, if appropriate management methods and attitudes were applied.[74]

Young, Hood, and Hamill have identified three phases in the relationship between host countries and multinationals: a 'honeymoon period' from 1950 to the mid-1960s, in which host nations welcomed the capital, management, and technology transfer applications of inward investment; a 'separation' period from the mid-1960s to late-1970s, in which host countries became more critical of overseas entrants (on both economic and political grounds); and a 'reconciliation' phase from the late 1970s, in which host nations competed for inward investment in the context of an increasingly globalized international market.[75] Britain's move to reconciliation was boosted by the election of its most radically neo-liberal post-war government in 1979. The Thatcher governments' vigorous privatization programme eventually allowed overseas-based firms to gain major stakes in a range of formerly public sector industries, despite initial provisions for a government 'golden share', designed to prevent undesirable takeovers (normally for a period of five years). Privatized car firms such as Jaguar and Rolls Royce eventually fell into overseas hands, followed by a switch of production out of Britain. The government's apparent indifference towards nationality of owner-ship, even in traditionally sheltered sectors such as defence, was thrown into sharp relief by the 1985 Westland Affair, when it allowed the sale of Westland, Britain's last helicopter manufacturer, to the American firm Sikorsky, despite a political storm that led to the resignation of two senior cabinet ministers.

Britain experienced a heavy fall in foreign-owned manufacturing employment during 1979–96, though this was mainly a reflection of the contraction of the domestic manufacturing base, especially during the early years of the Thatch-er governments. Foreign-owned manufacturing employment then experienced a limited recovery, which persisted during the 1989–92 recession. However, some of this increase reflected the transfer of UK companies to foreign ownership, during a boom period for takeovers of British companies by Western European and North American corporations.[76] Multinationals continued to 'punch above their weight' in the UK economy. In 1991, overseas-owned MNEs accounted for only 17.2 per cent of UK manufacturing employment, but comprised 22.5 per cent of net output, 21.7 per cent of gross value added, 33.5 per cent of net capital expenditure, and 20.5 per cent of gross salaries and wages. Net output per employee was 31 per cent higher than for all manufacturers and gross value added per employee was 26 per cent above the UK manufacturing average.[77]

Moreover, recent inward FDI has partially compensated for both the decline of traditional manufacturing sectors and the demise of 'mature' producers (some of which are themselves branches of overseas multinationals). A classic example of the latter effect concerns Japanese investment in the British motor vehicle industry, during a period which has witnessed both the final collapse of the British-owned industry and the decline of the long-established American-owned UK car producers Ford and General Motors (Vauxhall). The first significant inward investment occurred via a technical strategic alliance between Rover and Honda, initiated in 1979. Nissan commenced UK assembly in 1986, while Honda and Toyota followed (with both assembly and engine facilities) in 1992. Non-tariff barriers against Japanese car imports made barri-er-jumping FDI attractive, while the strong yen increased its financial attractions. Japanese producers agreed to informal voluntary agreements with the UK and other EU nations to achieve levels of local (EU) content of at least 80 per cent. In addition to Britain's more familiar language and legal system compared to continental Europe, low labour costs, and liberal attitude towards inward investors, it also offered generous financial incentives. For example, Nissan received £125 million in capital grants, plus training grants and infrastructure incentives.[78]

THE NEW SCEPTICISM TOWARDS OVERSEAS MNES

Britain's emergence as a stable and (by OECD standards) relatively high-growth nation over the past two decades has been accompanied by growing scepticism regarding the impacts of overseas MNEs on the British economy. Public concerns have been heightened by the growth, since the late 1970s, of entrants in the tertiary sector, including key suppliers of services as central to everyday life as mass media, high street catering, and groceries. Few examples are as extreme as the acquisition by News International of some of Britain's most important national newspaper titles and their more recent dominance of UK satellite TV (and a substantial stake in ITV). These interests have made their chief executive, Rupert Murdock, arguably one of the most powerful individuals in Britain, with the result that both the Conservative and Labour parties have openly courted his support (which proved important and, in some cases, possibly even decisive in successive national elections). Macdonald's expansion in Britain raised widespread concerns ranging from the health effects of its products, aggressive marketing to children, and the environmental and animal-welfare impacts of its sourcing policies (particularly following the notorious MacLibel trial). Similarly the recent acquisition of Asda by the American Wal-Mart group has raised fears regarding its alleged ruthless policies towards competing small businesses, the environment, and its workers – particularly female and ethnic minority employees.[79]

Academic opinion has also become much more sceptical regarding the magnitude of the economic benefits that inward investors bring with them. Studies conducted since the late 1980s have produced a broad consensus that, while the direct effects of inward investment into the UK and its regions have been positive, the spillover effects, especially with regard to local sourcing, have been very disappointing.[80] Turok has identified two scenarios put forward in the literature, summarized in Table 6.2. Under the optimistic, developmental scenario, economic pressures promote flexible, industrial district-type production structures, based around close collaborative relationships between multinationals and local suppliers. These encourage further geographical clustering to minimize transaction and transport costs, and foster a process of cumulative growth based around an exchange of technical ideas and information regarding market intelligence and corporate plans. Such a scenario would produce high spin-off benefits from the transfer of technology and expertise to local firms, operating as part of a network with embedded multinationals that are highly committed to long-term local linkages.

Meanwhile under the dependency scenario, 'flexibility' has a very different meaning. Market power is held by the multinationals, which move freely between local and global suppliers on the basis of short-term cost-minimization. Under this scenario suppliers do not participate in technical development, but produce standard components or other low value-added goods. They might also be used intermittently by multinationals, to manage periodic fluctuations in orders.

Table 6.2. Alternative local linkage scenarios for inward direct investment

	Developmental	Dependent
Nature of local linkages	Collaborative, mutual learning Based on technology and trust Emphasis on added value	Unequal trading relationships Conventional sub-contracting Emphasis on cost-saving
Duration of linkages	Long-term partnerships	Short-term contracts
Meaning of 'flexibility'	High-level interaction to accelerate product development and increase responsiveness to volatile markets	Price-cutting and short-term convenience for multinationals
Inward investors' ties to the locality	Deeply embedded High investment in decentralized, multi-functional operations	Weakly embedded Branch plants restricted to final assembly operations
Benefits for local firms	Markets for local firms to develop and produce their own products Transfer of technology and expertise strengthens local firms	Markets for local firms to make standard, low-tech components Sub-contracting means restricted independent growth capacity
Quality of jobs	Diverse including high-skilled, high-income	Many low-skilled, low-paid, temporary, and casual
Prospects for the local economy	Self-sustaining growth through cumulative expansion of the industrial cluster	Vulnerable to external forces and corporate decisions

Source: Turok, 1993: 402.

Such volatile market relationships would further encourage the type of low-skilled, labour-intensive, production methods that are already implied by the standardized nature of the sub-contracted tasks. Local suppliers would have no real control over product development, marketing, or strategic management, thus limiting their capacity to develop into stronger enterprises with deeper capabilities.

Turok found that even in Scotland's 'Silicon glen' – one of the longest-established and most successful enclaves of overseas multinationals in Britain – the dependency scenario appears to have become characteristic of relationships between electronics multinationals and local firms. Output growth during the 1980s had strongly out-paced value-added and employment growth, as multinationals concentrated on final assembly, with only around 12 per cent of material inputs being sourced within Scotland. Meanwhile local sourcing was biased towards standard components or items with a high bulk to value ratio, the main exceptions being products manu-factured by the branch plants of overseas suppliers.[81]

A related framework builds on Kindleberger's model of the enclave economy.[82] Phelps et al. contrast the 'embedded' multinational branch-plant with the 'en-clave' model in which it may provide high levels of direct employment but be poorly integrated into the local economy. Instead dedicated on-site suppliers dominate meaningful local linkages, others tending to be shallow. They also propose a third scenario between these archetypes, the 'extended enclave' in which MNEs develop partial connections with the local economy along a limited number of dimensions, perhaps encouraged by regional development agencies. Their empirical research, on manufacturing MNEs in Wales and the north-east of England, shows strong support for this 'extended enclave' scenario. Many plants are found to undertake on-site functions in addition to pure manufacturing, but levels of local sourcing remain low, collaborative R&D linkages are limited in scope, and relationships with regional organizations and firms are of minor importance in determining whether further investment will be made in the local affiliate. More important local linkages are largely limited to regional development agencies and vocational training schemes.[83]

Optimistic commentators have argued that 'Post-Fordist' changes in corporate structures, including organizational decentralization, the flattening of corporate hierarchies, and the devolution of authority and decision-making to plant-level management, might facilitate the development of embedded MNE branch plants. Initiatives by regional development agencies to encourage the formation of local supply chains, expand aftercare services for in-coming multinationals, and encourage technology transfer, could be expected to accelerate this process. However, the evidence reviewed above points in the opposite direction.

CONCLUSIONS

In 2002, Britain held an estimated 10 per cent of the world's inward FDI stock, second only to the US. Indeed in terms of its importance to the UK economy – equivalent of 40.8 per cent of GDP – Britain outranked even the US. Compared to the eve of the First World War, when it probably did not even rank among the top ten FDI hosts, or 1929, when it ranked eighth, Britain at the start of the twenty-first century was an outstanding success in the market for inward FDI.[84] Meanwhile the sectoral composition of foreign-owned manufacturing enterprises has remained biased towards capital and research-intensive sectors and branded consumer goods. Food products, chemicals, motor vehicles, and machinery still account for nearly half aggregate UK employment by foreign-based manufacturers.[85]

Yet the advantages conferred by foreign-ownership appear much less clear-cut than was the case in 1930 or 1970. In an open world economy, with strong international competition for inward investment, the bargaining power of the UK government to extract favourable deals from new entrants is much reduced compared to the autarchic world of the inter-war and early post-war years. Meanwhile the productivity gap between Britain and the source countries for FDI has narrowed and in the new, flexible, globalized economy of the early twenty-first century alternative channels for transmitting superior overseas methods and technology – such as licensing, partnership arrangements, and sub-contracting, have become increasingly attractive. The political attractions of inward investment have also diminished, in the light of evidence that (particularly in services) multinationals have come to enjoy monopoly or oligopolistic positions in key consumer markets. Meanwhile, globalization has also increased the exposure of Britain to international economic downturns, which can lead to heavy closures of multinational branch plants – often for reasons not directly connected with the financial performance of the branch. Overseas based MNEs still appear to constitute an asset to the British economy – but a much more problematic asset than was the case during the decades of Britain's relative decline.

NOTES

1. J. Stopford and L. Turner, *Britain and the Multinationals*, Wiley, Chichester, 1985: 1.
2. G. Jones et al., *Impact of Foreign Multi-National Investment in Britain since 1850* [computer file], ESRC Data Archive, Colchester, 1993; F. Bostock and G. Jones, 'Foreign Multinationals in British Manufacturing, 1850–1962', *Business History*, 36, 1994: 89–126; G. Jones and F. Bostock, 'US Multinationals in British Manufacturing before 1962', *Business History Review*, 70, 1996: 67–116. There are slight differences in the number of firms given in these sources, due to revisions of the database.
3. Some tariffs were abolished temporarily under the 1923–4 Labour government.
4. F. Capie, *Depression and Protectionism: Britain between the Wars*, Allen & Unwin, London, 1983: 44.
5. J.H. Dunning, 'The Growth of U.S. Investment in U.K. Manufacturing Industry 1856/1940', *The Manchester School*, 24, 1956: 245–69, p. 258; M. Wilkins, and F.E. Hill, *American Business Abroad: Ford on Six Continents*, Detroit, 1964: 46–7, 102, 111–12, and 134.
6. M. J. French, 'The Emergence Of a U.S. Multinational Enterprise: The Goodyear Tire and Rubber Company, 1910–39', *Economic History Review* 2nd ser., 40, 1987: 64–79; J. Marshall, *The History of the Great West Road: Its Social and Economic Influence on the Surrounding Area*, Heritage Publications, Hounslow, 1995: 54.
7. D.C. Coleman, *Courtaulds: An Economic and Social History*, Clarendon, Oxford, 1969: 265–66.
8. Jones and Bostock, 'US Multinationals': 223–4.
9. House of Commons, *Parliamentary Debates*, 266, 1932: 1331–4; 273, 1932: 734–7; 278, 1933: 917–19. In a small proportion of cases the firms involved were not 'multinationals' as there was no continuing element of overseas control. However, the union movement and most other contemporaries did not make any clear distinction between migrant and foreign-controlled firms.
10. P. Scott and T. Rooth, 'Protectionism and the Growth of Overseas Multinational Enterprise in Interwar Britain', *Journal of Industrial History*, 3, 2: 31–50, p. 39.
11. P. Scott and T. Rooth, 'Public Policy and Foreign-based Enterprises in Britain prior to the Second World War', *The Historical Journal*, 42, 2: 495–515.
12. Stopford and Turner, *Britain and the Multinationals*: 60.
13. Scott and Rooth, 'Public Policy': 497.
14. R. McCulloch, 'New Perspectives of Foreign Direct Investment,' in K.A. Froot, ed., *Foreign Direct Investment*, Chicago, 1993: 37–53, p. 43; S. Lall, *Multinationals, Technology and Exports*, Macmillan, New York, 1985: 7.
15. Lall, 'Multinationals': 2–3.

16. Jones and Bostock, 'US Multinationals': 79.

17. Scott and Rooth, 'Protectionism': 41.

18. Jones, 'Foreign Multinationals': 439–42.

19. S. Tolliday, 'The Rise of Ford in Britain: from Sales Agency to Market Leader, 1904–1980', in H. Bonin, Y. Lung, and S. Tolliday, eds., *Ford, 1903–2003: The European History*, Vol. 2, Plage, Paris, 2003: 10.

20. E.D. Smithies, 'The Contrast between North and South in England 1918–1939: A Study of Economic, Social and Political Problems with Particular Reference to the Experience of Burnley, Halifax, Ipswich, and Luton', PhD thesis, Leeds, 1974: 65.

21. C.M. Law, *British Regional Development Since World War 1*, David & Charles, Newton Abbot, 1980: 177.

22. J.H. Dunning, *Multinationals, Technology, and Competitiveness*, Unwin Hyman, London, 1988: 38.

23. M. F. W. Hemming, C. M. Miles, and G. F. Ray, 'A Statistical Summary of the Extent of Import Control in the United Kingdom since the War', *Review of Economic Studies*, 26, 1958–59: 75–109.

24. J.H. Dunning, *American Investment in British Manufacturing Industry*, Allen & Unwin, London, 1958: 48.

25. The Sterling Area by the early 1950s consisted of the British Commonwealth (except Canada), Burma, Iceland, Iraq, Jordan, Libya, and the Persian Gulf Territories. These members maintained exchange controls against the rest of the world but largely unrestricted current and capital account payments between the United Kingdom and themselves. Catherine R. Schenk, *Britain and the Sterling Area: From Devaluation to Convertibility in the 1950s*, Routledge, London, 1994: 7–12.

26. N. Tiratsoo and J. Tomlinson, 'Exporting the "Gospel of Productivity": United States Technical Assistance and British Industry, 1945–1960', *Business History Review*, 71, 1997: 41–81.

27. OEEC, *Private United States Investment in Europe and the Overseas Territories*, OEEC, Paris, 1954.

28. D. J. Teece, 'Firm Organization, Industrial Structure, and Technological Innovation', *Journal of Economic Behavior and Organization*, 31, 1996: 193–224, p. 196; R.R. Nelson and S.G. Winter, *An Evolutionary Theory of Economic Change*, Belknap, Cambridge, MA, 1982.

29. M. Hodges, *Multinational Corporations and National Government: A Case Study of the United Kingdom's Experience, 1964–1970*, Saxon House, Lexington, MA, 1974: 12–13.

30. OEEC, *Private United States Investment*: 18.

31. Max. D. Steuer et al., *The Impact of Foreign Direct Investment on the United Kingdom*, HMSO, London, 1973: 204 [based on US Dept. of Commerce data].

32. Statistics Canada, *Canada's International Investment Position: 1926 to 1967*, Statistics Canada, Ottawa, 1971: 164–65.

33. Hodges, *Multinational Corporations*: 24.

34. G. Jones, 'The British Government and Foreign Multinationals Before 1970', in M. Chick, ed., *Governments, Industries and Markets. Aspects of Government-Industry Relations in the U.K., West Germany and the U.S.A. since 1945*, Elgar, Aldershot, 1990: 200; R. W. Gillespie, 'The policies of England, France, and Germany as Recipients of Foreign Direct Investment', in F. Machlup, W. S. Salant, and L. Tarshis, eds., *International Mobility and Movement of Capital*, NBER, New York, 1972: 399.

35. J. C. R. Dow, *The Management of the British Economy, 1945–60*, CUP, Cambridge, 1964: 149–53.
36. T. Rooth and P. Scott, 'British Public Policy and Multinationals during the "Dollar gap" Era, 1945–1960', *Enterprise & Society*, 3, 1, 2002: 124–61, pp. 140–1.
37. C. R. Schenk, 'Exchange Controls and Multinational Enterprise: The Sterling-Dollar Oil Controversy in the 1950s', *Business History*, 38, 4, 1996: 21–40.
38. Rooth and Scott, 'British Public Policy': 142–3.
39. Dunning, *American Investment*: 49.
40. Ibid.: 86–8; Bostock and Jones, 'Foreign Multinationals': 115.
41. Tolliday, 'Rise of Ford in Britain': 38–9.
42. National Archives: T231/809, Treasury note on US investment in British industry, for the guidance of overseas posts, Jan. 1954.
43. Ibid., Treasury brief on screening inward investment, for United Kingdom representatives at meeting of Commonwealth officials, Dec. 1952.
44. Rooth and Scott, 'British Public Policy': 144–5.
45. Bank of England Archives, EC5/236, note, 21 Oct. 1954; EC5/232, note, c. Oct. 1957.
46. National Archives, T231/922, minute by Robert J. Painter (Treasury), 26 Jun. 1957.
47. Bank of England Archives, EC5/233, memorandum, 30 Jul. 1958.
48. Ibid., Glaves-Smith (Treasury) to G. H. Tansley (Bank of England), 30 Jul. 1958.
49. National Archives: T231/817, Treasury brief for Chancellor regarding Parliamentary debate of 29 Jun. 1959 on acquisition of control of United Kingdom firms by Americans.
50. 'Capital Questions,' *The Economist*, 16 May 1959: 647–8.
51. Hodges, *Multinational Corporations*: 33–7; J. H. Dunning, *Studies in International Investment*, Allen & Unwin, London, 1970: 313–85.
52. Steuer et al., *Impact of Foreign Direct Investment*: 196.
53. J. N. Behrman, *National Interests and Multinational Enterprise: Tensions among North Atlantic Countries*, Prentice-Hall, New Jersey, 1970: 14–15.
54. Dunning, *American Investment*: 197.
55. T. G. Belcher, 'American Factory Operation in Scotland Successful', *Foreign Commerce Weekly* 53, 17 Jan. 1955. Another response was to manufacture items that, other things being equal, could be purchased more economically externally, in order to ensure accurate quality control and production scheduling.
56. Bostock and Jones, 'Foreign Multinationals': 119.
57. Jones and Bostock, 'U.S. Multinationals': 208.
58. Hodges, *Multinational Corporations and National Government*: 286.
59. A. E. Safarian, *Multinational Enterprise and Public Policy. A Study of the Industrialised Countries*, Edward Elgar, Aldershot, 1993: 349.
60. Hodges, *Multinational Corporations and National Government*: 112–15.
61. G. Jones, *Multinationals and Global Capitalism. From the Nineteenth to the Twenty-First Century*, OUP, Oxford, 2005: 206.
62. Hodges, *Multinational Corporations and National Government*: 165.
63. Steuer et al., *Impact of Foreign Direct Investment*.
64. S. Young, N. Hood, and J. Hamill, *Foreign Multinationals and the British Economy. Impact and Policy*, Croom Helm, London, 1988: 159–61.
65. Safarian, *Multinational Enterprise and Public Policy*: 339.
66. Jones, *Multinationals and Global Capitalism*: 208.
67. J. Taylor and C. Wren, 'UK Regional Policy: An Evaluation,' *Regional Studies*, 31, 9, 1997: 835–48.

68. Safarian, *Multinational Enterprise and Public Policy*: 360–1.
69. Young, Hood, and Hamill, *Foreign Multinationals and the British Economy*: 118 and 127.
70. Stephen Young, Neil Hood, and James Hamill, *Foreign Multinationals and the British Economy. Impact and Policy*, Croom Helm, London, 1988: 80–1 and 122–3, summarize these studies.
71. Stopford and Turner, *Britain and the Multinationals*: 135.
72. S. Young, N. Hood, and J. Hamill, *Foreign Multinationals and the British Economy. Impact and Policy*, Croom Helm, London, 1988: 148.
73. Stopford and Turner, *Britain and the Multinationals*: 5.
74. Stopford and Turner, *Britain and the Multinationals*: 153.
75. Young, Hood, and Hamill, *Foreign Multinationals and the British Economy*: 33–4.
76. N. Driffield and M. Munday, 'Industrial Permormance, Agglomeration, and Foreign Manufacturing Investment in the UK', *Journal of International Business Studies*, 31, 1, 2000: 21–37, pp. 21–2.
77. N. Hood and S. Young, 'The United Kingdom,' in John H. Dunning, ed., *Governments, Globalization, and International Business*, OUP, Oxford: 1997: 246.
78. Hood and Young, 'The United Kingdom': 265.
79. See, for example, http://www.walmartmovie.com/
80. For a review of these studies, see S. Young, N. Hood, and E. Peters, 'Multinational Enterprises and Regional Economic Development', *Regional Studies*, 28, 7, 1994: 657–77, p. 658.
81. I. Turok, 'Inward Investment and Local Linkages: How Deeply Embedded is "Silicon Glen"?', *Regional Studies*, 27, 5, 1993: 401–17.
82. C.P. Kindleberger, *American Business Abroad*, Yale, New Haven, CN, 1969.
83. N. A. Phelps, D. Mackinnon, I. Stone, and P. Braidford, 'Embedding the Multinationals? Institutions and the Development of Overseas Manufacturing Affiliates in Wales and North East England', *Regional Studies*, 37, 1, 2003: 27–40.
84. Jones, *Multinationals and Global Capitalism*: 256–7.
85. Driffield and Munday, 'Industrial Performance': 22.

7

British Management Since 1945: 'Renaissance' and Inertia, Illusions and Realities

Nick Tiratsoo

In recent years, it has become increasingly commonplace to argue that British management has experienced something of a renaissance. Writing in 1999, the ex-editor of the *Financial Times*, Geoffrey Owen, opined: 'There is no doubt that some British companies were badly managed in the 1950s and 1960s and that there was a significant improvement in the 1980s and 1990s'.[1] Perhaps the world's most influential authority on management, Harvard's Michael Porter, also appears to have noticed a sea change. In his 1990 magnum opus, *The Competitive Advantage of Nations*, Porter claimed that British managers lacked motivation; that British management culture worked against innovation and change; and that anyway this was a country where the best talent invariably chose other vocations.[2] Yet when, a dozen years later, he was asked by the UK government to investigate management's responsibility for the nation's poor productivity performance, his judgement was relatively benign. Britain's managers could do better, Porter now believed, but they were certainly not the seat of the problem.[3] Predictably, managers themselves have voiced similar claims, and with growing confidence. Thus, when *Management Today* celebrated its fortieth anniversary in 2006, the mood was decidedly upbeat. British managers, it was suggested, had recovered from the dark days of previous decades, and were now more professional, more technically adept, more thoughtful, and even more socially responsible than ever before.[4]

Given that much modern discourse about Britain's economic performance has been about the phenomenon of decline, this tale of apparent redemption is at first glance rather seductive, a heart-warming coda to an uncomfortable past. Yet, in reality, what is being asserted turns out to be little more than wishful thinking. Britain has some outstanding managers, and it may be that overall standards in some areas are improving. But the truth is that, whatever the statements to the contrary, British management *as a whole* continues to suffer from a range of debilitating pathologies, which are much the same today as they were forty or fifty years ago. Indeed, as will be suggested, what appears most notable about British management in an historical perspective is precisely this unfortunate continuity, which in turn begs questions about why real change has been so difficult to engineer.

To begin with, it is sensible to carefully review the relevant literature, principally the various assessments of British management quality that have appeared sporadically over the years since 1945. A few words of caution are prudent before proceeding. The sources discussed here all yield insights, to be sure, but none are wholly unimpeachable. Investigators have varied considerably in the way that they have approached their subject. Some have contented themselves with only very limited samples. Others have accepted management's evaluation of itself without question. Wider factors ranging from political exigencies to academic insularities have foreshortened perspectives. More fundamentally, accurately evaluating a national management cohort is intrinsically difficult. Judgements inevitably contain some element of comparison, and this is rarely unproblematic. Time-based evaluations have to cope with the fact that management is to a greater or lesser degree effected by context, so there is a danger of not contrasting like with like. The use of some other country as a yardstick continues to be popular, but is equally fraught with difficulties. The waxing and waning of enthusiasm for supposed exemplars – Japan is, of course, the most obvious recent example – tells its own story. Even appealing to some more abstract concept or theory does not necessarily solve the problem, because what actually constitutes 'good management' is to some extent in the eye of the beholder. The approach taken here is to define success in terms of productivity growth, broadly defined, since this has usually been the major government concern, and so features in much of the literature. Nevertheless, it is worth noting that narratives could easily be written using other criteria – for example, shareholder value or stakeholding – and these would no doubt yield rather different conclusions. Each of these points needs to be born in mind during the following discussion.

EVALUATIONS OF BRITISH MANAGEMENT
FROM THE 1940s TO THE 1980s

The first major survey after the Second World War that illuminated management quality was presided over by the government supported Anglo-American Council on Productivity (AACP) between 1948 and 1952.[5] The AACP's *modus operandi* was to send a series of expert investigative teams, sixty-six in all, to the United States in order to discover why American business was so vibrant. These teams had a broad remit, and reported on everything from macroeconomic conditions to the minutiae of particular industrial processes, but in the course of their deliberations, many looked, too, at US management, and made comparisons with that found at home. The contrast rarely flattered the British. A common finding was that superior American productivity did not depend on new technology, but rather on systematic application of the best that was already available. Thus, the Materials Handling team, for example, reported: 'Factory managements in the United States review continuously and study intensively all matters affecting the transfer of materials and products to, through, and from the manufacturing unit. This policy is directly responsible for increased productivity and major reductions in costs'.[6] The key question, therefore, was why British managers seemingly failed to behave with the same alacrity. The teams usually recognized that part of the explanation had to do with difference in factors like market size and overall business conditions. But they also often concluded that more could be achieved even given the existing context, and explicitly linked this to management failing. The widely shared judgement was that American managers were simply better at their jobs. A summary volume of 1953, which sought to spell out what the AACP programme as a whole had discovered, put the matter as follows: 'All qualified observers agree that American industrial management is on average more effective than British management. It is different; in many ways it might even offend British ideas or susceptibilities; but it is demonstrably more effective'.[7] The policy recommendation that followed from this was that urgent action should be taken to improve UK standards, for example by radically increasing management training and education.

In the following decades, the literature on British management gradually proliferated. Some studies concentrated on managers themselves, either in Britain[8] or in a comparative context;[9] while others focused on specific management or production techniques, and tried to measure how far they were being deployed, and what variables governed their uptake.[10] Alongside all of this were periodic assessments by economists or economic historians, for example, studies of growth or productivity, which disaggregated key components, and thus contained judgements about management and its overall contribution.[11] Taken together, this body of work proved illuminating on several different counts.

First, there seemed to be little doubt that, in general, British managers continued to be relatively deficient in technical skills. The judgements offered here were more or less robust. In discussing residual components of British productivity performance, the respected economic historian, Edward Denison, considered that 'management knowledge, competence, and vigor', might well explain 'an important part' of why the country was lagging behind America.[12] On the other hand, those who produced micro-studies of firms or processes tended to be considerably less circumspect. The potential for improved productivity in the United Kingdom, they argued, was enormous. Much could be achieved through the introduction of relatively simple innovations which had already been proven to work. The problem was that managers remained blind to the opportunities that were available to them, simply insufficiently attuned to what might be achieved. After completing various intensive investigations of the Midlands metals sector in the 1960s and 1970s, the academic, N.A. Dudley, encapsulated this position succinctly:

Companies are being urged to employ new techniques and bring their equipment up to date. Much more critical is the development and advancement of industrial skills and, in particular, of managerial skills. In general, the 41 companies now included in these studies appear to be typical and representative of their industries as a whole and yet they are not employing modern production planning and control techniques, applying modern principles of plant layout, work design, and quality control and operational research techniques. There is a lack of adequately trained personnel at middle management level, particularly of executives concerned with engineering production, and, as a result, a lack of awareness of the benefits that could accrue from the employment of modern methods.[13]

Second, it appeared that British managers also had some ongoing problems forging constructive labour relations. In the 1950s and 1960s, it was commonplace for informed outsiders to point out that management thinking revolved around the idea of 'the right to manage', and that attitudes to the workforce could be brusque, even peremptory. Indeed, the experienced social psychologist J.A.C. Brown went so far as to argue that the regime in an average factory was less 'tolerant, broad-minded, progressive and fair' than was the case in the British army.[14] Recalling his time in a bottle factory during the 1950s, the author Anthony Glyn described a rare – but far from untypical – brush with one of the hierarchy:

Shortly before Christmas, he came along the factory floor, shaking hands with each operator in turn. I pulled off my gloves and shook hands with him.
'Merry Christmas', he said.
'Merry Christmas, sir', I replied.
'Happy New Year'.
He moved on . . . I found the foreman standing beside me. 'Well, that's your Christmas present', he said, smiling. 'Don't spend it all at once'.[15]

Subsequent detailed explorations suggested that such reflexes persisted. Investigating attitudes to joint consultation at the end of the 1970s, a team from the University of Wales found that managers clearly preferred schemes 'which implied only a very limited erosion of decision making prerogatives'; and that, anyway, only about a third of the 1,058 questioned agreed with the statement: 'There is need for greater employee participation in my organization'.[16] A series of case studies reinforced this rather bleak picture. For example, academics researching ChemCo, 'a giant, British-owned multinational chemical producer', found that some managers were prone to think of the workers as pieces of machinery ('You've got to jump on them now and then to make sure they don't seize up'), while others revelled in being 'hard'. The general impression was of a cadre determined to get its own way, virtually whatever the consequences.[17]

Finally, several reports emerged which looked at managers' education and skill levels, and pointed to some significant shortcomings. Early snapshots, based upon comparatively small samples, discovered that many managers had little more than basic schooling.[18] Subsequently, with education and training receiving more and more political attention, the true scale of the problem began to emerge.

Crockett and Elias reworked data from the government's large-scale National Training Survey of 1976 and discovered that as many as half of the managers in this sample had no qualification at all, and that managers as a whole were 'only marginally more qualified than the general population'.[19] Dovetailing in with this at the end of the 1980s, Charles Handy and colleagues published a widely noticed review of management training and education systems in the elite industrialized countries which showed that, as far as Britain was concerned, although there had been some obvious progress during recent years, notably a profusion of business schools, provision in general was simply '*too little, too late for too few*'.[20]

EVALUATIONS OF BRITISH MANAGEMENT IN THE 1990s AND 2000s

From the mid-1990s onwards, as has been noted, there were some who argued that British management was changing, evolving in a new and more progressive direction. From a distance, the signs could certainly appear propitious. The rise of high-profile figures like Richard Branson and Anita Roddick implied that the corporate world was becoming less stuffy, and more attuned to wider social realities. There was a boom in management education and training. Britain now had over 100 business schools, with the business and management subject area accounting for about one in seven of all students at university, and one in five of all postgraduates.[21] All the broadsheet newspapers produced significant business sections, and these grew in size. Management books periodically appeared in the best seller lists. 'Gurus' like Charles Handy became famous and influential. And, above all else, the United Kingdom entered a prolonged period of economic growth, which apparently confirmed that 'the British disease' – in whatever form conceptualized – was firmly a thing of the past.

However, digging a little beneath the surface reveals that the picture was in fact considerably less satisfactory than many imagined. To begin with, British managers, taken as a whole, still seemed loath to introduce new techniques. Two investigations were particularly revealing. In 2000–1, the Engineering Employers Federation (EEF) produced a report on US–UK productivity, which explicitly looked at, amongst other things, the utilization of 'lean manufacturing'.[22] The research methodology employed was impressive. The EEF team had conducted in-depth interviews with senior managers in manufacturing companies on both sides of the Atlantic, and also commissioned a special survey of 352 EEF members. The major findings contained many echoes of the past. The 'lean manufacturing' approach was proven to work. It had been widely and successfully adopted in the United States. Yet in Britain, its take up was patchy. Perhaps, a third of companies reported that they were using 'lean' principles across the whole of their organization, while over 40 per cent stated that they were not, and, further, had no plan to.[23] The question for the EEF team, therefore, was why

Britain lagged behind. A number of different possible causes were cited. However, when the UK companies which had introduced 'lean' methods were quizzed, they emphasized that their main difficulties had been internal – 'a lack of understanding', 'a lack of lean skills (at the management/supervisor/workforce level)', or 'cultural issues'.[24] The ball, in other words, was firmly in management's court. Little wonder that when the *Economist* commented upon these findings, its headline was 'Blame the Bosses'.[25]

The second investigation was conducted jointly by the London School of Economics' Centre for Economic Performance (CEP) and McKinsey & Company, and published in 2005. This reported on more than 730 manufacturing firms in France, Germany, the United Kingdom, and the United States, and attempted to measure how far they had adopted good management practice. The approach used was unusually encompassing: the CEP–McKinsey team examined eighteen specific management activities under four main headings – shop-floor operations, performance monitoring, target setting, and incentive setting – and scored them on a 1–5 scale. The findings presented a familiar picture. British companies ranged from the 'world class' to the mediocre. But when all the material was aggregated into a national league table, Britain came a distinct fourth, scoring 3.08 compared to the United States' 3.37 – a fact that, it was claimed, accounted for as much as 10–15 per cent of the overall productivity gap between the two countries.[26]

Alongside these two impressive pieces of research, other evidence pointed in a similar direction. Proudfoot Consulting analysed global productivity performance on a regular basis in the early 2000s, and confirmed that, for Britain, management inattention to routine – though unarguably essential – activities like operations planning was imposing serious costs.[27] Various other consultants made essentially the same point. Corporate performance, they demonstrated, could often be substantially improved by the systematic implementation of relatively simple measures: what prevented this from happening in many cases was simply the myopia of those at the top.[28]

Meanwhile, it appeared that British management had also failed to fully overcome its longstanding difficulties about how to relate to the workforce. The rhetoric, it is true, had evolved – and dramatically so. An avalanche of literature and advice now maintained that a firm's 'people' were its most precious asset, and urged employers to cultivate partnership and trust, provide enhanced training, and assiduously seek to maximize engagement and foster a 'passion for work'.[29] 'Human relations' professionals of all sorts proliferated. Yet when researchers turned to study practice, it quickly became clear that the extent of real change could easily be exaggerated. In a report of 2006, the Chartered Institute of Personnel and Development estimated that only 'one in five UK organizations' was actually implementing the new insights 'in a consistent way'.[30] In fact, as other research showed, many corporate strategies clearly continued to be shaped to a surprising degree by highly traditional assumptions. Employee training was frequently viewed as little more than a luxury. In a downturn, or when it was necessary to trim costs, the payroll was invariably cut regardless of long-term consequences. If profitable survival could be guaranteed by operating at a low-skills–low-wage equilibrium, then so be it.[31] Fairly typically, when UK business leaders were questioned in 2007 about the idea of dismissing a fixed quota of staff each year – as Jack Welch had controversially done at General Electric – some 61 per cent declared themselves in favour.[32]

Given such circumstances, what tended to be strike outside observers most about UK employees was not their 'passion for work' but their sense of alienation from corporate goals. In 1997, a survey for the British Social Attitudes series concluded:

In the eyes of employees, the working environment has clearly deteriorated since the early 1980s. Nowadays employees are more likely to feel that the gap between the high and low paid at their workplace is too large, that management and employee relations are poor, that their jobs are insecure, that their workplaces are not being managed as well as they could be, and that they do not have much say over how their work is organised.[33]

Eight years later, the Gallup Employee Engagement Index showed that just 16 per cent of those questioned were loyal and committed, compared to 24 per cent who were 'actively disengaged'. In a relative context, according to consultants ISR, this placed the United Kingdom at seventh in a league table of the world's ten largest economies.[34] BBC's 'Back to the Floor' series of 2001–2, which followed various leading executives doing a week's work alongside their employees, captured the prevailing attitudes in particularly stark form. In one episode, the new head of Wedgewood's Stoke factory, Brian Patterson, was filmed helping an experienced decorator, Yvonne Morrall, as she went about her tasks. Their conversation began with some innocuous banter but soon deteriorated sharply:

Yvonne: When people have been here two, three and five years and they don't even know what you look like, then they're only going to get one impression of you aren't they? People on the shop floor feel that people like yourself are all about profits – less people, more machines, more profits.
Brian: And that's it? Nothing else?
Yvonne: They just feel as though they're not worth anything anymore. Why bother . . . It feels as though you drive off in your BMWs and that's it . . .
Brian: We don't care?
Yvonne: You don't care.
Brian: Listen . . . I've had enough. I've had enough [walks away].[35]

Finally, the much hyped boom in management education and training was also not quite what it seemed. British business schools might be turning out increasing numbers of MBAs, but the big majority were from overseas.[36] Indeed, the links between the business school sector as a whole and the home economy often appeared rather tenuous. All schools of course assiduously assembled networks of influential corporate contacts, and promoted themselves as aiding competitiveness. But evidence that their activities actually produced any sustained impact in the wider economy was, to say the least, meagre. When questioned about business school research in 2002, one group of UK employers fairly typically dismissed it as 'published in academic journals in inaccessible language', with 'little or no relevance to practice'.[37] The situation as regards management training was equally circumscribed. More firms than ever, it is true, were sending their managers on courses, and there was an enormous growth of provision. Yet, if all this activity was evaluated in an international context, it looked far less impressive. Thus, a Chartered Management Institute report of 2004 noted that, not only did the United Kingdom spend significantly less on executive education than either Germany or France, it even failed to match the European average of 2,513 euros per manager per annum.[38] In these circumstances, it was little surprise to find that, when analysts tried to assess the broader question of how far British managers were 'qualified', they often came to the same rather pessimistic conclusions as their predecessors. Examining the issue in 2005, the Leitch Review of Skills reported: 'a greater proportion of those classified as "managers" by the Labour Force Survey hold low-level qualifications than in other "higher" level occupations such as professional occupations'.[39] The notion that managers are 'born not bred' – a staple of much commentary in the 1940s and 1950s – clearly lived on.

To conclude, a review of the literature concerning UK management since 1945 indicates a considerable degree of continuity. It would be unwise to suggest that there was no change during these years, or a complete lack of progress. But, on the other hand, it is striking how the same flaws and difficulties are identified again and again, right up to the present day. British managers, it seems, have continued to be relatively backward in terms of technical proficiency, deficient in their relations with the shop floor, and largely lukewarm about the whole matter of education and training. In short, they have too often underperformed in essential aspects of their calling, passing up opportunities to implement proven solutions to the riddles of productivity.

EXPLAINING INERTIA

All this raises some obvious questions. As has been shown, no one could describe UK management's inadequacies as a secret. So what has prevented them from being addressed? Why has genuine advance been difficult to contrive? If, as is often argued, catch up and convergence have been such notable features across the modern world economy, how is it possible that they appear to have remained so weakly evident in this particular case? The following paragraphs consider various possible explanations.

One hypothesis is that the United Kingdom's business environment has been so constrained in terms of both competition and regulation – formal and informal – that managers have in effect had neither the incentive nor the power to exercise their talents. This is certainly plausible. Various authorities have argued that, for possibly four decades after 1945, the British economy was unusually sheltered from competition. Organizations like the Federation of British Industries – later the Confederation of British Industry (CBI) – have consistently railed against red tape and government bureaucracy. Moreover, it has often been asserted that the situation on the shop floor in many British work places has been deeply inimical to progressive innovation, with trade unions enforcing crippling restrictive practices, and strikes called at the slightest provocation. Those who see managers as essentially hamstrung, therefore, appear to have a case.

However, on closer inspection, little of this is, in fact, very compelling. The British economy may have been relatively protected and highly regulated in the immediate post-war period – opinions about this differ[40] – but as time has passed, the unequivocal trend has been towards liberalization. Thus, for example, calculations by the Fraser Institute show that Britain's 'level of economic freedom' index rose from 5.9 out of 10 in 1970 to no less than 8.1 out of 10 in 2004, placing the country joint sixth in the world league table.[41] Assertions about workforce intransigence also need to be treated with caution. Interest in the subject peaked during the 1970s, when denunciations of the closed shop and strikes, amongst other things, regularly made the headlines. In 1976, Cambridge University's C.F. Pratten appeared to provide credible substantiation. His study established that the productivity performance of UK operating units in international companies was often comparatively poor, and argued that, in an 'important minority' of instances, one of the causes was 'the lower performance of labour'. He observed: 'Some firms have lower output and productivity because of a worse strike record in the U.K., and some firms have lower productivity because of severe restrictive practices ... More generally, managers claim to have difficulty in implementing changes and achieving high productivity in the U.K.'[42] However, when, a few years later, the sociologist Theo Nicholls forensically examined Pratten's methods and conclusions, he exposed them as less than convincing.[43] Other purportedly authoritative studies, before and after, met much the same fate. Reviewing the evidence anew is sobering. A handful of economic sectors have no doubt continued to suffer from significant difficulties over work organization, occasionally right down to the present.[44] There have been some high-profile strikes, and also times when the number of disputes rose far above the average. But, even in the worst years, none of this remotely amounted to what could be called a general malady.[45] And, of course, here as elsewhere, the long-term trend has been towards less and less restraint, with increasingly flexible labour markets, a diminution of trade union power, and a sharp downturn in industrial relations friction of any kind.[46] Significantly, the very term 'restrictive practices' is today by and large an anachronism.

It is difficult to argue, therefore, that the broad sweep of managers somehow have been discouraged from change by material circumstances. In fact, the major source of inertia almost certainly lies elsewhere, in the rather more amorphous sphere of ideas. British managers have not acted on a whim. Indeed, most of their fundamental decisions have continued to be guided by the same corpus of very characteristic values and assumptions – notions, as already suggested, about education and labour relations, but also many other important topics and issues.[47] What needs to be explained, then, is why this edifice has proved so enduring. Of course, longevity itself must be one source of resilience, in the sense that over time particular ways of thinking inevitably become ever more entrenched. But in this case, it is also necessary to give due weight to the surprising fact that – despite all the reports and inquiries detailing failings – there seems to have been no very strong challenge to the status quo in management practice, no real build-up of pressure, inside or outside business, for a different way. The following paragraphs first briefly explore this notable 'absence', and then try to account for it.

The main players involved in discussions about how to improve British management have included, at one time or another, the government, professional associations (including progressive practitioners), and a range of different pundits. This looks, at first glance, like a formidable combination, but the truth is very different. Whitehall interest has only ever flickered. The AACP enjoyed some success, no doubt, but its much longer running successor, the British Productivity Council, was largely anonymous, and is now almost completely forgotten. More recently, the Blair administrations produced several interesting reports, and a handful of modest initiatives, but that is all. The tentativeness of a 2006 Department of Trade and Industry judgement – that 'there is a general perception of UK management weakness, but . . . little evidence to enable an objective international comparison to be made'[48] – speaks for itself. Turning to the professional associations, it cannot be denied that some of the specialists (those dealing exclusively with engineers, marketeers, and accountants, for example) have prospered. But when attempts have been made to involve management as a whole, and spread best practice across the spectrum, the results have been generally disappointing. One example is particularly telling: the Chartered Management Institute, which can trace its history back to 1946, currently has a membership of about 100,000, which sounds impressive, but is in fact a mere 2.5 per cent of those eligible to join.[49] Finally, as regards the pundits, they have no doubt occasionally produced best sellers and a legacy of comment, but, again, their real impact is questionable. Both the 'airport management' book and the broadsheet management column are fairly recent phenomenon. Different authors take contrasting viewpoints on even fundamental questions. The whole field is renowned for its susceptibility to quickly passing fads and fashions. Besides which, little of what has been written actually deals with the specificities of Britain.[50] Authors and their agents might want to claim that they have made a difference, but this remains to be substantiated.

Outside of this inner circle, the management question has barely registered. There have been occasional diatribes from polemicists,[51] and various contributions from the media, in formats that range from the serious to the satirical. In the early 2000s, the BBC comedy series *The Office* focused upon the day-to-day working life of a dysfunctional manager, David Brent, and in no time at all spawned a popular cliché, 'Dave Brent-style management', which encapsulated everything that was bad about the profession.[52] Yet, what is most striking is how rare such comment has been. Research for the Royal Commission on the Press in the late 1970s, which analysed industrial relations coverage, underlined that most stories focused on trade unions, and that employers and managers remained almost completely 'invisible'.[53] Since, then, as has been noted, things have changed in several different ways, but it is still comparatively unusual to find management *per se* treated as an issue. Significantly, an authoritative 2007 internal review observed that, over recent years, the BBC had come to examine business stories largely from the viewpoint of the consumer, and as a result overlooked much of what was occurring in the workplace.[54]

An objection might be that, prior to the late 1990s, Britain endlessly debated its alleged decline, and in this context, at least, management must have featured. But in fact the silences here were nearly as marked as elsewhere. Most commentators were greatly influenced by what amounted to the then current party lines of the Left and Right, and this invariably meant that the stock in trade of alleged villains, too, was very limited – essentially 'the trade unions', 'finance capital', 'the state', 'the working class', or 'the ruling class', according to taste.[55] Iconoclasts remained few and far between. When the campaigning television producer, Glyn Jones, broke from the pack in 1968, and delivered a *Tuesday Documentary* which placed UK management incompetence at the heart of the country's problems, the *Evening Standard*'s distinguished television critic, Milton Schulman, was so astonished that he called it 'that rare TV phenomenon', a programme which had 'challenged preconceived attitudes' and 'forced you to question your own prejudices'.[56]

What explains this relative silence about management? A full answer to this question would require a book in its own right, but some of the main contributing factors can be briefly encapsulated as follows. One obvious point is that comment about British managers has often been drowned out by competing discourses. An insistent theme from the 1940s to the 1990s, for example, emanating from the Conservative Party, right-wing think tanks, and also a variety of peak organizations, was that industry had been a victim, sacrificed on the alter of politics. The culpable, then, were a succession of post-war ministers who had consistently neglected the crucial importance of wealth creation – certainly not managers.[57] In 2006, business organizations such as the Institute of Directors and the CBI still spent much of their time 'griping about the government'.[58] With such powerful voices repeating a similar mantra at every opportunity, it has been difficult for others to get a look in.

Meanwhile, it is also noticeable that many of those standing outside the immediate worlds of government and business have, to a surprising degree, overlooked management, too. Before the late 1990s, the Labour Party and business were largely estranged, so that, though a few leading figures like Stafford Cripps and Ian Mikardo on occasion showed an interest in management, they had very little impact.[59] Subsequently, the situation has changed somewhat, in that Labour has engineered a rapprochement with business at some levels, and become much more interested in public service delivery. Nevertheless, across the Left as a whole, practical knowledge about how *commercial* organizations function has remained notoriously hazy.[60] Many of those within relevant academic disciplines have been equally blinkered. The growing influence of the neoclassical school has curtailed economists' interest in 'the black box'. The study of industrial relations tended until very recently to be largely about trade unions. Sociologists have often studied work, but their sympathies have frequently led them to view it 'from below'.[61] Indicative of the whole mindset, Crafts and Woodward's otherwise comprehensive student textbook of 1991, *The British Economy since 1945*, included no dedicated chapter on management, and only scant reference to the subject in any shape or form.[62] Of course, the recently arrived business schools have to some extent filled these gaps, though, as already noted, whether they have actually bridged the gulf between academia and everyday corporate life remains at best debatable.

Finally, it appears that the public's interest in management has also been rather shallow. The Conservative-voting middle classes have often shared the view that government meddling is the real cause of British business's problems, not corporate incompetence.[63] Their more liberal counterparts have tended to be interested in the public services rather than commerce. Working-class attitudes are less easy to précis. Employed on the shop floor of a printing firm during the 1970s, the journalist, Martin Leighton, was struck by the ambiguities:

In the maintenance shop, bitterness erupted from time to time with remarks like 'They only speak to you when they want something done. The rest of the time they treat you like dirt'. And management's own performance was monitored and criticised . . . Yet there was at the same time a certain tolerance which was expressed frequently in the word 'fiddle'. The managing director's new Jaguar was a tax 'fiddle', such and such a director got his job because of some 'fiddle', the sales representative's expense account was a 'fiddle', as, indeed, were all management perks and privileges. A 'fiddle' was not necessarily something to condemn.[64]

What is clear, though, is that popular antipathy and cynicism has rarely triggered concern about management as such, or sustained belief that something should be done to change things.

CONCLUSION

In the last decade or so, there has been an ongoing re-evaluation of British economic performance since 1945. Older interpretations that emphasized an all-embracing 'decline' are now judged unhelpful, and there is general consensus that the story has in fact been far more nuanced. This is welcome. However, it would be a mistake to move from one extreme to the other, and now claim that the country's economic actors have simply played out the role that was allotted to them. The UK management cohort has certainly underperformed. The challenge for the future is to develop strategies which will allow this fact to be addressed. Necessarily, given that the barriers to change in the past have been so multifaceted, this will mean dragging management from the shadows out into the limelight of national debate.

NOTES

1. G. Owen, *From Empire to Europe*, HarperCollins, London, 1999, 422.
2. M. Porter, *The Competitive Advantage of Nations*, Macmillan, London, 1990, 502–3.
3. M.E. Porter, and C.H.M. Ketels, UK *Competitiveness: Moving to the Next Stage*, Department of Trade and Industry, London, 2003; and N. Tiratsoo, and J. Tomlinson, *The Porter Report on British Productivity*, EBK Working Paper, 2004/1, 2004.
4. *Management Today*, September 2006: *passim.*
5. N. Tiratsoo, and J. Tomlinson, 'Exporting the "Gospel of Productivity": United States Technical Assistance and British Industry 1945–1960', *Business History Review*, 71, 1997, 41–81.
6. Anglo-American Council on Productivity Materials Handling Team, *Materials Handling in Industry*, Anglo-American Council on Productivity, London: 1949, 9.
7. G. Hutton, *We Too Can Prosper*, George Allen & Unwin, London, 1953, 35.
8. For example, R. Lewis, and R. Stewart, *The Boss. The Life and Times of the British Business Man*, Phoenix House, London, 1958; I. McGivering, D. Mathews, and W.H. Scott, *Management in Britain*, Liverpool University Press, Liverpool, 1960; and Political and Economic Planning, *Attitudes in British Management*, Penguin, Harmondsworth, 1966.
9. For example, J. Dunning, *Studies in International Investment*, George Allen & Unwin, London, 1970; D. Granick, *Managerial Comparisons of Four Developed Countries: France, Britain, United States and Russia*, MIT Press, Cambridge, 1971; and R. Dore, *British Factory–Japanese Factory*, George Allen & Unwin, London, 1973.
10. For example, Department of Scientific and Industrial Research, *Productivity in Letterpress Printing*, Her Majesty's Stationary Office, London, 1961; R. Wild, and K. Swann, 'The Small Company, Profitability, Management Resources and Management Techniques', *Journal of Business Policy*, 3, 1972: 10–21; Department of Industry Committee for Material Handling, *Materials-Handling Costs: A New Look at Manufacture*, Her Majesty's Stationary Office, London, 1976; and K.G. Lockyer, J.S. Oakland, and C.H. Duprey, 'Quality Control in British Manufacturing Industry: A Study', *Quality Assurance*, 8, 1982, 39–44.
11. For example, C.F. Pratten, *Labour Productivity Differentials within International Companies*, Cambridge University Press, Cambridge: 1976; and R.E. Caves, 'Productivity Differences among Industries', in R.E. Caves, and L.B. Krause, eds., *Britain's Economic Performance*, George Allen & Unwin, London, 1980, 135–98.
12. E.F. Denison, 'Economic Growth', in R.E. Caves, and Associates, eds., *Britain's Economic Prospects*, George Allen & Unwin, London, 1980, 275–6.
13. N.A. Dudley, 'Comparative Productivity Analysis-Study in the United Kingdom West Midlands Engineering and Metalworking Industries', *International Journal of Production Research*, 8, 1970, 402.
14. J.A.C. Brown, 'Surveying the British Scene', in F. A. Heller, ed., *New Developments in Industrial Leadership*, Polytechnic Management Association, London: 1955, 10–28.
15. A. Glyn, *The Blood of a Britishman*, Readers Union, Newton Abbott, 1971: 204.
16. M. Poole, R. Mansfield, P. Blyton, and P. Frost, 'Participation: The Manager's Viewpoint', *Employee Relations*, 3, 1981, 10–1.

17. N. Nichols and H. Beynon, *Living with Capitalism. Class Relations and the Modern Factory*, Routledge & Kegan Paul, London: esp. 33–4; and see also, for example, G. Cleverley, *The Fleet Street Disaster. British National Newspapers As a Case Study in Mismanagement*, Constable, London, 1976.

18. D. S. Clark, *The Industrial Manager*, Business Publications, London, 1966, 40.

19. G. Crockett and E. Elias, 'British Managers: A Study of Their Education, Training, Mobility and Earnings', *British Journal of Industrial Relations*, 22, 1984, 36.

20. C. Handy, 'Great Britain', in C. Handy, C. Gordon, I. Gow, and C. Randlesome, *Making Managers*, Pitman Publishing, London, 1988, 168.

21. C. Ivory, P. Miskell, H. Shipton, A. White, K. Moeslein, and A. Neely, *UK Business Schools: Historical Contexts and Future Scenarios*, Advanced Institute of Management Research, London, 2006, 9 and 12.

22. The EEF published interim and final versions of this report – Engineering Employers Association, *Lessons from Uncle Sam*, Engineering Employers Association, London, 2001; and Engineering Employers Association, *Catching up with Uncle Sam*, Engineering Employers Association, London, 2001.

23. Ibid., 29.

24. Ibid., 32.

25. Anon., 'Blame the Bosses', *Economist*, 10 Oct. 2002.

26. N. Bloom, S. Dorgan, J. Dowdy, T. Rippin, and J. Van Reenen, 'Management Practices: The Impact of Company Performance', *CentrePiece*, Summer 2005, 2–6; and see also, P. Thornton, 'David Brent-Style Managers "Have Widened UK Productivity Gap with US"', *Independent*, 8 Sept. 2005.

27. See, for example, Proudfoot Consulting, *Untapped Potential. The Barriers to Optimum Corporate Productivity*, Proudfoot Consulting, London, 2002, 13–14.

28. For one interesting example, see S. Joynson, and A. Forrester, *Sid's Heroes*, BBC Books, London, 1995.

29. R. Taylor, *Britain's World of Work – Myths and Realities*, Economic and Social Research Council, Swindon, 2002, 11.

30. Chartered Institute of Personnel and Development, *Smart Work*, Chartered Institute of Personnel and Development, London, 2006, 22.

31. See, inter alia, P. Geroski and P. Gregg, *Coping with Recession: UK Company Performance in Adversity* Cambridge University Press, Cambridge, 1997; and R. Wilson, and T. Hogarth, eds., *Tackling the Low Skills Equilibrium: A Review of Issues and Some New Evidence*, Institute of Employment Research, Coventry, 2003.

32. Hudson, *Cull or Cure: The Secret of an Efficient Company* Hudson, London, 2007.

33. A. Bryson and S. McKay, 'What about the Workers?' in R. Jowell, J. Curtice, A. Park, L. Brook, K. Thompson, and C. Bryson, *British Social Attitudes the 14th Report. The End of Conservative Values?*, Ashgate, Aldershot and Brookfield Vermont, 1997, 38.

34. S. Caulkin, 'What Sort of Boss Gives a Monkey's about His Staff?', *Observer*, 28 Jan. 2007; D. Thomas, 'Most UK Employees Enjoy Their Jobs But Don't Care about the Success of Their Employer', posted at www.PersonnelToday.com 16 Apr. 2007; and, more generally, Chartered Institute of Personnel and Development, *How Engaged Are British Employees*, Chartered Institute of Personnel and Development, London, 2006.

35. This is an edited version of the transcript, taken from the BBC's website.

36. Ivory et al., *UK Business Schools*, 12.

37. Council for Excellence in Management and Leadership Business Schools Advisory Group, *The Contribution of the UK Business Schools to Developing Managers and*

Leaders, Council for Excellence in Management and Leadership, London, 2002, 26; and, more generally, K, Starkey and N. Tiratsoo, *The Business School and the Bottom Line*, Cambridge University Press, Cambridge, 2007.

38. C. Mabey and M. Ramirez, *Developing Managers: A European Perspective* Chartered Management Institute, London, 2004, 3.

39. The Leitch Review of Skills, *Skills in the UK: The Long-Term Challenge. Interim Report*, Her Majesty's Stationary Office, London, 2005, 109.

40. See Jim Tomlinson's chapter in this volume.

41. See material at www.freetheworld.com and S. Caulkin, 'The Red Herring of Red Tape', *Observer*, 29 May 2005.

42. C.F. Pratten, *Labour Productivity Differentials within International Companies*, Cambridge University Press, Cambridge, 1976, 66.

43. Nichols, T., *The British Worker Question* Routledge & Kegan Paul, London, 1986, 44 and 55.

44. N. Tiratsoo and J. Tomlinson, 'Restrictive Practices on the Shopfloor in Britain, 1945–60: Myth and Reality', *Business History*, 36, 1994, 65–82.

45. R. Richardson, 'Trade Unions and Industrial Relations', in N.F.R. Crafts and N.W. C. Woodward, eds., *The British Economy since 1945* Oxford University Press, Oxford, 1991, 416–42.

46. M. Cully, S. Woodland, A. O'Reilly, and G. Dix, *Britain at Work*, Routledge, London, 1999.

47. For enduring elements of British management culture, see *inter alia* Lewis and Stewart, *The Boss*; J. Child, *British Management Thought*, George Allen & Unwin, London, 1969; and J-L. Barsoux, and P. Lawrence, *The Challenge of British Management*, Macmillan Education, Basingstoke, 1990.

48. Department of Trade and Industry, *UK Productivity and Competitiveness Indicators*, Her Majesty's Stationary Office, London 2006, 44.

49. For this organization's early history and travails, see N. Tiratsoo, 'High Hopes Frustrated: the British Institute of Management as an Agent of Change, 1947–63', in F. Amatori, A. Colli, and N. Crepas, eds., *Deindustrialization and Reindustrialization in 20th Century Europe*, Franco Angeli, Milan, 1999, 143–54.

50. A.J. Huczynski, *Management Gurus* Routledge, London and New York, 1993.

51. A recent example of this genre is R. Protherough and J. Pick, *Managing Britannia. Culture and Management in Modern Britain* Brynmill Press, Denton, Norfolk, 2002.

52. See http://www.bbc.co.uk/comedy/theoffice/

53. Cmnd. 6810–4, *Analysis of Newspaper Content. A Report by Professor Denis McQuail*, Royal Commission on the Press, London, 1977.

54. T. Conlan, 'BBC Business Needs Wider View', *Guardian*, 25 May 2007.

55. D. See Coates and J. Hillard, 'Introduction', in D. Coates, and J. Hillard, eds., *The Economic Decline of Modern Britain. The Debate Between Left and Right*, Wheatsheaf Books, Brighton, Sussex, 1986, xi–xii.

56. M. Barnes. 'Glyn Jones', *Independent*, 22 Oct. 1999. Jones subsequently used the research for this film in G. Jones and M. Barnes, *Britain on Borrowed Time*, Penguin Books, Harmondsworth, 1967.

57. For a classic example, see Sir Keith Joseph, 'Inflation, De-capitalizing British Industry', speech delivered at Leith, 8 Aug. 1974, posted at www.margaretthatcher.org/archive

58. Anon., 'Cameron Preferred Soldiers', *Economist*, 2 Dec. 2006; and R. Wilson, and M. Harris, *Who Do We Think We Are? A profile of IoD Membership*, Institute of Directors, London, 2006.
59. For Cripps and Mikardo, see, respectively, N. Tiratsoo and J. Tomlinson, *Industrial Efficiency and State Intervention: Labour 1939–51* Routledge, London and NewYork, 1993; and I. Mikardo, *Back-Bencher*, Weidenfeld and Nicolson, London, 1988.
60. See, for example, C. Landry, D. Morley, R. Southwood, and P. Wright, *What a Way To Run a Railroad. An Analysis Of Radical Failure* Comedia Publishing Group, London, 1985.
61. A. H. Halsey, *A History of Sociology in Britain*, Oxford University Press, Oxford, 2004.
62. Crafts and Woodward eds., *The British Economy since 1945*.
63. See, for example, R. Scase and R. Goffee, *The Real World of the Small Business Owner*, Croom Helm, London, 1980.
64. M. Leighton, *Men at Work*, Jill Norman, London, 1981, 72.

8

Not 'Decline and Revival': An Alternative Narrative on British Post-War Productivity[1]

Jim Tomlinson

From the late 1950s until the 1980s the dominant narrative of post-war British economic history was one of 'decline'. Originating as a commentary on contemporary events in the very specific circumstances of the late 1950s, 'declinism' entered the historiography soon after, and swept almost all before it.[2] The narrative was always heavily politicized. Having originated on the Centre-Left, declinism was taken up across the political spectrum, but deployed with most effect by the Right.[3] Above all, Mrs Thatcher staked her claim to power on a declinist account of modern Britain, from which dire fate, of course, only her policies could offer rescue.[4] Unsurprisingly, when in power the Conservative government under Mrs Thatcher was anxious as soon as possible to assert that decline had been halted and a revival initiated – and as early as 1982 this was exactly what the Chancellor, Nigel Lawson, was proclaiming.[5]

Among academics, until recently, the dominant narrative on post-war British economic history was also one of 'decline', but of late this has been challenged from a whole variety of directions. One attack has come from a questioning of the meaning of the term decline, however 'relative' it is asserted to be, when applied to an almost continuously expanding economy.[6] A second has been to historicize the term as a product of a very particular context.[7] A third is work which questions the thesis of failure (particularly in manufacturing industry) which usually accompanies the discussion of 'decline'.[8] Fourth, is work which criticizes the declinist assertions about the nature of the British state, and its alleged unconcern with technological and scientific progress.[9] Finally, and most broadly, is the work which questions the benefits of the post-war enthusiasm for economic growth, and therefore by clear implication suggests that in welfare terms a focus on 'decline' (which by most accounts means 'slow' growth) is highly problematic.[10]

Recognition of the weakness of declinism, as applied specifically to productivity, is growing, with Stephen Broadberry, for example, arguing in his contribution to the Cambridge Economic History that 'In considering the performance of British manufacturing since the Second World War, it is important to avoid

Table 8.1. Labour productivity in manufacturing, 1960–95

	1960–73	1973–9	1979–95
Britain	4.1	1.0	4.3
France	6.6	4.4	3.1
Germany	5.7	4.2	2.2

Source: Owen, *From Empire to Europe*: 4.

the excessive pessimism of the "declinists" who undoubtedly dominated the literature of the 1980s'.[11] Despite these challenges to declinism, the 'decline and revival' story remains popular. The purpose of this chapter is to criticize that narrative as applied to productivity (especially in manufacturing industry), which commonly provides a key underpinning for broader 'decline and revival accounts', and to provide an alternative more helpful story.

One of the best examples of a declinist account applied to industry is Geoffrey Owen's book, *From Empire to Europe*, whose subtitle is *The Decline and Revival of British Industry since the Second World War*.[12] Owen's book is a good place to start because it is not 'extreme' in its declinism, and is aware of at least some of the problems with that narrative. Within a broad story of British manufacturing falling behind other European countries in the 1960s and 1970s and reviving from the 1980s, the book gives productivity performance a key role, with Table 8.1 acting as a starting point of the argument for the book.

After a scene-setting 'decline and revival' introduction, Owen's book consists of case studies of ten industries. These case studies do not consistently disaggregate productivity comparisons, so that it is not that easy to judge from the book how many of the cases fit the overall story. But my reading of Owen's own account suggests the British decline and revival story applies to only a minority of his cases – cotton textiles (where Britain failed to find a niche within a general context of declining European production), steel, cars, and paper. Of the others, electronics was 'a shared European failure', as was shipbuilding.[13] Aerospace, chemicals, and pharmaceuticals were successes. The most difficult to assess is engineering, which is a huge amalgam of diverse activities, where, unsurprisingly, some parts did better than others. But an overall 'decline and revival' story is not borne out by, for example, Owen's data on 'shares of world machinery exports', which shows Britain's share as significantly ahead of France and Italy (but behind Germany) as late as 1980.[14]

The picture conjured up by Owen's case studies is one of some industries doing well and some doing badly, rather than an aggregate story of 'decline and revival'. The lack of a compelling story of across the board decline in the pre-1970s period is underlined by the summary given for the declines of textiles, steel, cars, and paper. In each case the book assesses how far three very standard reasons identified in the declinist literature – the financial system, training, and education and labour relations – applied. The results are summarized in Table 8.2. Owen's conclusion conforms to the story in this table by discounting all three factors as

Table 8.2. Causes of decline?

	Financial system	Education	Labour relations
Textiles	No	No	No
Cars	No	No	'Contributed but not central cause'
Steel	No	No	'Subsidiary factor'
Paper	No	No	No

Source: Owen, *From Empire to Europe*: 88–9, 250–2, 149–50, 170–1.

crucial to the 'decline and revival' story.[15] Owen's own explanation therefore effectively dismisses many traditional declinist diagnoses, and focuses instead on a transition in public policy from 'consensus to competition' as the explanation for moving from decline to revival.

This explanation draws on the work of Crafts and Broadberry, whose arguments are returned to below. But it is useful to examine it in the context of Owen's own book. As noted, only four of Owen's industries fit the broad pattern of a British 'decline and revival'. How many of these four failures can be ascribed to an absence of competition? In the case of cotton textiles, there was huge competition for British producers from the free entry for Commonwealth imports until 1958, when voluntary restrictions were brought in. But as Owen notes, these restrictions were very generous to importers, so that Britain was much less highly protected than other European countries: 'In 1960 cotton textile imports accounted for 35 per cent of domestic consumption in Britain compared with 5 per cent in the six Common Market countries and only 1 per cent in the USA.'[16] It would seem difficult on that basis to tell a story of cotton's decline and revival based on a distinctly British attachment to protection.

In the case of cars, Owen's argument is linked to his broader thesis about the major error of Britain in not entering the EEC at its inception: 'the decision to opt out of European integration was the biggest missed opportunity of the 1945–60 period . . .'.[17] Specifically in relation to cars, the argument is that Britain delayed serious entry into European car markets until the 1960s, being previously overly concerned with Commonwealth, and to a lesser extent, American markets. But prior to Britain's entry into the EEC it is hardly the case that British producers did not face competition. While in the home market tariff protection was substantial, this protection had of course, since the First World War brought an influx of American car producers, so competition in the car market was substantial. Indeed, one of the reasons for the 'merger mania' in the industry in the 1960s was the recognition that the industry was more fragmented than in other European countries.[18] Decline there undoubtedly was in cars, but that cannot be ascribed to an absence of competition.

The competition explanation for a purported British decline has more plausibility in the case of paper, where the creation of EFTA opened up a previously protected industry to powerful Scandinavian competition.[19] But even here the link from competition to revival seems, by Owen's own account, not entirely straightforward – it was only twenty to thirty years after its onset that this competition yielded an improvement in paper's performance.[20] Finally, the steel industry has the 'best fit' with the decline and revival story, with competition as the key driver of performance.[21]

Overall, therefore, we can argue that of the ten industries investigated only two fit reasonably well into the story of a peculiarly British decline and revival largely caused by the degree of competition exerted on the industries. Such a low proportion of cases fitting the general narrative surely suggests this narrative is to be treated with considerable scepticism.

That many industries in Britain do not fit a story of decline and revival is clearly recognized in Broadberry's key text on manufacturing productivity. His disaggregated work 'helps to counter the tendency in much of the existing literature to dwell on the failures and ignore the successes, which has resulted in an overly negative view of British manufacturing performance over the long run'.[22] For him, the different performance of sectors is largely accounted for in a mass production versus flexible specialization framework, in which the failings of the period 1950 to 1979 'occurred largely as a result of an unsuccessful attempt to apply mass production techniques'. In addition, there were problems on the demand side relating to the initial post-war fragmentation of markets for British goods in Commonwealth countries, and the later need to adjust to European markets. It is in this context that Broadberry concurs with Owen in seeing an absence of competition as a problem, by adding to the difficulties of making adjustment to this shift.[23]

The mass production/flexible specialization framework is highly contestable, but is not our concern here.[24] Rather, the relevant issue is how far Broadberry's work is compatible with a 'decline and revival' narrative. The key problem here is timing. While Broadberry talks, as above, of a problem extending over the whole period from the beginning of the 1950s to 1979, at other points he spells out that as far as his key comparison with Germany is concerned most of the decline in Britain's performance was in the years 1973 to 1979. Thus: 'During the post-Second World War period, Germany began to pull ahead of Britain in manufacturing, although the major divergence between Britain and Germany in this sector did not occur until the 1970s, and was very much reversed during the 1980s.'[25] (The figures underlying this summary are given in Table 8.3, which

Table 8.3. Anglo-German labour productivity differences, 1938–89 (UK = 100)

	Manufacturing	Whole economy
1938	107.1	82.6
1950	96.0	65.8
1973	118.6	111.7
1979	140.3	123.9
1989	105.1	115.7

Source: Broadberry, *Productivity Race*: 68.

also underpin Broadberry's broad thesis that long run decline depended primarily on forces operating outside manufacturing). The concentration of the relative deterioration in manufacturing in the 1973–9 period seems evident here, and throws serious doubt on a manufacturing 'decline and revival' story which places decline within the golden age of the 1950s and 1960s.

To open up this issue of the timing of Britain's problems in matching German rates of productivity growth it is useful to look at the recent debate between Booth and Broadberry and Crafts on manufacturing performance in the golden age.

Booth offers a wide-ranging critique of the manufacturing failure hypothesis as applied to Britain in this period. In the current context what is particularly important is his discussion of the timing of the deterioration relative to West Germany. He uses Broadberry's data to point out that 'two-thirds of the total relative improvement of German manufacturing productivity between 1950 and 1973 had been secured by 1952, and from 1959 to 1973 British industrial productivity growth rates were virtually identical.'[26] However, because of his focus on the 'long boom' period, Booth makes much less of the point, evident in Table 8.3 above, that by far the sharpest Anglo-German relative deterioration was in 1973–9. He rightly notes the loss of competitiveness in the sector arising from exchange rate deterioration after 1977 and the fall in the share of manufacturing in the whole economy with which this deterioration was accompanied. He also makes the important point that 'the deterioration of manufacturing performance between 1977 and 1982 can be explained predominantly by forces operating within that period. It is unnecessary to invoke cumulative decline'. But he does not offer detailed analysis of productivity performance in the 1970s.[27]

In their reply, Broadberry and Crafts offer a re-statement of their view that there was indeed a failure in manufacturing productivity growth relative to Germany, which operated over the whole period from 1950 to 1979, but which 'culminated in the productivity debacle of the 1970s'.[28] They criticize Booth's attempt to challenge their own approach of starting the analysis in 1950, on the grounds that that year was a cyclical peak and therefore appropriate for the analysis of trends.[29] However, they do not address the question of what happened between 1973 and 1979, beyond asserting 1979 as the turning point, and the problems of the immediate preceding years as the 'culmination' of long run trends.[30] This absence of attention to the mid-1970s is especially interesting in the light of both Broadberry's account of the importance of this period in his book, as noted above, and the deployment of figures by Broadberry and Crafts which make this point very clearly – figures reported below as Table 8.4.

These figures surely show that if we measure from cyclical peaks, the turning point in British manufacturing productivity was 1973 not 1979. Before that date performance was marginally inferior to that of West Germany and respectable by any long-run standards. Between 1973 and 1979 it was indeed a 'debacle'. This suggests the beginnings of a possible alternative narrative of British post-war productivity which sees the events of the 1970s not as the 'culmination' of long run problems, but as largely the consequence of short run forces, and therefore

Table 8.4. Manufacturing labour productivity in Britain and West Germany, 1951–89 (% per annum per person engaged)

	Britain	West Germany
1951–64	4.50	5.32
1964–73	4.18	4.52
1973–9	0.68	3.47
1979–89	4.14	1.92

Source: S. Broadberry and N. Crafts, 'UK productivity performance from 1950 to 1979: a restatement of the Broadberry–Crafts view' *Economic History Review*, 56, 2003: 723.

undermines the idea of some profound malaise or decline, asserting instead highly contingent and particular factors causing a short-run crisis within a longer run picture of 'mildly disappointing'[31] performance in the golden age.

What happened in the 1970s? Analysing productivity over the period 1973 to 1979 is beset with difficulties.[32] We can avoid some of these problems by continuing to focus attention on manufacturing alone, though this significantly biases our understanding, given that productivity performance was much worse in manufacturing than for the economy as a whole.[33] In general, 'estimates of productivity change are notoriously fragile',[34] and this fragility is enhanced when the period looked at is both short and characterized by sharp fluctuations in output. Particular problems arise in measuring the productivity of capital at such times, because estimates of the capital stock rely heavily on stable trends in the utilization of capital and the scrapping of old capital goods, whereas we know that such scrapping is highly unstable in times of big changes both in output trends and in the economic environment. The 1970s seems to be a period when uncertainties on the scrapping issue are particularly intense.[35] As a result it seems wise to focus on labour productivity in trying to construct a plausible narrative which relates what happened to productivity to the economic and political events of the period. For good or ill, this accords with the concern of most of the debate.[36]

Table 8.5 shows some details on aggregate manufacturing productivity in these years. It is clear that the productivity stagnation is especially concentrated in the

Table 8.5. Manufacturing labour productivity, 1973–9

	Output/hour worked (1993 = 100)	Real output (1993 = 100)
1973	49.0	97.5
1974	49.0	95.8
1975	49.0	89.2
1976	51.0	90.9
1977	51.7	92.6
1978	52.7	93.2
1979	53.6	93.0

Source: Mary O'Mahony *Britain's Productivity Performance 1950–1996. An International Perspective*, NIESR, 1999: 96, 56.

Table 8.6. Employment in manufacturing, 1973–9

	Total persons engaged (1993 = 100)	Hours worked/person engaged
1973	7,993	1,870
1974	8,051	1,824
1975	7,669	1,783
1976	7,425	1,806
1977	7,480	1,800
1978	7,448	1,786
1979	7,424	1,756

Source: Mary O'Mahony *Britain's Productivity Performance 1950–1996. An International Perspective*, 1999: 87, 116.

first part of the period, the period when output was falling. In 1974 and 1975 the economy suffered from the consequences of OPEC I, with manufacturing output falling more than the economy as a whole, where the decline between 1973 and 1975 was from index 74.7 to 72.0.[37]

This fall in output was mild in comparison with what was to come in the early 1980s and 1990s, but it was the first significant fall in the post-war years (there was a tiny fall in 1951–2), following one of the fastest ever expansions.[38] The consequences of output changes for labour productivity require that we also look at employment, summarized in Table 8.6.

These figures show that employment actually grew in the first year of the recession, then fell for the rest of the period. The result was that, in the recession years, output in manufacturing fell by around 8.5 per cent, employment by 4 per cent. The figures are slightly complicated by changes in the hours worked. The productivity data given in Table 8.5, on the basis of hours worked smooth out the changes in productivity, as these hours move more closely with the cycle than 'numbers engaged', as indicated by the second column in Table 8.6. But the overall story does not much alter whichever measure is used – the fall in employment lagged the fall in output in the recession of 1974 and 1975, and when it did eventually fall it did not match the size of the fall in production.

How far does this aggregate pattern disguise divergent patterns at a more disaggregated level? Broadberry lists thirty different industries in his account of productivity change, and a sample of these is given in Table 8.7. The wide range of productivity experience is evident here. The first four cases are all the industries where productivity fell more than 10 per cent in the period. The second set are the four best productivity performers. When we compare productivity performance with output the general pattern is clear; the bigger the fall in output, the bigger the fall in productivity. The fit is not perfect, but the general point is clear if we note that of the ten sectors where Broadberry finds a fall in productivity, only one, distilling, records an increase in output.[39]

This suggests that the cause for the labour productivity problems of the mid-1970s was the hoarding of labour in the face of sometimes large falls in output; in

Table 8.7. Changes in output and labour productivity, 1973–9
(1973 = 100)

	Output in 1979	Labour productivity in 1979
Iron and steel	54.2	64.6
Aerospace	64.5	72.3
Bricks	66.6	87.3
Cement	84.0	88.8
Office machinery	131.7	174.4
Brewing	110	140.8
Soap and detergents	152.2	140.3
Clothing	115.3	135.8

Source: Broadberry, *Productivity Race*: 307, 325, 382, 381, 338, 357, 301, 352.

iron and steel the fall in employment was 16 per cent, aerospace 11 per cent, bricks 24 per cent, and cement 5 per cent, but these falls were still much smaller than the output falls recorded in Table 8.7.[40]

Why was labour hoarded on such a scale? First, it should be clear from the numbers in the previous paragraph that after the initial period significant cuts in employment were made; but they fell far short of the enormous falls in output. For such industries, this was a period of huge and unexpected trauma. The absence of a previous recession in the post-war period meant that expectations of continued growth had become deeply ingrained in British attitudes, including the attitudes of employers. Labour hoarding had been a consistent feature of the previous post-war episodes of slowing growth, and a substantial literature grew up seeking to explain it, with a variety of explanations offered.[41]

CBI data on firms' output expectations finds them consistently overestimating future output levels in the mid-1970s.[42] With such expectations, holding on to labour in the expectation of a rapid revival made sense, and surely can account for the initial maintenance of employment in 1974 and the slow decline thereafter. This interpretation seems to fit with data on expectations on 'numbers employed' in the CBI Industrial Trends Survey, which show no sharp downward movement until January 1975, by which time the recession was almost over.[43] It may also fit with a story which has employers only slowly recognizing the erosion of profits which was taking place in the recession, although the precise dimensions of this erosion remain clouded.[44]

These expectations can also be related to the wider political context. When Labour came to power in 1974 it was still taken for granted amongst almost everyone in the political class that a government that failed to deliver full employment would be electorally doomed. Only in 1983 was this key assumption of the 'post-war consensus' to be shattered.[45] In 1972, when unemployment had risen above a million the Heath government came under tremendous pressure, and famously inaugurated a 'U-turn' in policy.[46] Getting back to pre-OPEC

I levels of unemployment was a key objective for Labour in the 1974 elections. The October Manifesto described that produced for the February election as 'a programme for getting Britain back to work'.[47] In this climate, expectations that any recession would be vigorously counteracted by government action, especially by a Labour government, was fully justified. And, of course, initially that was what the new government's rhetoric suggested was the case, at least up until the budget of 1975, even though the actual policy stance is perhaps more accurately characterized as 'steady as she goes'.[48]

The argument so far suggests that a significant part of the productivity problem of manufacturing in the 1970s was a consequence of 'rational' expectations on the part of private employers that output would be maintained at a much higher level than turned out to be the case, and that hanging on to labour in this expectation would be a wise path to follow. But is this the whole story?

Narratives of the 1970s suggest that policy favoured employment at expense of productivity. To understand this we can look at the whole economy productivity story set out in Table 8.8, even though, as already noted, the biggest problem was in manufacturing. These figures do not show huge pattern of variations – except mining and oil-refining which largely reflects the huge expansion of 1960 to 1973 period, which then turned into over capacity after 1973.[49]

There is no sign here that productivity in the non-marketed public sector performed worse than the average of the economy. The figure for railways given here fits with Millward's account of productivity in the nationalized sector as a whole. He argues that, in line with long-run trends, the nationalized industries labour productivity performance in this period was superior to that of manufacturing industry, and better than the largely privately owned comparable sectors in the USA.[50]

Millward's analysis of public ownership excludes iron and steel and aerospace because of their changing ownership status within the years he discusses. Iron and steel was nationalized for the second time in 1967 and privatized in 1988; in

Table 8.8. Whole economy labour productivity, 1973–9 (output/hour worked: 1993 = 100)

	1973	1979
Agriculture, forestry, and fishing	41.6	52.8
Mining and oil refining	38.1	23.8
Electricity, gas, and water	40.4	48.6
Construction	50.2	56.9
Transport and communications	58.2	61.7
(of which, railways)	69.7	73.9
Distributive trades	73.5	75.4
Finance and business services	66.5	80.6
Non-market services	90.0	94.8
Market sector	59.0	67.3

Source: Mary O'Mahony, Britain's Productivity Performance: 116–17.

aerospace Rolls-Royce was taken over by the state in 1971, and the rest of the industry in 1977. The productivity of these two sectors, as noted above, was particularly bad in the mid-1970s, but it is hard to argue that this performance had much to do with nationalization. Both had been taken into public ownership as responses to already existing difficulties, and their problems in the 1970s reflected the particularly sharp downturn in global demand conditions post-OPEC I. Nationalized industries in the 1970s were not systematically used to sustain employment – and indeed, this had never been the case. The overall pattern in the industries in the 1950s and 1960s was huge labour-shedding, only marginally reduced by explicit slowing of, for example, pit closures, to sustain employment in particularly hard hit regions such as South Wales.[51] The financial problems of the industries in the 1970s derived from a combination of global demand problems in several of the constituent sectors, coupled to the consequences of the Heath government's holding down of nationalized industries prices to try and underpin incomes policy – a stance it was only able to slowly reverse.[52]

While macroeconomic policy became more restrictive from 1975, the use of subsidies to support employment expanded notably from the same year.[53] The numbers supported by such programmes were at their maximum in 1977 at around 190,000. The impact of these subsidies was relatively small as the proportion of workers affected, in any sector outside textiles and clothing where expenditure was concentrated, was tiny.[54] The short-run effects of such subsidies are likely to have been to reduce productivity, but we should be wary of exaggerating the idea that thousands of 'uneconomic' jobs were maintained by these subsidies, using as evidence, as Bowen does, what happened to employment in the subsidized sectors when their position was tested by the recession of 1980–1.[55] That recession was mainly driven by an extraordinary and unprecedented appreciation of the pound which unsurprisingly drove large swathes of British industry into severe decline. It was hardly a sensible test of underlying efficiency.[56]

Overall, the impact of public policy on productivity in the 1970s was likely to have been small. Certainly the recession, combined with the election of a Labour government, within the continuing political priority accorded to employment made job protection a more compelling issue than it had been in the 1950s and 1960s. But the evidence does not support the view that large numbers of jobs were being sustained in either the private or public sectors by policy measures.

The arguments above suggest an alternative narrative about post-war British productivity which focuses attention on the mid-1970s as an exceptional 'one-off' period of deterioration, rather than as a culmination of some long-run decline. In this story, the turning-point in productivity performance is 1975–6, following the output cycle. Before that date productivity at best stagnated, after that date it began to recover. This is shown in Table 8.5, and further emphasized by Britton's analysis, which divides 1974–9 into sub-periods of 1974–6 and 1977–9, and shows that for a wide range of selected industries the mean growth rate of productivity was minus 1.8 per cent in the first period and plus 2.3 per cent in the second.[57]

This picture conforms with our understanding of economic events and policy under the Labour government of the 1970s. Initially, stumbling to find a response to the stagflation unleashed by OPEC I, the government quickly found that to placate international financial opinion it had to give priority to cutting inflation and public borrowing. Beginning with the budget of 1975 it started down that road, and by early 1976 the economy had 'turned the corner' by most indices, and had started expanding again. The political crisis, later in 1976, surrounding the IMF loan, was not caused by the government being forced by the terms of the loan to change policy direction, but was instead because, having lost credibility for its policies in 1974–5, the government had to struggle hard to get the credibility that the IMF loan conveyed. As Burk and Cairncross put it: what 'financial markets . . . looked for was the acceptance by the IMF that enough had been done. Nothing less would have restored confidence in sterling'.[58] Thus what was negotiated in 1976 was a 'stamp of approval' that restored the international credibility of British policy and ended the outflow of capital and the downward pressure on the exchange rate. By 1977–8 the economy was on clear recovery path. Narratives of the 1970s which stress the 'Winter of Discontent' conflate the undoubted political importance of that event with its relative economic insignificance. Economically it was about the government trying to accelerate the decline in the rate of inflation by putting what proved to be unsustainable pressure on public sector money wage increases. The underlying performance of the economy was still moving in a favourable direction during the winter of 1978–9.[59]

The narrative given here is plainly in contradiction with that which sees the events of the mid-1970s as a 'culmination' of trends from the golden age.[60] The culmination story looks highly problematic if we look at the pattern of labour productivity within the golden age in Table 8.9.

These figures show no evidence of deceleration in productivity growth as a notion of 'culmination' would surely require. Without putting too much stress on one cycle, it is surely striking that 1968–73 saw the fastest growth of the whole golden age – not obvious evidence of an economy about to generate a crisis.

Table 8.9. Labour productivity in manufacturing within the golden age (average annual rates of growth in output per hour worked between cyclical peaks)

1951–5	3.6%
1955–60	4.6%
1960–4	4.7%
1964–8	4.0%
1968–73	5.7%

Source: Calculated from Mary O'Mahony, *Britain's Productivity Performance*: 116.

This picture of the golden age as one of dynamism accords with other evidence, not least with pace of structural change in that period. Structural change in manufacturing, measured as the 'weighted average dispersion of the rates of growth of output in individual industries around the overall growth rate' was significantly above the peace-time average in 1951–73: 'The generally high rate of expansion and pressure of demand in the post-war period made structural changes less conspicuous and less disturbing than they were in the inter-war period'.[61] These structural shifts were facilitated by enormous movements of labour out of the 'old staples' of coal, railways, plus agriculture and textiles and clothing, which shed around a million workers between 1959 and 1969 – and with practically no resistance on the part of those affected.[62]

Historians are rightly cautious about the term 'golden age' whatever era it is applied to. Nevertheless, it is hard to avoid this term when looking at British economic performance in the 1950s and 1960s in comparison with either preceding or succeeding years. As is well recognized unemployment and inflation were exceptionally low in this period. The balance of payments was seen as in recurrent 'crisis', but for most of the time (and again contrasting with other periods) Britain was running a current account surplus. The crises were not the result of an incapacity to finance a full employment level of imports – a sensible measure of balance of payments performance – but of the governments' expensive attempts to play a world role, to invest heavily abroad, and sustain the pound as a reserve currency.[63] If, as argued above, we also rescue British productivity performance in this period from the condescension of posterity, then we have a narrative of economic success not 'decline'. Conversely, for the period after 1979 we have a narrative of poor performance on inflation, unemployment, and the balance of payments combined with a productivity record which was better relative to our West European neighbours than in the golden age (because they had slowed down), but in absolute terms somewhat inferior to the story of the 1950s and 1960s. Between these eras lay the tribulations of the mid-1970s. Serious and important as these were, they are best seen as short-term and highly conjunctural, not evidence of some profound, long-running malaise.

NOTES

1. I am grateful to Alan Booth and Roger Middleton for comments on an earlier draft of this chapter.
2. J. Tomlinson, 'Inventing "Decline": The Falling Behind of the British Economy in the Post-War Years', *Economic History Review*, 49, 1996: 731–57.
3. J. Tomlinson, *The Politics of Decline*, Pearson, Harlow, 2000.
4. D. Cannadine, 'Apocalypse When? British Politicians and British "Decline" in the Twentieth Century' in P. Clarke and C. Trebilcock, eds, *Understanding Decline*, Cambridge University Press, Cambridge, 1997: 261–84.
5. N. Lawson, *What's Right with Britain*, Conservative Political Centre, London, 1982.
6. Clarke and Trebilcock, *Understanding Decline*.

7. Tomlinson 'Inventing "Decline"'.

8. A. Booth, 'The Manufacturing Failure Hypothesis and the Performance of British Industry During the Long Boom', *Economic History Review*, 56, 2003: 1–33.

9. D. Edgerton, *Science, Technology and the British Industrial 'Decline' 1870–1970*, Cambridge University Press, Cambridge, 1996; *Warfare State: Britain 1920–1970*, Cambridge University Press, Cambridge, 2006.

10. A. Offer, *The Challenge of Affluence* Oxford University Press, Oxford, 2006; R. Layardm, *Happiness: Lessons from a New Science*, Allen Lane, London, 2005.

11. S. Broadberry, 'The Performance of Manufacturing', in R. Floud and P. Johnson, eds, *The Cambridge Economic History of Modern Britain vol iii, Structural Change and Growth, 1939–2000*, Cambridge University Press, Cambridge, 2004: 58.

12. G. Owen, *From Empire to Europe*, Harper Collins, London, 2000.

13. Owen, *From Empire to Europe*: chapters, 10 and 2.

14. Ibid.: 205. On engineering see also Broadberry, *Productivity Race*: 316–45; Booth, 'Manufacturing Failure': 5–6. On using trade shares as indicators of performance see Ibid.: 23–7; Broadberry and Crafts, 'Re-statement': 732–3.

15. Owen, *From Empire to Europe*: chapters 14, 15, and 16.

16. Ibid.: 67.

17. Ibid.: 450.

18. Ibid.: 224. Note that despite Britain not being within the EEC, BMC made a strong attempt to enter EEC markets in the 1960s; ibid.: 226.

19. Ibid.: 156–7.

20. Ibid.: 170.

21. Ibid.: 149.

22. Broadberry, *Productivity Race*: 1–2.

23. Ibid.: 397–8.

24. K. Williams, T. Cutler, J. Williams, and C. Haslam, 'The End of Mass Production?', *Economy and Society*, 16, 1987: 405–39.

25. Broadberry, *Productivity Race*: 3. In relation to the USA, Britain saw a small catch-up in productivity in this period.

26. Booth, 'Manufacturing Failure', citing data from Broadberry, *Productivity Race*: table A3.1 (c), 49.

27. Booth, 'Manufacturing Failure': 12.

28. Broadberry and Crafts, '*Re-statement*': 720.

29. Ibid.: 721–5.

30. Ibid.: 720. Booth, 'Broadberry–Crafts View': 7.

31. Booth, 'Manufacturing Failure': 10.

32. For a discussion of productivity performance in industrial counties in this period, see C. Dow, *Major Recessions: Britain and the World, 1920–1995*, Oxford University Press, Oxford, 2000: 273–303.

33. C. Feinstein and R. Mathews, 'The Growth of Output and Productivity in the UK: The 1980s as a Phase of the Post-war Period', *National Institute Economic Review*, 1990: 84, has labour productivity in manufacturing growing at 1.1 per cent per annum 1973–9, whole economy productivity at 2.2 per cent. Some of this disparity is accounted for by the exceptionally rapid growth of North Sea oil and gas in this period.

34. R. Millward, 'The Nationalized Industries', in M. Artis and D. Cobham, eds, *Labour's Economic Policies 1974–79*, Manchester University Press, Manchester, 1991: 147.

35. J. Muellbauer, 'Productivity and Competitiveness in British Manufacturing', *Oxford Review of Economic Policy* 2, 3, 1991: i–xxii.

36. Though we should note how distorting the focus on labour productivity can be. For the general case, see T. Nichols, *The British Worker Question: A New Look at Workers and Productivity in Manufacturing*, Routledge and Kegan Paul, London, 1986 and for a highly important specific instance, T. Cutler, J. Williams, and K. Williams, 'The Aberystwyth Report on Coal', in D. Cooper and T. Hopper, eds., *Debating Coal Closures*, Cambridge University Press, Cambridge, 1988.

37. O'Mahony, *Britain's Productivity Performance*: 57.

38. Dow, *Major Recessions*: 295.

39. Broadberry, *Productivity Race*: 362. The rise in output in distilling was 4.2 per cent over the whole period.

40. Ibid.: 307, 325, 382, 381.

41. R. Nield, *Pricing and Employment in the Trade Cycle: A Study of British Manufacturing Industry, 1950–1961*, Cambridge University Press, Cambridge, 1963; J. Bowen, D. Deaton, and J. Turk, *Labour Hoarding in British Industry*, Basil Blackwell, Oxford, 1982.

42. S. Wren-Lewis, 'An Econometric Model of UK Manufacturing Employment Using Survey Data on Expected Output', *Journal of Applied Econometrics*, 1, 1986: 197–216.

43. The proportion of surveyed employers expecting a fall in numbers employed over the next four months rose from 26 per cent in October 1974 to 43 per cent in January 1975. CBI *Industrial Trends Survey, 1974 and 1975*.

44. M. Sawyer, 'Prices Policies', in Artis and Cobham, *Labour's Economic Policies*: 177–9.

45. J. Tomlinson, 'Mrs Thatcher's Macroeconomic Adventurism', *British Politics*, 2, 2007: 3–19.

46. Dow, *Major Recessions*: 276.

47. 'Britain Will Win with Labour: Election Manifesto for October 1974', Labour Party, London, 1974: 1.

48. Artis and Cobham, 'Backgound', in Artis and Cobham, *Labour's Economic Policies*: 7.

49. Broadberry, *Productivity Race*: 299.

50. Millward, 'The Nationalized Industries', 141–7. However, in coal-mining labour productivity did stagnate, following a recovery after the 1973–4 dispute. W. Ashworth, *The History of the British Coal Industry vol 5 1946–1982: The Nationalized Industry*, Oxford University Press, Oxford, 1986: 366–77.

51. Ibid., 279–80. See also M. Chick, 'The Marginalist Approach and the Making of Fuel Policy in France and Britain, 1945–72', *Economic History Review*, 59, 2006: 146–7.

52. Millward, 'Nationalized Industries': 148–52; K. Jones, 'Policy Towards the Nationalized Industries', in F Blackaby ed., *British Economic Policy 1960–74*, Cambridge University Press, Cambridge, 1978: 510–2.

53. Alex Bowen, 'Labour Market Policies', in Artis and Cobham, *Labour's Economic Policies*: 194–9.

54. Ibid.: 196–7.

55. Ibid.: 198.

56. Tomlinson, 'Mrs Thatcher's Economic Adventurism'.

57. A. Britton, *Macroeconomic Policy in Britain 1974–1987*, Cambridge University Press, Cambridge, 1991: 291.

58. K. Burk and A. Cairncross, *Goodbye Great Britain*, New Haven, 1992: 226; S. Ludlam 'The Gnomes of Washington: Four Myths of the 1976 IMF Crisis', *Political Studies* XI, 1992: 713–27.

59. Artis and Cobham, 'Background': 15–16.

60. Broadberry and Crafts, 'Re-statement': 720; compare Booth, 'Broadbery–Crafts view': 738.

61. C. Feinstein, R. Matthews, and J. Odling-Smee, *British Economic Growth 1956–1973*, Cambridge University Press, Cambridge, 1982: 255, 256.

62. J. Tomlinson, *The Labour Governments 1964–1970 vol 3 Economic Policy*, Manchester, 2004: 221.

63. J. Tomlinson, 'Balanced Accounts? Constructing the Balance of Payments Problem in Post-war Britain', *English Historical Review*, Forthcoming.

9

Marketing Management in Britain: What is the Evidence for 'Failure'?

Robert Fitzgerald

MARKETING AND NATIONAL ECONOMIC SUCCESS

The longer the case for British economic decline and managerial failure has been discussed, the more questions have been raised about the debate itself. In order to explain the poor performance of major industries from the 1870s onwards, or low national growth rates, historians blamed weakening entrepreneurship or a 'gentlemanly', anti-business culture.[1] Elbaum and Lazonick specifically hint at the inability of British firms to find market outlets that might have assisted the techniques of mass production, as pioneered by US enterprise.[2] Chandler is a well-quoted critic of British industrial leadership in the first half of the twentieth century. He believes that Britain adhered to forms of family or personal capital-ism, and responded inadequately to the scale and complexities of the new growth sectors. The relative strengths of US, German, or Japanese managerial enterprises are directly associated with their national economic success. Amongst several claims, Chandler notes how large-scale British businesses failed to develop and integrate marketing systems. As a result, they were competitively deficient in a key organizational capability.[3] By following Chandler's analytical approach, the case for British managerial and marketing failure, and especially in comparison to the United States, has been recently and strongly restated.[4] Others have ques-tioned the foundations on which these debates have been built. There has been a shift from why the British economy declined to whether it did decline in any meaningful sense.[5] In other words, how strong is the case to be answered? It is possible, furthermore, to note how performance has greatly varied between regions and industries. Since the diversity of British corporate organization and management is striking, the rationale of a systemic national managerial malaise is thrown into doubt.[6] The evidence from marketing history rarely enters into discussions of British managerial failure, and, when it does, it focuses on the operational aspects of distribution, ignoring the wider significance of marketing at many levels. It is pertinent to examine the development of marketing and distribution in Britain more fully, and to consider its changing purposes as a business function. Through international comparison, moreover, we can discover if British companies consistently failed to match trends or advanced practice elsewhere.

Before doing so, it is worth pondering the role and impact of marketing systems on the twentieth century and their relationship to consumption, living standards, and competitiveness. Those historians drawn to matters of economic well-being have tended to employ measures of GDP per capita or income, and sought explanations of changing national fortune in technology, efficient markets, or political economy. By focusing on the development of marketing and distribution, we might fairly ask if they are mistaken. Human beings gauge their welfare by how much they consume or by what they consume. Ultimately, the value of economic systems rests on their ability to provide goods and services that improve the lives of the population and not just a privileged few. Industrialization and market competition discouraged payments-in-kind in favour of monetized incomes, and increased the possibility of choices between goods. For modern societies, at a later stage, the means by which most people or families gained augmented discretionary incomes rather than sustenance wages is a transformation of equal significance. So, too, was the appearance of businesses that could meet mass expectations of consumption. The period after 1870 – once associated with British entrepreneurial failure, and still strongly linked to failures in corporate organization and management – saw the beginnings of 'modern' marketing systems.

The improvement in living standards, like the relative shift within industrialized economies from the production of capital goods to the supply of consumer products and services, is not suited to a single explanation. The trends, however, can be discerned. In the decades before the First World War, the combination of mass production and rising real wages enabled leading nations to satisfy more and more needs, improve product quality and choice, and extend the range of popular semi-luxuries. In the United States and Britain, and to a lesser degree in Continental Europe, long-term increases in living standards during the interwar years overcame several economic crises, and encouraged consumption and advertising based not on utility but on cachet, status, and choice. It is, surely, a remarkable feature of twentieth-century history that an international economic system could lose so much credibility in the Great Depression of 1929–31; undergo the destruction of the Second World War; and then, within a matter of years, initiate the era of post-war mass consumption. Critics fixed on the conversion of class-based producers into individual consumers, and questioned the values of materialism. They expressed, additionally, their suspicion of large corporations and advertisers, as they seemingly manipulated compliant populations into desiring previously unknown wants. They admitted, on the other hand, that mass consumption had revolutionized economics. No longer the dismal science of scarcity, it could ponder how people exercised choice in circumstances of such plenty.[7]

The enterprises that developed techniques of mass marketing and distribution did not respond passively to general trends in the economy and society. Success did not automatically follow the balancing of supply with available or rising demand, as economic theory might imply. The complexities of business entailed a proactive investment in consumer loyalty and in distribution networks; in other words, companies became concerned with the very creation and not just the 'optimization' of consumer markets. Changes in business strategy and managerial organization were needed to achieve and then sustain competitive success. The degree to which expenditure increases in relation to real income is only a measure of possibilities. It cannot account for the consumer's willingness to alter spending habits, and consider a new purchasing proposition. It cannot consider, furthermore, the consumer's evaluation of value over price, and the attraction of quality and cachet over quantity. It cannot explain complex consumption decisions between the increasing numbers of substitute goods that drove inter-firm competition and brought structural change to national economies. Companies did not accept cultural attitudes or lifestyle inertia, but had to 'educate' consumers on the advantages of manufactured soap, packaged foods, or electric appliances. They needed marketing systems that would enable their products to meet the needs of economies and societies undergoing transformation. By the beginning of the twentieth century, leading nations were hosts to mass consumption. Did US companies respond more effectively than those in Britain? Was there, amongst British firms, a general laggardness or failure in the increasingly important managerial competence of marketing?

Overall, American historians have proved more willing to provide general explanations of marketing's development and impact, so revealing the substantial progress of US companies. They have achieved some consensus for the period 1880–1920 on the arrival of large-scale companies, national markets, mass advertising, branding, department stores, and mail order, alongside critical improvements in distribution and storage. Some interpret these developments as the beginnings of 'modern' marketing. Pope, supported by Tedlow, notes the relationship between corporate policies, unitary mass markets, high volumes, low margins, and large profits. But he detects, after 1920, a further phase, with firms switching to greater market segmentation, more value-based pricing, and the use of emotive, associational advertising.[8] Other US historians have questioned the notion of discernable development stages.[9] In Britain, explanatory schemes seem to be more elusive. Moreover, although presumably taunted by well-known criticisms of British management, its historians have not so far exposed the facts to a transatlantic comparison of marketing capabilities.

US historians, on the other hand, have provided useful yardsticks by which to measure British marketing capabilities. Descriptions of production, product, sales, and marketing orientations offer a set of yardsticks by which to assess the strategic objectives of firms and degrees of organizational sophistication. It is tricky in practice to discern when a company moves from one orientation to another, and even trickier to detect general or national trends. Yet, however imperfect, descriptions of changing corporate emphasis are a workable device, and they can be used to detect the evolution of so-called 'modern' characteristics. Entrepreneurs concentrated, first, on improving production technology and factory operations, often seeking the twin objectives of better product quality and lower costs; second, they became more concerned with selling and distribution, as they coped with the effects of mass output; finally, the marketing-orientation gave priority to the wishes of consumers, ultimately guided by market research, and purchasing, product development, production, and finance were brought under the direction of the marketing department. For specific industries or nations, orientations might become common or dominant during a turning-point or period. A concern for production and products demonstrate, it is said, businesses driven by supply-side challenges that are 'internal' to the firm. At early stages of their growth, producers in the United States and in Britain could largely rely on mass manufacturing, new technologies, falling prices, and the quality of their products to achieve distribution and sales, although the tradition of travelling salesmen was long-established. Consideration of 'internal' exigencies was enough to generate success. As markets grew in size or became more competitive, companies had to divert more resources to advertising, transportation, and other sales activities, and adjust their mix of organizational skills. However, manufacturing was still seen as preceding the separate if increasingly important activity of sales, or 'marketing' as it became called in the United States and Britain of the 1920s. In contrast, the marketing-orientated company aims to discover consumer wishes, which are depicted as 'external' to the firm, and does so through market research, psychological understanding, and product development systems. To achieve its goals, it ends the segregation of business functions and integrates them in a manner best able to satisfy consumer desires. Management authorities, like Drucker, offered an idealistic vision: a thorough understanding of the consumer should enable goods to sell themselves, and 'best-practice' marketing would make the downstream activity of selling superfluous.[10] For the marketing-orientated company, it is consideration of 'external' exigencies that generates success. It is this relationship between unitary mass markets and corporate policies in the United States that interests Pope and Tedlow: first, due to the achievement of high volumes, low margins, and large profits by 1920; and, second, with the shift to market segmentation, value-based pricing, and associational advertising after 1920.

The origins of 'modern' marketing and the building of national markets are connected to increases in real wages, the choices generated by disposable incomes, transport and communication systems, and urbanization. If the economic and social opportunities were to be fulfilled, businesses needed to adapt products and systems, and they initially succeeded with the manufacturing and distribution of standardized goods. Production and product-orientations were initially complemented by a needed investment in downstream activities such as sales, distribution, and advertising. The continued growth in personal wealth and market size raised consumer expectations and stimulated competition. The assumption of the marketing-orientation, which started with the wishes of consumers, was a response by many leading enterprises to the greater individual spending power of the consumer. Instances of this approach are evident in the United States and in leading British companies during the inter-war period. In several important cases, it allowed the increasing segmentation of formerly

homogenous markets. Market research assisted the process of product development, and, in properly understanding the consumer, the use of psychological
analysis challenged the simplicities of 'narrow' economics. But, as we shall see,
it was a managerial 'philosophy' more commonly adopted during the consumer
boom of the 1950s and 1960s. Did British companies belatedly absorb the lessons
of dedicated sales organizations or the 'marketing orientation'? Did they, furthermore, learn these lessons from the United States?

MARKETING MANAGEMENT BEFORE 1920

In Britain, real wages increased by some 60 per cent between 1860 and 1900, and,
whereas 50 per cent of the population in 1851 had dwelt in towns with 20,000 or
more inhabitants, the percentage was 77 by 1901. Consumer industries and
extensive distribution networks were formed to meet the needs of a larger, richer,
and more concentrated population.[11] Imported wheat provided a necessity at
cheaper prices, and tea and sugar became popular semi-luxuries that attracted
a substantial portion of common incomes. The per capita consumption of
packaged, household goods, confectionery, pharmaceuticals, and tobacco expanded with the pursuit of leisure activities and spectator sports.[12] Urban
infrastructure, such as buildings and transportation, and mass newspapers offered greater opportunities for advertising, and packaging, labelling, and the
promotion of 'hidden' goods were symptoms of long-distances deliveries to
cities. Just as production technologies began to transform the size of operations
after 1870, approximately speaking, they also brought improved prices, product
qualities, and profits. These benefits were combined with significant rises in living
standards and consumption and with the urbanite's need to purchase all their
requirements. It is the opportunities for entrepreneurial initiative, the extending
range of consumer goods, the new scale of marketing and advertising, and their
greater importance to business strategies and organization that distinguishes
the middle from the end of the nineteenth century. Internationally high levels
of personal expenditure and well-developed product markets had by 1900
brought to Britain a number of expanding consumer goods industries, which
had not existed on the scale found thirty years previously.

Outlays on housing, utilities, transport, and household durables revealed
an improvement in living conditions for all classes in receipt of an income; yet
the differentials in individual expenditures, as well as purchases of insurance and
health services, emphasized the contrasts in middle-class and working-class lifestyles. The middle class, which mainly accounted for the expansion of suburbia,
were more likely to buy household durables such as carpets, curtains, furniture,
and fixtures, all of which supported significant industries, usually regionally
based.[13] Seebohm Rowntree, in his famous study of working class living standards, delved into a very different Britain, and estimated that some 30 per cent
of the British population in 1900 lived in primary poverty, for whom diet was

inadequate for physical efficiency. Between 1900 and 1913, when living standards did not improve as quickly as they had in the last three decades of the nineteenth century, the percentage of national product attributed to personal and household consumption continued to rise.[14]

In what ways do the business histories of British companies validate and elucidate measures of economic and social change? For consumer goods manufacturers, mass production brought mass advertising, and transformed business policies. Initially, the rapid growth of markets and the appropriation of new technologies had placed an emphasis on production processes and supply, but some companies safeguarded capital investments and consumer loyalty by concentrating on quality, product identity, and branding. Many of the firms that evolved into leading advertisers of nationally recognized brands gained a long-lasting first-mover advantage. Most brewers preferred to secure outlets in the form of tied public houses rather than resort to advertising. But companies like Bass, Whitbread, and Allsopp did place a heavy emphasis on trademarks and their promotion, and the Anglo-Irish firm of Guinness was one of the country's largest advertisers, deciding, exceptionally, not to own drinking venues. Pharmaceutical companies were early and giant advertisers, making dubious claims about the efficacy of their medicines. Thomas Holloway was the most important, before being superseded by Beecham. Some chocolate and confectionery manufacturers – especially Cadbury and Fry – were noted practitioners of advertising, and they were joined by Rowntree, and then Mackintosh. Soap firms, including Lever Brothers; Reckitt in household chemicals; Wills and, its successor Imperial Tobacco; the Bryant and May matchmakers; and food companies such as Colman, Bovril, Huntley and Palmers, and Liebegs were all prominent. Swiss chocolate and food manufacturers such as Cailler or Nestle and the goods of Dutch margarine enterprises, Jurgens and van den Bergh, were equally visible on the posters seen along British streets. At Cadbury, in 1910, conferences amongst sales staff and commercial travellers demonstrated a high understanding of advertising and its impact. Personnel unanimously supported the use of illustrations as a means of appealing and communicating to consumers, and they argued that slogans and catchphrases were more effective than the traditional wordy 'argument'.[15]

Grocers Liptons, the Maypole Dairy Company, Home and Colonial, Boots the chemist, and the newsagent and railway outlet shop W.H. Smith were all large retail chains by 1914.[16] Clothing and general stores such as Marks and Spencer; the grocer Sainsbury; shoe seller Freeman, Hardy and Willis; the butcher Dewhurst; tailor Montague Burton; and W.H. Smith's rival, John Menzies, were also well established. Above all, there was the network of retail Cooperative Societies, backed by the supplies and products of the Cooperative Wholesale Society, one of Britain's largest manufacturers. Department stores such as Harrods, Selfridges, and John Lewis were important presences in city centres, but they were not so important to the nation as a whole, and served a high-class market. Sewing machine maker, Singer, was unusual in Britain as a manufacturer that depended highly on its own retail outlets, a result of its US origins, the novelty of its product, and the need to provide expert advice.[17] One other exception was the purchase of tobacconist Salmon & Gluckstein by the giant Imperial Tobacco Company, aiming in 1901 to secure its oligopoly against the invasive American Tobacco Company. Salmon & Gluckstein by this point owned the famous Lyons tearooms, and their products and afternoon teas became associated with something intrinsically English. It might be added that, in the pre-war period, retailers such as Burton and Boots did undertake backwards integration into manufacturing.[18] British circumstances were favourable to smaller, more special-ist wholesaler. Market mechanisms and established trading relationships between distributors thrived through their low transaction costs and locational external-ities, such as advanced transport systems and concentrated, urban populations.

Were circumstances in Britain, the first industrial nation, especially suited to the development of mass marketing? Chandler lists the opportunities that concentrated, urbanized markets and highly evolved transport and distribution systems made available to British companies.[19] These advantages explain the early emergence of numerous competitors, each making a diverse range of products and brands that rapidly won consumer recognition and loyalty. Economies of scale could be achieved by several competitors in pursuit of a national market that was, consequently, more segmented than the one that emerged in the United States. On the other hand, Tedlow asserts that, '[m]ore than any other nation in the history of the world', Americans constitute a 'nation of consumers'. Lebergott states that the size and homogeneity of the US home market were internationally unmatched assets. The subsequent standardization of products improved both quality and price and required an innovation in distribution as well as produc-tion. To understand how Americans began to associate their needs with the new factory goods is to emphasize the central role of mass marketing in the economy and society. While Veblen had already identified the New York elite that could indulge in 'conspicuous consumption',[20] other commentators were pointing by 1914 to a new mass consumer consciousness.[21]

In 1913, the US population reached 97.2 million, significantly larger than Britain's 45.6 million. Total GDP, roughly equivalent to Britain's in 1870, was 2.4 times larger in 1913. By 1903, GDP per capita in the United States had caught up with Britain's, and, from 1918, it assumed a permanent lead. The building of the railway and telegraph system underpinned an emerging national market: 46,800 miles of track in 1869 had been extended by 1913 to 240,000. Considering the vast distances of North America, frozen winter waterways, and population spread, railways had a bigger economic impact in the United States than in Britain. In 1870, 26 per cent of Americans lived in towns of 2,500 plus, and, by 1910, the figure was still only 46 per cent. It was not until 1960 that half of the US population resided in towns of 5,000 plus, whereas half the British, 110 years earlier, could be found in towns of at least 20,000.[22]

Geographic and demographic factors in the United States had three major marketing implications. First, in comparison to British companies, manufac-turers placed greater emphasis on distribution and wholesaling, and vertical integration was more usual. Second, general rather than specialist shippers were more dominant, and economies of scope were needed to carry a variety of products over large distances. Changes in wholesaling were neither so extensive nor so necessary in Britain. Third, mail order was an important means of purchase in the United States compared to the British case. Mass production and product standardization assisted rising living standards and demand. Rural household and disposable income improved during this period, and the demand for foods was income-elastic enough to benefit the sale of other consumables. The growing number of urban dwellers, who had to purchase all their requirements, was another spur to mass manufacturers and distributors, and to the replacement of regional by national markets. The local general store, not surprisingly, remained the focal point of small town communities and rural areas, and retailing was not as transformed as the manufacturing and wholesaling sectors. Exceptions were the emergence of department stores and chain stores in cities, most obviously in the highly populated northeast, and the mail order enterprises that reached the United States' more scattered populations.[23]

Manufacturers adopted production and product-orientated strategies based on new technologies, higher output, lower price, and better quality. Guarding their investments in manufacturing capacity, companies created distribution systems, secured access to consumers, and gained their repeated loyalty. They used branding as marks of quality, and advertised the characteristics of their brand to a mass and distant population. Packaging facilitated branding and transportation and offered assurances against adulteration. As in Britain, mass advertising urged consumers to demand manufactured brands, undermined the appeal of unpackaged goods, and lowered per unit distribution costs. By threatening retailers with withdrawal of popularized products, manufacturers could exercise greater control over final prices. In many cases, and in furtherance of product diversification and corporate growth, advertising convinced consumers into accepting products that had uses previously unknown to them.

There were numerous examples of food and household goods manufacturers that emerged as mass advertisers of packaged lines. By 1900, Coca-Cola was an intensively advertised national line. Its travellers attended their first sales convention in 1905, and discussed the company's mission, advertising strategy, and sales schemes. It was the launch of Ivory Soap in 1879 that constituted Procter & Gamble's watershed. As well as slogans and illustrations showing happy, clean families, Ivory became, as the 'soap that floats', a novelty product. By 1914, the advertising of soaps had moved from a product-orientated approach to a consumer-orientated emphasis on values, status, and cachet. While Ivory was a fortuitous product subsequently mass marketed, the company consciously tested and, in 1911, developed the cottonseed cooking oil Crisco. As well as food and soap, instances of nationally advertised lines could be found in tobacco, matches, detergents, and household products. Their success was rooted in distinctive brands, standardization, affordable price, national distribution, packaging, large sales teams, convenience purchasing, and advertising.[24] Manufacturers recognized the need to educate consumers about factory goods and unfamiliar products. Colgate, which introduced its Ribbon Dental Cream in 1905, had to prove the advantages of dental hygiene to sceptical consumers. While most advertising was filled with often prolix product information, many major brands had revealed a trend towards storylines, distinctive personalities, emotional appeals, and an association with desirable lifestyles and values.[25] Overall, corporate cases demonstrating the existence of planned marketing campaigns and 'emotional' advertising undermine, to some extent, the argument for a definitive turning point in strategy and techniques after 1920.

Manufacturers increasingly sought success through the 'pull' marketing of advertising and branding rather than the 'push' of distribution. But, compared to Britain, more difficult distribution problems did encourage US firms to establish their own wholesaling networks.[26] Chain stores, department stores, and mail-order companies did emerge. Nevertheless, one survey, in 1923, records that two-thirds of purchases were still made at the general store.[27] The greater dependence on mail order and a less concentrated retailing sector in the United States were major differences with Britain, and can be explained by demographic characteristics. There were, moreover, early signs that US companies were leading the development of advanced techniques in product development and statistical planning. Yet it is the similarity of the United States and Britain in overall living standards, product development, branding, advertising, and the role of the consumer goods industries – and not British managerial 'failure' – that is striking. In terms of marketing management and consumption patterns, it is the continued lag in Continental Europe that is noteworthy. Before the First World War, contrary to the situation in Britain and the United States, consumer goods providers did not feature amongst the largest enterprises in Germany and France, where levels of GDP and urbanization were less pronounced. Britain and the United States, despite differences, had national mass markets, whereas marketing developments amongst the nations of Continental Europe remained more regional. Chandler exaggerates the marketing capabilities of chocolate manufacturer Stollwerck, notably in relation to Britain's Cadbury.[28] Dutch margarine makers Jurgens and van den Bergh, which later merged with Lever Brother to form Unilever, supplied the demands of Germany's urban workers from the late 1890s.[29] But there were, of course, exceptional cases. In France, by the early 1900s, Michelin was a leader in advertising and promotions.[30] In Italy's northern industrial 'triangle', there was a market for advertised brands such as Borsalino, Cinzano, and Campari.[31]

MASS MARKETING IN BRITAIN AFTER 1920

The Great War ultimately proved, in Britain, a fillip for standardizing products, cheapening production, and raising real wages, yet these advances should not detract from the importance of the inter-war period to living standards, consumer opportunities, and marketing practice. Between 1922 and 1938, consumer expenditure grew in real terms by 32 per cent, and, as food and drink sales rose by 14 per cent, there was a shift in the Engel's Coefficient. For many goods, unit costs fell dramatically, and the variety of products expanded. The composition of personal expenditure shifted towards consumer durables, but statistics conceal important trends towards more expensive, branded foods and clothing.[32] Although improvements in management and business organization were not as pronounced as those in the United States, they were advanced enough to transform living standards and consumption patterns. Amalgamations and rationalization continued after the First World War, and, throughout the 1920s, improved technology use, scale, and organization. Firms gained first-mover advantages, such as distribution, advertising, price, and consumer recognition, and products that were increasingly standardized and mass-produced were capable of mass advertising and branding. Interwar deflation maintained the real wages and earnings of the industrial working classes, and the middle class continued to enhance their lifestyles, by investing in their homes, and by purchasing products demonstrative of their status. Despite the decline of Britain's staple and heavy industries, notably in export markets, economic dynamism came from consumer goods and domestically orientated concerns.[33]

Comments in the financial press by the end of the 1920s reflected the discussions of employers and consultants, asserting that the 'manufacturing problem' was largely solved. Efforts could be focused, instead, on the selling or marketing 'problem'. Considering the recent advances in production technology, products and business organization, it was the state of the consumer market that demanded new managerial skills. Whether it was cigarettes, or confectionery, or canned goods, what for many had been, a generation before, an occasional indulgence or a considered choice were converted into frequent semi-luxuries and impulse purchases. By the 1930s, for example, 90 per cent of all classes purchased chocolate, and regulars bought two or three bars every week. Corporate capabilities and entrepreneurship in distribution and marketing were needed to take advantage of what were market opportunities, not certainties. Just as consumers moved towards high value, branded items in food and household goods, the growth in consumer durables expenditure suggests greater wealth and a higher income elasticity of demand. The range of electrical goods – from irons to hotplates, cookers, boilers, heaters, and kettles, as well as lighting – was highly developed by the 1920s. Britain's own General Electric Company (GEC), sold household durables under its Magnet brand, and its large-scale advertising competed against the Cosmos range, made by the General Electric of America subsidiary, Associated Electrical Industries.[34]

British electrical manufacturers remained reliant on the co-operation of well-entrenched wholesalers and retailers, often owned by regional generators and, therefore, city authorities, and they did not directly own distribution outlets. Their market was at an earlier stage of development than food and household goods, and every branch of the industry had to promote the installation of electricity, demonstrating its value and life-transforming effects. Generators, contractors, manufacturers, and distributors tended to coordinate through trade associations, which prohibited trespassing and vertical diversification within the industry. On the other hand, clothing, footwear, brewing, pharmaceuticals, food, toiletries, and the cooperatives all witnessed the combination of manufacturing and retailing, usually, with the exception of the brewing industry, by backward integration. In the 1920s, the Co-op still dominated with 20 per cent of the retail market, with grocers Allied Suppliers, formed by merger in 1929, leading the competition.[35]

Case studies reveal that, in the 1920s, leading firms in the confectionery industry became increasingly interested in the collection and use of statistics as a means of assessing future demand, estimating output, and organizing distribution. Cadbury and Rowntree both renamed the 'sales' department as the 'marketing' department. Firms re-conceived 'marketing' as an activity based on scientific planning, rather than intuition, and as a complement to the detailed and technical task of manufacturing and factory organization. Their activities strengthened sales efforts, but grew out of management's inherent production-orientation. Although the actual word 'marketing' was clearly a US import, changes in technique and business organization were markedly indigenous rather than transatlantic in origin. The use of statistics and psychological insight could be found in the last years of the First World War, although knowledge of the United States and the influence of agencies such as J. Walter Thompson were to have a significant influence by the end of the 1920s.[36] There is no doubt, moreover, that US companies in Britain – including Shredded Wheat, Quaker Oats, Kellogg, and Proctor & Gamble's Thomas Hedley – made their mark on British consumers.[37] By the 1930s, a few leading firms consciously adopted what became labelled in the post-war boom as the 'marketing orientation', in which the marketing department's anticipation and satisfaction of consumer wants were, in theory, given priority over the wishes of production. The preferences of consumers could be gauged through market research, and targeted product development replaced trial-and-error and short production runs. Confectionery makers Rowntree and the soap and food conglomerate Unilever both acknowledged and absorbed this change of approach. The idea of the marketing-led company was undoubtedly brought from the United States, most notably through J. Walter Thompson. Levels of advertising intensified during the 1930s. They were restrained by the public service ethic of the BBC, which did not carry advertising, but manufacturers could turn instead to continental stations such as Radio Luxembourg and Radio Normandie.[38]

The early development of British markets and capabilities meant that the decades following the Second World War did not bring substantial marketing innovation, but did see, naturally, an enlargement in the scale of operations, and the further spread of 'best-practice' management techniques. Many companies were understandably concerned, after so many years of austerity, with simply re-establishing their well-known brands, although new products and especially electricals extended the horizons of the consumer. Per capita consumption grew by 1.9 per cent per annum between 1946 and 1973, compared to the 1.6 achieved between 1922 and 1938. There were social implications, too, as a housing boom, rising real wages, and freed output made the metaphor of the Englishman's 'castle' more of a reality. Life became increasingly comfortable and 'home centred' for both the working and the middle classes. In 1951, 10 per cent of British homes were still without electricity, over a quarter had outdoor toilets or shared one indoors, and 38 per cent lacked a fixed bath. In 1955, 51 per cent of households had a vacuum cleaner; the figures for refrigerators and televisions were 8 and 35. By the 1970s, the 'fridge', washing machine, television, and telephone were accepted as standard equipment. Admittedly, in comparison to the United States, a smaller domestic market, higher prices and lower living standards lowered the diffusion rate of durables. Yet the widespread ownership of electricals and cars amongst British households did occur during the 1960s and 1970s, and, if generally behind the United States, Britain was ahead of Europe. For many, the British had lost an Empire, or looked enviously at United States or German growth rates; in truth, the average Briton had never lived better.[39]

The total spent on advertising rose from 1.1 to 1.3 per cent of GDP between 1956 and 1966. One associated occurrence was the founding of commercial television in November 1955. Another incident of note was the introduction of a self-service grocery store at St Albans, England, in 1947, by the grocery chain Tesco. Change was not always willingly accepted. An angry, and presumably confused, customer at the first self-service Sainsbury is reported to have thrown the innovation of the shopping basket in the direction of the proprietor. The growing oligopoly of the retailing multiples and particularly supermarkets such as Tesco and Sainsbury was a phenomenon recognized by the 1950s, and nationally established by 1970s, when they took over 40 per cent of the grocery market. Even department stores such as Debenhams, House of Fraser, and John Lewis became chains and no longer provided just for the more exclusive customer. The greater concentration of retailing outlets challenged the control that manufacturers had deliberately forged over distributors. As in the United States, market power had come through the ownership of proprietary brands, which were especially reliant on mass advertising and pull marketing. The multiples' competitive advantages in logistics, bulk purchase, and price by the 1960s weighed to an important extent against the manufacturers' emphasis on cachet and image.[40] Contemporary survey evidence suggests that the marketing-orientation gained wider acceptance amongst British consumer goods companies during the post-war boom of the 1950s and 1960s. By the end of this period, therefore, this marketing approach by itself was too commonplace to offer a competitive lead. In any case, the new power of the supermarkets and multiple retailers called for an investment in supply-chain management, organization-to-organization relationships, and push marketing rather than the creative development of products and brand image. Leading producers, no longer gaining competitive advantage from marketing-orientation policies that had become widespread, began the switch to business strategies based more on merger, acquisition, and corporate restructuring.[41] The concentration and power of UK retailers increased in the 1980s, and became internationally notable. In fashion goods, long production runs were not suited to greater market segmentation and rising youth sales, and new arrivals such as Next were beginning to

exploit the vulnerability of clothing giant Marks and Spencer. Yet, British consumers did not abandon their desire to buy from the national supermarkets,
and especially Tesco, which emerged as the country's largest retailer.[42]

MARKETING AFTER 1920 COMPARED

During the 1920s, US firms increased the scale of their marketing operations, the
number and size of advertising agencies spread, and a key business function was
established as an identifiable profession. The use of demographics and statistical
testing assisted the planning of distribution, and greater understanding of the
consumer further supported the design of 'emotional' advertising. These techniques originated from earlier decades. The founding of the Harvard Graduate
School of Business in 1908 bore witness to the American tradition of pragmatism,
and, by 1920, both Harvard and New York Universities hosted a Bureau of
Business Research. Large-scale companies, undertaking or completing essential
reforms in production management and business organization, responded to the
booming consumer demand of the 1920s. Market research agencies, such as
Nielsen and Gallup, burgeoned. Having founded a market research department,
and departments in planning and statistics, J. Walter Thompson became the
United States' most influential advertising agency. Its use of surveys to discover
the cognizant and hidden wishes of consumers complemented the arrival of a
bigger and richer market, which emphasized quality and cachet over price, and
facilitated greater product segmentation.[43] Large-scale companies strove for the
'scientific' organization and coordination of product development, branding,
advertising, and distribution, and replaced the 'entrepreneurial intuition' of
small firms with the managerial objective of the marketing orientation.

   Although electrical domestic appliances were available before the First World
War, it was the 1920s that marked the era of the toaster, water and room heaters,
and refrigerators, in addition to powered vacuum cleaners and washing machines. Manufacturers were supplying the means to transform the home-life
of Americans. In the auto industry, it was General Motors that set trends in
distribution, promotion, and product development. To surpass Ford, it extended
the range of its products and price, and advertised intensively. It formed a credit
company, and exclusive retailers with set locations enhanced its distribution
network. In the 1920s, only food and beverages and then drugs and toiletries
outdid autos in terms of promotional outlay. US firms, in 1928, spent some $2
billion on all forms of advertising, with General Motors, American Tobacco,
Coca-Cola, and Procter & Gamble determining the pace.[44] Department stores
were still mainly located in the cities of the east and Midwest, but chains
had national prominence, including A&P, Woolworth, and J. C. Penney. Sears
and Montgomery Ward used the fame of their catalogues to open stores that
could serve growing urban markets.[45]

While consumer goods companies and retailers did become more prominent as corporate enterprises in inter-war Germany, their scale remained small compared to British and US counterparts.[46] Siemens began to develop and promote consumer appliances, but its corporate bias towards a mix of technology, product and production-orientations, economic crises, and re-armament soon pulled the firm back to its well-recognized expertise in heavy engineering.[47] Change was more evident in France, where consumption expanded more quickly in the 1920s. Advertising agencies, such as Agence Havas, furthered the use of slogans and illustrations, and devised concerted advertising plans.[48] Leading Italian firms similarly adopted innovative approaches to branding and advertising.[49] Throughout Europe, including Britain, American products, brands, machinery, and cars were well-established by the inter-war decades, and J. Walter Thompson had twenty-two overseas offices by 1939.[50]

The United States maintained its international lead in marketing techniques during the post-war decades. While the depression years and wartime circumstances had restrained innovation, the period 1950–73 brought a consumer boom of unprecedented opportunity. Increases in market size and disposable incomes drew manufacturers to particular income levels or income groups. Marketers had, from the 1920s, already revealed their interest in the science of psychology, but, by the late 1940s, greater emphasis on psychological insight was beginning to replace a reliance on statistical planning techniques. Companies and agencies were attracted to 'Motivational Research' as the era of affluence seemingly erased the concerns of 'rational' economics. It seemed to be the age of the suburbs and the automobile, with Buick and Oldsmobile drivers portrayed as would-be Cadillac owners. Motivational Research inspired Vance Packard, in 1957, to write *The Hidden Persuaders*, in which a quiescent people were unknowingly manipulated. If true, Americans were easily persuaded to consume more and more.[51] By the 1960s, low cost chains and discount stores, such as Korvette, posed problems for the traditional multiples. Moreover, in the United States, the shopping mall grew into a centrepiece of life outside the home: there were eight in 1945, and 3,840 by 1960.[52] Wal-Mart, founded as late as 1962, was by 1990 the largest retailer in the United States, offering the proprietary brands of manufacturers at discount prices. By 2002, its worldwide sales were three times larger than its next biggest rival, France's Carrefour, and its 30 per cent control of household staples expenditure in the United States had major implications for the supply-chain and consumer choice.

In the period of post-war reconstruction, the populations of Europe were inevitably concerned with life's basic necessities, but, by the late 1950s and the 1960s, there were already indications of rising expectations. Personal consumption was linked to concepts of modernity, and therefore to closing the gap with US lifestyles. West European companies and retailers absorbed American techniques in marketing management, and the consumer culture and modern lifestyles began to move out of particular cities, regions, or income groups.[53] During the inter-war period, in Japan, the manufacturers of new products had already concluded that traditional distribution systems provided inadequate levels of sales exposure, product information, or after-sales service. These producers established, instead, directly owned or tied wholesalers and retailers. Through these distribution *keiretsu*, they had unfiltered access to consumers, and, in a developing market, they needed to demonstrate the benefits of their goods.[54] Rapid growth and industrialization in the post-war decades put an emphasis on product development and production management, but needed also downstream marketing solutions. As demand outstripped supply, marketing strategies continued to emphasize the expansion of distribution *keiretsu*.[55] In Japan, the term 'marketing' is contrasted with the supply-side challenges of 'distribution', and implies a 'managerial science' of statistical techniques, product testing, and psychological models, imported from the United States. Amongst Japanese manufacturing companies, the marketing function was comparatively weak, in part because *keiretsu* sales companies or agents assumed these responsibilities, in part because general trading companies or *sogoshosha* had a key role in the national economy. The approach continued to be production or product-driven, with economic conditions and federated business structures being comparatively less amenable to the more integrated marketing-orientation. New types of retailers and independent multiples began to provide greater competition from the 1970s,[56] and slower growth rates and corporate reconstruction since the 1990s have raised interest amongst manufacturers in pull marketing techniques and branding strategies.

MARKETING SYSTEMS AND BRITISH ECONOMIC FORTUNES

The existing evidence does not reveal a failure in British marketing management, or even a harmful lag in the adoption of new approaches. It is difficult to see how poor practice in marketing might have contributed to comparative national decline over the twentieth century. Historians have detected important trends in the United States over the decades before 1920, leading to the emergence of 'modern' marketing. If we look for these yardsticks in Britain during the same period, we can find the same combination of unitary national markets, large-scale manufacturing companies, volume, high profits, mass advertising, branding, and improved distribution and storage. Leading companies had gained oligopolistic advantages by successfully creating standardized goods and services with unique characteristics. Product and production-orientations were originally adequate, but firms took up the challenge of sales and distribution in order to manage rising throughput. They needed, moreover, to increase competitiveness, and exercise control over goods and services that were increasingly trademarked. In doing so, firms were active in the formation of national markets, and established dedicated sales or distribution departments. In Britain and the United States, 'early' industrialization had been followed towards the end of the nineteenth century by the emergence of consumer goods and service sectors, in which advertising, branding, and product choice were characteristic. The marketing systems honed by United States and British companies responded positively to structural changes in the economy, expenditure patterns, and social trends.

The vertical integration of sales and distribution by firms appears to have occurred more strongly in the United States, as did the expansion of mail-order. Differences in transport distances, urbanization, population concentration, and the relative efficiencies of wholesaling offer explanations. Dissimilar demographics and geography account for the greater level of change in British retailing, most apparent in the rise of large multiple stores, and the slower transformation of shopping in the United States. In comparing strategies of vertical integration, or retailing developments, we do not need arguments of British management weakness in the first case, nor US failings in the second.

The available corporate studies point to greater market segmentation, more value-based pricing, and the extensive use of emotive, associational advertising after 1920 in both the United States and Britain. There exists too the leading practice of linking product development, production, sales, and advertising, in what was later called the marketing-orientation, with firms employing market research by which to guide their decisions. The United States by this stage was the generator of new marketing ideas and techniques, as in many areas of management, and American advertising agencies began to establish themselves in Europe during the inter-war decades. Boom years in the 1920s further assisted change within US companies. But there is enough case evidence to trace the adoption of new ideas by British companies, some of which were indigenous, and the successful growth of major consumer industries throughout the inter-war period.

In determining changes in marketing, and the incidence of best practice, we almost inevitably encounter problems. The evidence does not fall neatly into periods determined by key turning-points. On both sides of the Atlantic, many companies had already perceived the advantages of associational advertising before 1920. Despite brands and value-pricing continuing, after 1920, to become a greater influence on consumer decision-making, the trend had been a long-term one, and falling prices in the inter-war period were vital to the expansion of mass markets and rising discretionary incomes. The wider adoption of the marketing-orientation in the United States and Britain, even amongst the consumer goods industries, was a lengthy process for which the post-war boom of the 1950s and 1960s was important. In interpreting broad trends, and comparing between countries at particular dates, the case evidence is good but not wholly conclusive. Were prominent examples of US or British marketing typical, or just puzzling outliers? The main mistake is to construct one homogenous national managerial system or pattern and to compare it with another. Comparative analysis has often been too quick to assume significant national patterns of management. Historically, variations within national marketing systems were notable, and differences between industries remained critical. Nor should we assume that nations will undergo the same stages of economic development, and that industrial organization and required managerial competencies will be easily comparable.[57]

While, therefore, case studies illustrate the emergence of marketing within major companies, it is difficult to judge the impact on less-studied companies and whole industries. The importance of marketing to consumer goods firms, and later to providers of services, might be assumed, but the selling of industrial goods is rarely considered in the historical literature. Ideas about 'advanced' marketing may be useful only or especially to providers of mass consumer goods and services. In addition, the marketing-orientation is possibly better suited to understanding rich economies, which possess high standards of living, support multiple consumer choice, and encourage the growth of consumer goods and service industries. Where the satisfaction of basic wants is the overriding political and social question, then manufacturing systems, price, and distribution have greater relevance, in a manner more closely associated with a production and product-orientation.

On the other hand, while we should be wary of assuming an 'average' national experience, and we can note some important differences between the United States and Britain, levels and patterns of consumption before the Second World War do show much comparability. The available corporate case evidence lends further support to this interpretation. After 1950, for several decades, the scale of US economic leadership over all other national economies is undeniable. Yet the consumer goods and retailing industries were amongst those in which Britain retained a general competitive advantage. Again, corporate case evidence from the post-war consumer boom reveals significant progress in British marketing management, not failure.

It is, historically, a lag in Continental Europe that is conspicuous. The growth of large-scale consumer goods companies, the formation of national markets, and lower average income levels all hindered the development of marketing and retailing systems (compared to the United States and Britain). It is pertinent, however, to remember differences between city and country, and between regions within nations, plus examples of leading enterprises with notable marketing achievements. During the post-war consumer boom, European marketing systems gradually closed the gap perceived to exist with American lifestyles. The Japanese case highlights development patterns that differ even more markedly with US and British experience. The nature of Japanese industrialization and urbanization necessitated a greater emphasis on distribution and 'push' marketing, and consumers acquired deep loyalty to the highly advertised brands of well-known companies. Japanese business was receptive to 'best practice' from the United States in the post-war period, but the variations in Japan's marketing system were necessary adaptations to its economic circumstances.

Historians do not view mass consumption as 'natural', but see it as a 'cultural' or 'social construction' fashioned in the past. The social transformation that accompanied mass consumption was built upon an economic base and formed by conscious business policies. While part of a modern human's upbringing is the process of consumer socialization, in the past the majority could not assume the availability of consumption choices and expanding consumption opportu-nities. Conceiving these circumstances is an act of historical imagination. At the beginning of 'modern' marketing and distribution, rising real wages and falling prices were not sufficient causes. If the increasing rate of product innovation was to succeed, it was necessary to alter entrenched ideas, life habits, and customary product choices. Methods reflected learning from global, best practice, but they were important adaptations to national circumstances. By initiating and implementing mass marketing and advertising, the actions of companies had far-reaching consequences. For the historian, the macroeconomic, social, psycho-logical, and business factors involved present a Herculean research agenda. It is reasonable to conclude that there is much research work to be done. For the moment, the case of historical failure in British marketing management – and then a later needed renaissance – is not strong.

NOTES

1. P. L. Payne, *British Entrepreneurship in the Nineteenth Century*, McMillan, London 1998; B. Collins, and K. Robbins, eds., *British Culture and Economic Decline* Weidenfeld and Nicolson; London 1990; D. H. Aldcroft, 'The Entrepreneur and the British Economy, 1870–1914', *Economic History Review* 1964: xii; A. Levine, *Industrial Retardation in Britain*, New York 1967; W. J. Wiener, *English Culture and the Decline of the Industrial Spirit*, 1850–1980. London, 1985.

2. B. Elbaum, and W. Lazonick, *The Decline of the British Economy*, Oxford University Press, 1986.

3. A. D. Chandler *Scale and Scope: The Dynamics of Industrial Enterprise*, Harvard University Press, Cambridge, MA, 1990.

4. J. F. Wilson and A. Thomson *The Making of Modern Management: British Management in Historical Perspective*, Oxford University Press Oxford, 2006.

5. D. N. McCloskey 'Did Victorian Britain Fail?', *Economic History Review*, 1970: xxii; D. N. McCloskey *Economic Maturity and Entrepreneurial Decline: British Iron and Steel*, 1870–1913, Harvard University Press, Cambridge, MA, 1973; B. Supple 'The Decline of Declinism', *Economic History Review*, 47, 1994: 441–58; P. Clarke, and C. Trebilcock, eds., *Understanding Decline: Perception and Realities of British Economic Performance*. Cambridge University Press, Cambridge, MA, 1997.

6. Y. Cassis, *Big Business: The European Experience in the Twentieth Century*, Oxford University Press Oxford, 1997.

7. J. K. Galbraith, *The Affluent Society*, London, 1958.

8. S. Strasser, *Satisfaction Guaranteed: The Making of the American Mass Market*. Smith-sonian Institution Press Washington, DC, 1995; D. Pope, *The Making of Modern Advertising*, Basic Books: New York; R. Tedlow and G. Jones, eds, *The Rise and Fall of Mass Marketing*, Routledge: London; R. Tedlow, *New and Improved: the Story of Mass Marketing in America*, Heinemann Professional: Oxford, 1990; P. Baird *Advertising Progress: American Business and the Rise of Consumer Society*, John Hopkins University: Baltimore, T. Nevett, and S. C. Hollander, eds., *Marketing in Three Eras*, Michigan, 1987.

9. R. Fullerton 'How Modern is Modern Marketing? Marketing's Evolution and the Myth of the "Production Era"', *Journal of Marketing*, 52, 1988: 108–25; S.C. Hollander, and R. Germain, *Was there a Pepsi Generation before Pepsi Discovered It? Youth Segmentation in Marketing*, IL, 1991 NTC Business Books, Lincolnwood.
10. P.F. Drucker, *The Practice of Management*, London 1974: 64–5.
11. R. Fitzgerald, *Rowntree and the Marketing Revolution*, Cambridge University Press, Cambridge: 1995 17–9.
12. Fitzgerald 1995: 17–9; J.B. Jefferys *Retail Trading in Britain, 1850–1950*, 1954: Cambridge University Press, Cambridge: 1–93 and 254; P. Mathias, *Retailing Revolution: A History of Multiple Retailing in the Food Trades, Based on the Allied Suppliers Group*, Longman: London: 3–31.
13. J. Benson, *The Rise of Consumer Society in Britain, 1880–1920*, Longman, London, 1994: 1–34; A.R. Prest and A.A. Adams, *Consumers' Expenditure in the United Kingdom*, Cambridge, 1954: 122–47.
14. B.S. Rowntree, *Poverty and Progress: A Second Social Survey of York*, London, 1941: 150–1; B.R. Mitchell, *British Historical Statistics*, Cambridge, 1990: 823–50.
15. Fitzgerald, 1995; C.H. Wilson, *The History of Unilever: A Study in Economic Growth and Social Change*, Vols. I&II, Cassell London: T.R. Nevett, *Advertising in Britain: A History*, Heinemann London; R. Fitzgerald 'Markets, Management, and Merger: John Mackintosh & Sons, 1890–1969', *Business History Review*, 74, 2000: 555–609; W.H. Fraser, *The Coming of the Mass Market*, 1880–1914, MacMillan, London; Benson, 1994; R. Fitzgerald, 1981 'Products, Firms and Consumption: Cadbury and the Development of Marketing, 1900–39', *Business History*, 47, 2005; B.W.E. Alford, *W.D. & H.O.Wills and the Development of the UK Tobacco Industry, 1786–1965*, London, 1973; T.A.B. Corley, *Quaker Enterprise in Biscuits: Huntley and Palmers of Reading, 1822–1972*, London, 1972; T.A.B. Corley, 'Consumer Marketing in Britain, 1914–60', *Business History*, 29, 1987: 65–83; T.R. Gourvish and R.G. Wilson, *The British Brewing Industry, 1830–1990*, Cambridge, 1994.
16. Mathias, 1967; S. Chapman, *Jesse Boot of Boots the Chemist: A Study in Business History*, London, 1974; C.H. Wilson, *Unilever, 1945–1965: Challenge and Response in the Post-War Revolution*, Cassell London, 1968.
17. Fraser, 1981.
18. Alford 1973; E.M. Sigsworth, *Montague Burton and the Clothing Trade, 1885–1952*, Manchester University Press, 1990; Chapman, 1974.
19. Chandler, 1990.
20. T. Veblen, *The Theory of the Leisure Class; an Economic Study of Institutions*. London, 1924.
21. L.B. Glickman, *Consumer Society in American History: A Reader*. Cornell University Press: New York; S. Lebergott, *Consumer Expenditures: New Measures and Old Motives*, Princeton University Press, 1996; Tedlow 1990.
22. Tedlow, 1990; Chandler 1990; J.D. Norris, *Advertising and the Transformation of American Society*, 1865–1920, Greenwood Press: New York.
23. Tedlow, 1990; Norris 1990; Pope 1983; Baird 1998.
24. J. Sivulka, *Soap, Sex and Cigarettes: A Cultural History of American Advertising*, Wadsworth Publishing Company: Belmont, CA, 1998; Tedlow 1990; Norris 1990; Pope 1983.
25. Strasser, 1995; Sivulka 1998; Norris 1990; Pope 1983.
26. Strasser, 1995; Tedlow 1990; Pope 1983; Sivulka 1998; Norris 1990.
27. Norris, 1990; Tedlow 1990; Strasser 1995; Pope 1983.

28. C. Wischermann, and E. Shore, *Advertising and the European City: Historical Perspectives*, Ashgate Publishing: Aldershot, 2000; J. Benson, and G. Shaw, *The Evolution of Retail Systems, c. 1800–1914*, Leicester University Press, 1992; Y. Cassis, *Big Business: The European Experience in the Twentieth Century*, Oxford, 1997.

29. J. H. van, Stuyvenberg, ed, *Margarine: an Economic, Social and Scientific History, 1869–1969*, Liverpool University Press Liverpool; Wilson, 1954.

30. S. Harp, *Marketing Michelin: Advertising and Cultural Identity in Twentieth-Century France*, Johns Hopkins University Press: Baltimore.

31. J. Morris, *The Political Economy of Shopkeeping in Milan*, Cambridge University Press, Cambridge, 1993; A. Arvidsson, *Making Modernity: Italian Advertising from Fascism to Postmodernity*, Routledge London.

32. *The Economist, Economic Statistics 1900–1983*, Economist Publications Unit, London, 1985: 16; Mitchell 1990: 823–50; A. Maddison, *Dynamic Forces in Capitalist Development*, Oxford University Press: New York, 1995.

33. Fitzgerald, 1995; Fitzgerald 2000; Corley 1987; Benson 1994.

34. Fitzgerald, 2005; Mitchell 1990: 823–50; Marconi archives.

35. Marconi archives; Chapman 1974; Gourvish and Wilson 1994: 267–313; Mathias, 1967; Sigsworth 1990; Jefferys 1954: 16–8.

36. Fitzgerald, 1995; Fitzgerald 2005.

37. V. Ward, 'Marketing Convenience Foods between the Wars', in G. Jones, and N.J. Morgan, eds., *Adding Value: Brands and Marketing in Food and Drink*, Routledge London; F. Bostock and G. Jones, 'Foreign Multinationals in British Manufacturing, 1850–1962', in G. Jones, ed., *The Making of Global Enterprise*. Frank Cass & Co.: London; E. J. T. Collins, 'Brands and Breakfast Cereals in Britain', in G. Jones and N.J. Morgan, eds, *Adding Value: Brands and Marketing in Food and Drink*, Routledge: London; G. Jones, 1994 'Foreign Multinationals and British Industry before 1945', *Economic History Review*, 1988: xli.

38. Fitzgerald, 1995: 1–42 and 277–346; Unilever annual report 1932.

39. Fitzgerald, 1995; Corley, 1987; Nevett, 1982; Fitzgerald, 2000.

40. Jefferys, 1950; Fitzgerald, 1995.

41. Fitzgerald, (2000).

42. G. Jones and N.J. Morgan, eds., *Adding Value: Brands and Marketing in Food and Drink*, Routledge London; Fitzgerald 1995; Corley 1987; Nevett 1982; Fitzgerald 2000; Tedlow and Jones 1993: 58–92; Jones and Morgan 1994: 310–35.

43. P. Schuwer, *History of Advertising*, Edito-Service S.A.: Geneva, 1966; Tedlow 1990; Schuwer 1966; Sivulka 1998; Morris 1993.

44. Norris, 1990; Sivulka 1998; Tedlow 1990; Pope 1993; Schuwer 1966.

45. Tedlow, 1990; Pope 1983; S. Strasser, ed., *Commodifying Everything: Relationships of the Market*, Routledge: New York, 2003.

46. Cassis 1997.

47. W. Feldenkirchen, *Siemens*, 1918–1945, Ohio State University Press: Columbus, 1995.

48. Cassis 1997; Harp 2001; Schuwer 1966; R.H. Williams, *Dream Worlds: The Middle Classes in Late 19th Century France*, University of California Press: Berkeley, 1982.

49. Arvidsson 2003; Sivulka 1998.

50. G. Jones 'Foreign Multinationals and British Industry before 1945', *Economic History Review*, 1988: xli; G. Jones, *Renewing Unilever: Transformation and Tradition*, Oxford University Press Oxford, 2005; G. Jones and N. J. Morgan, eds., *Adding*

Value: Brands and Marketing in Food and Drink. Routledge London; Wischermann and Shore 2000.
51. Sivulka, 1998.
52. Glickman 1999; Tedlow 1990.
53. Cassis 1997; Arvidsson 2003; Jones 2005; Harp 2001; Jones and Morgan, 1994; Tedlow 1990; Jones 2005.
54. N. Kawabe 'The Development of Distribution Systems in Japan before World War II', *Business and Economic History*, 18, 1989: 33–44; N. Kawabe 'The Development of the Retailing Industry in Japan', *Entreprises et Histoire*, 4, 1993: 13–25; K. Maeda 'The Evolution of Retailing Industries in Japan', in A. Okochi and K. Shimokawa eds., *The Development of Mass Marketing: the Automobile and Retailing Industries*, Tokyo University Press, 1981: 265–92.
55. Y. M. Yoshino *Marketing in Japan: a Management Guide*, Praeger: New York; M. Shimotani 'The Formation of Distribution Keiretsu', in E. Abe and R. Fitzgerald, eds., *The Origins of Japanese Industrial Power*, Frank Cass: London: 54–62; A. Okochi and K. Shimokawa, eds., *The Development of Mass Marketing: The Automobile and Retailing Industries*, Tokyo University Press, 1981.
56. Y. M. Yoshino, *The Japanese Marketing System: Adaptations and Innovations*, MIT Cambridge, MA, 1971; Yoshino 1975; M. Y. Yoshino and T. B. Lifson, *The Invisible Link: Japan's Sogoshosha and the Organization of Trade*, Cambridge, Massachusetts: MIT; S. Yonekawa, ed, (1990) *General Trading Companies: A Comparative and Historical Study*, United Nations University: Tokyo; S. Yonekawa and H. Yoshihara, eds., *Business History of General Trading Companies.* University of Tokyo Press, 1987.
57. C. Smith, B. McSweeney, and R. Fitzgerald, eds., *Global Management Practice*, Cambridge University Press: Cambridge, 2008.

10

British Retail Banking in the Twentieth Century: Decline and Renaissance in Industrial Lending

Lucy Newton

The financial sector has been crucial to the economic development of the United Kingdom; from the early development of banking in seventeenth century London, to the industrial revolution of the eighteenth and early nineteenth century and on to the modern corporate era of the twentieth and twenty-first centuries. The financial sector, and banking in particular, has made a positive contribution to the overall economic performance of the UK, for example in terms of balance of payments, contributions to GDP, and as a generator of employment. In addition it has provided finance and financial mechanisms that support other sectors of the economy. In 1997, the banking industry as a whole contributed about £25 billion in value terms to UK national output; in 1998, it provided £15 billion in net overseas earnings; in 2001, it generated 4.3 per cent of GDP; and in 2002, it provided 459,000 jobs in addition to being a net exporter of £3.2 billion.[1] In February 2005, assets of the UK banking sector reached to £4.969 billion; three times the 1993 total.[2] The twentieth century ended with the UK banking sector flourishing.

Within this sector the role of domestic retail banks has been significant. These clearing banks[3] have provided services to commercial and personal customers that have supported Britain's overall economic activity and stability. They have also proved to be successful businesses in their own right. Yet the performance of these institutions throughout the twentieth century has not always been without criticism. They were the subject of two government enquiries at the beginning of the century. The Colwyn Committee in 1918 questioned the highly concentrated structure of the British banking sector, and the Macmillan Committee from 1929–31 was critical of its provision of finance to industry. The century ended with the launch of an investigation in 1998 into the UK banking sector – at levels of innovation, competition, and efficiency in the industry, and how well it served the needs of business, other consumers, and the UK economy – which ended in a highly critical report by Dan Cruickshank in 2000.[4]

This chapter aims to examine the development of domestic UK banks during the twentieth century. Within this period, did British banking experience a decisive decline and renaissance or were the fluctuations in the fortunes of British retails banks more complex than this? How well did British retail banks serve their customers, especially businesses?

BRITISH RETAIL BANKING, 1900–39: DOMINANCE AND STABILITY

The beginning of the twentieth century saw Britain's retail banking sector in the throws of an ongoing merger movement. This had gathered pace from the 1880s until, by 1918, the 'Big Five' clearing banks came to dominate the sector – Lloyds, Barclays, Midland, National Provincial, and Westminster banks. British retail banks had become large-scale, centralized, and bureaucratic organizations, focused upon a London head office, and had began to operate what became a very effective oligopoly. Local or regional ties had been loosened.[5] It has been accepted by historians that this process of concentration and decline of ties in the British 'regions' led to two distinct developments in the lending behaviour of the 'Big Five' banks. First, an increase in risk aversion in lending, and second, an growing unwillingness to lend to industry, especially for long periods. By 1914 the absorption of regional banks by national banks had led to the nurturing of a highly liquid industrial loans portfolio, a decline in credit provision to the private sector and an overall rise in bank liquidity.[6] While banks were often prepared to continue support for distressed borrowers, they maintained an arms length approach even during general crises. Rather than intervention, their key strategy for minimizing bad debts was avoiding entering into relationships with potentially problematic clients. British banks were the epitome of 'market-orientated' institutions, as opposed to the customer-facing, universal banks that existed on the Continent.[7]

Concentration in the banking sector caused political and public disquiet which resulted in the formation of the Colwyn Committee in 1918.[8] The report of this committee summarized the main areas of unease: the potential reduction of competition resulting from amalgamations, and the danger of the concentration of the entire banking facilities of the country into one powerful institution.[9] Such a banking combine was referred to as a 'Money Trust' and the Committee were vocal in their opposition to its potential formation, due to the power it could place in the hands of a few. Bankers repeatedly countered such criticism, maintaining that amalgamations had led to increased competition amongst the remaining banks;[10] that larger banks were better able to meet the needs of postwar industrial recovery and the demands of large-scale industrial customers;[11] and that big, stable clearing banks had the advantage of being able to loan funds based on national, rather than local, pools of deposits.

As a result of the Colwyn Committee, it was the necessary for banks to obtain Treasury approval for every bank amalgamation that took place after 1918. Bank amalgamations still occurred after this date but there was no combination among the 'Big Five' until the 1960s. Yet British bankers had been allowed to undertake a process of concentration that was largely over by the time that the Colwyn Committee ensured that consequent fusions would be regulated and supervised.

The impact that market concentration by the clearing banks had upon industrial lending was significant. It was a vital influence upon the attitudes of clearing bank managers towards their industrial customers and their lending practices. Bank lending had traditionally been short-term in nature. Lending policies had developed in an era when the long-term capital needs of industry were moderate and those running businesses mainly required loans for working capital and cash flow purposes.[12] The merger movement accentuated this emphasis on liquidity.[13] London-based head offices imposed more restrictive lending criteria than their provincial-based predecessors had implemented. For example, rigorous screening procedures of loans and of clients were implemented and collateral security upon accommodation was required.[14]

Lending practices varied between banks; the Midland, National Provincial, and Westminster banks adopted a centralized policy, while Lloyds was somewhat less centralized with local committees providing opinions on loan applications.[15] Barclays adopted the most decentralized vetting system among the major banks with its system of 'local boards', which had discretion relating to advances below £20,000.[16]

Amalgamation was accompanied by a centralization of decision-making, a more 'mechanical' approach to vetting loan applications and a switch in emphasis from assessment of the borrower to that of the security offered.[17] Such a mechanical approach was necessitated by centralized decision-making. It is not easy to adapt local, embedded knowledge to a form that can be easily codified and assessed. In contrast, basing lending on criteria such as appropriate collateral allowed the development of clear rules that could be easily communicated from head office to branch managers.[18]

The emergence of nationally based banks thus resulted in a transformation of the banking system towards 'transaction banking'. The making of decisions at a centralized Head Office in a bureaucratic fashion; lending undertaken on a short-term basis; potential borrowers undergoing rigorous screening; active borrowers being monitored; and collateral security increasingly required for accommodation to be granted – all were classic strategies of transaction banking by which banks attempted to control the risk and information asymmetries inherent in lending contracts.[19] British banks maintained long-term relationships with their borrowing customers but did not become involved with the running of client's firms, or take ownership interests in them, as had traditionally been the case in the German or Japanese systems in which relationship banking was prevalent.[20] For the British banker in the twentieth century, a form of transaction banking was an attempt to reduce the dangers of defaulting customers and to ensure 'safety first'. Bankers defended this stance in the face of criticism by pointing out that they had an essential obligation to their depositors. Besides, as the Economic Advisor to the Bank of England declared in the 1930s, there was 'ample credit available to those who have the confidence to use it'.[21] Historians of Barclays Bank, for example, have shown that the bank repeatedly renewed overdrafts, thus supplying long-term credit.[22]

What of the perspective of British firms? After the First World War banks lent heavily to British industry, but mainly as they were 'locked' into doing so – to pull out of such lending was likely to cause the collapse of many firms. Also, this lending was usually short-term in nature, albeit becoming longer in term through the rollover in overdrafts. British banks faced criticism from contemporaries (and since from some historians) for not intervening with the running of firms that were in financial distress.[23] Yet historians have found many examples of the clearing banks supporting industrial customers during the 1920s and 1930s through substantial financial provision and/or involvement in the reorganization of industrial customers.[24] British retail banks and their lending to industry offered a flexible service in a specialist financial system, a system that had developed over the centuries and that offered alternative sources of finance in addition to that available from retail banks.[25] Moreover, a policy of non-intervention by banks was often preferred by their borrowing customers.[26]

Bank lending to trade and industry was viewed as problematic by some contemporaries in the corporate sector. H. E. Levitt of the Institute of Bankers visited the Bradford and Manchester Chambers of Commerce and reported that:

There is undoubtedly a general feeling of dissatisfaction with the Banks . . . Many people stated that Foreign Banks in London were far more enterprising than English Banks and were anxious to help even the small businessman. There were also many complaints against the policy of centralisation. It was said that not only was the banking system being mechanised, but that local managers were being turned into machines for the transmission of requests to Head Office.[27]

Some began to press for change. This led to the formation of the 'Macmillan Committee' in 1929 to investigate finance and industry. Having carried out its investigation and published its report in 1931, the Committee saw no reason to alter the existing system of banking in Britain and no radical amendments were proposed. However, it did identify a deficient provision of long-term finance to small and medium-sized enterprises (SMEs), which became known as the 'Macmillan gap':

Great difficulty is experienced by smaller and medium-sized business in raising the capital which they may from time to time require, even when security offered is perfectly sound.[28]

It should be emphasized that the lack of credit available to small business in the UK, as identified by the Macmillan Committee, was not merely a result of bank deficiencies but has since been identified as arising from difficulties in acquiring funds from the UK capital market as a whole.[29]

As a response the Bank of England established the Special Areas Reconstruction Association (SARA) as a political gesture to help firms located in areas facing industrial distress to obtain medium and long-term finance. Other ventures were also established, including the Charterhouse Industrial Development Co. (CID), established in June 1934; and Leadenhall Securities, launched in July 1935 by the merchant bank J. Henry Schroder & Co. Both of these firms sought to lend to concerns that would be suitable for a public issue within a few years. Credit for Industry (CFI) was established with finance from United Dominions Trust (UDT) (the HP firm) and genuinely attempted to breach the Macmillan Gap. UDT had received the backing of the government in 1930 when the Bank of England provided £250,000 to double UDT's paid-up ordinary share capital in an attempt to encourage lending to small- and medium-sized manufacturers.[30] The Governor of the Bank of England tried to persuade the clearing banks to provide financial support for CFI but was unsuccessful. CFI aimed to assist established concerns whose capital requirements were too small to be served economically via the ordinary capital market.[31] However, CFI, SARA, CID, and Leadenhall Securities all had limited impact of the provision of funding to SMEs. The British clearing banks maintained such a tight hold on the market for industrial lending that it was difficult for smaller institutions to encroach and make inroads into this business. Further government action was limited. Bankers had established good relations with the government during the First World War and thereafter the London clearing banks formed a powerful lobby group which successfully protected their own interests.

Despite the stifling of competition for industrial lending and in spite of the perceived deficiencies in bank lending to industry, the centralization of retail banking in Britain into large-scale organizations brought institutional stability. Such stability and control of the British retail domestic market meant that Britain survived the economic downturn of the 1930s without any bank failures and customers did not experience losses, whereas US and European banking systems experienced catastrophic failures. Indeed there was no major risk of failure by a large British retail bank until Northern Rock in the Summer of 2007.

BRITISH RETAIL BANKING, 1945–71: DECLINE

The Second World War brought a complete change of conditions for banking and industry. During the Second World War, banks supported the war effort by supplying finance to the British government and to vital sectors, such as the armaments industry and agriculture. In the immediate aftermath of the war, banks supported the reconstruction of industry and infrastructure through finance largely directed by the government. Yet after 1945 banking activity was severely restricted, in terms of lending by government controls, both qualitative and quantitative. The government itself required finance from the banks to aid the post-war recovery and service its debts, but also wished to direct bank lending towards those industries involved in exports (in order to generate much needed 'hard' currency), defence, and general reconstruction. They wished to maintain stable and high employment levels and suppress inflation. They also had to finance foreign policy, such as the Korean War and the Suez in the 1950s. Balance of payments crises occurred in 1961, 1964, and 1967, which led to further control by the British government. The result was to freeze the oligopolistic structure of the banking sector.

The period from 1945–71 saw bankers frustrated in their desire to increase lending, and a frustrated public who wished to borrow. During the 1950s consumer goods were in short supply (some rationing continued until 1954) and consumer borrowing was very limited. By the 1960s, the British economy had generated both employment and higher incomes, and the public wished to spend their money on consumer goods. It was not until July 1958 that official restrictions on bank lending were lifted for the first time since 1939. But even then, freedom from credit restraint only came in short bursts – July 1958 to July 1961, October 1962 until December 1964, and a few months in 1967 – with no real change being made until 1971. Bankers made requests to government to increase their lending ability, but with no success.[32] Within this environment it was extremely difficult for British banks to behave in an innovative or entrepreneurial fashion.[33] British clearing banks were in effect being used as a tool for government fiscal and monetary policy.[34]

In terms of the structure of the banking industry, there was little change between 1918 and the 1960s. The 'Big Five' banks dominated retail banking, along with the other members of the Committee of London Clearing Bankers.[35] The 1960s witnessed a merger movement whereby these eleven banks were reduced to six – William Deacon's and Glyn Mills merged to become William Glyns (becoming Royal Bank of Scotland in 1985); National Provincial merged with the Westminster Bank to become National Westminster (which was absorbed into the Royal Bank of Scotland Group in 2000); Barclays merged with Martin's Bank and retained the name Barclays. The other three banks were Midland, Lloyds, and Coutts. District Bank had been taken over by the National Provincial in 1962. Barclays, National Westminster (later NatWest), Lloyds, and Midland became the 'Big Four'. These mergers were not opposed by government nor prevented through regulation. Rather they were viewed positively, as they could provide potential benefits in terms of rationalizing branch provision through branch closures (and thereby reduce costs) and also providing large-scale institutions that could meet the demands of large-scale corporations at both the national and multinational level.[36] Yet a proposed merger between Barclays, Lloyds, and Martins had been a step too far and was prevented by the Monopolies Commission in 1968.[37] After 1968 Barclays and the National Westminster were the largest two banks and together possessed nearly 60 per cent of total clearing bank liabilities. Lloyds and Midland accounted for just below 40 per cent of liabilities and Williams and Glyns 3 per cent.[38] Between 1945 and 1968 there had been little change in market share between the major clearing banks. Only the mergers of 1968 resulted in a significant change as Barclays and the National Westminster took the lion's share of the market.

In terms of deposits, clearing banks experienced growth throughout the 1950s and 1960s. Lending activity, despite qualitative and quantitative restrictions, continued in a similar vein to that before the war. Relations with industrial customers were arms-length, and lending was provided mainly in the form of overdrafts and short-term bill advances. Overdrafts to industrial customers were rolled over to form longer-term credit. However this could still be recalled at short-notice. Medium-term fixed loans to industry were also available. Lending policy in this period remained risk-averse. British bankers wished to lend to customers that were likely to repay and at rates that would generate comfortable profits. They did not wish to accept higher risk customers, even by charging them higher interest rates. This risk aversion was demonstrated in the low levels of bad debt experienced during this period.[39] In a position of asymmetric information, whereby the borrower has more information about the potential risk than the lender, the position of the British clearing bank policy may be considered understandable. Bankers also wished to maintain high quality customers and not to encourage existing customers to take higher risks on loans with higher interest rate charges. Yet in taking such a low risk option, the banks were likely to have missed some profitable business opportunities. The system benefited large, stable industrial customers, often ones that had long-standing relationships with the main clearing banks. It discriminated against smaller firms, enterprises without a credit history at a clearing bank, and those firms wishing to take risks with an unusual or untried business venture or project. All such firms were more difficult and expensive for banks to assess and to monitor. It was difficult for such firms to seek out finance at an alternative bank as there was a tacit agreement between the main clearers that they would not offer an advance to a customer that had been refused by another bank. It was also far more expensive for small firms to seek alternative forms of finance, for example, on the stock exchange, and they also often lacked the assets that large firms would possess with which they could secure finance at a reasonable cost from alternative financial institutions.

Thus the main British clearing banks were constrained in their industrial lending in the period from 1945 to 1971 by government restrictions but also by restrictions of their own making. In this environment they lost market share to competitors. As such the British clearing banks may be viewed as being in 'decline' during this period but stagnation is probably more accurate. British retail banks maintained respectable profits, not a sign of a sector in decline, yet stagnated in terms of innovation of their products and services. Savings banks, building societies, insurance companies, and hire purchase (HP) organizations encroached upon the traditional market of the clearing banks. These institutions competed with the banks by offering lower interest rates for borrowing and adopting a much stronger customer focus than the banks. The percentage contribution of building society assets to total assets of UK financial institutions increased from 1.9 per cent in 1920 to 11.7 per cent by 1962 and that of banks and discount companies decreased from 59.5 per cent of the total assets to

33.1 per cent during the same period.[40] In 1968, the new Post Office GiroBank opened for 'personal' customers. Overseas banks, especially from America, also entered the British market to compete for corporate customers. Such new entrants were freer from the post-1945 official lending controls that were applied to the clearing banks.

HP companies led developments in the provision of consumer credit – most clearing banks were reluctant to become involved in this area of business. Bankers viewed such consumer lending as unprofitable and really not part of their traditional business.[41] HP firms provided credit, to be repaid in instalments for not only consumer goods but also for industrial equipment and plant. The UDT, founded in 1919, was one of the most successful HP companies. Government lending restrictions meant that the provision of credit via HP was very limited immediately after the war. These restrictions were lifted in 1954, but it was not until general credit restrictions, including limits on minimum deposit and repayment periods, were eased in 1958 that this type of lending increased. The Commercial Bank of Scotland had pioneered banking participation in HP schemes in 1954 by acquiring the Scottish Midland Guarantee Trust. It was the only bank with an HP association in the summer of 1958, yet by the end of September 1958 all of the London Clearing banks (apart from Coutts) possessed an HP subsidiary.[42] In 1960 controls on HP interest were re-introduced by the British government. This, together with the higher cost of money, increased competition and a growing number of bad debts, meant that returns from HP business suffered throughout the 1960s.[43]

The clearing banks were also forced to face competitions from institutions supported by government initiatives. The Industrial and Commercial Finance Corporation (ICFC) was established in 1945 by the Bank of England, with subscriptions from the clearing banks, as a new vehicle for bridging the Macmillan Gap. The ICFC model was based on a mixture of equity and debt, with a ceiling on investments of £200,000. Headed by Lord Piercy, a pioneer in the unit trust movement, and by John Kinross, a specialist in small-scale share issues, ICFC formulated an innovative modus operandi, based on risk and personal assessment. ICFC also established a regional branch network, again counter to the trend of centralization in mainstream banking. Despite early losses which were somewhat grudgingly covered by the banks at the insistence of the Bank of England, ICFC went on to become an independent institution in the 1970s, successfully providing venture capital to industry as Investment for Industry.[44]

The 'Big Five' banks attempted to meet competition from non-banking financial institutions and, to a certain extent, compete between each other through increasing their marketing and advertising activities. During the 1960s the main clearing banks developed corporate identities and logos, and developed 'branding' through corporate architecture. They also competed in the provision of service to their customers, especially through the provision of bank branches. The number of branches increased. Thus the number of possible points at which banks could interact with the customer grew and, potentially, the opportunity to expand their business.[45]

Despite losing market share and experiencing 'decline' relative to other non-bank financial institutions (or some may say stagnation), the British clearing banks still overall maintained a profitable and safe business in this period. They retained their oligopoly to the benefit of senior bankers and those employed in the banking sector. Was this of benefit to industrial firms and the broader British economy? This is debatable. An unadventurous, 'safe' but stable financial system meant that customers, both personal and commercial, were at a low risk of losing any money. Post-war economic recovery was aided and the government was able to successfully assert fiscal and monetary controls via the banking sector, leading to low inflation and low interest rates which benefited many in the economy. Yet, customers experienced very limited benefits from innovation in products or services. Also, those 'outside' the system of established industrial lending, such as small firms or those seeking funding for riskier but potentially successful enterprises, were limited in the alternative avenues for finance that they could pursue, despite the efforts of ICFC. This was likely to have a broader negative impact on innovation and success in the UK economy. Such a failure to fully serve some sections of British industry may be blamed upon the inherently conservative senior management of the British banks. Yet these senior bankers were also constrained by the context in which they were operating and in which they had been operating for some time. What happened when such constraints were lifted? In the 1950s and 1960s when lending restrictions were temporarily lifted British retail banks leapt at the chance to meet pent-up consumer demand by introducing new lending products for personal customers, such as personal loans (Midland) and a credit card (the Barclaycard).[46] They took over HP institutions in order to expand their lending. There is also evidence that they increased lending to small-scale businesses.[47] But what happened to bank lending policy when liberalization went further and lasted longer?

BRITISH RETAIL BANKING, 1971–2000: RENAISSANCE

It was not until 1971 that regulation was loosened and a new system of lending was introduced, following the Bank of England's publication of its paper 'Competition and Credit Control', whereby quantitative constraints on bank lending were removed and the allocation of credit to bank customers was primarily dependent upon interest rates and the ability of customers to repay. The system also reduced banks' liquidity requirements and ended the interest rate cartel. Retail banks were able to compete and lend more freely alongside other financial institutions. 'Corset' controls on bank lending were re-introduced in 1972 and 1974 in order to curb credit booms, but these were temporary and were abandoned completely in 1980. British retail banks were far freer to lend than they had been at any time since 1945 and able, potentially, to make higher profits from their resources. In response to this freedom to lend, these institutions began to borrow on inter-bank markets and in the Eurodollar markets. Following a period between 1945 and 1970 of what may not be classified as full-scale 'decline' but certainly one of stagnation, the British banking sector now entered a period of 'Renaissance' in terms of innovation and competition.

The final three decades of the twentieth century were certainly not plain sailing for British clearing banks, however. This was a period of tremendous change and bankers had to face fierce competition. The clearing banks' share of total deposits in UK financial institutions fell from 50 per cent in 1963 to 28 per cent in 1973.[48] Corporations and personal customers increasingly deposited with building societies, HP companies, and other non-bank institutions as they offered higher interest rates than the clearing banks. During the 1970s building societies were able to take advantage of the growth in personal savings in the UK. Personal savings as a percentage of GDP more than doubled to just below 11 per cent in 1979, whilst corporate and public sector savings fell. The number of building societies had fallen as a result of mergers (from 480 in 1970 to 270 in 1980) but the number of branches had grown from 2,500 in 1970 to 6,000 in 1980 (the latter number being about half of total clearing bank branches). In terms of deposits, building societies took market share from savings banks, national savings certificates, and bonds but also from the London clearing banks. Building society deposits rose five-fold between 1967 and 1978 as they offered favourable interest rates. They were also able to offer competitive mortgages as the demand for home ownership grew in the 1970s. They achieved this from branches that were easily accessible for customers, and by providing a variety of products that were simple (in terms of charge structures).

The election of a Conservative government in 1979 meant the lifting of the supplementary special deposits scheme which restricted bank lending, and the result was the entry of retail banks into the market of home mortgage provision. But legislative freedom was also applied to building societies during the 1980s, whose managements were given more freedom to raise outside funds and thus were able to offer a new range of financial services and to compete more vigorously with the clearing banks. Traditionally building societies had competed for deposits with the retail clearing banks but now they competed by offering banking services, such as cheque accounts (following their admittance to the London Clearing House), credit cards, and insurance services. Dominance of the mortgage market by building societies was a particular advantage in the house price boom of the 1980s. Some demutualized and floated on the stock exchange.[49] For example, Abbey National became a bank in 1989 but retained its name and, by association, its previous identity as a building society.[50] Halifax, Northern Rock, and Alliance & Leicester building societies floated on the stock exchange in 1997, and the Bradford & Bingley in 2000; these institutions presented British retail banking with very direct competition.[51]

Trustees savings banks (TSBs) and the National GiroBank were less competitive during the 1970s. They did not provide such a wide range of services as building societies and their interest rates remained uncompetitive as they were compelled to invest in public sector debt. TSBs and National GiroBank deposit share fell from 8 per cent of total deposits in the mid-1960s to approximately 5 per cent in 1978. This situation changed in 1976 with the passing of the Trustee Savings Bank Act which loosened restrictions on the way in which they conducted business. As a result TSBs merged and subsequently provided a greater range of competitive services, such as chequing accounts, credit cards, and consumer credit.[52] The TSB was floated as a corporation in 1986 and was able to develop to challenge retail banking, only to merge with one of the major clearers, Lloyds, to form LloydsTSB Group plc in 1995. This demonstrates one way in which clearing banks dealt with competition, as witnessed between 1880 and 1918, the 1960s and the 1990s – through merger.

The 1980s and 1990s witnessed competition from non-bank financial institutions. For example, the retailer Marks & Spencer provided services such as charge cards, insurance polices, and personal loans; and American car manufacturers offered credit cards and HP services. The 1990s saw new entrants into UK retail banking – internet banks and supermarkets' banks made very successful inroads into the sector. Retail banks responded by developing electronic delivery channels such as ATMs, internet banking facilities, and telephone banking. They also developed more aggressive marketing and advertising campaigns, redeveloped branches, extended opening to Saturdays, and invested in technology in order to decrease costs.

Competition also increased amongst the clearing banks and overseas entrants. Both the Royal Bank of Scotland and the Bank of Scotland (which merged with the Halifax Building Society to form HBOS in 2001) moved south from Scotland during the 1980s to successfully compete with the London-based clearing banks. The clearing banks faced increasing competition for commercial customers from US banks that had moved to London to take advantage of the Eurodollar markets and from British merchant banks, institutions that offered both competitive corporate lending and depositing facilities. US banks in particular offered new and innovative products to their corporate customers. They also marketed their services heavily and in the 1970s were successful in winning business from the British clearing banks. Profits of the clearing banks were under pressure. By 1980, one-third of all banks loans to British industry were made by overseas banks.[53] In the 1990s there was a new challenge from abroad as foreign banks took over a variety of UK banks. In the retail sector the most prominent acquisition was HSBC's take over Midland Bank in 1992, moving its head offices form Hong Kong to London in the process. In this increasingly competitive environment corporate and personal customers could and did move banks.

In terms of corporate lending, the lifting of restrictions after 1971 led to lending to a greater variety of types of company by British retail banks. More funds were lent to service sector companies and less to manufacturing enterprises, reflecting the restructuring of the economy as a whole. This is a trend that has continued into the twenty-first century. Fewer restrictions also led to riskier lending and the level of bad debts grew in between 1971 and 2000, especially during the early 1970s and the recessions of 1979–81 and 1989–93. Some corporate lending remained at arms-length – even when corporate customers experienced difficulties clearing banks provided financial support but refrained from involvement in the management of a company. Yet there was also evidence of close involvement by banks with industrial companies in difficulties, such as Midland's support of Rolls-Royce in the early 1970s and the role of Barclays in the replacing the board of Dunlop in 1984 and forcing the sale of Clive Sinclair's electronics business to Amstrad in 1986. Barclays also occasionally took equity interests or placed directors on corporate boards, both in the case of companies in difficulties but also when it had provided venture capital, for example, to the management buyout of the National Freight Corporation in 1982. Corporate finance divisions were established by banks, for example, at Midland in 1974, taking corporate lending decisions away from branches. During the 1980s and 1990s it became more culturally acceptable for banks to become involved in restructuring companies and to participate in directing corporate behaviour. Corporate lending was now a profitable business but inherently risky, and bank managements wished to protect their interests by becoming more involved with their corporate clients.[54]

By the 1990s the tradition of borrowing short and lending had long ended. Lending to corporate clients became medium or long-term, as rather than relying on deposits for liquidity, clearing banks could turn to the inter-bank market. This led to more fixed rate, fixed term lending to firms rather than the traditional borrowing method of the overdraft. Innovations also occurred in corporate lending. Factoring was introduced, a method whereby cash could be immediately raised upon unpaid invoices. Instalment credit for and leasing to corporate customers were also increasingly undertaken by the clearing banks from the 1970s onwards. Change was stimulated by the lack of segmentation of financial services. UK retail banks offered services that had previously been the preserve of merchant banks or building societies and had to successfully innovate and compete with a variety of financial institutions in order for such services to remain profitable. Such competition put pressure upon the margins of all those competing in the financial services market.

What of lending to SMEs? The Wilson report of 1980 had criticized the provision of credit and financial services to SMEs, as had the Macmillan Committee and the Radcliffe report before it. These firms got a better service and access to credit in the enterprise culture of the 1980s, usually through loans rather than overdrafts. But the 1989–93 recession hit small businesses hard and led to losses by the banks.[55] Credit became harder to come by for all in the early 1990s, but by the start of the twenty-first century the performance of banks with regard to SME lending had been improved. Between 2000 and 2002 bank borrowing accounted for 52 per cent of external finance for UK SMEs, far higher than that provided by leasing (25 %), factoring and shareholders (both around 6 %) and venture capital (3 %).[56]

Industry and commerce, large or small, was not the only recipient for bank funding in the post-1971 era. This period experienced the importance of financing in the property sector. Borrowing by manufacturing sector had been slow to increase in the early 1970s but there was a boom in borrowing for property development that was funded by the (less regulated) secondary banks. When the property market slowed in 1973, combined with rising oil prices and industrial unrest, a secondary bank crisis followed. This crisis threatened the liquidity of the entire banking system. The concept of a 'Lifeboat' fund for threatened institutions was launched by the Bank of England and financially supported by the main clearing banks in an attempt to stem the crisis. By mid-January 1974 over £200 million had been lent by the Lifeboat Committee to shore-up the depleted balance sheets of the secondary banks that were illiquid but remained solvent. Commitments of the Lifeboat fund peaked in March 1975 at £1.29 billion. Not all companies survived. Those that were insolvent were allowed to go under. By the end of the 1975 demand on the Lifeboat for support lending was declining and by the end of 1976 it had fallen to £783 million.[57] The stability of the banking system had been preserved. The over-commitment of banks during the property boom of the late 1980s and early 1990s resulted in losses for the clearing banks and had an adverse impact on their profits, but it did not lead to a crisis as in the early 1970s. More recently, risky credit provision in the mortgage market led to the 'credit crunch' of 2007–8 and a subsequent financial crisis. At the time of writing (October 2008) the outcome of this crisis is as yet unknown, but, once again, it seems that it was lending in the volatile property markets that precipitated the turmoil.

The secondary banking crisis had followed liberation in the banking sector in 1971. Was there a need to tighten regulation again? 'Corset' controls on bank lending were re-introduced in 1972 and 1974 but there was no return to the tight governmental controls of the 1950s and 1960s. The Wilson Committee investigated the operation of financial intermediaries and reported in 1980. It was generally satisfied with the operation of the clearing banks, despite a lack of finding for small-scale industrial enterprise having been identified. The report did not recommend further regulation. The 1980s witnessed a further loosening of regulation of the financial sector in general. The year 1981 saw the end of the Bank of England setting minimum lending rates but also the end of the requirement of banks to maintain set cash ratios or reserve asset ratios.[58] HP controls were lifted in 1982. In 1986, the 'Big Bang' relaxed regulatory controls on the stock exchange and banks were permitted to own jobbers and brokers firms, thus entering a new market.

Lending increased during the 1970s and 1980s as incomes rose and correspondingly demand for personal and corporate credit increased. Expansion in credit provision was controlled not by the setting of lending levels by banks nor by government rationing or control but by interest rates set by the market. As a result, British retail banks became more complex organizations offering a greater variety of services. They offered new products, facilitated by developments in technology. These institutions had the advantage of having thrown off the shackles of credit rationing but, conversely, were no longer protected from competition as they had been in the oligopoly of the 1950s and 1960s. This required some adjustment. The 'club-like' atmosphere of co-operation and self-regulation between the 'Big Four' London banks and the Bank of England had to change. Self-regulation was formalized. The Committee of London Clearing Bankers was replaced by the Governors' Advisory Group. This preserved communication between the 'Big Four' banks and the Bank of England but the large clearing banks no longer possessed the market control they once had. This was demonstrated by the admission, following public pressure, of building societies and foreign banks to the London Clearing House (LCH), an organization once owned by the clearing banks. In 1985, the LCH was renamed the Association of Payment Clearing Services (APACS) and open to relevant applicants.

The 1979 Banking Act defined banking in the UK and provided insurance for depositors. The Bank of England still monitored the capital adequacy of financial institutions, a role that was formalized at an international level with the Basle Accord of 1988. Investors and depositors were protected through the Financial Services Act of 1986. Under this Act the Securities and Investment Board (SIB) was established as the regulatory authority for investment business. Banking supervision and investment services regulation were eventually merged in 1997 and the SIB formally changed its name to the Financial Services Authority (FSA). The FSA took over the traditional regulation of banks and other financial institutions from the Bank of England. Also in 1997 the Bank of England gained independence from government in setting interest rates. Thus the 1980s and 1990s witnessed the movement away from banking self-regulation towards preventative supervision from outside financial institutions.

During the 1980s and 1990s bankers lobbied for reduction in regulation and freedom to offer services and products. Their wishes were granted but a laxer system also increased the potential for moral hazard. In 1991, the failure of the Bank of Credit and Commerce International (BCCI) demonstrated this risk. Clearing banks had to cover the losses of depositors in BCCI through an insurance fund.[59] Competition also increased pressure on margins and correspondingly pressure to sell products and services which could lead to outcomes that were not beneficial to customers. An example was pensions mis-selling by Barclays' staff.[60] Under-performing products such as endowment mortgages were also heavily marketed during the 1980s and 1990s. Concern grew at the end of the century about mounting levels of personal debt, the part that banks played in the 'selling' of credit to individuals and their eventual responsibility for those who faced difficulty in making repayments. It was clear that open competition could result in bad behaviour. In the press it was also clear that such open competition could lead to negative publicity and even levels of public animosity towards banking institutions and those that managed them.

Therefore, after 1971, on the one hand deregulation occurred and a more competitive market-orientated system was permitted to develop in UK financial services, along with the risks of moral hazard and failure that this entailed. On the other hand, more formalized controls were introduced to replace the informal regulatory culture that had prevailed in UK financial services but especially in the banking sector. The result for the customer, both corporate and personal, was a greater variety of services and products from a wider range of providers than ever before. This competitive environment brought with it risks and potential for negative outcomes as banks and non-banks alike fought in an overcrowded marketplace.

The century ended with a period of consolidation in UK retail banking as the number of banks began to fall from the mid-1990s as a result of mergers and acquisitions. For example NatWest (National Westminster) was acquired by the Royal Bank of Scotland in 2000 and in 2001 Halifax (the former building society) and the Bank of Scotland merged to form HBOS. At the start of the twenty-first century the largest UK retail banks (by capital) were HSBC, Royal Bank of Scotland, HBOS, Barclays, and Lloyds TSB Group. Two of the original 'Big Five' are still in this list, in updated form, and the other three form constituent parts of the new largest five banks. These new 'Big Five' dominated the current account market at the start of the twenty-first century with over two-thirds of the 71 million UK accounts in 2003 and over half of the credit cards and personal loans.[61]

CONCLUSION

Large-scale British retail banks entered the twentieth century in a position of dominance. In 1918 the 'Big Five' were very profitable and successfully dominated the market for corporate and personal lending in the UK. During the 1920s and 1930s bankers experienced difficult economic conditions yet retained their dominance of UK banking through oligopolistic practices. It was after the Second World War that these institutions experienced if not decline then certainly stagnation. This was due to a mixture of constraints imposed by government but also reinforced by the behaviour of senior bankers. It was only during the final three decades of the twentieth century, following the lifting of restrains and loosening of regulation in 1971, and again during the 1980s, that the large British clearing banks were able to compete freely and develop into extremely successful businesses in their own right. As such, the post-1971 period can be viewed as a Renaissance period for British banking. Freedom to compete stimulated competition and innovation in the sector and led to large profits for banks at the end of the twentieth century. In terms of longevity and stability, UK retail banks could be considered successful by the end of this century. Their contribution to the UK economy during this period, as businesses in their own right as well as in the provision of finance to commercial customers, remained significant.

The flip-side of this has been an increase in the levels of bad debt. Also, as competition in UK financial services during 1980s and 1990s became fierce, there was over-capacity and as a result, there was a decrease in margins for those in this sector, including the retail banks. There was a certain amount of 'bad behaviour' as pressurized selling techniques entered the financial services sector and products were sold which were not necessarily the best for the customer.

At the end of the twentieth century retail banks could look back on two decades in which they had undergone a renaissance, both in commercial terms and in terms of innovation. Yet a very high price was to be paid in the twenty-first century as deregulation and fierce competition culminated in the financial crisis of 2008. Although the outcome of this crisis is as yet unknown, it is clear that regulation has been too soft, or not applied rigorously enough; the 'light touch', combined with the growing complexity of financial markets, has meant that the UK banking system has come under very severe strain. Government intervention has been necessary and key bankers have lost their positions. The future is likely to see tighter regulatory control to protect government funds and ensure stability in the financial sector; the prospects for the global financial system – of which the British banks are all part – are, however, still not clear.

NOTES

1. Duncan McKenzie and Marko Maslakovic, 'City Business Series 2000', *Statistical Update: Banking*, British Invisible, London, 2000; and Marko Maslakovic and Duncan McKenzie, 'City Business Series, 2004', *Banking*, International Financial Services, London, 2004.
2. UK Trade and Investment, Financial and Legal Services Sector Team, 'Financial Services – An Overview', Nov. 2005.
3. Those banks that are members of a national cheque clearing system.
4. Don Cruikshank, 'Competition in UK Banking: A Report to the Chancellor of the Exchequer', HM Treasury, Mar. 2000.
5. An exception to this was Barclays Bank which maintained local 'boards' with decision-making powers to lend. Margaret Ackrill and Leslie Hannah, *Barclays. The Business of Banking 1690–1996*, Cambridge, 2001: 63, 130–3, 147.
6. Mae Baker and Michael Collins, 'English Commercial Bank Stability, 1860–1914', *The Journal of European Economic History*, 31, 3, 2002: 510; Mae Baker and Michael Collins, 'Sectoral Differences in English Bank Asset Structures and the Impact of Mergers, 1860–1913', *Business History*, 43, 4, 2001: 19.
7. Continental universal banking has been traditionally been viewed as supportive of the financial requirements of industry (including long-term lending) and involved in its operation.
8. The year 1918 also saw the investigation by the Cuncliffe Committee into currency and finance.
9. 'The Report of the Treasury Committee on Bank Amalgamations', *Bankers Magazine* [*BM*], 1918: 49–50.
10. *BM*, 108, 1919: 618.
11. *BM*, 117, 1924: 683.
12. Capie and Collins, 'Banks, Industry, and Finance, 1880–1914'; Capie and Collins, 'Industrial Lending by English Commercial Banks, 1860s–1914'; Baker and Collins, 'English Commercial Bank Stability, 1860–1914'; Baker and Collins, 'English Industrial Distress before 1914 and the Response of the Banks'; Collins and Baker, *Commercial Bank and Industrial Finance in England and Wales, 1860–1913*.
13. Michael Collins and Mae Baker, 'English Commercial Bank Liquidity, 1860–1913', *Accounting, Business & Financial History*, 11, 2001: Part 2, 171–91; Collins and Baker, 'Sectoral Differences in English Bank Asset Structures': 7.

14. For a review of this literature, see Lucy Newton, 'Government, the Banks, and Industry in Inter-war Britain', in Terry Gourvish ed., *Business and Politics in Europe, 1900–1970. Essays in honour of Alice Teichova*, Cambridge, 2003: 156.

15. W. A. Thomas, *The Finance of British Industry, 1918–1976*, London, 1978: 57.

16. Ackrill and Hannah, *Barclays*: 91.

17. F. Lavington, *The English Capital Market*, London, 1921: 143.

18. Francesca Carnevali and Leslie Hannah, 'The Effects of Banking Cartels and Credit Rationing on U.K. Industrial Structure and Economic Performance Since World War Two', in Michael D. Bordo and Richard Sylla eds., *Anglo-American Financial Systems. Institutions and Markets in the Twentieth Century*, Burr Ridge IL, 1995: 65–88, p. 75.

19. Michael Collins and Mae Baker, 'English Bank Business Loans, 1920–1968: Transaction Bank Characteristics and Small Firm Discrimination', *Financial History Review*, 12, 2, 2005: 136–8.

20. See J. Edwards and K. Fischer, *Banks, Finance and Investment in Germany*, London, 1994; M. Collins, 'British Bank Development Within a European Context, 1870–1939', *Economic History Review*, 51, 1998; W. Lazonick and M. O'Sullivan, 'Finance and Industrial Development. Part I: The United States and the United Kingdom', *Financial History Review*, 1997: 4; W. Lazonick and M. O'Sullivan, 'Finance and Industrial Development. Part II: Japan and Germany', *Financial History Review*, 1997: 4.

21. *BM*, 132, 1931: 86–7.

22. Ackrill and Hannah, *Barclays*, 95; and A. W. Tuke and R. J. H. Gillman, *Barclays Bank Limited 1926–1969: Some Recollections*, 1972: 48.

23. For an overview of the debates in the inter-war period see Newton, 'Government, the Banks, and Industry': 145–168; and Peter Scott and Lucy Newton, 'Jealous Monopolists? British Banks and Responses to the Macmillan Gap During the 1930s', *Enterprise and Society Enterprise & Society*, 8, 4, 2007: 881–919.

24. R. A. Church, *Herbert Austin: The British Motor Car Industry to 1941*, London, 1979; J. Foreman-Peck, 'Exit, Voice and Loyalty as Responses to Decline: The Rover Company in the Interwar Years', *Business History*, 23, 2, 1981; E. Green and M. Moss, *A Business of National Importance. The Royal Mail Shipping Group, 1892–1937*, 1982: Chapters 7–8.

25. Duncan M. Ross, 'Commercial Banking in a Market-Orientated Financial system: Britain Between the Wars', *Economic History Review*, XLIX, 2, 1996: 314–35; Katherine Watson, 'Banks and Industrial Finance: The Experience of Brewers, 1770–1913', *Economic History Review*, XLIX, 1, 1996: 58–81.

26. S. Tolliday, *Business, Banking and Politics: The Case of British Steel 1918–1939*, Cambridge, 1987: 179.

27. LTSBGA: File 2327, General Management files.

28. Macmillan, *Report of the Committee on Finance and Industry*, 1931: para. 404. See R. Coopey, and D. Clarke, *3i: Fifty Years Investing in Industry*, Oxford, 1995.

29. For the latest arguments see Scott and Newton. 'Jealous Monopolists?'; and Francesca Carnevali, *Europe's Advantage. Banks and Small Firms in Britain, France, Germany, and Italy since 1918*, Oxford, 2005.

30. BLPES, Pamphlet Collection, J. Gibson Jarvie, 'Credit for Industry', text of a speech delivered to the LSE Banking Society, 21 Nov. 1935: 18; and Sue Bowden and Michael Collins, 'The Bank of England, Industrial Regeneration, and Hire Purchase Between the Wars', *Economic History Review*, XLV, 1, 1992: 134.

31. Scott and Newton. 'Jealous Monopolists?'.

32. Ackrill and Hannah, *Barclays*: 117.
33. Geoffrey Jones, 'Competition and Competitiveness in British Banking, 1918–71', in Geoffrey Jones and Maurice W. Kirby, eds., *Competitiveness and the State: Government and Business in Twentieth-Century Britain*, Manchester, 1991: 120–40.
34. Thomas, *The Finance of British Industry*: 185–6.
35. The other six members were: District Bank, Martins Bank, William Deacon's and Glyn Mills and Co., all owned by the Royal Bank of Scotland; Coutts, owned by National Provincial; and the National Bank.
36. Collins, *Money and Banking*: 398–400.
37. Monopolies Commission, 'Barclays Bank Ltd, Lloyds Bank Ltd and Martins Bank Ltd: A Report on the Proposed Merger', HMSO, London, 1968: 44–63; and Winton, *Lloyds Bank*: 194–200.
38. Collins, *Money and Banking*: 401.
39. Ackrill and Hannah, *Barclays*: 142; and Homes and Green, *Midland*: 244–5.
40. D. K. Sheppard, *The Growth and Role of Financial Institutions, 1880–1962*, London, 1971: 3.
41. The Chairman of Barclays was particularly against bank involvement in HP business during the 1950s and 60s. Ackrill and Hannah, *Barclays*: 149–50.
42. For the cases of Lloyds, Midland, and Barclays see (respectively) Winton, *Lloyds*: 162–3; Holmes and Green, *Midland*: 226–9; and Ackrill and Hannah, *Barclays*: 149–51.
43. Winton, *Lloyds*: 162–3.
44. Coopey and Clarke: *3i*.
45. Lucy Newton, 'A Favourable Impression of Banking? British Banks and their Consumers, 1920–1970', forthcoming.
46. Holmes and Green, *Midland*: 222; and Ackrill and Hannah, *Barclays*: 185–9.
47. Ibid.: 147.
48. Ibid.: 165.
49. Collins, *Money and Banking*: 388–90; and Ackrill and Hannah, *Barclays*: 215–7.
50. Abbey National plc changed its named to Abbey in 2003 and became part of Grupo Santander in 2004.
51. http://www.bsa.org.uk/mediacentre/simple/demutualisation.htm
52. Collins, *Money and Banking*: 391.
53. Ibid.: 411.
54. Holmes and Green, *Midland*: 274–6, 277; and Ackrill and Hannah, *Barclays*: 225–9, 233–6.
55. Ackrill and Hannah, *Barclays*: 239–40.
56. Maslakovic and McKenzie, *Banking*, 2004: 9.
57. Margaret Reid, *The Secondary Banking Crisis: Its Causes and Course*, Palgrave Macmillan, Basingstoke, 1983; and Peter Scott, 'The New Alchemy: Veblen's Theory of Crisis and the 1974 British Property and Secondary Banking Crisis', *Journal of Economic Issues*, 30, 1996: 1–11.
58. Collins, *Money and Banking*: 438–9.
59. Nikos Passas, 'The Genesis of the BCCI Scandal', *Journal of Law And Society*, 23, 1, Mar. 1996: 57–72; and Richard J. Herring, 'BCCI: Lessons for International Bank Supervision', *Contemporary Policy Issues*, 11, 2, 1993: 76–84.
60. Ackrill and Hannah, *Barclays*: 368.
61. Maslakovic and McKenzie, *Banking*, 2004: 5.

11

The Decline and Renewal of British Multinational Banking

Geoffrey Jones and Lucy Newton

Britain was the home of multinational banking. From the 1830s, British commercial banks, the primary focus of this chapter, had established branches in colonial and foreign markets. By 1914, they owned thousands of overseas branches. They proved highly flexible when faced by the changing political and economic environment of the mid-twentieth century, but their performance and that of other British banks was less impressive as banking was transformed by the emergence of global capital and money markets from the 1960s. They restructured slowly, incurred heavy losses during the world debt crisis, and made costly and unsuccessful acquisitions in the United States. However, from the 1990s there was major restructuring and a much improved performance, until the global financial crisis that began in 2007 raised challenging questions about the trajectory of the entire global financial system.

DECLINE

In the nineteenth century, British banks had been at the heart of the first global economy. London had been the world's financial centre. Its merchant and investment banks such as Barings and Schroders were financial giants. Meanwhile British-owned overseas banks operated several thousand branches worldwide, primarily in Asia, Africa, Latin America, and Australasia.[1]

The inter-war years had been extremely difficult for financial institutions, but British banks had proved far more robust than those of, for example, the United States or Germany. During the 1950s, the weakened British domestic economy, the resulting weakness of Sterling, and the unwinding of the British Empire, appeared to doom London and British banks to a much reduced role in the world economy. However, this proved not to be the case when, from the late 1950s, international banking underwent a transformation which began with the emergence of the Eurodollar market.[2] This new international money market was largely unregulated, and rapidly captured a rising share of financial intermediation from sheltered and conservative domestic banking markets. The birth of Eurobonds in 1963 resulted in a similarly unregulated capital market.[3]

London emerged as the rather unexpected leading home of these new global financial markets. As is well-known, the key factor was regulation, or rather the lack of it. While the United States and most European governments sought to closely control and regulate their financial systems, the Bank of England opted to create a regulatory framework for this new type of banking which was far more flexible. Foreign banks were allowed to establish London branches, which did not require separate capitalization, and the Bank of England pursued a flexible approach to foreign currency operations with non-residents. There were no reserve requirements or maturity constraints. The contrast with the highly regulated American system was particularly striking. The result was that a growing proportion of dollar-denominated financial transactions began to take place 'offshore' in London rather than in the United States.[4]

British banks including the Midland Bank, the Bank of London and South America, and Warburgs were early pioneers of the new Euromarkets. However, British banks rapidly lost their pre-eminence. American banks in particular took the lead in the new era of international banking; in the process, the banking system of the United States was transformed from being essentially local in character to being highly integrated with the world financial and banking system. In 1960, eight American banks operated a total of 124 foreign branches. By 1980, 159 American banks had 799 foreign branches. Japanese and continental European banks expanded their multinational activities on a large scale also.[5]

During the late 1970s, competition for international banking business intensified as New York and Tokyo grew in importance as financial centres. When in 1979 the newly elected government of Margaret Thatcher finally abolished British exchange controls, over four-fifths of all foreign exchange transactions in London were carried out by foreign-owned firms. The City appeared to lag in financial innovation. The Stock Exchange's historic specialization of functions – market-makers were split into 'jobbers' and 'brokers' and restrictions existed on the ownership of member firms – provided a major constraint on innovation.

On 27 October 1986, the London Stock Exchange was deregulated in a series of measures that came to be known as the 'Big Bang', eliminating the minimum scales of commission on security transactions; combining the responsibilities of 'jobbing' and 'broking'; and reducing membership requirements to the Exchange, which allowed financial institutions to buy jobbers and brokers. The London Stock Exchange also shed into self-regulatory status. London was the first European market to experience such a major deregulation.[6]

However, the Big Bang failed to establish strong, British-owned institutions to take on the heavily capitalized US investment banks. As barriers fell and competition increased, British-owned firms exited the market while foreign firms replaced them.[7] Citibank, Chase Manhattan, and Shearson Lehman were among the US banks which paid large sums for London stockbroking firms, largely for 'goodwill'.[8] Over the following decade most of Britain's merchant banks were also acquired by foreign firms. In 1995, Warburgs was acquired by the Swiss Bank Corporation and Kleinwort Benson was taken over by Dresdner Bank. In 1997, Hambros was bought by Société Générale. In 2000, the investment banking business of Schroders was acquired by Citicorp's Salomon Smith Barney and Robert Fleming was acquired by Chase Manhattan. In 1997, the commercial bank Barclays also abandoned its expensive attempt to exhibit its affiliate Barclays de Zoete Wedd (BZW) as a global investment bank. A number of banks were also overwhelmed by management failure. In 1995, Barings was sold to the Dutch bank, ING for £1 after one of its Singapore-based traders, Nick Leeson, was found to have covered up over £800 million in losses.[9] By the new century there was little British presence in investment banking. Overall, the share of foreign banks of total UK cross-border bank assets reached 75 per cent.[10]

British-owned commercial banks also struggled to respond to the new global financial system. The British banking system still reflected the inheritance of the highly specialized structure of the nineteenth-century British banking. This made a sharp distinction between the clearing banks and overseas banks. The clearing banks were primarily concerned with the domestic British market, while the overseas banks had specialized in different foreign markets.

The advent of the global capital and money markets, a simultaneous sharp fall in the cost of transmitting electronic information, and the institutionalization of household savings, which created a pool of professionally managed capital, rendered such segmentation highly problematic. The large corporate customers of banks increasingly expected to be serviced on a worldwide basis, for example, but this was not a service that the traditional structure of British banking was well placed to provide. The clearing banks, with the partial exceptions of Barclays and Lloyds, had largely relied on correspondent relationships abroad to provide the trade finance and exchange operations required by their corporate clients, but the speed and complexity of the new financial markets shifted the weight of advantage towards internationalization rather than the use of market mechanisms. Meanwhile the overseas banks had almost no clients among the large British corporations, or, rather, they often served as bankers to individual subsidiaries of British multinationals in particular markets but had weak links with their head offices in Britain.[11]

It proved very difficult to overcome this structural legacy. The clearing banks sought to become 'global banks'. Barclays, the largest of the clearing banks, had a long history of multinational banking, especially through its Barclays DCO affiliate founded in 1926, which had a vast branch network all over Africa and the West Indies. In 1971, Barclays merged all its overseas banking interests in the wholly owned Barclays Bank International (BBI). This combined its businesses in developing countries, many of which had taken local shareholdings due to political pressures, with wholly owned affiliates operating in developed market economies, including small ventures in California, New York, and Canada.[12] During the 1970s, BBI expanded into wholesale banking and into related financial services including leasing, merchant banking, and corporate finance.

In 1984, Barclays merged BBI into the parent domestic bank to form a unified bank able to offer its customer services on a global basis. After the deregulation of the London market in 1986 – the 'Big Bang' – Barclays also invested heavily to build-up a presence in investment banking with the creation of a subsidiary, BZW, which sought to become a multinational bank in its own right, establishing offices in other international financial centres.

There was a striking geographical re-allocation. Most of Barclays' retail business in the developing world was sold, as was the residual shareholding in the South African bank in 1986. The United States and Europe became the location for most of Barclays' assets outside the United Kingdom. In France and Spain, Barclays pioneered interest-bearing accounts, marketing its services from a low-cost base of a limited number of profitable branches. In the United States, Barclays built up its Californian and New York affiliates through small bolt-on acquisitions. In 1979, it also bought the American Credit Corporation, a consumer finance, leasing and factoring, and mortgage loan company active in twenty-three states, and other acquisitions followed.[13]

During the 1990s, much of this global business was abandoned. Barclays investment in investment banking yielded poor returns. In 1997, BZW's equities business was sold. The attempt to develop a large retail and consumer finance business in the United States was abandoned. Although Barclays remaining retail branches in Africa and the Caribbean were financially successful, in the developed world and the Pacific Rim Barclays could only achieve low returns. Barclays became focused on its core British domestic market, with a strategy of building retail and commercial business elsewhere in Western Europe and seeking private banking, credit card, and other niche opportunities more widely.

Lloyds was the second British clearing bank with a long history of multinational banking, but it also struggled to create a new global business. Many of its foreign businesses had minority shareholders. In 1973, it had brought them out to form the wholly owned Lloyds Bank International (LBI) which owned an impressive multinational branch network spanning Latin America and Western Europe. Lloyds also had investments in banks in California, New Zealand, and Asia which remained outside LBI.

During the 1970s, LBI adopted an aggressive global growth strategy. There was a particular emphasis on expansion to the Far East, with branches and representative offices being opened in all the leading regional financial centres. An entrepreneurial culture flourished, encouraged by a substantial staff recruitment, at middle and senior levels, of bankers from other institutions. The outbreak of the world debt crisis in 1982 all but doomed LBI, however, as it had engaged in massive cross-border lending, especially in Latin America. It was merged into the domestic bank four years later. A failed attempt to acquire Standard Chartered in that year led to a progressive withdrawal from multinational banking, except in niche products and activities. The bank withdrew from commercial banking in the United States and in the Far Eastern financial centres except Tokyo.

Lloyds focused on the domestic British market. It diversified into estate agency business, following a pattern seen in the United States, innovated in retail banking products, and in 1988 merged with a leading British life assurance company, Abbey Life Insurance Company, to create Lloyds Abbey Life. In 1995,

Lloyds also acquired Cheltenham & Gloucester, a former building society (providing a stronger presence in the mortgage market), and in the same year merged with TSB Group to form Lloyds TSB Group. In 2000, the Scottish Widows insurance company was acquired. By then the once-global Lloyds TSB had 86 per cent of its total assets in the United Kingdom.

Midland and National Westminster, the two remaining 'Big Four' English clearing banks had few pre-existing interests in multinational banking. They had initially taken stakes in 'consortium' banks which were formed in London by European banks without substantial international business which were searching for an appropriate competitive response to the large American money centre banks. However, within a decade this network of consortium banks and clubs had been dismantled. Many partners in the consortium banks decided to establish their own multinational branches, causing conflicts of interest.[14]

National Westminster and Midland turned to developing multinational banking on their own account. National Westminster had inherited a small subsidiary which operated a small number of branches in France and Belgium and this was transformed into the International Westminster Bank, which developed a presence in wholesale and Eurocurrency markets. During the 1970s, branches were also established in New York, Chicago, and San Francisco, in leading continental centres such as Frankfurt, and in Bahrain, Singapore, and Tokyo.

During the mid-1970s the Midland Bank, alarmed about its dependence on Britain for its profits, also began establishing its own branches.[15] Between 1979 and 1982 Midland embarked on a series of foreign acquisitions, culminating in the acquisition of 51 per cent of Crocker National, one of California's largest banks. The acquisition made Midland Bank the tenth largest banking organization in the world.[16] A few months previously, National Westminster Bank also purchased a large American bank on the East Coast.

There was little joy as a result of these bold moves. Heavy losses eventually forced Midland Bank to sell Crocker National in 1986, minus most of its bad debts and all its Latin American loans, which Midland was obliged to retain. The bank's total losses in California were estimated at around £1 billion. The Midland Bank, which had been the world's largest bank in 1914, became a takeover target. In 1987, Hongkong Bank acquired 14.9 per cent of Midland's shares, but their burgeoning relationship stalled three years later in a climate of mounting losses and weak share prices. In 1990, Midland became the first British clearing bank to cut its dividend for fifty years. A new chairman and a new CEO were appointed, the latter imported from Barclays Bank.[17] Midland almost reached a merger agreement with Lloyds, but ultimately it was Hongkong Bank which reached an agreed takeover deal.[18]

National Westminster's involvement in investment banking led to a major financial scandal which led in 1989 to the resignation of National Westminster's chairman and three other directors. Its investments in the United States also resulted in substantial financial losses. NatWest USA lost $140 million in 1989 and $352 million in 1990: the 1990 loss (equivalent to £167 million) was larger even than Crocker National's record loss in 1984.[19] National Westminster sold its US business – which had become the biggest foreign-owned bank in the United States with $31 billion of assets – in 1995.

While the British clearing banks had sought and largely failed to transform themselves into successful multinational banks, the descendants of Britain's overseas banks also struggled with their difficult organizational inheritance. ANZ, for example, had a board of directors and an international banking business located in London, but the rest of its business was almost entirely confined to Australia and New Zealand. In 1976, ANZ solved the conundrum by leaving Britain altogether, transferring its domicile to Australia, even though over 95 per cent of ANZ's shareholders were residents of the United Kingdom.[20]

The three other surviving British overseas banks were not able to take the ANZ route. The host economies of Standard Chartered and Grindlays in Africa and Asia did not offer hospitable locations to transfer domicile, while even the Hongkong Bank's base in Hong Kong was subject to political uncertainties. In the reverse process to the clearers, during the 1970s and 1980s all three banks sought to develop financial activities in Britain.

Grindlays experienced major managerial problems, in part because of joint ownership by Lloyds Bank and Citibank, and in part through the acquisition of a London merchant bank in the mid-1960s that incurred heavy losses through property loans. Finally in 1984, Grindlays was acquired by ANZ, which wanted to acquire its branch network in Africa, Asia, and the Middle East. However, ANZ lacked the skills to manage the bank effectively. There were heavy losses from securities dealings in India in 1992 and divestitures began. In 1992, ANZ Grindlays sold all its African operations to Stanbic, the successor in South Africa to Standard Bank of South Africa. The European branches of Grindlays were also sold. Finally, in 2000, ANZ sold the remainder of Grindlays to Standard Chartered.[21]

During the 1970s, Standard Chartered also began to turn away from its past in Africa and Asia. Created through the merger in 1969 of the Standard Bank of South Africa and the Chartered Bank of India, Australia, and China, the bank inherited two distinctive corporate cultures, developed over the previous century and influenced by the nature of their host economies. Chartered's staff were skilled in trade finance and exchange banking, while Standard's past focus had been in retail banking.

During the 1970s, branches were opened in countries as varied as Australia and Sweden, to Colombia, Panama, and Nepal. However the main focus was the United States and Britain. In the United States, a series of acquisitions of small Californian banks culminated in the acquisition of Union Bank. In Britain, a joint venture merchant bank was begun in 1973 and brought under full control in 1977, when it was renamed Standard Chartered Merchant Bank. Standard Chartered also acquired a large shareholding in the Mocatta Group, leading bullion-dealers.[22] In 1973, it acquired the entire capital of the Hodge Group, a British retail operation extending mainly small-scale credit to, and attracting deposits from, individuals through a large UK branch network. The acquisition proved ill-fated, for it was a difficult period for British finance houses, with low levels of consumer demand, volatile interest rates, rising costs, oil price shocks, and bad debts. The diversified Hodge Group suffered a particularly high incidence of bad debts, and a considerable management effort was required to divest the group of many of its non-core businesses. The consumer finance operation was renamed Chartered Trust in 1979, but further extensive bad debts were made during the 1979–82 recession.[23]

During 1980, Standard Chartered's management concluded that the only way to radically improve its banking presence in Britain was by acquisition. In March 1981, Standard Chartered announced a £334 million agreed bid for the Royal Bank of Scotland Group one of the 'Big Three' Scottish clearing banks, and a small English clearing bank.[24] There appeared a near-perfect synergy between the Royal Bank, whose business was largely domestic banking, and Standard Chartered. Three weeks later the Hongkong Bank, anxious to diversify away from Hong Kong, made a higher counter-bid for the Royal Bank. The Monopolies and Mergers Commission reported against both bids, largely on the grounds of the need to retain an autonomous Scottish banking system, with ultimate decisions taken in Scotland.[25]

The performance of both Standard Chartered and the Hongkong Bank weakened after the Royal Bank affair, but it was the former that suffered the most. Initially, Standard Chartered appeared to recover from the defeat of its British strategy. In 1984, it acquired clearing bank status in Britain, while in the following year agreement was reached to purchase United Bank of Arizona, which represented a further geographical diversification within the United States. Meanwhile, the historic reliance on Africa continued to decline as subsidiaries were localized and, partly for political reasons, the bank reduced its involvement in South Africa. In 1985, Standard Chartered did not participate in a rights issue by the South African holding company Standard Bank Investment Corporation Ltd (SBIC), and as a result the British parent's shareholding fell to 39 per cent. Meanwhile, growing debts led in April 1986 to the hostile takeover bid from Lloyds.

Standard Chartered's management were determined to maintain the independence of their bank and this was achieved three months later when a number of prominent Far Eastern and Australian business groups, which were customers of the bank, assumed the role of 'white knights', taking a large shareholding amounting to 40 per cent of the equity, sufficient to defeat Lloyds.[26] Although preserved as an independent bank, Standard Chartered's problems became acute. The unusual shareholding structure created constant uncertainty about its future and its shares became a speculative stock. Asset sales and a management purge followed. In 1987, the group's residual investment in SBIC was sold, and in the following year Union Bank and United Bank of Arizona were sold, ending the bank's American strategy. Meanwhile, in March 1988, shortly before the 1987 results were declared, the head of the Bank of England's banking supervision was appointed executive chairman. A rights issue was made to boost further the group's capital strength and the bank sold its head office in London and its Singapore headquarters. Over time the bank's unusual shareholding structure was resolved, with most of the equity held by the 'white knights' being sold.[27]

The Hongkong Bank avoided the traumas of Standard Chartered. Like Standard Chartered, its response to the failure of the Royal Bank bid was to seek diversification elsewhere. In 1980, it paid $314 million for 51 per cent of a large New York state bank, Marine Midland.[28] The remainder was acquired in 1987. This doubled the bank's total assets, though the retention of Marine Midland's senior management delayed a full restructuring of the business.[29] It also entered Canada and Australia as these countries deregulated their banking systems.

As the 1980s progressed, however, it became evident that the Hongkong Bank faced a serious problem. In 1984, the British government negotiated an agreement under which the colony was to be returned to China in 1997, but with a guarantee of continuity in the territory's economic life-style for a further fifty years beyond 1997. Although the diversification strategy had given it over 1,300 offices in around fifty countries and about one-quarter of its assets in the United States and Canada, Hong Kong remained the jewel in the crown. The British colony accounted for 87 per cent of the bank's profits before tax in 1991.[30]

The overall performance of the British commercial banks during these decades was not impressive. The clearing banks, despite their strong retail franchises in their domestic market, stumbled repeatedly when they ventured into other activities, whether investment banking or acquiring foreign retail banks. The overseas banks, with the exception of Hongkong Bank, were so concerned to escape the political risks in developing countries that they rushed to invest in highly competitive and mature markets where they had no expertise.

The United States in particular proved a graveyard for the ambitions of British banks. They had a tendency to pay a lot of money for banks which no one else wanted, or which had management problems, and then sold them once economic conditions deteriorated. British banks, in their initial stages at least, attempted to penetrate a whole range of markets – retail, investment banking, and wholesale corporate – in which they lacked both the size and managerial expertise to be successful in such a competitive market as the United States. The British banks wholly underestimated the problems of multinational retail banking in a developed market economy, especially one as competitive and rule-bound as the United States. They held no real advantage in the United States beyond an ability to finance acquisitions, and inadequate management had rapidly led to difficulties in a competitive and complex market.[31]

Between 1986 and 1990 British multinational retail banking was completely eliminated from California, with the sale of two of the British-owned banks to Japanese banks and of the remaining two to Wells Fargo, a local Californian bank. The terms of several of the sales indicated the poor conditions of the British banks. Midland sold Crocker at book value, but only after taking over $3.5 billion (£2,502.5 million) of Crocker's less desirable assets – including Latin American debt, and non-performing Californian property loans.[32] By 1990 Standard Chartered, Lloyds, and Midland had abandoned branch banking in the United States. They were left with corporate banking and treasury business largely managed by New York offices, which was effectively the position with which they had started the 1970s. Barclays withdrew from Californian retail banking and also from its large consumer finance business, which became seriously loss-making. In 1992, it withdrew completely from American retail banking when it sold its sixty-five branches in New York. In 1994, Barclays sold its asset-based lending business in the United States, Barclays Business Credit. Loans and advances to customers booked through Barclays' US offices fell from over £9,000 million in 1992 to under £3,000 million in 1996. The start of the 1990s did not see British multinational retail banking in a strong position.

RENEWING

In view of the erratic performance between the 1960s and 1990, the subsequent renewal of British multinational banking was surprising. The structure of British banking was substantially transformed by mergers and the demutualization of most of the country's building societies. Royal Bank of Scotland's (RBS) acquisition of National Westminster in 2000 made it, at the end of 2002, the second largest bank in the United Kingdom and the seventh largest in the world by Tier 1 capitalization. Lloyds TSB and Barclays were the remaining survivors of the old English clearing banks (fifth and fourth largest banks in the United Kingdom and sixteenth and fourteenth largest in the world by the end of 2002), while in 2001 the Bank of Scotland merged with the Halifax to form HBOS which was larger than both Lloyds and Barclays.[33] HBOS's sudden collapse in September 2008, two days after the bankruptcy of Lehman Brothers in the United States, created worldwide financial panic, and its subsequent acquisition by Lloyds Bank, was one of the central events during an extraordinary period which at times appeared to threaten the entire British financial system.

The new era of multinational banking was led by three institutions – Standard Chartered, HSBC, and RBS. Standard Chartered's recovery was based on reverting to the business which it knew best, or rather its core competencies. The Far East-Pacific and Africa were the main areas of operation, with a focus on traditional business such as trade finance. The bank reverted to seeking to become what it had been in 1970: an institution which combined London-based international banking activity with an extensive commercial bank branch network inherited from Chartered Bank in the Asia-Pacific region, and a profitable banking business in parts of English-speaking Africa. Most of Standard Chartered's operations in developed markets were sold, including the British consumer finance business Chartered Trust, which was sold to Lloyds TSB for $950 million in 2000. Residual offices in Europe and the United States engaged in wholesale banking and trade finance.

During the 1990s, Standard Chartered sought to position itself as a specialist 'emerging markets bank'. Branches were opened in Vietnam in 1990, Cambodia and Iran 1992, Tanzania in 1993, and Myanmar in 1995. In 1998, a controlling share was purchased in Banco Exterior de Los Andes, an Andrean Region bank involved primarily in trade finance. In 1999, a 75 per cent shareholdings was also acquired in Nakornthon Bank, a victim of the Asian financial crisis of two years previously which the Thai government had rescued.[34] This gave Standard Chartered over fifty branches with a substantial retail banking presence in Thailand. In 2000, Standard Chartered made the two largest acquisitions in its history when it acquired the Chase Manhattan consumer business in Hong Kong for $1.32 billion and Grindlays for $1.74 billion.[35] This latter acquisition made Standard Chartered the largest international bank in India measured by assets.

Standard Chartered's business was not without risks. In 2001, the banks' loses in Argentina forced it to reduce its business in Latin America, and to restructure its business by increasing its penetration of consumer banking markets and focusing its wholesale business on higher-margin products. However the bank's focus on emerging markets – in 2007 a third of its revenue were derived from Hong Kong, and a further 10 and 9 per cent from Singapore and India, respectively – made it less immediately exposed when the global financial crisis swept over the American and European markets during 2008.[36]

At Hongkong Bank, a key development was getting a resolution to the political risks of being dependent on Hong Kong. A new group holding company called HSBC Holdings was created, based in London. The structure appeared to give the Hongkong Bank the safety of British citizenship without a British tax burden. At the end of March 1991, the Hongkong Bank's shares disappeared off the Hong Kong and London markets, reappearing in early April as those of HSBC Holdings.[37] In 1992, Midland Bank was finally acquired (and renamed HSBC Bank in 1999). In contrast to the previous case of Marine Midland, senior HSBC executives were immediately installed at the top of the bank.

The acquisition of the Midland Bank was transformative because it dramatically broadened HSBC's geographical scope. In a broader sense it was a crucial stage in the creation of a global financial services group which combined the provision of international banking services with extensive retail banking franchises in Britain, North America, and Asia. In 1993, HSBC Group head office moved to London. The group's traditional emphasis on local accountability meant that this head office provided only central functions, such as corporate strategy and financial control. HSBC began to expand in both developed and emerging markets. In 1999, HSBC was established as a uniform international brand name across the world. The corporate image was of 'the world's local bank'. It expanded in South America, taking over the ailing Banco Bamerindus in 1997 and in the same year acquired full control of Banco Roberts in Argentina. In 2002, $1.1 billion was paid for GF Bital, Mexico's fourth largest financial services group with some 1,400 branches in that country. In the following year, HSBC acquired the asset management business of Bank of America in Brazil. In 2000, HSBC also acquired CCF, one of France's largest banks, for $11 billion. This was a notably expensive acquisition for HSBC, which had a history of making low cost deals, and was the outcome of a bidding war with ING of the Netherlands. In 2001, HSBC acquired Barclays Bank branches and a fund management company in Greece, while CCF began acquiring small regional banks in France.[38]

HSBC was characterized by a culture which many considered thrifty, risk-averse, and highly disciplined.[39] However it could also not resist the siren call of the United States. In 1999, it acquired Republic New York Corporation, and three years later it acquired Household International for $15 billion, its largest ever acquisition. Household International was the leading independent non-bank financial company in the United States with $107 billion of total managed loans, fifty million customers, and 1,400 offices in forty-six states. Its dominant business was consumer lending to 'sub-prime' customers with unsatisfactory or non-existent credit history. It also had a large private label credit card business, including GM (General Motors) and a range of store cards.

The fateful consequences of bundling together individual sub-prime mortgages in ways which appeared to make them less risky, and the sales of these opaque financial instruments to banks worldwide, became fully apparent within a few years, but at the time Household appeared to offer HSBC the opportunity to greatly expand its business in the United States, given that one-third of the American population was 'sub-prime'.[40]

The acquisition of Household continued the long tradition of misfortunes experienced by British banks in the United States. The British bank first failed to install its own management to integrate Household properly into HSBC. Household began to buy up large amounts of sub-prime mortgages in the belief that it could assess and underwrite risks better than other lenders. When interest rates began rising and house prices failing in 2006, Household began to experience growing defaults and found itself centrally located in the emerging of the sub-prime lending crisis. In 2007, HSBC was obliged to issue its first ever profits warning.[41] In that year the bank was obliged to set aside $12.2 billion for bad loans in its North American divisions. Although one-fifth of its business was in North America, it made no profits.[42]

It was RBS that made the most spectacular entrance into multinational banking. The Royal Bank had become the largest bank in Scotland in 1969 with a 40 per cent market share. During the 1980s it began to diversify, establishing an innovative car insurance company called Direct Line in 1985, offering low cost insurance via the telephone, and later launched Britain's first comprehensive online banking service over the internet in 1997. However the most important event in its growth was its successful hostile takeover bid for National Westminster, which was nearly three times its size, but far less efficient. The $34 billion acquisition was the largest acquisition in British banking history.[43]

In 1988, the Royal Bank – previously the owner of only a small number of foreign branches and offices – had also acquired Citizens Financial, the largest state-chartered bank in Rhode Island, and subsequent small acquisitions over the next two years gave it over fifty branches in the state.[44] Citizens grew through incremental growth and the use of small bolt-on acquisitions to build a substantial regional bank. During the first half of the 1990s, Citizens made a series of acquisitions of moderately sized New England banks. In 1995, it also began operating supermarket branches in partnership with Shaw's Supermarkets, then a wholly owned affiliate of the large British retailer J. Sainsbury. In 1996, Citizens merged with the First New Hampshire Bank, owned by the Bank of Ireland, in an agreement which gave the Irish Bank a 23.5 per cent share of Citizens. In 1998, after further small acquisitions, Royal Bank re-acquired full control.

In 2001 Citizens purchased, for over $2 billion, Mellon Bank's banking business in the mid-Atlantic, for the first time taking its retail franchise into Pennsylvania, Delaware, and New Jersey. By 2003, Citizens was ranked one of the United States' twenty largest commercial bank holding companies, with $55 billion in assets and 740 branches in seven states. Royal Bank also obtained ownership of Greenwich Capital from National Westminster when it was acquired in 2000. This became Royal Bank's US-based debt markets business, and was a recognized leader in the US asset-based securities market. Citizens was also persistently profitable. In 2004, Citizens acquired Charter One Financial group, a Cleveland, Ohio bank operating in six states in the Midwest and Northeast.[45]

In 2007, the Royal Bank's new global stature was confirmed when it led a consortium of Santander of Spain and Fortis of Belgium in a successful hostile takeover bid to break up ABN Amro, one of Europe's largest banks, defeating its rival Barclays in the process. The Royal Bank secured global and wholesale clients in the Netherlands, Latin America, and Asia. The major problem was timing. As the global financial crisis gained momentum, Royal Bank's exposure to the developed markets at the heart of the storm took a heavy toll. In August 2008, the Royal Bank announced a pre-tax loss of £680 million for the first six months of the year, which was the second largest in British banking history. The subsequent collapse of Fortis, and the acquisition of most of its assets by France BNP Paribas, was indicative of how much the financial world had changed in just a few months.[46]

In retrospect, the apparent caution of Barclays Bank during these years seemed the wiser path. After its divestments from investment banking and the American banking market, Barclays Bank resumed international growth on a more modest scale. After 2000 the bank expanded its investment and fund management divisions. By 2006, the bank made half its profits outside Britain. On a smaller scale, it also resumed multinational commercial banking. It acquired control of Absa, the South African bank, between 2005 and 2006, and elsewhere began to expand new branches.[47] In September 2008, it was sufficiently well-capitalized to pay $1.75 billion for the core North American assets of stricken Lehman Brothers.

During the two decades after 1990, therefore, there were some remarkable growth stories. HSBC became the third largest commercial bank in the world by assets through a series of acquisitions in both developed and developing countries. Standard Chartered, another old overseas bank whose survival had been in doubt throughout the 1970s and 1980s, repositioned itself as a highly successful emerging markets bank. The Royal Bank built through a series of bolt-on acquisitions one of the ten largest commercial banks in the United States.[48]

Why was the performance of British-owned multinational banks better than their predecessors over the last twenty years? It might in part be explained by broader political and economic circumstances. First, the improved performance of the British economy as a whole from the 1980s played a part. There was a sustained period of UK economic growth with GDP growing two to three per cent per annum at constant prices.[49] Much of this expansion was stimulated by a growth in global economic activity and trade which British multinational banks were able to service.

Second, while emerging markets between the 1960s and 1980s featured growing state intervention, political instability, anti-foreign policies, etc. – with Hong Kong as one of the rare exceptions – over the last twenty years their economies boomed as political circumstances changed. In China, economic and trade liberalization since 1979, but particularly since the 1990s, stimulated spectacular economic expansion. This was aided by political stability and policies aimed at encouraging international trade and foreign inward investment.[50] China's GDP increased from 1,854,790 billion Chinese Yuan in 1990 to 7,830,807 billion Chinese Yuan in 2005, with annual increases ranging between 8 and 14 per cent.[51] India also saw extraordinary economic expansion following economic liberalization and reform beginning in 1991. By 2008, it was Asia's fourth largest economy.[52] British multinational banks, especially those such as Standard Chartered and HSBC that operate in Asia, benefitted from the increase in demand for their services generated by such spectacular growth in India and China.

However, there was also a change in leadership within key multinational banks. It was striking how the leaders of the successful banks came from beyond the London banking establishment. At HSBC a succession of the chairmen who transformed the bank had spent most of their careers in Hong Kong or elsewhere in Asia. Michael Sandberg, Chairman and Chief Executive HSBC between 1977 and 1986, was a bold, entrepreneurial figure who acquired the US-based bank Marine Midland in the 1980s. He spent his banking career in Asia. William Purves, Chairman and Chief Executive of HSBC from 1990 to 1998, led the bank in its acquisition of Midland in 1992, which has been an undeniable success. He was a Scot but spent the majority of his banking career with HSBC in Asia, only moving to London in 1992. John Bond oversaw several large acquisitions by HSBC after becoming Chairman in 1998, including that of Household. Having joined the bank as a teenage trainee he spent 30 years in Asia and in the United States before returning to London in 1993 to become Chief Executive following HSBC's takeover of Midland Bank.[53] Stephen Green, who became HSBC Chief Executive in 2003 and Chairman in 2006, worked in the civil service and at the consultants McKinsey before entering banking.[54]

Iconoclastic Scotsmen George Mathewson and Fred Goodwin transformed RBS from a primarily domestic bank to a global institution. They followed unconventional and bold strategies, such as taking over a far bigger bank (National Westminster in 2000) and breaking up ABN Amro.[55] Mathewson grew up and was educated in Scotland and worked for Bell Aerospace, the venture capital organization 3i and the Scottish Development Agency before joining RBS in 1987, becoming Chief Executive in 1992 and Chairman of the bank in 2001. His career progression was not a conventional one for a banker.[56] Goodwin was also born and educated in Scotland and qualified and worked as an accountant before entering banking in 1995. He joined RBS in 1998, became Chief Executive Officer in 2001, and built a reputation for cost saving and an unusually abrupt style of negotiating. In October 2008 he was obliged to resign after a liquidity crisis left RBS largely owned by the British government.

At Standard Chartered Mervyn Davies did not even speak English until he was 8 (his first language being Welsh), and worked for Citibank for a decade. He went to Standard Chartered in 1993, joined the board as a Group Executive Director in 1997, became Group Chief Executive in 2001 and Chairman of the bank in 2006. Although working in banking all his life, Davies spent a large part of his career in Asia, especially Honk Kong. Peter Sands grew up in Asia and worked for the consultants McKinsey before joining Standard Chartered, working his way upwards to become Group Chief Executive in 2006. Neither man came from the conventional London banking establishment.

British multinational banks, therefore, underwent a renewal of fortune from 1990 onwards that was supported by a benign era of economic growth, despite major political upheavals and regional wars, and of fast globalization. This external environment was combined with internal benefits in the form of leaders who were not entrenched in a conservative banking tradition but rather took a global, innovative, and often very ambitious programme of expansion. The key problem, however, was exogenous, for they succeeded within a global financial system which was structurally flawed and inadequately regulated. They became, as a result, vulnerable to major shocks and contagion that could and did threaten even the most well-managed bank. Going forward, the nature of opportunities in multinational banking was likely to be changed considerably by the restructuring of the global financial markets and the intervention of governments to nationalize banks and support liquidity. It remains to be seen how British-based banks would fare in this new context.

CONCLUSION

The multinational banking industry was transformed from the 1960s. The advent of global financial markets changed the industry almost beyond recognition. Britain, or rather the City of London, retained a position of great international importance, for many of the new markets were physically located in the resurgent City, but British-owned banks rapidly lost significance. The growth of American and, later, Japanese multinational banking, reflected the size of their economies, their relative importance in the world economy, and the strength of their currencies. The shrinking of British-owned multinational banking was, in this sense, 'inevitable'.

British banks were also weakened by problems in their strategies and structures. They entered the era of global banking from the 1960s with a heritage based on segmented markets, specialist institutions, and strong corporate cultures. Strategic misjudgements hindered the ability of these banks to take full advantage of their location in the reborn City of London. The banks pursued expensive acquisitions in the United States, which they proceeded to poorly manage, whilst failing to build on their own strengths. It was only when these institutions focused on their core competencies, specifically in geographical areas in which they had a record of success, and were led by bankers who had experience in such regions, that they were able to enter a period of renewal. A new generation of executives were able to take advantage of globalization after 1990.

Yet in the search for yield, British multinational banks entered new markets and once again forays into the United States have proved challenging. Above all, the global financial crisis beginning in 2007 with the sub-prime lending market in the United States exposed the structural and regulatory weakness of the existing global financial system in which the British banks had become major players. British multinational banks had appeared more robust and well-managed than their predecessor institutions between the 1960s and 1980s, but the events of 2008 were of sufficient magnitude to cast great uncertainty on the future direction of the entire global financial industry, and with it the prospects for the British banks.

NOTES

1. Stanley Chapman, *The Rise of Merchant Banking*, London, 1984; Philip Ziegler, *The Sixth Great Power. Barings, 1762–1929*, London, 1988; Richard Roberts, *Schroders, Merchants and Bankers*, London, 1992. On the overseas banks, see Geoffrey Jones, *British Multinational Banking 1830–1990*, Oxford University Press, Oxford, 1993. The first part of this chapter draws heavily on this book.

2. Eurodollars are US-dollar denominated deposits at banks outside of the United States. See Catherine Schenk, 'The Origins of the Eurodollar Market in London: 1955–1963', *Explorations in Economic History*, 35, 2, 1998: 221–38.

3. Ian M. Kerr, *A History of the Eurobond Market – The First 21 Years*, Euromoney Publications/Amro Bank, 1984.

4. A vast literature on the history of London as a financial center includes David Kynaston, *The City of London*, Volumes 1–4, London, 1994, 1995, 2000, and 2002; and Youssef Cassis, *Capitals of Capital: A History of International Financial Centres, 1780–2005*, Cambridge University Press, Cambridge, 2006.

5. Mae Baker and Michael Collins, 'London as an International Financial Centre 1958–1980' in Youssef Cassis and Éric Busssière, eds., *London and Paris as International Financial Centres*, Oxford University Press, Oxford, 2005; Michael Darby, 'The Internationalization of American Banking and Finance,' *Journal of International Money and Finance*, 5, 1986: 405–7; Mark S. Mizruchi and Gerald F. Davis, 'The Globalization of American Banking, 1962–1981', in Frank Dobbin, ed., *The Sociology of the Economy*, 2004; Lawrence G. Goldberg and Denise Johnson, 'The Determinants of US Banking Activity Abroad,' *Journal of International Money and Finance*, 9, 1980: 126–7; Thomas F. Huertas, 'US Multinational Banking: History and Prospects,' in Geoffrey Jones, ed., *Banks as Multinationals*, Routledge, London, 1990: 254.

6. C.A.E. Goodhart, 'The Economics of Big Bang,' in Ranald C. Michie, ed., *The Development of London as a Financial Centre*, Vol. 4: 1945–2000, I.B. Tauris, London, 2000: 261.

7. 'The City of London Now Belongs to the World – The Once-Staid District is Fast Becoming the Go-Go Capital of Global Finance,' *Business Week*, 2 June 1986, available from Factiva, http://www.factiva.com accessed 8 Oct. 2003.

8. David Kynaston, '"Banks and Yanks": Towards a History of the Restructuring of the London Securities Industry in the 1980s', in Manfred Pohl, Teresa Tortella, Herman Van der Wee, eds., *A Century of Banking Consolidation in Europe: The History and Archives of Mergers and Acquisitions*, Ashgate, Aldershot, 2001: 135–45.

9. David Kynaston, *The City of London: A Club No More, 1945–2000*, Chatto & Windus, London, 2001: 764–8; and Stephen Fay, *The Collapse of Barings*, W.W. Norton Company, New York, 1997.

10. Richard Roberts, 'London as an International Financial Centre, 1980–2000: Global Powerhouse or Wimbledon EC2?', in Eric Bussière and Youssef Cassis, eds., *London and Paris as International Financial Centres in the Twentieth Century*, Oxford University Press, Oxford, 2005: 287–312; Philip Augar, *The Death of Gentlemanly Capitalism: The Rise and Fall of London's Investment Banks*, Penguin, London, 2000.

11. For an extended discussion of the events discussed in the next section, see Jones, *British Multinational Banking*: chapters 8 and 9.

12. Margaret Ackrill and Leslie Hannah, *Barclays: The Business of Banking*, Cambridge University Press, Cambridge, 2001: 301–26; Derek F. Channon, *British Banking Strategy and the International Challenge*, Macmillan, London, 1977.

13. Derek F. Channon, *Cases in Bank Strategic Management and Marketing*, Wiley, Chichester, 1986: 286; Ackrill and Hannah, *Barclays*: 313–18.

14. Richard Roberts with Christopher Arnander, *Take Your Partners: Orion, the Consortium Banks and the Transformation of the Euromarkets*, Palgrave, London, 2001; Alberto A. Weissmüller, 'London Consortium Banks,' *Journal of the Institute of Bankers*, 95, Aug. 1974: 203–16; Derek F. Channon, *Global Banking Strategy*, Wiley, Chichester, 1988.

15. Channon, *Global Banking Strategy*: 257–60 and 287. Chairman's Statement, 1979 Report of the Directors and Accounts, Midland Bank.

16. 'How Midland was Struck by a Californian Earthquake', *Financial Times*, 25 Jan. 1988; 'Crossing the Atlantic Can End in Oblivion', *FT.com*, 24 Feb. 2003.

17. 'McMahon to Quit Midland', *Financial Times*, 6 Mar. 1991; 'A Look Back at Years of Living Dangerously,' *Financial Times*, 12 Mar. 1991.

18. 'Lloyds and Midland Merger was Blocked by Threat to Quit', *Financial Times*, 25 Mar. 1992.

19. Lex Column, *Financial Times*, 5 Apr. 1991.

20. David Merrett, *ANZ Bank*, Allen and Unwin, Sydney, 1985: 295–301.

21. D.T. Merrett, 'The Internationalization of Australian Banks', *Journal of International Financial Markets, Institutions and Money*, 12, 2002: 385; http://www.rbs.com/about03.asp?id=ABOUT_US/OUR_HERITAGE/OUR_ARCHIVES/ONLINE_ARCHIVE_-GUIDE/THE_ARCHIVE_GUIDE/GRINDLAYS_BANK_PLC accessed 2 Aug. 2008.

22. Margaret Reid, *The Secondary Banking Crisis, 1973–75*, Macmillan, London, 1982: 145. There is a study of the history of Wallace Brothers before 1973 by A.C. Pointon, *Wallace Brothers*, Oxford University Press, Oxford, 1974.

23. Standard Chartered Bank, *A Story Brought Up to Date*, date unknown: 29; and Timothy O'Sullivan, *Julian Hodge: A Biography*, Routledge & Kegan Paul, London, 1981: 89–96.

For contemporary discussion of the affair of the consumer credit licence, see *Daily Express*, 18 Dec. 1978; *Financial Times* and *Guardian*, 21 Dec. 1978.

24. Monopolies and Mergers Commission, *A Report on the Proposed Mergers of the Hong Kong and Shanghai Banking Corporation, Standard Chartered Bank Limited and the Royal Bank of Scotland Group Limited*, London, Jan. 1982: 4 and 62.

25. Monopolies and Mergers Commission, *Report on the Proposed Mergers of the Hongkong and Shanghai Banking Corporation*: 84–7.

26. The three key 'white knights' were Sir Yue-Kong Pao, a leading Hong Kong magnate and shipowner, who acquired 14.9 per cent of the equity; a Malaysian businessman, Tan Sri Khoo Teck Puat, who purchased 5 per cent; and the Bell Group of Australia led by Robert Holmes à Court, which acquired 7.4 per cent.

27. 'Bond Sells £165m Bank Stake,' *Financial Times*, 5 Nov. 1988; 'Y. K. Pao Sells 10% Stake in Standard,' *Financial Times*, 20 June 1989. By 2002, only Tan. Sri Knoo remained a significant shareholder, with around 13.9 percent of the equity, which he held until his death in 2004.

28. Frank King, *The History of the Hongkong and Shanghai Banking Corporation*, 4, Cambridge University Press, Cambridge, 1991: 776–848.

29. Tarun Khanna and David Lane, 'HSBC Holdings', Harvard Business School Case No. 9–705–466, 2006.

30. 'The Beginning of an Era of Change for Hong Kong Investors', *Financial Times*, 15 Apr. 1992.

31. 'Crossing the Atlantic Can End in Oblivion', *FT.com*, 24 Feb. 2003.

32. 'Midland Bank Sells Crocker for £715m. to Wells Fargo', *Financial Times*, 8 Feb. 1986.

33. Marko Maslakovic and Duncan McKenzie, *Banking*, City Business Series 2004, International Financial Services, London, 2004: 5 and 26.

34. 'Standard Chartered Finally Buys Nakornthon', *Banker*, 149, 884: 71.

35. 'SC lands Grindlays for $1.34 bn.', *Banker*, 150, 892, Jun. 2000: Oct. 40.

36. http://www.standardchartered.co.jp/home/global.html (accessed 3 Aug. 2008) and Maslakovic and McKenzie, *Banking*: 26.

37. 'The Bank Does a Bunk', *Far Eastern Economic Review*, 27 Dec. 1990; 'Bank Seeks to Retain its Privileges', *Financial Times*, 18 Jan. 1991.

38. http://www.hsbc.com/1/2/about-hsbc/group-history/group-history-1980-1999 and http://www.hsbc.com/1/2/about-hsbc/group-history

39. Khanna and Lane, 'HSBC Holdings': 5.

40. 'HSBC Focuses on Household Integration', *Financial Times*, 4 Mar. 2003.

41. 'A Year of Living Dangerously', *Financial Times*, 21 May 2007.

42. 'HSBC Counts the Cost of its Subprime Foray', *Financial Times*, 4 Mar. 2008.

43. Nitin Nohria and James Weber, 'The Royal Bank of Scotland: Masters of Integration', Harvard Business School Case No. 9–404–025, 2005.

44. Linda S. Tissiere, 'Citizens Financial Group, Inc.: From the Past to the Present', *The Royal Bank of Scotland Review*, 171, Sept. 1991.

45. Rajiv Lal and Arar Han, 'Citizens Bank', Harvard Business School Case No. 9–505–034, 2005.

46. 'ABN Takeover Beat the Odds But Tests Await', *Financial Times*, 17 Oct. 2007; 'Ex-RBS Boss Says ABN Buy "A Bad Mistake",' *Financial Times*, 11 Feb. 2009.

47. 'Barclays Extends Global Horizons', *Financial Times*, 21 Feb. 2007; 'Barclays Plans Integration after Absa Bank Deal', *Financial Times*, 10 May 2005; 'South Africa:

Barclays – ABSA Merger', *Africa Research Bulletin: Economic, Financial & Technical Series*, 12/16/2005, 42, 12: 16796.

48. 'Royal Bank of Scotland to Buy Charter One', *FT.com*, 4 May 2004.
49. GDP at constant prices. Figures provided by IMF at http://www.imf.org/external/pubs/ ft/weo/2006/01/data/dbcselm.cfm?G=2001 (accessed 3 Aug. 2008).
50. 'China's Economic Boom Goes on', *Financial Times*, 25 Oct. 2007.
51. GDP at constant prices. Figures provided by IMF at http://www.imf.org/external/pubs/ ft/weo/2006/01/data/dbcselm.cfm?G=2001 (accessed 3 Aug. 2008).
52. 'Doing Business in India: Tax and Business Guide', Ernst & Young, India, 2006.
53. 'Once Again Replacing the Irreplaceable', *Financial Times*, 29 Nov. 2005; and 'HSBC's Elder Statesman Sticks to His Thrifty Line', *The Independent*, 11 Aug. 2003.
54. 'The Low Key Rise of Stephen Green', *Financial Times*, 28 Nov. 2005.
55. 'RBS Aims to Repeat NatWest Trick', *Financial Times*, 16 Oct. 2007.
56. 'Rise and Rise of a Scottish Iconoclast', *Financial Times*, 3 Jun. 2007.

12

Back to the Future: The Aircraft and IT Industries in Britain since 1945

Richard Coopey and Peter Lyth

This chapter looks at two sectors of 'advanced technology', or 'science-based' industry in Britain in the post-war period: airframe and aero-engine manufacturing, and IT. In many ways both sectors were 'born' in this period. Though they both have longer lineages, depending on precisely which aspect we choose to take as their genesis, their real period of growth in both complexity and scale, and their real foundation as modern industries, are characteristically post-war. The two industries share many common features – both were identified early on as key components of a new wave of science, technology, and industry, and essential pillars of any economy hoping to survive in the new international struggle for comparative and competitive advantage as the world recovered and readjusted after 1945. From the perspective of the 1950s computers, aerospace, and nuclear industries were increasingly seen as the triumvirate of modernity – sectors of the future. Moreover, Britain seemed uniquely placed to exploit these future industries – the first computers were built here, the first jets (shared with Germany) likewise, and the Queen was about to cut the ribbon on the first civil nuclear power station. British genius was poised to lead the economy and country into a new renaissance.

So where did it go wrong? Or, indeed, did it go wrong? The following sections outline the fate of the aircraft and IT industries from the 1950s onwards. In many ways it is a story of strong parallels: of the weight or necessity of government policies and priorities, civil and military; of mistaken or unrealistic ambitions; of corporate structural weaknesses; and of a new world of international competition. But it is also a story of contrasts – of failures and successes, and a cautionary tale against accepting blanket explanations of decline which so often attribute the failure of high technology industries in Britain to simplistic, unicausal explanations such as 'good at inventing, no good at mass producing', or the debilitating effects of an alleged 'binary' culture.

BRITISH AIRCRAFT AND AERO ENGINE
MANUFACTURING SINCE 1945

As this chapter was being written, news came from Seattle that the aircraft manufacturer Boeing, one of America's most prominent national champions, was launching the latest addition to its family of airliners: the 787 *Dreamliner*. According to the advance publicity, the 787 will be cleaner, more fuel-efficient, and an altogether smarter aircraft. This is partly thanks to its use of novel construction materials such as plastic and carbon fibre, which make it lighter and more aerodynamic than earlier models using metal alloys. But it is also partly because its two Trent 1,000 jet engines, made by the British manufacturer Rolls-Royce, allow it to fly further, on less fuel and with fewer carbon emissions. What is significant in the context of this chapter is that Boeing's selection of the Trent 1,000 to power its new aircraft is an expression of trust in one of the few remaining British-owned, high technology manufacturing firms and not surprisingly it was a decision which led to justifiable celebration in Rolls-Royce's home town of Derby. By outlining Rolls-Royce's history against the broader canvas of the British aircraft industry in the twentieth century, this section considers how Rolls came to find itself one of the few survivors in this field of British manufacturing companies at the beginning of the twenty-first century.

1915–45: A British Industry Ascending

In 1919, Britain had the largest aircraft industry in the world.[1] This industry was actually two industries, manufacturing airframes and aero-engines. Some firms like Bristol and de Havilland performed both functions. More often they were separate and British airframe constructors like A.V.Roe, Blackburn, Fairey, Handley Page, Hawker, Short Brothers, and Vickers used power plants made by British engine companies like Armstrong–Siddeley, Napier or Rolls-Royce, which built engines for both cars and planes. Production was craft-based, often using skills from car manufacturing, marine engineering or cabinet making.[2] The aircraft produced were reliable in operation but generally not advanced in terms of aerodynamic theory drawn from academic science.[3] As the wartime boom gave way to the more modest levels of demand associated with a peacetime economy, the airframe industry contracted, with a considerable degree of merger between firms.[4] Thereafter, the remaining airframe companies cruised comfortably through the 1920s and early 1930s producing in small batches a diverse range of military and civil aircraft.[5]

British aero-engine manufacturers did rather better. Because there was a close connection between high-performance car engines and power plants for aircraft, engine makers were not obliged to cut capacity in the post-war period to the same extent as the airframe companies. By the 1930s the British aero-engine industry was probably the world's largest and the Air Ministry was supporting five main engine manufacturers ('the family'), consisting of Armstrong–Siddeley, Bristol, de Havilland, Napier, and Rolls-Royce. Rolls-Royce was already the leader in engines for military types, having made its name with the 'R' engine which powered the Supermarine seaplanes in the 1929 and 1931 Schneider Cup speed trials.[6] Within a few years development of the 'R' had led to the 'Merlin', the engine which eventually powered a wide range of British fighters and bombers during the Second World War as well as the North American P.51 Mustang.[7] As aircraft flew higher and faster, and piston engines and propellers gave way to gas turbines, Rolls-Royce became quickly involved in jet engine technology.[8] By the winter of 1944 Rolls was test running the most powerful jet engine in the world (the 'Nene') and within months of the end of the war the company had switched production entirely from piston engines to turbines, underlining the strength of its conviction that the future lay in jets.[9] Meanwhile on the civil airframe side the government had launched the ambitious Brabazon Programme under whose auspices British airframe companies began work on a range of airliners for the post-war period. Most of these reached some sort of fruition in the ten years after 1945, but only two can claim to be successful or celebrated: the Vickers-Armstrong Viscount equipped with four Rolls-Royce 'Dart' turbo-prop engines and the de Havilland Comet, originally powered by de Havilland's own 'Ghost' engine, later by the Rolls-Royce 'Avon'.[10]

1946–76: Comet to Concorde

In the period between the end of the war and the 1970s the British airframe industry struggled and eventually gave up the effort to maintain a coherent national identity. To some extent its history in these years reflects the general trend within British manufacturing, for example, lower levels of investment and labour productivity than in the United States, western Europe, or Japan, and an unwillingness to face the need for concentration among a large number of small or medium-sized firms. But in other respects the aircraft industry was different. It was, after all, a high technology industry which had experienced very rapid expansion in the war years, indeed benefited to an extraordinary degree from the war and done so with the sustained and lavish support of government. And this government was well aware of the aircraft industry's potential to assist in Britain's vital post-war export drive.[11]

The period began with a victorious but bankrupt Britain still expecting to fulfil a wide range of international strategic commitments and provide from its own depleted resources the military hardware needed to do the job.[12] The years from 1945 to 1960 also witnessed an unparalleled increase in the technological complexity of airframe and aero engine construction. Aircraft manufacture now required such high expenditure on R&D that, besides a sympathetic government with deep pockets, firms needed to combine or cluster in order to remain internationally competitive. Britain had such clusters in aircraft manufacturing but they were locked into a domestic procurement process where the purchaser (the RAF or the national air corporations, BOAC and BEA) failed to set specification standards that would have made their products competitive at the international level.[13] The only competitor of the British industry in these years was the United States, where, besides large manufacturing and R&D contracts from the Defence Department, American firms benefited from vastly greater economies of scale in manufacturing and in their use of domestic networks for component supply.[14] Britain needed to achieve similarly long production runs in aircraft manufacturing to cover the design and development costs of new aircraft and if it could not, commercial failure was almost inevitable.[15] Moreover it now needed to limit its aircraft procurement objectives to a small number of projects where there was a strong likelihood of success and where the high value-added quotient stemming from those fields where it still excelled technologically, for example jet engines, would yield the highest return in the form of export orders. Yet, instead of taking this approach, the Labour government's planning instrument, the Ministry of Supply (MoS), continued from the 1930s the strategically less risky but commercially doomed policy of maintaining a broad, general capacity in the airframe industry. It did this because, lacking the resources to adequately research the future course of aeronautical science and therefore unable to 'pick winners', it simply backed everybody's projects with the limited resources it had at its disposal.[16] In civil aircraft procurement, for example, instead of awarding contracts to the few firms with a proven record, like de Havilland and Vickers, the MoS spread its favour widely; according to one authority it was 'insufficiently selective and ruthless in its approach to either contract allocation or the cancellation of ailing projects' and as a result delayed by at least ten years the process of rationalization and concentration around the strongest companies.[17] In general Britain's civil airframe industry remained a community of prototype builders rather than mass producers of aircraft using substantial production orders to recoup the heavy costs of research and development.[18]

As in the inter-war period, British aero-engine builders were usually more successful. This was partly because aero-engines could go either in civil or military aircraft and manufacturers had a larger potential market over which to spread development costs. Of greater importance, however, was the trump card they possessed in the gas turbine.[19] Jet engines led the post-war British aircraft industry, particularly on the civil side where American airlines were reluctant to abandon the radial piston engines of Pratt & Whitney and Wright. The de Havilland Comet and the Vickers Armstrong Viscount exemplify this spearhead role for gas turbines. Indeed it is hard to exaggerate the symbolic power of the Comet at the time of its introduction into airline service in 1952; the nation's belief in a British economic recovery based on science and technology seemed almost to be riding on its wings.[20] Beyond the triumphalism of the Comet, three British companies were working on jet engines: de Havilland, Armstrong–Siddeley, and Rolls-Royce. Rolls-Royce was undoubtedly the brightest star, but de Havilland was a strong contender in engines, besides being a very important airframe producer, and Armstrong–Siddeley had built probably the most powerful engine in the 'Sapphire'. Rolls-Royce was developing two jet engines in the 'Avon' and the 'Conway', the latter a 'by-pass' engine. The history of the 'Conway', which powered British military aircraft as well as early versions of the Boeing 707 and Douglas DC.8 jet airliners, is as revealing an episode in British science-based industry in this period as it was a salutary experience for Rolls-Royce. No sooner had the company begun to take orders for the 'Conway' than their American rival Pratt & Whitney produced their own bypass engine, the JT3D, which, with a higher 'bypass ratio' than the British engine, was both more powerful and more efficient. Rolls sold no more 'Conways' for Boeing or Douglas airframes and learnt the hard lesson that in competition with an American industry that was capable of rapid commercial response to a technological challenge, it was vital to have an engine's successor already on the drawing board, if not actually in development.[21]

Meanwhile the Chandlerian rationalization of the British airframe industry, discouraged by indiscriminate MoS nurturing under Labour, was delayed further by the laissez-faire regime of the Conservatives after 1951. With the Comet and the Viscount promising to win the 'race' with the Americans, the industry looked strong enough to stand on its own feet and the new government decided to halt further state-financed launch aid.[22] But greater exposure to market forces did not enhance the industry's ability to 'pick winners', or encourage it to unite around any winners which did emerge. And although there is evidence of increasing frustration on the part of civil servants at the lack of rationalization in the industry, strategic mergers did not begin until 1958.[23] In that year, when there were still twenty-four airframe and six aero-engine producers in Britain, the government used its powers as the industry's dominant customer to force through concentration with the objective of achieving greater international competitiveness. Launch aid of up to 50 per cent of development costs was restored for selected projects and the industry coaxed and coerced with the promise of that aid into two pairs of airframe and engine groups. Of the airframe makers Hawker Siddeley Aviation (HSA) was formed out of Armstrong Whitworth Aircraft, Armstrong–Siddeley Motors, Gloster, Hawker, and A.V.Roe with Folland, Blackburn, and de Havilland joining shortly afterwards; and the British Aircraft Corporation (BAC) was assembled in 1960 out of Bristol, English Electric, Hunting, and Vickers-Armstrong.[24] Of the engine makers Rolls-Royce now found itself with a sizeable and potentially serious competitor in Bristol Siddeley Engines which emerged between 1959 and 1961 from the union of Bristol Aero Engines with the engine interests of Armstrong–Siddeley Motors, Blackburn, and de Havilland.[25]

Space does not allow a lengthy analysis of how the British civil airframe industry shrank to a fraction of its former glory in the years between the government-induced rationalization of the early 1960s and the formation of the nationalized enterprise, British Aerospace (BAe) in 1977, but looking at the history of three programmes, involving both airframes and engines, allows us to pick out the critical milestones.

The BAC One Eleven and Two Eleven

BAC worked on three major projects within the company's lifespan, two for the government, and one as a private venture. They were the TSR2 strike aircraft, which was cancelled to the accompaniment of much public gnashing of teeth in 1965, the supersonic Concorde airliner and the BAC One Eleven short-haul airliner. The One Eleven, which first flew in 1963 and enjoyed 50 per cent launch aid, was built on the strength of unprecedented (for a British company) market research amongst the airlines. It was also produced, unusually, on the basis of an order from an independent airline, British United Airways, as opposed to one of the nationalized air corporations (BEA or BOAC). Eventually over 200 One Elevens were sold, including important sales to American airlines, thus making it, along with the Vickers Viscount, one of the very few international commercial success stories of the post-war British airframe industry.[26]

The BAC One Eleven was important not only for the acuity of its market positioning but also for its role in the history of Airbus and the European aircraft industry which challenged and eventually eclipsed the British one. The Airbus concern was created in 1966 as a consortium of aircraft firms from Britain, France, and Germany, brought together by their governments to build the wide-body, twin-jet A-300. Within three years the British government had had second thoughts on 'European co-operation' and pulled out, leaving France and Germany to relaunch the project as equal partners. The British airframe industry stayed in Airbus, however, in the form of private participation by HSA, which designed and built the A-300's wings. Thus a substantial part of the British airframe industry now became a contractor to an embryonic, government-subsidized Franco-German concern. For a while Airbus had difficulty in finding any customers for the A-300, which made its first flight in 1972, but a subsidized deal with the American airline Eastern finally led to a break-through, and substantial international orders followed in the late 1970s.[27] The British alternative to the A-300 was the BAC Two Eleven, a wide-body 'Airbus' and a natural progression from the One Eleven. But the Two Eleven never got off the drawing board because without maximum launch aid from the government, BAC lacked the resources to build it. The government for its part felt it was already spending enough on the Concorde and the troubled Rolls-Royce RB211 engine (see below).[28]

The background to the BAC Two Eleven/Airbus story is revealing of the changing environment in international aircraft manufacturing; three aspects of that environment are important. First, aircraft manufacturing had in the space of the two decades since the end of the Second World War become extremely demanding and expensive, to such a degree that very few airframe makers could now produce a new model without some sort of government assistance.

Second, military procurement, the bedrock of the aircraft industry since the First World War, was in long-term decline. While across the Atlantic the Pentagon was busy escalating its Cold War spending, a sizable chunk of which was going to the aircraft industry, the post-war 'peace dividend' in Britain had caused a steady reduction in military budgets and in the amount of tax-payers' money which governments were prepared to spend on building new fighters and bombers. This meant a greater role for civil aircraft in the strategic planning of firms like BAC and Hawker Siddeley, and a greater need for those companies to find out more precisely what the world's airlines wanted. Third, and stemming from the first two, trans-national collaboration was vital if the bigger aircraft projects stood any chance of taking off. These features of the new reality in aircraft manufacturing were recognized in the 1965 Plowden Report which called for the British industry to be reduced to a size 'compatible with future demand'. The report, while stopping short of recommending the merger of the two airframe and engine groups to create one of each, nonetheless acknowledged that such a move was the only way to provide 'scope for economizing in overheads and design facilities, and for rationalizing production'.[29] Plowden also advocated a 'comprehensive programme of collaboration' with international partners – an association with the European industry being preferred to one with the Americans.[30] In the event Britain had to wait until 1977 and the next Labour government for Plowden's doctrine to be enforced, at the time of the nationalization of BAC and Hawker Siddeley, and their merger in BAe. In the 1960s there still remained a lack of agreement on which direction to take: should the British industry continue to try and maintain its national identity, with or without help from the government, should it embrace Airbus fully and accept a share of growing European success in place of dubious national ambitions, or should it look across the Atlantic and make the best deal possible with the Americans?

The Concorde

Although it was called the Anglo-French *Concorde*, the supersonic aircraft designed and built by BAC and Sud Aviation should be seen as a French-led project, brought to fruition within a highly politicized context at French insistence, in the face of erratic support from Britain and fierce condemnation from environmental lobbyists and parts of the US Congress. The aircraft itself undoubtedly possessed an iconic beauty and was exceptionally fast, indeed with a speed of 2,230 km/h it had more in common with military aircraft than other commercial airliners. However, it was also small and narrow, and, despite the best efforts of British Airways and Air France, it was not especially comfortable. The 'military' nature of the Concorde was exemplified by its engines which were Bristol Siddeley Olympus 593s, originally designed, complete with afterburners, to power the British Vulcan V-bomber. These thirsty engines were the antithesis of what was required by a civilian airline and their use meant that every inch of the airframe not dedicated to carrying fare-paying passengers had to carry fuel. For BAC, Concorde was a job for the government which was expensive in terms of opportunity cost, depriving aircraft with real commercial prospects like the 'Airbus-type' BAC 2–11 of precious government resources. By contrast, for the French it was an opportunity to benefit from cross-Channel technology transfer and consolidate an expertise which they later invested in Airbus.[31]

Perhaps more than a milestone in the history of the British airframe industry, Concorde represents a fork in the road: Europe or America, Airbus or Boeing? British ambivalence towards Airbus, under both Conservative and Labour governments in the 1970s, reflects the broader confusion in both parties as to how far Britain should be 'in Europe'. Plowden had already indicated that consolidation in the British aircraft industry should go further, as should international collaboration on future aerospace projects, preferably with the Europeans. The consequence of this erosion of national identity, or loss of the famous names in British aircraft manufacturing, was a stark choice between being a major stakeholder in Airbus, with its opportunity to absorb French and German know-how as well as passing knowledge to them, or retaining nominal independence for the British industry at the price of being reduced to the status of subcontractor to the Americans. It is hard to resist the conclusion that Concorde, with its huge non-recoverable R&D costs, as well as its interminable political wrangling, soured the British airframe industry's relationship with 'Europe' to the extent that it drifted down the latter course in a state of disillusioned sour grapes.

The Rolls-Royce RB.211

Whereas the need to make a choice between America and Europe was pressing in the airframe industry by the end of the 1960s, in aero-engines it had already been made in favour of America. Rolls-Royce, already the leading engine maker, consolidated its position in 1966 by taking over Bristol Siddeley Engines, giving it an effective monopoly in Britain and making it one of the select few jet engine manufacturers in the world.[32] It was at this stage that Rolls began design work on an advanced new bypass engine known as the RB.211. This engine and similar turbofans from Pratt & Whitney and General Electric represented the first of a new generation of high by-pass ratio (HBPR) engines which would power the equally new wide-bodied airliners which came into airline service after 1970. The RB.211 was an exceptionally ambitious engineering challenge, even for Rolls-Royce, and the enormous cost involved in its development drove the company into bankruptcy. However with the benefit of hindsight, it is also possible to see the RB.211 as the product of a crucial piece of long-term strategic decision-making by Rolls-Royce. With prospects for its current engines (the Dart, Avon, Conway, and Spey) looking poor for the 1970s, the company decided to invest in a massive new engine whose only application (unlike the earlier engines) was in civil airliners, and do so at a time when many other British manufacturing companies were giving up civil work for the more congenial and less competitive atmosphere of defence contracting.[33]

The story of the RB.211 begins in 1968 when Rolls-Royce won the contract to supply the engines for the American Lockheed L.1011 Tristar airliner. Rolls had decided that it must penetrate the US market, independently of British airframe exports, if it was to have a serious future as a supplier of large jet engines.[34] The Tristar order was a major step towards achieving that goal and was 'the largest single export order in British history'.[35] To get the Lockheed order, however, Rolls had signed a tough contract with the Americans which stipulated a fixed price for each engine as well as a fixed charge for the engine's development. Inevitably development costs on the engine, which used very advanced carbon-fibre construction to save weight and a revolutionary triple shaft construction design, overran its budget and did so at a time of rising inflation.[36] The financial arrangement for the RB.211 became a crippling burden for the company and by 1970 Rolls-Royce was facing acute cashflow problems. The new Conservative government of Edward Heath advanced £42 million in subsidy but this proved inadequate and the company was forced to declare bankruptcy in February 1971. The Heath government, having only months before declared that it would abandon Labour's industrial policy initiatives and no longer prop up 'lame duck' British industries, was forced to do a widely condemned 'U-turn' over Rolls-Royce and the RB.211.[37] Having established that the engine was as good as the company said it was, and actually meeting its test-bed performance goals, the government nationalized the firm's engine production, hived off the famous motor car division, and set about renegotiating a deal with the Americans to save the RB.211.[38] What can now be seen as an inspired piece of government intervention was justified at the time on the grounds that Rolls could not be allowed to fail: it was one of the few remaining British manufacturing firms at the cutting edge of aerospace technology, it employed thousands of highly skilled workers and represented a significant share of the nation's export effort. It was also, and this may have been critical to the government's decision, an important defence contractor and supplier to NATO forces. As a highly-placed observer noted not long afterwards, 'it could not be allowed to disappear as if it was a corner shop'.[39] Eventually the government nationalized the major part of Rolls-Royce and reached a deal with the Nixon Administration which included higher prices for Rolls, higher prices from the airlines Eastern, TWA, and Delta for the Tristar's manufacturer, Lockheed, and a $250 million bridging loan to that company from the US Congress. Like no other example since the end of the war, the RB.211/Tristar saga demonstrated how 'political' aircraft manufacturing had become.[40]

The conclusion and long-term consequences of the saga are important not only for a judgement on the British aero-engine industry but also a wider evaluation of the British manufacturing economy in the second half of the twentieth century. For while the Tristar's disappointing sales caused Lockheed to leave civil aviation to concentrate on military hardware, Rolls-Royce went on over the next 35 years to become the world's second largest civil jet engine manufacturer (behind GE).[41] The RB.211 engine, rescued with tax-payers' money by a Conservative government in 1971, attained its specification power and weight, and eventually became the basis of an expanding family of Rolls-Royce engines stretching down to the present 'Trent' series. Rolls-Royce itself was returned to the private sector in 1987 and is now a successful multinational corporation producing gas turbines for aerospace as well as competing success-fully in the marine and energy fields. Rolls-Royce is one of Britain's few remain-ing national champions.[42]

1977–2007: A Shrinking British Industry

The late 1970s was a time of transformation for the British aircraft industry: in 1976 Concorde entered service with British Airways and Air France, in 1977 BAC and Hawker Siddeley were nationalized and merged to form BAe, in 1978 Freddie Laker launched the era of low cost flying with *Skytrain*, and in 1979 BAe re-joined Airbus, consolidating Hawker Siddeley's experience, building wings for the Europeans. Of these events, *Skytrain* was indicative of the future course of civil aviation, Concorde was not. With the deregulation of the airline industry, mass air travel would become a reality and 'flying people-carriers' like the Boeing 747 and the Airbus A-300 series would represent the growth sector of the industry. By contrast, military aircraft production would become ever more complex and expensive, condemned to short produc-tion runs and endless political wrangling. In this environment, Rolls-Royce, adding value to its core product line through the exercise of an 'art' perfected over three quarters of a century, was in a much stronger position than BAe, now dependent, on the civil side, on work for a company (Airbus) where the strategic decisions were taken not in Bristol but in Toulouse and Hamburg. For the British airframe industry, Airbus had replaced the British government as paymaster, policy-maker, and chief customer. Moreover from a technological perspective too, the future looked more promising for engine makers than airframe produ-cers. While the civil airframe designs of 2008, including the Boeing 787 *Dreamli-ner* and the Airbus A.380, look much the same as the Boeing 707 and Douglas DC-8 of 1958, a real change has taken place in engine design and manufacture. Indeed it is the technological evolution of aircraft engines that have made air-liners more efficient and low cost airline operations from Skytrain to Ryanair possible.

In 1981, BAe was privatized by the Conservative government of Margaret Thatcher and began a strategic shift towards military production, exemplified by the enormous, and now infamous, Al Yamamah contract with Saudi Arabia in 1985.[43] The privately-owned BAe of the 1980s, now highly diversified (it owned the Rover Group car manufacturer at this stage, as well as property companies like Arlington Securities), could hardly offer a more striking contrast to Rolls-Royce: the one clearly focused on a single core technology of which it was the master, the other unable to see its core business amongst the muddle of interests that sheltered under the BAe umbrella. BAe's shift towards defence manufacturing and the American market accelerated after the company missed the last chance to build stronger links with Europe: in 1998 it came close to merging with the German DASA concern before abandoning negotiations at the last moment to acquire GEC's defence electronics subsidiary, Marconi. In despair at the British, DASA turned to the French and Aérospatiale to create a European answer to Boeing in EADS; BAe merged with GEC to become BAE Systems, turning its back on Europe to concentrate on the American defence market.[44] Indeed so wholeheartedly did they do this that by 2007 BAE Systems was selling more defence equipment to the US Defence Department than it was to the British Ministry of Defence.[45] The final chapter in the history of the British airframe industry came in 2006 when BAE Systems sold its share of Airbus and ownership of the two British factories at Broughton and Filton, which made wings for the Airbus 'family', passed to Airbus UK. Thus eighty years of British civil airliner production drew unceremoniously to a close.

How can we summarize the history of the British aircraft industry in the twentieth century? A 'declinist' view might agree with the commentator Will Hutton that the airframe industry had suffered since the Second World War from 'endemically weak strategic thinking . . . infected by Euroscepticism'. While the British dithered or changed their minds, the French and the German governments played 'the role of long-term, patient and engaged owner', finally reaping the harvest of a major segment of the international market for airliners as the long, thirty-year cycle of investment in Airbus reached fruition.[46] An alternative and more charitable view might point out that an industry that is so critically dependent on government money – whether in the form of launch aid, 'captive' state-owned airlines, or the general largesse flowing from an overblown defence budget – was bound to run into difficulties as the government, for political reasons, had to turn off the flowing cash tap. That explanation, of course, does not fully explain why Rolls-Royce managed to survive, and prosper, after turning its relationship with the government to its advantage after its bankruptcy in 1971. A third, 'anti-declinist' view might ask a different question, arising from a reappraisal of declinism's 'very particular pictures of Britain, its elite, its businesses, its armed forces, its culture'.[47] Instead of asking why did the British airframe industry ultimately fail, or why did it not seize more wholeheartedly the opportunities arising in Continental Europe after the mid-1960s, or why did it not perform as well as the British aero-engine industry, it might ask why it chose to reinvent itself as an international weapons manufacturer when faced with the emergence of a global market where the largest customer was the United States Department of Defence. When that question is asked, one might answer that rather than decline, it simply struck out on a new path.

THE BRITISH COMPUTER INDUSTRY

If we are considering questions of relative decline and the British economy, all the revisionist zeal we can muster cannot disguise the fact that, in the manufacture of IT, Britain's record was that of failure. We might tinker about with periodization of decline – certainly not post-1870 (obviously) – not until the later 1960s perhaps, but nevertheless decline there was. And it was absolute, not relative decline. At the end of the 1960s Britain's computer manufacturing industry came to be represented by the national champion, ICL.[48] By the 1990, this firm was in the hands of the Japanese corporation, Fujitsu, and along with most other European computer manufacturers had been eclipsed by US and nascent Japanese competition.[49] How did this situation come about? A series of 'problems' have been put forward – a 'declinist' agenda, not dissimilar to other fields, but also bearing traits unique to the 'high technology' sectors. These will be weighed in due course, first we need a brief profile of the development of the computer manufacturing industry and one or two comments on the application of computing in post-war Britain.

The Early Years – Invention, Science, and the Military

Though many interpretations vie for the origins of the modern computer, the IT industry can reasonably be identified as a child of World War Two. Without being overly reductionist, the impact of military imperatives is crucial in understanding the trajectories of the first phases of the sector – particularly in the British and American cases. Early British machines grew partly from academic programmes, notably at Cambridge and Manchester, but also fed off developments in signals processing, code-breaking, weapons design calculations, and so on. As it became clear, or at least clearer, to manufacturing industry that there was a market for digital computers, then manufacturers began to emerge in numbers. These can be largely grouped under two headings – electronics firms, and firms with a background in business machines.

Electronics companies included GEC, Ferranti, Elliott Automation, Marconi, English Electric, and EMI. These companies had expertise in manufacturing sophisticated electronic devices, equipment, and apparatus and saw the electronic computer as a logical extension, or sub-division of this activity. Sometimes the computer was part of a very diverse product range indeed. EMI, for example, also produced gramophones and recorded music, English Electric made the Lightning, an iconic jet fighter. Such diversification did not lead to vertical integration however – later to be pointed out as a weakness in comparison to Japanese IT firms for example.[50] Integration tended to be horizontal, with other divisions within the group. The second group of computer manufacturing companies comprised those with a background in business machines. Briefly, these emerged out of the punched card based equipment manufacturers and converged in the 1950s through BTM, and Powers Samas into ICT.[51] Added to this list of companies was perhaps the oddest diversification in the history of business – or so it might seem on the face of things. Lyons, the national teashop chain, diversified into computer manufacture in the late 1950s, building on their expertise in office automation. The diversification starts to make sense when considering the firm's systems of stock control and accounting which were the foundations on which the business was built. They recognized early on the potential of computing to empower their systems further and collaborated with Cambridge to develop their own business computer. This proved so successful they then went into the manufacturing business as LEO computers. It may be worth dwelling on the Leo example, not least because it has been claimed, with some justification, that this was the world's first business computer.[52]

It is clear then that the British computer industry stemmed from a world technological lead, and developed across a range of companies, with a variety of backgrounds, each producing its own machines and systems, and, of course, software. Engineers and scientists involved in development formed a complex network spanning government, industry, and academic activities, sometimes with strong connectivity, sometimes weak. All the companies involved experienced some success, though as the 1950s wore on it became clear that US companies, led by an exponentially growing IBM, were capturing markets abroad, and in the UK. There had been early attempts to rationalize the industry, led by the National Research Development Corporation (NRDC) under Lord Halsbury.[53] These had foundered in the face of impracticality and more importantly perhaps, the manufacturers' intransigence and lack of compulsive powers by the government. A more serious attempt came in the 1960s with the move to rationalize the sector, principally by merging the computer manufacturing components of all the various firms into one national champion – International Computers Limited (ICL). ICL was effectively a direct response to the growing hegemonic position of the US firm IBM.[54] IBM had dwarfed the other US manufacturers, using a strategy of innovation (through its 1,400, and 360 series computers), built in upgradeability, software and engineering support systems, and leasing and sales strategies.[55] Many of the latter factors were embedded in the firm from its pre-computer era, and have been pinpointed by Usselman as particularly important in giving IBM a comparative advantage over US and particularly, European firms.[56]

IBM formed a central part of the fears over the growing power of US multinationals in the 1960s, led by the OECD report into 'technology gaps', and the popularity of Servan-Schreiber's book highlighting the 'American Challenge', which posited a Europe increasingly dependent on US advanced technology.[57] This development also reflected the growing power of the idea that advanced technology industries were the future, and that the computer was an enabling technology at the centre of all other advanced technologies and industries. It was therefore imperative that a computer manufacturing industry should be nurtured. This thinking was reflected in the priorities of the Ministry of Technology, set up by the Wilson government in 1965, and was carried through to the thinking behind the largely fruitless Alvey programme of IT support, and marginally more successful Inmos transatlantic chip manufacturing project, funded in the teeth of Thatcherite withdrawal of state intervention.[58] Simply put, computers were the future. Britain had invented them. High technology was what Britain was best at. So, we couldn't be allowed to lose the race. But lose it we did. Why?

Empires and Warfare States?

One important factor in the development of the computer manufacturing industry in Britain was its relationship with the state. The sector was born out of state sponsorship, either directly through research and development in government establishments, or indirectly, through R&D carried out in academic centres or under contract in private sector firms. Added to this, much of this work was directly or indirectly related to military priorities. This was overwhelmingly the case during the earliest years when cryptanalysis, ballistics, nuclear weapons design, etc., were a wartime priority, but it seamlessly spilled over, and intensified into the cold war decades, and on into the vital later stages of microprocessor development.[59] As David Edgerton has argued, Britain's technological effort in the twentieth century, should, first not be underestimated, or uniformly bracketed under 'relative decline', but, second, should be recognized as strongly under influence of military priorities. This 'warfare state' effect may be most notable in the aircraft industry, but is equally to be found in the computer sector.[60] The effects of such a relationship are complex. It is tempting to ascribe a simple negative effect to such a relationship in the long run. Cost-plus culture may have pervaded the manufacturer's thinking, on the one hand, and a lack of will to force efficiency or rationalization may have prevailed in government departments. There may well have been a preference for a multiple of firms from a government perspective, to preserve diversity and perhaps competition, or to maintain basic capacity in an uncertain and unpredictable military environment. Technologies developed under military priorities have their own market dynamics including the privileging of performance over the ability to mass produce, secrecy rather than diffusion of knowledge, poor R&D-production feedback, bureaucratic decision-making, and so on. However, set against all these negatives, we should remember that there are positives perhaps. These days it is a commonplace that the Pentagon wasted vast amounts of money on military contracts during the post-war period. But firms such as IBM did benefit greatly from the money provided, and civil commercial spin offs were real. This might not have been the cheapest and most direct way to get the US computer (or aircraft and nuclear) sector into a position of world leadership, but it worked nevertheless.[61]

The problem in Britain may have been that much of the early research capability was within government establishments such as the Royal Aircraft

Establishment, nuclear centres at Harwell and Aldermaston, the Royal Radar Establishment and so on – which constituted the largest high technology research centres, civil or military, in Western Europe in the 1950s and 1960s. It was this compartmentalization which the Ministry of Technology attempted to reconcile in the later 1960s, but which proved to be too intractable a problem within the limits of Labour's political economic strategy.[62] Even if we accept Agar's notion that the state 'machine' in Britain lent itself to the development and promotion of the computer in Britain,[63] the structures of the industry, its cultures, its different sub-trajectories, meant that the task of effective rationalization was beyond the capabilities of the most enlightened of state policies. In reality even the Japanese struggled to find policy led growth in IT, even with MITI as the paragon of intervention during the crucial formative years of the IT industry. Their approach, led through the Japan Electronic Computer Corporation (JECC) which operated a system of leasing and finance, had its closest parallels with the National Enterprise Board (NEB) in Britain perhaps. It is widely accepted that the latter was hamstrung by political diversions, it did have some successes when moving away from a strategy of creating or fostering national champions, and instead promoting smaller-scale ventures.[64] In the end it was Japanese corporations alone, without overt government support, which bridged the gap in some later large-scale IT areas, particularly semiconductor-based control and memory technologies. Japanese firms also took production onto a global platform.[65] In contrast, by the mid-1980s the British and European semiconductor industry was 'extremely weak'.[66]

Fragmentation and Corporate Cultures

Tempting though it is to lay the blame on the dead weight of government (military) involvement for the problems of the computer industry, there are a range of other factors to be taken into account, however. A key feature of the sector was its fragmentation, both between and within companies. As noted above, it was clear from an early date that there were too many manufacturers in the sector. This meant duplication of R&D, and lack of economies of scale in R&D through to production. In an industry characterized by rapid product development in processor and memory technologies – moving from vacuum tubes, mercury tubes through to transistors, magnetic media, and on to various forms of semiconductors – keeping abreast of developments required a very high proportion of resources to be directed to R&D. It also led to difficult product planning strategies. Often, by the time a system was determined upon and carried through to the production stage it might well be obsolete in general market terms. Set against this was the fact that computers rapidly developed into systems, where components could be upgraded or bought in. This again went against ideas of individual firm sovereignty which was strong among the early British producers. In addition, R&D activities in IT could be diverse to say the least, and herein lies one of the early critiques of the sector. A broad range of activities within a firm can be beneficial of course – cross-fertilization of ideas between departments or divisions can pay dividends – if ideas are allowed to circulate. Information may not always flow between divisions, however, and also a diversity of interests may lead to a dissipation of market knowledge in one sector. This may not have been perceived as a problem while the industry was tied to government funding, as much of the early industry was, but when standing alone, facing global competition, these factors are crucial.

Generally speaking, in this turbulent product environment, the more coordination from R&D through to marketing within firms, and the more co-operation and networking between firms, the better chance British firms had to compete on the domestic and global stage. Unfortunately the opposite seems to have been the case. There was a basic rift between the electronics firms and the business machine firms in terms of market knowledge and technical ability. There were rifts within the large electronic firms as divisions failed to communicate. As highlighted by Kidder's study of IT research cultures in *Soul of a New Machine/* the structure and organization – the culture perhaps – of a firm can be replicated in the product it produces. Moreover, the 'social structure and traditions' of firms are a central component, or possible barrier, when trying to foster co-operation between departments or companies.[67] This is particularly the case in IT industries where tacit knowledge is disproportionately important. An example of the lack of synergy in these terms can be found in the LEO example, when LEO and English Electric's computer manufacturing division merged in 1963, producing a profound 'culture shock' for the LEO engineers and managers.[68] And yet the imperative of merging companies to achieve both a critical mass of R&D capability and achieve production and marketing economies of scale was clear. Synergy problems bedevilled LEO and English Electric, they bedevilled ICL after the government finally brokered a general merger in 1968; they bedevilled the trans-European Unidata initiative of the early 1970s which saw (German company) Siemens, (Dutch company) Phillips, and (French company) CII attempt to construct a global-scale European manufacturer to challenge IBM.[69] They persisted through programmes such as the European Strategic Programme for Research in Information Technologies (ESPRIT) in the 1980s.[70] In almost all cases, despite concerted and urgent attempts to stem the growing decline in comparative IT capability, management, and engineering teams had their own ways of working and their own preferred technological trajectories. Strategies could never be effectively implemented nor markets accurately predicted or met. Rivals, notably IBM had been a unified entity, capable of redirection under strong leadership, for many years. By the era of the modern PC, networks and the internet, etc., the growth of these industries was no longer dependent, or boosted by government support, in whatever form, but rather sprang from a specific combination of youthful entrepreneurial zeal, and academic/venture capital enabled clusters and networks, creating and reacting to markets which were rapidly evolving and mutating in frequently unpredictable ways.[71] This was no longer an environment where anyone should have suggested that intervention was feasible or sensible, except in the most lightly handled *Porteresque* fashion.

First Mover Disadvantages: Finance and Market Failures

In some ways the computer manufacturing sector in Britain was a victim of its own success, in the early stages of the technology. The arguments continue over what comprised the first computer, and who the 'inventor' might be. Teleological and Whiggish history gravitates towards a series of figures from Babbage to Eckert and Mauchly to Wilkes and so on.[72] Certainly there was strong impression that Britons had a disproportionate claim to some of these firsts, an attitude which dovetails with the ubiquitous and persistent notion that Britain is good at inventing, no good at developing – jet engines being the other glaring example in the context of this chapter. Quite whether this idea bears scrutiny or not need not concern us here. What is clear is that this *idea* of elitism, of advanced scientific and technological prowess, when combined with the other legacies of Empire and global economic leadership, often shaped decisions over which research and development paths to follow. This is visible in ICL's technology strategies for example, based on trying to supersede or overtake IBM, rather than following a strategy of compatibility. It is found in the Alvey programmes ambitions to supersede the Japanese fifth generation computing programme.[73] Ironically the Japanese had their greatest success during this period in copying rather than challenging IBM.[74] In all these cases the idea of prestige triumphed of pragmatism and marketable products, in what might be termed 'TSR2 syndrome'. Even if ambitious prototypes could be made to work they were often a long way from reliable, manufacturable products which could command a global market.

Another reason for the decline in British IT manufacture might lie in the perennial declinist villain, the city-industry divide. Briefly, this analysis would say that the banking system in Britain from the start of the twentieth century at least, had little interest in industry and was overly concerned with security and liquidity, and gravitated towards a cosy cartel dominated by London banks. The other half of the financial picture, the stock market, similarly militated against high technology, R&D led investments – preferring various forms of global commercial investment instead, or being dominated by short-term thinking or the pull of speculative investment.[75] Could the computer manufacturing sector's eclipse be attributable to the structure of the Britain's banks or capital markets? It is certainly the case that several of the leading emergent technologies in the USA were funded through the emergent venture capital sector from the 1950s onwards. Britain's venture capital sector by contrast was relatively poorly developed, and when it did emerge into the 1980s, was diverted into management buy-out funding rather than high risk – high reward technology investments.[76] It is also the case that the dominance of the capital market by the large institutions – and consequent control by a relatively small group of pension and insurance fund managers – led to an aversion to knowledge intensive investments in technology sectors. By the time we get to the era of the PC and the internet, the British IT industry is largely out of the picture. In Tim Berners-Lee, we see again a celebrated British first, but the story is really about Google, Yahoo, Cisco, Microsoft, Apple, Intel, etc. – all from a culture connecting the academic, we might even say nerdy, to a venture capital sector, based largely in the USA. Where the British capital market can be seen to be active in the sector it is in the headlong rush to inflate the speculative bubble which emerged in the dot.com boom of the 1990s.

Yet another factor hampering the growth of the computer manufacturing sector in the UK was the configuration of markets. The pull of Empire markets in the early days was clearly not an asset in a sector such as this. Domestic markets were an alternative, and there is a strong case that in an industry such as this, a sophisticated domestic market will have a pull effect both on sales and innovation. Evidence suggests that some sectors of the British economy were well advanced in their affinity for computer systems from the earliest emergence of business machines. This is particularly true of the banking and other service sectors, some of whom were world leaders in their adoption of realtime computing and teleprocessing in the 1970s.[77] However, this advanced marketplace did not equate with any sense of loyalty to British computer manufacturers. Unreliability and costs of many British made computer systems meant that IT systems buyers would often go for IBM. In a turbulent and unpredictable IT environment, where expensive hard copy back-up systems were still the norm, IBM was the safe option. It was a commonplace in business that 'no one ever got fired for buying IBM'. Moreover once an IBM system was installed, it was difficult for domestic manufacturers to get a customer to convert to another system. Software, and the language it was written in, was specific to manufacturers during the 1950s and 1960s. A switch of machines meant expensive retraining and recruitment programmes, in a world where IBM had pursued an extensive policy deep into the education system, where programmers were brought up in culture of IBM. Again, the decision by ICL to pursue an independent path meant resisting rather than capitalizing on this trend. In the event, firms such as ICL were to rely on a disproportionate amount of sales to the public sector, where a sense of national loyalty could be imposed on IT purchasing departments and where reliability and accountability were less of an issue perhaps. It should perhaps be noted at this point, however that national loyalty in this sector is a complex issue. As soon as machines became systems, they often became technologically multinational. While IBM retained a high proportion of US manufactured and sourced components, others manufacturers were less patriotic. Honeywell, an American firm, built its computers in Scotland using a majority of British made parts. ICL, in contrast, used a large number of foreign components. In effect Honeywell was far more 'British' than ICL. It is doubtful whether users were aware of this.

If we turn to the software sector, we can see that this follows a similar path of 'decline' in the UK, though it is different in essence since the industry itself never came close to any kind of world lead in the first place, if we consider the software industry in terms of its true origins as a separate sector of IT activity. While computer software was an integral part of each IT system, then it was part and parcel of any competitive position Britain might have held. If ICL mainframes became competitive, then the software to run them was part of the same picture. As software became traded – as applications became discrete from particular machines and manufacturers – then the US took an early lead and kept it.[78] The pattern in Britain is similar to that of hardware if we look at government aspirations. Software is the thinking end of a thinking industry, so logically, as far as policy makers thought (and still think) that is where the British future lay. Instead of the workshop of the world, Britain might become the 'software house of the world'. Such ambitions, started early with deep education strategies, and were again prevalent in programmes such as Alvey, and on a European scale in ESPRIT.[79] Such ambitions did reflect the domestic prowess in custom written software, but against an industry fast becoming dominated by traded software giants, Britain's software sector became rightly categorized as a cottage industry. It may have been very sophisticated, but it was a cottage industry nonetheless.[80] As the packaged software industry grew to prominence on the global stage, Britain's tradition of small custom software development was never likely to give it a platform on which to build.

To conclude this section on IT in Britain; the legacy of wartime efforts and the nature of early computing as essentially a scientific endeavour, based in universities or research establishments, meant that Britain could secure an early lead or parity with developments elsewhere, notably in the USA. As the 1950s wore on, however, two broad trends became noticeable. The first was the move towards the almost mass-produced, business machine market, which though in some ways led by LEO, in reality soon became dominated by the US makers from Remmington/Sperry Rand's Univac early start to the dominance of IBM. IBM's dominance of global markets reflected the growing confidence in US production, and the successful strategies of the US firms in marketing, model, and range coherence, and reliability and support. When IBM emerged as a leader it did so on the basis of a long-term knowledge of the business user, allied to considerable development support from the US government. IBM went on to establish a platform, or springboard for other major players, notably Microsoft and Intel, when it switched from proprietary manufacture to bundling as it moved to counter Apple's lead in the PC market. In this we see an interesting confounding of the Chandlerite paradigm – a large corporation with rationalized internal structures, adapting in a radical way to a market change by adopting symbiotic relationships with newer, more flexible or creative firms. The situation in the UK was markedly more complex and haphazard. There was no IBM at the core. Computer manufacturing firms came from a range of backgrounds, some multidivisional electronics military/civil firms, some from the business machine sector, and LEO the teashop oddity of course. Added to these was the considerable R&D, and in some cases manufacturing, in the government sector at the big research establishments. Early recognition of the fragmented nature of the industry by the NRDC was more visionary than practical and rationalization of the sector had to wait until the impact of the American Challenge in the 1960s. And by this time IBM had established a dominance and an effective business model which was all but unassailable. The only thing in favour of domestic producers was governmental determination to save the industry – a mixture of legacy, pragmatism, political imagery, and the perceived imperative of an economic future centred on a technological comparative advantage. Despite the assets which seemingly lay at its disposal, a series of initiatives turned into at best rearguard actions, at worst bungled and misconceived policies – chasing last year's trends, or vainly trying to second guess the trend after next. National independence – taking on IBM rather than going with IBM compatibility was the product of national pride, the same nationalism that spurned the pan-European Unidata initiative. Inmos, Alvey, and similar initiatives proved the cherished notion of IT at all costs was still strong enough even in the 1980s to fly in the face of Thatcherite market forces ideology, still trying to leapfrog into the next phase of technology, irrespective of market trends. Eventually of course the IT industry grew in ways no-one (not even Bill Gates) could predict. New companies grew in an environment which often combined extremes of capital market faddism, geeky entrepreneurialism and unpredicted, de novo, mass markets for auction sites, on-line retailing, internet search engines, social network sites, etc. The networked PC at work and at home continues to be driven by Mooresque reductions in size and increases in power, as applications and hardware across a range of media converge and mutate, enveloping laptops, Blackberries, mobile phones, cameras, TV systems, etc. These developments are allied to a new international division of labour, the latest phase of which has seen the ascendance of Chinese manufacturing capabilities. Interestingly, a relatively high proportion of Apple's latest iPhone (almost certainly superseded by the time this goes to press) were developed by British companies. However, these are mostly smaller niche players in a component driven industry. British IT companies operating on a global scale effectively never made it out of the 1960s. Perhaps we should be charitable in recognizing the prescience of those who, from the NRDC onwards, recognized that this was indeed an industry of the future, even if there was little that could be effectively done to save it.

Conclusions

Corelli Barnett's caricature of post-war Britain turning its back on industrial and technological modernization in favour of social welfarism is clearly nonsensical if we look at the trajectory of the aircraft industry in the round, or if we widen the scope to include other 'high technology' sectors.[81] Britain emerged into the 1950s with a range of technological leads and competencies, and moreover with ambitions to resituate its economy in a new global future, underpinned by a series of burgeoning science and technology-based industries. In the case of the aircraft industry, or to be precise the aircraft engine industry, there is a notable success story to be told. We should also not lose sight of the fact that British producers held their own in world markets for many years, even if they did lose ground eventually. A different picture emerges, however, in IT. Again, we should acknowledge that firms did produce computers that were innovative and did sell, but the longer term picture has few high spots. Both aircraft and IT sectors had similar structures, trajectories or impediments. Both were more or less tied to government either in terms of origins, R&D funding, military duality, monopsonistic markets or policy ambitions. Both sectors struggled to compete with the burgeoning US producers, or to penetrate US markets. In relation to this, both sectors suffered some degree of fragmentation and efforts to overcome this were beset by synergistic difficulties. National champions were fostered, but never achieved the ambitions set out for them, though in the case of Rolls-Royce, credit should perhaps be given for a policy which was derided at the time, and subsequently given less credit than is due. Both sectors were wooed by pan-European initiatives, which in many cases were rejected with a lofty disdain, in some cases leading to expensive failure, and in yet others to long-term success. In many respects, perhaps, the expectations placed on both sectors were their undoing. Time and again plans were made based on ideas of world leadership, of forging beyond the competition or outdoing rivals through the next generation of technologies. We can see this in aircraft in the military sector with TSR2, and in the civil sector with Concorde. The future in fact lay in the more prosaic technology of the wide-bodied 'jumbo jet'. The Alvey programme – a quest for fifth generation computing – was described in the 1980s as an 'information technology Concorde', and ICL's earlier refusal to come into line with IBM technology, all exhibit this 'leapfrog' mentality, which in all cases ended in technological dead ends or enormous and unrecoverable R&D bills. In popular conception there remains, unfortunately, the idea of British genius – from Whittle to Wilkes – failed by British industry, or by some nebulous cultural malaise. The truth is more complex. There are success stories in British high technology industries – Rolls-Royce is certainly one, British pharmaceuticals (another R&D intensive sector) is another. But we could also add to the list of high technology failures, the example of the nuclear sector which fell well short of expectations. What is clear is that the picture is complex and multi-faceted, a picture in which both decline and renaissance often co-exist, and where they both have multivariate causes and effects.

NOTES

1. Peter Fearon, 'The British Airframe Industry and the State, 1918–35', *Economic History Reviewnomic History Review*, 2nd Series, 27, 2, May 1974: 236; also S. B. Saul, 'Research and Development in British Industry from the End of the Nineteenth Century to the 1960s', in T. C. Smout, ed., *The Search for Wealth and Stability. Essays in Economic and Social History presented to M. W. Flinn Search for Wealth and Stability. Essays in Economic and Social History presented to M. W. Flinn*, Macmillan, London & Basingstoke, 1979: 114–15, 119.

2. R. McKinnon Wood, *Aircraft Manufacture: A Description of the Industry and Proposals for its Socialisation,* Victor Gollancz/New Fabian Research Bureau, London, 1935: 3–5.

3. It is probably fair to say that up until 1945, and certainly up until 1930, Germany was the leading centre for the development of aerodynamic theory. See T. A. Heppenheimer, *Turbulent Skies: History of Commercial Aviation,* John Wiley & Sons, New York, 1995: 141–3.

4. G. Simonson, 'The Demand for Aircraft and the Aircraft Industry, 1907–58', *Journal of Economic Historyrnal of Economic History,* 20, 1960: 361–82.

5. For a comprehensive account of both engine and airframe industry before 1945, see Keith Hayward, *The British Aircraft Industry,* Manchester University Press, Manchester, 1989: 9–45, also Fearon, *The British Airframe Industry:* 248–51. For British civil aircraft manufacturing and its weaknesses, see Peter J. Lyth, 'The Empire's Airway: British Civil Aviation from 1919 to 1939', in Guy Vanthemsche, ed., *Revue Belge de Philologie et d' Histoire,* 78, 2000: 879–80.

6. Bristol's air-cooled engines were generally favoured for *civil* aircraft before the war.

7. See Ian Lloyd, *Rolls-Royce, The Merlin at War,* Macmillan, London & Basingstoke, 1978. For a technical account of developments between the wars, see Charles Harvard Gibbs-Smith, *Aviation: An Historical Survey from its Origins to the end of World War II,* HMSO, London, 1970: 180–204.

8. The first jet engines were tested in the late 1930s simultaneously in Britain and Germany. See Peter Lyth, 'Reverse Thrust: American Aerospace Dominance and the British Challenge in Jet Engines', in Helmuth Trischler, ed., *Tackling Transport,* Science Museum, London, 2003: 1–18. Also valuable is Edward W. Constant III, *The Origins of the Turbojet Revolution,* Baltimore, 1980.

9. Lloyd, *Rolls Royce:* 132. Inexplicably the government had no airframe for the 'Nene' although the American company Pratt & Whitney used it (as the J-42) to get started in the jet engine business and the Russians built nearly 40,000 of them to power the Mig. 15 fighter. See Jeffrey A. Engel, *Cold War at 30,000 Feet: The Anglo-American Fight for Aviation Supremacy,* Harvard UP, Cambridge, MA, 2007: 53–124.

10. Hayward, *The British Aircraft Industry:* 43–8; also Keith Hayward, *Government and British Civil Aerospace: A Case Study on Post-War Technology Policy,* Manchester University Press, Manchester, 1983: 12–38.

11. In 1952, Reginald Maudling reckoned the solution to Britain's economic problems lay in the export of high value engineering products like aircraft. Reginald Maudling, Parl.Sec, MCA, 29 Sept. 1952, to Low MoS, Exports of British Civil Aircraft, 1952, PRO FO.371/99735.

12. See Mark Harrison, 'Resource Mobilisation for World War 2', *Economic History Review,* 41, 2, 1988; also Thomas Balogh, 'The International Aspect', in G.D.N. Worswick and P.H. Ady eds., *The British Economy 1945–1950,* Oxford University Press, 1952: 476–510.

13. Michael Porter, *The Competitive Advantage of Nations,* Basingstoke, Palgrave, 1998: 168–70. The notable exception here was the Vickers Viscount where the input of the Canadian airline TCA raised the aircraft's specification to a level acceptable to North American carriers. The Viscount also enabled Rolls-Royce to gain knowledge (with the Dart engine) of what American airlines expected from an engine supplier by way of support with service and spares. Charles Gardner, *British Aircraft Corporation: A History,* London, Batsford, 1981: 71.

14. Keith Pavitt, 'Technology in British Industry: A Suitable Case for Improvement', in Charles Carter, ed., *Industrial Policy and Innovationustrial Policy and Innovation,* Heinemann/National Institute of Social and Economic Research, London, 1981: 107.

15. This, and the fact that Britain had only a small domestic market and the aircraft industry needed to export if it was to survive, was recognized in the 1965 Plowden Report: *Report of the Committee of Inquiry into the Aircraft Industry*, HMSO, Cmnd. 2853, London, 1965.

16. Britain's lack of large scale wind tunnels for testing both airframes and engines held it back in aeronautical R&D. A lot of British aeronautical development in the 1950s depended on wind tunnel results obtained from the United States under various exchange agreements stemming from the Second World War. *The State of Aeronautical Research and Development in the United Kingdom in Relation to that in the USA*, 4 Nov. 1953, Public Record Office, Kew, AVIA 65/14.

17. Hayward, *Government and British Civil Aerospace*: 17.

18. It was even worse in defence procurement where the Labour government has been accused of frittering away Britain's limited resources on too many projects, the logic being that 'a large number of projects (was bound to) lead to one workable design'. Peter Burnham, *The Political Economy of Post-war Reconstruction*, St. Martin's Press, New York, 1990: 151. See also Till Geiger, 'The Next War is Bound to Come', in Anthony Gorst et al., eds., *Contemporary British History, 1931–1961: Politics and the Limits of Policy*, London, Pinter, 1991: 95–118.

19. The speed of the jet engine's technological development was striking on both sides of the Atlantic. It was aided by the influx of German scientists and know-how into American and, to as lesser extent, British laboratories and research facilities. Lyth, *Reverse Thrust*: 3.

20. It was a hope cruelly dashed by the fate of the Comet, which first flew in 1949, entered service with BOAC in 1952 and was withdrawn from service after a series of crashes in 1953 and 1954. After the Comet crashes, BOAC turned against jet operation for 'a short but crucial period'; whereas the Americans were undeterred and simply waited until more powerful jet engines could make economic Atlantic crossings possible. Hayward, *Government and British Civil Aerospace*: 20–1.

21. The advantage of the by-pass engine is that is both quieter and more economical – both features attractive to commercial airlines. The head of Pan American Airways, Juan Trippe, visited Rolls-Royce in 1955 to have a look at the Conway, with a view to using it to power Pan Am's new Boeing 707s and Douglas DC.8s. His visit seems to have galvanized Pratt & Whitney into action and the launching of their JT3D. See Heppenheimer, *Turbulent Skies*: 187–90.

22. Hayward, *Government and British Civil Aerospace*: 19.

23. In 1954, it was noted that the American aircraft industry, five times as big as the British, employing four times the labour and producing eight times as many aircraft, had 'no more firms than here . . . our design resources are divided up into too many pockets, some of which are inevitable weak'. *The Size and Shape of the British and American Aircraft Industries*, 25 Nov. 1954, PRO, Kew, AVIA 65/14.

24. A third helicopter group emerged in 1960 led by Westland and incorporating the helicopter operations of Saunders-Roe, Bristol, and Fairey. For details on the mergers, see Hayward, *The British Aircraft Industry British Aircraft Industry*: 63–82; and *Government and British Civil Aerospace*: 38–46.

25. Bristol Siddeley Engines (BSE) was anxious to be independent from its former parent airframe makers in HSA and able, like Rolls-Royce, to handle orders from anywhere, *Economist*, 'Change Partners', 7 Feb. 1959: 517.

26. Gardner, *British Aircraft Corporation*: 65–79.

27. In the 1980s, Airbus expanded its product line, with airliners both larger (A-330/340) and smaller (A-320) than the A-300. By the 1990s, having become a corporate entity in Airbus Industrie, it had gained at least 30 per cent of the world market for airliners, putting the American number two, McDonnell-Douglas, out of the airliner business and closing the gap on the number one, Boeing. Heppenheimer, *Turbulent Skies*: 302.
28. Gardner, *British Aircraft Corporation*: 166–8.
29. *Plowden Report*: chapter 34, para. 440.
30. Ibid.: chapter 22, para. 262–3.
31. Seven years before the Concorde was introduced into airline service, the head of BAC, Sir George Edwards, thought that because of the aircraft's clear lead over its American rival, the SST at that time, 'at least 250 could be sold during the 1970s', *Flight International*, 21 Aug. 1969: 287. When the SST was cancelled in 1971, the fate of the Concorde was also sealed. British Airways and Air France ordered nine in 1972, but they were alone; the seventy-four options to purchase Concorde, garnered from sixteen different airlines, all melted away once Pan American and TWA decided not to buy any. Heppenheimer, *Turbulent Skies*: 257–8.
32. In 1963 over half of the world's civil aircraft fitted with gas turbines had Rolls-Royce engines. Department of Trade & Industry (DTI), *Rolls Royce Limited*, Investigation under Section 165 (a) (i) of the Companies Act 1948, (Bankruptcy), HMSO, London, 1973: 5.
33. David Smith, 'Defence Contractors and Diversification into the Civil Sector: Rolls-Royce, 1945–2005, *Business History*, 49, 5, Sept. 2007: 674–5.
34. Keith Hayward, *International Collaboration in Civil Aerospace*, Francis Pinter, London, 1986: 35; John Newhouse, *The Sporty Game*, Alfred Knopf, New York, 1982: 119.
35. Donald M. Pattilo, *Pushing the Envelope*, University of Michigan Press, Ann Arbor, 1998: 256.
36. For the technical details of the RB 211, see Sir Stanley Hooker, *Not Much of an Engineer: An Autobiography*, Airlife, Shrewsbury, 1984: 183–98.
37. Aubrey Silberston, 'Industrial Policies in Britain, 1960–80', in Charles Carter, ed., *Industrial Policy and Innovation*, Heinemann, London, 1981: 46.
38. Heppenheimer, *Turbulent Skies*: 249–51.
39. Michael Stewart, *The Jekyll and Hyde Years: Politics and Economic Policy since 1964*, Dent, London, 1977: 135.
40. Heppenheimer, *Turbulent Skies*: 233–7, 253–4; Hayward, *Government and British Civil Aerospace*: 99–123; Newhouse, *Sporty Game*: 173–83. For the official account of the RB.211 story, see DTI, *Rolls Royce Limited*.
41. Pattilo, *Pushing the Envelope*: 257–8; Smith, *Defence Contractors and Diversification into the Civil Sector*: 684.
42. For the details of Rolls-Royce's civil sector-led recovery, including the strategic alliances it entered into with other engine makers during the 1980s, the development of modular engines in the Trent 'family' since 1990 and the diversification into power generation and marine applications, see Smith, *Defence Contractors and Diversification into the Civil Sector*: 679–86.
43. By 1990 BAe's revenue from military sales was three times that from civil aircraft, see Philip Gummett, 'Civil and Military Aircraft in the UK', *History and Technology*, 9, 1992: 203–22.
44. *Economist*, 'Getting it Together?', 20 Jul. 2002; Peter Spiegel, 'End of an Era at BAE'. *Financial Times*, 17 Jul. 2004. An account of the deal by the BAe chief executive can be found in Richard Evans, *Vertical Take-off*, Nicholas Brealey, London, 1999.

45. *The Times*, David Robertson, 'Milestone for BAE as its Trade with America Outstrips MoD Business', 10 Aug. 2007.

46. *Observer*, Will Hutton, 'Why We Are on the Wrong Flight Path?', 23 Jan. 2005: 30.

47. David Edgerton, *Warfare State: Britain, 1920–1970*, Cambridge University Press, 2006: 5.

48. For a history of ICL see Martin Campbell-Kelly, *ICL: A Business and Social History*, Oxford University Press, 1989.

49. Peter Wells and Philip Cooke, 'The Computer Hardware Industry in the 1980s: Technological Change, Competition and Structural Change', in Philip Cooke, Frank Moulaert, Eryk Swyngedouw, Oliver Weinstein, and Peter Wells, eds., *Towards Global Localisation: The Computing and Telecommunications Industries in Britain and France*, UCL, London, 1992: 129–31, 137–43; Tim Kelly, *The British Computer Industry: Crisis and Development*, Croom Helm, London, 1987.

50. Paul Jowett and Margaret Rothwell, *The Economics of Information Technology*, Macmillan, London, 1986: 21–32. Michael Borrus, *Competing for Control: America's Stake in Microelectronics*, Ballinger, Cambridge, MA, 1988: 4–5.

51. Campbell-Kelly, *ICL*: 144–203.

52. Peter Bird, *LEO: The First Business Computer*, Hasler, Wokingham, 1994; David Caminer, John Aris, Peter Hermon, and Frank Land, *LEO: The Incredible Story of the World's First Business Computer*, McGraw-Hill, New York, 1998.

53. John Hendry, *Innovating for Failure: Government Policy and the Early British Computer Industry*, MIT, Cambridge, MA, 1989.

54. Richard Coopey, 'Empire and Technology: Information Technology Policy in Postwar Britain and France', in Richard Coopey, ed., *Information Technology Policy: An International History*, Oxford University Press, 2004: 144–57.

55. Martin Campbell-Kelly and William Aspray, *Computer: A History of the Information Machine*, BasicBooks, New York, 1996: 131–44.

56. Steven Usselman, 'IBM and its Imitators: Organisational Capabilities and the Emergence of the International Computer Industry', *Business and Economic History*, 22, 2, Winter 1993: 1–35; Campbell-Kelly and Aspray, *Computer*: 48–50, 151–3.

57. J.-J. Servan-Schreiber, *The American Challenge*, Hamish Hamilton, London, 1968; Organisation for Economic Cooperation and Development (OECD), *Gaps in Technology: Electronic Computers*, OECD, Paris, 1969. For a later contextualization of this crisis and responses see Paul Gannon, *Trojan Horses and National Champions: The Crisis in the European Computing and Telecommunications Industry*, Apt-Amatic Books, 1997.

58. Mick McLean and Tom Rowland, *The Inmos Saga: A triumph of National Enterprise?*, Pinter, London, 1985; Brian Oakley and Kenneth Owen, *Alvey: Britain's Strategic Computing Initiative*, MIT, Cambridge, MA, 1989. For Ministry of Technology initiatives see Richard Coopey, 'Restructuring Civil and Military Science and Technology: The Ministry of Technology in the 1960s', in Richard Coopey, Matthew Uttley, and Graham Spinardi, eds., *Defence Science and Technology: Adjusting to Change*, Harwood, Chur, Switzerland, 1993: 65–84.

59. Erik Arnold and Ken Guy, *Parallel Convergence: National Strategies in Information Technology*, Pinter, London, 1986: 114–17.

60. David Edgerton, *England and the Aeroplane*; the other part of the triumvirate of high technology military civil industrial sectors is of course that of nuclear power and weapons. In many ways the computer sector forms a foundation technology to the other two.

61. Arthur Norberg and Judy O'Neill, *Transforming Computer Technology: Information Processing for the Pentagon 1962–1986*, Johns Hopkins, Baltimore, 1996; Paul Edwards,

The Closed World: Computers and the Politics of Discourse in Cold War America, MIT, Cambridge, MA, 1996; Kenneth Flamm, *Targeting the Computer: Government Support and International Competition*, Brookings Institution, Washington, DC, 1987: 93–124.

62. The ultimate public–private transfer in this sector was that of the sale of the vestigial Mintech establishments including the RAE and RRE, re-badged as QinetiQ in 2001. The very rapid escalation in profitability and value of this now private firm has caused a major controversy over the ability of government even to value its high technology assets accurately, let alone effectively exploit them. National Audit Office, *The Privatisation of QinetiQ*, HC52, Nov. 2007.

63. Jon Agar, *The Government Machine: A Revolutionary History of the Computer*, MIT, Cambridge, MA, 2003.

64. Martin Campbell-Kelly and Ross Hamilton, 'From National Champions to Little Ventures: The NEB and the Second Wave of Information Technology in Britain, 1975–1985', in Coopey, *Information Technology Policy*: 169–86.

65. Martin Fransman, *Japan's Computer and Communications Industry: The Evolution of Industrial Giants and Global Competitiveness*, Oxford, 1995. Joseph Grunwald and Kenneth Flamm, *The Global Factory: Foreign Assembly in International Trade*, Brookings Institute, Washington, DC, 1985: 39–134.

66. Borrus, *Competing for Control*: 195.

67. Jon B. Thornberry, 'Competition and Cooperation: A Comparative Analysis of Sematec and the VSLI Research Project', *Enterprise and Society*, 3, 4, Dec. 2002: 657–86; Tracy Kidder, *The Soul of a New Machine*, Allan Lane, London, 1982.

68. Caminer et al., *LEO*: 98–102.

69. Eda Kranakis, 'Politics, Business and European Information Technology Policy: From the Treaty of Rome to Unidata, 1958–75', in Coopey, *Information Technology Policy*: 209–46.

70. Dimitris Assimakopoulus, Rebecca Marschan-Piekkari, and Stuart MacDonald, 'ESPRIT: Europe's Response to US and Japanese Domination in Information Technology', in Coopey, *Information Technology Policy*: 247–63.

71. Campbell-Kelly and Aspray, *Computer*: 233–82; Robert Cringely, *Accidental Empires: How the Boys of Silicon Valley Make Their Millions*, Viking, London, 1992; AnnaLee Saxenian, *Regional Advantage: Culture and Competition in Silicon Valley and Route 128*, Harvard, 1994.

72. Martin Campbell-Kelly and William Aspray, *Computer: A History of the Information Machine*, Basic, London, 1996: 53–104.

73. Arnold and Guy, *Parallel Convergence*: 7–8; Oakley and Owen, *Alvey*.

74. In this sense there are strong parallels with the nuclear industry, the failed fast breeder at Dounreay being only the most notable of several attempts at intellectual 'leapfrog', as is Concorde, of course.

75. Forest Capie and Michael Collins, *Have the Banks Failed British Industry? An Historical Survey of Bank Industry Relations in Britain 1870–1990*, Hobart, London, 1992; Will Hutton, *The State We're In: Why Britain is in Crisis and How to Overcome It*, Vintage, London, 1996.

76. Richard Coopey and Donald Clarke, 3i: *Fifty Years Investing in Industry*, Oxford University Press, 1995; Bygrave and Timmons, *Venture Capital and the Crossroads*, Harvard, Cambridge, MA, 1992.

77. Richard Coopey, 'Management and the Introduction of Computing in British Industry, 1945–1970', *Contemporary British History*, Vol 13, No. 3, (Autumn 1999).

78. For a general history of the software industry see Martin Campbell-Kelly, *From Airline Reservations to Sonic the Hedgehog: A History of the Software Industry*, MIT, Cambridge, MA, 2003. For an international perspective see David Mowery, ed., *The International Computer Software Industry: A Comparative Study of Industry Evolution and Structure*, Oxford, 1996.

79. Jowett and Rothwell, *The Economics of Information Technology*: 57–86.

80. Peter Grindley, 'The Future of the Software Industry in the United Kingdom: The Limitations of Independent Production', in Mowery, ed., *The International Software Industry*: 197–239.

81. Corelli Barnett, *The Audit of War: The Illusion of Britain as a Great Nation*, Macmillan, 1986.

13

Industrial Research and the Employment of Scientists in British Industry before the 1970s

Sally Horrocks

In a recent discussion of the relationship between science and the state in Britain, scientist Sir Herman Bondi suggested that during the 1950s and 1960s the nation was gripped by an 'engineering megalomania'.[1] His remarks have been reflected in writing on the history of British science and technology during this period that has frequently stressed the widespread extent of technological enthusiasm that underpinned a significant increase in the resources devoted to these activities. This narrative of British technological enthusiasm runs counter to the widely held view that neglect of science and technology by British business contributed to the relative decline of the British economy, but fits closely with the assessments of those historians who have argued that British industry in fact invested heavily in the application of science and in research and development (R&D) when compared with most of its competitors until at least the late 1960s. In this chapter I draw on these insights to reappraise chronologically the history of industrial research and the application of science in British industry before the 1970s. I will argue that this history demonstrates not only an extensive enthusiasm for the integration of science, technology, and industry among British business leaders that started during the nineteenth century and persisted for much of the twentieth century, but also the extensive translation of this enthusiasm into action. This perspective allows us to develop a better understanding of the role of scientific expertise and R&D in British business history than a narrative that is dominated by discussions of relative economic decline.

BEFORE WORLD WAR I

Extensive research has revealed the significant commitment of large British firms to utilizing the fruits of scientific, particularly chemical, expertise before World War I. Studies of industries as diverse as food, railways, and brewing, as well as the chemical industry itself, have shown clearly that a narrow focus on activities labelled 'research and development' is anachronistic during a period before the term had come into regular use, and that such a focus has led to a serious underestimate of the scientific and technological capabilities of British firms. Instead, we need to look closely at how and why trained scientists were employed by firms and the important roles they came to play across manufacturing industry and beyond. Although W. Bernard Carlson has called this period of industrial innovation before the designated R&D laboratory and organized innovation within the firm the 'prehistory' of industrial research, it is important to remember that many of its features persisted long after some, particularly larger, firms had established organizations with the title research and development as an integral part of their activities. This was particularly the case with smaller firms and in those industries that were not among the pioneers of industrial research.[2]

The use of scientific expertise and the employment of scientists by British firms were stimulated by a range of factors. In many cases it emerged from the use of scientists, primarily chemists, for analytical purposes. Initially, firms looked to chemical consultants for the necessary expertise. The growth in demand for scientific expertise in industry is suggested by the growth in the number of chemical analysts and consultants able to make a living by offering their services to firms for a fee. The 1870 Post Office London Directory contained thirty-eight entries under the heading 'Chemists: Analytical'. By 1891 this had risen to ninety-eight and there were separate listings for 'Chemists: Agricultural' and 'Chemists: Consulting'. There was some overlap between the categories, but this still represents a substantial increase in just over two decades. Other manufacturing centres had their own contingent of experts. In the 1873 Lancashire Directory there were seven analytical chemists in Manchester, six in Liverpool, and a further five in other key industrial towns such as Wigan, Barrow, and Blackburn.[3] In addition to these independent practitioners, many of the staff at the rapidly expanding number of institutions of higher education offered their services as consultants.[4] A number of recent studies of the lives of William Ramsay, William Crookes, and Edward Frankland have shown clearly the importance of consulting activities in their careers.[5] Catherine Watson's detailed analysis of Sir William Ramsey's consulting activities shows clearly the diversity of firms that sought his expertise as well as the importance of the fees earned from this work for the financial health of his department at University College London and its ability to carry out research in other areas of chemistry. Industrial consultancy became increasingly remunerative for Ramsay during the latter part of the nineteenth century and especially after he was awarded a Nobel Prize in 1904. He took on a diverse range of projects, many of them with little or no connection to the research work in which he was engaged and he frequently worked with longstanding friends, including the consultant Otto Hehner. Despite the extensive nature of these activities, Watson notes that there is a 'relative reticence of the records on consulting and expert witnessing'. This suggests both that Ramsay did not see these activities as being as important to his long-term legacy as some of his other achievements and that it may well be the case that other academic scientists were more heavily engaged in such activities than the surviving records might indicate.[6]

This decision to make use of professional scientific expertise was often stimulated by circumstances peculiar to individual industries where the imposition of analytical control was of particular economic significance. Railway companies had started to make use of consultant analysts to examine water supplies during the 1830s, and by the 1840s this was common practice. In the food industry the trigger was new legislation on food quality in the 1870s.[7] The advent of the Bessemer process for steel production was another major stimulus for the employment of chemical expertise. Consultant analysts rapidly discovered inadequacies in the existing knowledge of the materials they were called on to examine and in the analytical techniques at their disposal and started to undertake research that led to new knowledge and new techniques. Some consultants specialized in particular industries or commodities. Edward Frankland became the leading water analyst, while in the food sector Otto Hehner specialized in dairy products and *Butter, Its Analysis and Adulterations Specially Treating on the Detection and Determination of Foreign Fats* appeared in 1877. William Jago specialized in food analysis and published widely on the topic, collecting his contributions in 1886 as *Chemistry of Wheat, Flour, Bread and Technology of Bread Making.*

The employment of consultants led the management of some firms to the conclusion that scientific expertise was so important to the success of their business that it warranted a permanent place within the firm. Until recently it tended to be assumed that relatively few firms employed qualified scientists before World War I, and that those that were employed were primarily engaged on routine analytical work. In his 1972 article, Michael Sanderson listed fifteen firms known to have been doing research.[8] More recent research has revealed that not only were there far more qualified chemists employed across a diverse range of sectors in manufacturing industry by this date, but that a significant number of them spent at least some of their time on research.[9] The absence of systematic data on these activities and their location in departments with a diverse range of labels should not obscure their ubiquity or their economic importance. Examples from two industries that have been studied in detail suggest just how widespread the employment of chemists had become. In brewing there were five major laboratories before 1900, when the arsenic scare encouraged a much larger number of firms to employ their own scientists. By 1910 it is estimated there were almost sixty laboratories in the industry with identifiable chemists in charge. Indeed, by 1908 complaints from brewers were growing that their expertise was being ignored in favour of that of the chemists.[10] The railway industry could boast fourteen laboratories by 1915, and although the number of companies in the sector was far larger, most of these without their own facilities had access to scientific expertise through links to those companies that had invested in it.[11] In addition to this data at the sectoral level, it is also possible to see the very large number of firms across a broad range of sectors that employed chemists as a result of the construction of a Biographical Database of British Chemists. This documents the careers of a cross-section of the profession active from the second half of the nineteenth century. This database also reveals the range of other ways in which the work of chemists supported industry. Unfortunately it is not possible to use it to ascertain the number of scientists employed in industry or the amount of money spent on research or related activities.[12]

We do know that some of the research carried out in industry made a significant contribution to knowledge, leading its authors to achieve some of the highest honours available to the scientific community, including election to a Fellowship of the Royal Society and the award of its Copley Medal. Particularly prolific were the Burton-Upon-Trent brewery chemists, Peter Griess, Cornelius O'sullivan, and Horace Tabberer Brown. Crosfields, a margarine and soap manufacturer, employed two future fellows, Edward F. Armstrong and Thomas P. Hilditch, on its staff during its dispute with Lever Brothers over the fat hydrogenation process shortly before World War I.[13] While the majority of scientists employed in industry devoted much of their time to routine analytical work, the achievements of this group demonstrate clearly the important role of research well before World War I.

Two further features of the relationship between science and industry that were already firmly established before World War I are also worthy of mention. The first is the extent to which British firms not only drew on local knowledge and expertise, but also relied on the international exchange of personnel and information. British firms acquired patents from overseas and overseas firms operated in the UK. The movement of staff between countries, particularly Britain and Germany, was a regular occurrence.[14] Perhaps the first example of recognized research activities by an overseas multinational in the UK is that of British United Shoe Machinery Company, based in Leicester and associated with the United Shoe Machinery Company of Boston, MA. The British company was underpinned by access to the patents of the US operations, but it established an Experimental Department in Leicester in 1899 to work on modified designs for British and Commonwealth markets.[15]

The second area that has been highlighted by Stephen Sambrook's recent study of the optical munitions company Barr and Stroud is the role of the major armaments manufacturers as employers of scientists and as centres of innovation. Vickers, Nobel, and Marconi all employed teams of scientists, as did the steel manufacturers, many of whose key innovations were armaments related. In the case of Barr and Stroud, a partnership which began when the two founders were professors at the Yorkshire College, had, by 1914, developed a 'hegemonic position in the international market place' in range finders, able to 'supply not only all the nation's own peacetime demands, but many of those of foreign powers besides.'[16] This work is also important for the effective challenge it presents to one of the most enduring 'myths' regarding the technological failure of British manufacturing during World War I, which focuses on the optical industry. Sandbrook argues that it was difficulties in the procurement process, rather than any backwardness of the industry, that were at the heart of problems of industrial mobilization, exacerbated in the case of the army by its pre-war failure to take optical munitions seriously or to develop a relationship with suppliers.[17] Indeed, prior to World War I the only countries that had an optical munitions industry were Britain and Germany and it was the British firm of Barr and Stroud that were manufactures of range-finders to the world other than Germany.

This example highlights both the involvement of armaments manufacturers as important members of the group of companies that employed qualified scientists and took innovation seriously, and the longstanding debates about the extent to which British firms lagged behind other nations in their investment in science and technology in the years preceding World War I. Given the ubiquity of scientists in industry by World War I, it seems surprising that historians have been so reluctant to recognize that this was the case. This failing can be attributed to two factors. The first is that undue credence has been accorded to the writings of those contemporary commentators that lambasted the level of investment and castigated both entrepreneurs and the state for their failure to make effective use of new knowledge. These writings have been accepted as accurate representations of reality, rather than being placed firmly in their context, which was that of campaigns for greater resources for science and scientists. As Andrew Hull has argued, drawing on the work of Frank Turner,

the rhetoric painted an overly dismal picture of contemporary British science, and linked this to contemporary fears of declining industrial performance and national power (in comparison with Germany). The hope was to create public pressure on the executive to fund scientific activity.[18]

The rhetoric of inadequacy needs to be seen not as an accurate assessment of the situation, but instead it can be read as evidence of the high level of enthusiasm for science.

The second reason is that these published critical commentaries have been far more easily accessible to historians than the often fragmented evidence of the actual work that scientists did in industry. There were no systematic studies of the extent to which scientists were employed in industry before the 1930s and the records of industrial science in company archives are often fragmentary or non-existent. Other sources, particularly the technical press, can yield significant quantities of information, but identifying it can be extremely laborious. Only a very small proportion of the hundreds of scientists employed in industry before 1914 left their mark in the form of published papers or were deemed important enough to warrant published obituary notices, which renders them very difficult to identify. The lack of interaction between historians of science and of business has also contributed to the persistence of these views.

WORLD WAR I

World War I has been described by one scholar as having a 'peculiarly scientific and technological character'[19] and as we have seen above in relation to optical munitions, it was also a period when the scientific and technological capabilities of British industry came under a great deal of scrutiny. Much of the literature on this topic has painted a rather negative picture, stressing inadequacies and shortages without balancing them with material that points to a more optimistic assessment. The extent to which industry successfully drew on existing capacity has frequently been ignored. In addition the negative emphasis has led to a failure to consider the performance of British industry in the context of the conflict as a whole, or to recognize that the nature and longevity of the war was unprecedented and unanticipated. There has also been a concentration on just a few sectors where shortages were particularly acute, rather than looking across manufacturing industry as a whole.

When we do this we see that firms made extensive use of their existing staff and facilities in order to continue to trade in the new conditions presented by the war. Many firms directly involved with munitions production and with supplying other goods to the armed services expanded their research effort or initiated new ones. Those in other sectors with existing scientific staff generally lost at least some of their employees to war research elsewhere but were able to use those that remained to help sustain production in the face of raw materials shortages. Indeed for some of them the war provided scientists with an unprecedented opportunity to carry out new research and to demonstrate their value to their employers.[20] It also provided qualified women scientists with their first opportunities to secure employment in industry or in Royal Ordnance Factories. Although many of the specific wartime posts created for women did not survive beyond 1918, women continued to form part of the labour force in industrial science throughout the inter-war period, albeit primarily in very subordinate positions.[21]

Wartime conditions favoured large, well resourced firms who were better able to withstand the difficult trading conditions and served as an example to others. It is not surprising that a number of large firms established their own laboratories either during the conflict or very soon afterwards.[22] Regular exhortations by commentators and government officials aimed at fostering stronger links between science and industry may have played a part, but the practical realities faced by firms, their experience of employing consultants and specific circumstances peculiar to each case were probably of much greater significance. What these exhortations do indicate is a belief in the value of such links and they should certainly not be seen as indicating that they did not already exist.[23]

BETWEEN THE WARS

The expansion of industrial research in the years immediately after World War I, and its continued increase during the inter-war period, has been well documented. There was considerable growth, both by those firms already involved, and by new entrants who had been persuaded of the value of research during the conflict. The activity became increasingly visible as a growing number of books and articles were published on the subject and there was enthusiasm from both scientists and leading industrialists for an expansion in industrial research. Some of the publications on industrial research appeared under the auspices of the DSIR, but the majority were private initiatives. One of the most significant was A.P.M. Fleming and J.G. Pearce's 1922 volume, *Research in Industry: The Basis of Economic Progress*, which appeared as part of Pitman's Industrial Administration Series.[24] The extensive bibliography attests to the growing enthusiasm for industrial research and its planning during the preceding decade and the acceleration of interest during and after the war. The text itself contained several eloquent pleas for more scientific research in industry, as well as confidence that Britain stood to gain from its expansion:

If it is undertaken systematically there is no doubt that Britain will reap a reward from research in industry comparable with, and possibly exceeding, that of other great industrial nations.[25]

This enthusiasm for industrial research, evident here and in numerous other texts, was translated into action and industrial research in Britain expended despite the difficult economic conditions. The main contours of this expansion have already been documented elsewhere, but a number of additional features have become apparent from recent scholarship, which reinforce the picture of enthusiasm that is the focus of this chapter.[26] The first of these is the extent of interest among small firms. A significant number of these were members of the Research Associations that were established under the auspices of the DSIR. While these have frequently been criticized for their failure to make significant contributions, the number of small firms that joined them can be taken as an indication of the extent to which the message promoted by authors such as Fleming and Pearce had permeated beyond large enterprises.[27] Even in an industry such as chocolate and confectionary, where there was considerable concentration after 1918, the research association attracted many members. Of the 111 members of the British Association of Research for the Cocoa, Chocolate, Sugar Confectionary and Jam Trades listed in 1924, 52 had less than a hundred employees and ninety-four less than 500.[28] In milling the Research Association of British Flour Millers had seventy-nine members in the early 1920s. This later decreased with further concentration in the industry, but the research association was later successful in persuading the two largest firms in the sector, Rank and Spillers, to join.[29] This enthusiasm is also evident from the large number of firms that reported small expenditures on industrial research during the 1930s to the

Federation of British Industries when they were surveyed during World War II. It is also worth noting that many more firms employed scientists than carried out their own research, indeed many reported this fact to the FBI.[30] Many of these firms supplemented the work of their own employees with the continued use of commercial consultants or staff at universities and technical colleges. The continued existence of a large number consultancy practices across the country is further evidence of the demand for scientific expertise by those firms who did not themselves employ scientists. Very little research has been carried out on this group, but we do know that that 75 practices supplied replies to the FBI survey in 1946 and 103 were listed in a directory published in 1947. The obituaries of leading consultants active during this period suggest that they needed to offer specialized services in order to compete, on the one hand with in-house teams carrying out routine analyses, and on the other with research associations who offered access to research on problems generic to their industries.[31] Perhaps the clearest indicator of the extent to which British manufacturing firms had embraced scientific expertise was the extent to which the presence of scientists in many industries ceased to provoke comment by the late 1920s. While there are no definitive figures on the number of scientists in industry during this period, in 1933 the *Industrial Chemist* estimated that there were between 10,000 and 12,000 chemists in industry. This suggests that the total number of scientists was much larger.[32]

A second important feature was the growth in the international links, despite the tendency towards economic nationalism. These occurred in at least three ways. As British firms expanded their operations overseas they also established research and particularly development facilities to adapt products to local markets. The Dunlop-Perdriau Rubber Co Ltd, the Australian affiliate of Dunlop, for example, included among the laboratory equipment at its Montague factory a two-ton truck that was used to test tyres in Australian conditions.[33] The British operations of overseas multinationals did the same in the UK, and it has been estimated that over thirty of them had laboratories by the mid-1930s. Thirteen of these responded to the FBI industrial research survey in 1943 and accounted for 4.9 per cent of the total expenditure and 4.5 per cent of the qualified scientists and engineers reported for 1935. These figures did not include the electrical engineering industry, where American companies held substantial stakes in many of the leading firms. Were these to be included, the proportion of expenditure attributed to overseas affiliates would be in excess of 10 per cent during the mid-1930s, a figure it did not reach again until the late 1960s. This included some of the largest research operations in the UK with Mond Nickel, Kodak, and the British United Shoe Machinery Company all among the most prominent.[34] In addition to the internationalization of research within the firm, scientific societies with strong industrial links became more international in character, and improvements in transport meant that the organization of overseas meetings became more practical than they had previously been. The Society of Chemical Industry held its 1938 annual meeting in Canada and its Food Group embarked on a regular series of European tours starting with Paris and Brussels in 1935.[35]

Table 13.1. Treasury estimates of government-funded 'scientific research', 1925

	Expenditure
Air Ministry (Air force)	1,373,000
Admiralty (Navy)	983,000
War Office (Army)	495,000
Total Defence	2,851,000
DSIR	380,263
Ministry of Agriculture	348,756
Other	464,609
Total Civil	1,193,628
Total Government	4,044,628

Source: R. MacLeod and K. Andrews, 'The Committee of Civil Research: Advice for Economic Development, 1925–1930', *Minerva*, 7, 1969: 699.

The third feature of the inter-war period that is worth considering here is the development of organizations for weapons development. This aspect of industrial research has received considerable attention during the years after World War II and the important role played by private industry in Cold War defence research has drawn attention to the extent of continuity with the inter-war period. Unfortunately only limited data is available on this topic. We do have information on the overall levels of expenditure by the service ministries on scientific research during the 1920s (Table 13.1).

Unfortunately there are no figures which indicate the extent to which the supply ministries channelled R&D funding to industry. Nor do we have a clear indication of the R&D expenditure of the main armaments manufacturers, who are conspicuous by their absence from the earliest extensive surveys of industrial research, being either unable or unwilling to disclose this information. There is clear evidence from elsewhere of their high level of expenditure and the extent to which state support helped to sustain them. During the 1930s, for example, the companies in the Vickers Group undertook extensive R&D projects, many of which received funding from the state (Table 13.2).

It is likely that at least part of the decline suggested by these figures between 1930 and 1935 is a consequence of the end of the airship programme that ran

Table 13.2. Vickers Group R&D expenditure noted in archives compared to expenditure reported to FBI survey, 1930 and 1935

	Vickers Group R&D expenditure	Vickers companies reported to FBI survey	Total reported to the FBI (number of firms)
1930	299,000	1,000	1,736,000 (422)
1935	127,000 (1934)	19,000	2,696,000 (484)

Sources: Details of expenditure for individual firms from University of Warwick, Modern Records Centre, CBI Predecessor Archive, MSS 200/F/3/T1/127 c. Vickers Group figures from Cambridge University Library, Vickers Archives, 88, Particulars and Correspondence Regarding Research and Experimental Expenditure, 1930–4.

from 1924 until 1930 and which had an R&D budget of £0.41 million divided between the Air Ministry and the Vickers Group.[36] They also indicate the very large sums of money that were being spent in this sector, and the extent to which this went under-reported to the FBI even when firms did provide some data to the survey.

While much of the evidence from this period points towards the consolidation and expansion of industrial research, it is important to note that laboratories were closed as well as opened, and staff lost their jobs when businesses failed or suffered hardship. In addition, mergers led to the loss of some laboratories and the downgrading of others.[37] The most well known case is probably that of Standard Telephone and Cables, whose laboratories in Hendon employed 420 when they were closed in 1930.[38] In the railway industry consolidation led to a reduction in the number of facilities, while stagnation and decline in the brewing industry undermined the strong position that scientific staff had acquired before World War I. The industry as a whole reported just fifty qualified research staff in 1938, a figure lower than that for 1910.[39]

An indication of the extent to which scientific expertise resided in industry, and its significance, came during planning for wartime food supplies initiated in 1936. The Food (Defence Plans) Department rapidly established that research was needed in a number of fields in order to carry out its remit and it sought advice as to the most appropriate way to proceed with the necessary projects. Thomas P. Hilditch, Professor of Industrial Chemistry at Liverpool University was consulted on the issues relating to edible fats and replied that 'the people who can give the best advice on the practicability of this proposal are the edible fat manufacturers themselves'. Director of Food Investigation, E. Barnard, noted that, 'there is a great deal of research carried out by the highly organised industry', and wondered, 'how is government research to be added so as to make an effective and harmonious whole?'[40] This situation was the result of the sustained enthusiasm of manufacturers for investment in the service of scientists and the facilities to house them.

WORLD WAR II

World War II has frequently been presented as a conflict during which British scientific and technological prowess contributed decisively to the success of the armed forces of both Britain and her allies. Radar, code breaking operations, aircraft design, jet engines, penicillin, and the atomic bomb are all regularly cited as examples of this prowess. Although this positive assessment appears to contrast strongly with many assessments of World War I, in fact there are significant similarities. In both cases wartime achievements were underpinned by considerable enthusiasm for industrial research and a belief that it could make a vital contribution to the war effort. This could be put into practice because of the extensive facilities that already existed in private industry. Many firms, with the support of the state, enlarged their research facilities significantly to accommodate the demands which came from the Ministry of Supply and the Admiralty to carry out R&D contracts as the system already in place before the war expanded dramatically.[41]

Although we do not have figures for the firms most closely involved in the aircraft and electronics industries, we do know that they received considerable sums from the supply ministries. By December 1942, the Ministry of Supply was operating 186 R&D contracts with 114 different firms.[42] Leading firms in industries such as steel, engineering, and photography experienced significant increases in the number of research staff they employed between 1938 and 1941. Some, such as Colvilles, doubled their staff. On the other hand, firms whose output was for domestic consumption lost scientists – fully half the total in the case of brewing for example.[43] The Ministry of Labour through its scientific and technical register had considerable powers to direct scientists to those areas deemed most important to the war effort. There were also measures to increase the output of graduates in those areas regarded as most essential to the war effort through the use of shortened courses, bursaries, and the threat of the call-up for those not taking the designated courses.[44] This led to a dramatic increase in the output of scientists. In 1942 Ministry of Labour officials surveyed universities and university colleges to ascertain the number of students who had started chemistry courses since 1939. In the first year of the war the number was just 136, but this had risen to 351 in 1940 and 649 the following year. The expected intake for 1942 was 840.[45]

1945 TO THE 1970s

Such was the enthusiasm for the expansion of both industrial- and government-funded research after the conflict, that the increased wartime output of scientific manpower was quickly seen to be wholly inadequate for the nation's needs.[46] During the latter years of World War II and the period immediately afterwards there was considerable enthusiasm for the idea that industrial research was essential to the future of the British economy and to national well-being. This was expressed by politicians from all political parties, by leading industrialists and by scientists, in speeches, newspaper articles, and in the scientific and technical press. Dissenting voices are conspicuous by their absence, and while advocates sometimes differed in the emphasis they placed on the roles of different elements of the research system, they were united in their calls for expansion and in their faith that the successful exploitation of new ideas would also help to win the battle of the peace, ensuring long-term economic stability.[47] The Minister of Supply John Wilmot, who stated in 1946 that 'upon the response which the masses of British industrialists make to the tremendous opportunities offered to them by science depends our industrial future',[48] was just one voice of many that assumed that investment in science by industry was the route to long-term success.

The response was indeed enthusiastic, despite the shortages of both human and material resources that firms faced. Spending by British industry on R&D grew significantly. When the Federation of British Industries Industrial Research Committee repeated their 1945/6 survey of research expenditure and employment in 1950/1 they concluded that their sample was actually too small to generate an estimate of total expenditure, but were confident that the increase since the previous survey was between 50 and 100 per cent.[49] In subsequent years more detailed data was collected by the Department of Scientific and Industrial Research, and later the Central Statistical Office, reflecting an increasing scrutiny of industrial R&D and a belief in the important role that it had to play. This means that rather than the fragmented data that we have for the period before 1930, there is much more comprehensive evidence available for this period. It reveals that the period from 1945 to 1955 was one of particularly rapid growth. During the early 1960s, however, the rate of growth slackened and it slowed yet further in the second half of the decade (Table 13.3).

What these figures also show clearly is the extent to which the state was an important source of funds for R&D carried out by private industry. State spending on defence R&D was the single largest source of finance for R&D in 1955, but by 1961 it had been overtaken by private industry. There was also a shift in the orientation of state resources away from defence projects towards civilian projects, but this took place over a longer time-scale. It was in place well before the changes in the machinery of government and administration of policy for science and technology that took place during the mid-1960s. State funding was significantly more important for some sectors than others (Table 13.4).

Table 13.3. Expenditure on R&D by manufacturing industry, £ million at current prices

		Government funded		
	Total expenditure	Company funded	Total	Of which defence
1955	187	60	127	118
1958	266	112	154	142
1961	378	223	155	
1964	458	296	162	
1966	585	390	195	151
1967	609	413	196	131
1968	639	435	204	124
1969	679	457	222	129

Notes: The figures from 1955 to 1964 are not as comprehensive as the later figures. For 1967–9 the figures include the state-owned British Steel Corporation. The company funded column includes a small amount of expenditure from overseas.

Source: *Economic Trends*, 1974: xxxiii.

Table 13.4. Proportion of R&D carried out within private manufacturing industry and financed by the British government by sector, 1959–70

	1959	1964–5	1966–7	1967–8	1968–9	1969–70
Aerospace	86	84.1	78.1	71.0	75.3	80.4
Electronics	42	47.6	43.4	45.0	40.0	38.7
Other electrical		3.2	5.8	4.1	4.0	0.8
Chemicals	3	0.5	2.5	1.2	2.3	1.6
Machinery	16	15.2	13.8	18.6	14.3	15.8
Ships and marine Engineering	9	52.6	35.4	32.0	30.1	63.3
Motor vehicles		1.2	2.2	1.7	3.2	0.5
Instruments	40	23.2	19.4	16.6	19.0	17.5
Non-ferrous metals		2.6	2.6	2.7	2.3	4.0
Metal products		0.1	4.5	0.5	0.9	0.4
Other manufacturing		6.6	0.0	0.1	0.1	0.0
All R&D in private industry	47	35.0	33.0	32.4	32.0	32.8

Notes: These figures refer to private manufacturing industry only and do not include public corporations or research associations. They include all government funding, both military and civil. The 1959 figures give a total of 11 per cent for Freeman's Group B sectors: rubber, ferrous metals, non-ferrous metals, metal products, stone, clay, and glass and paper, and 13 per cent for the Group C sectors: food, textiles and apparel, lumber and furniture, and other manufacturing. In 1964–5, aerospace was classified as aircraft. Chemicals here includes all categories classed under this heading in each year, with the omission of petroleum products which are disaggregated for all years. Further minor adjustments in classification occurred for 1969–70. Categories previously aggregated have been added together. The following sectors received less than 2 per cent of R&D funding from the government throughout the period covered above and are omitted: petroleum products, paper, food, textiles and apparel, timber and furniture, rubber, ferrous metals, stone, and clay.

Sources: For 1959, C. Freeman, 'Research and Development: A Comparison between British and American Industry', *National Institute Economic Review*, 20, May 1962: 21–39. Other years, CSO, *Research and Development Expenditure*, 1973.

The impact of government defence funding on the distribution of R&D is evident if we consider the distribution by sector of expenditure funded by industry itself (Table 13.5).

While the upward trend in investment by firms in R&D suggests a continued high level of enthusiasm for the activity, there were already some commentators

Table 13.5. Distribution of private manufacturing industry funded R&D by sector, 1959–70

	1959	1964–5	1969–70
Aircraft/aerospace	10.6	5.1	5.1
Electronics	22.0	11.6	15.9
Other electrical		8.5	7.8
Chemicals	26.0	23.2	25.0
Vehicles	7.4	11.9	12.8
Non-electrical engineering and shipbuilding	14.4	10.5	9.1
Food, drink, and tobacco		5.3	5.4

Notes: Chemicals included petroleum products.

Source: For 1959, Freeman and CSO, *Research and Development Expenditure*, 1973: table 16.

urging caution by the mid-1950s. Leading industrialist Sir Charles Renold suggested in 1954 that:

We hear that the chief need for British industry is for more science and more research. That may be, but it will not be met merely by increasing the number of scientists. If the contributions of science are to be put to work and bear fruit in industry, management must provide the opportunities, the organisation and the procedures. The immediate bar to more science in industry is the failure to make full use of what we already have: it is a failure of management.[50]

There were also concerns about the way in which R&D in industry were managed, and that expansion had taken place without the imposition of proper controls. The editor of *Administrative Science Quarterly* noted in 1956 that 'such devices as cost accounting face enormous problems when applied to research activities'.[51]

Four years later, a survey of industrial research carried out by the Federation of British Industry in collaboration with the NIESR in 1960 found that the majority of firms contacted did not normally use specific criteria such as profit forecasts in selecting research projects. Some firms 'categorically denied the possibility of measuring the return on research'. When asked to assess whether research work had been applied commercially, firms calculated that on average 16 per cent had not been used and was not anticipated to yield useful results. This average concealed considerable variation, with the proportion in some cases exceeding one-quarter.[52]

These findings echoed the concerns that had been raised by economists Charles Carter and Bruce Williams in their work. They were dismayed to discover that 'in the majority of firms we visited . . . we felt certain that little thought had been given to the question of deciding the level of research expenditure'[53] and that 'cost consciousness' was not well developed in the planning of research programmes. They were impressed by the high proportion of companies that 'do not attempt an economic assessment before embarking on research projects, or choosing between alternative projects.' and noted how rarely decisions between projects were based on the results of market analysis. Indeed the planning of research programmes, or more precisely the lack of attention given to this was a major concern. Somewhat paradoxically the evidence provided by one research director of a large firm, who admitted that 'at the moment we work on a programme partly determined by tradition, history and personalities, and I am certain that some of the aspects of our programme are not well conceived'[54] was taken as evidence that attention was increasingly being paid to the criteria for planning research programmes. There was also concern about the poor deployment of scientists, technologists, and technicians.[55] 'The "art of using scientists"' Carter and Williams made clear, 'is not a highly developed one'[56] The enthusiasm for employing scientists had not, it seemed, been translated into their effective deployment.

In the introduction to the final volume which emerged under the auspices of the Science and Industry Committee, *Policy for Progress*, they informed readers that some of their suggestions might seem obvious, but they had been included because, 'the simple, elementary, and obvious things are not universally practiced . . . we know of many who need to be reminded of them'.[57]

During the 1960s there was increasing disillusionment with the expectation that simply spending more on R&D and providing scientists with freedom to do research was the most effective route to innovation. The British literature on industrial R&D increasingly emphasized managing and controlling the activity. Research management was discussed at British Institute of Management seminars and came under renewed academic scrutiny. Collinson's book, published in 1964 and aimed at those taking the management papers of professional bodies such as the Institute of Chemistry or Institution of Mechanical Engineers summed up this shift: 'research is not a mysterious form of ju-ju, and neither are research workers witch doctors'.[58] It blamed the poor management of R&D projects for the apparent shortage of qualified scientists and engineers in the UK and went on to outline techniques for organizing and managing research more efficiently based on careful project selection, coordination, and budgetary control, the effective use of staff, including appraisal and attention to career development, and the constant evaluation of results.

This new spirit of scrutiny, both by scholars and by R&D managers marked the end of an era in British industrial R&D. Unbounded enthusiasm that 'more would always be better' was replaced by an emphasis on control and coordination and a growing awareness that despite the high levels of investment in R&D the British economy had not grown as fast as that of many of her leading industrial competitors who spent less on this activity. Bruce Williams summed this up when he stated in 1963 that, 'There is, however, more to growth through science than investment in innovation. However brilliant the technical innovation, however well timed the investment, if it is not managed well the growth potential will be squandered. There is no doubt that this has been a factor of significance in the United Kingdom.'[59]

By the time J. Allen undertook a survey of R&D evaluation and control procedures used by British firms in 1966/7, the effects of this change had started to be felt. Two-thirds of the firms he surveyed had a formal system for the evaluation of R&D projects – a significant increase over the FBI survey of seven years earlier, although the samples were different. Of these firms one-third made use of mathematical models and/or weighted checklists or project ranking indices as elements of their project evaluation. The extent to which Allen was able to obtain detailed information on project evaluation and review is perhaps testimony to the rapid growth of its importance.[60] There is evidence too at the level of the firm that greater attention was paid to the control of R&D expenditure and the freedom that had been given to those scientists recruited by firms to staff 'fundamental' laboratories in the aftermath of World War II was curtailed. An early and particularly symbolic example was Courtaulds, where Cyril Kearton, himself a Fellow of the Royal Society chose to close the firm's fundamental research laboratory at Maidenhead as one of his first acts upon assuming control.

This had failed to generate new fibres as conspicuously as it had succeeded in producing papers for academic journals.[61]

This evidence suggests that by the late 1960s the R&D 'monster' had begun to be both tamed and transformed.[62] This process was accompanied by a reduction in the rate of growth of R&D expenditure by firms, and during the early 1970s by declining expenditure. In 1975 this was 11 per cent below the peak of the late 1960s and total R&D employment had declined even more significantly.[63] This decline took the level of expenditure on R&D in the UK below that of several leading industrial competitors, provoking some anxiety among those who continued to regard high levels of expenditure on R&D as important to economic growth.[64] This decline meant that concern over effective management was replaced by one for lack of overall investment which came to be taken by many commentators as indicative of the post-war period as a whole. The anxiety over underinvestment can itself be seen as indicative of the persistence of enthusiasm for R&D that characterized British industry for the first seventy years of the twentieth century. Unfortunately some of the scholarly work that it generated had a profoundly unhelpful impact on the historiography of British industrial R&D, deflecting attention away from the high levels of investment during earlier periods.

NOTES

1. This comment was made at a witness seminar, 'Talking off the Record: Conversations between Government and Scientists', Churchill Archives Centre, 11 May 2005.
2. W. Bernard Carlson, 'Innovation and the Modern Corporation', in J. Krige and D. Pestre, ed., *Science in the Twentieth Century*, Amsterdam, 1997: 203–26.
3. *Post Office London Directory, 1870*, London, 1869; *Post Office London Trades Directory for 1891*, London, 1891; ER Kelly, *The Post Office Directory of Lancashire, Liverpool and Manchester*, London, 1873.
4. An overview of some of these activities can be found in Michael Sanderson, *The Universities and British Industry, 1850–1970*, London, 1972: 83–94.
5. Katherine D. Watson, 'The Chemists as Expert: The Consulting Careers of Sir William Ramsay', *Ambix*, 42, 1995: 143–59; William H. Brock, *William Crookes (1832–1919) and the Commercialization of Science*, London, 2008; Colin Russell, *Edward Frankland: Chemistry, Controversy and Conspiracy in Victorian England*, Cambridge University Press, 1996.
6. Katherine D. Watson, 'The Chemists as Expert: The Consulting Careers of Sir William Ramsay', *Ambix*, 42, 1995: 143–59 p. 156.
7. S.M. Horrocks, 'Consuming Science: Science, Technology and Food in Britain, 1870–1939', PhD thesis, University of Manchester, 1993.
8. Michael Sanderson, 'Research and the Firm in British Industry, 1919–39', *Science Studies*, 2, 1972: 107–51.
9. James Donnelly, 'Industrial Recruitment of Chemistry Students from English Universities: A Revaluation of its Early Importance', *British Journal for the History of Science*, 24, 1991: 3–20.

10. Ray Anderson, 'Chemists in the Brewing Industry', paper presented at the Royal Society of Chemistry Historical Group Meeting, 28 Oct. 2008.

11. John Hudson, 'Chemists in the Railway Industry', paper presented at the *Royal Society of Chemistry Historical Group Meeting*, 28 Oct. 2008; and 'Chemistry and the British Railway Industry, 1830–1923', unpublished PhD thesis, Open University, 2005. BLDSC DX237386.

12. Gerrylyn Roberts and Robin Mackie, 'Biographical Database of British Chemists', http://www5.open.ac.uk/Art/chemists, 2nd edition 2006, updated 2 Oct. 2008.

13. Anderson, n. 10 above, C.S. Gibson and T.P. Hilditch, 'Edward Frankland Armstrong', *Royal Society Obituary Notices of Fellows*, 5, 1945–8: 619–33; and R.A. Morton, 'Thomas Percy Hilditch, 1886–1965', *Biographical Memoirs of the Fellows of the Royal Society*, 12, 1966: 259–90. Certificates of election for Fellows can be viewed at www.royalsociety.org

14. G.K. Roberts and A.E. Simmons, 'The Overseas Dimensions of British Chemical Societies, c.1890–c.1950', in Y. Furukawa, ed., 'Special Issue: Globalization and Diversity in Chemical Sciences', Historia Scientiarum, 16, 2007: 1–20.

15. Sally M. Horrocks, 'The Internationalization of Science in a Commercial Context: Research and Development by Overseas Multinationals in Britain before the Mid-1970s', *British Journal for the History of Science*, 40, 2007: 227–50, p. 230.

16. Stephen Curtis Sambrook, 'The Optical Munitions Industry in Great Britain, 1888 to 1923' PhD thesis, University of Glasgow, 2005: abstract and p. 114. Accounts of the 'failure' of the industry rely heavily on R.M. MacLeod and K. MacLeod, 'War and Economic Development: Government and the Optical Glass Industry in Britain 1914–1918', in J.M. Winter, ed., *War and Economic Development Cambridge*, 1975: 165–203.

17. Sambrook, *Optical Munitions Industry*: 116–19.

18. Andrew Hull, 'War of Words: The Public Science of the British Scientific Community and the Origins of the Department of Scientific and Industrial Research, 1914–16', *British Journal for the History of Science*, 32, 1999: 461–81. See also Frank Turner, 'Public Science in Britain, 1880–1919', *Isis*, 71, 1980: 589–608.

19. Keith Vernon, 'Science and Technology', in Stephen Constantine, M.W. Kirby and Mary B. Rose, eds., *The First World War in British History*, Edward Arnold, London, 1995: 81–105, p. 81.

20. This was certainly the case at Cadbury and Rowntree, see Horrocks, thesis.

21. Marelene and Geoffrey Rayner-Canham, *Women in Chemistry: Their Changing Roles from Alchemical Times to the Mid-twentieth Century*, Chemical Heritage Foundation, 1998: pp. 166–9. On women in industrial chemistry more generally, see Sally M. Horrocks, 'A Promising Pioneer Profession? Women in British Industrial Chemistry before 1939', *British Journal for the History of Science*, 33, 2000: 351–67.

22. D.E.H. Edgerton and S.M. Horrocks, 'British Industrial Research and Development before 1945', *Economic History Review*, 47, 1994: 213–38.

23. Examples of this encouragement are A.P.M. Fleming, *Science and Industry: Industrial Research in the USA*, London, 1917; and A.P.M. Fleming and J.G. Pearce, *Research in Industry: The Basis of Economic Progress*, Pitman's Industrial Administration Series, Pitman, London, 1922.

24. Ibid.

25. Fleming and Pearce, *Research in Industry*: 220.

26. The main overviews have been presented in Sanderson '*Research and the Firm*'; and Edgerton and Horrocks, '*British Industrial Research and Development*'.

27. Ian Varcoe, 'Co-operative Research Associations in British Industry, 1918–34', *Minerva*, 19, 1981: 433–63; and David C. Mowery, 'Industrial Research in Britain, 1900–1950', in B. Elbaum and William Lazonick, eds., *The Decline of the British Economy*, 1986: 189–222.

28. TNA PRO DSIR 16/250 Report of inspection of the BARCCSCJT, Apr. 1924: appendix 1.

29. TNA PRO DSIR 16/148.

30. University of Warwick Modern Records Centre, CBI Predecessor Archive, MSS 200/F/3/T2/7/1.

31. Obituaries of H. E. Cox and Thomas Crosbie-Walsh, *Chemistry and Industry*, 71, 1952: 71; and 73, 1954: 1255. Research on careers in chemistry suggests that consultancy declined in relative importance as a career destination for chemists, Robin Mackie and Gerrylynn K. Roberts, 'Career Patterns In the British Chemical Profession during the Twentieth Century', D. Mitch, J. Brown, and M. H. D. van Leeuwen, eds., *Origins of the Modern Career*, Aldershot, 2004: 317–36, esp. table 15.2.

32. *Industrial Chemist*, 8, 1933: 37.

33. Australian National University, Noel Butlin Archives Centre, 31/13, 'The Story of the Test Truck', *Dunlop Gazette*, Nov. 1936: 7.

34. Sally M. Horrocks, 'The Internationalization of Science in a Commercial Context: Research and Development by Overseas Multinationals in Britain before the Mid-1970s', *British Journal for the History of Science*, 40, 2007: 227–50.

35. Horrocks, thesis: 290.

36. P. Masefield, *To Ride the Storm: The Story of Airship R101*, 1982: 486.

37. After the takeover of Crosfields by Lever Brothers the latter lost its research oriented members of staff who feared the level of influence that their new boss would seek to exert. See Sally M. Horrocks, 'Industrial Chemistry and its Changing Patrons at the University of Liverpool, 1926–1951', *Technology and Culture*, 48, 2007: 43–66, p. 50.

38. Peter Young, *Power of Speech: A History of Standard Telephones and Cables, 1883–1983*, London, 1983: 67.

39. Anderson, 'Brewing'; Hudson, 'Railway Industry', MSS 200; etc.

40. TNA PRO DSIR 6/106, E. Barnard, 'Notes on Research on Processing'.

41. Sally M. Horrocks, 'Enthusiasm Constrained? British Industrial; R&D and the Transition from War to Peace, 1942–1951', *Business History*, 41, 1999: 42–62; and ' Defence Research and Private Industry: Finding Capacity for Research in the Electronics Industry, 1945–55', *Yearbook of European Administrative History*, forthcoming.

42. J. D. Scott and Richard Hughes, *The Administration of War Production*, London, 1956: 284.

43. MRC MSS 200/F/3/T1/127 c.

44. TNA PRO LAB 6/149. Question of the Distribution of Technical and Scientific Students between Industry and the Armed Forces.

45. TNA PRO LAB 6/251.

46. 'Scientific Manpower', Report of a committee appointed by the Lord President of the Council Cmd 6824, 1946.

47. Sally M. Horrocks, 'Enthusiasm Constrained? British Industrial R&D and the Transition from War to Peace, 1942–51', *Business History*, 41, 2000: 42–4.

48. FBI, *Industry and Research*, 1946: 63.

49. Ibid., *Research and Development in British Industry: A Survey of Expenditure on Industrial Research and Development in the Year 1950–1*, 1952: 6.

50. Sir Charles Renold, 'Training for Management', *Advancement of Science, X*, 1954: 299, quoted in Ronald S. Edwards and Harry Townsend, *Business Enterprise: Its Growth and Organisation*, London, 1958: 545–6.
51. 'Editor's Critique', *Administrative Science Quarterly*, 1, 1956: 382–5.
52. FBI, *Industrial Research in Manufacturing Industry: 1959–60, Results of a Survey Including Commentaries and a Statistical Report*: 58–9.
53. C. F. Carter and B. R. Williams, *Industry and Technical Progress: Factors Covering the Speed of Application of Science*, London, 1957: 50–1.
54. Ibid.: 54.
55. Ibid.: 104.
56. Ibid.: 134.
57. *Science in Industry: Policy for Progress*, London, 1959: introduction.
58. Harold A. Collinson, *Management for Research and Development*, London, 1964: 15.
59. Bruce R. Williams, 'Assessing the Economics of Innovation', in B. R. Williams, ed., *Technology, Investment and Growth*, London, 1967: 57–63.
60. J. M. Allen, 'A Survey into the R&D Evaluation and Control Procedures Currently Used in Industry', *Journal of Industrial Economics*, XVIII, 1969–70: 161–81.
61. Sally M. Horrocks, 'R&D In British Industry', in Michael J. Lynskey and Seiichiro Yonekura, eds., *Entrepreneruship and Organization: The Role of the Entrepreneur in Organizational Innovation*, Oxford, 2002: 303–29.
62. F. Clive De Paula, 'Control of the Monster', review of Warran C. Lothrop, *Management Uses of Research and Development*, in *The Manager*, Aug. 1965: 44.
63. 'Research and Development in 1975', *Trade and Industry*, 38, 6 Apr. 1979: 35.
64. OECD, *Patterns of Resources Devoted to Research and Experimental Development in the OECD Area, 1963–1971*, Paris, 1975.

14

Increasing Value?

Modern British Retailing in the Late Twentieth Century

Carlo Morelli

The rise of large-scale retailing represents arguably one of the success stories of British business in the second half of the twentieth century. Growing consumer prosperity after the Second World War saw rising demand for an ever widening array of consumer products, leading Prime Minister Harold Macmillan to famously suggest that the public had 'never had it so good'. To match these changes innovations from the United States were adopted by leading British retailers from the 1950s, especially in the fields of store size and layout, product packaging, and marketing. A new wave of innovation emerged, this time generated from within, during the 'Golden Age' of retailing from the mid-1970s to the mid-1990s, when further advances in new store development, supply chain management, and the use of information technology became widespread. Thus, over the period of half a century British retailing had become a leading sector for innovation within British business. As a result by the 1990s British retailing had not only become oligopolistic, and the subject of repeated anti-monopoly investigation, but the largest retailers were now turning to internationalization as they themselves began to transfer their own technological know-how into new markets.

Historians and other scholars had little to say with regard to modern retailing prior to the 1990s. The focus of much of the literature was upon the predominance of small scale, family-owned, and independent shopkeepers in the nineteenth century which were increasingly undermined by multiple retailing organizations, variety and department stores along with cooperative retailing.[1] More recently, however, business historians' and geographers' interest in retailing has grown substantially. Issues of organizational capabilities and the nature of competition have been the focus of much attention, with particular reference to the growth of retailers' own-brands,[2] logistics and distribution,[3] market structure,[4] and the post-war challenge to manufacturer-imposed resale price maintenance.[5] By the twenty-first century retailing had become a main stream area of academic research with internationalization,[6] competition and policy,[7] trade,[8] and innovation[9] to name but a few areas of contemporary interest.

This chapter does not seek to review all of this growing body of work, rather it sets itself a more modest, yet arguably more important, task. As recently as 1995

Akehurst could hope that 'a general theory of competition in retailing may be developed'.[10] Unlike competition between firms within manufacturing industry retail competition has never simply resulted in competition between retailers over price or quality for substitutable goods. Retail competition has at each stage in its development centered upon competition between differing forms of retail format and businesses' organizational form rather than over substitutable goods. Thus, the approach of adopting concepts of competition from manufacturing and simply applying them to retailing has proven problematic. It is therefore to the question of providing a theoretical understanding of the economic role of retailing and competition that this chapter addresses. This chapter explains innovation, in the form of organizational structures and retail format, as central to understanding competition in the retailing environment, especially in the second half of the twentieth century. It suggests that innovation, in particular the way in which it impacts on the supply chain, is central to understanding competition within retailing and that the importance of innovation lies with the market power innovation provides retailers over the supply chain in relation to manufacturers.

This chapter therefore seeks to develop a framework, available to business historians, for an understanding of the business function of retailing and provide an explanation for the dynamic nature of the sector in contrast to much of manufacturing in the period. The unique importance of retailing's economic function, in realizing value rather than simply creating value, is suggested to lie at the economic heart of the retailing function. This has allowed retailers to successfully change the balance between markets and hierarchies at different times in their development. It is these changes that have given rise to new retailing formats. In so doing retailers provide an example of organizations where the boundaries between markets and hierarchies are increasingly blurred and are themselves perhaps more accurately understood within a transaction cost framework of a nexus of contracts. Using new institutional economics and an understanding of market power, contracting is shown to adapt to changes in the importance of manufacturer branded goods, retailer own-label goods, and asset specific investment in retailing outlets, computer technology, and logistics. Finally, this chapter examines these changes in more detail through the history of Britain's largest food retailer, Tesco plc. Food retailers, most notably Tesco, led the changes in retailing that this chapter identifies are key to understanding the dynamic relationships that retailers have managed to create in the late twentieth century.

THE RISE OF RETAILING

Retailing in Britain has undergone numerous 'revolutions' as new forms of retailing challenged existing methods for marketing goods to consumers. Competition within retailing became characterized not simply by competition over price and location between similar organizations, referred to as intra-type competition, but also by competition between very different retailing formats, referred to as inter-type competition.[11] So, itinerant merchants faced competition between themselves and between their form of retailing and that of fixed store retailing for the provision of goods to consumers by the nineteenth century, full-service provision was challenged by self-service retailing after the Second World War, small stores by large supermarket retailing by the 1960s and town-centre by out-of-town hypermarket retailing by the 1980s and still more recently e-retailing in the 1990s. Thus competition in the context of the history of retailing is typically a history of competition between forms of organization as between firms themselves.

Internally, firms were emerging by the mid-nineteenth century in the United Kingdom that moved beyond the single store structure with multiple store organizations establishing themselves by the 1850s with WH Smith and John Menzies in the book trade; followed shortly afterwards in dairy products and dry packaged goods with firms such as the Maypole Dairy Co., Lipton Ltd, and the Home and Colonial Tea Company; in footwear with Freeman Hardy & Wilis; tobacco with Finlay & Co.; oil and paint retailing with George Mence Smith; and pharmacy with Boots Pure Drug Co. to name but a few.[12] Large city centre department stores and mail order firms were similarly all in existence before 1900 with Schoolbred being dated back as far as 1820.[13] Most significantly of all, the Co-operative Wholesale Society (CWS), originating in 1844 but by 1900 already responsible for between 6 and 7 per cent of retail sales, had established international purchasing and warehousing facilities in Ireland, the US, the East Indies, France, Denmark, Germany, Canada, and Australia.[14] The CWS had also diversified beyond retailing of foodstuffs and into food manufacturing, clothing, footwear, soap, and furniture. By the First World War the CWS was by far and away the largest retailer in the world.

In the area of consumer marketing, retailers were also developing new forms of competition before the twentieth century. The development of the co-operatives spread fixed price retailing and 'honest dealing', leading to quality and service becoming the hallmark of consumer marketing for the rising numbers of multiple firms. The development of the Co-op's 'dividend' emerged as retailers sought to establish loyalty between consumers and retailers, and was in many respects a precursor to the relationship marketing that retailers would focus upon in the 1990s.

The inter-war years saw, as in other industries, a merger movement occur which introduced both new scale economies and new forms of specialization. The number of firms with twenty-five or more branches grew continuously from fifty-eight in 1920 to eighty-nine by 1939 with the number of stores operated by these multiples rising from 6,719 to 12,062.[15] Whereas multiple retailing had emerged in a number of important areas of retailing before 1900 it had by the inter-war period become commonplace across all sectors. The largest multiples now achieved national coverage while many regional multiples also emerged. Jeffrey's seminal study details the growth of multiple retailing across a wide range of trades including: grocery and provision; meat, bread, and flour confectionary; milk;

fruit and vegetables; fish; chocolate and sugar confectionary; tobacco; newspaper; stationary and books; clothing; footwear; chemists and druggists; sewing machines; bicycles; electrical goods; jewellery; toy and sports goods; and furniture and household goods trades.

These large-scale retailers, focusing upon a narrow range of goods, developed further specialization by buying in bulk and integrating their warehousing and distribution within the firm.[16] The inter-war era also brought co-operation between retailers and manufacturers aimed at restricting price competition with the spread of resale price maintenance on branded goods.[17] Price maintenance, although successfully introduced, did not go unchallenged during the 1930s as discounting retailers emerged in food retailing with Tesco and in clothing Marks & Spencer avoiding branded goods by producing own-label clothing.[18]

The Second World War reduced competition still further and by the time rationing ended in 1954, retailing was ready to see rapid changes in the retailing industry. By the 1950s, discounting retailers, particularly in food retailing, had broken manufacturer-imposed resale price controls and begun to introduce new forms of retailing with self-service and supermarket retailing formats. While the co-operative movement led in the introduction of self-service stores it was with the private multiple food retailers, such as Sainsbury and Victor Value, where supermarket retailing emerged most strongly.[19]

Rising spending power and the rise of consumer society saw significant changes in patterns of consumption. While food expenditure fell as a proportion of total expenditure from 29.1 per cent of consumer expenditure to 17.2 per cent between 1950 and 1980 the volume of food consumption could still rise by 40 per cent. Over the same period expenditure on motor vehicles and fuel could rise from 1.9 per cent of consumer expenditure to 10.4 per cent.[20] The spread of consumer durables including refrigerators, washing machines, and other domestic electrical devices along with the mass ownership of cars all contributed to this rapid growth of consumer society.

This growing consumer society together with retailers' locational advantages through ownership of limited high street sites helped contribute to the dominance of larger retailers in high streets across Britain. Retailing firms themselves, it should be stressed, were not however uniform in their responses to the opportunities a new consumer society brought. While some larger retailers, such as Tesco, made use of public liability ownership structures to gain access to capital market finance, others, such as Sainsbury, preferred continued family control and incremental growth. The growing importance of retailing in the supply chain continued until the next 'retail revolution', with hypermarket retailing, the emergence of out-of-town shopping and one-stop shopping in the 1980s. During this 'Golden Age' deregulation of land use and planning controls permitted the rapid expansion of new, out-of-town development.[21] The largest retailers now increased the scale and scope of their operations, with food retailers moving into clothing, household durables, electrical goods, and even financial services while in clothing retailers such as Laura Ashley and Next moved into household furnishings and decorations, and financial services. In the 1990s, retailers began to look at internationalization as domestic saturation and limited new sites threatened to stall further expansion while increased government concerns over large multiples impact on competition led to repeated anti-monopoly investigations by the Monopolies and Mergers Commission in 1981, the Office of Fair Trading in 1985, and the Competition Commission in 2000.[22]

By the turn of the century British retailers were turning to internationalization as a major route to future growth. By 2003, the leading British retailer, Tesco, had moved into twelve foreign markets in west Europe, eastern Europe, and East Asia. In internationalizing, however, British retailers were attempting to catch up with much larger US and European firms, most notably the US retailer Wal-mart with stores in eleven countries, the Dutch retailer Ahold with stores in twenty-seven countries, and the French retailer Carrefour with stores in thirty-two countries. Nevertheless, by 2003, Tesco was the only UK retailer listed in the top fifteen international retailers by sales.[23]

While this picture of the growth of big business has dominated academic work the continued prevalence of small-scale retailing organizations has continued, despite attempts to write its obituary.[24] The existence of low barriers to entry has made this a sector open to new entrepreneurial immigrant populations and those excluded from wider labour markets, whether bringing new forms of restaurant in the form of Indian cuisine to indigenous consumers or satisfying the demands of newer immigrant populations. Thus during the twentieth century retailing became a more complex industry with a range of distinct sectors. Within each sector a process of polarization between larger multiple retailers and smaller local niche markets emerged limiting competition.

In the development of large-scale retailing, however, evolutionary quantitative change gave way to fundamental qualitative changes with the development of new forms of inter-type competition. Retailers were able to develop new forms of market power and challenge manufacturers' price setting abilities. This shift was further aided with government's intervention from the banning of resale price maintenance from 1956 to the increasing role in regulation given to retailers by government in the 1990s.[25] The emergence of multiple retailers' market power derived from increased levels of asset specificity; as scale increased and new technology was adopted, so new economies of scope emerged. As the following section aims to show, explaining these changes requires recognition of the uniqueness of the retailing function.

RETAILING THEORY AND BUSINESS HISTORY

As highlighted above, because competition within retailing encompasses more than simply price, quality, or location, and includes form it has been recognized that retailing requires alternative theoretical developments to be developed within business history.[26] Yet retailing creates some difficulties for business historians in attempting to develop theories for its development and growth.

Business history has typically represented retailing within an eclectic theoretical framework, one in which elements from disparate and even conflicting theories are moulded to specific needs. Yet there remains a deep, yet rarely acknowledged, polarization between approaches which use either transaction cost or value chain analysis. In what follows I seek to highlight this divergence and outline a resolution that enables a consistent theory of retailing to emerge based upon retailing's role in value realization.[27]

Chandlerian business history rooted within a transaction cost approach, derived from Coase and Schumpeter, developed through Williamson and Casson, and extending into an evolutionary tradition of Langlois and Robertson rests on the neo-classical recognition of profit maximization, and productive and allocative type efficiencies.[28] While these theories are far from uniform and conflict over important issues, not least the role of entrepreneurship and the explanation for the development of hierarchical organization, they nevertheless share a series of common concerns relating to production cost structures and most importantly the use of information.

It is information, in the form of tacit or implicit knowledge, which provides the rationale for internalization and a theory of the firm within a Coasian framework. The heroic ability of Schumpeterian entrepreneurs, derived from this unique knowledge, finds expression through the innovative development of production orientated organizations. Alternatively, the less visible, but more extensive, market making opportunities of Casson-type entrepreneurs create investment opportunities within culturally based contexts of high or low trust market economies. Finally, Langlois and Robertson maintain that dynamic information costs provide a rationale for internalization. As Langlois and Robertson make clear:

Ultimately, the costs that lead to vertical integration are the (dynamic) transaction costs of persuading, negotiating with, coordinating among, and teaching outside suppliers in the face of economic change or innovation.[29]

While dynamic transaction costs provide encouragement to hierarchy over markets it is not the case that the transaction cost analysis deterministically maintains the superiority of hierarchy over markets for coordination. Indeed the classical school from Smith to Stigler would maintain that in the long-run markets predominate as tacit information, in the form of capabilities, becomes transformed into codified information in the form of routines, and thus become transferable between organizations.[30] Within retailing innovation is particularly liable to transfer due to the limited role of patenting or copyright within the industry, such that only branding provides some control over property rights of innovation. Thus, while innovatory firms make cost savings through internalization, in the long-run, market-based learning encroaches into the idiosyncratic firm specific capabilities.

The conclusion deriving from this literature, when applied to an industry such as retailing, is that it is production efficiency, technological change, and innovation which lead to relative price change. Thus, we have a theory of dynamic change but not one which provides predictions on the degree to which vertical integration or disintegration may take place.

Within the management literature a wider concept of value is used to evaluate firm development. Value, combining elements of price, consumer's desire, and satisfaction is used to move away from economist's narrow preoccupation with product homogeneity in markets. Value clearly has some similarities to economist's knowledge of utility in that it is through consumption that value is understood. Individual consumers value branded and unbranded goods differentially and base their decisions on purchasing on this knowledge. However, in contrast to utility value is considered to be constant for each good irrespective of how many are consumed by an individual whereas consumers from an economic perspective are considered to face declining marginal utility rates. Therefore value is closer to price in that it is the commodity itself which embodies the property of value rather than the consumer and, as with property rights, value may then be transferred through exchange.[31]

Commodities are said to gain value through the operations of the firm from production to marketing and sales. An understanding of value-adding is then used to examine the degree to which firms are successful in adding value in the production process. Porter's value-chain approach thus provides a core component of management literature on firm behaviour.[32]

Through the choice between markets and hierarchies firms are able to capture a greater or lesser degree of the value added. A clear similarity exists here in the conceptual understanding of transaction cost economics and value-chain analysis. The greater degree of ownership of value-adding activities within the firm ensures a greater degree of idiosyncratic capabilities emerge, allowing value to be created and retained within the hierarchy.

However, while a significant overlap exists within the two approaches there remains a fundamental problem in combining the two, namely value and price are demonstrably different. For example, changes in technology leading to relative price changes in computing has led to rapid declines in relative prices while simultaneously further value has been added to these commodities. Price and value are distinct and typically have a negative relationship.

In the case of retailing Johnson and Schols maintain that firms such as the furniture retailer IKEA are able to utilize changes in the supply chain to create competitive advantage. Through the adoption of modern styling, durable design, and immediate availability IKEA have been able to revolutionize the home and office furnishing markets. One of the key changes within IKEA's development was the shift of responsibility to consumers for specific manufacturing and retailing tasks. Consumers purchased flat-pack furniture from the store, transported it, and assembled it themselves. While we can recognize this as a cost minimization approach adopted by IKEA within a value-chain context it is suggested that removing these tasks from the firm's value chain permits still further value to be added. Thus, Johnson and Schols maintain that

IKEA... econourag(ed) customers to create value for themselves by taking on certain tasks traditionally done by the manufacturer and retailer, for example the assembly and delivery of products to their homes.[33]

The fundamental problem with this approach is the suggestion that consumption adds value. If value is not synonymous with price and measured in a monetary form it is just a short step to suggest that value can be continually added even after commodities are consumed. In so doing the concept of value and the suggestion that all activity, even consumption, adds value removes all analytical content to the term 'value'.

Nowhere is this conceptual problem more acute than in a study of retailer supply chains. Elsewhere I have argued that the division between manufacturer, wholesaler, and retailer has been neither static nor mono-directional over time.[34] Currently, particularly within food retailing, the movement is towards sub-contracting and disintegration. However, this is not on the basis of classical or simple bilateral contracting. As Foord et al. make clear, relationships are much more extensive, relational, and reflect a wider balance of power between retailer and manufacturer.[35] The crucial question posed by this movement towards disintegration is: what has happened to the understanding of value-adding in this process?

While it is theoretically consistent to suggest that retailers are minimizing transaction costs through discrete bilateral trading it cannot be readily maintained that retailers have added value through disintegration. Disintegration has either passed value-adding functions to suppliers or removed functions that add no value (or in extreme even destroyed value) from their own organization. In the case of value-adding functions being passed further down the supply chain we can readily invoke transaction cost analysis to suggest that specialization and idiosyncratic capabilities are developed by specialist manufacturing, warehousing, and logistics firms which retailers are able to recognize but not duplicate. Certainly, Casson would suggest that all economic activity leading to problem solving is productive activity:

In practice... problem identification and problem investigation are also productive – they add value and are, indeed, indispensable to the wealth-creation process.[36]

Indeed there is some *prima facie* evidence here for the movement towards disintegration and the linkages between food retailers and specialist warehousing firms. British food retailers lead the world in stock turnover and minimizing the time from manufacturing to customers' kitchens.[37] However, again, this value adding takes place against a background of falling relative prices bringing into question the mechanisms for realizing this value.

The management-focused literature on retailing in recognizing the role and importance of vertical integration, development of multi-national corporations and marketing, in certain respects sits very easily within the business history framework. However, its adoption of the value-chain as a mechanism for understanding the development of competitive advantage gives rise to a departure from a more economistic approach of transaction cost analysis.

In cases where value-neutral or even value-destroying functions have been passed down the supply chain a theoretical understanding of vertical disintegration is not so straightforward. We can readily recognize within transaction cost approaches retailers removing themselves from elements of the warehousing and distribution systems which they are unable to develop the capabilities to add value and suggest retailers have therefore retreated into their core competence of realizing the value of the commodities sold. This, however, poses the theoretical problem of how do the specialist disintegrated firms exist if they themselves do not create value? Under such circumstances transaction cost and value-chain analysis diverges in its understanding of retailing.

By reintroducing a distinction between value-creating and value-realization functions it is, however, possible to rethink the role of the supply chain. The actions associated with processing and manufacturing products need to be distinguished from the costs incurred in ensuring goods reach markets and their value realized though their sale to consumers. The retailing function should be understood not as creating value in commodities, but in ensuring the value generated in the production processes can be released, through consumption. Retailing is an intermediary market function required for value to be realized.

Retailing's growth, decisions on the use of hierarchies or markets then becomes one in which the transaction cost minimization strategies developed by retailers seek to maximize retailers' share of revenue derived from the sale of commodities whose value has been generated in previous areas of the production process. Retailers are thus intermediary forms of organization creating market environments between manufacturers and consumers. Within this view inter-type competition emerges precisely because retailers seek to develop innovatory methods of sales and marketing to consumers in order to maximize their share of the value previously generated. Developments in scale and scope, format, and location, and IKEA's removal of assembly functions are all examples whereby retailers attempt to maximize their share of the value embodied in the product at the expense of manufacturers as well as other retailers.

Much of the contemporary geography approach to retailing is rooted in such a framework.[38] Derived from Marx and classical economists who recognized the labour theory of value, contemporary writers including Thompson, Braverman, and Marglin have all focused on the importance of control, power, and the division of labour as determinants in the development of the firm and organizational structure.[39] In this approach profit maximization derives from a firm's ability to maximize labour output while simultaneously minimizing labour costs. Retailers act as increasingly powerful intermediary institutions in a process whereby labour's output can be sold to consumers. Retailers' market power thus derives from arbitrage opportunities between manufacturers and consumers.

Issues of power within relationships between labour and capital, as well as between organizations are of central importance to much of the recent retailing literature within the field of human geography.[40] From this viewpoint markets and hierarchies are understood as interchangeable structures for the maximization of economic power by the dominant organizations. Such an approach fits closely with the more sophisticated transaction cost approach favoured by Pitelis which recognizes the firm not as a black box structure delineated by ownership criteria but as a fluid coordinating organization delineated by a nexus of contracts.[41]

THE CASE OF TESCO

As the rest of this chapter now demonstrates an examination of the changing approach taken by Tesco in the late twentieth century appears to fit within such an approach. Tesco, established by Jack Cohen in London, was a store which from its beginning in 1931 specialized in the sale of dry packaged branded goods. Although being a publicly limited company, the Cohen family, particularly the founder Jack Cohen, dominated the running of the company as a highly centralized family firm. Family connections also played an important part in the management of stores, with Jack Cohen using family members as managers for Tesco stores.

Initially established through price cutting, Tesco rapidly adopted agreements over prices with manufacturers in order to maintain supplies in the 1930s.[42] However, with the challenge to manufacturer imposed Resale Price Maintenance and its banning by government in 1956 Tesco began to re-establish its reputation for 'pile it high: sell it cheap' food retailing. After 1964, following the announcement of the Resale Prices Act to reinforce the earlier 1956 Act and outlaw individual resale price agreements, Tesco further challenged price maintenance in non-food goods.[43] Like most other grocery retailers Tesco specialized in retailing, rather than wholesaling and manufacturing, and as a result did not develop extensive own-brand capabilities. A concentration upon own-brand groceries began to develop from the 1960s onwards but even as late as 1980 Tesco own-brand share as a proportion of turnover was only, at 22 per cent, in line with the industry average.[44]

Tesco adoption of public limited status by 1949 to gain access to capital markets ensured that Tesco led the adoption of self-service and supermarket retailing from the late 1950s.[45] Tesco was also thus able to gain the necessary capital for growth through take-overs such as Irwins and later Victor Value so that by 1990 Tesco had developed a large branch network extending to 371 stores.[46] Despite this growth Tesco were still largely a regional concentrated multiple retailer. It was not until the mid-1990s that a majority of its stores were to be found outside the south-east and south-west of England.[47]

Thus until the mid-1970s Tesco looked similar to other large multiple retailers. It was the changes brought about from the late 1970s onwards that saw Tesco emerge as the most significant food retailer in the UK by the mid-1990s. In 1977,

Tesco launched the first of a series of innovations within food retailing with its 'Check Out' campaign of deep price discounting in order to develop first mover advantages and catch up with the market leader Sainsbury. Heavy investment in increasingly large scale, high-street-based, supermarket retailing also occurred such that the average selling space in Tesco stores increased to 9,900 sq.ft by 1980 in contrast to the 2,000 sq.ft that supermarkets had been on their introduction into the UK in the 1960s.[48] This was followed by the building of superstores, of over 25,000 sq.ft, in locations on the edge of towns and further centralization of Tesco warehousing such that 95 per cent of goods, by value, were passing through centralized, retailer controlled distribution warehouses.[49] However, multiple retailers, who previously had undertaken warehousing and distribution operations, now found that the complexity of the retailing environment had increased to such an extent, with Tesco's product lines increasing to over 31,000 items, that they turned to partnerships with specialized independent logistics companies for the management of these processes. By 1992 an average of 51 per cent of stocks, by volume, were supplied to the four leading retailers, Sainsbury, Tesco, Dee (Gateway), and Argyll (Safeway) direct from third party's warehousing operations.[50] Together these changes ensured that Tesco was able to achieve stock turnover rates of 24 times per annum, the highest in the industry and raise their pre-tax margins between 1985 and 1990 from 3.7 to 5.9 per cent, exceeding that of Sainsbury the market leader.[51]

Innovative investment strategies, aimed at creating competitive advantage, were based upon turning high fixed cost into low unit costs while also raising adaptive firms' costs of adaptation, as a barrier to entry.[52] However, in a rapidly moving and innovative sector, such as retailing, the danger for the innovative firm is that fixed costs for adaptive firms will fall rather than rise as idiosyncratic knowledge becomes tacit and transferable and first mover firms' capabilities become contestable. Thus the discussion of the competitive environment at Tesco's 1995 Chairman's Conference began with the recognition that,

we have learnt from experience that we cannot afford to be complacent, superficially, all superstores are looking more similar, and unique differentiation is a prize that can only be won by *continually* being first. (original emphasis)[53]

Innovation continued into the 1990s with a greater focus upon the consumer. Tesco introduction of 'Clubcard' loyalty cards in 1995, despite the cost of half of 1 per cent of sales stemmed, from a recognition of the importance of the 'primary' shopper.[54] The primary shopper, spending over 50 per cent of their grocery budget in one store was now increasingly important for the success of the larger, less accessible, out-of-town superstores.[55] From 1985, Tesco recognized the need to focus upon primary shoppers and 'who they are'. They were already aware that primary shoppers represented 2.5 million (33%) of Tesco weekly shoppers and that they were responsible for 80 per cent of sales. Below this key group were the 1.6 million (22%) of secondary shoppers who were spending over 10 per cent of their weekly food budget within the store but only accounting for 16 per cent of turnover. Finally there were 3.4 million (45%) of tertiary shoppers accounting for 4 per cent of turnover.[56] Tesco, were able to use loyalty cards to collect unique computerized information on customers' purchasing patterns. In return customers collect points, based upon spending within stores, which can then be redeemed against future spending on a range of other goods and services. One recent estimate suggests there are some 25 million Clubcards in existence of which some 10 million are active.[57] Tesco produces separate magazines for its Clubcard members, based upon the categories students, young adults, families, older adults, and pensioners.[58] As Tesco's Director of Corporate Marketing acknowledged early on, the company had 'only scratched the surface' with the accumulated data.[59] Nevertheless they recognized the 'key importance [of the primary shopper] to the business' and the need to 'increase the percentage of primary shoppers'.[60] Finally, from the mid-1990s Tesco took a strategic decision to internationalize its retailing operations and, as described above, rapidly became one of the top fifteen retailers in the world.[61]

CONCLUSION

The importance of these innovations for our understanding of retailing is the recognition that Tesco's innovative strategy was based on the need to increase the firm's market power. Innovations, in the form of increased scale and developing information databases on customers from the Electronic Point of Sale (EPoS) technology provided the company with inter-type forms of competitive advantage over rival retailers and importantly increasing influence over suppliers. Vertical integration, and disintegration, within the supply chain altered as firms gained increased influence and control over the supply chain. In doing so margins could be increased, not through adding value but through the forcing of lower unit cost operations on firms higher up the supply chain. Tesco, and other retailers, could vertically disintegrate their supply chains and instead resort to contracting with external warehousing and logistics companies for warehousing and distribution functions, without any loss of control. Simultaneously innovation in inter-type hypermarket retailing formats reduced consumer's ability to substitute goods in a more monopolistic retailing environment. Thus Tesco could integrate forward towards consumers using direct marketing via their Clubcard information systems to increase their proportion of primary shoppers and hence raise margins.

Finally, it is necessary to recognize that none of these changes can be automatically assumed to have increased 'value'. Indeed, increased monopoly powers and the growth of consumer protest against continued expansion suggests perhaps the opposite. Tesco's operations may indeed be detrimental to consumer welfare, that is, value destroying, if their market power is sufficient to prevent competitive rivalry from emerging.

NOTES

1. D. Davis, *A History of Shopping*, Routledge, London, 1966; J. B. Jeffreys, *Retail Trading in Britain 1850–1950*, University Press, Cambridge, 1954; Mathias, *Retail Revolution*; Longman, London, 1967; M. Winstanley, *The Shopkeepers World 1830–1914*, Manchester University Press, 1983.
2. B. Williams, *Best Butter in the World*, Ebury Press, London, 1994.
3. L. Sparks, 'Food Retailing in Great Britain since 1960', in R. S. Tedlow and G. Jones, eds., *The Rise and Fall Of Mass Marketing*, Heinemann Professional Publishing.
4. C. Moir and J. Dawson, *Competition and Markets: Essays in Honour of Margaret Hall*, MacMillan, London, 1990; M. Winstanley, 'Concentration and Competition in the Retail Sector c.1800–1990', in M. W. Kirby and M. B. Rose, eds., *Business Enterprise in Modern Britain: From the Eighteenth to the Twentieth Century*, Routledge, London, 1994.
5. C. J. Morelli, 'Constructing a Balance Between Price and Non-Price Competition in British Food Retailing 1954–64', *Business History*, 40, 2, 1998: 45–61.
6. A. Godley and S. Fletcher, 'Foreign Entry into British Retailing, 1850–1994', *International Marketing Review*, 17, 2000: 392–400. N. Wrigley, 'The Globalisation of Retail Capital: Themes for Economic Geography', in G. L. Clark, M. P. Fieldman and M. S. Gertler eds., *Oxford Handbook of Economic Geography*, Oxford, OUP, 2000: 292–313.
7. J. Blythman, *Shopped: The Shocking Power of Supermarkets*, Fourth Estate, London, 2004; N. M. Coe, 'The Internationalisation/Globalisation of Retailing: Towards and Economic–Geographical Research Agenda', *Environment and Planning A* 36, 2004: 1571–94; A. G. Hallsworth and D. Evers, 'The Steady Advance of Wal-Mart Across Europe and Changing Government Attitudes Towards Planning and Competition', *Environment and Planning C*, 20, 2004: 297–309; C. Hines, *Localisation: A Global Manifesto*, Earthscan, London, 2000; A. Hughes, 'Corporate Strategy and the Management of Ethical Trade: The Case of UK Food and Clothing Retailers', *Environment and Planning A*, 37, 2005: 1145–63; C. J. Morelli, 'Explaining the Growth British Multiple Retailing during the Golden Age 1976–94', *Environment & Planning A*, 36, 4, 2004: 667–84; C. J. Morelli, 'Further Reflections on the Golden Age in British Multiple Retailing 1976–94: Capital Investment, Market Share and Retail Margins', *Environment & Planning A*, 39, 12, 2007: 2993–3007.
8. C. Dolan, and J. Humphrey, 'Changing Governance Patterns in Fresh Vegetables between Africa and the United Kingdom', *Environment and Planning A*, 36, 2004: 491–509.
9. A. Alexander, G. Shaw, and L. Curth, 'Promoting Retail Innovation: Knowledge Flows During the Emergence of Self-service and Supermarket Retailing in Britain', *Environment and Planning A*, 37, 2005: 805–21.
10. G. Akehurst and N. Alexander, eds., *The Internationalisation of Retailing*, Frank Cass, London, 1995: 43.
11. G. Shaw, A. Alexander, J. Benson, and D. Hodson, 'The Evolving Culture of Retailer Regulation and the Failure of the 'Balfour Bill' in Inter-war Britain', *Environment and Planning A*, 32, 2000: 1977–89.
12. J. B. Jeffreys, *Retail Trading*, 23–5.
13. G. Shaw, 'The Evolution of Large-scale Retailing in Britain', in J. Benson and G. Shaw, eds., *The Evolution of Retail Systems, c.1800–1914*, University Press, Leicester, 1992: 134–65.

14. J. Birchall, *Co-Op: The People's Business*, MUP, Manchester, 1994; J. B. Jeffreys, *Retail Trading*: table 7.
15. Ibid.: 137.
16. C. Fulop, *Competition for Consumers: A Study in the Changing Channels of Distribution*, IEA, London, 1964.
17. B. S. Yamey, *Resale Price Maintenance*, Weidenfeld and Nicolson, London, 1966.
18. C. Fulop, *Competition*: 72.
19. C. J. Morelli, 'Constructing a Balance Between Price and Non-Price Competition in British Food Retailing 1954–64', *Business History*, 40, 2, 1998: 45–61.
20. S. Pollard, *The Development of the British Economy, 1914–80*, 3rd edition, Edward Arnold, London, 1983: table 7.32.
21. N. Wrigley, 'Is the "Golden Age" of British Grocery Retailing at a Watershed?' *Environment and Planning A*, 23, 1991: 1545–60.
22. P. Langston, G. P. Clarke, and D. B. Clarke, 'Retail Saturation: The Debate in the Mid-1990s' *Environment and Planning A*, 30, 1998: 49–66.
23. N. M. Coe and Y. S. Lee, 'The Strategic Localization of Transnational Retailers: The Case of Samsung-Tesco in South Korea', *Economic Geography*, 82, 1, 2006: 61–88.
24. H. Raven and T. Lang, *Off Our trolleys? Food Retailing and the Hypermarket Economy*, Institute for Public Policy Research, London, 1995.
25. T. Marsden, and N. Wrigley, 'Regulation, Retailing and Consumption', *Environment and Planning A*, 27, 1995: 1899–1912.
26. G. Akehurst, and N. Alexander, eds., *Retail Structure*, Frank Cass, London, 1996. J. Benson, *The Rise of Consumer Society in Britain 1880–1980*, Longman, London, 1994.
27. C. Doel, 'Market Development and Organizational Change: The Case of the Food Industry', N. Wrigley and M. Rowe, eds., *Retailing, Consumption and Capital: Towards a New retail Geography*, Longman, Essex, 1996: 48–67.
28. A. D. Chandler, *Scale & Scope: The Dynamics Industrial Capitalism*, Harvard University Press, Cambridge, MA, 1990. R. H. Coase, 'The Nature of the Firm', *Economica*, 4, 1937. J. A. Schumpeter, *Capitalism, Socialism and Democracy*, Unwin Allen, London, 1965. O. E. Williamson, *Economic Organisation, Firms, Markets and Policy Control*, Brighton, 1986, M. Casson, 'Information and Economic Organisation', *Reading University Discussion Papers In Economics*, No. 317, 1995. M. Casson, *Enterprise and Competitiveness: A Systems View of International Business*, OUP, Oxford, 1990. R. Langlois and P. L. Robertson, *Firms, Markets and Economic Change: A Dynamic Theory of Business Institutions*, Routledge, London, 1995.
29. Langlois and Robertson, *Firms*: 37.
30. A. Smith, *The Wealth of Nations*, Penguin, London, 1986; G. J. Stigler, *The Organisation of Industry*, Richard Irwin, Illinois, 1968.
31. D. Adcock, R. Bradfield, A. Halborg, and C. Ross, *Marketing Principles and Practice*, 3rd edition, Financial Times Management, London, 1998: 218.
32. M. E. Porter, *Competitive Advantage: Creating and Sustaining Superior Performance*, Free Press, New York, 1985.
33. G. Johnson, and K. Scholes. *Exploring Corporate Strategy: Texts and Cases*, 5th edition, Prentice Hall, London, 1999: 6.
34. C. J. Morelli, 'Information Costs and Information Asymmetry in British Food Retailing', *Service Industries Journal*, 19, 3, 1999: 175–86.

35. J. Foord, S. Bowlby, and C. Tillsley 'The Changing Place of Retailer–Supplier Relations in British Food Retailing', in N. Wrigley and M. Lowe, eds., *Retailing, Consumption and Capital*, 1996: table 4.1.

36. M. Casson, *Enterprise and Competitiveness: A Systems View of International Business*, OUP, Oxford, 1990: 53.

37. J. Fernie, 'International Comparisons of Supply Chain Management in Grocery Retailing', in G. Akehurst and N. Alexander, eds., *The Internationalisation of Retailing*, Frank Cass, London, 1995.

38. N. Wrigley, M. Lowe, eds., *Retailing, Consumption and Capital*, 1996; A. G. Hallsworth, 'Rethinking Retail Theory: Circuits of Power as an Integrative Paradigm', *Geographical Analysis* 29, 1997, 329–38.

39. K. Marx, *Capital: A Critique of Political Economy*, vol. I, Lawrence & Wishart, London, 1972. E. P. Thompson, *The Making of the English Working Class*, Penguin, Harmondsworth, 1991. H. Braverman, 'Labor and Monopoly Capital: The Degradation of Work in the Twentieth Century', Monthly Review Press, New York, 1974. S. A. Marglin, 'What Do Bosses Do? The Origins and Functions of Hierarchy in Capitalist Production', *Radical Review of Political Economics*, 6, 2, 1974.

40. N. Wrigley, M. Lowe, eds., *Retailing, Consumption and Capital*, 1996; A. G. Hallsworth, 'Rethinking Retail Theory'.

41. C. N. Pitelis, *Market and Non-market Hierarchies: Theory of Institutional Failure*, Blackwell, Oxford, 1993.

42. D. Powell, *Counter Revolution: The Tesco Story*, Grafton, London, 1991: 31–41.

43. M. Corina, *Pile it High: Sell it Cheap*, 1972: 30–1. J. F. Pickering, *Resale Price Maintenance in Practice*, George Allen & Unwin, London, 1966.

44. Euromonitor, *The Own Brands Report*, 1986: table 5.3, p. 28. Tesco Archive, A2.4, 'Tesco in the Market Place: A Top Line Survey', Aug. 1990: 5.

45. M. Corina, *Pile it High: Sell it Cheap: The Authorised Biography of Sir John Cohen, Founder of Tesco*, Weidenfeld and Nicolson, London, 1972: 127. C. J. Morelli, 'Constructing a Balance': 45–61.

46. M. Corina, *Pile it High*, 1972. Simms, A., *Tescopoly: How One Shop Came Out on Top and Why it Matters*, Constable, London, 2007: 88. Tesco Archive, A2.4, 'Tesco in the Market Place', 1990. B. Williams, *Best Butter*, 1994: 219.

47. Institute of Grocery Distribution, 'Tesco Plc', *Account Management Series*, Letchmore Heath, 1996: 61–2.

48. C. Gardner, and J. Sheppard, *Consuming Passions*, Unwin Hyman, London, 1989: 177.

49. Institute of Grocery Distribution, *Retail Distribution*, Letchmore Heath, 1996: 14.

50. D. Carter, *Retailer Distribution Profiles*, IGD, Letchmore Heath, 1986. Institute of Grocery Distribution, *Retail Distribution*, 1996: 6. A. McKinnon, 'The Distribution Systems of Supermarket Chains', in G. Akehurst and N. Alexander, eds., *Retail Structure*, Frank Cass, London, 1996.

51. Institute of Grocery Distribution, *Food Retailing*, Letchmore Heath, 1991. Institute of Retail Studies, *Distributive Trades Profile 1991: A Statistical Digest*, Stirling, 1992: table 54. J. Kay, *Foundations of Corporate Success*, Oxford University Press, Oxford, 1993: table 2.1,

52. W. Lazonick, *Business Organisation and the Myth of the Market Economy*, Cambridge, MA, 1991: 95–101.

53. Tesco Archive, G13.10, 'The Competitive Environment', Chairman's Conference, 20 Nov. 1995: 1.

54. Institute of Grocery Distribution, Tesco Plc, 1996: 6.

55. Tesco Archive, A.201, No. DK/568, 'The Consumer's View of Tesco', Jun. 1988: section 3.3.
56. Tesco Archive, B.1.1, 'A Qualitative Assessment of Customer Service in Tesco Super-markets', Nov. 1985. Tesco Archive, A.2.4, No. JR.382, 'An Introduction to Tesco and its Performance in the Marketplace', Feb. 1989: 3.
57. A. Simms, *Tescopoly*, 2007: 96.
58. *Retail Week*, 1996: 3.
59. Institute of Grocery Distribution, 'Tesco Plc', 1996: 94.
60. Tesco Archive, A.2.4, No. JR.382, 'An Introduction to Tesco and its Performance in the Marketplace', Feb. 1989: conclusion.
61. N.M. Coe, and Y.S. Lee, 'The Strategic Localization of Transnational Retailers', 2006: 61–88.

15

Predicting, Providing, Sustaining, Integrating?

British Transport Policy since 1945

Mike Anson and Gerald Crompton

Transport services, involving both goods and people, have been indisputably important, if not critical, to the performance of the UK economy since 1945. This chapter deals with inland surface transport – roads, railways, and inland waterways – for both passengers and freight. It examines some of the main changes in the provision of these services since the Transport Act of 1947. This covers issues of both ownership and management, with particular emphasis on the impact of public policy. Even in periods when public ownership has been in retreat, government has been continuously involved, whether directly or indirectly, through legislation, planning, regulation, or investment decisions. After identifying some key statistics, the chapter considers the context and consequences of nationalization in the early post-war period. It then outlines the main trends in infrastructure provision and operation of railways and road haulage, and, more briefly, buses and waterways. After an assessment of the causes and effects of privatization, the conclusion draws out some key public policy issues.

TRANSPORT TRENDS

Since the early 1950s Britain has seen a tremendous increase in the movement of both people and goods. Passenger transport has grown from 218 billion passenger kilometres to 781 billion passenger kilometres in the early twenty-first century. Beneath these totals are some significant modal shifts. Road transport has remained dominant, increasing its share from 82 to 94 per cent, while rail travel fell from 18 to 6 per cent. Important shifts have occurred within road transport: at 677 billion passenger kilometres cars now account for 87 per cent of the total, whereas fifty years earlier the figure was 27 per cent. On the other hand, bus and coach use has more than halved in terms of passenger kilometres, and its share has fallen from 42 to 6 per cent. Motor and pedal cycle use has also declined dramatically. Data for passenger journeys made by public transport tell a similar story: bus use falling from more than sixteen billion in 1950 to 4.5 billion five decades later. More recently journeys using rail, London Underground, and other urban light rail systems have shown some growth.

Goods moved in the UK in 1953 totalled eighty-nine billion tonne kilometres. This had doubled by 1983, and had reached 252 billion tonne kilometres by 2003. Again there have been modal shifts. Rail freight has declined from thirty-seven to nineteen billion tonne kilometres, while at the same time road haulage increased from thirty-two to 162 billion tonne kilometres. In 1953, 42 per cent of freight was carried by rail, 36 by road: in 2003 the shares were 8 per cent and 64 per cent, respectively. The remaining domestic freight has been moved by pipeline or water. In the latter case estuarial and coastal shipping remains significant.[1]

To some extent, the above trends are also mirrored in other data, most notably the fact that the number of private cars has increased from two million to twenty-five million. Other figures are less clear. Despite the fall in public road passenger transport, the total number of buses and coaches has been surprisingly stable, at something over 70,000 during the entire period. Goods vehicles grew from around 450,000 to a peak of 593,000 in 1967, thereafter falling back to 425,000. This reflects more productive use, and the increase in permitted lorry weights. Transport undertakings have often been large employers. When the British Transport Commission was established it had a workforce of 873,000, with 649,000 of these on the railways. Current figures show over one million people are currently employed in the transport sector: 54,000 in the railway industry, and over 450,000 in other land transport. The total also includes more than 300,000 transport related jobs such as handling and storage, and 200,000 in airlines and travel operators.[2]

COMMANDING HEIGHTS

It was World War II and the Labour election victory of 1945 which brought much of land transport, and indeed a substantial part of the economy, into public ownership. A number of related factors, virtually all of which were applicable to the railways, explained the selection of industries for nationalization. They were sectors with potential for gains through economies of scale and the integration of operations on a national basis. Often, like railways, existing private operators were already cartelized or heavily regulated or in local authority ownership. Private capital was usually not attracted to these industries, or there was a perceived danger of private monopoly. In the case of the railways, after prolonged under-investment and low profitability in the inter-war years, the need for modernization was so pressing as to justify description of the 1947 Transport Act as 'a national rescue act'.[3] A further motive for nationalization was the belief that utilities providing essential services to other sectors of the economy, both private firms and individual consumers, had a duty to supply them on a cheap, efficient and universal basis. Nationalized transport was therefore explicitly expected to be 'efficient', 'adequate', and 'properly integrated'.[4]

In several important respects transport nationalization was implemented in forms which had not been anticipated by its supporters. It had been assumed, first, that the purpose of public ownership was to integrate transport as a whole and, second, that the public sector would be used as a major planning instrument in shaping the development of the economy. The second assumption was soon dropped as the Attlee government retreated from ambitions of either constructing a socialist economic system, or even of devising a coherent industrial policy under capitalism. It relied instead for planning purposes on short-term physical controls and Keynesian budgetary methods, and conceded considerable autonomy to the public corporations in charge of each nationalized industry. The first assumption was undermined by the decision to exclude most of road haulage from the scope of nationalization and not to impose mileage limits on the 'C' licences (own account haulage). Only about 34,000 road vehicles were acquired by the state in 1948, of which 14,000 came from the railway companies. At least 100,000 A and B licensed vehicles remained in private ownership.[5]

A major unresolved ambiguity was that the nationalized industries were expected not to act as profit-maximizers, but nevertheless to combine commercial efficiency with public service. This was not identified as a significant contradiction at the time, but the later emergence of persistent deficits posed the issue of which of the two basic objectives ought to be given the higher priority. Official guidance was occasionally formalized, as in the White Papers of 1961 and 1967, which supplied cost-benefit criteria for investment projects and encouraged greater use of marginal cost pricing.[6] It is, however, surprising that, despite the government's clear entitlement to give 'directions of a general character', relatively little advice seems to have been offered by ministers on long-term goals and strategic matters. On the other hand, intervention flourished at lower and more ad hoc levels, especially in relation to proposed price increases, cuts in service, or possible industrial disputes. The financial problems of the railways were repeatedly aggravated by the propensity of government to scale down or delay price increases recommended by management.

A third problem arising at the end of the war was how to find an appropriate organizational structure. The public corporation model did not provide a blueprint, and plans had to be produced hastily in 1947. The British Transport Commission (BTC) was set up as a single body in charge of all state-owned railways, road transport, docks and inland waterways. The Railway Executive (RE) was one of five subordinate authorities established under the BTC. It had a functional, vertical managerial structure, and was given the onerous task of unifying the railway network, where it had to cope with some still strong regional identities. Relations between the BTC and the RE were often strained. One judgement on the first five years is that 'the nationalization period got off on the wrong organizational foot, and the structure erected in 1947 was the first of several defective solutions'.[7] The Conservatives' Transport Act of 1953 passed judgement on the 1947 'solution' by removing the Railway Executive, partly denationalizing the Road Haulage Executive and leaving the BTC with the double brief of running the railways and overseeing all nationalized transport. The implementation of the rather imprecise 1953 Act took eighteen months and resulted by 1955 in what has been described as 'a great semi-military bureaucratic edifice', confusingly lacking a clear chain of command, 'cumbersome and rather remote', and 'ill-conceived' in relation to its railway functions.[8] Apart from this dubious organizational restructuring, the 1953 Act introduced a number of specific policy changes, such as reducing the BTC's licensing powers and abolishing the 25-mile limit on private hauliers. It did nevertheless mark the formal abandonment of some of the key perspectives of post-war nationalization, replacing regulated monopoly with 'a mixed system of active competition and partial monopoly'.[9]

THEY TRIED TO RUN A RAILWAY

During most of the 1950s, the revival of the railways was still seen as central to national transport problems. Optimism persisted that with the right equipment, traffic would return and the profitability of the system could be restored. These assumptions were tested in the Modernisation Plan of 1955, an ambitious scheme to invest £1.24 billion over fifteen years.[10] It was more a statement of intent than a precise plan, and the details had been drawn up in some haste. The 'plan' was riddled with errors and massive excesses in several directions, particularly the huge marshalling yards and variety of diesel prototypes. It 'used a scattergun approach to fire investment at all parts of the railway with little sense of overall objectives or priorities'.[11] Accordingly, the vast expenditure yielded results which were disappointing in both technical and financial terms.[12] The expectation of breaking-even on the operating account by the early 1960s was no doubt illusory from the start, but failure of such scale and transparency was nevertheless damaging to the industry. This episode represented probably the worst failing by management during the whole period of nationalization. It certainly helped the Treasury, who did not need much assistance in this respect, to acquire 'almost a pathological dislike of large public sector projects'.[13]

Mounting losses in 1960–2 lifted the annual deficit to £100 million. The crisis generated significant changes in both policy and structure. The 1962 Transport Act wrote down railway debt and replaced the BTC with five autonomous boards, including the British Railways Board (BRB). The BRB's first chairman was Dr Richard Beeching, earlier recruited from ICI at the unprecedented salary of £24,000. Beeching, though keen to present himself as a railway champion, became intimately associated with the principle of solving the financial problem through systemic cuts. *The Reshaping of Britain's Railways*, published in 1963, recommended drastic surgery on the more marginal parts of the network, in the hope of restoring the remaining core to financial health.[14] Over 5,000 miles of track and 2,000 stations were intended for closure, and less than half of the surviving mileage was earmarked for development. The simple idea was to concentrate resources on key routes, encouraging 'dense flows of well-loaded through trains'. In this way the railways could focus on objectives 'for which they offer the best available means' and would 'cease to do things for which they are ill-suited'.[15] It rested on a fragile statistical base, however, and was arguably excessively concerned with improving the productivity of capital rather than of labour.[16] Although the strategy was implemented, in a diluted form, over the rest of the decade, it proved unsuccessful in its principal aim of restoring profitability. The accumulated losses of £775 million for the ten years after the report were higher than the £560 million for the previous fourteen. Nevertheless, the concept of the 'commercial railway' continued to exert a negative influence long after Beeching's resignation in 1965. Though some specific closures, for instance the Great Central route, later came to be regretted, there was an overwhelming case for trimming the network. But there was a damaging tendency through the 1960s and into the 1970s to pursue a chimera of financial stabilization via further pruning, even though it was unlikely that additional closures could ever produce sufficient savings to eliminate the overall deficit. This illusion proved a distraction from the need to control total costs and to promote greater efficiency through higher productivity, which often required targeted investment. Treasury resistance to investment proposals made this look impossibly difficult and encouraged persistence with network reduction. Net disinvestment on a considerable scale occurred between 1963 and 1973, with a trough in 1969.[17] Successive chairmen, especially Peter Parker, argued in vain for major investment and by the late 1970s the Board was highlighting the problem in its annual reports, most famously in the phrase the 'crumbling edge of quality'.[18] For a time there appeared to be consensus on the desirability of maintaining a network of around 11,500 miles, but the severe economic depression of the early 1980s instigated a new crisis. As losses reached £1 billion, the Serpell Committee produced a resolutely negative report, recommending reductions in current expenditure and a range of options for cutting the network. Option A, which became the best known, would have limited route mileage to little more than 1,000.[19] This archaic reversion to an extreme form of the commercial railway concept generated a powerful backlash from public opinion.

Against this background, the Board had embarked on a major organizational change, sector management. This saw the creation, in 1982, of five separate businesses: Inter-City, London and South East, and Provincial on the passenger side; Railfreight; and Parcels. The concept facilitated a more business-led approach, gave sector directors both greater entrepreneurial freedom and bottom-line responsibility, and diminished the autonomy of the once-powerful regions. This all took time, and the full flowering occurred under the banner of Organising for Quality (OfQ) in 1992.[20] By then a combination of Treasury parsimony, effective decentralized management, and clearer objectives had turned British Rail into a lean organization, employing only 115,000 by 1993. During this period its productivity performance, in terms of train-kilometres run per member of staff, was comfortably ahead of the European average. Arguably it was also the most financially successful operator, receiving the lowest ratio of subsidy. Though such figures were undoubtedly impressive in purely business terms, there was still cause for some dissatisfaction: British Rail's fares were higher and investment levels were lower than those found on other European railways.[21]

One positive post-Beeching development was the concept of the 'social railway'. Under a complex formula, special grants were made for loss-making routes considered necessary on public service grounds. In 1969, 302 lines and services received grants amounting to £361 million. The 1974 Railway Act replaced the route-specific subsidies with a block grant system, the Public Service Obligation (PSO). This was influenced by the BRB's arguments for a 'necessary', as opposed to a merely 'viable' railway. The PSO increased rapidly in the second half of the 1970s, peaking at around £1.3 billion, nearly half of passenger revenues, in 1982. Thereafter, economic recovery, and the benefits of sector management, allowed the PSO to fall to a low point of only £495 million in 1989/90. Even the final grant of £930 million in 1993/4, when the economic climate was again unfavourable, was lower than subsequent support payments made to the privatized railway.

A key aspect of BRB's case for investment in the network was railway electrification. On this, the Modernisation Plan had been suitably ambitious, with projected expenditure of £135 million.[22] Over 780 route miles were added between 1959 and 1965: the electrified proportion of the network reached 12 per cent by 1965 and 21 per cent by the mid-1970s. Pressure for a major expansion of electrification received additional impetus from the oil price shocks of the 1970s. A joint BRB and Department for Transport (DfT) document proposed in 1981 that substantial electrification would be financially viable, particularly if the largest schemes were pursued. The Government responded by asking for a ten-year plan for electrification, fully costed on a line-by-line basis.[23] The only big electrification project to be approved was the East Coast main line, which was completed by 1991. London to Wales and the West Country, the Midland Mainline, and others remained unfulfilled and large-scale electrification has stayed firmly off the agenda.[24]

If it was difficult to modernize existing routes, dedicated high-speed passenger lines, on the French TGV model, were an even remoter prospect. The one exception to this was the Channel Tunnel Rail Link (CTRL). After the abandonment of an earlier project in the 1970s, the Tunnel itself was opened in 1994 as a joint Anglo-French venture. The Thatcher Government had determined that the Channel crossing should be funded entirely by the private sector. Yet through the provision of associated road and rail infrastructure the state contributed significant amounts: Gourvish estimates £3 billion prior to the opening of the Tunnel, and at least a further £4 billion spent or committed since then.[25] The rail link was important to the success of the Tunnel, although it proved difficult to find an acceptable route through Kent and Sussex. Plans were not finalized until January 1994, only a matter of months before the Tunnel was officially opened.[26] The official opening of the full CTRL route between St Pancras and the

Tunnel finally took place in November 2007. In the meantime the finances of both the Eurostar train service and of Eurotunnel remained precarious, despite indirect public sector assistance.

THE ROAD TO NOWHERE?

In 1958, Prime Minister Harold Macmillan opened the first stretch of motorway in Britain, the eight-mile long Preston bypass. The following year the first section of the M1 Leeds-London motorway was completed, at a cost of over £28 million, just before the autumn general election. Before these symbolic inceptions of the motorway age, progress in modernizing Britain's roads had been slow, but far more ambitious thinking was now the order of the day. In 1960 the Minister of Transport, Ernest Marples, introduced his ten year 'Master Plan' including a further 800 miles of motorway and total expenditure of £1.5 billion. Two years later the commitment to 1,000 miles of motorway was added, and this was delivered by 1972, with more new roads promised.[27] In 1950 there were nearly four million licensed vehicles in use: Marples justified his 1960 plans on the basis that there were then 8.5 million vehicles on the roads, and by 1975 there would be sixteen million.[28] Environment Minister Peter Walker employed a similar argument in 1971, pointing out that the number of vehicles was expected to rise from fifteen million to twenty-two million in 1980. At this time it appeared self-evident that the main transport problem was that more cars and lorries were entering an inadequate road system and that the principal solution was an accelerated programme of trunk-road construction. 'Predict and provide' seemed a logical strategy. Also important was Colin Buchanan's 1963 report *Traffic in Towns*. This had a seminal impact on the nature of road planning in urban areas, but also provided further support for those who argued that continuing traffic growth had to be accepted.[29] The decline in the railways' share of the transport market merely supplied another argument in favour of this policy orientation.

The mid-1950s saw the development of a close relationship between successive transport ministers and the roads lobby. This had not always been the case. The main coordinating organization, the British Roads Federation, had been at work since 1932. Its constituents and allies at various times included the AA (Automobile Association) and RAC (Royal Automobile Club), the Society of Motor Manufacturers and Traders, and latterly the Road Haulage Association, the Freight Transport Association, and the major oil and civil engineering companies.[30] These bodies gained in weight as the number of their members, employees and customers grew, and by the mid-1950s the poor state of British transport had opened up unprecedented opportunities for them. Harold Watkinson, minister between 1955 and 1959, took a significant role as 'the unofficial leader of the roads advocacy coalition'.[31] He understood that there were 'votes in roads'. Watkinson presided over a doubling of government roads expenditure, dismissed the principle of tolls, and took an unusually close interest in the details of policy implementation. In addition, he strengthened the roads division within the Ministry, ensuring that there was continuing institutional support for the new priorities.[32] There was never much doubt about the sympathies of his successor. Marples was a major shareholder in the family civil engineering firm Marples Ridgeway, which was awarded public contracts during his tenure of office.

One important factor in the strong post-war expansion of road haulage was an increase in the size, capacity, and speed of commercial vehicles. Technological advances facilitated this, but there was also intense lobbying to have legal limits relaxed. This was more easily accomplished because a generally sympathetic ministry merely had to justify a more permissive official attitude without needing to raise public expenditure. Maximum lorry weights were increased in 1955, from twenty to twenty-four tonnes, and the speed limit was raised to thirty mph in 1957, when the British Road Federation's celebration dinner featured Watkinson as guest of honour. Further advances came quickly: thirty-two tonnes was sanctioned in 1964, with extensions to permitted width and length; in 1966 the speed limit went up to forty mph; maximum length was raised in 1968 to fifteen metres to allow the carriage of the largest international containers. In 1973 it was decided to leave the thirty-two tonne maximum unchanged for articulated lorries but to allow an extra two tonnes for smaller lorries with three or four axles. From this point onwards additional pressure for higher weights came from the EEC (European Economic Community) which favoured standardization on forty tonnes. Environmental campaigners then managed to delay the inevitable until 1982 when thirty-eight tonnes was permitted, if the weight was spread over five axles. A year later 'an administrative sleight of hand' effectively raised the weight to forty tonnes.[33] A forty-four tonne standard was adopted in 2001, with the formal justification that this was in harmony with the limit for rail freight wagons.

In the 1970s the road-building programme suffered a loss of momentum on several occasions. The economic circumstances were not propitious with the first oil crisis and accelerating inflation. Future traffic forecasts looked less secure and there was pressure on public spending. Both Conservative and Labour governments announced standstills or cuts in roads expenditure. Apart from economic troubles, there was the emergence of an 'environmental advocacy coalition' meaning that for the first time the roads lobby faced an organized, though less well-funded, opposition.[34] This included new bodies such as *Friends of the Earth, Transport 2000*, and older organizations like the *Civic Trust* and the *Council for the Protection of Rural England*. There was resistance to controversial proposals, for instance, the 'motorway box' scheme for London, which threatened the demolition of 20,000 houses, and had to be abandoned in 1972. Disruptions to public enquiries into roads schemes, led by individual campaigners such as John Tyme, gained publicity. The net effect was that environmental, or 'green' issues, were regularly raised in the context of road building and the case for public transport received a boost. However, following the Conservative election victory of 1979, the roads lobby was able to re-establish its influence. Margaret Thatcher was notoriously antipathetic to public transport, especially railways, and environmental considerations received little support from successive transport ministers, or the departmental permanent secretary. The real price of petrol resumed a downward trend, and from 1983 the economy entered a sustained recovery. Thus by 1988 there were predictions of an alarming increase in traffic of between 83 and 142 per cent by 2025.[35] All this culminated in the 1989 White Paper *Roads for Prosperity* which called for a 'step change' in the size of the roads programme in order to relieve inter-urban congestion, and proposed a doubling of the trunk roads programme.

The policy climate then changed again quite rapidly, and to such an extent that many soon perceived road building to be more of a problem than a solution. Early influences included the Earth Summit in Rio de Janeiro in 1992, which popularized the theme of 'sustainable development'. The acceptance of explicit obligations to reduce the level of carbon emissions was important in the adoption, in 1993, of a strategy for annual 5 per cent real term increases in fuel duty. Two significant documents appeared in 1994: the Houghton report, *Transport and the Environment*, recommended, inter alia, that expenditure on trunk roads should be reduced to about half its current rate and that fuel duty should be raised sufficiently to double the price of petrol within ten years; the Standing Advisory Committee on Trunk Road Assessment produced evidence that new roads designed to relieve congestion were themselves generating additional traffic. This 'induced traffic' factor had been omitted in the past from cost–benefit studies, and its inclusion in the future was likely to inflict further damage to the 'predict and provide' approach.[36] At the end of 1995 many road schemes were scrapped, with spending planned to fall from over £2 billion to £1.41 billion by 1998–9. The 1997 Labour administration appeared to set the seal on these trends by promising to improve maintenance on existing roads before building new ones, giving approval in principle for road pricing, and establishing a Commission for Integrated Transport.[37]

In 2000, a ten-year plan, *Transport 2010*, envisaged that £180 billion would be shared roughly equally among rail, road, and public transport. This apparent balance depended on highly optimistic assumptions about the ability of the railways to attract private investment, whereas the funding for roads was to be sourced almost entirely from the public sector. The plan partly restored earlier cuts in road building, and similar steps were taken in subsequent years. In 2004, *The Future of Transport* White Paper boasted of twenty major road schemes completed since 2002 and contained widening plans for two motorways. Moreover, enthusiasm for road pricing within the DfT remained fixed in a very long-term perspective, and a charging scheme for lorries, which had been expected to start the process, was postponed indefinitely. The only advance in this direction was the successful introduction in 2003, without much encouragement from central government, of the congestion charge on traffic in London, whose mayor was prepared to take the necessary political risk.

A 2006 study has concluded that 'the most striking feature of New Labour's transport policy since 2000 has been its growing resemblance to the Conservative policies of the 1980s and 1990s.[38] More recently still, this resemblance has grown. By July 2007 a number of expensive road schemes were either underway or under consideration, and the White Paper, *Delivering the Sustainable Railway,* announced a new policy of reducing subsidy and raising fares until passengers carried 75 per cent of the total burden, a rise from £5 billion a year in 2007 to £9 billion by 2014. There are only a few proposals for major schemes to increase capacity, and no commitments to new high-speed lines or greater electrification.[39] The downward revision of earlier intentions for higher petrol tax has completed a formidable set of factors discouraging a change in the balance in favour of rail. After the roads lobby had apparently been defeated in the debates of the 1990s, few, if any, believed there were still votes in roads. Since then renewed pressure from vehicle numbers, from congestion, and from towns wanting by-passes, has reasserted the economic case for further construction. Meanwhile the long-term cost of motoring has continued to be stable or declining. It has been realized that greater priority for public transport is incapable, at least in the short run, of suppressing this demand.

DRIVEN BY DOGMA

Privatization became increasingly a matter of fact rather than of debate in the course of the 1980s. In the case of transport, the first sell-off was the National Freight Corporation, which was proposed in 1979 and accomplished in the form of an employee buy-out in 1982. Associated British Ports followed in 1983, and then a number of the subsidiary railway businesses such as hotels, ferries, station catering, and railway workshops.

The bus sector was affected by both sale and deregulation. Since the 1968 Transport Act, bus services had been largely under public control. The Act created self-managing Public Transport Authorities in four (later increased to six) metropolitan areas, with the ability to subsidize and specify fare structures, and integrate bus, and train, services. Most other buses were run either by municipal operators, or the publicly owned National Bus Company (NBC). The NBC was also a creation of the 1968 Act, being formed initially from ninety-three companies.[40] In 1985 legislation authorized the privatization of NBC, which was implemented between 1986 and 1988, realizing £323 million for a total of seventy-two subsidiaries. Road service licensing was removed outside London, and local authorities were expected to put out tenders for subsidized services. All this met with little resistance. The bus industry had few influential supporters and had come to be seen as 'transport providers for those too poor to own a car'.[41] Transport secretary Nicholas Ridley justified the 1985 act by claiming that 'its purpose was to halt the decline that [had] affected the bus industry for more than twenty years' and that 'the key to increasing patronage' was competition. It did nothing to arrest the decline in bus usage and passenger journeys fell from five billion in 1985–6 to 3.8 billion in 1993–4. Deregulation did achieve a striking decline in operating costs, which fell between 1983 and 1993 by 87 per cent in the former metropolitan counties, and 58 per cent in the shire counties. This was based on cuts in both the numbers and the pay of employees. Over the same period fares rose: by an average of 10 per cent above retail prices in the shires, and 33 per cent in metropolitan areas.[42] Subsidy reductions were also achieved. After several years of stability, there was a modest increase in bus use, to 4.1 billion journeys by 2005–6.[43] This rise was, however, entirely accounted for by London where bus patronage grew by 59 per cent, to 1.81 billion, in the twenty years after 1985–6, mostly after 1993.[44] Although London Buses Limited was privatized in 1993, this was, crucially, not accompanied by deregulation and London Transport retained control of services and fares.

The increase in competition promised by privatization was short-lived, as the bus industry rapidly consolidated. By 1996 the three largest companies controlled 54 per cent of the market, with the next three taking a further 20 per cent.[45] Resale and merger often led to bus executives realising large financial gains, which implied that the original sell-off had been under-priced. This anticipated what happened in more spectacular fashion with the railway rolling stock companies. The newly dominant companies in the bus industry, such as Stagecoach, First Group, and Go Ahead, later won train operating franchises, having demonstrated their efficiency in reducing labour and other costs in a declining sector.

The railways eventually became the last major nationalized industry to be sold. This decision was announced in a White Paper in 1992 and approved by the Railways Act of 1993. Despite worries about the difficulties in selling a loss-making industry, John Major's government was anxious to press ahead, and received support from sympathetic civil servants, especially the 'hyper-active privatization unit' in the Treasury.[46] Armies of consultants were also employed, at a cost of £450 million, during the preparations. The model eventually adopted, which split the infrastructure from train operation, 'did not have the support of the railway professionals', and BR had to acquiesce in dismembering itself.[47] The British version of privatization introduced a unique degree of fragmentation. By 1997 the former BR had been split into about a hundred companies, which included Railtrack, the monopoly infrastructure provider, twenty-five passenger train operating companies (TOCs), three rolling stock companies (ROSCOs), thirteen infrastructure maintenance and renewal companies (INFRACOs), each employing numerous subcontractors and six freight companies (soon reduced to two). A correspondingly complex regulatory system was required. Apart from the DfT, the main supervisory institutions were the independent Office of the Rail Regulator (ORR), and the Office of Passenger Rail Franchising (OPRAF), which later become the Strategic Rail Authority (SRA). The SRA in turn only had a short life before its responsibilities were transferred to the DfT in 2004.

Prominent among the objectives of privatization was the injection of competition and the supposedly superior skills of private sector management. Ambitions for on-track competition did not survive long, as it was realized that in order to attract bidders the TOC franchises had to be virtual local monopolies. Thus, the only feasible element of competition was 'for', not 'on' the ground. Letting the franchises proved costly for both bidders and judges, and the decision-making lacked transparency and consistency. The elimination of subsidies was another major Treasury aim. Some TOCs, particularly the early franchise winners, enjoyed a combination of subsidies and comfortable profits whilst others struggled. This situation was usually resolved either by increasing the subsidies, a process by which half the TOCs benefited, or by putting the franchise on cost-plus management contracts, which were in force on nine out of twenty-five by 2003. In these cases the TOCs simply following detailed specifications imposed by the SRA, undermining the pretence that private management was supplying a creative input. Together these two devices for the bailing-out of unprofitable operators emphasized the token nature of the supposed transfer of risk to the private sector. It had been envisaged that subsidies to the TOCs would taper off and eventually disappear by 2005. In fact they were stabilized in the late 1990s and then began to rise substantially, reaching £2.5 billion by 2003–4. Track access fees to Railtrack accounted for more than half of the outgoings of TOCs, which partly explained the need for subsidies.[48] As over 90 per cent of these charges were fixed, with no variation in proportion to use, Railtrack lacked the incentive to spend adequately on maintenance or improvement of the infrastructure. However, the company was atypically efficient in negotiations with the ORR over its funding requirements. By 2001, it had been promised direct subsidies of £1 billion a year in addition to the indirect subsidies it received via the TOCs. Thus the vision of a subsidy-free railway faded rapidly. Indeed, subsidies had increased to several times the level of BR days.

Rising costs were also a critical issue for the privatized railway, and again the new fragmented structure had contributed to this. One justification offered at the time was that the devolution of BR's role to a large number of separate firms would 'replace command relationships with British Rail by contractual relationships between free-standing autonomous bodies'.[49] But reliance on contractual relationships between profit-seeking independent units quickly generated 'friction at the interfaces' and led to an uncontrollable escalation of costs.[50] An analysis of Railtrack's investment projects concluded that they were two to three times as expensive in real terms as under BR, because of the need to reward layers of contractors and to compensate TOCs.[51] The company's lack of engineering skills and poor project management were also relevant. All of this was conspicuous in the fiasco of the upgrading of the West Coast Main Line, where estimated costs spiralled from an initial £2.1 billion to over £10 billion by 2001. This precipitated the collapse of Railtrack in 2001 and its eventual replacement by a 'not-for-dividend' organization, Network Rail, which was effectively in the public sector, although its massive debts were not classified as such.[52]

Total leakages from the railway between 1995/6 and 2000/1 have been estimated at about £3.8 billion. Apart from the redistributed profits of Railtrack and the TOCs, most went to the ROSCOs. These three companies were initially sold for £1.8 billion, only to quickly change hands again for £2.7 billion, leading to criticisms that they had been undervalued in the first place. The ROSCOs were not subject to regulation, and 80 per cent of the revenue obtained from leasing trains to the TOCs was guaranteed by government. Between 1996 and 2002, profits in most years were equivalent to over 30 per cent of turnover, amounting in all to £1.8 billion, or roughly the sum for which they were sold at privatization. Dividends of £1.3 billion have been paid out, and the parent companies also received interest payments as finance providers. In 2007 the government finally decided to refer the issue of ROSCO leasing charges to the Competition Commission.

Rail privatization delivered none of the benefits claimed for it. It has not increased efficiency, it has not improved the quality of services, it has not solved the problem of capital shortages, it has not reduced subsidy, it has not relieved government of responsibility for the industry, and its regulatory system has been unable to cope with the fragmentation of the system. Only the unstated aim of the transfer of wealth from the public to the private sector has been accomplished. It has transpired that Foster's characterization 'complicated, inefficient, ineffective and bureaucratic' was more applicable to the privatized than to the nationalized structure.[53]

Finally, mention should be made of the one component of the former BTC that still remains in public ownership, British Waterways. So far, privatization of canals has been avoided, despite the potentially attractive property portfolio. The BTC acquired around 2,000 miles of canal and inland waterways in 1947. As with railways, the approach was to identify a viable network of waterways on which freight carrying would still be viable. In fact only about 350–400 miles fell into this category. Some investment, for instance larger locks, was made in these waterways, and the process continued up to the early 1980s. But it was distinctly limited, and there has been nothing comparable to the scale of expenditure on inland waterway transport infrastructure on the continent.[54] On the other hand, substantial amounts of money have been spent in regenerating and reopening canals and waterways for leisure use.

CONCLUSIONS

In the UK, as in all modern economies, there was a reciprocal relationship between transport and economic growth. Effective transport methods were important inputs into the growth process; continuing growth required in turn the regular extension of transport capacity. The large scale and high cost of many transport projects, the major implications for land use, and the inevitable divergence between private and social rates of return determined the involvement of government. Individual citizens had a growing interest in capturing some of the benefits of mobility. Such benefits, for both business and leisure, have been spread more widely, though unequally, during this period, especially through the newer transport modes. These fundamentals guaranteed that transport policy issues would often be urgent and contested.

Over the last few decades a number of more contingent factors have created additional demands. Although some changes can be identified which reduced pressure on transport, such as the decline of the traditional industries and of their exports, these were comfortably outweighed by developments which had the opposite effect. The huge and unprecedented boom in consumer goods, many of them imported, was clearly one of these. Related trends in the retail sector, such as the growth of out-of-town shopping centres, and the more recent surge in e-commerce, belong to the same category, and made heavier demands on the roads in particular. Greater car use was also virtually dictated by some basic social trends, such as the higher proportion of single households, increased longevity and the allied tendency for more old people and more women to hold driving licences. High urban property prices, especially in the larger conurbations, encouraged longer-distance commuting. The continuing pattern of relatively low density urban housing, by comparison with more compact continental cities, also magnified transport requirements. Several further factors of an essentially negative variety are also relevant, such as slow progress in developing possible solutions, or at least ameliorating measures, like staggered working hours, increased working from home, and, perhaps most critically, road pricing.

During the post-war decades, public policy was conducted in a clear framework in which rail and bus transport were essentially public sector operations, and cars and road haulage belonged to the private sector, though obviously dependent on government for infrastructure provision. From the late 1940s integration was a merely token objective. Transport infrastructure was, in any case, neglected in comparison with other countries. A Treasury estimate of 1956 indicated that Britain had the lowest proportion of investment in transport and communications, but the highest traffic densities, in the West European economies in the sample. This disadvantaged both road and rail. Railway investment was among the weakest in Europe as a proportion of either GDP or railway revenue, and train speeds often below 1930s standards. In 1955 only 0.09 per cent of national income was spent on roads, as against 0.69 per cent in France and 0.75 per cent in West Germany. Until the mid-1950s governments seemed indifferent to the developmental potential of transport investment. The Treasury was concerned mainly with macroeconomic stabilization and the Transport Ministry, lacking trained economists or such instruments as cost-benefit studies, was ill-equipped to argue with it. The main political priorities appeared to be defence, agriculture, and housing.[55] When it came to be accepted that transport expenditure had been suboptimal, the principal beneficiary was the road sector. One of the most powerful secular trends in policy was the decisive swing in favour of roads from the later 1950s. This mode enjoyed a long period of benign economic and political conditions, with the falling real cost of oil, subject to two interruptions in the 1970s, an outstanding advantage. Substantial technical improvements in vehicle efficiency were also clearly beneficial to a high degree. Rail in contrast experienced a large-scale decline in market share, which was inevitable within the parameters of any likely government strategy, and furthermore suffered from a crucial decline in ministerial confidence at the end of the 1950s. Governments were held responsible for the performance of the nationalized railways and their management, and frequently responded to problems with declining financial generosity and unhelpful detailed interventions. It was much more straightforward for ministers to sanction funds for building roads, where operation was in other hands, especially in times when this was universally seen as positive.

Just as British governments had been reluctant to appreciate the positive relevance of improved transport to economic growth rates in the early post-war period, they can also be considered slow in taking action to prevent growing congestion and lack of capacity from imposing handicaps on the economy in the last few decades. The weak response has sometimes brought a measure of unity to otherwise opposed interest groups. Sir Rod Eddington warned that the UK had 'nearly reached the point of no return at which its transport infrastructure became so bad that it deterred foreign investment'.[56] The Director of the Campaign for Better Transport complained that 'we can't go on like this. Traffic is destroying our communities, our health and our environment'.[57] There has also been greater recent awareness, sometimes in surprising places, of relatively poor British performance on transport policy. An AA spokesman has argued that 'UK citizens know the transport system lags behind those in Europe. The UK's congested network would do better with a dose of European medicine, showing how to run a truly joined-up transport system'.[58] This was realistic in its assumption that various national governments in Europe have more progressive transport policies than the UK, but excessively optimistic if there was an expectation of effective initiatives from the European Commission. Under current EU rules, heavy freight vehicles are charged only for use of road infrastructure. The only breach so far of this principle is a directive of May 2006 that the environmental costs of heavy lorries should be included in toll charges. The idea of allowing freight companies to be taxed for their contribution to global warming appears to have been dropped.[59]

Policy debates certainly acquired greater complexity when environmental considerations were granted a place on the transport agenda from the 1970s onwards. Awareness of the dangerously negative impacts of some well-established forms of investment made a qualitative difference. Before the end of the century the concepts of integration and sustainability both commanded attention, the former having undergone a long-delayed revival in popularity. Together they pointed unequivocally to concerted action to boost public transport and to reduce reliance on the roads. However, not only were the two concepts difficult to operationalize, but in vital respects the goals they implicitly required cut against the grain. In every other area of economic policy, a renewed emphasis on central planning and systematic priority for the public sector over the private were unacceptable to all governments after 1979. The bus industry had been privatized in the 1980s, and outside London, languished in deregulated decline and stagnation. Railway privatization was the very opposite of an integrating mechanism, creating multiple interfaces within the network among companies with different functions. Although privatization generated both higher subsidies and more detailed government intervention than had been normal under nationalization, it certainly diminished the scope for integration, within both the rail sector and transport more broadly. A comparable regression occurred in the case of the London Underground between 1998 and 2003, when Labour's preference was for both vertical separation and for division of the private sector participation into three very long term contracts, one of which has already ended disastrously.[60] With DfT policy entering a new cycle of subsidy reduction and fare increases, it is not clear how the railways can contribute substantially to a shift away from roads. Passengers are currently scheduled to pay 75 per cent of rail costs by 2014 (£9 billion instead of £5 billion). The government has also proved reluctant to support the extension of urban tram networks, despite their success in several cities. The Commission for Integrated Transport has conceded in the past that the UK lags behind best continental practice (particularly Germany), where there are lower modal shares for cars, and where public transport is usually more subsidized, better in quality, and more likely to be run by a single organization.[61] More recently, it has consoled itself by merely emphasizing points of improvement in the UK's record – the safest roads in Europe, above-average progress in reducing carbon emissions, and freight tonnage growing more slowly than the economy.[62]

The official travel survey for 2007 shows that 80 per cent of all journeys by Britons are by car, despite a fall in average speeds on trunk roads over the last decade – a proportion virtually unchanged over twenty years.[63] This confirms Britain's status as one of the most car dependent societies in the world. Key statistics on relative travel costs show that average bus and coach fares were 42 per cent higher and rail fares 39 per cent higher than in 1980, whereas the overall cost of motoring (including car purchase and servicing, petrol, tax, and insurance) has not increased at all, and may even have fallen slightly, despite a 16 per cent rise in the real cost of fuel.[64] Transport has become an integral component of the modern economy. Tarmac, wheels, and rails in all their various forms are the outward manifestation of the desire for travel and mobility of both goods and of people. In the second half of the twentieth century this was a demand fuelled by the availability of cheap oil. This path is surely becoming increasingly unrealistic. Yet the opposition to higher vehicle excise duty, to road pricing schemes, and the panic engendered by fuel price increases and isolated instances of fuel shortages, all demonstrate the degree to which expectations about the right to private transport have become embedded in society. Furthermore, while people may eschew public transport, but it is not clear that unbridled market solutions will be politically acceptable. Much determined and purposive government action would be needed to change these trends and attitudes before integration and sustainability can become more than slogans. It cannot be said that the pursuit of transport policy in Britain since 1945 offers many grounds for optimism.

NOTES

1. The data in this section is taken from Department for Transport (DfT), *Transport Statistics Great Britain*, The Stationery Office, London, 2007; Department of the Environment Transport and the Regions, *Focus on Public Transport: Great Britain*, The Stationery Office, London, 1999; DfT, *Waterborne Freight in the United Kingdom: 2006*, The Stationery Office, London, 2007.

2. *Transport Statistics Great Britain*: table 1.17.

3. R. Millward and J. Foreman-Peck, *Public and Private Ownership of British Industry 1820–1990*, Oxford University Press, Oxford, 1994: 291.

4. R. Millward, 'State Enterprise in Twentieth Century Britain', in P. A. Toninelli, ed., *The Rise and Fall of State Enterprises in Western Countries*, Cambridge University Press, 2000: 167.

5. British Transport Commission, *Report and Accounts for 1948*, HMSO, London, 1949.

6. *The Financial and Economic Obligations of the Nationalised Industries*, Apr. 1961, Cmnd.1337; *Nationalised Industries. A Review of Economic and Financial Objectives*, Nov. 1967, Cmnd.34377.

7. T. R. Gourvish, *British Railways 1948–73. A Business History*, Cambridge University Press, 1986: 129–30.

8. Ibid.: 157, 171.

9. A. M. Milne, and A. Laing, *The Obligation to Carry* Institute of Transport, London, 1956: 37.

10. British Transport Commission, *Modernisation and Re-equipment of British Railways*, London, 1955.

11. C. Wolmar, *Broken Rails. How Privatisation Wrecked Britain's Railways*, Aurum Press: London, 2001: 41.

12. Gourvish, *British Railways*: 274–5.

13. T. Gourvish, *British Rail 1974–97. From Integration to Privatisation*, Oxford University Press, Oxford, 2002: 3.

14. British Railways Board (BRB), *The Reshaping of British Railways*, HMSO, London, 1963.

15. Ibid.: 57.

16. R. Pryke, *The Nationalised Industries: Policies and Performance Since 1968*, Robertson, Oxford, 1981: 74.

17. C. Loft, *Government, the Railways and the Modernization of Britain: Beeching's Last Trains*, Routledge, London, 2006: 121.

18. BRB, *Annual Report and Accounts*, 1976: 7.

19. *Railway Finances*, Report of a Committee chaired by Sir David Serpell, HMSO: London, 1983; P. S. Bagwell, *End of the Line? The Fate of Public Transport Under Thatcher*, Verso; London, 1984: 124–41.

20. T. R. Gourvish, 'British Rail's "Business-led" Organization, 1977–1990: Government-Industry Relations in Britain's Public Sector', *Business History Review*, 64, Spring 1990; Gourvish, *British Rail*: 103–40, 374–83.

21. J. D. Shires, et al., Rail Privatisation: 'The Practice – An Analysis of Seven Case Studies'. Working Paper 420, Institute for Transport Studies, Leeds, 1997. Gourvish, *British Rail*: 291–2.

22. BTC, *Modernisation*: 13–8.

23. Department of Transport/British Railways Board, *Review of Main Line Electrification: Final Report*, London, 1981; Gourvish, *British Rail*: 92–3, 154–5.

24. A recent reworking of the 1981 scheme show electrification remains viable. R. Ford, 'Should We Have a Rolling Programme of Electrification', *Modern Railways*, 63, 692, May 2006: 28–32.

25. T. Gourvish, *The Official History of Britain and the Channel Tunnel*, Routledge, London, 2006: 366, 385.

26. Gourvish, *British Rail*: 319–28, 328–40; *Channel Tunnel*: 330–46.

27. G. Dudley, and J. Richardson, *Why Does Policy Change? Lessons from British Transport Policy, 1945–99* Routledge, London, 2001: 119, 128.
28. Dudley and Richardson: 114.
29. C. Buchanan, *Traffic in Towns: Reports of Steering Group and Working Group*, Department of Transport, London, 1963.
30. M. Hamer, *Wheels Within Wheels – A Study of the Road Lobby*, Routledge and Kegan Paul, London, 1987. T. Gibson, *Road Haulage by Motor in Britain: The First Forty Years*, Ashgate, Aldershot, 2001: 274–8.
31. Dudley and Richardson: 96.
32. Ibid.: 97, 108.
33. Hamer, *Wheels Within Wheels*: 1, chapter 7.
34. Dudley and Richardson: 121.
35. Ibid.: 148–9.
36. S. Glaister, J. Burnham, H. Stevens, and T. Travers, *Transport Policy in Britain* 2nd edition, Palgrave Macmillan, Basingstoke, 2006: 30.
37. 1998 White Paper, *A New Deal for Transport.*
38. Glaister et al. *Transport Policy*: 36, 236–8.
39. *Guardian*, 31 July 2007; DfT, *Delivering a Sustainable Railway*, 2007.
40. National Bus Company, *Annual Report, 1969.*
41. Dudley and Richardson: 204; F. Poole, 'Buses', House of Commons Library, Research Paper, 99/59, 1999; P. Bagwell, and P. Lyth, *Transport in Britain. From Canal Lock to Gridlock*, Hambledon and London, London, 2002: 182–5.
42. Glaister et al. *Transport Policy*: 195–8.
43. *Transport Trends 2006*, Department for Transport, London, Feb. 2007: 27.
44. Ibid.: 28.
45. Bagwell, 1996: 174–5; *Guardian*, 19 Jun. 1996.
46. Wolmar, *Broken Rails*: 61–3, 88.
47. W.P. Bradshaw, 'The Rail Industry', in D. Helm, and T. Jenkinson, eds., *Competition in Regulated Industries*, University Press: Oxford, 1998: 179.
48. G. Crompton, and R. Jupe, '"A Deficient Performance?" The Regulation of the Train Operating Companies in Britain's Privatised Railway System', *Critical Perspectives on Accounting*, 17, 2006: 1035–65.
49. C. Foster, *The Economics of Rail Privatisation*, Centre for the Study of Regulated Industries, London/Bath, 1994: 7.
50. G. Crompton, and R. Jupe, '"A Lot of Friction at the Interfaces": The Regulation of Britain's Privatised Railway System', *Financial Accountability and Management*, 19, 4, 2003: 397–418.
51. R. Ford, 'Railtrack "Investment" – Money into a Black Hole?', *Modern Railways*, Jul. 2000: 19–21.
52. G. Crompton, and R. Jupe, 'Network Rail – Forwards or Backwards? "Not-for-Profit" in British Transport History', *Business History*, 49, 6, 2007.
53. Foster, *Economics of Rail Privatisation*, 1994.
54. G. Crompton, '"The Tortoise and the Economy": Inland Waterway Transport in International Economic History', *Journal of Transport History*, 25, 2, 2004.
55. P. Scott, 'Public Sector Investment and Britain's Post-War Economic Performance: A Case Study of Roads Policy', *Journal of European Economic History*, 34, 2, 2005: 406, 412, 415.
56. J. Eaglesham, 'Business Urges Transport Investment', *Financial Times*, 6 Jan. 2006.
57. D. Milmo, 'Warning of Gridlock with 6m More Cars by 2031', *Guardian*, 10 Sept. 2007.

58. R. Smithers, 'Britons Reply on Their Cars for 80% of Travel', *Guardian*, 31 Aug. 2007.
59. T. Barber, 'Road Hauliers Face Pollution Toll', *Financial Times*, 7 Jul. 2008.
60. Glaister et al. *Transport Policy*: 212–17.
61. *European Best Practice in Transport – the German Example*, Report. Commission for Integrated Transport, London, May 2000.
62. *Are We There Yet? A Comparison of Transport in Europe*, Report, Commission for Integrated Transport, London, Apr. 2007.
63. *National Travel Survey 2006*, DfT, Aug. 2007.
64. *Transport Trends 2006*: 24.

16

The Film Industry in Twentieth Century Britain: Consumption Patterns, Government Regulation, and Firm Strategy

Peter Miskell

> Well, to put it quite bluntly, isn't there a certain incompatibility between the terms 'cinema' and 'Britain'?[1]

In the decades since Francois Truffaut posed this question to Alfred Hitchcock in 1966, an extensive literature on British film history has emerged which has helped to rescue the reputation of British cinema among film scholars. Leading British producers, directors, actors, studios – not to mention the films themselves – have been subject to detailed scholarly analysis and reappraisal.[2] The same cannot so confidently be said for the companies responsible for managing the production, distribution, and exhibition of British films. The publications of former film executives do offer an insight into the development of some firms,[3] but the absence of archival records has prevented a detailed historical examination of the enterprises that dominated the British film industry for much of the twentieth century. A comprehensive business history of the British film industry remains to be written.

While this chapter cannot provide such a comprehensive history, it will at least attempt to sketch out a framework on which such a history might be based. It draws heavily on the existing British cinema history literature, but in doing so re-assesses the evidence from the perspective of British firms. The aim is to explain how both the structure of the industry and the strategies pursued by leading firms evolved through the twentieth century, and to offer some explanation as to why the industry developed in the way that it did.

This chapter is divided chronologically into five sections. The first deals with the industry in its infancy, and briefly charts the evolution of the systems of production, distribution, and exhibition. The second section, covering the period from c.1910 to 1927, examines the functioning of the industry within Britain under broadly liberal free-market conditions. The third section, from 1927 to c.1960, explores the impact of government intervention and the emergence of a (protected) domestic industry. Section four charts the decline of that domestic industry during a period of falling cinema attendance. The final section, covering the period since c.1980, examines how the industry reacted to the revival of the film market on the one hand, and the removal of government protection on the other. The periodization is designed to highlight changes in industry structure and firm behaviour, and to illustrate how these changes have been shaped by changing patterns of film consumption as well as government legislation.

THE EMERGENCE OF AN INDUSTRY: 1896–1910

The business of projecting moving images onto a screen, and presenting before a paying audience, began in Britain in 1896. The public appetite for this novel form of entertainment was at least as strong in Britain as anywhere else, and entrepreneurs were quick to see the commercial opportunities offered by this new media. It took at least a decade, however, for the film industry to begin to develop the systems of production, distribution, and exhibition on which it would be based for most of the twentieth century.

In terms of film production, the now ubiquitous feature film did not emerge until around 1910. In the industry's early years films tended to be very short (usually running for not more than a few minutes) and for the most part were produced at relatively little expense. The majority of films made by British producers at this time were 'topical' or 'actuality' films showing scenes of local people or events (such as sporting fixtures, ceremonial events or public appearances of various dignitaries).[4] Some of the more innovative film-makers were beginning to employ narrative devices in story films from around 1905, while others were experimenting with colour, but the use of professional actors, the promotion of 'stars', and the filming of well known plays or major works of fiction remained some years ahead. While there were a number of professional production companies with their own 'studios' at this time, there was still scope for the amateur cinematographer or showman to make films that could compete with the very best – and reach a worldwide audience. As such, film production was not concentrated in one place, and a number of producers operated quite successfully in different parts of the country.[5]

The emergence of longer and more sophisticated (and more expensive) feature films was bound up very closely with changing patterns of film distribution. In the industry's first decade it was commonplace for films to be sold directly to exhibitors for a flat rate fee (which fell from around 1s. per foot in 1899 to about 4d. or 5d. a foot by 1907–8).[6] Under this system films were traded as a basic commodity, and if exhibitors did find themselves in possession of a particularly popular film, their incentive was to screen it as many times as possible – until the print deteriorated and public demand was exhausted. Producers actually stood to gain relatively little if their films (once sold) were highly popular, and they had little incentive to invest large sums of money to give their pictures a distinctive appeal. Exhibitors potentially stood to gain most under this system. They often commissioned films from producers and even took a hand in the making of films themselves.[7]

The system of renting films to exhibitors for limited time periods coexisted alongside the practice of direct sale, with some leading distributors offering films on both a sale and a rental basis.[8] The crucial development, however, was the creation of a system whereby films were rented on an exclusive basis to certain exhibitors in any given area. The shift from outright selling or unrestricted renting of film, to renting on an exclusive basis was gradual, with distributors for a time offering selections of both exclusive and non-exclusive films.[9] Once the system of exclusive rental was established, however, it became possible for distributors to control the release pattern of films, and thus maximize revenues. The largest and more prestigious venues in any town, which usually charged the highest admission prices, typically rented films first (becoming known as first-run halls), with smaller and less salubrious venues screening films for their second, third, or fourth run. By this simple process of market segmentation, distributors were able to charge higher prices to their highest value customers (those prepared to pay more to see the latest films in the best venues) while still retaining the custom of lower value patrons. The incentive for distributors was no longer to sell as many films as they could to as many exhibitors as possible, but to obtain control of the most popular and successful pictures. Rather than being sold as a basic commodity, film came to be treated more like a fashion product, with the latest and most appealing pictures commanding the highest prices. This prompted leading film producers to embark on a 'quality race',[10] not only to create increasingly sophisticated and spectacular pictures, but also to market them more aggressively – with particular prominence given to the leading players or 'stars'.[11] The increasing length and technical sophistication of films, along with the rapidly rising salaries paid to the leading stars, drove up the cost of film production at an astonishing rate. Cecil Hepworth's *Rescued by Rover*, made at the end of 1905, was an internationally successful film of its day. It ran to just 425 feet in length, and cost £7 13s. 9d.[12] By 1913, it was being reported that the producer W.G. Barker had spent around £8,000 just on artists' salaries during the making of *Sixty Years A Queen* (a film which was 6,000 feet in length).[13]

For the first ten years of the industry's existence the processes by which films were made and distributed meant that the type of films audiences saw were very different from those experienced by later generations. As well as watching very different types of films, these early audiences also consumed their entertainment in very different surroundings. Working class audiences were attracted to film shows in fairground booths, or converted shops (known as penny gaffs), while those a little further up the social scale were more likely to watch films as part of a wider programme of entertainment in music hall or public hall shows. The first permanent structures given over exclusively to the showing of films (buildings that we might think of as 'cinemas') did not emerge until around 1907–8. Although these first cinemas proved to be highly popular with audiences, concerns were raised about the safety of these venues, as well as the long term viability of this form of popular entertainment. Safety concerns (specifically the fire risk associated with inflammable film stock) were largely allayed with the introduction of the Cinematograph Act of 1909, which regulated cinemas as places of entertainment.[14] The perception that film-going was no more than a passing fad, however, proved more difficult to overcome.

If the film business in 1906 remained in its infancy, influenced as much by traditions of fairground showmanship as by modern industrial enterprise, we can still identify features of the industry in Britain that would become familiar to later observers (and critics). The presence, for example, of foreign producers and distributors in Britain was as much a feature of the early film industry as it would be later in the twentieth century. As early as 1897, the American Muto-scope Company established a British affiliate, called the British Mutoscope and Biograph Company, which was by some margin the largest film enterprise in Britain at the turn of the century. With nominal capital of around £1 million, the company was able to build its own indoor film studio in London's Regent Street in 1900.[15] The French company, Gaumont, established a British subsidiary in 1898, initially for the purpose of distributing its own films in Britain, but its London office soon became one of the most important international film ex-changes, selling films from many of the leading British and international film producers.[16] Pathe, another French film multinational, also operated a British sales and distribution subsidiary, although it did not begin film production in Britain (apart from newsreel footage) until 1911.[17] One of the leading British film distributing companies at this time, the Warwick Trading Company, was founded and controlled by an American, Charles Urban (who had first come to Britain to manage the London office of yet another early multinational film distributor – the New York based Maguire & Baucus).[18]

Yet while the British industry was influenced quite significantly by inward foreign investment, there is much less evidence of British film companies invest-ing overseas. The British Mutoscope and Biograph Company does appear to have been the hub of an extensive international network of Biograph companies, with affiliates in many European and British imperial markets, but whether this can be classed as British multinational activity is questionable.[19] British films were certainly exported to foreign markets, but British producers did not typical-ly control the distribution of their films abroad, and they seldom undertook production in foreign countries. The London office of the Gaumont Company was the principal outlet through which British films made it into foreign markets. Even very small producers could (and did) reach a worldwide audience if their films were picked up by Gaumont. *The Salmon Poachers* (1905), for example, one of the most internationally successful pictures of its day, was made by a travelling fairground showman.[20] The larger British producers of the time (Charles Urban, Cecil Hepworth, R. W. Paul) were more involved in the selling of other producers' films in Britain, than in establishing foreign distribution centres for their own pictures. In the first decade of the industry's development British film-makers had demonstrated an ability to produce pictures with a broad international appeal, but this was not matched on the part of British companies by a supporting infrastructure of multinational investment.

AMERICAN DOMINANCE IS ESTABLISHED: 1910–27

By 1910, the viewing of moving pictures had been an established form of popular entertainment for about a decade-and-a-half. During that time significant developments had been made in the length and sophistication of films produced; a system of distribution based on film rentals had evolved; in terms of film exhibition, purpose built cinema buildings had appeared and were regulated by their own specific Act of Parliament. Despite these developments, however, the perception that cinema was no more than a passing fad proved difficult to overcome – particularly in the City of London. Investors remained highly sceptical about the long term prospects for the industry, often likening it to the popular craze for skating, which had proved short-lived.

Entrepreneurs who sought to build cinema chains in Britain between 1910 and 1914 (of whom there was no shortage) found it difficult to attract finance. In order to signal to investors that their businesses were sound, they resorted to paying out extraordinary dividends (up to 40% in some cases), which left little scope for further reinvestment and expansion.[21] The aversion of the London financial markets to the film business helps to explain why, despite being one of the largest film markets outside the US, Britain had such a fragmented film exhibition sector until the end of the 1920s.[22] Only one chain, Provincial Cinematograph Theatres (PCT), which controlled eighty-five cinemas by 1927, had anything approaching a nationwide coverage.[23] Other circuits were regional and tended to be very small. In 1920, there was only one circuit (other than PCT) with 20 or more cinemas, and by 1927 there were still just four. At the time the 1927 Films Act was passed, the largest twenty-three cinema circuits in the country controlled just 408 cinemas – little more than ten per cent of the national total.[24] There was little evidence of any vertical integration in the industry.

Scepticism towards the film industry on the part of city financiers may also partially account for the lack of overseas investment by British film distributors, and for the inability of British firms to keep pace with European and American rivals in film production. French and Italian firms had been pioneers of feature films in the early 1910s, but were unable to compete with American producers as the 'quality race' in film production continued through the First World War.[25] British film-makers, in contrast, had been less than competitive, even in their domestic market, well before the onset of the War. By 1909–10 not more than 15 per cent of the films shown in Britain were made by British firms (36% were French). As Rachael Low puts it, 'the myth that the British led the world until 1914 and lost their lead through no fault of their own must be recognised as a convenient excuse.'[26]

By the 1920s, cinema-going had become an established feature of British popular culture. Attendances boomed during the First World War, reaching 20 million per week, and then stabilized at somewhere between fifteen and twenty million per week for the remainder of the inter-war period.[27] As a cultural form the (popular) cinema may not have gained intellectual respectability, but as an industry it was at least recognized as more that a temporary 'craze'. By this time, however, US firms had established themselves as global leaders. The US market was by far the largest in the world, and having established powerful vertically integrated organizations in this market, American firms were better positioned than foreign companies to exploit its potential. From their strong domestic base, the leading American firms expanded abroad in the early 1920s (in some cases earlier), creating distribution subsidiaries in foreign markets, and making limited investments in cinema exhibition. By the mid-1920s, American films accounted for a large share of box-office takings in countries around the world, and even the once powerful European film industries could not compete.[28]

The difficulties faced by European film multinationals, however, did provide some opportunities for British investors looking for a way into the industry. Gaumont's London-based film distribution subsidiary was acquired by British interests in 1922 (with the financial support of a London merchant bank run by brothers Isidore and Maurice Ostrer). The British distribution arm of Pathe was similarly brought under British ownership.[29]

By the mid-1920s, the British market for films was strong and firmly established. The cinemas that served this market were owned by British firms, but cinema ownership was widely dispersed among a large number of small, local firms. British firms were also active in film distribution, handling the release of most British-made films as well as those of smaller foreign producers. The films of the major US studios, however, were typically distributed through their British-based subsidiaries.

GOVERNMENT PROTECTION AND THE CREATION
OF NATIONAL FILM INDUSTRY: 1927–60

The extent to which American firms had come to dominate the global film industry by the mid-1920s was a cause of considerable concern within Britain, for cultural as well as economic reasons.[30] Responding to such concerns, in 1927 the British Government introduced a protective quota, to reserve a certain proportion of screen time in British cinemas for British-made films (the quota rose from 5% in 1928 to 25% by the mid-1930s). Along with an exhibition quota there was also a distribution quota. This meant that all film distributors operating in Britain (whether British or American) had to offer a minimum proportion of British made films.[31] The Act triggered not just a period of growth in the British film industry, but a fundamental restructuring of that industry.

The size of the British film market did not change significantly during the inter-war period, but with British films suddenly guaranteed a growing share of this market (the largest outside of the US), film producers found it easier to attract finance.[32] The more ambitious producers were also keen to secure access to the largest and most prestigious 'first run' cinemas, while the managers of cinema chains were anxious to secure supply of the best quality British films. Within a year or so of the passing of the 1927 Act, vertically integrated British film companies began to emerge.[33]

British International Pictures (BIP) was the creation of John Maxwell – a solicitor by training, who had built up a circuit of around twenty cinemas in Scotland in the 1910s, and subsequently moved into film distribution, taking control of Wardour films in 1923. When, in 1927, Maxwell bought out the consortium behind the construction of Elstree studios to form BIP, he controlled production, distribution, and exhibition assets. With only a modest chain of cinemas (mainly restricted to Scotland), however, Maxwell moved swiftly to expand the exhibition arm of the business. A new public company was established in 1928, Associated British Cinemas Ltd. (ABC), which by 1931 controlled around 160 cinemas across the country, and continued to expand throughout the 1930s. In 1933, Maxwell merged ABC cinemas, BIP, and the distribution arm Wardour Films into a single corporate entity called the Associated British Picture Company (ABPC). Maxwell had financed his move into film production, and the later expansion of his cinema circuit, by issuing shares: first in BIP and then in ABC cinemas. ABC Ltd. was formed with a capital of £1 million, and this had doubled to £2 million by 1929. By the mid-1930s the authorized capital of the ABPC group stood at £4 million, of which £3.5 million was issued.[34]

The Gaumont-British Picture Corporation Ltd., was registered as a public company in March 1927. It brought together the production and distribution interests of the Gaumont Company, with two other leading British distributors (Ideal Films Ltd. and W & F Film Service Ltd.). With a capital of £2.5 million, and the financial backing of the Ostrer Brothers, the new company quickly began expanding its film exhibition interests, controlling a circuit of 187 cinemas by 1928. That year also saw the formation of Gainsborough Pictures Ltd., a production subsidiary with studios at Islington and Shepherd's Bush, under the management of Michael Balcon. By 1929, a private holding company had been established which controlled the Gaumont-British group, in which the Fox Corporation acquired a 49 per cent share. This injection of American investment increased the company's capital to £3.75 million, enabling it to expand its cinema chain (to 287 cinemas), by acquiring the PCT circuit.[35]

The creation of these two vertically integrated firms with strong financial backing is evidence that the British film industry was, at last, becoming established on a more secure footing. Both firms operated modern and well equipped film studios, and both were able to guarantee that their films would obtain a national distribution in the country's leading cinemas. ABC and Gaumont-British, however, were not the only firms to build national cinema chains in the 1930s. The first Odeon cinema was built by Oscar Deutsch in Birmingham in 1930, and by 1937 Odeon had grown into a national circuit consisting of some 250 halls.[36] In 1936, another well-capitalized film company was registered, the General Cinema Finance Corporation (GCFC), under the control of J. Arthur Rank. This organization controlled newly built film studios at Pinewood, along with a distribution firm called General Film Distributors (GFD) – it also gained a minority shareholding in the American film company Universal (with this studio's films being distributed through GFD in Britain). Towards the end of 1938 Rank's GCFC group made its first investment in the Odeon chain, and by 1941 this circuit had come under Rank's direct control.[37]

As well as the creation of these large and well-capitalized organizations, the 1930s also witnessed large amounts of investment in the British film industry that was more speculative in nature. By guaranteeing a share of the domestic market for British films, the 1927 legislation made film production a viable investment. If one of these films was to become popular internationally, however, the returns to investors could be very high indeed. When Alexander Korda's *The Private Life of Henry VIII* became just such a 'hit' in 1933, it appeared to demonstrate that British films could compete with the best that the American studios could produce. With the potential market for British films conceived as an international one, new investment poured into the industry.[38] In 1928, the floor space on the stages of British film studios amounted to 105,200 square feet, by 1938, this had risen to 777,650 square feet. Over the same period the estimated value of film production rose from around £500,000 to over £7 million.[39] The investment boom was short lived. Korda's success proved extremely difficult to repeat, and investors lured by the prospect of further international hits were to be disappointed. Even access to the domestic market was far from guaranteed for some British producers by the late 1930s. In the year to March 1938, 228 British films were registered, far more than the minimum number required for the quota. Many were never screened in the major cinema chains and thus stood no chance of recouping their production costs.[40]

For the new British film enterprises the strategic question was whether to concentrate on the production of films that could recoup their costs in the domestic market, or to develop films with international audiences in mind. ABPC's production arm followed a domestically oriented strategy. At its formation BIP had (as its name suggests) initially set out to make high quality films that could be sold in international markets, but the focus was on Europe more than the US. As talking pictures replaced silent pictures, however, it became clear that BIP's output would have limited appeal in the rest of Europe, and from this point the company would ensure that film budgets were restricted to a level which could be recouped from a British release. Such a strategy, of course, did nothing to address popular rhetoric about creating an industry to rival Hollywood that would help to spread British values and ideals around the world, and, as such, it won Maxwell few political friends. It was, however, the most economically rational response to the market conditions that had been created by government policy, and it enabled BIP to maintain a consistent output of films, and to ensure regular employment for British film actors and technicians, well into the 1950s.[41]

BIP's main British rival in the early 1930s, Gaumont-British, followed the alternative path. It produced a series of high budget epics in the mid-1930s 'with an eye on the American market', but found that while popular with British audiences these films failed to earn sufficient revenue in overseas markets to cover their production costs.[42] At this point the Ostrer brothers (the London-based merchant bankers who controlled Gaumont-British) began looking for a way out of the industry. Gaumont's head of production, Michael Balcon, also left the company and from 1938 embarked on a much more successful tenure as head of Ealing Studios, which concentrated on the production of more modestly budgeted pictures 'projecting Britain and the British character.'[43]

The only British-based producer to achieve any notable international success in the 1930s was Alexander Korda.[44] Following the success of *Henry VIII*, Korda acquired a 25 per cent stake in the US distributor United Artists, but this firm was unable to release his films in the types of US cinemas where they stood their best chance of success.[45] Korda, who built Denham studios in 1936 and produced a series of big budget costume films in the following years (intended to appeal to international audiences) found that while these pictures were highly popular in Britain, their failure to replicate the global success of *Henry VIII* meant that they consistently lost money.[46] By 1939, Korda had been forced to sell Denham Studios, and by 1943 he had broken off his association with United Artists.

The financial losses of Gaumont-British and Korda's London Films were to be J. Arthur Rank's gain. Assets of both companies were acquired by his GCFC. By the end of 1941 Rank controlled two of the three major cinema circuits in Britain (Gaumont and Odeon), he owned production studios at Pinewood, Denham, Islington, and Shepherd's Bush, and his distribution company (General Film Distributors) was the most powerful in the country. As the dominant force in British film production in the 1940s, what strategy did Rank pursue: domestic focus or global reach?

We can see evidence of both approaches within GCFC during the 1940s. At Gainsborough Studios, the former Gaumont-British subsidiary, film production was run along similar lines to BIP. Over twenty films were made at Gainsborough during the war years at a combined cost of £1.3 million, and these pictures brought in double that amount at the box-office.[47] Elsewhere within GCFC, however, film studios were not run by a general production manager as was the case at Gainsborough – as well as at BIP and Ealing. Rather, Rank secured the services of a variety of 'independent' British producers, who rented space in his studios and whose films he then distributed and exhibited. Arrangements with producers were often informal, based on trust and mutual respect rather than written contracts. Rank provided finance for these producers, but seldom interfered in the production process itself, he also allowed his producers a share of their films' profits. By offering what were, by the standards of the film industry, unusually generous terms, Rank was able to secure the services of just about all the leading British film producers. Even Michael Balcon at Ealing, who was not reliant on Rank for studio space, agreed to distribute through Rank from 1943.[48]

The films made by Rank's 'independent producers' formed the basis of what is often regarded as a 'golden age' of British film production.[49] These producers, however, did not restrict their costs to levels that could be recouped from the domestic market. Rank, in fact, embarked on a strategy of international expansion. He established an international distribution organization, Eagle-Lion, which set up sales offices around the world and made direct investments in foreign cinema chains. In the largest and most important market of all, however, Rank owned no cinemas and the influence of Eagle-Lion in the US was limited.[50] Rank's pictures were not without success in the US market, but hits such as *Henry V*, and *In Which We Serve* remained relatively rare. The majority of Rank's films failed to make any significant impression in the US, yet the sums being spent by his independent producers could not be recovered in the British market alone. The inevitable financial losses on the film production side of the business were offset, for a while, by profits from the major cinema chains. By 1948, however, cinema attendance in Britain had already peaked, and production losses were becoming unsustainable. At this point Rank's chief accountant, John Davis, instituted a maximum budget of £150,000 for any feature film. Rank's independent producers were being told that they could retain their creative autonomy, but they were now subject to strict financial control. Many chose to leave, to join Alexander Korda whose London Films was revived (again without lasting success) around this time.

Largely as a result of government legislation introduced in 1927, the 1930s and 1940s did witness a renewal of the British film industry, which came to be dominated by large vertically integrated firms. The hope was frequently expressed that these firms would compete alongside Hollywood studios in the global marketplace, but the economic reality was that unless they restricted themselves to producing films that could recoup their costs domestically, they would not be financially sustainable. By classifying as 'British' films made by UK subsidiaries of foreign companies, British film policy actually did more to encourage inward investment by American firms than it did to support British companies pursue a strategy of outward expansion.

For much of the 1930s, inward investment in film-making was restricted to the production by US firms of sufficient lengths of film footage in Britain to meet their quota requirements. In 1938, the quota legislation was amended so that films made in Britain by foreign firms could count double (or triple) for quota purposes if sufficient sums were invested in their production.[51] MGM did make a small number of relatively high budget films in Britain on this basis, but the outbreak of war soon curtailed such activities.[52]

The post-war years saw further refinements to British film policy. Concerns about imports of US films intensified as Britain's dollar reserves diminished, and in 1947 the Treasury imposed a 75 per cent duty on all imported films – a punitive measure which triggered a boycott of the British market by American firms.[53] The Anglo-American film dispute was resolved the following year when the import duty was scrapped and the quota restored (at a higher level), but to this was added a new feature of film policy. The Eady levy (named after the Treasury official Wilfred Eady), was an attempt to redistribute film industry revenues from exhibition to film production. Under the scheme, introduced in 1950, film exhibitors agreed to pay a small share of their box office receipts into the newly established British Film Production Fund. Films classified as British automatically received a payout from the fund in proportion to their success at the box-office, with the most successful films receiving the highest

subsidy. In addition to the production fund, a National Film Finance Corporation (NFFC) was also created at around this time to provide a source of
financial support for British film projects that commercial investors considered
too risky.[54]

For US firms operating in Britain by the 1950s, the legal requirement to
distribute a proportion of 'British' films remained in place, but the incentive
to meet this requirement by producing good quality films in Britain were much
stronger than in the 1930s, and not just because of the subsidy on offer from the
British Film Production Fund. Investment in film production in Britain was
a means of utilizing blocked sterling balances, exploiting lower labour costs
and (for some) escaping the McCarthyite witch hunts back in Hollywood.
As the decade progressed, US firms became increasingly willing to produce
films in foreign markets, and Britain was firmly established as the most popular
foreign location.[55] The influx of investment kept British film studios active, and
actors and technicians in employment, but what did it mean for the domestic
firms?

FROM NATIONAL INDUSTRY TO HOLLYWOOD COLONY? 1960–80

Between the late 1950s and the early 1980s cinema attendance in Britain underwent a steep decline. Average weekly admissions had peaked in 1946, but until
1957 remained higher than they had been in the 1930s. As television ownership
became more widespread, however, and commercial broadcasting emerged in
competition with the BBC, the weekly cinema-going habit faded. Attendances fell
from over twenty-one million per week in 1956 to barely more than one million per
week by 1984. While attendance levels plummeted, revenue from film exhibition
held up slightly better. Box office takings did fall in the 1960s (though less sharply
than total admissions), and by the end of the 1970s revenues were actually higher
than they had been in the 1950s before adjusting for inflation.[56] Falling admissions
were, to some extent, offset by rising prices, and the abolition of entertainment
duty in 1960 (though in real terms box-office takings were far lower in the 1970s
than they had been in the 1950s). A new pattern of cinema consumption was
emerging. The public appetite for filmed entertainment remained strong, but
cinemas were now competing against a much wider range of alternative forms of
popular youth oriented entertainment. As such, audiences became more selective
in the films they went to see. This, in turn, made firms rather more selective in the
types of films they would make and distribute. Low budget films or supporting
pictures could no longer be relied upon to find an audience. Only the most
popular 'hit' films (usually with big budgets and well known stars) were able to
generate substantial profits – though predicting which films would become each
year's hits was fraught with uncertainty.[57] As the film industry came to rely

increasingly on the success of a few 'hit' films that audiences paid high prices to see, the smaller neighbourhood cinemas (which had typically charged low prices for older or less prestigious films) gradually became obsolete. Between the mid-1950s and the late 1970s the number of cinemas open in Britain fell from around 4,500 to 1,500 (with most of the closures occurring in the 1960s). The demise of the small, local cinema only served to reinforce the decline in film-going as a habit.[58]

In economic terms, film distribution and exhibition had in effect become more efficient. Revenues were now generated by screening fewer films in fewer cinemas and charging higher prices. Film exhibition, though much reduced by declining audiences, remained a profitable area of activity. Film production on the other hand, though still potentially highly profitable, became increasingly risky. The strategy of producing low or medium budget films that could be relied upon to cover their costs became gradually less viable. In order to maintain profitability, film companies needed produce 'hit' pictures, and the risk associated with this could not be offset by making other (less risky) types of films.[59]

Despite these changes in the nature of film consumption and the economics of the film industry, government regulation of the industry in Britain remained almost unchanged in this period. The tax levied on cinema admissions in the form of the Entertainment Duty was finally abolished in 1960, but the core elements of government film policy (the protective quota, the Eady levy, and the NFFC) remained intact. The aim of these policies was to promote British film production and to ensure that a market existed for British made films. Until the 1950s British film policy was broadly successful in stimulating investment in British film production and helping to develop a domestic industry. Admittedly, some of the films made by British producers ended up being marketed by US distributors, and it was also possible for films made (in Britain) by US firms to qualify as 'British' under the terms of the legislation. Government legislation certainly did not enable British firms to compete on equal terms with the Hollywood majors in international markets, but it did make British film production viable, and its benefits were more apparent to British producers, than to American firms based in the UK.

By the 1960s, however, it was no longer so evident that British producers were the primary beneficiaries of British film policy. From the 1950s, US firms began to increase their investments in film production in Britain, and in doing so came to control the distribution of 'British' films. For most of the 1960s, the majority of British films shown in the main cinema circuits in the UK were either partly or wholly US financed. Whereas in 1950 only 10 per cent of films made in Britain were distributed by US companies, by 1970 this figure had increased to 60 per cent.[60] With good reason is the term 'Hollywood England' used to describe the British film industry in this period.[61]

For policy-makers concerned about maintaining a steady output from British film studios, and for independent British producers looking for financial backing, the influx of American capital was a welcome development. The danger of over-reliance on US investment, however, became apparent in the 1970s as

American firms became more reluctant to finance film production in Britain. In the period 1965–9 the average level of investment in British film production by US firms stood at £21.6 million per year. During 1970–4, this figure halved to £10.6 million per year, and for the years 1975–9 it almost halved again to £5.6 million.[62] With American capital disappearing almost as rapidly as it had arrived, British firms were either ill-equipped or unwilling to finance and support a revival in domestic film production.

As the 1960s and 1970s progressed, the two leading firms (Rank and ABPC), both came to rely increasingly on their cinema chains, rather than production activities for profits. With prospects for growth in film exhibition appearing to be very limited, however, these firms did not offer much promise of long term shareholder value.[63] Unless they could tap into new (and more profitable) sources of revenue, both firms were likely to become victims of Britain's 1960s merger wave. Rank did find such a new line of business in its Rank-Xerox subsidiary – which grew rapidly in the 1960s and by the end of that decade accounted for 90 per cent of corporate profits.[64] ABPC did not diversify, and in 1968 the company was acquired by EMI (which in turn became Thorn-EMI a decade later).

While neither the Rank group, nor EMI could be described primarily as film companies in the 1970s, these firms had increased their control over film exhibition in Britain since the 1940s. Both ABC and Rank were forced to close or sell some of their cinemas as attendances dropped (and Rank consolidated their Odeon and Gaumont chains into a single one), but it was the smaller, independently owned, neighbourhood halls that accounted for the majority of cinema closures. In 1950 the circuits controlled by Rank and ABC accounted for 20 per cent of British cinemas (and around 44% of box office revenues). By the end of the 1970s these firms controlled 37 per cent of cinemas (and were responsible for around 50% of cinema admissions).[65]

As British cinema exhibition became increasingly concentrated in the hands of the two leading circuits, however, the vertically integrated structure of the industry began to break down. Far from exploiting their control over cinema exhibition by filling their screens with in-house productions, the Rank and ABC organizations gradually cut back on film production. As we have seen, the majority of British films shown in Rank or ABC cinemas in the 1960s were US backed productions (made by independent British producers or British subsidiaries of American firms). Why were British firms increasingly reluctant to invest in film production?

The strategic question facing British producers in the 1960s and 1970s was an entirely familiar one: whether to focus on the production of relatively low budget films that could recoup their costs in the domestic market, or to embark on a more ambitious programme of high budget pictures aimed at international audiences. As we have seen, no British firm before the 1960s had been able to operate a viable business model on the basis of the latter approach. Making big-budget films for international audiences was a risky undertaking even for the major US studios, but without control over distribution in the largest international market, the position of British producers was significantly undermined. The experiences of Gaumont-British, Korda, and Rank all point to the same conclusion.

The problem for the likes of Rank and ABC in the 1960s and 1970s, however, was that the alternative (domestically oriented) production strategy, was also becoming problematic. Whereas the likes of BIP, Ealing, and Gainsborough Studios had shown it was possible to operate successfully on this basis through the 1930s and 1940s, the following decades saw film production costs continue to rise while the size of the domestic market contracted. Under such circumstances, a purely domestic production policy became increasingly difficult to sustain. Firms did what they could by way of creating and exploiting popular film 'franchises' (such as the *Carry On, Doctor,* and *St. Trinians* series), in which costs were kept to a minimum for pictures with a known popular appeal. British film-makers wishing to take on more ambitious (and expensive) projects, however, were more likely to be backed by American distributors in this period than by the vertically integrated domestic firms.[66]

For Rank and ABPC/EMI, profits from film exhibition were far more important than those from production, so the imperative was to book the most popular pictures for their cinemas rather than to provide preferential treatment to their own productions. If popular American-backed films qualified as 'British' under the quota, it made economic sense to screen these and to cut back on in-house productions.

Rank's involvement in film production steadily diminished through the 1960s and 1970s, and in 1980 the firm announced its complete withdrawal from film-making activity. ABPC, likewise, became far less committed to producing films for the domestic market following the removal from office of their head of production at Elstree studios in 1958.[67] After their acquisition by EMI, the firm did embark on an international production strategy in the 1970s, in which it provided backing for a number of high profile pictures made in the United States. There were some early successes (most notably *The Deer Hunter*), but in the long run this high risk venture proved no more sustainable than earlier attempts at the international market. Thorn EMI Screen Entertainment did continue to make films into the 1980s, but on a reduced scale. The other significant British firm to enter the market in this period was ACC, headed by the charismatic entrepreneur Lew Grade. Grade had enjoyed a long and successful career as a theatrical agent and then television executive by the time he turned his attention to films in the 1970s. His attempts to revive the British film industry by backing major international projects, however, proved no more successful than those of EMI. There were individual successes, but not enough to compensate for the failures. Grade withdrew from film production (at least on a large scale) after the spectacular failure of the 1980 film *Raise the Titanic*. As he put it at the time, 'it would have been cheaper to lower the Atlantic'.[68]

RENAISSANCE OR RETRENCHMENT? THE BRITISH
FILM INDUSTRY SINCE THE 1980S

By 1980, the prospects for the British film industry looked decidedly unpromising. Cinema admissions continued to fall, which meant that the British market was too small to enable British films to recoup their costs on the basis of a domestic distribution. Attempts at producing films for wider international audiences, meanwhile, continued to prove unsustainable. The leading cinema chains continued to be owned by British firms, but these companies had become less interested in film production and were increasingly reliant on the pictures of US film distributors to fill their screens. British firms had ceased to be major players in either film production or distribution, and while they continued to control leading cinema circuits in the early 1980s, even their grip on cinema exhibition loosened as the decade progressed. This was the context in which Dickinson and Street published their history of the British film industry in 1985. Understandably, perhaps, the authors predicted a 'black future', in which 'British film production may finally lose its protracted but tenacious struggle for survival'.[69]

That British film production did survive through the 1980s and 1990s must be attributed in no small measure to the remarkable revival of the market for filmed entertainment. The renewal of this market has been an international phenomenon, and by no means restricted to Britain. It has been based partly on an increase in cinema attendance (associated with the development of 'multiplex' cinema venues), but more importantly on the growing importance of ancillary (post cinema release) distribution channels such as cable and pay TV and video/DVD. These developments have meant that, in real terms, the revenues earned by films in the British market are now broadly comparable with the levels of the 1930s and 1940s.

Figure 16.1 charts the decline, and subsequent (modest) revival in real revenues generated at the British box office since the 1930s. Before adjusting for inflation the growth in box office income since the mid-1980s appears to be quite spectacular. When we present the data in constant prices, however, we see that while revenues did more than double between 1984 and 1997, they remained four times smaller than they had been at their peak in the 1940s. The revival of the market for feature films in Britain, and internationally, was not based on box-office takings alone, but on the growing value of additional revenue streams from television and home video.

Precise figures for the amounts of revenue generated from different distribution channels in the British market are difficult to obtain, but an indication of the relative importance of each sector can be obtained by looking at the (international) sources of revenue of the major film distributors. Table 16.1, above, charts the change over time in the relative importance of these market sectors. Two sets of data are provided from recently published books that analyse the international film industry. There are discrepancies in the two sets of figures, but in terms of the relative share of the market accounted for by box-office cinema takings, the

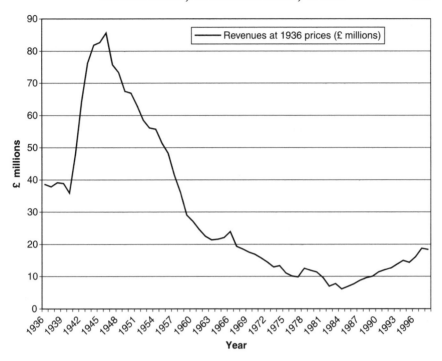

Figure 16.1. Annual revenues from cinema admissions in Britain (at 1936 prices)

trend over time is very clear. In Britain, where the growth of cable TV and home video did not take-off until the 1980s, the relative importance of cinema takings to overall revenues would have been much higher in 1980 than is indicated here. By the turn of the century, however, it is reasonable to assume that the relative importance of box-office income would have been broadly consistent across developed markets.[70]

Taking the information from Figure 16.1 and Table 16.1 together, and assuming that by the end of the 1990s cinema revenues accounted for somewhere between 20 and 25 per cent of the total market for films in Britain, we can see that in real terms, the total size of the British market had by the end of the century returned to (perhaps even surpassed) the levels of the 1940s. This is without taking into account revenues from film-related merchandising. As far as the British film market is concerned, the period since 1980 has indeed witnessed something of a renaissance – but can the same be said of the British film industry?

The size of the market for films in Britain may have returned to the levels of the 1940s, but a crucial difference between this earlier period and the 1990s, was that British films were no longer granted privileged access to their domestic market. The film quota that had, since 1927, reserved a certain proportion of screen time

Table 16.1. Worldwide sources of revenue for distributors of feature films (percentages)

Year	Cinema box office		Broadcast TV (inc. basic cable)		Pay TV		Home video/DVD	
	Vogel	Waterman	Vogel	Waterman	Vogel	Waterman	Vogel	Waterman
1948	100	100	0	0	0	0	0	0
1980	53.3	60.7*	39.7	16.2*	4.6	11.0*	2.4	12.1*
1985	24.8	39.0	46.86	12.7	8.7	10.4	19.6	37.9
1990	25.7	32.4	37.0	18.4	8.1	10.7	29.2	38.5
1995	21.1	27.2	29.9	14.5	8.8	9.6	40.2	48.6
2000	18.7	26.0	34.2	17.8	9.9	12.3	37.2	43.9
2004	16.5	23.9**	28.1	12.9**	8.9	10.4**	46.5	52.8**

* These figures refer to 1981.
** These figures refer to 2003.

Sources: Harold L. Vogel, *Entertainment Industry Economics*, Cambridge, 2007: 91; David Waterman, *Hollywood's Road to Riches*, Cambridge, MA, 2005: 290–1.

in British cinemas for films made in Britain, was eventually abolished in 1984. No consideration was ever given to regulating the proportion of British made films screened on television or released on video.

The decision to abolish the film quota, along with the Eady levy, aroused *relatively* little opposition. Both measures had been introduced to support and promote British film production, but as the economic viability of film-making for British firms became increasingly questionable in the declining market of the 1960s and 1970s, there was little by way of a domestic industry for the state to support. Many of the films classified as 'British' for the purposes of both the quota and the British Film Fund were financed and distributed by US firms. The single biggest payout from the Film Fund in 1978, for example, was £123,000 for a short film called *Hot Wheels* which was screened as part of the supporting programme for the hit film *Grease*.[71] With the chief beneficiaries of British film policy often being US rather than British firms, the argument for a change of policy was compelling.

What policy-makers in the early 1980s could not have predicted, of course, was that the film market was set for a period of rapid expansion which would have made the production of British films for the domestic market a viable strategy once again had some form of quota remained in place. As it was, with the British film market returned to the sort of free-trade conditions last seen in the 1920s, British firms were less able to benefit from the resurgent market of the 1980s and 1990s in the way that their predecessors had in the 1930s and 1940s. It was certainly possible for a modestly budgeted film to recoup its costs in the British market by the 1990s, but unlike in earlier periods, there was much less certainty that such a film from an independent British producer would make it onto British cinema or television screens.

At this point it should be emphasized that even though takings at the cinema box-office constituted a diminishing proportion of total film industry revenues in the 1980s and 1990s, the importance for any individual film of a successful cinema release remained crucial. If we were to compare patterns of film distribution in the 1990s with those of the 1940s, we could say that a cinema release in the later period was broadly equivalent to a screening in 'first run' cinemas. Similarly, the release of a film on DVD or pay-per-view television was similar to a 'second run', with subsequent screenings on cable or terrestrial television constituting third or fourth runs. While these secondary distribution channels may have brought in proportionately much more revenue in the 1980s and 1990s than third or fourth run cinemas ever did in the 1940s, a film's ability to tap into these lucrative markets was very much dependent on the strength of its popularity with cinema audiences. Films that proved unsuccessful on their cinema release, or which failed to get a cinema distribution at all (thus being released 'straight to video') were typically unable to attract anything like the same revenues from secondary markets as those with stronger box-office appeal. If British film producers were to benefit from the revival of the market, therefore, it remained as important as ever that they were able to gain access to the screens of the leading cinema chains.

For British production companies, the problem was not just that UK cinemas were no longer required to screen their films, but that they had no direct control over film distribution or exhibition in their domestic market. The firms which owned and controlled the major British cinema chains in the 1980s and 1990s were no longer important producers or distributors of British films. The Rank Group continued to run the Odeon chain of cinemas until 2000, but the company was never persuaded to go back on its decision to withdraw from film production in 1980.[72] The ABC cinema chain passed through the hands of several owners, including the Cannon Group in the 1980s and MGM and Virgin in the 1990s before being acquired by a private equity firm and eventually merged with the Odeon chain in 2000. By the 1990s these two cinema chains were no longer the dominant force in film exhibition that they had once been. The pioneers of multiplex cinema venues in Britain were American firms such as Warner Bros. and UCI, and these chains (owned and controlled by American producer–distributors) became at least as important as the older Odeon and ABC circuits.[73] In the 1990s, US film producers and distributors had arguably acquired greater control over film exhibition in Britain than at any time in their history.

While US firms integrated forward into film exhibition in Britain, there was less inclination on the part of British firms to (re)create a vertically integrated industry structure. Independent film production companies in Britain were in no position to build or buy their own cinema chains, while the owners of the main British cinema circuits had little desire to become active in production. The only evidence of vertical integration in the British industry at this time came from television broadcasting organizations, such as the BBC and Channel 4, which did make investments in feature film production. While such firms were in a position to guarantee television screenings for the films they backed, they had little or no influence over the all important (first run) cinema release. The revival in the market for filmed entertainment may have made a domestically oriented film production strategy viable once again, but even firms interested in making films mainly for the British market were now increasingly reliant on US film distributors to handle the release of their pictures.

In the early 1980s, with cinema audiences in decline and large film companies in both Britain and America cutting back on their film-making investments in Britain, the prospects for British film producers looked decidedly unpromising. Yet a glance at the list of Academy Award winners and nominees for this period tells a different story. Films such as *Chariots of Fire, Gandhi, A Passage to India, The Killing Fields*, and *A Room With a View* figure prominently. 1985 was the fourth year in a row, according to one observer, that 'the Oscar nominations look like a benefit night for the British film industry.'[74] Not since the 1960s had 'British' films been so critically and commercially successful in the US. The difference this time was that the films in question relied mainly on British, rather than American, backers. How had this happened? And for how long could it last?

By far the most important investor in British film production at this time was Goldcrest Films. The firm had started out with the modest intention of providing 'development finance' for potentially promising projects.[75] After becoming associated with some high profile successes, Goldcrest eventually became part of the Pearson Group, and began its involvement in film financing on a much larger scale. Its first major investment was in the film *Gandhi* (a project which Richard Attenborough had spent twenty years trying, unsuccessfully, to find backers for), to which worldwide distribution rights were eventually sold to Columbia. By the time *Gandhi* was awarded its eight Oscars, Goldcrest appeared to have carved out an interesting market niche. It invested in films which were distinct from Hollywood adventure, romance or comedy pictures, yet which had a clear international appeal, often being based on real historical events and touching on important social issues. After some notable successes, however, the strategy began to unravel. Fundamentally, the problem was that Goldcrest had no control over film distribution or exhibition. It relied on selling the distribution rights for its pictures to US firms (which gave the firm only a share of the distributor's share of the box-office revenue). Even if Goldcrest succeeded in keeping production costs on its films under control, they still needed to be very successful in order for the firm to make money. Very little needed to go wrong in order for the firm to lose money, and before long it did. By the beginning of 1986 the company was struggling for survival, and by 1987 that struggle was finally lost. The latest heroic attempt by a British firm to compete in the international market had ended as all earlier efforts had done.[76]

Goldcrest's sudden rise to prominence helped to rekindle the interest of the major US studios in British film-making talent, and a number of British producers were able to form agreements with US distributors in the 1980s.[77] Goldcrest's failure, however, was yet another reminder that without an international film distribution network, no British company was in a position to compete with those US firms on a long-term basis. The 1990s did witness a serious attempt on the part of a British-based enterprise to establish such an international distribution network. The company was Polygram Filmed Entertainment (PFE), and it briefly looked as though it might become the first European film distributor to challenge the international dominance of US firms since the 1910s.

PFE is better thought of as a European enterprise rather than a British one. It was based in London and headed by a British manager, but it was ultimately owned and controlled by the Dutch electronics multinational Phillips. Its aim was to establish a major European centre for film production and distribution to rival the US studios. It did handle the distribution of some prominent US film-makers (such as the Coen brothers), but many of its films were made by European producers and part-financed by various European media organization such as Canal+, Channel 4, and the BBC. Of the European production units that supplied PFE with product, much the most important was a London-based company called Working Title. Its film, *Four Weddings and a Funeral*, provided PFE with its first major success, and it remains the most consistent producer of popular British films at the time of writing.

PFE appeared to have developed a viable business model. It had built up a network of production companies, for which it supplied financial backing, but to which it also allowed creative autonomy. PFE's manager likened the system to that of record labels in the music industry, but it was also strikingly similar to the system of 'independent producers' operated by Rank in the 1940s. The key difference between PFE and Rank (apart from the latter's lack of a US distribution arm) was that PFE exercised much tighter financial control over their producers.[78]

Whether PFE's business model would have proved any more sustainable than Korda's, or Rank's, or Goldcrest's, will never be known. In 1999, Phillips decided to sell its nascent film distribution subsidiary to Vivendi (which merged it into its own US film subsidiary, Universal). With projects such as *Billy Elliot* and *Notting Hill* in the pipeline, however, at the time of its sale PFE was a promising enterprise and not a failing one. Following PFE's sale, Working Title went on to form a close relationship with Universal, with the US distributor acquiring a 67 per cent stake in the firm. Universal now provides the financial backing and distribution for its films – which have included *Bridget Jones's Diary, Pride and Prejudice,* and *Atonement,* along with more specifically British oriented pictures such as *Hot Fuzz*.

CONCLUSIONS

In the middle decades of the twentieth century the global film industry was essentially dominated by an oligopoly of vertically integrated US firms, with various national European film industries functioning effectively within their (protected) domestic markets. By the end of the twentieth century the vertically integrated structure of the industry had broken down to a large extent, but the same US firms remained at the heart of global film distribution networks. During the 1930s and 1940s British firms had tried and failed to compete with the major American studios in international markets. The firms that had prospered in this period had been those restricting their ambitions to the protected domestic market. By the end of the twentieth century, no British firm had managed to establish a global distribution network of its own. With the domestic market no longer protected, the firms which survived and prospered did so not so much by eschewing international markets, but by finding a distinctive position within the (US dominated) global film distribution networks.

Does this constitute a story of decline, or of renaissance? It is certainly not difficult to cast the history of the British film industry as a tale of decline. By focusing on the operation of the domestic film industry within Britain from the 1930s onwards, we can chart the emergence of powerful vertically integrated firms under dynamic (and patriotic) British entrepreneurs which, as the post-war decades progressed, reduced their commitment to film production and gradually lost control over film distribution and exhibition as well. If we are to look at the industry over a slightly longer historical period and from a broader international perspective, however, a slightly different picture begins to emerge. It perhaps makes more sense to judge the contemporary film industry not in comparison with the 1930s and 1940s, but with the 1910s and 1920s, when broadly comparable free market conditions existed. In both periods the demand for filmed entertainment within Britain was strong, and most of this demand was satisfied by imported US product (much of which was distributed by American firms). Rather than a process of steady decline, perhaps we have seen the industry return to something like its existing form before the introduction of Government protection that supported it in its so-called heyday.

Did half a century of Government support for the British film industry really leave no longer lasting benefits? In terms of domestic film distribution and exhibition, arguably not. British firms probably have less control over the way in which films are today presented to the British cinema going public than was the case in the 1920s. In terms of film production, however, British firms are now better equipped to compete in a competitive global market than in the pre-1927 period. British producers may be dependent on global distribution networks that they do not own or control, and some of the most popular 'British' films may actually be co-productions with major US studios, but films made by British firms and based on British themes or characters continue to be made and enjoyed by audiences in the UK and beyond. British films actually achieved a 27 per cent market share of the domestic box-office in 2007 (up from 19% in 2006).[79] Had the British film industry been able to achieve this level of success in the 1920s there would have been little need for protective legislation.

NOTES

1. F. Truffaut, *Hitchcock*, London, 1966: 100.
2. For an introduction to some of this literature see, J. Curran and V. Porter, eds., *British Cinema History*, London, 1983; C. Barr, ed., *All Our Yesterdays*, London, 1986; R. Murphy, ed., *The British Cinema Book*, London, 1997; J. Ashby and A. Higson, eds., *British Cinema: Past and Present*, London, 2000.
3. For example, J. Eberts and T. Ilott, *My Indecision is Final: The Rise and Fall of Goldcrest Films*, London, 1990; M. Kuhn, *One Hundred Films and a Funeral*, London, 2002.

4. V. Toulmin, S. Popple, and P. Russell, eds., *The Lost World of Mitchell and Kenyon*, London, 2004.

5. R. Low and R. Manvell, *The History of the British Film, Vol. I, 1896–1906*, London, 1948.

6. R. Brown, 'War on the Home Front', *Film History*, 16, 2004: 28–36.

7. R. Brown, 'New Century Pictures', in Toulmin et al., eds., *The Lost World*: 69–82.

8. Brown, 'War on the Home Front'.

9. Political and Economic Planning (PEP hereafter), *The British Film Industry*, London, 1952: 27–8.

10. For a fuller explanation see G. Bakker, 'The Decline and Fall of the European Film Industry', *Economic History Review*, 58, 2005, 310–51.

11. G. Bakker, 'Stars and Stories', *Enterprise and Society*, 2, 2001, 45–76.

12. Low and Manvell, *History of the British Film, Vol. I*: 108.

13. R. Low, *The History of the British Film, Vol. II, 1906–1914*, London, 1948: 119.

14. A. Kuhn, *Cinema, Censorship and Sexuality, 1909–1925*, London, 1988.

15. R. Brown and B. Anthony, *A Victorian Film Enterprise*, Trowbridge, 1999.

16. Low and Manvell, *History of the British Film, Vol. I*: 21.

17. Low, *History of the British Film, Vol. II*: 132.

18. Low and Manvell, *History of the British Film, Vol. I*: 25–7.

19. Brown and Anthony, *Victorian Film Enterprise*.

20. The showman was Walter Haggar, see Low and Manvell, *History of the British Film, Vol. I*: 21.

21. Low, *History of the British Film, Vol. II*: 20.

22. J. Burrows, 'Folly, Fraud and Failure? Evaluating the Hostility of the Financial Press Towards the Early British Film Exhibition Industry, 1910–1914', Paper presented at the University of Reading, Jun. 2006.

23. PCT was unusual in that it did have strong financial backing (from the industrialist Sir William Bass).

24. PEP, *British Film Industry*: 37.

25. Bakker, 'Decline and Fall'.

26. Low, *History of the British Film, Vol. II*: 54, 133.

27. N. Hiley, 'Let's Go to the Pictures', *Journal of Popular British Cinema*, 2, 1999: 39–53; H.E. Browning and A.A. Sorrell, 'Cinemas and Cinema-Going in Great Britain', *Journal of the Royal Statistical Society*, 117, 1954: 133–65.

28. W.V. Strauss, 'Foreign Distribution of American Motion Pictures', *Harvard Business Review*, 8, Apr. 1930; H. Lewis, *The Motion Picture Industry*, New York, 1933; K. Thompson, *Exporting Entertainment*, London, 1985.

29. PEP, *British Film Industry*: 45–7; M. Dickinson and S. Street, *Cinema and State: The Film Industry and the British Government 1927–84*, London, 1985: 34–5.

30. M. Glancy, 'Temporary American Citizens? British Audiences, Hollywood Films and the Threat of Americanization in the 1920s', *Historical Journal of Film, Radio and Television*, 26, Oct. 2006; 461–84; R. Low, *The History of the British Film, 1918–1929*, London, 1971.

31. R. Low, *Film Making in 1930s Britain*, London, 1985; Dickinson Street, *Cinema and State*; J. Sedgwick, *Popular Film-Going in 1930s Britain: A Choice of Pleasures*, Exeter, 2000.

32. F.D. Klingender and S. Legg, *Money Behind the Screen*, London, 1937.

33. T. Ryall, 'A British Studio System: The Associated British Picture Corporation and the Gaumont-British Picture Corporation in the 1930s', in R. Murphy, ed., *The British Cinema Book*, London, 1997.

34. See Vincent Porter's introduction to W. Mycroft, *The Time of My Life*, Oxford, 2006: xix–xx; *The Times*, 4 Oct. 1940: 9; Klingender and Legg, *Money*: 30–2; PEP, *British Film Industry*: 47–8.

35. Klingender and Legg, *Money*: 23–9; PEP, *British Film Industry*: 45–7.

36. See Robert Murphy, 'Deutsch, Oscar', in D. Jeremy, ed., *Dictionary of Business Biography*, London, 1984: 89–93. Other fast growing cinema chains in the 1930s included Union cinemas and the County circuit, both of which were acquired by larger vertically integrated firms.

37. Geoffrey Macnab, *J. Arthur Rank and the British Film Industry*, London, 1993: 17–34; PEP, *British Film Industry*: 61–6; Klingender and Legg, *Money*: 37–41.

38. Klingender and Legg, *Money*.

39. PEP, *British Film Industry*: 67.

40. PEP, *British Film Industry*: 67–75; Klingender and Legg, *Money*: 53–5.

41. V. Porter, 'Film History of Cinema History: The Case of John Maxwell', Paper presented at the University of Reading, Jun. 2006.

42. Sedgwick, *Popular Filmgoing*: 211–29; Ryall, 'A British Studio System'.

43. See Charles Barr, *Ealing Studios*, London, 1977.

44. Karol Kulik, *Alexander Korda: The Man Who Could Work Miracles*, New Rochelle, 1975.

45. Peter Miskell, '"Selling America to the World"? The Rise and Fall of an International Film Distributor in its Largest Foreign Market: United Artists in Britain, 1927–1947', *Enterprise and Society*, 7, 4, Dec. 2006: 740–76.

46. Sedgwick, *Popular Filmgoing*: 232–5.

47. Macnab, *J. Arthur Rank*: 115.

48. Ibid.: 82–120.

49. For more on the British films of the 1940s see R. Murphy, *Realism and Tinsel*, London, 1989; A. Aldgate and J. Richards, *Britain Can Take It*, Oxford, 1986; C. Drazin, *The Finest Years*, London, 1998.

50. Macnab, *J. Arthur Rank*: 51–81.

51. Dickinson and Street, *Cinema and State*: 89–102.

52. M. Glancy, *When Hollywood Loved Britain*, Manchester, 1999: 81–8.

53. I. Jarvie, *Hollywood's Overseas Campaign: The North Atlantic Movie Trade, 1920–1950*, Cambridge, 1992; Murphy, *Realism and Tinsel*: 219–23; J. Trumpbour, *Selling Hollywood to the World*, Cambridge, 2002: 200–8.

54. Dickinson and Street, *Cinema and State*: 211–26.

55. I. Bernstein, *Hollywood at the Crossroads*, Hollywood AFL Film Council, 1957: 48–61.

56. L. Wood, *British Film Industry*, London, 1980.

57. J. Sedgwick, 'Product Differentiation at the Movies: Hollywood, 1946–1965', *Journal of Economic History*, 62, 3, 2002: 676–705; A. de Vany, *Hollywood Economics: How Extreme Uncertainly Shapes the Film Industry*, London, 2004.

58. J. Spraos, *The Decline of the Cinema*, London, 1962.

59. Sedgwick, 'Product Differentiation'.

60. Dickinson and Street, *Cinema and State*: 234.

61. A. Walker, *Hollywood England: The British Film Industry in the Sixties*, London, 1974.

62. Based on data presented in Dickinson and Street, *Cinema and State*: 240.

63. It should be noted that the most important shareholder in ABPC at this time was the US firm Warner Bros., with 37.5 per cent of the shares.

64. Macnab, *J. Arthur Rank*: 227–8.

65. PEP, *British Film Industry*: 80; Wood, *British Film Industry*, Leaflet E: 3.

66. Walker, *Hollywood England*; R. Murphy, *Sixties British Cinema*, London, 1992.

67. V. Porter, 'All Change at Elstree: Warner Bros., ABPC and British Film Policy, 1945–1961', *Historical Journal of Film, Radio and Television*, 21, 1, 2001: 5–35.

68. P. Waymark, 'Grade, Lew', in H.C.G. Matthew and B. Harrison, eds., *Oxford Dictionary of National Biography*, 23, Oxford, 2004: 160–3.

69. Dickinson and Street, *Cinema and State*: 247–8.

70. David Waterman estimates that in foreign (non-US) markets, takings at cinemas contributed 84 per cent of total revenues in 1981, while the figure for the US domestic market was just 50 per cent. In 2000, by contrast, cinema takings were estimated to be 26 per cent of total revenues in both US and foreign markets. Waterman, *Hollywood's Road to Riches*: 290.

71. Second Report of the Interim Action Committee on the Film Industry, *The Financing of the British Film Industry*, HMSO, London, 1979: 7.

72. A. Walker, *Icons in the Fire*, London, 2004: 214–16.

73. The development of the UCI cinema chain in Britain (and later other foreign markets) was actually a joint venture between the Paramount and Universal film companies based in the United States. The chain was sold to the private equity group Terra Firma in 2004, and merged with the Odeon chain (which had itself been merged with the old ABC cinema circuit in 2000).

74. J. Eberts and T. Ilott, *My Indecision is Final: The Rise and Fall of Goldcrest Films*, London, 1990: 445.

75. This involved relatively small sums of money to fund the preparation and polishing of scripts or screenplays which producers could subsequently pitch to potential investors.

76. Eberts and Ilott, *My Indecision is Final*.

77. For example, Richard Attenborough with Universal and Palace Pictures with Miramax. Columbia even (briefly) made a British producer (David Putnam) its chief executive in the mid-1980s.

78. Kuhn, *One Hundred Films and a Funeral*.

79. UK Film Council, *Research and Statistics Bulletin*, 5, 1, Oct. 2007: 4.

17

British Sport Transformed: Sport, Business, and the Media since 1960

Dilwyn Porter

Sport is not a game. It is a business. (*Financial Times,* 21 Jul. 1997)

If there was ever any doubt that football was more than a game, the press coverage generated by England's failure to qualify for the final stages of Euro 2008 would have settled the issue. While the sports pages criticized a disappointing performance against Croatia, there was an abundance of news and comment reflecting the relationship between sport, business, and the media. The Football Association (FA) was said to have missed out on £150 million in revenue to have been derived from licenses to manufacture and sell endorsed products – items ranging from replica shirts to inflatable hands, soft toys, and beer – that would not now be taken up. The negative impact of England's defeat on consumer spending was estimated to be over £1 billion. At Independent Television (ITV), which had bought the rights to screen the tournament, England's exit was estimated to have cost between £10 and £12 million in lost advertising revenue, perhaps £14 million if England had reached the final. Some consolation, however, could be derived from the news that a better than expected World Cup performance by England's rugby union team a few months earlier along with Lewis Hamilton's bid for the Formula One drivers' championship had generated huge viewing figures for ITV so that advertising revenues still showed an increase over the previous year.[1]

Thus the events of a single year in modern sport demonstrate how a goalkeeping error, a refereeing decision, or a mechanical failure can impact on businesses located well beyond the boundaries of sport itself. They are also indicative of the way in which sport in Britain has been transformed since 1960. There is, of course, a long-standing relationship between sport and business. What has happened since sport established itself as a form of commercialized entertainment in the late nineteenth century is that this relationship has become progressively more structured and more visible, a process in which the growth of business sponsorship has played a major part. In the 1930s, according to the FA's Sir Frederick Wall, the 'financial side' of the game was likely to arise wherever football was discussed. By the end of the twentieth century, its importance was such that it had changed the way in which football was talked about. 'Gone were the game's familiar terms and phrases', observed James Walvin. 'The game which had for a century been the people's game was now discussed as an 'investment vehicle'.[2] There was an element of hyperbole here – excusable on account of the rapidity with which change had occurred in the 1990s and the relatively new phenomenon of an active market in the shares of leading clubs – but there was certainly an increasing tendency to discuss football and other sports as if they were branches of commerce. 'What newspapers call sports sections nowadays', one journalist recently observed, 'often look as though they should be tacked onto the financial page'.[3]

If its relationship with business has changed sport and the way we think about it, so too has its relationship with the media. Again, the connection goes back a long way. Sport and the media have had a symbiotic relationship since the late nineteenth century. 'There was never any doubt in the minds of both newspaper proprietors and editors that racing results and tips sold newspapers', Tony Mason has argued. 'Football coverage probably helped too'.[4] The rapid transmission of sports news was the activity on which the British sporting press was founded. Results, statistics, match reports, and transfer gossip – the formula popularized by the newspaper industry's sporting 'pinks' and 'greens' – now constitute the stock-in-trade of Sky Sports News, their direct descendant. The advent of radio and then television changed the relationship between sport and the media and eventually raised it to a new level of interdependence. Whereas the publicity provided by the press was an unqualified benefit in that it generated and sustained public interest in the entertainment on offer, coverage by the broadcast media (especially live coverage) was more problematic in that it offered new ways of consuming sport without the inconvenience of leaving home and having to pay for entrance. Though there was variation from sport to sport, the relationship with television evolved gradually up to the 1980s. 'After at first being barred from many sports events because of its likely impact on crowd attendances', one media historian has observed, 'and then admitted only on the strictest conditions, television has gradually begun to take them over, in some instances adapting them to its own particular requirements by changing the way in which they are played'.[5] It is commonplace, for example, for major sporting events to be timed to meet the requirements of television, rather than for the convenience of paying spectators. It is often argued now that the relationship with the media has effectively changed the nature of sport itself. 'For many people', as Garry Crawford has suggested, '(and for most of the time) sport is television sport'. This fusion of sport and communications has led some social scientists to refer to 'a new genetic strain called MediaSport'.[6]

Though there are difficulties in defining the limits of the sports business, it is clear that consumer spending on sport and sports-related goods and services grew steadily through the twentieth century, accelerating rapidly from the mid-1980s. John Benson has estimated that expenditure by active participants in sport was four times greater in real terms at the start of the 1980s than it had been in the 1920s while non-participant expenditure doubled over the same period. He concludes that 'as players, spectators and as gamblers, those interested in sport became active, and often enthusiastic consumers of the sporting and sports-related goods and services made available to them'.[7] The Leisure Industries Research Centre noted that consumer expenditure on sport surged by 30 per cent in real terms between 1985 and 1995 when it reached a total of £10.4 billion, 2.33 per cent of total consumer expenditure. Over the same period, the number employed in sport and sports-related services grew from 324,470 to 415,000, 1.61 per cent of total employment. Total consumer expenditure on sport stood at £15.2 billion by 2000, its high rate of growth in the late 1990s being in part attributable to a surge in satellite television subscriptions.[8] The sustained long-term growth indicated generally benign market conditions across the twentieth century. During the last two decades, when sports-related expenditure grew faster than the economy of the United Kingdom as a whole, they were especially favourable as consumers were in a position to spend more on 'luxuries' than on 'essentials'.[9] Another way of looking at this is to view expenditure on sport as a function of ongoing developments in modern consumer societies. When people define themselves by what they consume rather than by what they produce an increasing proportion of income is spent on 'experiential commodities', such as holidays, leisure activities, and sport.

This suggests that it is best to work with broad rather than narrow definitions of the sports business. 'Sport' straddles a wide range of competitive and recreational activities in the market and non-market sectors of the economy. In addition, it tends to spill over from one business sector to another, blurring the boundaries by which they might otherwise be recognized. The line between sportswear and fashion is increasingly hard to discern.[10] Stephen Hardy has provided a way of negotiating this territory by defining sport as 'a three-part commodity'. 'These parts', he explains, 'which can exist in isolation but which reach full expression in combination, are as follows: the activity or game form, the service, and the goods'. Once a game form with recognized rules has become established, it is subject to a 'period of discovery' when the willingness of consumers to pay in order to play, watch, or otherwise engage in it – 'in essence exchanging money to derive their personal use-value from their own form of involvement' – is determined. This phase in the economic development of sport is characterized by the emergence of a variety of sports-related services, including the media. Finally, having argued that sport is commodified via the development of related services, 'sports goods' are defined rather narrowly as 'the physical objects necessary to the game form' (e.g. balls, bats, sports clothing) that are indicated by the rules'.[11] British sport in the second half of the twentieth century saw significant developments in game forms, as it adapted to an increasingly competitive commercial climate; it saw a huge development of sports services for participants and spectators, most evident in golf courses, sports centres, fitness clubs, new stadia, and the broadcast media. Finally, the manufacture and sale of equipment and clothing have grown enormously. Hardy's definition of the sports product is helpful; it recognizes a dynamic relationship with the market and embraces both competitive and recreational sport. This is important when considering an era that saw darts, once a recreational game played in pubs, acquire a world championship, a commercially sponsored professional circuit and a substantial television audience.

The intention here is to focus on the way in which sport has been transformed since the early 1960s. During this period, the bodies governing British sport were subject to pressures that led them to abandon the amateur, anti-commercial ethos that had shaped their activities since the mid-nineteenth century, thus removing many of the constraints that had inhibited the development of sports business. Though modernization was slow and uneven – arguably it was incomplete until rugby union went 'open' in 1995 – the institutional changes that occurred made it possible for sport to benefit from a closer relationship with business, to become more businesslike in the way it conducted its affairs and eventually to be recognized as a business in itself. Aside from the stimulus of competition with other forms of entertainment, the process of transformation in British sport was shaped by two external influences – business sponsorship and television, the latter being the most powerful factor determining the nature of the sports product by the end of the century. At the same time, it is important to recognize that the growth of the sports business reflects long-term trends in consumer expenditure. In the ten years after 1985, the era which saw the advent of football's Premier League and open rugby, the fastest growing areas of consumer expenditure on sport were participants' fees and club subscriptions (up 115 per cent) and spending on clothes and footwear (both up 105 per cent).[12] Selling recreational sport and leisure services, along with associated sportswear and equipment, to recreational joggers or to women keeping fit and losing weight at local sports centres, was as important a feature of sports business as the much publicized corporate romance between the Premier League and British Sky Broadcasting (BSkyB).

OPENING UP: BRITISH SPORT IN THE 1960s

In the late 1950s and early 1960s, Britain succumbed to anxious introspection. Readers were submerged under a wave of 'state-of-the-nation' literature; a series of Penguin 'specials' asked 'What's Wrong with Britain?' If a unifying theme was discernible, it was that the people running the country were out-of-touch and that its institutions were out-of-date: 'the fusty Establishment, with its Victorian views and standards of judgement, must be destroyed'.[13] The institutions that had governed British sport since the middle of the nineteenth century were also called to account. Most of them appeared to be the very embodiment of Victorianism, not least in the importance they assigned to amateurism and the anti-commercial ethos that it encompassed. 'Even sports in which professionals played a prominent part', as Richard Holt has noted, 'were frequently run by amateurs'.[14] It did not help that British sportsmen and women often appeared to underperform in international competition or that sports which had once attracted large crowds were losing their appeal.

In these circumstances the 'amateurs' who governed British sport were fair game. According to an *Economist* survey of the state of British sport in 1960, cricket's governing body, the Marylebone Cricket Club (MCC) 'did very much as it likes', even if it was not always in the best long-term interests of the game. The Rugby Football Union (RFU) – 'old farts' many years before Will Carling applied the label – was condemned for its continuing vendetta against rugby league and the Football League, where England's ninety-two full-time professional clubs were located, for looking inwards and backwards at the same time.

The League's objective is the familiar one of many small trade associations (once very prevalent in manufacturing but now declining there thanks to the Restrictive Trades Practices Act) – that of keeping as many small and inefficient firms as possible in being. To this end it operates a rigid system of dividend limitation (which prevents any dynamic commercial types coming into the business and building attractive new stadia) and an even more rigid system of wage limitation (which keeps bright young men out of professional football and is one reason why England nowadays is beaten by teams like Brazil, who do not have to rely on the typically bovine 'failed eleven-plus' types that League football so largely depends on).[15] Like the MCC and the RFU, the football authorities – both the Football League and the FA – had autocratic tendencies. Critics were subject to 'a dubious form of censorship' and disciplined if they spoke out.[16]

These criticisms seemed especially relevant at a time when many British sports, especially those that relied heavily on gate receipts, appeared to be failing. Attendances at Football League matches fell from forty-one million in 1948–9 to twenty-eight million in 1961–2; 'Soccer's Missing Millions' became a sports page cliché. Some other sports fared even worse. Rugby league attendances declined even more dramatically from 6.8 million in 1949–50 to below three million in 1959–60. Clubs struggled to find the money for wages, ground maintenance and, until they were mercifully released from the burden in 1957, a 16 per cent Entertainment Tax on their declining gate receipts. They increasingly depended on funds raised by supporters' clubs through football pools, lotteries, and raffles.[17] Greyhound racing, another working-class entertainment that enjoyed a boom in the immediate post-war period, also suffered declining attendances in the 1950s and 1960s. Here the downward trend was accentuated by the impact of the 1960 Betting and Gaming Act which legalized off-course betting.[18]

The problem was especially evident in the lower reaches of the Football League, though here the clubs were offered a degree of protection by the imposition of a maximum wage. 'The real hope of the smaller clubs at present', noted the *Economist*, 'is to discover a youthful star, and sell him for a large transfer fee to a bigger'. If a percentage of the transfer fee was paid to footballers, as their union was demanding, 'or if higher clubs were allowed to lure players away by the offer of higher maximum wages, this system of finance would collapse'. With two-thirds of the ninety-two League clubs in the red, the situation was indeed precarious as Accrington Stanley was to discover when its cash flow dried up during the grim winter of 1961–2 leading to its resignation from the competition in midseason. 'The existing organisation and wage restrictions', the *Economist* had observed earlier, '. . . are designed to keep a host of small clubs in small towns like Accrington barely alive'. Now, it seemed, the achievement of even this modest objective could not be guaranteed and the football authorities were advised to embrace rationalization before market forces made it inevitable.[19]

The suggestion was sometimes made that winter-season sports businesses, should switch to summer so as to take advantage of lighter evenings and warmer weather, but the experience of county cricket clubs during this period was hardly encouraging. In English cricket, cash-strapped clubs were playing in front of dwindling crowds from May to September, down from two million in 1950 to 750,000 in 1960. It did not help that summer was the time of year when opportunities to pursue other leisure activities were maximized. 'Accepting the principle that cricket never has and never will be a money-making concern', the Essex and England all-rounder Trevor Bailey wrote in 1961, 'there is every reason to suppose that the game in its present form will continue for years to come'.[20] As it turned out, he was wrong, but his attitude of resignation was illuminating for it seemed that many had given up any hope of making first-class cricket pay. Significantly, Warwickshire's reputation as the most enterprising of the seventeen first-class county clubs in the 1950s was due largely to its success in developing a weekly football pool.[21]

The crisis conditions that many sports were experiencing by the early 1960s did generate a series of reforms which were of long-term significance for the business development of sport, even though they were often undertaken reluctantly. Where reform was most radical, as in cricket and tennis, it involved a decisive breach with the amateur traditions that had kept commerce at a distance. In this respect the symbolic significance of the MCC's abandonment of the class-based distinction between gentlemen (amateurs) and players (professionals) in 1962 was hugely important even though it might be seen simply as a rational response to a decline in the number of cricketers with sufficient time, money and talent to play as amateurs at the top level. 'At the time', as Derek Birley has argued, 'the outside world, on the brink of the Beatles era, no doubt regarded it as a sign that even the MCC saw the need for change. In fact, their pre-occupation, then as afterwards, was for the preservation of the obsolete pattern of county cricket'.[22] Within these constraints the professionalization of county cricket's labour force helped to underpin the era of commercialization that was to follow. In order that the game form to which traditionalists were devoted (three-day county matches) might continue, it was necessary to subsidize it via the revenue that could be derived from what was often referred to as 'instant cricket'; firstly the Gillette Cup (1963) and later the John Player League (1969) and the Benson and Hedges Cup (1972), each offering a variety of 'limited-overs' matches that guaranteed a result at the end of a single day's play. Professionalization facilitated the transition to a regime which imposed new and greater demands on cricketers as they travelled the county circuit, often having to adapt to two or three versions of the game within a week, which included play on Sundays from 1966. It was, in the parlance of the trade, 'a lot of hard yakka', a working life rather than a gentlemanly pursuit.[23]

The arrival of open tennis at Wimbledon a few years later supplied another symbolic breach with sport's amateur past. As in cricket, tennis was subject to the overriding influence of a private members' club, the All England Tennis and Croquet Club, whose annual tournament at Wimbledon was a money-spinner. At the start of the 1960s, Wimbledon was an amateur tournament. This meant that many of the world's best players were excluded. Paying spectators and a growing television audience continued to find it attractive – perhaps as much for its social ambience as for the tennis – and this helped to sustain elements within the game resistant to change. The pressure of external competition appears to have been critical here. The International Lawn Tennis Federation had come very close to sanctioning open tennis in 1960; major championships in the United States, Australia, and France were considering moving in that direction. 'If Wimbledon does not follow them', noted *The Economist*, 'it could then no longer claim to be one of the top tournaments of the world'.[24] By 1967, the steady drift of top amateurs into the professional ranks proved decisive. Disguised payments in the form of generous allowances for expenses were proving insufficiently attractive. When the All England Club announced that the 1968 tournament would be open, it was in the knowledge that 'not merely the reigning Wimbledon champion (John Newcombe) but an entire supporting cast [was] disappearing into the professional ranks'.[25] That this represented 'game, set and match' for professionalism and the intensified commercialism that came with it was evident by 1972 when Lamar Hunt's World Championship Tennis demanded a fee for its contracted players to participate at Wimbledon. Thereafter the commercial success enjoyed by professional tennis ensured that it was sometimes singled out as an example for other sports businesses to follow. In a highly competitive climate its tournament promoters were driven to exploit all available sources of revenue – paying spectators, sales of television rights, advertising, and sponsorship.[26]

While cricket abandoned the 'gentlemen' and tennis went open, football's symbolic breach with the past came when the Football League, under pressure from the Professional Footballers' Association (PFA), agreed to abolish the maximum wage system in 1961. It is possible to overstate the backwardness of British football at the start of the 1960s. Top clubs, with Hibernian leading the way in 1956 and Manchester United following in 1957, now engaged in European competition; the two-legged ties played under floodlights in mid-week offering an exotic variation on the customary domestic game. Floodlights were an important innovation enabling matches to kick-off at times that spectators might find more convenient. Most professional football clubs in England and Scotland installed them between 1958 and 1961, often using funds supplied by supporters' clubs. There was some resistance; 'I don't think there is any future in it at all', complained Gillingham's chairman. Other clubs saw it as a marketing opportunity: at Stockport County, where fans might be tempted by a short trip to see one of the Manchester clubs on a Saturday afternoon, the local club relaunched itself with floodlights under the slogan 'Friday Night is County Night'.[27] Rebranding and a greater attention to customer care was especially evident at Coventry City whose enterprising chairman, Derek Robins, and manager, Jimmy Hill, promoted the 'Sky Blue Revolution', transforming the club's fortunes on and off the field in the process.[28]

Yet, despite these signs of enterprise, the structures that had characterized professional football since the late nineteenth century remained unchanged. This was especially evident in the League's determination to defend its maximum wage regulations along with terms of employment ('retain and transfer') weighted heavily in favour of the employers. 'It is not too fanciful', Dave Russell has observed, 'to argue that football symbolised the world of industrial relations as the businessmen who largely ran the clubs would have liked it to be'.[29] As the League's dispute with the players' trade union came to a head in 1960–1, the abandonment of its restrictive practices was often regarded as a test of football's willingness to modernize. With strike action threatened by the PFA, the *Economist* came down firmly on the side of reform, linking the maximum wage to wider issues of competitiveness and changing consumer expectations:

... professional football is no longer a sport, it is an entertainment. To keep star players' wages artificially low is to condemn this entertainment to remain at the level of a third-rate repertory performance rather than where it should be, on the level of high-class West End (or Eurovision) drama. The day of the cloth-capped, faithful supporter of the local professional team has passed. Now that he can afford to travel to the nearest city to see a really good game – or to watch one on television (screening of star matches for a fat fee should be part of the League's reform) – the old-fashioned fan has not so much died as been transported to a higher sphere.[30]

It was also clear that the labour market for star footballers was now international. The wage ceiling, which applied in both the Football League (England) and the Scottish League, increased the possibility that the best players would be tempted by the salaries and non-wage benefits on offer in Italy, following the example set by John Charles, who had moved from Leeds United to Juventus in 1957. Thus when the PFA secured an agreement to end the maximum wage, it seemed an especially significant breakthrough. *The Economist* welcomed the news that England captain Johnny Haynes was to earn £7,000 a year playing for Fulham, 'just like any other valuable entertainer'.[31] The future of retain and transfer took longer to resolve and the PFA was reluctant to push the outcome of the case brought by George Eastham against Newcastle United in 1963 to its logical conclusion. Thus, though the courts ruled that it was 'unreasonable and therefore illegal' for a club to retain a player's registration at the end of his contract, a compromise was reached allowing them to protect their financial interest in transfer values while mitigating the hardships of 'soccer slavery'. This was not the freedom of movement later achieved via the Bosman ruling of 1995 but, as John Harding has argued, 'the professional player was now in a significantly better position vis-à-vis his employer than he had been all century'.[32] The collection of mainly small businesses huddling under the protective umbrellas provided by the Football and Scottish Leagues were thereafter less likely – and less able – to retain players against their will than before.

By the 1970s British sport had begun to shake off its nineteenth-century legacy. The transition, however, was incomplete and the pattern of development uneven. Motor racing, where the commercialization of sport was most advanced, was something of a special case on account of the level of investment required to design, build, and race Formula One cars. It was already a sport dominated by manufacturers: cars were plastered with advertisements, mainly for oils and other motoring-related products. The demise of Hesketh Racing in 1975 marked the end of sponsorship by the wealthy 'amateur' at this level. Lord Hesketh's ambitions to win the world championship with an all-British car had foundered 'on the costly realities of Grand Prix racing'.[33] Some sports, especially tennis and golf, had been revolutionized and, at least in terms of elite performers and tournaments, were highly commercialized. Wimbledon, it was noted in 1979, eleven years after the first open tournament, was 'an incongruously amateur shrine for the sport which can boast the largest number of teenage millionaires. In fact, it is run as an extremely successful business'.[34] British golf followed a similar route in 1971 via the Professional Golfers' Association (PGA) whose tournament director, Eric Jacobs, raised the prize money available on the professional circuit by determining which days of the golfing calendar were most valuable and stipulating that tournaments played on them should offer at least £15,000. 'The business point of view has moved into British golf', purred the *Economist* approvingly, 'and the results are spectacular'. By 1976, the PGA had established a separate Tournament Players' Division, under Jacobs's direction, with a remit to promote all professional golf tournaments in Britain.[35] This strategy was designed to ensure that top players committed themselves to the British tournament circuit thus making it more attractive for spectators, viewers, and sponsors alike.

There was, it seems, more awareness than before of the need to make the sports product attractive to newly affluent consumers who might now be inclined spend their leisure time in other ways. From 1965, it was the policy of the Jockey Club, long regarded as a citadel of diehard conservatism, to promote horse racing 'by making the spectator once more the focus of the sport'. Improving facilities for spectators became important. The British tendency to see sport as 'character-building', *The Economist* observed dryly in 1973, was because facilities for players and spectators were 'invariably so primitive that only the strongest characters could survive them'. It went on to praise the facilities offered by the new grandstand at Sandown Park which recognized 'that the trend in leisure activities is for people to trade up'.[36] In rugby league the mid-1960s had seen 'probably the biggest collective investment in stadia since the 1890s'.[37] Modifying the basic game form was another sign of a more consumer-aware attitude. This was, perhaps, most evident with one-day cricket but there were changes elsewhere designed to enhance spectator appeal. Allowing substitutes (rugby league 1964; football 1965), for example, reduced the incidence of one-sided contests when players were injured. The repeal of the Sunday Observance Act in 1969, though some restrictions remained in place, opened the way for more sport to be played on what was becoming an increasingly secularized Sabbath. Football took a step in this direction by sanctioning Sunday matches for the first time during the fuel crisis of 1974, an initiative that enjoyed a good deal of popular support that was reflected in higher attendances.[38]

Elsewhere amateurism, and the indifference to business that went with it, remained relatively intact. Major Olympic sports, like athletics and swimming, were reluctant to abandon the amateur ideal though it was increasingly compromised; *The Economist* urged them to take 'the tennis-golf route'.[39] Rugby union, whose officials lived and died by the amateur code, continued to resist modernization across the board. In Wales, where leading players were nominally amateur but 'blindside remuneration' was an open secret, clubs worked their way through a time-honoured fixture list comprised largely of friendly matches against each other. There were as yet no knock-out cup and no leagues. The 'friendly match', as D. J. Taylor has recently observed, remained 'the *locus classicus* of the amateur ethic'.[40] In England, the RFU remained attached to it, thus keeping professionalization, commerce, and the late twentieth century at a distance. 'We were', former Bedford and England international Derek Wyatt later recalled while reflecting on rugby union the mid-1970s, ' . . . happy in the tradition of the game. Coaching was still a dirty word; training was largely unscientific and progress something that happened in America'.[41] Likewise, professional football, despite the changes that had occurred in the 1960s, was still in the age of maximizing utility rather than profit. FA regulations dating from the era of amateur hegemony, especially rule 43 which limited dividends to 7.5 per cent before tax and outlawed the direct remuneration of club directors, were said to 'show a distaste for anyone seeking as a director to make a profit out of professional soccer'.[42] The end of the maximum wage may have changed the environment in which football's small businesses operated but 'Victorian views and standards of judgement' lingered.

AGENTS OF TRANSFORMATION: BUSINESS SPONSORSHIP AND THE MEDIA

Though the process of change was uneven and protracted it was sufficient to allow sport to develop closer links with business and to become more businesslike in the way that it conducted its affairs. This connection was especially clear in cricket where the abolition of status distinctions was quickly followed by deal with the razor and men's grooming product manufacturer Gillette to sponsor a new one-day knock-out competition from 1963. The phenomenal growth of commercial sponsorship in British sport since the 1960s has proved an especially important agent of transformation. While sports sponsorship 'hardly existed' before 1970, by 1999 it was estimated to be worth around £350 million annually.[43]

Indeed, this figure was an underestimate in that it failed to capture arrangements between small businesses and local clubs which may account for as much as a quarter of the total. A recent history of a local table tennis association recalled such an arrangement with a local firm in the 1970s; 'they gave us a new table, a good room and paid our registration fees the only proviso being that we played under their name'.[44] A glance at junior football coverage in any local newspaper indicates that no self-respecting parks side takes to the pitch these days in an unsponsored shirt. In addition, available estimates tend to measure only what is visible. Firms have often allocated significant time and human resources to servicing their sponsorship activities. Indeed, in some circumstances, it may well have been a major aspect of the work undertaken in relation to promotions and advertising. This would have applied especially to cigarette manufacturers forced to turn their attentions to sports sponsorship when they were prohibited from direct advertising on television in 1965.

British companies had long been alive to the advantages of associating themselves with sport, not least because of its appeal to male consumers. In both football and rugby league it was commonplace for beer to be advertised on perimeter fences and in match programmes as local suppliers 'aimed to secure the same allegiance to their brews as to the team on the field'.[45] Product endorsements by sports personalities also had a long history. Stanley Matthews, then England's most famous footballer, was paid £15 a week in the early 1950s ('more than I earned with Blackpool') to advertise the Cooperative Wholesale Society's football boots. Cricketer Denis Compton's relationship with Brylcreem has been well documented.[46] Sponsorship, however, has generally involved a systematic rather than an opportunistic business relationship with sport. It has proved especially attractive to companies seeking to improve their image by association with a healthy activity that attracts public attention or to increase brand awareness with a view to securing improved market share. The 'name awareness' of Cornhill Insurance rose by 18 per cent in four years after the company began sponsoring test cricket in 1977. Sponsorship might also be used to enhance the appeal of a product by association with a particular sport. Gillette's investment in county cricket was designed to overcome consumer resistance to the company's 'American' image by linking it with a sporting activity deemed quintessentially 'English'. In addition, there were companies that sought links with particular sports in order to secure their position in a niche market. Beefeater Gin's sponsorship of the Oxford and Cambridge Boat Race, an event with an elite social cachet, seemed to fall into this category, along with Sanatogen's sponsorship of bowls, where elderly participants were deemed to be in particular need of cod liver oil and other dietary supplements.[47]

Although it is difficult to quantify precisely the benefits derived from sponsorship, it is clear that the business community learned to regard them as useful and significant. The trickle of money into sport – only £2.5 million according to the Sports Council in 1971 – had become a hugely important revenue stream by the end of the 1980s when sponsorship was running at over £200 million annually. Not all sports were equally favoured. 'Small events', it was noted in

1971, 'usually have to go looking for sponsors. Big events, with mass interest, have sponsors looking for them'. Thus the British Show Jumping Association, with their 'big TV appeal', could 'dictate terms' to potential sponsors while other governing bodies were 'glad to take what they can get'. The Amateur Wrestling Association was reported to have approached thirty firms when seeking sponsorship for an international match but its efforts had produced only a bottle of whisky.[48] The exposure offered by television was recognized as critical. Colonel Whitbread, brewer and former National Hunt rider, was one of the first to recognize the importance of this connection when he chose to sponsor a Gold Cup at Sandown Park rather than buy airtime on commercial television in 1957.[49] This established an important trend. Companies increasingly viewed sports sponsorship 'as a more effective way of reaching their desired audience than plain advertising'.[50]

By the 1980s, sponsorship had become ubiquitous in British sport. The Sports Council, which set up a Sports Sponsorship Advisory Service in 1981, identified 714 active commercial sponsors in 1981, 927 in 1982, and 1,067 by mid-1983.[51] Though a few diehard amateur sports remained aloof, most were prepared to reach some accommodation with the new paymasters. The RFU, along with its Welsh counterpart, had argued in 1971 that 'commercial sponsorship is contrary to amateur principles'; by 1975, however, it had sold its new knock-out competition to John Player for £100,000.[52] The Jockey Club was moving decisively in the same direction, changing its rules in 1975 so that companies could own race-horses and advertise themselves by racing them under company names. Over 450 firms had taken advantage of this dispensation by 1979.[53] By the mid-1980s, it was commonplace for a sponsor's name to be linked to classic races such as the Holsten Pils St Leger and the Ever Ready Derby. The development of cricket sponsorship had been especially striking. The initial £6,500 invested by Gillette in 1963 had marked 'the beginning of formal modern cricket sponsorship and the rebirth of active public interest in the sport'. When Gillette relinquished its sponsorship of the major one-day knock-out competition in 1981, the National Westminster Bank took over, agreeing to pay an index-linked £250,000 a year for the privilege. The bank added a further £25,000 in 1982 to help cover the cost of extending the competition to the top thirteen minor counties, Scotland and Ireland. Yet the Nat West Bank Trophy was only one of six sponsored competitions in English first-class cricket by 1982. In addition to test matches and one-day internationals sponsored by Cornhill (£255,000) and Prudential Assurance (£120,000) respectively, there was a fifty-five-over, early season cup competition sponsored by Benson and Hedges (£207,000), a forty-over league competition sponsored by John Player (£300,000), along with the traditional three-day County Championship sponsored by Schweppes (£218,000).[54]

This trend accelerated throughout the 1980s. The unique status of the FA Cup, the oldest competition of its kind in the world, ensured that it remained unsponsored until 1994 but the Football League Cup, dating only from 1960, was renamed the Milk Cup in 1982 in recognition of its first sponsors, the Milk Marketing Board. The Football League accepted sponsorship from office equipment manufacturers Canon in 1983; the Scottish League from supermarket chain Finefare two years later. For spectators, one of the most obvious changes was that players were increasingly likely to wear the name of the club sponsor on their shirts. This was permitted in rugby league from 1974 and arrived in the Football League in 1979, though the growth of this practice was inhibited by the BBC's insistence that the advertisements be removed if a match was to be televised, a somewhat perverse requirement in view of the free airtime it made available to sponsors of sports events, notably test cricket and snooker. Despite this constraint, removed in 1984, it was still possible to raise some useful money in this way. Hitachi paid £50,000 in 1979 to sponsor Liverpool's shirts. As *The Economist* commented, they were buying, 'mobile billboards closely observed by 30,000 people for 90 minutes each week'.[55] At club level sponsorship helped to compensate for diminishing revenue from gate receipts as attendances continued their downward trend, accelerated in the 1980s by the impact of recession and the perception that there were safer places to spend a Saturday afternoon than at a football stadium in the company of hooligans. It was, however, increasingly possible for corporate sponsors to insulate themselves and their match-day guests from these grim realities in private boxes, first introduced by Manchester United at Old Trafford in 1964, and a feature at thirty-four British club grounds by 1986.[56] The proliferation of such facilities was an indication of the increasing importance of corporate hospitality, a development that was closely linked to business sponsorship of sport. The Sports Council noted that one company that allocated £50,000 annually to sports sponsorship – a major commitment in 1971 – dedicated half of this sum to entertaining customers.[57] In this context, it made sense for sports businesses to supply these facilities themselves. At Wimbledon, the All England Club, recognizing that 'companies are an important source of cash', was soon providing BP, IBM, Barclays Bank, and other corporate clients with 'up-market entertainment in the shape of hospitality marquees plus tickets'.[58]

When, some years later, the *Financial Times* declared unequivocally that sport was a business, it was prompted by the news that Merchant Asset Management (MAM), the United Kingdom's largest fund-management group, were sponsoring cricketer Brian Lara who had just scored a world-record 501 for Warwickshire against Durham. MAM was seeking 'to draw a connection between the excellence at sport of Lara . . . [and] its fund management skills'. It was also using cricket to target potential clients; 31.7 per cent of the television audience for cricket, it was noted, were classified in the socioeconomic group AB.[59] This underlined the nature of sponsorship as a hard-nosed commercial transaction. As far as British sport was concerned, it undoubtedly made a difference and cash was not the only consideration; there were perceived benefits 'in associating with experience, know-how and p.r.' (sic).[60] Given the importance of sponsorship as a lifeline, sports became more attuned to the requirements of business; it was important 'to produce an idea – a product – worthy of the sponsor's money'.[61] If this meant changing the game form, then so be it. In yachting, where powerful organizations like the Royal Ocean Racing Club were 'sniffy' about commerce, Admiral's Cup competitors were prohibited from any kind of advertising display while racing. 'Sponsors', it was reported, 'trust that such pettifogging restrictions will soon be swept away'. Frustrated race organizers circumvented these constraints in 1985, upstaging the main event by a race for 'maxis', replete with sponsors' logos. 'By starting the big boats 10 minutes earlier than the rest of the fleet, it was noted, "the organisers sidestepped the ban on advertising under existing rules"'.[62] Arguably, sponsorship encouraged enterprising behaviour of this kind. It was also clear that seeking, securing, and sustaining relationships with businesses imposed important disciplines. At county cricket clubs like Surrey, where even the drains were sponsored by the early 1980s, it was reported that 'the need for cricket to go commercial and adopt business procedures is not in dispute'.[63]

Yet, though the impact of commercial sponsorship on British sport since the 1960s was financially beneficial, it was insufficient in itself to bring about the structural changes that have created the modern sports business. It became clear in the 1970s and 1980s that the sporting revolution, such as it was, was incomplete. Indeed, there was something to be said for the argument that sponsorship, by offering sports a lifeline, had sometimes perpetuated inefficiency and died-in-the-wool conservatism. In English cricket, despite injections of sponsor's cash and the introduction of various forms of 'instant' cricket, the sums still did not add up, especially at county level. Reviewing the 1974 season *Wisden's Cricketer's Almanack* noted that several county clubs were 'in serious financial difficulties'.[64] Their precarious financial circumstances were indicative of a sport that was still walking backwards into the future. The announcement, in 1977, that Australian entrepreneur Kerry Packer had contracted fifty-one test cricketers (including the England captain, and three of his colleagues) for his World Series Cricket (WSC) organization, administered a profound external shock. The prospect of alternative, 'unofficial', test and one-day international matches, threatened an important revenue stream, especially as star players contracted to Packer would be unavailable for England. The Test and County Cricket Board (TCCB), responsible for the administration of first-class cricket since 1968, responded by threatening any player who signed for WSC with a ban, a stance which proved unsustainable (and expensive) when it was challenged in court as an unreasonable restraint of trade.[65]

Throughout this affair, which might be seen as something of a watershed in the development of modern British sport, *The Economist* threw its weight behind Packer. This was consistent with its support for free markets where inefficient industries would be exposed to the discipline of competition. Cricket's Establishment came under renewed attack. It seemed that the arguments of the 1960s still applied:

... committees of gentlemen have proved the wrong bodies to seize sport's new financial bonanza. Big money does not now come mainly from gate receipts ...; nor from television fees (although gentlemanly committees can kill the golden goose by demanding too large ones.) But when millions of like-minded people all over the world are gazing fixedly at internationally televised sport, there is a huge market for all sorts of advertising: whether by direct television advertisements, or placards on the grounds, or sponsorship, or by saying that folk-hero Fred bowls faster because he eats shredded wheat.[66]

The outcome of the affair seemed to justify this stance. In need of cash to outbid Packer in the market for elite cricketing talent the TCCB was forced to seek sponsorship for the traditional version of test cricket that it valued so highly. Before the close of the 1977 season, it had secured a lucrative deal with Cornhill and with it the future of test cricket in its traditional form. 'Once there was front-page publicity about competition between "respectable" and "commercial" cricket', *The Economist* crowed, 'the sponsorship of respectable cricket was bound to become more attractive to those seeking the image of the respectable establishment's St George'.[67] Test cricket, it should be noted, had previously been deemed too prestigious to sell to a commercial sponsor.

One aspect of the Packer affair that did not attract much comment at the time was that it illustrated the capacity of the media to transform sport. As Graeme Wright has observed, the TCCB was certainly alive to the commercial opportunities generated by their sport 'but whereas for them the business was cricket, for Packer the business was commercial television'.[68] The origins of the episode that wrought such profound change in cricket could be traced to the commercial rivalry between Packer and Rupert Murdoch, and the respective television channels that they owned in Australia. There was soon evidence from closer to home of the way in which television could make or break modern sport. Professional snooker, a downmarket entertainment with a limited audience, had entered a new era with the spread of colour television in the 1970s. Suddenly, as the telegenic properties of coloured balls on green baize became apparent, snooker began to attract major sponsors. 'Only Wimbledon and the World Cup', noted the *Economist*, can now compete as television sports with snooker'; scheduled television coverage rose by around 80 per cent, from 120 to 218 hours between 1980 and 1982.[69] Snooker and other popular television sports provided companies with opportunities to expose their products to a mass audience at a relatively low cost. Wills Embassy cigarettes, sponsors of the World Professional Snooker Championship from 1976, according to one contemporary estimate, achieved media coverage in 1982 – the tournament was covered for eighty-one hours over a seventeen-day period – that would have cost £68 million at average television advertising rates for an outlay of only £200,000.[70] Ironically, this was delivered by the BBC whose public-service remit precluded advertising. Television coverage and the sponsorship opportunities it generated helped snooker move upmarket, from small halls to prestige venues; from modest winnings (£6,000 for the world championship winner in 1979) to prize money comparable to tennis or golf (£105,000 in 1989). Enhanced levels of competition underpinned snooker's popularity with television audiences, thus helping to attract more sponsors. The audience of 18.5 million viewers for the final frame of the 1985 World Championship was at the time the largest ever British audience for any programme screened after midnight. It helped to secure the Embassy connection until 2005, when sponsorship of sporting events by tobacco companies was prohibited. Sports promoters, fearing that it would cause attendances to fall, had once sought to restrict television coverage; they now complained if they did not get enough of it.[71]

Rapid development of media technology ensured that the media, and television in particular, was powerfully placed to bring about a further instalment of major structural change in British sport by the early 1990s. Cable TV, a beneficiary of the development of fibre optics from the late 1970s, was widely available as an alternative to terrestrial broadcasting from 1983, offering up to twenty additional channels, though take-up was relatively slow. In part this was because of parallel developments in Direct Broadcasting by Satellite (DBS) pioneered by Sky from 1989 and British Satellite Broadcasting (BSB) from April 1990. Huge start-up costs coupled with the initial reluctance of British consumers to buy satellite TV led to a restructuring of provision with Sky absorbing BSB when it collapsed in November 1990 to form BSkyB. By the end of 1991, BSkyB was offering six channels to subscribers. It soon became clear that sport was a highly significant commodity as terrestrial, cable, and satellite channels competed for viewers and advertising revenue in an increasingly competitive market. Sky Sports investment in exclusive rights to screen cricket's 1992 World Cup generated increased sales of satellite dishes. 'Ever since England beat India in the first match...', it was noted, 'installation has grown dramatically'; the monthly sales figure of 78,000 was almost double the 41,000 bought in the corresponding month a year earlier; the 94,000 dishes bought the following month simply underlined the point that sport could play an important strategic role as rival channels competed for market share. 'The availability of cricket', the FT Satellite Monitor reported, 'increased dish sales among the over 45s and the AB social group of managers and professionals – groups which were less likely in the past to install satellite television'.[72]

Sport had established a significant place in television programming during the 1960s, especially after 1964 when BBC's *Grandstand* and ITV's *World of Sport* were scheduled against each other on Saturday afternoons and *Match of the Day* made its debut on BBC2. Though this may now be seen as a critical phase in the transition of elite sport into an experience most often encountered at home via television the limited number of channels inevitably imposed constraints. By 1992, these had largely disappeared. Christopher Dunkley, television critic of the *Financial Times*, supplied a powerful impression of the sporting feast on offer to armchair spectators.

The amount of sport now being delivered to British sitting rooms by television is unprecedented. This is particularly noticeable, of course, for those with satellite dishes since there are three entire channels dedicated to sport. Eurosport, running 24 hours a day; Screensport, which provides 18 hours a day during the week and 24 hours at weekends; and Sky Sports which is on screen for about 20 hours virtually every day. True, most viewers have no dish but even they can find more sport than ever before, delivered by the terrestrial channels. The BBC alone in the next couple of months will be showing, in addition to its routine sports programmes, the rest of the Five Nations Championship, the fifth and sixth rounds of the FA Cup, the European Indoor Athletics Championship, the World Figure Skating Championship, the Grand National, the Boat Race, the start of a new season of

Grand Prix motor racing, the US Masters, the women's hockey cup final, and the London Marathon.

What this indicated, apart from a high level of consumer demand, was the arrival of a sports product shaped to meet the requirements of sponsors (and other advertisers) and media interests. 'As with every other aspect of life touched by television', Dunkley concluded, 'sport is not merely conveyed to us by the medium, it is changed by it'.[73]

The transforming power of the media became increasingly clear during the 1990s as the process of sports modernization begun in the 1960s was completed. This was especially evident in the radical structural change experienced by professional football, rugby league, and rugby union. Professional football had seen some important changes since the 1960s, not least with the advent of sponsorship, yet by the 1980s it was widely perceived to be in a state of crisis. After rallying briefly to reach thirty million after England's World Cup win of 1966, Football League match attendances declined steadily to an all-time low of 16.4 million in 1985–6. In view of the disasters at the end of the previous season – notably a fire at Bradford City (fifty-six fatalities) and the disturbances involving Liverpool fans at the Heysel Stadium in Brussels (thirty-eight fatalities) – and the negative publicity that had long been generated by football-related hooliganism, this was hardly surprising. Though it remained by some distance the country's most popular spectator sport, football's image was badly damaged. It was, according to one press critic at the time, 'a slum sport, played in slum stadiums, increasingly watched by slum people, who deter decent folk from turning up'.[74] What is noticeable when revisiting the 'state of the game' analyses that inevitably followed is the extent to which they echo criticisms that had been made in the 1960s.[75] These were repeated, with minor variations, after the Hillsborough disaster (ninety five fatalities) in 1989. 'For complacency and incompetence there is nothing like a cartel; and of Britain's surviving cartels, the Football League is one of the smuggest and the slackest', thundered the *The Economist*; its ninety-two clubs comprised 'a gazetteer of Victorian industrial England'. Football's biggest liability, however, was 'rank bad management' which had failed to capitalize on a huge fan base and world famous brand names, like 'Liverpool' and 'Manchester United'.[76] It was even suggested that the basic requirements of sound financial management – being able to provide an account of current income, expenses, liabilities, and assets – were beyond the capacity of most football clubs.[77]

Though the denouement, when it arrived in 1992, was sudden, these circumstances ensured that the League's historic cartel was under severe pressure throughout the 1980s. In retrospect, the FA's decision in 1982 to abandon the 7.5 per cent limit on dividends payable to club shareholders, was an indication of the growing severity of the crisis and the need to bring new ideas, as well as new money into the professional game. When Irving Scholar, the kind of profit-driven entrepreneur that the FA were now anxious to attract, floated Tottenham Hotspur on the Stock Exchange in 1983, it seemed that a new era might have arrived with clubs looking to the capital markets to finance their ambitions rather than to 'businessmen keen to be associated with the local team'. Six years later, as soccer's fortunes plunged again after Hillsborough, Spurs shares were trading at only 18 per cent of their flotation price.[78] Launching football clubs as public companies was, however, an important development in that it represented a decision to transfer ownership to people primarily interested in financial performance rather than performance on the pitch'.[79] Other professional clubs, albeit a minority, later followed Tottenham's lead, especially as football's fortunes revived in the 1990s, thus subjecting themselves to the disciplines imposed on companies by Stock Exchange regulation. In a sector where the payment of dividends to shareholders had been an infrequent occurrence, this was a significant change.

It was during this period that 'new directors', like Scholar and Martin Edwards at Manchester United, began to pull their clubs away from their partners in the Football League and draw closer to those media interests that seemed to offer the best prospect of restoring the cash flows that had dried up when top English clubs were banned from competing in Europe after the Heysel Stadium incident. England's 'Big Five' (Arsenal, Tottenham, Everton, Liverpool, and Manchester United) – seen at the time as the core of any prospective 'Superleague' – successfully used the threat of secession in 1981, 1985, and 1988; first bringing to an end the time-honoured arrangement by which gate receipts were equally shared between home and away teams; then securing for First Division clubs 50 per cent of the money derived from sponsorship and television and a reduction in the end of season levy on gate receipts; and finally securing a live television deal with ITV worth £44 million over four years. As Scholar explained:

We wanted to be able to compete in Europe and build our clubs up without being constantly held back by the rest of the Football League.[80]

Most of all, they wanted to engineer a decisive shift towards profit maximization, a change that became imperative for all First Division clubs as they contemplated the cost of the transition to all-seat stadia required by the 1990 Taylor Report on ground safety.

'The pressure within the League has been building up for years', noted *The Economist*, as England's First Division clubs, aided and abetted by the FA, prepared to break away to form the Premier League in 1992. The secessionists were seeking 'to squeeze more out of television contracts, advertising royalties and sponsorship'.[81] It was fortunate that the hour of their greatest need coincided with the beginning of serious competition between BSkyB and the terrestrial broadcasters after 1990 and Rupert Murdoch's decision to use sport to persuade British viewers, who had proved somewhat reluctant to buy satellite dishes, to become subscribers. After years of dealing with what was effectively a BBC/ITV cartel, the clubs were now faced with two suitors determined to outbid each other for exclusive rights to screen live Premiership football for the next four years; ITV's £262 million being trumped at the eleventh hour by a bid of £304 million from BSkyB (including £4.5 million from the BBC for the rights to screen highlights on *Match of the Day*). As far as the top twenty clubs and those who aspired to join them were concerned, the sudden availability of this kind of money – the 1997–2001 deal was worth £743 million – justified the decision to break up the organization that had underpinned the professional game since 1888.[82]

Arguably, Rupert Murdoch's decision to use televised sport as a 'battering ram' as he sought to expand News Corporation's global network had an even profounder impact on rugby league which had experienced similar tensions to football in the 1980s as the more successful clubs, like Wigan, sought a larger share of the money coming into the game at the expense of the league's minnows. Rugby league's relationship with television had been problematic. Eddie Waring's match commentaries on BBC's *Grandstand* had exposed the game to a national television audience while simultaneously emphasizing a rather dated, 'northern' image that many rugby league insiders considered unhelpful.[83] Yet, arguably, rugby league had shown itself more willing to accommodate the media than many other sports. Television had already influenced the basic game form when the four-tackle rule (later changed to six) had been introduced to encourage attacking play in the BBC2 Floodlit Trophy in 1966.[84] BSkyB's offer of a five-year deal worth £77 million in 1995 initiated even more fundamental changes – a fourteen-team European Super League which would play in the summer rather than the winter. Faced, like their counterparts in soccer, with the expense of modernizing stadia to meet the requirements of the Taylor Report, this was an offer that hard-pressed club chairmen could hardly refuse. They were dazzled by the sums on offer. 'I believe', wrote one journalist, 'that they would have agreed to anything – indeed, several of them voted for things with which, it later emerged, they profoundly disagreed'.[85] Thus another Victorian institution, in this case dating from 1895, was abandoned.

Almost simultaneously, rugby union, a sport steeped in the amateur tradition went open. Amateurism, at the highest levels of the game, had long threatened to expire, crushed by the weight of its own contradictions.[86] Given the increasing demands on top players as rugby union began to market itself as a global game after its first World Cup competition in 1987 the diehard stance of the RFU Establishment became increasingly difficult to defend, especially when they were failing to maximize potential revenue. 'The old Freddies who still dominate England's rugby bureaucracy', *The Economist* noted in 1987, 'insist that players should make sacrifices for the love of the game'. They were proposing to pay a miserly £15 a day to players on World Cup duty in Australia and New Zealand at a time when the potential revenue from international matches at Twickenham was unrealized because tickets were underpriced.[87] As in football and rugby league, media money underwrote the transformation, the contest between BBC and ITV for the UK rights to screen the 1991 World Cup – won by ITV with a bid of £3 million – marking a watershed in this respect. The cost to ITV was minimized by a secondary arrangement with Sony to sponsor its coverage, an early example of what became known as 'ambush marketing' that irritated the tournament's eight official sponsors. 'The reason we went after the sponsorship', explained Sony's project sponsorship manager, 'is the same as why ITV went after the rugby – to reach the notoriously light-viewing ABC1 males'.[88] The most important – and most controversial – deal, however, was struck in 1996 when BSkyB agreed to pay £87.5 million for exclusive rights to cover England's rugby internationals for the next five years, leading to a temporary rift between England and its opponents in the Five Nations championship (France, Ireland, Scotland, and Wales). As in football and rugby league, the RFU was in no position to resist Murdoch's advances having taken on a £34 million loan to redevelop its stadium at Twickenham. The other home nations subsequently made their own arrangements with the BBC and ITV/S4C.[89] The revenue from television, along with money derived from the sponsorship of domestic and European club competitions, helped the game negotiate a somewhat disorderly transition to professionalism over the next five years. This marked the completion of the modernization of British sports institutions that had begun in the 1960s.

IN CONCLUSION

While this process of transformation was under way consumption of sports-related goods and services expanded rapidly and it may be useful to conclude by touching on the links between sport as commercialized entertainment and the wider sport/leisure market. Key long-term trends supported the growth of this sector in the second half of the twentieth century and beyond. Britain's population, it has been observed, 'benefited from significant increases in the resources needed to enjoy leisure – more free time, higher real incomes, and improved access to leisure enhancing equipment such as the motor car, the television set and the washing machine'. This led to wider participation in sport generally with one estimate for 1983 indicating that 21.5 million adults and seven million children participated in some kind of sporting activity at least once a month.[90] The number of people playing squash regularly grew from around one million in 1975 to three million in 1985; it was now 'a mature market wherein clubs must compete for members in the same manner as supermarkets compete for shoppers'.[91] This reminds us that consumers in this sector, as in others, exercise choice and it is here that the change from utility- to profit-maximization in the commercialized sports sector has been influential. Business sponsorship and the media, by sustaining a wide range of sports activities and making them more widely accessible via television have a significant impact on consumer choice. This is especially evident in areas such as the consumption of sports leisurewear where brands effectively advertised by sports personalities as they go about their work, are critical. 'We will never sell anything other than brands', explained David Whelan, chairman of sports goods retailers JJB. 'It's what people want'.[92]

The metamorphosis of sportswear into various forms of fashionwear implies that sport itself is fashionable, an assessment that reflects simultaneously the successful marketing campaigns of its various sponsors and the power of media communication. Profit-maximizing sports businesses have increasingly sought to influence consumer behaviour outside the realm of sport itself, especially via merchandising. Manchester United ('Merchandise United') sold 850,000 replica shirts in 1996, 250,000 more than any other club and 200,000 more than England. The growth of this market indicated that consumers had come to see football in a new light since the dark days of hooliganism, Heysel and Hillsborough. 'Demand', it was noted, 'has been further fuelled by increased media coverage, with the birth of satellite TV channels dedicated to sports and a rise in coverage by other media'.[93] All this suggests a business sector with ever-expanding boundaries where the stadium, the traditional location is giving way to the 'tradium', a commercialized space in which sport, sports-related business, and consumers interact and where leisure is linked to spending.[94] The chief executive of Coventry's Ricoh Arena explained it neatly:

Our main selling point is our versatility because guests can say in our high-quality hotel, watch Coventry City in action or attend a trade exhibition or conference, eat in the restaurant, enjoy a concert and then try their luck in the casino – without leaving the Ricoh.[95]

Over the forty years or so since the 1960s Britain's sports businesses had learned from their relationship with sponsors to become more businesslike. The timing of Kevin Keegan's exit as Newcastle United's manager in 1997 was dictated not by what was happening on the pitch but by the need to ensure a successful stock market flotation. It was an episode indicative of 'a degree of convergence between the worlds of football and business'.[96] At the same time sport was learning to adapt to the requirements of a market the limits of which were largely determined by the media, especially television. Such developments underpinned the location of commercialized sport within an increasingly integrated sports-leisure sector.

NOTES

1. '£2.5m Payoff for McClaren and a 1bn Hit for Leisure Industry', *Guardian*, 23 Nov. 2007: 2; 'Phone-ins and Footie put the Boot into Grade's ITV', Business and Media, *Observer*, 25 Nov. 2007: 11.
2. Sir F. Wall, *Fifty Years of Football, 1884–1934*, Soccer Books Ltd, Cleethorpes, 2006: 105 (first published in 1935); J. Walvin, *The Only Game: Football in Our Times*, Longman: London, 2000: 200. See also Alan Sugar's comments on Tottenham D. Hotspur in Conn, *The Football Business: The Modern Football Classic*, Mainstream, Edinburgh, 1997: 31.
3. 'A Dirty Old Game', *Guardian*, 18 Sept. 2007: 38. For coverage of football in the business press, see S. Morrow, *The New Business of Football: Accountability and Finance in Football*, Macmillan, Basingstoke, 1999: 1–2.
4. T. Mason, *Association Football and English Society 1863–1915*, Harvester Press, Brighton, 1981: 194–5; see also M. Huggins, *The Victorians and Sport* Hambledon and London, London, 2004: 141–66.

5. A. Crisell, *An Introductory History of British Broadcasting*, Routledge, London, 1997: 164; see also J. Williams, *Entertaining the Nation: A Social History of British Television*, Sutton Publishing: Stroud, 214–5.

6. G. Crawford, *Consuming Sport: Fans, Sport and Culture*, Routledge, London, 2004: 8; L. Wenner, ed., 'Preface', *MediaSport* Routledge, London, 1998: xiii. See also the perceptive overview of the relationship between sport and the media in G. Jarvie, *Sport, Culture and Society: An Introduction* Routledge, London, 2006: 138–41.

7. J. Benson, *The Rise of Consumer Society in Britain, 1880–1980*, Longman, Harlow, 1994: tables 5.1, 5.2, and 5.3, pp. 112–14, p. 135.

8. C. Gratton, and P. Taylor, *Economics of Sport and Recreation* Spon Press, London, 2000: 19–20; J. Horne, *Sport in Consumer Culture*, Palgrave Macmillan, Basingstoke, 2006: 24–7.

9. See Henley Centre, *The Economic Impact of Sport in the United Kingdom in 1990*, Sports Council, London, 1992: 33.

10. 'There's No Business Like Sports Business', *Financial Times*, 23 Sept. 1996: 14. 'Sports apparel', it notes while reflecting on the range of product groups, 'includes obviously common or garden sportswear (soccerwear, cricketwear, swimwear) but also aerobicswear, dancewear, beachwear, surfwear, sports fashionwear, fitnesswear, activewear, musclewear, bodywear, many types of leisurewear . . . and – for the cool – various types of streetwear'.

11. S. Hardy, 'Entrepreneurs, Organizations and the Sports Marketplace: Subjects in Search of Historians', *Journal of Sports History*, 13, 1, 1986: 17–9.

12. Gratton and Taylor, *Economics of Sport*: table 2.2, p. 20.

13. H. Thomas, 'The Establishment and Society', in H. Thomas, *The Establishment*, Anthony Blond, London, 1959: 18; see also M. Grant, 'Historians, Penguin Specials and State-of-the-Nation Literature, 1958–64', *Contemporary British History*, 17, 3, 2003: 29–54.

14. R. Holt, 'Amateurism and its Interpretation: The Social Origins of British Sport', *Innovation*, 5, 4, 1992: 19.

15. 'Sporting Offer?', *Economist*, 1 Oct. 1960: 21–2.

16. Sunderland's 'clown prince', Len Shackleton, had been punished in 1955 for a blank page in his autobiography headed 'The Average Director's Knowledge of Football'. See L. Shackleton, *Clown Prince of Soccer*, Nicholas Kaye, London, 1955: 78.

17. For falling attendances generally in this period see T. Collins, *Rugby League in Twentieth Century Britain: A Social and Cultural History*, London, Routledge, 2006: 87–100; D. Russell, *Football and the English: A Social History of Association Football in England, 1863–1995*, Carnegie Publishing, Preston, 1997: 131–6.

18. See K. Laybourn, *Working-Class Gambling in Britain, c.1906–1960s: The Stages of the Political Debate*, Edwin Mellen Press, Lampeter, 2007: 205–6.

19. 'Angry Young Men', *Economist*, 19 Nov. 1960: 69.

20. T. Bailey, *Championship Cricket: A Review of County Cricket since 1945*. Sportsmans Book Club, London, 1962: 12 and 214–5; for the problems afflicting the county game generally at this time see D. Birley, *A Social History of English Cricket*, Aurum Press, London, 1999: 292–3.

21. L. Duckworth, *The Story of Warwickshire Cricket*, Stanley Paul, London, 1974: 338–44.

22. D. Birley, *The Willow Wand: Some Cricket Myths Explored*, Aurum Press, London, 2000: 149. See also S. Wagg, '"Time Gentlemen Please": The Decline of Amateur

Captaincy in English County Cricket', *Contemporary British History*, 14, 2, 2000: 54–6.

23. For the working life of the modern professional cricketer see H. Blofeld, *The Packer Affair*, Collins, London, 1978; 96–8; R. Sissons, *The Players: A Social History of the Professional Cricketer*, Kingswood Press, London, 1988, 303–5; S. Hughes, *A Lot of Hard Yakka: Triumph and Torment in a County Cricketer's Life*, Headline, London, 1997: 191.

24. 'No Love Match', *Economist*, 2 Jul. 1960: 24.

25. R. Evans, *Open Tennis: The First Twenty Years*, Bloomsbury, London, 1988: 13.

26. See, for example, 'The Last Judgement?', *The Economist*, 3 Dec. 1977: 28. For a succinct account of these developments see R. Holt, and T. Mason, *Sport in Britain 1945–2000*, Blackwell, Oxford, 2000: 78–80.

27. S. Inglis, *The Football Grounds of Great Britain*, Willow Books, London, 1987: 43–5; 'Go, Go, Go County!!! Victor Bernard and the Rise of Stockport County in the 1960s', *Soccer History*, 19, Spring 2008: 32–3.

28. See 'Coventry City's Sky Blue Revolution', *Soccer History*, 18, Winter 2008: 3–6.

29. Russell, *Football and the English*: 151. The Football League, supported by the FA, appealed directly to club supporters in setting out its case for the maximum wage. See, for example, the 'Special Notice', signed by Joe Richards of the League and Arthur Drewry of the FA, Leyton Orient v. Brighton and Hove Albion match programme, 14 Mar. 1959. It argued, somewhat perversely, that players had opportunities to earn beyond the £20 a week maximum.

30. 'Up the Strikers', *The Economist*, 31 Dec. 1960: 1374.

31. 'Offside', *The Economist*, 22 Apr. 1961: 305–6.

32. J. Harding, *For the Good of the Game: The Official History of the Professional Footballers' Association*, Robson Books, London, 1991: 276–88. For the Eastham case and its consequences see 'Mr Wilberforce frees the slaves', *The Economist*, 13 Jul. 1963: 142–5; 'Back to the Slave Market?', *The Economist*, 9 Nov. 1963: 571.

33. 'Farewell Lap', *The Economist*, 22 Nov. 1975: 37.

34. 'Wimbledon's Money Machine', *The Economist*, 23 Jun. 1979: 120–1.

35. 'Prize Results', *The Economist*, 25 Dec. 1971: 75; R. Physick, and R. Holt, 'Big Money: The Tournament Player and the PGA, 1945–75', *Contemporary British History*, 14, 2, 2000: 76–7.

36. Cited in M. Polley, *Moving the Goalposts: A History of Sport and Society since 1945*, Routledge, London, 1998: 77; 'Half a Revolution', *The Economist*, 15 Sept. 1973: 38–9.

37. Collins, *Rugby League*: 92.

38. See C. Field, '"The Secularized Sabbath Revisited": Opinion Polls as Sources for Sunday Observance in Contemporary Britain', *Contemporary British History*, 15, 1, 2001: 6. A survey at the time indicated that 60 per cent of the public were in favour of having the option of Sunday football 'even when there is no energy crisis'. 'The Fans Say it Again', *The Economist*, 2 Feb. 1974: 26.

39. 'The Games They Play', *The Economist*, 9 Aug. 1980: 13–4.

40. D. J. Taylor, *On the Corinthian Spirit: The Decline of Amateurism in Sport*, Yellow Jersey Press, London, 2006: 50–1.

41. H. Richards, *A Game for Hooligans: The History of Rugby Union*, Mainstream, Edinburgh, 2007, 14; D. Wyatt, *Rugby DisUnion: The Making of Three World Cups*: 17.

42. 'Soccer's Financial Score', *The Economist*, 9 May 1981: 116–17.
43. Gratton and Taylor, *Economics of Sport*: 163–6; for a succinct survey of the growth of sports sponsorship in Britain see Polley, *Moving the Goalposts*: 67–84.
44. J. Bromhead, *Bromsgrove, Redditch & District Table Tennis Association: The First Fifty Years*, Bromsgrove, Redditch & District TTA, Redditch, 2002: 98.
45. N. Macrae, 'Football and Beer in the 1960s: Transformation of the British Brewing Industry and its Impact on Local Identity', *Sport in History*, 28, 2, 2008: 236–7; see also Horne, *Sport in Consumer Culture*: 22.
46. S. Matthews, *My Autobiography: The Way It Was*, Headline, London, 2000: 337–8; T. Heald, *Denis Compton, The Life of a Sporting Hero*, Aurum Press, London, 2006: 135–7; P. Hennessy, *Having It So Good: Britain in the Fifties*, Allen Lane, London, 2006: 92–3.
47. Polley, *Moving the Goalposts*: 73–5; Horne, *Sport in Consumer Culture*: 91.
48. *An Inquiry into Sponsorship*, The Sports Council: London, 1971: 8.
49. See the comments on the beginnings of sponsorship in Birley, *English Cricket*: 294.
50. 'Sports Sponsors to Weather the Gloom?' *BBC News Online*, 12 February 2002, http://news.bbc.co.uk/1/hi/business/1814335.stm accessed 26 Jun. 2008.
51. Committee of Inquiry into Sports Sponsorship (CISS), *The Howell Report* Central Council of Physical Recreation, London, 1983: para. 2.11, p. 13.
52. CISS, *Howell Report*: 6–7; Polley, *Moving the Goalposts*: 69.
53. 'Horse Sense', *The Economist*, 4 Jun. 1977: 127.
54. CISS, *Howell Report*: table headed 'First Class Cricket Sponsorship in 1982', p. 78.
55. 'Here Come the Sponsors', *The Economist*, 11 Aug. 1979: 20. See also Collins, *Rugby League*: 173.
56. Inglis, *Football Grounds*: 20–1.
57. CISS, *Howell Report*: 6.
58. 'Wimbledon's Money Machine', *The Economist*, 23 Jun. 1979: 120–1.
59. 'Game of Sponsorship', *Financial Times*, 21 Jul. 1994: 17.
60. This was the view of the Amateur Swimming Association; CISS, *Howell Report*: 9.
61. Ibid.: 5.
62. 'A Hull of a Place to Advertise', *The Economist*, 17 Aug. 1985: 58.
63. CISS, *Howell Report*, paras. 10.38–10.39, p. 7.
64. 'Notes by the Editor', *Wisden's Cricketer's Almanack*, Sporting Handbooks Ltd, London, 1975: 99. Middlesex had asked each of its 7,000 members for a donation of at least £10 in order to avoid bankruptcy.
65. For a contemporary account of the affair see Blofeld, *Packer Affair*; see also Birley, *English Cricket*: 316–20; M. Marquese, *Anyone but England: An Outsider Looks at English Cricket*, Aurum Press, London, 2005: 122–8; G. Wright, *Betrayal: The Struggle for English Cricket's Soul*, H. F. & G. Wetherby, London, 1994: 113–8.
66. 'Gentlemen v. Players', *The Economist*, 6 Aug. 1977: 18–9.
67. 'Er, That Dragon is St Kerry', *The Economist*, 3 Sept. 1977: 13.
68. G. Wright, *Betrayal*: 114.
69. 'Balls on the Green Baize', *The Economist*, 22 May 1980: 32; CISS *Howell Report*: table 10.2, p. 72.
70. See Gratton and Taylor, *Economics of Sport*: 171 and 174. For a more conservative estimate of the value of the time bought by sports sponsors see Williams, *Entertaining the Nation*: 222.
71. Williams, *Entertaining the Nation*: 214–15.

72. 'Cricket Helps to Boost Dish Installations', *Financial Times*, 19 Mar. 1992: 8; 'Cricket Boosts Dish Sales', *Financial Times*, 6 Apr. 1992: 9.
73. 'Sport of a Sort – But it May Not Sound Like Cricket', *Financial Times*, 19 Feb. 1992: 17.
74. *Sunday Times*, 19 May 1985, quoted in A. King, *The End of the Terraces: The Transformation of English Football in the 1990s*, Leicester University Press, London, 1998: 93. For declining match attendances and British football's mid-1980s nadir see J. Walvin, *Football and the Decline of Britain*, Macmillan, Basingstoke, 1985: 6–11; D. Conn, The Beautiful Game? Searching for the Soul of Football, Yellow Jersey Press, London, 2004: 150–74; M. Taylor, *The Association Game: A History of British Football*, Pearson Education, Harlow, 2008: 318–19.
75. See, for example, 'New Rules, New Ref?', *The Economist*, 18 May 1985: 32, which described the Football League as 'a self-perpetuating, ossified elite of 92 clubs, of which a third are technically bankrupt and all but a handful nearly so'.
76. 'Beleaguered', 'Playing at Management', *The Economist*, 22 Apr. 1989: 28–32; for a summary of these critiques see especially King, *End of the Terraces*: 88–96.
77. Walvin, *Football and Decline*: 20–4.
78. 'Spurred on to Market', 'Playing at Management', *The Economist*, 18 Jun. 1983: 86; 22 Apr. 1989: 29–32. For the 'new directors' of the 1980s see King, *End of the Terraces*: 120–32; see also the comments on Martin Edwards of Manchester United in Conn, *Football Business*: 143–4.
79. S. Szymanski, and T. Kuypers, *Winners and Losers*, Penguin, London, 1999: 73–4.
80. Quoted in Conn, *Football Business*: 144–5.
81. 'There They Go, There They Go', *The Economist*, 18 Jan. 1992: 31–2. For an account of the tensions that led to the restructuring of professional football in Scotland, see Morrow, *New Business of Football*: 25–7.
82. See Szymanski and Kuypers, *Winners and Losers*: 55–67; see also R. Nash, 'Television', in R. Cox, D. Russell, and W. Vamplew, eds., *Encyclopedia of British Football*, Frank Cass, London, 2002: 301–3.
83. See J. Williams, '"Up and Under": Eddie Waring, Television and the Image of Rugby League', *The Sports Historian*, 22, 1, 2002: 115–37.
84. Collins, *Rugby League*: 113.
85. See Ibid.: 181–4.
86. For a sense of these contradictions see especially the account of the evidence given by Dudley Wood, secretary of the RFU, to the National Heritage Select Committee inquiry in 1995 in D. Hinchcliffe, *Rugby's Class War: Bans, Boot Money and Parliamentary Battles*, London League Publications Ltd: London, 2000: 80–4.
87. 'Pay the Game', *The Economist*, 24 Jan. 1987: 30.
88. Wyatt, *Rugby DisUnion*: 72–3; for 'ambush marketing', see Gratton and Taylor, *Economics of Sport*: 168–70.
89. Richards, *Game for Hooligans*: 256–7; for the relationship between the television companies and rugby in this period generally, see A. Smith, 'Civil War in England: The Clubs, the RFU, and the Impact of Professionalism on Rugby Union, 1995–99', *Contemporary British History*, 14, 2, 2000: 152–8.
90. C. Brackenridge, and D. Woodward, 'Gender Inequalities in Leisure and Sport in Post-War Britain', in J. Obelkevich, and P. Catterall, eds., *Understanding Post-war British Society*, Routledge, London, 1994: 193, 196–7.

91. *Squash Participation Survey*, Squash Rackets Association, London, 1985: 4; 'Slimming Off the Pounds', *Economist*, 20 Jul. 1985: 32.
92. 'City Awards Gold to Sporting Heroes', *Financial Times*, 17 Oct. 1996: 24.
93. C. Brick, 'Misers, Merchandise and Manchester United: The Peculiar Paradox of the Political Economy of Consumption', in D. Andrews, ed., *Manchester United: A Thematic Study*, Routledge, London, 2004: 103–4; 'City Awards Gold to Sporting Heroes', *Financial Times*, 17 Oct. 1996: 24.
94. J. Bale, 'The Changing Place of Football, Stadiums and Communities', in J. Garland, D. Malcolm and M. Rowe, eds., *The Future of Football: Challenges for the Twenty-First Century*, Frank Cass, London, 2000: 93.
95. 'Why is it the Mix that Matters', *Birmingham Post*, Business of Sport Supplement, 20 Aug. 2007: 2.
96. 'Newcastle and the City Mourn King Kevin's Exit', *Financial Times*, 9 Jan. 1997: 1; 'Just Another Game', *Financial Times*, 10 Jan. 1997: 12.

18

Ethics, Religion, and Business in Twentieth Century Britain

David J. Jeremy

In the Judaeo-Christian tradition, religion and ethics have been intimately connected. Faith in a God who is invisible and eternal included the imperatives and ideals of social justice.[1] Both the Jewish law (Torah) and the teaching of Jesus, the founder of Christianity, on the one hand labelled as vices and condemned behaviours such as greediness, falsehood, the exploitation of the weak and poor, and the idolizing of material things. On the other hand they identified and praised as virtues personal characteristics such as humility, honesty, generosity, loyalty, self-sacrifice, and being a good neighbour.[2] At first sight such teaching about individual and social morality would seem inimical to the goals and methods of an acquisitive, entrepreneurial society. Adjustment came with the rediscovery during the Protestant Reformation of the sixteenth century, of the doctrine of stewardship, Christian teaching with antecedents in Judaism. The stewardship accommodation informed all the varieties of Protestant, as well as Catholic, Christianity by the early twentieth century. In Britain, Christian stewardship was a widely taught ideal, until at least the 1960s. However, in the last thirty or so years of the twentieth century, Britain emerged as a highly secularized and pluralistic society. For most people religion no longer guided their ideas of the good and the right. As one Archbishop of Canterbury pointed out in the 1990s, in Britain belief and behaviour had become privatized matters.[3] His views arose partly because of the decline in churchgoing: reportedly, from a peak of 33 per cent in 1900 (church membership in the British population as a whole), the figure moved down to 25 per cent in 1950, 23 per cent in 1965, and then 12 per cent in 2000.[4] In fact, since the social disillusion wreaked by the killing machines of the First World War, the universal absolutes of religion competed with diminishing success against relativism, materialism, and self-interest.

Starting with an indication of the scope of business ethics, this chapter addresses a number of questions designed to explore long term trends, like decline and renaissance, in the interactions between religion, ethics, and business. Can ethical behaviour in business be measured? Have there been discernible long-run patterns in ethical behaviour in business, when ethical standards in business seem to have been better or worse than at other times? What have been the sources of ethical standards in business in twentieth-century Britain? How have debate and prescription about business ethics been transformed into action and performance? When religion has informed ethics, have religious convictions preserved business leaders from ethical dilemmas and irresponsible choices? Have business people charged with the management of their churches' business affairs demonstrated an ethical record superior to that of the wider UK world of business? Are there any connections between ethical behaviour in business and business performance? Can business history illuminate the boundary between business, ethics, and religion?

BUSINESS ETHICS

If business ethics is about the right, the good, the just in the realm of business,[5] directors and managers (with whose perspective this chapter is mostly concerned) face in two directions at once.[6] They face inwards, looking at inter-personal issues and problems within their company. They face outwards, towards the company's social and natural environment. Two sets of ethical issues occur. Within the company these include relations between directors and shareholders (method and amounts in rewarding directors for example); fairness between employees (gender and ethnic issues); health and safety; or the ethical dimension of corporate culture formation. Externally there are relations with customers, suppliers, and competitors; truth in advertising; the corporate impact on the community and the natural environment; corporate activities in politics (party donations, lobbying for industry or company interests, for example). In the former (inward interface), directors and managers are creating a moral environment within the corporation. In the latter (outward interface) the corporation is situated within society's prevailing moral environment and directors/managers are steering their business in response to the expectations and demands set by that society. At the firm level, observance of high ethical standards in business relationships lent an organization, or a business leader, a reputation which engendered public trust and respect.[7]

CAN ETHICAL BEHAVIOUR IN BUSINESS BE MEASURED?

In any precise way, the answer to this question is no. However, there are proxies that can be used as indicators. For example, measures of philanthropic giving might be constructed. But these would have to be associated with business activity. The Companies Act of 1967 required the disclosure of charitable dona-tions in the annual report and accounts. Under-reporting of donations has forced researchers to discover the dimensions and directions of corporate philanthropy by recourse to other sources such as Charities Aid Foundation data. They show that between 1979 and 1986, company charitable giving never exceeded a quarter of 1 per cent of the collective pre-tax profits (or about £40 million to £60 million) of the 200 top companies.[8]

From the perspective of this chapter, the major weakness of these post-1967 data is that they are limited in time. More promising for a long-run view of business ethics are estimates of unethical business. One relatively consistent measure is the annual number of cases of compulsory windings-up. Circumstances under which company winding-up could be enforced were defined in the Companies (Winding-up) Act of 1890, and were preserved over the century in the Companies Acts of 1908, 1929, and 1948, and the Insolvency Act of 1986.[9]

Compulsory, as opposed to voluntary, liquidation invariably arose from forms of unethical behaviour. The Inspector General in Companies Liquidation observed in his first report to the Board of Trade in 1891,

On the whole it would be a difficult, if not an impossible task, to select out of the whole number of cases wound up by the Court during the year, a single case in which it could be said that the objects of the company were reasonable, that its promotion and management were honest, and that its failure was due chiefly to misfortune.[10]

Over a century later, but this time referring to Section 122 of the Insolvency Act, legal commentators could observe that 'by far the most important ground for winding up a company is that the company is unable to pay its debts, and the next most important ground, that the court is of the opinion that it is just and equitable that the company should be wound up'.[11]

Spanning such a long period of time, inevitably there are problems with this metric. First and foremost, compulsory winding-up might be due to technical incompetence rather than moral failure. In addition, unethically-run companies succeeded in evading legal penalties. Third, the law might have been applied unevenly. Little is known about the Registrar General of Companies and the thoroughness, or lack of, with which the tens, and later hundreds, of thousands, of companies were monitored. There were a number of courts, so there may have been some variation in the application of the law. While the statutory criteria for compulsory liquidation have remained constant, their interpretation by the courts will have varied, in one direction or another. Until a detailed examination of the matter is made, the series seems to offer a useful long-term barometer of unethical activity in business. Of course, grounds for winding-up were not the only reasons for bringing directors into the courts. Nor, if the data were available, is it clear whether the investigator should tally numbers of companies, their shareholders' capital plus what they owed their creditors, or numbers of directors involved. Here numbers of companies has been the chosen measure.

The Companies Acts of 1907, 1929, 1948, 1980, 1981, and 1985 increased the range of misdemeanours for which an individual could be fined, disqualified, or brought into the criminal courts, or his companies be dissolved. To provide some indication of their effect, numbers of failures to observe the law, reported annually by the Registrar of Companies, without distinguishing between large or small violations or between companies and individuals, may be counted. This has also been attempted below.

Another way of measuring unethical activity is to assemble a chronological table of scandalous cases. This has the weakness of being confined to cases of high public interest, rather than the general level of unethical behaviour; and the selection of cases, directed by the need to sell newspapers, cannot be objective. Nevertheless, it is used here in conjunction with the long-run data on compulsorily liquidated companies.

HAVE THERE BEEN DISCERNIBLE LONG-RUN PATTERNS IN ETHICAL BEHAVIOUR IN BUSINESS, WHEN ETHICAL STANDARDS IN BUSINESS SEEM TO HAVE BEEN BETTER OR WORSE THAN AT OTHER TIMES?

Unsurprisingly, in view of Sir Francis Bacon's aphorism that 'prosperity doth best discover vice, but adversity doth best discover virtue', some of the lowest levels of unethical business behaviour appear to have been experienced during the First and Second World Wars – and the highest levels in the prosperous decades at the end of the century. The Chart reveals the relative situation according to two metrics. Measured by compulsory liquidations as a proportion of the numbers of companies in existence, it seems that the incidence of corporate misbehaviour in the 1890s was not exceeded again until 1982–6 and 1989–96. Including all corporate offences (kinds of which were increased over the course of the century), the 1890s levels were briefly equalled in 1938–9 but not reached again until 1973. From then until the end of the century, mid-1890s levels were exceeded almost every year. Between 1973 and 2000 the numbers of corporate violations as a proportion of the number of companies in existence was above 1 per cent in 17 out of 28 years.

If absolute figures (not shown in the Chart) are used, the picture is worse: no more than 150 compulsory liquidations per annum in the 1890s; no more than 300 p.a. in the 1920s; no more than 400 p.a. in the 1930s. Until 1967 no more than 1,000 compulsory liquidations per annum were recorded. Levels of over 5,000 per anum were reached in 1983–7 and in every year 1990–2000 bar one (1999). An absolute height of 9,861 compulsory liquidations per annum came in 1992.

Evidence in Table 18.1 shows the extent and cost of cases of the grossest kinds of corporate misbehaviour. It needs to be interpreted with care and many caveats. These cases are the tip of the iceberg: many smaller cases were investigated by the authorities and of course many escaped prosecution. The dates relate to company collapse, rather than the outcome of any trial. The individual named here was often not the only defendant. The estimate of gross loss has been taken from public domain reports and has not been subjected to consistent criteria. Estimates of financial loss (whatever their level of accuracy) do not reflect the true

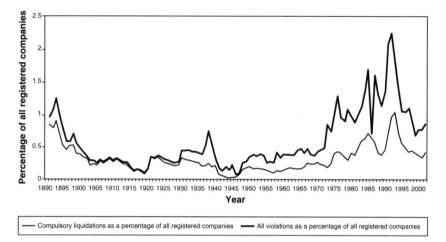

Figure 18.1. Company liquidations and violations from 1890 to 2002

extent of human misery and suffering. After the 1960s, the law and the rules governing misbehaviour in the City were strengthened. Consequently people operating in an innovative and entrepreneurial fashion were more likely to fall foul of the law, for example, insider trading was criminalized in 1980. In short, this is an impressionistic portrait until a badly needed definitive and exhaustive analysis of twentieth century white collar crime appears. In the meantime, the data summarized in the Chart and Table 18.1 provide a relative and roughly consistent, long-term measure of the extent to which company directors adhered to the law of their day.

Noticeably, prior to 1950, four corporate collapses each lost over £100 million, two of them over £500 million (at real 1998 prices); all were in the services sector, most in financial services. By comparison, in the 1980s and 1990s seventeen cases of corporate collapse incurred losses of over £100 million each. They included nine which lost over £500 million, and of these six which lost over £1,000 million. Again, a majority were in financial services.

Aside from high-profile fraud trials, perhaps nothing did so much to bring boardrooms into disrepute as spiralling directors' salaries. By 2000, the UK's highest CEO remuneration of £6.175 million a year was nearly 1,800 times greater than the state old-age pension, close to the differential of 1908, but six times that of the differential of 1970.[12]

These data raise the obvious question, why did ethical standards in business look low in the 1890s, and less than a century later plummet into unprecedented collapse? The 1890s and the 1980s–90s had much in common. In both periods, markets, business organizations, and the technology of business experienced rapid change. Yet there were major differences between the two periods. State intervention was far more evident in the late twentieth century than in the late

Table 18.1. Cases of gross unethical behaviour in British business, 1890s–1990s

Date of exposure or trial	Main individual held responsible	Company	Industry	Nature of unethical behaviour	Impact on company	Estimated gross losses incurred* (£ million)	1998 purchasing power (£ million)
1892	Balfour, Jabez	Liberator	Building soc	Forgery and conspiracy	Winding-up	3.4	199
1898	Hooley, Ernest Terah	Hooley & Rucker	Company promotion	Obscure	Collapse	1	58
1900	Wright, Whitaker		Finance	Share rigging	Insolvency	7.5	436
1902	Pease, Sir Joseph	J & J W Pease	Banking	Illiquidity	Insolvency	1.3	74
1903	Burnand, Percy	Lloyd's underwriter	Insurance	Fraud	Losses to names	0.1	6
1923	Harrison, Stanley	Lloyd's underwriter	Insurance	Fraud	Losses to names	0.4	9
1927	White, James	Beecham Trust	Company speculator	Share rigging	Receivership	0.5	10
1929	Hatry, Clarence Charles	Austin Friars Trust	Finance	Fraud	Collapse	14	507
1931	Kylsant, Baron	Royal Mail group	Shipping	Issuing false prospectus	Reconstruction	50	1,810
1931	Turner, Samuel	Turner & Newall	Asbestos	Denial of health hazard	Survival	n, continuing	
1962	Ellis, Sir Charles	BAT	Tobacco	Denial of health hazard	Survival	n, continuing	
1964	Bloom, John	Rolls Razor	Washing machine mfg	Issuing false information	Bankrupt	13	143
1968	Lord, Cyril	Cyril Lord Carpets Ltd	Carpets	Unproven?	Collapse		
1974	Poulson, John	Ropergate Services	Architectural services	Conspiracy and corruption	Winding-up		
1975	Slater, James	Slater Walker	Corporate take-over bidder	Financed purchase of own shares	Slater's resignation	1	6
1982	Grob, Kenneth	Alexander Howden	Lloyd's broker	Alleged theft	Disgrace	40	98
1982	Calvi, Roberto	Banco Ambrosiano	Banking	Currency offences	Collapse	790	1,588

(Continued)

Table 18.1. (Continued)

Date of exposure or trial	Main individual held responsible	Company	Industry	Nature of unethical behaviour	Impact on company	Estimated gross losses incurred* (£ million)	1998 purchasing power (£ million)
1982	De Lorean, John	De Lorean Motors	Motorcar manufacturer	Alleged theft	Collapse	78	157
1982	Wallrock, John	Minet Holdings	Lloyd's broker-underwriter	Alleged theft	Reputation dented	30	60
1983	Cameron-Webb, Peter	PC-W	Lloyd's broker-underwriter	Theft	Reputation dented	300	576
1984	Fraser, Ian	Johnson Matthey Bankers	Banking	Fraud and bribery	Bank of England rescue	100	183
1986	Saunders, Ernest et al.	Guinness	Drinks	Share rigging	Successful takeover of Distillers	100	167
1988	Clowes, Peter	Barlow Clowes International	Fund management	Fraud and theft	Collapse	190	289
1989	Reed, David et al.	Blue Arrow	Employment agency	Conspiracy to rig shares	County Natwest Securities losses	837	1,180
1989	Guerin, James	Ferranti	Electronics-defence	Fraud	Receivership in 1993	215	303
1990	Levitt, Roger	Levitt Group	Financial services	Fraudulent trading	Collapse and receivership	34	44
1990	Nadir, Asil	Polly Peck International	Electronics to fruit	Theft and false accounting	Liquidation	1,000	1,290
1991	Naviede Muhammed	Arrows	Short-term loans	Fraud and deception	Collapse	100	122
1991	Naqvi, Swaleh and Gokal, A. K. el al.	Bank of Credit & Commerce International	Banking	Fraud	Closure	10,000	12,200
1991	Maxwell, Robert	Maxwell Communications Corporation	Media	Theft and deception	Collapse	1,000	1,220

Year	Name	Business	Offence	Consequence		
1991	Botnar, Octav and Hunt, Michael et al.	Nissan UK	Motor vehicle importers	Conspiracy to cheat the Revenue	Survival	195	238
1992	Lovelock, Sir Douglas	Church Commissioners	Clergy stipends and pensions	Gross mismanagement	Reorg'n of CofE	695	820
1993	Government-insurance cos	Insurance companies	Personal pensions	Deception	600,000 defrauded	4,000	4,640
1994	Anderson, Donald	Brent Walker Group plc	Leisure	Falsification of documents	Loss of reputation	164	185
1995	Leeson, Nick	Barings Bank	Banking	Concealment of losses	Collapse and receivership	860	937
1996	Young, Peter	Deutsche Morgan Grenfell	Investment banking	Deception	90,000 customers' investments jeopardized	250	268
1996	Lines, Richard	MTM plc	Fine chemicals mfr	False information	Collapse	250	268
1997	Feld, Robert	Resort Hotels	Hotels	False statements, forgery	Collapse	140	144
1999	Cresson, Edith; Marin, Manual	European Commission	Business support programmes	Bribe-taking, fraud, nepotism	Reputation dented		
1999	Ganga, Jean-Claud	International Olympic Committee	Sport	Bribe-taking	Reputation dented		
2000	Taubman, Alfred	Sotheby's	Auction house	Criminal collusion in price-fixing	Fine	31	30
2000	Lay, Kenneth; Skilling, Jeffrey	Enron	Global energy	Fraud	Collapse	$102 million	

*Assets of business before creditors were paid.

nineteenth century and international business had been transformed by globalization by the late twentieth century. How might these changes have lowered standards of business ethics? With change came new opportunities for high risk financial behaviour and for lowered personal integrity. But this does not explain why opportunities for corrupt or morally questionable behaviour in one age were eschewed in another. At present more detailed studies are needed from which to draw generalizations about the impact of economic expansion on ethical behaviour.

WHAT HAVE BEEN THE SOURCES OF ETHICAL STANDARDS IN BUSINESS IN TWENTIETH CENTURY BRITAIN?

From an empirical standpoint, several domains have shaped concepts of business ethics. Philosophy, law, custom, political theory, theological understanding, and foreign exemplars were the main ones. Over the course of the twentieth century the impact of ideas from these sources has varied. For example, while a classical education might have introduced a public-school or university-educated director to the virtue theory of the ancient Greeks (as it did in the case of Sir George Schuster[13]), by the last decade of the century British business schools were introducing their MBA students to the goal-based utilitarianism of Bentham, the rights-based contractarianism of Rousseau, and the duty-based ethics of Kant, as well as to John Rawls's reinterpretation of virtue ethics.[14]

In theory, if not always in practice, the parameters and standards of business ethics were set by the law, which in Britain was a combination of statute and case law. The overarching purpose of the law was not to define an ethical solution to every boardroom problem but to establish broad principles whereby directors could perceive their rights and responsibilities in any particular situation. English law (especially the law of agency by which relations between principal and agent were governed), from the eighteenth century, evolved the concept of duties (or rules), legally enforceable obligations carrying liability for loss or damage resulting from failure to meet the obligation. These duties obliged directors always to act in the interests of the shareholders.[15] For company directors at the beginning of the century fiduciary duty was foremost – to act honestly and in good faith in the interest of their principal, the members (shareholders) of the company.[16] Under the Companies Act of 1929, directors' fitness to hold office encompassed filing annual returns, producing audited accounts, and keeping proper accounting records. Failure to do so was a criminal offence.[17] Administrative incompetence amounted to dereliction of duty.

Yet the law was not an infallible guardian of socially responsible standards in the boardroom. A prime obstacle to directors' ethical behaviour, secrecy, was enhanced by the Companies Act of 1908 which gave private companies an inordinate degree of corporate secrecy.[18] Unsurprisingly, a rush to convert partnerships and small public companies into private companies followed.[19] Coupled with and intensified by concentration of boardroom control over labour and capital, cloaking directors' activities was worrisome because secretiveness enhanced chances of boardroom mismanagement, financial or otherwise. The Companies Act of 1929 required publication of an annual balance sheet, but otherwise left boardroom decisions still cloaked in much secrecy.

Largely responding to the unsatisfactory situation left by the Royal Mail case (1931), the Companies Acts of 1947–8 forced companies to disclose more accounting information about their true assets and profits. The Act of 1947 finally outlawed secret reserves, while the larger Act of 1948 further opened up boardroom decisions, chiefly via the auditing standard of 'true and fair', rather than 'true and correct', and by requiring holding companies to publish accounts covering all the subsidiaries in their group.

Another way in which lawyers found legal means of defending the corporate interest against the public interest in the early twentieth century was by invoking the 'corporate veil' principle – separating the legal identities of parent firm and its subsidiaries. The device proved highly advantageous to some late twentieth century multinationals seeking to avoid liability for toxic hazards like asbestos.[20]

Custom, which can hardly be touched upon here, was a further powerful source shaping ethical standards in business, a topic which raises the large question of ethics and culture. One example suffices. Stanley Baldwin MP, Prime Minister, recalled the customary ethic of his family firm of E. P. & W. Baldwin, iron and tinplate manufacturers of Stourport, Worcestershire: 'It was also a place where nobody ever "got the sack".'[21]

The most radical challenge to rethinking boardroom relationships, both internal and external to the firm, in the first decades of the century came from the Left. Socialists, particularly advocates of nationalization of whole industries (like the Labour Party after 1918), offered the most far-reaching alternatives. Between the wars, central planning was in vogue because of its apparent success in the Soviet Union. Less drastic, but still radical, the Liberal Party in 1928, recommended that public companies in Britain, as in Germany, should have a supervisory council to oversee the board of directors. Such a supervisory council 'would consist of members directly representing shareholders and, in some cases, the employees.'[22] Admission of employees to the boardroom was the litmus test of willingness to adjust the board's relationships within the firm.

In the first half of the twentieth century the churches produced some of the sharpest critiques of economic behaviour. Adam Smith, in proclaiming the sovereignty of the market, effectively separated economics and business from religion and ethics. The nineteenth century subsequently saw a theological struggle to recapture economic systems and business behaviour for the religious, Christian domain. All denominations, from Quakers to Catholics, by the end of the First World War had moved, or were moving, towards agreement with the report of the Archbishops Fifth Committee of Inquiry, *Christianity and Industrial Problems* (1918): 'we think it our duty to point out that Christianity claims to offer mankind a body of moral teaching which not only is binding upon individuals in their personal and domestic conduct but also supplies a criterion by which to judge their economic activity, their industrial organization and their social institutions.'[23] John Lee, a Post Office executive and director of the Automatic Telephone Manufacturing Co,[24] in a work published in 1922 by the Student Christian Movement, offered an elevated view of a new generation of professional managers: they 'may provide a priesthood in industry, just as there is a priesthood in worship.'[25]

Two figures in the 1930s and 1940s, William Temple and Joseph H. Oldham, played a key part in aligning the attitudes of English churches with the rising orthodoxy of socialism. Temple, successively Bishop of Manchester, Archbishop of York, and Archbishop of Canterbury, had in 1918 joined the Labour Party, where his public school and university friend, the Oxford historian R.H. Tawney, was a shaper of policy. Most influential was Temple's *Christianity and Social Order* (1942) which in a few months sold 139,000 copies.[26] This expounded 'middle axioms', or maxims for conduct which mediated between fundamental Christian principles and the jungle of ethical dilemmas confronting society. Starting from Christian understandings of God and His purpose and of human-kind's dignity, tragedy, and destiny, he argued that 'The primary principle of Christian Ethics and Christian Politics must be respect for every person simply as a person'. The trouble was that the individual's selfishness all too often got in the way. So 'the art of government in fact is the art of so ordering life that self-interest prompts what justice demands'.[27]

Oldham, missionary statesmen and ecumenical pioneer, concerned at spreading unbelief and twin threats from Right and Left, mobilized Christian laity as part of the ecumenical project. He launched the *Christian News-Letter* (1939) and in wartime formed the Christian Frontier Council (CFC) in 1942.[28] Among the prominent and powerful men in business drawn into CFC conferences and study groups were Alan Campbell Macdiarmid, chairman and managing director of Stewarts & Lloyds, steelmakers; third Viscount Hambleden, Chairman of W.H. Smith & Sons, newsagents; and Samuel Courtauld, Chairman of Courtaulds, the highly successful rayon manufacturers.[29]

Out of the CFC came some of the radical ideas that shaped thinking about business legitimacy, ownership, and structure in the second half of the twentieth century. Courtauld, of Unitarian stock and a shy millionaire, lent respectability to some remarkably radical ideas published posthumously as *Ideals and Industry* (1949).[30] He favoured worker directors (1943); thought the best directors regarded themselves as servants of the shareholder, the worker, and consumer (1944); and emphasized the need for directors and managers to 'make themselves realize and sympathize with the natural feelings, needs, and aspirations of their workers, not only because it is the only possible thing for a decent man to do once the idea has crossed his mind, but because there is no other road to industrial efficiency' (1943).[31] Rejecting nineteenth century notions that the worker was no more than a machine, he asserted the necessity for healthy, contented workers who take pride in their work. For the last-named quality, the worker 'must have the right to know all about the administration, policy, and finance of the company for which he works; he must know how the company's income is distributed; he must be able to criticize inefficient management – for, after all, his own investment in the business – his body and brain – is dependent on that management . . .' (1943).[32] This was strong medicine for management. Whether Courtauld would have recommended it had there been no war, or had his company's profits suffered long-term decline, is another matter.

One important source of ethical ideas for directors emerged from the importation of American management techniques and the efforts of British pioneers of management education and the professionalization of management. The unique handbook edited by John Lee (above), *Pitman's Dictionary of Industrial Administration* (2 vols., 1928), encapsulated this new management thinking. With ninty-nine contributors, including engineers, managers, directors, civil servants, consultants, and academics, the volumes publicized a wide selection of management philosophies, from the Taylorist to the human-relations-in-industry schools of thought and practice.[33]

If the most radical, and innovative, ideas about ethical behaviour in business boardrooms in the first half of the century came from Left-wing views of churchmen, in the last four decades of the century, the intellectual legacy of social Christianity has been most important in generating new approaches to boardroom relationships. This is not to deny the significance of company law or of political influence. The ascendancy of Thatcherism and the Chicago school of economics reinstated a measure of market-oriented values, regarded as necessary for reviving a competitive, and entrepreneurial society. However, this tended to depreciate moral codes in business: 'The social responsibility of business is to increase its profits,' in the words of Milton Friedman.[34]

A recent study, examining the opinions of business leaders, identified three views of the political economy and ideology of business between the 1950s and the 1990s. One was a revisionist view, seeing business as the co-partner with other political and social institutions. Liberationists sought maximum influence and freedom of action for business enterprise in relation to the state. Thirdly, reconstructionists, the most radical group, wanted the recasting of social structures and cultures, including the corporation.[35]

In the long run the ideas of reconstructionists prevailed. The most reasoned and articulate of these was George Goyder, managing director of Newsprint Supply Co in wartime and a member of the Church of England's Church Assembly in the 1950s. In his seminal studies, 'Socialism and Private Industry: A New Approach' *Fabian News* (Nov. 1949) and *The Future of Private Enterprise* (1951), he developed the view, derived from Samuel Courtauld and the CFC group of which he had been a member, that the company had responsibilities to the consumer and to the community as much as to shareholders and employees.

From the model of the Carl Zeiss *Stiftung* (Foundation), established by Ernst Abbe at Jena in 1896, Goyder, learning from Archbishop William Temple about the scheme, took the concept of trustees (equivalent to a supervisory board, exercising ultimate corporate control), quite separate from managers or workers.

This structure he regarded as superior to profit sharing, or Wilfred Brown's experiment at the Glacier Metal Co (in which management shared control with 1,500 workers), or the John Lewis Partnership, (which left ultimate plenary powers in the hands of Spedan Lewis, the founder).[36] By 1961, Goyder wanted changes to British company law that would legalize the Zeiss 'participating company' as a halfway house between a public limited company and a nationalized industry.[37] Goyder's *Future of Private Enterprise* triggered a dramatic and oft-cited experiment, the Scott Bader Commonwealth founded by the Quaker Ernest Bader in 1951. Bader's example was admiringly described by Fritz Schumacher, formerly economist to the National Coal Board and a newly converted Roman Catholic, in his influential *Small Is Beautiful: A Study of Economics as if People Mattered* (1973).[38]

The early 1970s saw a renewed and broad interest in the social responsibility of business (SRB). This seems to have arisen from the lobbying for better management training, culminating in the foundation of the Manchester Business School and the London Business School in 1965–6. Such training would now include broad social perspectives as well as technical and strategic skills.[39] Another factor was the rising volume of debate about SRB on both sides of the Atlantic, with American commentators being increasingly heeded, not least because of the postwar spread of American multinational business to Europe.[40] Third, Britain's entry to the European Economic Community on 1st January 1973 demanded that British business leaders work towards harmonization with Continental patterns of corporate structure.[41] Among them was the two-tier board pioneered in Germany and publicized by Goyder in 1951 and again in 1961 when he proposed (as did Professor W.A. Robson of the LSE) that companies should issue a regular social audit.[42]

Industry's acceptance in principle of the new SRB was signalled in 1973 with the publication of the Confederation of British Industry's *The Responsibilities of the British Public Company* and, later that year, a government White Paper on *Company Law Reform* (Cmnd. 5391). The former originated in consultations on business ethics at St George's House, Windsor, started in 1967, and driven forward by revisionists then heading the CBI.[43] The White Paper was primarily concerned with issues left over from the 1962 Jenkins committee report on *Company Law* (Cmnd. 1749). One was the problem of insider dealing and, beyond that, the legitimacy of private enterprise. Both papers addressed employee participation in company affairs, two-tier boards, non-executive directors, and institutional shareholders. In addition the CBI paper brought the local community into the picture.

Hopes of enshrining industrial democracy in company law dwindled when the Royal Commission on Industrial Relations, set up by Harold Wilson's Labour government in 1975 and chaired by Lord Bullock, in 1977 split on the issue. The majority report recommended trade union directors on main boards; the minority report, representing the CBI, advocated worker participation on supervisory boards (with shareholder and independent representatives).[44] All proposals were dropped by the incoming Thatcher government. Concurrent attempts to introduce voluntary codes of business ethics elicited managerial support but until the USA's Sarbanes-Oxley Act of 2002 (below) have been of questionable value.[45]

ETHICS AND THE AGE OF MARKET FORCES

Boardroom issues came to the fore in a very public way in the 1980s and 1990s when the public sense of what was right and fair was offended by the consequences of the Conservative governments' determined application of market-centred economic policy – evidenced by the deregulation of the Stock Exchange of 1986; a succession of massive privatizations; and a number of major demutualizations. Several consequences incurred the wrath of newspapers and public opinion: a pay explosion and a series of corporate scandals (listed in Table 18.1). Trust in business diminished and demands for corrective legislation intensified. Christian voices, some from inside the City, ranged between the absolutist condemnation of markets to a qualified defence of the City.[46]

In the 1980s and 1990s the focus of ethical concern outside the boardroom moved back to poverty and on to the natural environment. The unemployed of Britain's deindustrialized regions and cities and the starving millions of the world's global 'South', brought into the affluent living rooms of the global 'North' by television, demanded a moral response from the churches if they were to fulfill their prophetic function as independent and critical voices in each new generation. Three episcopal publications epitomized their ethical challenges to boardrooms: *Bias to the Poor* (1983) by David Sheppard, the cricketing parson and Bishop of Liverpool; *Faith In The City: A Call for Action by Church and Nation* (1985) by the Archbishop of Canterbury's Commission on Urban Priority Areas; and *Grace and Mortgage: The Language of Faith and the Debt of the World* (1997) by Peter Selby, Bishop of Worcester. All confronted contemporary problems: poverty, unemployment, debt. All embraced broad, global perspectives. All drew on ecumenical Christian literatures. All ventured into controversial areas, arousing political passions and *Faith in the City* the hostility of the current Prime Minister Thatcher. All three acknowledged a necessary dependence on wealth creating capitalism while denying economic sovereignty over human values. And all three suggested some form of practical solution to the problems they addressed: Sheppard could point to his own activities (with the Roman Catholic Archbishop Derek Worlock) in the rejuvenation of the depressed city of Liverpool; the Archbishop's Commission established the Church of England's Urban Priority Fund; and Selby's volume gave additional theological teeth to the Jubilee 2000 campaign for debt relief for the world's poorest countries.

For Roman Catholics the demand for social action was stiffened by the papal encyclical *Populorum Progressio* (1967). The parallel epiphany for Protestant evangelicals was the National Evangelical Congress held at the University of Keele that same year.[47] Added to these were the investigations of development specialists and international statesmen, the most influential of which was the Independent Commission on International Development Issues chaired by Willy Brandt, whose report appeared in 1980 as *North–South: A Programme for Survival.*

Environmental issues arrived on boardroom agendas in the 1980s because of the mounting evidence accumulated and sometimes published by the scientific community. Victorian concerns about smoke abatement, pure drinking water, and sewage disposal gave way to threats arising from the intervening chemical and transportation revolutions of the early twentieth century. Two dates marked new turning points. In 1962, Rachel Carson, an American marine biologist, published *Silent Spring*, alerting the world to the hazards of chemicals in agriculture. In 1987, scientists discovered that the destruction of the Earth's protective ozone layer by the global release of carbon was causing the phenomenon of global warming.[48] Christian consciences seem to have awoken to the environmental crisis in the 1980s and 1990s.[49]

Changes in the social environment of business increasingly intruded into UK boardrooms in last two decades of the twentieth century. The women's rights movement exposed the gross under-representation of women among company directors.[50] Immigration had diverse repercussions. On the one hand Afro-Caribbean ethnic groups were left outside big business boardrooms. On the other hand, immigrant culture, most prominently that of Islam, challenged Western values with very different social and ethical standards.[51] Globalizing business brought British corporate behaviour into the orbits of European Union and United States laws, and into the ethical issues of developing countries. While these changes had mixed ethical impacts on British business, domestic or foreign terrorism, not least the atrocities of 11th September 2001, gave company directors additional ethical agendas.

HOW HAVE DEBATE AND PRESCRIPTION ABOUT BUSINESS ETHICS BEEN TRANSFORMED INTO ACTION AND PERFORMANCE?

A variety of agents and circumstances have aspired to promote high standards of business ethics in the twentieth century. In potential extent of their influence, foremost were accountants. Their numbers exploded from 5,000 at the beginning of the century to 190,000 at its close but, in terms of companies per accountant, their average distribution across the economy remained remarkably stable (Table 18.2). As auditors or as directors (and by 1931 nearly a third of accountants were in business, as opposed to professional practice), their ethical influence, instilled in their articled-clerk training, was, prima facie, benign, given their knowledge of company law and their function as annually required gatekeepers.[52] On the other hand, not until 1947 was it a statutory requirement for an auditor of a limited company to be a professional accountant, not until the following year that the

Table 18.2. Companies, directors, accountants in Britain, 1900–2000

	Companies total	Private cos	Private cos as % of total	Accountants	Number of companies per accountant
1900	29,730			5,188	5.7
1910	51,787			9,072	5.7
1920	79,541	**62,600**	79	12,926	6.2
1930	111,861	**95,598**	85	21,897	5.1
1940	**153,512**	**141,089**	92	30,335	5.1
1950	**258,265**	**241,063**	93	37,238	6.9
1960	379,975	**376,789**	99	55,251	6.9
1970	559,497	**503,232**	90	77,109	7.3
1980	828,496	**751,642**	91	114,399	7.2
1990	1,031,900	**998,700**	97	153,015	6.7
1995	1,036,200	**1,024,700**	97	186,826 (1995 accts)	5.5

Note: Bold from Matthews et al. 1998: 90; accountants from Matthews et al. 1998: 62. See note 52.

'true and fair' criterion was imposed. Consequently varying degrees of deceit and secrecy with balance sheets and profit-and-loss accounts were practised.[53] After 1970, the spread of audit committees and non-executive directors aimed to diminish chances of corporate misbehaviour, but with disputed effect.[54]

Equally important, but in a different way, were exemplary paternalists. Perhaps the most widely admired was George Cadbury. George and his brother Richard viewed their cocoa and chocolate manufacturing business not as a means of making a fortune but as a 'social experiment . . . , and their underlying purpose was to show that business success was not only consistent with a high regard for the welfare of the work people, but the corollary of it.' Their views arose from their Quaker convictions. 'The central doctrine of Christianity, as George Cadbury understood it, is that men and women, rich or poor, are infinitely valuable, and that their lives should not be squandered. Let wages be handsome, but save labour wherever possible – these were the twin axioms.'[55] Because he chose to be a Christian paternalist, a steward of large material resources, Cadbury (eventually employing over 3,000 people) declined to sell a controlling interest in his business to the shareholding public, fearing that, reduced to a manager, he would lose his steward's powers.[56]

In the dispersion, as in the accumulation, of his wealth George Cadbury sought the goal of redeeming society. He set up the Bournville Trust in 1900 with a gift of £172,000 to establish a model housing estate for his employees and local people (where, in contrast to William Lever's Port Sunlight, his homes were not tied to the job) with the object of pioneering social arrangements that other capitalists or the state might copy. In so doing he disposed of 'the bulk of my property outside my business', believing 'Great wealth is not to be desired, and in my experience of life it is more a curse than a blessing to the families of those who possess it. I have 10 children. Six of them are of an age to understand how my actions affect them, and they all entirely approve'.[57] At the same time he recognized the limits of private philanthropy and favoured a social redistribution of wealth via death duties.[58]

Still involving the element of ex gratia beneficence in their philanthropy, were the corporate paternalists. Where they enjoyed natural monopolies, they could offer secure employment and large internal labour markets. For example, the railway companies funded industrial welfare in order to gain the loyalty of their permanent workforce.[59] To a firm disciplinary code they added a rational, rather than *ex gratia*, system of benefits. When the welfare provisions of the state and the power of the unions increased appreciably after 1906, and when the railways were merged into four companies in 1922–3, some changes became necessary. Arrangements with numerous provident societies, into which both employers and employees had paid funds, needed to be rationalized. The London, Midland & Scottish Railway, for instance, tried to preserve the practices of its enlightened predecessor, the London & North Western Railway, establishing a welfare department with divisional welfare officers who oversaw educational and recreational as well as medical arrangements. In competitive industries the rationalization of welfare was predicated on the rationalization of economic structures, as seen in the cases of ICI and Unilever. The gas companies, and a number of large manufacturers, like the United Steel Cos, Richard Thomas, Dorman Long, and Stewarts & Lloyds (all in steel) and Brunner, Mond (one of the constituents of ICI) were also at the forefront of providing company welfare.[60]

Few industrialists with Christian convictions went as far as Cadbury. Even his co-religionists did not always see eye-to-eye with him. As a group, Quaker employers (some of them, religious leaders of their non-clerical denomination and most of them paternalists), in their decennial conferences between the wars, struggled with the question of employee-directors. In 1918, they decided that if workers were admitted to the boardroom, they should not deal with financial or commercial matters. In 1928, they could see no way by which boardroom decisions and contracts could be shared with employees. In 1938, it was decided that 'share in management should depend upon capacity, and capacity alone.'[61]

One strong voice raised against the notion that economics should be subordinated to ethics was that of Josiah Stamp, perhaps the best known Methodist laymen of the inter-war years and, as president of the London, Midland & Scottish Railway Company, possibly the most distinguished professional manager produced by Nonconformity.[62] He disagreed with John Lee in 1926 and was still citing him without approval in 1936.[63] Stamp believed in the Christian conversion of individuals rather than the Christian transformation of economic systems.[64] Mindful of American examples, he considered 'payment on results, or profit sharing, [as] so much nearer a scheme in which Christian principles may have part'.[65]

Until the early 1970s, entrepreneurs and businesses chiefly limited their social action to the provision of paternalistic company towns, or philanthropic enterprise designed to promote education (e.g. the civic universities of the late nineteenth and early twentieth centuries), medicine (e.g. the Wellcome Trust), or the advancement of learning (e.g. the Nuffield and Leverhulme Trusts). Exceptionally,

Marks & Spencer, headed by the Jewish dynasties of the Marks and Sieff families, sourced their merchandise in the UK not least to create British jobs: by 1939 some 94 per cent of their merchandise came from British suppliers.[66]

Corporate engagement in society widened in the 1970s and by the end of the century had achieved two significant innovations. The first arose from the disturbing restructuring of the British economy. The big step forward came in 1978 with the formation of the first enterprise agency, the Community of St Helen's Trust on Merseyside. Supported jointly by Pilkington Brothers (the town's main employer, then rapidly shedding jobs), other manufacturing firms, banks, accounting firms, the trade unions, the Town Council, the Chamber of Commerce, and government agencies, the independent Trust in its first six years created 320 new businesses and between 6,000 and 8,500 jobs. Such was its success that the concept was promoted by the Thatcher government, which faced acute urban problems on Merseyside (where the Toxteth riots occurred in 1981) and elsewhere. By 1986, the UK target of 300 such enterprise agencies was reached.[67] The innovation was a major one: small firm creation was seen by the Conservatives as the engine of innovation in their enterprise economy.

The second innovation was the social audit and social accountability. Proposed first in the US by Harold R. Bowen in 1953 and then in Britain by George Goyder in 1961, social audit was begun in an ad hoc, self-regulated way, promoted by Michael Young's Social Audit Ltd (1971) and explored by a United Nations conference (1972). Environmental disasters in the 1980s and early 1990s, such as the dumping of toxic waste on the west coast of Africa, Union Carbide's chemical plant explosion at Bhopal (1984), Chernobyl (1986), or the *Exxon Valdez* Alaskan oil spill (1989) brought demands for company environmental disclosure and accountability from pressure groups as wide-ranging as Friends of the Earth, Greenpeace, the Consumers' Association, Pensions and Investments Research Consultants (PIRC), and the World Bank.[68]

EEC/EU and UK company legislation brought fragmentary or weak forms of social audit. They were exceeded by Anita Roddick who made a virtue out of sourcing 'green' materials for her Body Shop toiletries, producing Values Reports in 1995 and 1997; and by the Co-op Bank which in 1998 added to ethical investment (1992) an impressive social audit policy. In 1998 also, Royal Dutch/Shell Group, the British based oil major, added the publication of its first values report, *Profits and Principles: Does There Have to Be a Choice?* to its six other corporate reports. This was a direct response to the deluge of criticism it received in 1995 for its perceived lack of intervention in the case of Ken Saro-Wiwa, the executed Nigerian activist, and for its proposed Atlantic disposal of the Brent Spar off-shore storage buoy.[69] Significantly, Shell announced five 'areas of responsibility': shareholders, customers, employees, suppliers, and society. While profitability had priority, the declared principles by which it was achieved comprised business integrity; a-political dealings with states; improved health, safety, and environmental management; constructive interest in society; and the promotion of free enterprise. BP, another oil major, formulated its social policy in 1997. By the end of the century stakeholding and values, not least human rights and green issues, were established in global capitalism's bellwether businesses.[70]

Paradoxically, SRB, though not its radical Continental version, triumphed in the Thatcher years. SRB became corporate social responsibility (CSR) in the late 1970s and early 1980s and Goyder's 'four parties'[71] or 'interests'[72] (shareholders, employees, consumers, community) were now hailed as 'stakeholders' in newly formulated corporate governance theory of the late 1980s and 1990s.[73] The reasons? Membership of the EEC/EU was one energizer. Spreading global enterprise, which brought American and Continental practices into British industry, was another. Above all, perhaps, stakeholding was deployed to shore up the reputation and defend the legitimacy of business in the late 1980s and early 1990s when business scandals shook the business community and the whole country.

A powerful antidote to these ills was perceived to be improved corporate governance. Dominant business interests in almost every major economy in the 1990s adopted a code of best practice for the structuring and conduct of systems for company direction (board) and control (shareholders): in the UK, the Cadbury report on financial aspects of governance (1992); the Greenbury report on directors' remuneration (1995); the Hempel report on governance of listed companies (1998); and the Turnbull report on internal control (1999).[74] Governance was one issue, stakeholding another, though both were intimately connected. Stakeholding, sharply contested by right-wing academic economists, was, by the end of the century, a widely recognized concept deployed in various guises by many of Britain's largest businesses. This was especially the case in those industries popularly challenged by the Left – oil, pharmaceuticals, and nuclear energy, for example.[75]

Boardroom instruments by which SRB was translated into practice after 1970 included audit committees and non-executive directors. Their efficacy was much disputed. Beyond the boardroom, more unethical behaviour was criminalized. For example, the Companies Act of 1980 made insider dealing illegal. The proliferation of business frauds in the 1980s demanded more than a Board of Trade investigation, the customary legal response to corporate wrongdoing. In 1987–8 the Serious Fraud Office, unifying police, legal, and accountancy functions, was established to deal, not always successfully, with large, often international, and complex frauds like BCCI and Maxwell[76] (see Table 18.2). However, nothing so much concentrated boardroom minds on ethical issues as the US's Sarbanes–Oxley Act (2002), passed following the catastrophic collapses of Enron and WorldCom. Affecting companies reporting to the Securities and Exchange Commission, it required many UK multinationals to tie up large resources in SOX compliance (including the adoption of a code of ethics and monitored adherence thereto), in order to spare directors, managers, and employees the swingeing penalties awaiting those convicted of violating the Act.[77]

WHEN RELIGION HAS INFORMED ETHICS,
HAVE RELIGIOUS CONVICTIONS PRESERVED
ENTREPRENEURS AND EXECUTIVES FROM
ETHICAL DILEMMAS AND IRRESPONSIBLE CHOICES?

The answer is – not always. Two cases at the beginning of the century illustrate polar situations. Jabez Spencer Balfour, Congregationalist and MP, developed the Liberator Building Society into the largest of its kind in the late nineteenth century by forming around it a property group with land and banking companies. Among his techniques, he made loans for chapel as well as house building and he recruited church and chapel halls as Liberator 'branch offices'. Behind the pious facade (he 'opened Board meetings with prayer') his later success rested on one very dubious stratagem which, when the property market collapsed, had to be covered by fraud: 'interest to Liberator shareholders was being paid out of current receipts on share and deposit accounts'.[78] In 1892, his crooked corporate pyramid collapsed; Balfour had to be extradited from Argentina to serve fourteen years' imprisonment; and over 11,000 Liberator shareholders, including many poor widows, lost £1.66 million.[79]

In the other case, that of Cadburys, the possibility of covering up unethical behaviour (an opportunity which Balfour seized) was rejected. Like Balfour, the Cadbury board were at first unwitting as the situation developed – in their case, reports that their West African cocoa suppliers were using slave labour. However, unlike Balfour, they immediately took steps to withdraw: as Quakers they abhorred slavery; their forefathers had fought for its abolition; and even the rumour of it would be disastrous for their business. George Cadbury's political enemies impugned his reputation and a libel case followed. However, he was awarded a derisory 1 farthing in damages because the court judged that the firm had taken too long in collecting evidence and making the decision to switch cocoa suppliers.[80]

Further examples could be given: Harold Morland, Quaker, and the auditor in the Royal Mail case; the Turner family, Methodists, members of whom denied the pernicious effects of asbestos exposure, continued for decades to expand asbestos production, and left employees, installers, and consumers unprotected; or, more recently, James Guerin, evangelical Christian, found criminally guilty in the Ferranti scandal.[81] Nor should it be forgotten that Robert Maxwell, media mogul and plunderer of the Mirror Group's pension fund, was born an Orthodox Jew and buried in Israel[82]; or that the century's most damaging case of financial fraud (larger even than WorldCom) was perpetrated by the managers of the Bank of Credit & Commerce International, an Islamic bank.[83] (See Table 18.1 for all these cases.)

Falls from grace in the boardroom or in executive management should not be surprising. Entrepreneurial decision making is hazardous. Boardrooms typically deal with imperfect information, privileged knowledge, risk, reliance on subordinates, fine judgements, and large amounts of capital and finance, to say nothing of dependent employees.[84] With the best will in the world and the highest ethical standards in view, individuals were sometimes drawn into the first stages of unethical activity. Circumstances conspired to create those first stages. The difference between the marginally guilty, as in the Cadbury case, and the thoroughly guilty, as in the Liberator, Turner & Newall, Ferranti, Maxwell, and BCCI cases, was the speed with which individuals realized their moral hazards and decided to break out of their situation. Delay, indecision, acquiescence, risked an ethical dilemma becoming a criminal circumstance.

HAVE BUSINESS PEOPLE CHARGED WITH THE MANAGEMENT OF THEIR CHURCHES' BUSINESS AFFAIRS DEMONSTRATED AN ETHICAL RECORD SUPERIOR TO THAT OF THE WIDER UK WORLD OF BUSINESS?

In the first half of the century businessmen played an important role in their denominations by creating national structures. These included economic structures, spanning church building, fund-raising, and investment in property and equities. Sir William Hartley, the jam manufacturer, was particularly effective among the Primitive Methodists in raising money and overseeing its use. Sir Josiah Stamp used his experience of multi-divisional organization and finance when Methodist reunion in 1932 required the merging of three sets of denominational funds. In the Church of England in the 1920s, Sir Robert Kindersley played a key role in the development of the Church Assembly's Central Board of Finance.[85]

Much less happy have been more recent decades. In Nonconformist churches, people in business have withdrawn from national leadership. On the other hand, Charles Jacob, stockbroker, widened the ethical investment policy of the Methodist Church; and David Wigley, a former Procter & Gamble executive director, oversaw the expansion of Methodist Homes.[86]

Woeful depths were reached in the Church of England. In the 1980s, Sir Douglas Lovelock, as First Church Estates Commissioner in charge of the central investments of the Church of England, pursued policies resting on the premise that the Commissioners were a pension fund, set up for profit maximization, rather than a charity, set up for the 'work of the Gospel'. Instead of reducing Church investments in the South African economy during the apartheid years, he increased them. In addition, he allowed his asset manager, James Shelley, to reduce the Commissioners' agricultural and housing portfolios and instead, with the aid of £250 million of loans from the NatWest, to pile into urban, commercial property, particularly giant shopping centres. When the property market collapsed in 1991 the Commissioners were left with geared investments incurring losses of £624 million by 1992 on gross assets of almost £3 billion

(1989). With repercussions for clergy stipends and pensions, this led to an overhaul of the Church's central structures.[87]

HAVE RELIGIOUS AND ETHICAL COMMITMENT INDUCED BETTER NATIONAL ECONOMIC PERFORMANCE?

In the first six decades of the century, churchgoing diminished, but not precipitously so; levels of unethical behaviour in the boardroom seemed to be at historically low levels; and the British economy, as measured by relative international GDP rates, exhibited persisting decline. In the last thirty years of the century the picture changed drastically. Churchgoing went into freefall. Boardroom misbehaviour rates rose from hundreds to thousands of cases. Economic decline reached a crisis point and then miraculously reversed. In contrast to Victorian Britain, economic growth now appeared to be associated with secularization and boardroom malpractice. How may this be explained?

One suggestion centres on the unleashing of consumerism. Begun in the 1960s and continued under Mrs Thatcher and her successors, consumer capitalism devoured the nationalized industries, some components of the welfare state, and the old good neighbour ethic. Materialism subverted the religious faith of society and good behaviour in the boardroom.

In theory, ethics and economics may be linked via leadership, as Casson argues.[88] Unethical leadership destroys trust in a particular firm, demolishing its market and perhaps ruining the firm. One classic case was Ratner's, once the world's largest jewellery retailer, whose head, Gerald Ratner, in 1991 publicly and intemperately described his firm's products as 'total crap': by the end of the following year the firm's shares at 10p were almost worthless, Ratner had resigned, and the name departed the high street.[89] More widely, the post-privatization controversy over directors' pay indicated a failure of socially responsible behaviour among business leaders in the 1980s and 1990s.

Firms are the building blocks of an economy. The proliferation of the kinds of unethical business practices catching headlines in the 1980s and 1990s, if unchecked, eventually reduces trust in market relationships, erodes the efficiency of markets, and eventually may lead to a failing economy. If there is causation between ethics and economic performance in Britain it must be diffused and delayed, perhaps inter-generational – operating through formal and informal institutions as Casson suggests.

A distinction should be drawn between the theory and practice of ethical business. The most notable contribution made in this area by followers of the Christian faith was not in the behaviours of individual paternalists but at the level of theoretical models. From theory, especially the formulation of ethical standards, came better boardroom practice by the end of the century. Out of the ashes of industrial democracy (derived in part from socialist and Christian principles, in part from Continental examples) came in the last decades of the century the phoenix of stakeholding. Stakeholding has been a very, perhaps the most, powerful tool deployed to advance the concept of corporate social responsibility in many FTSE companies. Its line of development ran across the twentieth century from socialism to William Temple, Samuel Courtauld, George Goyder, and, last, to American business school professors and CSR.

CAN BUSINESS HISTORY ILLUMINATE THE BOUNDARY BETWEEN BUSINESS, ETHICS, AND RELIGION?

Many of the questions raised in this chapter require further exploration. To deal with them adequately will need intellectual resources from several disciplines, from economics to ethics and theology. Business History, demanding long-term perspectives, an exhaustive quest for primary evidence, and a persistent scepticism of the facile judgements beloved of management gurus, offers scope for this sort of eclectic approach. In addition, it allows the combination of both quantitative and qualitative evidence. Perhaps the greatest opportunity in pursuing the ethics of business lies in twinning individual firms with localities and regions. In this way one of the least explored aspects of business ethics, the company and the community, may best be tackled. What is clear is that, to date, few business historians have bitten the bullet of analysing unethical business behaviour.[90]

NOTES

1. I am grateful to Christopher Tonge FCA and Rebecca Mon-Williams CA for their professional comments on the financial aspects of this essay, and to Geoff Tweedale for keeping me up-to-date on the history of unethical behaviour in industrial health and safety. In no way are they responsible for any of my assessments. In addition, Duncan Knox and Daniel Middleton gave me some valuable computing help.
2. Summarized in the injunction to 'love your neighbour as yourself', declared in both the Old and New Testaments: Leviticus 19: 18; Matthew 19: 19.
3. Archbishop Carey, 'Standards in Public Life' House of Lords speech, 22 Nov. 1994, and other speeches in 1996. My thanks to Jessamy Sykes of Lambeth Palace Library for the references to the 1996 speeches.
4. Peter Brierley, 'Religion in Britain, 1900 to 2000', in Heather Wraight and Peter Brierley, eds., *UK Christian Handbook, 2000/2001*, HarperCollins Religious, 1999: 25. Peter Brierley, 'Religion', in A.H. Halsey, ed., *British Social Trends Since 1900* Macmillan, 1988: 540, does not agree with the more pessimistic figures of Callum G. Brown, *The Death of Christian Britain: Understanding Secularisation, 1800–2000*, Routledge, 2001: 164.
5. A definition which simplifies wide and complex philosophical, cultural, and case issues: see Tom L. Beauchamp and Norman E. Bowie, eds., *Ethical Theory and Business*, 5th edn, Prentice Hall, Upper Saddle River, NJ, 1997, one of a number of introductory texts.

6. Kenneth E. Goodpaster, *Ethics in Management*, Harvard Business School, Boston, 1984: 4–5.

7. David Sunderland, *Social Capital, Trust and the Industrial Revolution, 1780–1880*, Routledge, 2007.

8. M. Marinetto, 'The Historical Development of Business Philanthropy: Social Responsibility in the New Corporate Economy', *Business History*, 41, 4 Oct. 1999: 7, 13.

9. The six reasons, found in these Acts, why a company might be wound up by the Court were the following:

   1. if the company has by special resolution resolved that it be wound-up;
   2. if default was made in filing the statutory report or in holding the statutory meeting;
   3. if the company did not commence its business within a year of its incorporation, or suspended its business for a whole year;
   4. if the number of members was reduced, in the case of a private company, below two, or in the case of any other company, below seven;
   5. if the company was unable to pay its debts;
   6. if the court was of opinion that it was just and equitable that the company should be wound up.

10. *First Report by the Board Of Trade under Section 29 of the Companies (Winding-Up) Act, 1890*, HMSO, London, 1893: 9. For the background to this 1890 act see George Robb, *White-Collar Crime in Modern England: Financial Fraud and Business Morality, 1845–1929*, Cambridge, 1992: 147–54.

11. Paul L. Davies, ed: *Gower's Principles of Modern Company Law*, 6th edn, Sweet & Maxwell, 1997: 835. To this may be added confirmatory evidence from the late 20th century scene in the US: see Henry N. Pontell, 'White-collar Crime or just Risky Business? The Role of Fraud in Major Financial Debacles', *Crime, Law and Social Change*, 42, 2004: 312.

12. Author's data.

13. George Schuster, *Christianity and Human Relations in Industry*, Epworth Press, 1951: 22–3.

14. See for these philosophical ideas, Tom Sorrell and John Hendry, Butterworth, Business Ethics Oxford, 1994, or most modern college texts on business ethics.

15. From the eighteenth century and, later, the *Foss v. Harbottle* decision of 1843, the company members (shareholders) in general meeting were regarded as the 'supreme governing body' of the company and the board their agent, the servant, of the company. Laurence C. Gower, *The Principles of Modern Company Law*, Stevens, 1954: 122n.

16. In the oft-cited dictum of Cairns L.C., in *Parker v. Mckenna*, 1874: 'No man can in this Court, acting as agent, be allowed to put himself in a position in which his interest and his duty will conflict'. Francis Beaufort Palmer, *Company Law*, Stevens, 1901: 130–3, 140.

17. 19 & 20 Geo. 5, c. 23, para. 122. See also Davies, *Gower's Principles*: 686–8.

18. 7 Edw. 7, c. 50, paras. 37, 121. Though it could not have more than fifty shareholders and might not offer its shares for sale to the public, the private company required directors only to file a statement (instead of a prospectus) with the Registrar of Joint Stock Companies and placed them under no obligation to file an annual balance sheet.

19. Between 1908 and 1950 the number of private companies increased from 19,190 to 235,307, an twelve-fold increase – compared to the increase in public companies from 4,395 to 11,920 between 1907 and 1955, less than a trebling from a much lower baseline. Of 66,000 companies in 1917, 50,000 were private companies. *PP*, Reports from the Registrar of Companies (whose various statistical tables sometimes diverged).

20. Geoffrey Tweedale and Laurie Flynn, 'Piercing the Corporate Veil: Cape Industries and Multinational Corporate Liability for a Toxic Hazard, 1950–2004' *Enterprise and Society*, 8 June 2007: 268–96.

21. Stanley Baldwin, *Peace and Goodwill in Industry*, Allen & Unwin, 1925: 8.

22. *Liberal Industrial Inquiry, Britain's Industrial Future*, Benn, 1928: 91.

23. *Report of the Archbishop's Fifth Committee of Inquiry, Christianity and Industrial Problems*, 1918: 9. John Oliver, *The Church and Social Order: Social Thought in the Church of England, 1918–1939*, 1968; Edward R. Norman, *Church and Society in England and, 1779 to 1970: A Historical Study*, Clarendon Press, Oxford, 1976; Adrian Hastings, *A History of English Christianity, 1920–2000*, SCM Press, 2001: 65–85, 193–212.

24. Harold Perkin, *The Rise of Professional Society. England since 1880*, Routledge, 1989: 294–306; *WWW*; *The Times*, 28, 29 Dec. 1928.

25. John Lee, *The Social Implications of Christianity*, Student Christian Movement, 1922: 109, 114–15.

26. David J. Jeremy, *Capitalists and Christians: Business Leaders and the Churches in Britain, 1900–1960*, Clarendon Press, Oxford, 1990: 65–72; F.A. Iremonger, *William Temple, Archbishop of Canterbury*, Oxford University Press, 1948: 435.

27. William Temple, *Christianity and Social Order*, 1942, repr. 1976: 65, 67.

28. From which the nascent ecumenical movement sprang. Jeremy, *Capitalists and Christians*: 196–209.

29. Ibid.: 196–209; D.C. Coleman, 'Samuel Courtauld IV', in David J. Jeremy and Christine Shaw, eds., *Dictionary of Business Biography*, 6 vols, 1984–6; hereafter *DBB*.

30. Jeremy, *Capitalists and Christians*: 201–3.

31. Samuel Courtauld, *Ideals and Industry*, 1949: 37, 45, 95, 126.

32. Ibid.: 23–4.

33. Lee's own position was clear from two of his other writings: *Management: A Study of Industrial Organization* (1921); and *Letters to an Absentee Director* (1928). He was not the only one in the 1920s to write about the new management techniques. Nor were his ideas always rigorously organized, well defined, or conclusive. However, what he lacked in clarity, Lee made up in the range of new management methods which he publicized. In addition, he included directors within the scope of his remarks.

34. *New York Times*, 13 Sept. 1970. Like many others, I take issue with this view: David J. Jeremy, *A Business History of Britain, 1900–1990s*, Oxford University Press, 1998: 526–7.

35. Jonathan Boswell and James Peters, *Capitalism in Contention: Business Leaders and Political Economy in Modern Britain*, Cambridge University Press, 1997.

36. George Goyder, *The Future of Private Enterprise*, Blackwell, Oxford, 1951: 73; George and Rosemary Goyder, *Signs of Grace*, Cygnet Press, 1993: 71–5. Geoffrey Tweedale, 'John Spedan Lewis', *DBB*. John Lewis Partnership, *John Spedan Lewis 1885–1963*, John Lewis Partnership, 1985: 11.

37. George Goyder, *The Responsible Company*, Blackwell, Oxford, 1961: 79–86.

38. Susanna Hoe, *The Man Who Gave His Company Away: A Biography of Ernest Bader, Founder of the Scott Bader Commonwealth*, Heinemann, 1978; Hastings, *History of English Christianity*: 573.

39. Michael P. Fogarty, 'Management Education and Values', in Michael Ivens, ed., *Industry and Values: The Objectives and Responsibilities of Business*, Harrap, 1970.

40. For example H.F.R. Catherwood, *The Christian in Industrial Society*, Tyndale Press, 1964; and Michael Ivens, *Industry and Values*: a collection of essays by 17 contributors to the debate in Britain. Others are noted in Marinetto, 'Historical Development'. On the American side see Harold R. Bowen, *Social Responsibilities of the Businessman* Harper: New York, 1953; Raymond Baumhart, *An Honest Profit: What Businessmen Say about Ethics in Business,* Holt, Reinhart & Winston: New York, 1968.

41. White Paper on 'Company Law Reform' Cmnd. 5391. 1973, 18–19; Christel Lane, *Management and Labour in Europe: The Industrial Enterprise in Germany, Britain and France*, Edward Elgar, Aldershot, 1989: 224–48.

42. Goyder, *Responsible Company*: 109–11; R. Edward Freeman, 'A Stakeholder Theory of the Modern Corporation', repr. in Beauchamp and Bowie, *Ethical Theory*.

43. Boswell and Peters, *Capitalism in Contention*: 116–19.

44. Lord Bullock (chairman), 'Industrial Democracy: Report of the Committee of Inquiry' Cmnd. 6706, 1976–7.

45. Simon Webley, *An Enquiry into Some Aspects of British Businessmen's Behaviour*, Industrial Educational and Research Foundation, 1971: 37–45; Tom Sorrell and John Hendry, *Business Ethics*, Butterworth-Heinemann, 1994: 11–16. However, see Adrian Cadbury, 'The Role of Voluntary Codes of Practice in Setting Ethics', in Ian Jones and Michael Pollitt, eds., *The Role of Business Ethics in Economic Performance*, Palgrave, Basingstoke, 1998.

46. Margaret Reid, *All-Change in the City: The Revolution in Britain's Financial Sector*, Macmillan, 1988; Timothy Gorringe, *Capital and the Kingdom*, SPCK, 1994; Stephen K. Green, *Serving God? Serving Mammon?*, Marshall Pickering, 1996. Stephen Green, an HSBC manager and an ordained clergyman in the Church of England, in 2006 became Group Chairman of HSBC. My thanks go to Mr Green for a photocopy of his (now scarce) book.

47. Hastings, *History of English Christianity*: 553–4, 573.

48. Brian W. Clapp, *An Environmental History of Britain since the Industrial Revolution*, Longman, 1994.

49. See sources in Ghillean Prance, *The Earth under Threat: A Christian Perspective*, Wild Goose Publications, Glasgow, 1996, a study by a former Director of the Royal Botanic Gardens, Kew.

50. See publications of the International Centre for Women Business Leaders at Cranfield University School of Management.

51. Jamal Badawi, 'Islamic Teaching and Business', in Oliver F. Williams, ed., *Business, Religion, and Spirituality*, Notre Dame Press, 2003.

52. See Derek Matthews et al., *The Priesthood of Industry: The Rise of the Professional Accountant in British Management*, Oxford University Press, 1998: 26, 35, 158, 276. John Richard Edwards, *A History of Financial Accounting*, Routledge, 1989: 152–5, 259–75.

53. Railways, public utilities, and financial institutions were better regulated than commercial and industrial companies according to R.H. Parker, 'Regulating British Corporate

Financial Reporting in the Late Nineteenth Century', *Accounting, Business and Financial History*, I, 1, Oct. 1990, but collusion between auditors and large insider investors and management (to the exclusion of small shareholders) is evidenced in Josephine Maltby, '"A Sort of Guide, Philosopher and Friend": The Rise of the Professional Auditor in Britain', *Accounting, Business and Financial History*, IX, 1, Oct. 1999.

54. Paul Collier, 'The Rise of the Audit Committee in UK Quoted Companies: A Curious Phenomenon?' *Accounting, Business and Financial History*, VI, 2, Sept. 1996.

55. Alfred G. Gardiner, *The Life of George Cadbury*, Cassell, 1925: 73, 80.

56. When the firm became a public company in 1912 only preference shares were offered to the public. Basil G. Murray, 'George Cadbury', *DBB*.

57. Gardiner, *Cadbury*: 103.

58. Ibid.: 105.

59. Robert Fitzgerald, *British Labour Management and Industrial Welfare, 1846–1939*, Croom Helm, Beckenham, 1988: 26.

60. Ibid.: 42–7, 115–36; Jonathan Boswell, *Business Policies in the Making: Three Steel Companies Compared*, Allen & Unwin, London 1983.

61. Jeremy, *Capitalists and Christians*: 166–8.

62. Michael Bywater, 'Josiah Charles Stamp', *DBB*; Jeremy, *Capitalists and Christians*: 178–83.

63. Josiah C. Stamp, *The Christian Ethic as an Economic Factor*, Epworth, 1926: 60–6; Josiah C. Stamp, *Motive and Method in a Christian Order*, Epworth 1936: 165.

64. Ibid.: 40.

65. Jeremy, *Capitalists and Christians*: 167–8; Stamp, *Christian Ethic*: 60–1.

66. Goronwy Rees, *St Michael: a History of Marks & Spencer*, Weidenfeld and Nicolson 1969: 108.

67. Ian Hamilton Fazey, *The Pathfinder: The Origins of the Enterprise Agency in Britain*, Financial Training, St Helen's, 1986: 91; Marinetto, 'Historical Development': 12–17.

68. Richard C. Warren, *Corporate Governance and Accountability*, Liverpool Academic Press, Bromborough, 2000: 80–93.

69. Considering the temper of the times perhaps it was no coincidence that Shell in the late 1990s produced a coffee-table company history, rather than a scholarly one like that of BP, to celebrate its centenary: Stephen Howarth, *A Century in Oil: The 'Shell' Transport and Trading Company 1897 to 1997*, Weidenfeld and Nicolson, 1997.

70. Warren, *Corporate Governance*: 94–109.

71. Goyder, *Future*: 93.

72. Goyder, *Responsible Company*: 85, 91.

73. E. Freeman and D. Reed, 'Stockholders and Stakeholders: A New Perspective on Corporate Governance', in C. Huizinga, ed., *Corporate Governance: The Definitive Exploration of the Issues*, UCLA Extension Press, Los Angeles, 1983.

74. Adrian Cadbury (chairman), *Report of the Committee on the Financial Aspects of Corporate Governance*, Gee, 1992; Sir Richard Greenbury (chairman), *Directors' Remuneration: Report of a Study Group*, Gee, 1995; Ronnie Hempel (chairman), *Committee on Corporate Governance: Final Report*, (Gee, 1998; Nigel Turnbull (chairman), *Internal Control: Guidance for Directors on the Combined Code*, Institute of Chartered Accountants in England and Wales, 1999. Jonathan Charkham, *Keeping Good Company: A Study of Corporate Governance in Five Countries*, Oxford University Press, 1995; Jonathan Charkham and Anne Simpson, *Fair Shares: The Future of Shareholder Power and Responsibility*, Oxford University Press, 1999.

75. The classic free-market statement is by the Chicago economist Milton Friedman, 'The Social Responsibility of Business is to Increase Its Profits' *New York Times Magazine*, 13 Sept. 1970. For 1990s debate see, on anti-stakeholding: Elaine Sternberg, *Corporate Governance: Accountability in the Marketplace*, Institute of Economic Affairs, 1998; on pro-stakeholding: Will Hutton, *The State We're In*, Cape, 1995. See also Warren, *Corporate Governance*.

76. Mark Killick, *Fraudsters: The Inside Story of the Serious Fraud Office*, Gollancz, 1998.

77. See, for example, Freshfields Bruckhaus Deringer, *The Sarbanes–Oxley Act and US Regulatory Developments: A Summary*, Apr. 2004; *idem, Code of Ethics: Requirements under the Sarbanes–Oxley Act*. Feb. 2003.

78. Esmond J. Cleary, 'Jabez Spencer Balfour', *DBB*; Henry Osborne O'Hagan, *Leaves from My Life*, 2 vols, Bodley Head, London, 1929, I, 141.

79. John Armstrong, 'The Rise and Fall of the Company Promoter and the Financing of British Industry', in J. J. van Helten and Y. Cassis, eds., *Capitalism in a Mature Economy* Elgar, Aldershot, 1990; Cleary, 'Balfour', *DBB*.

80. Lowell J. Satre, *Chocolate on Trial: Slavery, Politics and the Ethics of Business*, Ohio University Press, Athens, OH, 2005; Jeremy, *Capitalists and Christians*: 145–52.

81. For the Royal Mail case: Edwin Green and Michael Moss, *A Business of National Importance: The Royal Mail Shipping Group, 1902–1937*, Methuen, 1982; Edgar Jones, *True and Fair. A History of Price Waterhouse*, Hamish Hamilton, 1995: 145–57; John Richard Edwards, *A History of Financial Accounting*, Routledge, 1989: 148–54. For asbestos: Geoffrey Tweedale, *Magic to Killer Dust: Turner & Newall and the Asbestos Hazard*, Oxford University Press, 2000; Jock McCulloch and Geoffrey Tweedale, *Defending the Indefensible: The Global Asbestos Indusry and Its Fight for Survival*, Oxford University Press, 2008; David. J. Jeremy, 'Corporate Responses to the Emergent Recognition of a Health Hazard in the UK Asbestos Industry: The Case of Turner & Newall, 1920–1960', *Business and Economic History*, 24 1995. For Ferranti and Gueron: *The Times*, 30 Sept. 17, 18 Nov. 1989, 12 Aug. 1991, *Independent*, 25 Jan. 1990.

82. Tom Bower, *Maxwell, the Outsider*, Mandarin, 1991.

83. 'Behind Closed Doors', *Financial Times*, 1991; James Ring Adams, *A Full Service Bank: How BCCI Stole Billions around the World*, Simon & Schuster, New York, 1992; Nick Kochan and Bob Whittington, *Bankrupt: The BCCI Fraud*, Gollancz, 1991; Lord Justice Bingham, *Inquiry into the Supervision of the Bank of Credit and Commerce International*, House of Commons Paper 198, 22 Oct. 1992.

84. Mark Casson, *The Entrepreneur: An Economic Theory*, 2nd edn, Elgar, Cheltenham, 2003, emphasizes the judgemental nature of entrepreneurial decision-making.

85. Jeremy, *Capitalists and Christians*: 245–352.

86. David J. Jeremy, 'Twentieth Century Protestant Nonconformists in the World of Business', in Alan P. F. Sell and Anthony R. Cross, eds., *Protestant Nonconformity in the Twentieth Century*, Paternoster Press, Carlisle, 2003.

87. Terry Lovell, *Number One Millbank: The Financial Downfall of the Church of England*, Harper Collins, 1997; Andrew Chandler, *The Church of England in the Twentieth Century: The Church Commissioners and the Politics of Reform, 1948–98*, Boydell Press, 2004. Lovelock admitted that he was partly to blame, not least for failing to probe and stop the property deals that proved disastrous: Douglas Lovelock, *While I Remember: Christmas Island, Customs & Excise and the Church Commissioners*, Pentland Press, Edinburgh, 1998: 90.

88. Mark Casson, 'The Economics of Ethical Leadership', in Jones and Pollitt, eds., *Role of Business Ethics.*

89. See entry in David J. Jeremy and Geoffrey Tweedale, *Dictionary of Twentieth Century British Business Leaders*, Bowker Saur, 1994, though Ratner himself has made a recent comeback.

90. Geoffrey Tweedale, 'Researching Corporate Crime: A Business Historian's Perspective', in Steve Tombs and Dave Whyte, eds., *Unmasking the Crimes of the Powerful: Scrutinising States and Corporations* Peter Lang Publishing, New York, 2003. Recent confirmation of this blind spot is the inexplicable absence of more than a phrase or two about health and safety or business ethics in the 25-chapter *Oxford Handbook of Business History* edited by Geoffrey Jones and Jonathan Zeitlin (Oxford University Press, 2008). But the wider problem goes beyond neglect. Modern corporate battles over issues of business ethics demonstrate again the ancient and persisting appetite of powerful patrons for control of the historical process. As in the past, the mighty often succeed, and the independence and integrity of historians may be undermined, for a time at least. See Geoffrey Tweedale, 'Discovering "Discovery": The Pleasures and Perils of Litigation Archives', *Business Archives*, 97, Nov. 2008. For convergences between business ethics and business history, see R. Warren and G. Tweedale, 'Business Ethics and Business History. Neglected Dimensions in Management Education', *British Journal of Management*, 13, 2002.

Index

Figures and notes are indexed in bold.

AACP, *see* Anglo-American Council on Productivity
Aaronovitch, S. 87
ABC, *see* film companies, Associated British Cinemas Ltd. (ABC)
Abe, T. 74
accountants 88, 91, 370–1, 371**t18.2**
accounting 17, 141, 237, 265, 364, 365, 370–1
Ackrill, M. 190, 191, 192, 194, 195, 196, 197, 200, 202, 208, 210
acquisitions 26, 59, 117, 179
  banks 203, 213, 214, 215–16, 218, 219, 221
  by foreign competitors 125, 126
  UK acquisitions in USA 207, 210, 211, 212, 214, 217–19
  in UK 117, 123, 126
  see also mergers
Adams, A. A. 172
Adams, J. R. 375
Adcock, D. 276
advertising 24, 169, 171, 172, 176, 178, 179, 180, 196, 199, 330, 336, 340, 357
  mass 170, 173, 175–6, 177, 179, 182
  sports 341–2
aero-engine manufacturers 62–3, 225, 226–7, 228, 232, 233
aerospace 77, 154, 161–2, 225, 226
Agar, J.239
agency 35, 68
aircraft industries 50, 226–8, 231, 233, 244
  Airbus 54, 55, 57, 230, 231, 234, 235
  Anglo-French Concorde 51, 54, 230, 231–2, 234, 245
  jet engines 5, 51, 226, 228–9, 230, 232, 233–4, 241, 261
  procurement process 228
  sales 230, 233, 237, 242
  see also Boeing; British Aerospace; British Aircraft Corporation; aero-engine manufacturers; Hawker Siddeley; Rolls-Royce; USA, aircraft industries
airframe industry 225, 226, 228, 229, 230–2, 234
Akehurst, G. 272, 275
Aldcroft, D. H. 168
Aldgate, A. 314
Alexander, A. 271, 273
Alexander, N. 272, 275
Alford, B. W. E. 22, 31, 173, 174

Allen, J. A. 266
Allen, S. 105, 106
Amatori, F. 91
America, *see* USA
American Tobacco Company 22, 24, 25, 29, 30, 174
Anderson, R. 254, 255, 261
Anderson, S. 98, 102, 103, 106, 107
Anglo-American Council on Productivity (AACP) 138–9, 145
Anglo-American productivity gap 120, 123
Anglo-German productivity differences 156**8.3**
Anthony, B. 309
APACS, *see* Association of Payment Clearing Services
Argentina 15–16
Aris, J. 237, 240
armaments manufacturers 193, 255–6, 260
Armstrong, J. 375
Arnold, E. 238, 241
Artis, M. 161, 163
Arvidsson, A. 176, 181
asbestos 365, 375
Ashby, J. 306
Ashworth, W. 161
Aspray, W. 237, 240, 241
Assimakopulus, D. 240
Association of Payment Clearing Services (APACS) 202
Associated British Cinemas Ltd. (ABC), *see* film companies, Associated British Cinemas Ltd.
Associated British Picture Company(ABPC), *see* film companies, Associated British Cinemas Ltd.
Augar, P. 208
automobiles, *see* cars
Australia 15, 16, 21, 214, 259
  tobacco subsidiaries 23, 24, 29

BAC, *see* British Aircraft Corporation
Badawi, J. 370
BAe, *see* British Aerospace
BAE Systems 235
Bagwell, P. 291, 296, 297
Bailey, T. 335
Baird, P. 170
Baker, M. 87, 91, 190, 208

Bakker, G. 308, 310
balance of payments 61, 123, 164, 189, 194
balance sheets 3, 20, 26, 201, 365, 371, 379–80
Baldwin, Stanley 365
Bale, J. 350
Balogh, T. 227
Bank of England 50, 192–3, 196, 197, 201–2, 208
banking 126, 189 235
Banking Act 1979 202
bankruptcy 2, 53, 59, 215, 232, 233, 235
banks 85, 87, 190–1, 196, 203–4, 207, 208–9,
        220–1
    clearing 189, 190, 193, 196, 199–200, 201,
        202, 209, 210, 212, 214, 215
        market share 194, 195, 197, 198
    competition 203, 208
    deregulation 208
    investment 207, 209, 210, 211, 214, 218
    liquidity 190, 197, 200, 241
    merchant 83, 193, 199, 200, 208, 212
    mergers 191, 194–5, 212, 215
    multinational commercial 207, 208–9, 210,
        211, 212, 214, 215, 218, 219–20
    overseas 196, 199, 207–15
    trustees savings 198–9
    see also lending; under individual banks;
        retail banking; USA, banks
Barber, T. 301
Barclays Bank 209–10, 211, 215, 216, 218
Barker, H. 99
Barnard, E. 261
Barnes, M. 147
Barnett, C. 244
Barr, C. 306, 314
Barsoux, J.-L. 145
Bartlett, C. 76
Basle Accord 1988 202
BAT, *see* British-American Tobacco Company
Baumhart, R. 368
Beachy, R. 99
Beard, C. 31
Beauchamp, T. L. 357
Beeching, Dr. Richard 290, 291
Behrman, J. N. 123
Belcher, T. G. 124
Benson, J. 273, 275, 331, 332
Benson, T. 172, 176, 177
Berghoff, H. 90
Bernstein, I. 316
Beynon, H. 140
Big Bang 201, 208, 209–10
biotechnology 59–60, 65
BIP, *see* film industry, British International
        Pictures
Birchall, J. 273
Bird, P. 237
Birley, D. 335, 341, 343

Birley, S. 105, 106, 107
Blackford, M. 98
Blair, Tony 48, 60, 146
Blanchflower, D. 102
Blofeld, H. 336, 343
Bloom, N. 142
Blythman, J. 271
Blyton, P. 139
BMW (Germany) 56, 58
Board of Trade 123
Boeing 50, 54, 226, 234
Booth, A. 153, 157, 158
borrowing 107, 111, 163, 191, 194, 195, 200–1
Borrus, M. 236, 239
Bostock, F. 117, 118, 119, 122, 124, 125, 178
Boswell, J. 367, 368, 372
Bowden, S. 193
Bowen, A. 162
Bowen, H. R. 368, 373
Bowen, J. 160, 162
Bower, T. 375
Bowie, N. E. 357
Bowlby, S. 278
Bracken, P. 67
Brackenridge, C. 349
Bradfield, R. 276
Bradshaw, W. P. 297
Braidford, P. 132
brands 170, 173, 174, 175–6, 177, 178, 179,
        180, 181, 182–3, 184, 277, 340
    retailing own brands 271, 272
Brautaset, C. 93
Braverman, H. 279
brewing industry 178, 254, 255, 261, 262
Brick, C. 350
Brierley, P. 356
Britain, *see* UK
British Aerospace (BAe) 229, 231, 234–5
British Aircraft Coporation (BAC) 229–32,
        234, 248
British Railways 291–292, 297
British Roads Federation 293
British Steel Corporation 59
British Technology Group 56
British Telecom (BT) 58–9
British Transport Commission (BTC) 289, 299
British Waterways 299
British-American Tobacco Company (BAT)
        23, 28, 29
Britton, A. 162, 163
Broadberry, S. 35, 71, 85, 153, 154, 155, 156,
        157, 159, 160, 161, 163
Brock, W. H. 253
Bromhead, J. 340
Brown, Gordon 57, 59
Brown, J. 110, 259
Brown, J. A. C. 140

Brown, J. 307
Brown, R. 307, 308, 309
Browning, H. E. 310
Brush, C. 108
Bryson, A. 143
BT, *see* British Telecom
BTC, *see* British Transport Commission
Buchanan, C. 293
building societies 85, 198, 200
    demutualization 215
Bullock, Lord Alan 368
Burk, K. 163
Burnham, J. 295, 297, 302
Burnham, P. 228
Burrows, J. 310
bus industry 297
    deregulation 296–7, 301
    fares 302
    privatization 297, 301
    subsidies 297
    see also transport
business 87, 98, 110, 139
    and gender 97
    social responsibility 368
    see also women, in business/enterprise
Business Cycles (Schumpeter) 31
business elites 82–4, 85, 87, 89, 90, 91, 92
    education 88
        university 90–1
    integration with upper classes 89, 91
    social origins 87–8
business ethics 111, 356, 359, 364, 370, 378
    behaviour in 356–7, 359
    and law 364, 370
    and religion 356–7, 367, 369, 375, 377
    unethical behaviour in 358, 359, 360–1,
        370–1, 374, 378
    UK business 361–3t18.1, 364, 375–6
    voluntary codes of 368–9
    see also Christianity; Judaism
business machines 236–7, 240, 243
business schools 141, 143–4, 364, 368
'buy British movement' 118
Byers, S. 58
Bygrave, W. D. 241
Bywater, M. 372

Cadbury, A. 369, 374
Cadbury, George 371, 372
Cadburys 32, 375
Cain, P. 89
Cairncross, A. 163
Calico Printers' Association (CPA) 33
Callaghan, J. 54
Caminer, D. 237, 240
Campbell-Kelly, M. 52, 236, 237, 239, 240,
    241, 243

Canada 15, 22, 24, 29, 214
    FDI in Britain 121
    incentives to investors 126
Cannadine, D. 153
Cannon, T. 103
Capie, F. 117, 191, 241
capital 107, 125, 168
    access to 106–7
    lock-in 71
    removal of exchange controls 56
capital gains 26, 59
capital markets 23, 69, 118, 192, 208, 209,
    241–2, 274
capitalism 17, 30, 35, 84, 90
    family 90, 168
    personal 69, 90, 168
carbon emissions 295
Card, D. 60
Carey, Lord George 356
Carl Zeiss *Stiftung* (Foundation) 367–8
Carlson, W. B. 253
Carnevali, F. 18, 70, 72, 87, 191, 192
cars 54, 57, 58, 74, 274, 288, 300, 302
    decline 154, 155
    European markets 155
    see also motor vehicles
Carter, C. F. 265, 266
Carter, D. 281
Carter, S. 98, 102, 103, 106, 107
Cassis, Y. 32, 82, 83, 84, 85, 86, 87, 88, 89, 90,
    91, 168, 176, 181, 208
Casson, M. C. 73, 276, 278, 375, 376, 377
Catherwood, H. F. R. 368
Caulkin, S. 143, 145
Caves, R. E. 149
CBI, *see* Federation of British Industry
CFI, *see* Credit for Industry
Chandler, A. 377
Chandler, A. D. 15, 16, 18, 19, 20, 21, 22, 25,
    30, 31, 32, 33, 34, 35, 69, 84, 90, 91,
    119, 168, 174, 176, 229, 243, 276
Channel Tunnel Rail Link (CTRL) 292–3
Channon, D. F. 91, 208, 210, 211
Chapman, R. 67
Chapman, S. 173, 178, 207
charity donations (companies) 357–8
Charterhouse Industrial Development Co.
    (CID) 193
chemicals 59, 67, 86, 118, 119, 123, 132, 154,
    370
chemists 253, 254–5, 259, 274
Chick, M. 162
China 22, 23, 24, 59, 219, 244
Christianity 356, 365–6, 367, 371, 372, 375, 376
    paternalism 371, 372
    and socialism 366
    see also business ethics, religion

Church, R. 31
Church, R. A. 192
Church of England 376–7
CID, *see* Charterhouse Industrial
    Development Co.
cigarettes; *see* tobacco
cinemas, *see* film industry, cinemas
Cinematograph Act 1909 309
City of London 87, 89, 91, 119, 220–1
Clapp, B. W. 370
Clarke, D. 241
Clarke, D. B. 275
Clark, D. S. 140
Clarke, G. P. 275
Clarke, P. 153, 168
Clarkham, J. 374
clearing banks, *see* banks, clearing
Cleary, E. J. 375
Cleverly, G. 140
clusters 8, 12, 60, 65–7, 71, 74, 75–6, 78, 119,
    130, 227, 240
  renaissance of 73, 75, 76
Clutterbuck, D. 102, 106
Co-operative Wholesale Society (CWS) 273
coal 50, 65
  nationalization 73
Coase, R. H. 276
Coates, D. 147
Cobham, D. 161, 163
Coe, N. M. 271, 275, 281
Cold War 231, 238, 260
Coleman, D. C. 117, 366
collaboration 51, 54, 62, 76, 130, 231,
    232, 265
Collier, P. 371
Collins, A. 90
Collins, B. 168
Collins, E. J. T. 178
Collins, M. 87, 91, 190, 191, 193, 194, 198,
    199, 201, 208, 241
Collins, T. 334, 338, 342, 348
Collinson, H. A. 266
Colwyn Committee (1918) 189, 190–1
Committee of London Clearing Bankers 194,
    202
commodities 20, 67, 254, 277, 332
Common Market, and Britain 56
communication technology 65
companies 371**t18.2**
  charity donations 357–8
  liquidation 360**f18.1**
  violations 360**f18.1**
  voluntary liquidation 358–9
  welfare 372
  winding-up 358
  see also business ethics; public companies

Companies Act 1908 358, 364
Companies Act 1929 364, 365
Companies Act 1947–8 365
Companies Act 1967 357
Companies Act 1980 374
Companies Acts (1907, 1981, 1985, 1986–9)
    357–9, 364, 365, 374
Company Law Reform (White Paper Cmnd.
    5391) 368
competition 23, 26, 48, 56, 60, 66, 67, 71, 74,
    75, 118, 122, 144, 155, 156, 170, 178,
    182, 190, 208, 229, 236, 238, 245, 296,
    297, 333
  global 20, 30, 58, 240
  retail banking 201, 202, 203, 271, 275
  retailing 271–3, 274, 275, 279
Competition Commission 175, 299
competitive advantage 11, 28, 53, 70, 74, 90,
    118, 179, 184, 225, 244, 277, 279, 281,
    282
  regional business 66–8, 70–1, 72, 74
Competitive Advantage of Nations, The
    (Porter) 137
competitiveness 57, 73, 75, 78, 169, 170, 182
  decline in 74, 157
components 52, 54, 103, 109, 117, 130, 131,
    237, 239, 242
computer manufacturers 51, 125, 225,
    236–40, 242
  government intervention in 238, 240–1
  see also International Computers
    Limited
computer software 62, 237, 242–3
Conlan, T. 147
Conn, D. 346, 347
Conservative governments 125, 294, 369
  (1951) 122, 289–90
  (1970–74) 52, 126, 234
  (1979–97) 56, 60, 126, 128–9, 198, 234, 294,
    295
Conservative Party 48–9, 50, 51, 56, 57, 60,
    147, 373
  and industrial policy 51–2, 53, 55
Constant, E. W. 227
consultancies 257
  scientific 253–4, 259
consumer 274
  electronics 54, 73
  goods 172, 173, 176, 177, 181, 184, 194, 273,
    299–300
  loyalty 170, 173, 174, 175, 273
  markets 170, 177
  products 69, 169, 177, 271
  spending 170, 176–7, 274
consumption 169
  levels of 184–5, 274

per capita 178–9
  and value 277, 278
Cooke, P. 76, 236
Cookson, G. 73
copper 19, 20–1, 22
Corina, M. 280
Corley, T. A. B. 173, 177, 179, 180
corporate governance 34, 92, 374
corporate social responsibility (CSR) 368,
  374, 378
corporations 118–19, 120, 132, 169, 209
  foreign ownership of UK 48–9, 53–6, 59,
    62–3
  large 16, 21, 34, 65, 78, 89
  structure 132
Cortauld, Samuel 366, 367, 378
costs; *see* transaction costs
cotton textiles 65, 154, 155
  Lancashire 68, 70, 71, 72–3
Cotton Industry Act 1959 52
CPA, *see* Calico Printers' Association
Cox, H. 22, 24
Crafts, N. F. R. 35, 145, 148, 155, 157, 163
Craig, B. 99
Crawford, G. 331
credit 69, 190, 192, 194, 195, 196, 197, 200,
  201
credit crunch 201
Credit for Industry (CFI) 193
cricket 335–6, 338, 339, 345
  commercial sponsorship 340–1, 342–4
  revenue stream 343–4
  see also sports
Crisell, A. 331
critical mass 67, 70, 71
Crockett, G. 141
Crompton, G. 298, 299
Cruikshank, D. 189 query spelling
CSR, *see* corporate social responsibility
CTRL, *see* Channel Tunnel Rail Link
Cuba 23
Cully, M. 145
Curran, J. 306
Curth, L. 271
Cutler, T. 156, 158
CWS, *see* Co-operative Wholesale Society

Darby, M. 208
Davidoff, L. 99
Davies, P. L. 358, 364
Davis, D. 271
Davis, G. F. 208
Davis, L. 32
Dawson, J. 271
DBB, *see* Dictionary of Business Biography
De Goey, F. 100, 102
De Long, B. J. 16

De Paula, F. C. 267
de Vany, A. 317
Deaton, D. 160
debt 202
  bad 190, 195, 196, 199, 203, 211, 213, 358
decision-making 27, 84, 132, 140, 191, 232,
    238, 297, 375–6
declinism 18, 34, 35, 61, 65, 82, 85, 137, 147,
    154, 153, 162, 168, 182, 197–8, 225,
    243
  causes 154–5, 155 **t8.2**
  relative 82, 90, 116, 133, 236, 238, 252
  revival 155–6, 157
Defence, Ministry of 51
defence 233, 235, 264
Delivering the Sustainable Railway 296
Dennison, E. 139
Denton, G. 54
Devereux, J. 16
Devine, M. 102, 106
Dickinson, M. 315, 316, 317, 318, 320
Dictionary of Business Biography (DBB) 84
directors 18, 83, 88, 291, 306, 357, 358, 365,
    366, 367, 371**t18.2**, 374
  company 86, 105, 360, 364, 370
distribution 67, 85, 168, 169, 170, 171, 172,
    174–5, 176, 177, 178, 180, 181–2, 185
  see also film industry, distribution
distribution networks 170, 172, 180
division of labour 61, 244, 279
Dix, G. 145
Doel, C. 276
Dolan, C. 271
dollar (US) 120, 121, 122, 123, 208, 221, 315
domestic markets 28–9, 179, 242
  banks 193, 210, 214
  see also film industry, domestic markets
Donnelly, J. 254
Dore, R. 139
Dorgan, S. 142
dot.com 108, 109, 242
Dow, C. 158, 159, 160
Dow, J. C. R. 121
Dowdy, J. 142
Driffield, N. 128, 132
Drucker, P. F. 171
DTI, *see* Trade and Industry, Secretary of State
  for
Duckworth, L. 335
Dudley, G. 293, 294, 295, 296
Dudley, N. A. 139, 140
Duke, James B. 22–30
Dunkley, C. 345, 346
Dunlavy, C. A. 32
Dunning, J. H. 76, 117, 120, 122, 123,
    124, 139
Duprye, C. H. 139

Durbin, S. 109
Durden, R. F. 22
Dyestuffs Act 1921 117

Eaglesham, J. 301
Eberts, J. 306
economics 55
    growth 48, 65, 125, 141, 153, 219, 377
    liberal policies 55
    patriotism 49
    performance 52, 55, 148, 164, 218–19
    theories 84, 169–70
economies of scale 66, 75, 76, 78, 228, 239,
        240, 273, 288
economies of scope 66, 70, 78, 175, 275, 279
Eberts, J. 323, 324
Eddington, Sir R. 301
Edgerton, D. 153, 235, 238, 257, 258
education 48, 63, 88, 89, 154–5
    UK managers 140–1, 145
    university 88, 89, 90
    see also business schools; public schools
Edwards, J. 191
Edwards, J. R. 370, 375
Edwards, P. 238
EEF, *see* Engineering Employers Federation
Elbaum, B. 168
Electrical and Plumbing Trades Union 128
electrical industry 19, 52, 77
electronics 75
    companies/firms 53, 236, 240
    European failure 154
Elias, E. 141
emerging markets 215, 216, 218, 219
employees:
    attitudes to work 142–3
    fairness between 357
    training 142
    as women 105
employment 60, 106, 118, 123, 125, 129, 160,
        189, 194
    constraints 106
    foreign-owned 127**t6.1**
    manufacturing 158–9, 159**t8.6**
    and nationalized industries 162
    service sector, by gender (1956–97) 100**t5.1**
        (1984–98) 101**t5.2**
enclave economy 131–2
engineering 62, 123, 140, 154, 252, 259, 262,
        293
Engineering Employers Federation (EEF) 141
Engel, J. A. 227
England:
    Home Counties 73, 74
    industrial regions 65–6, 70, 132
entrepreneurs 82, 84, 91–2, 119, 276
    and achievements 90, 92

and failure 90, 169
and business elites 87, 89
and upper classes 89
and women 97, 98, 99, 105
environment:
    campaigns 294, 295, 301
    disasters 373
    issues 110, 370
    transport 301
Epstein, T. 106
Erickson, C. 82, 84
ethics, *see* business ethics
Eurodollar 198, 199, 207; *see also* dollar
Europe 16, 17, 76, 77, 86, 91, 156
    aircraft industries 231, 235
    copper 19, 20
    FDI in UK 121
    film production 324–5
    transport policies 301
    women, in business 105
European Economic Community (EEC) 122,
        123, 125, 128, 294, 374
    and UK entry 155, 368
European Union (EU) 126, 128
Evans, R. 336
Evers, D. 271
Exchange Control Act 1947 121
exchange controls 123, 126
    abolishment of UK 208
exchange rates 61, 157, 163
expenditure, *see* research and development,
        expenditure
exports 17–18, 122, 125
    aircraft industries 227
    manufacturing 61
    tobacco 24–5

FA, *see* Football Association
family firms 26, 32, 90
fashion goods 67, 70, 179–8
Fazey, I. H. 373
FBI, *see* Federation of British
        Industry
FDI, *see* foreign direct investment
Fear, J. 34
Fearon, P. 226
Federation of British Industry (CBI) 144,
        147, 160, 259, 260–1, 263, 265, 368
Feinstein, C. 158, 164
Feldenkirchen, W. 181
female, *see* women
female-specific businesses 97, 102
Fenton, E. 76, 77
Ferli, E. 76
Ferni, J. 278
Field, C. 339
Filatotchev, I. 73

film companies 309, 310, 312–14, 318, 319, 325
  Associated British Cinemas Ltd. (ABC) 312, 318
  Associated British Picture Company (ABCP) 312, 313, 318
  British International Pictures (BIP) 312, 313–14, 319
  Ealing Studios 314, 319
  J. Arthur Rank 314–15, 318, 319, 323, 325
film industry 306–7, 315–16, 320, 322, 324, 325–6
  cinemas 308, 310–12, 315, 318, 320, 323
    attendance admissions 316–17, 320–1, 321**f16.1**, 322; first run 311–12, 323; mulitplex 320, 323; safety of 308–9
  distribution 307–8, 310, 311, 317, 318–19, 320, 322**t16.1**, 322–4, 325–6
  exhibition 306, 307, 310, 311, 312, 315, 316, 317, 318, 319, 320, 323, 324, 326
  feature films 307, 322**t16.2**, 323
  finance 310, 311, 312, 314, 316, 322, 324, 325
  investment 311, 313, 314, 316, 317, 318
    foreign 309, 311; inward 315; USA 317–18
  markets 307, 308, 309, 311, 315, 316, 320
    domestic 310, 314, 318, 321, 321**f16.1**, 322, 323, 325–6; international 313, 317, 319, 324, 325–6
  moving pictures 310
  policy 315, 317, 322
  production 307–8, 310, 313, 317–18, 319, 320, 323, 324–5
  revenues 308, 320, 321, 321**f16.1**, 322, 323, 324
  stars 308, 313, 315, 316, 317, 318, 320
  subsidies 315–16
  see also USA, film industry; vertical integration, film industry
film quota 321–2
Films Act 1927 310
finance industry 86, 87, 91, 121, 171, 189, 193
  women and discrimination 107
financial crises (2008) 204, 216, 221
financial markets 60, 69, 85, 163, 205
financial services, deregulation 202–3
Financial Services Act 1986 202
Financial Services Authority (FSA) 202
financial systems 154–5, 192, 197, 215
  global 204, 207, 209, 220, 221
  regulations 201, 208
First World War 17, 19, 29, 50, 85, 89, 117, 132, 169, 176, 177, 178, 192, 231, 252, 254, 255, 256, 257, 258, 261, 273, 288, 310, 359, 365
Fischer, K. 191
Fitzgerald, R, 172, 173, 177, 178, 179, 180, 372

Flamm, K. 238, 239
Fleming, A. P. M. 257, 258
Fletcher, S. 271
Flynn, L. 365
Fogarty, M. P. 368
food:
  expenditure 274
  manufacturers 132, 170, 173, 175, 177–8, 180, 252, 254, 272
  retailing 278, 280–1
  warehousing 278, 281
  wartime supplies 261
  see also Tesco
Foord, J. 278
football 336–7, 339, 340
  clubs as public companies 347
  commercial sponsorship 340–1, 342–8
  and finance 330–1, 334–5
  ground safety 347
  image of 346
  professionalism 337–8
  wages 336, 337, 339
  see also sports
Football Association (FA) 330, 334, 346
Foray, D. 109
Ford, R. 292, 298
Ford 56, 117, 119, 122, 125, 129
foreign direct investment (FDI) 117–19, 120, 128
  inward 117, 120–6, 128, 129, 132
  stock 121, 127–8
foreign exchange 120, 123
foreign-owned enterprises/plants 116–18, 120, 127–9, 132
Foreman-Peck, J. 192
Forrester, A. 142
Forson, C. 102, 109
Foster, C. 298, 299
France 15, 16, 88, 90, 142
  aircraft industries 235
  consumer goods 176
  film industry:
    in Britain 309; production 310
  industrial policy 49, 55
  nuclear industry 55
  social mobility 88
  tobacco 22
  see also aircraft industries, Anglo-French Concorde
Frankland, E. 254
Fransman, M. 54, 239
Fraser, W. H. 173, 174
free trade 24, 49, 117, 322
Freeman, E. 374
Freeman, R. 60
French, M. 98
French, M. J. 117
Friedman, M. 367, 374

From Empire to Europe (Owen) 154
Frost, P. 139
Fruin, M. 31
FSA, *see* Financial Services Authority
Fullerton, R. 170
Fulop, C. 274
Future of Transport (White Paper CM 6234) 295

Galbraith, J. K. 169
Gálvez Muñoz, L. 105
Gamber, W. 110
game theory 25
Gannon, P. 237
Gardiner, A. G. 371, 372
Gardner, C. 228, 230, 281
GDP 15, 32, 61, 189, 198, 219, 300
  inward FDI stock 132
  per capita 169, 169, 174
GEC, *see* General Electric Company
Geddes, K. 54
Geiger, T. 228
gender:
  in business 98, 109, 110
  convergence 105
  ethnicity 110
  gap 105, 110
  and ownership 102
General Electric Company (GEC) 34, 52, 54,
  58–9, 177, 235, 236
General Motors 56, 117, 129, 180, 217
Germain, R. 170
Germany 15, 18, 19, 23, 32, 32, 35
  aircraft industries 235
  banks 207
  business 30, 62
  business elites, education 88
  cigarettes 30
  consumer goods 176, 181
  education 90
  industrial firms 32, 34
  industrial policy 49
  large scale business enterprises 33, 168
  living standards 16
  manufacturing 49, 61–2, 142, 156
  nonferrous metals industry 20
  productivity growth 157
  social mobility 88
  in world markets 71
Geroski, P. 143
Gershenkron, A. 69
Ghoshal, S. 76
Gianetti, R. 32
Gibbs-Smith, C. H. 227
Gibson, C. S. 255
Gibson, T. 293
Giddens, A. 83, 84, 87
Gillespie, R. W. 121

Gillman, R. J. H. 192
Glaister, S. 295, 297, 302
Glancy, M. 311, 315
glass ceiling 105, 106
GlaxoSmithKline 63
Glickman, L. B. 174, 181
globalization 49, 60, 63, 85, 132–3, 220, 364
Glyn, A. 139, 140
Godley, A. 18, 272
Goffee, R. 106, 109, 148
Golborne, N. 60, 62
Goldberg, L. G. 208
golden age 157, 158, 163, 163**t8.9**, 164
Goodhart, C. A. E. 208
Goodpaster, K. E. 357
goods 70
  global demand for 70–1
  movement of 288
Gorringe, T. 368
Gourvish, T. 35, 82, 86, 91, 92, 173, 178, 289,
  290, 291, 292
governance 67–8
  corporate 34, 92, 374
  industrial districts 67, 70, 74–5
government policies 48, 225
  employment and productivity 161
    intervention in 50, 54–5, 120, 123
  computer industries 238, 240–1
  non-intervention 49
  transport 299
  US FDI 120
  see also research and development,
    expenditure; research and
    development, private industry
Gower, L. C. 364
Goyder, G. 367, 368, 373, 374, 378
Goyder, R. 368
Granick, D. 139
Granovetter, M. 74
Grant, M. 333
Gratton, C. 332, 333, 339, 344
Great Depression 169
Great War, *see* First World War
Green, E. 192, 197, 200, 375
Green, S. K. 369
Greenbury, Sir R. 374
Gregg, P. 143
Grindley, P. 243
Grunwald, J. 239
Gummett, P. 234
Guy, K. 238, 241

Hague, D. 52
Hakim, C. 100, 106
Halborg, A. 276
Hall, C. 99
Hallsworth, A. G. 271, 279

Halsey, A. H. 148
Hamer, M. 293
Hamill, J. 125, 128, 129
Hamilton, R. 293
Han, A. 218
Handy, C. 141
Hannah, L. 18, 22, 31, 32, 33, 34, 85, 87, 90, 91, 190, 191, 192, 194, 195, 196, 197, 198, 200, 202, 208, 210
Harding, J. 337
Hardy, S. 331
Harp, S. 176, 181
Harris, A. K. 110
Harris, M. 147
Harrison, M. 227
Harvey, C. 30, 84, 85, 88, 89
Haslam, C. 156
Hassink, R. 72
Hastings, A. 366, 368, 369
Hawker Siddeley 51, 54, 229, 231, 234
Hayward, K. 50, 226, 227, 228, 229, 233
Heald, T. 340
Heath, E. 52, 160, 162, 233
Hedlund, G. 76
Hehner, O. 253, 254
Hemming, M. F. W. 120
Hempel, R. 374
Henderson, P. D. 51
Hendry, J. 51, 237, 369
Hennessy, P. 340
Hentschel, V. 16
Heppenheimer, T. A. 226, 229, 230, 232, 233
Hermon, P. 237, 240
Herrigel, G. 32, 34
Herring, R. J. 202
Heseltine, Michael 57
heterarchy 65, 67, 76, 77
Hewitt-Dundas, N. 77
hierarchy 32, 33, 70, 76, 77, 87, 276, 277
high-technology industries 51, 54, 74, 77, 227
    research capability 238–9
Higson, A. 306
Hikino, T. 91
Hilditch, T. P. 255
Hiley, N. 310
Hill, F. E. 117
Hillard, J. 147
Hinchcliffe, D. 348
Hines, C. 271
Hirst, P. 91
Hitachi 54, 57
Hodges, M. 120, 121, 123, 125
Hodson, D. 273
Hoe, S. 368
Hogarth, T. 143
Hollander, S. C. 170
Hollywood England 317

Holmes, A. R. 197, 198, 200
Holt, R. 333, 336, 338
Honeyman, K. 99, 99
Hong Kong 214, 216, 219
Hongkong Bank 211, 212, 213–14, 216
Hood, N. 126, 127, 128, 129, 130
Hooker, Sir S. 233
Hopkins, A. G. 89
horizontal integration 70, 77, 125
Horne, J. 332
Horrocks, S. M. 254, 255, 257, 258, 259, 261, 262, 267
Hott, T. 306, 323, 324
household goods 172, 173, 175, 177, 179, 274
Howarth, S. 373
Howlett, P. 50
HP companies 196, 198, 201
HSBC 215, 216, 217, 218, 219
Huczynski, A. J. 146
Hudson, J. 254, 261
Hudson, S. 99, 143
Huertas, T. F. 208
Huggins, M. 331
Hughes, A. 271
Hughes, R. 262
Hughes, S. 336
Hull, A. 256
human rights 374
Humphrey, J. 271
Hutton, G. 139
Hutton, W. 235, 241, 374
hypermarkets 273, 274, 282

IBM 3, 51, 52, 237–8, 240, 241, 242–5, 342
ICFC, *see* Industrial and Commercial Finance Corporation
ICL, *see* International Computers Limited
IKEA 277–8
IMF, *see* International Monetary Fund
Imperial Tobacco Company 22, 23, 27–8, 30, 174
imports:
    from dollar area 120, 122
    tobacco 23
income 24, 169–70, 171, 172, 177, 181, 184, 194, 201, 300
    disposable 171, 175, 181, 332
India 24, 59, 219
Industrial and Commercial Finance Corporation (ICFC) 196, 197
industrial clusters, *see* clusters
industrial democracy 368, 377–8
industrial districts 67, 68, 70, 74, 76, 78, 79
    development of 69
    political lock-ins 72
industrial policy 48, 49, 51, 52–4, 57, 60, 63, 289
industrial relations 74, 147
Industrial Reorganization Act 1966 125

Industrial Reorganisation Corporation (IRC)
52, 58, 125
industrial research, *see* research and
development
industrialization 49, 65, 68, 69, 73–4, 169,
182–3
industry 256, 257
foreign control of 54, 61, 63
in France 55
lending, risk aversion 190
Industry Act 1972 53
Industry Act 1975 126
infant industries 49
inflation 163, 164, 194, 233, 254, 294, 316, 320
information 67, 118, 240
information technology (IT) 62, 65, 109, 225,
236, 239, 240, 241, 243, 245, 271
systems 242, 243
see also International Computers Limited
Inglis, S. 336, 337, 342
Inmos 53–4, 56, 238, 244
innovation 62, 67, 71, 77, 137, 139, 145, 178,
185, 253, 255, 256, 266, 276
retailing 271, 272, 281–2
see also retail banking, innovation
insider trading 348, 360, 368, 374
Insolvency Act 1986 358
institutions:
lack of support for women 107
weaknesses in 63, 69
interest rates 61, 195, 197, 198, 201, 202, 213, 217
International Computers Limited (ICL) 52,
53, 54, 56, 59, 236, 241, 243
International Monetary Fund (IMF) 163
internationalization 259, 271, 275, 282
Internet 102, 109, 199, 217, 242, 244
Invest in Britain Bureau 126
investment 19, 26, 84, 119
film industry, foreign 309
inward 63, 120, 121–2, 123, 125, 126,
127–8, 129, 132–3
local linkages 131t6.2; spillover effects 130
knowledge intensive, aversion to 241–2
railways 295
science 252
and women 111
see also banks, investment
IRC, *see* Industrial Reorganisation
Corporation
Iremonger, F. A.
IT, *see* information technology
Italy 15, 176, 310
Ivens, M. 368
Ivory, C. 141, 143

J. Arthur Rank, *see* film companies, J. Arthur
Rank

Jago, W. 254
Jaguar 56, 129
Japan 15, 56, 59
banks 220
computer manufacturers 236
distribution 181–2
industrial policy 54–5
information technology 239
investment in 28
incentives for 126
large scale business enterprises 168
management 138
marketing 184
partnerships 54
production techniques 75
subsidiaries 128
tobacco:
exports from 25; exports to 22; foreign
subsidiaries 23; tariffs 24
Japanese Ministry of International Trade and
Industry 54
Jarvie, I. 315
Jarvie, J. G. 193
Jarvie, G. 331
Jeffreys, J. B. 172, 178, 179, 271, 273
Jeremy, D. J. 74, 84, 86, 87, 108, 366, 367, 372,
375, 376, 377
John, R. 31
Johnson, A. 105
Johnson, D. 208
Johnson, G. 278
joint ventures 59, 65
Jones, E. 375
Jones, G. 30, 32, 91, 117, 118, 119, 121, 122,
124, 125, 126, 132, 170, 178, 180, 181,
194, 207, 208, 378
Jones, K. 162
Joseph, Sir K. 147
Jowett, P. 236, 2343
Joynson, S. 142
Judaism 356, 373–2
Jupe, R. 298
just-in-time production 75

Kay, J. 28
Kaelble, H. 87
Kawabe, N. 182
Kay, J. 281
Kelly, T. 236
Kennedy, W. 35
Kerr, I. M. 208
Ketels, C. H. M. 137
Khanna, T. 214, 217
Kidder, T. 240
King, A. 346, 347
King, F. 214
Kitson, M. 61

Kleinschmidt, C. 35
Ketels, C. H. M. 75
Killick, M. 374
Kindleberger, C. P. 131
Klingender, F. D. 311, 312, 313
Kluger, R. 22
knowledge sector 58, 59, 62, 76, 108–9
Kochan, N. 375
Kostova, E. 67
Kramer, D. C. 53
Kranakis, E. 240
Kuhn, A. 309, 325, 325
Kulik, K. 314
Kuypers, T. 347, 348
Kwollek-Folland, A. 102, 110
Kynaston, D. 208

Lamoreaux, N. R. 31
labour:
    hoarding 160–1
    lock-in 71
    market 60, 109
        flexible 145; segmentation 100; and
        women 99–100, 105
    output 160–1, 161**t8.8**, 164, 171, 279
    movement 164
    productivity 154**t8.1**, 158, 158**t8.5**, 159–60,
        160**t8.7**, 161, 161**t8.8**, 162–3
        Anglo-German differences 156**t8.3**;
        golden age 163, 163**t8.9**, 164; West
        Germany 158**t8.4**
    relations 154–5
        and UK managers 128, 140, 142, 145
    surplus 118
Labour, Ministry of 262
Labour Force Survey (LFS) 102–3
Labour governments 76, 88, 163, 228, 229, 294
    (1945) 288
    (1964–70) 52, 124–5, 238
    (1974–1979) 53, 54, 126, 160–1, 162, 163,
        231, 299, 368
    see also Blair, Tony; Brown, Gordon;
        Wilson, Harold
Labour Party 48, 60, 147
    government intervention 50
    non-invention 58, 59
    industrial policy 52, 54, 59, 60, 239
labour theory of value 279
Laing, A. 290
Lal, R. 218
Lall, S. 118
Land, F. 237, 240
Landes, D. 31, 32, 90
Landry, C. 147
Lane, D. 214, 217
Lang, T. 275
Langlois, R. 276

Langston, P. 275
Lavington, F. 191
law 22, 358, 360, 364
    company 367, 368, 370
Law, C. M. 119
Lawrence, P. 145
Lawson, Nigel 56, 153
Layardm, R. 153
Laybourn, K. 334
Lazonick, W. 168, 191, 281
LCH, *see* London Clearing House
Leadenhall Securities 193
leadership, unethical 377
lean manufacturing 141–2
Lebergott, S. 174
Lee, J. 366, 367, 372
Lee, Y. S. 275, 281
Legg, S. 311, 312, 313
legislation 75, 117, 126
    film industry 313, 315, 316
Leighton, M. 148
lending 191, 196, 200, 201
    industrial 192–3, 195, 197, 199
    retail banks 193–5, 197–8
    risk aversion 190, 195
Leung, T. 35
Levine, A. 168
Lévy-Leboyer, M. 84
Lewis, H. 311
Lewis, M. J. 73
Lewis, R. 139, 145
LFS, *see* Labour Force Survey
liberalization 56, 145, 197, 219
life cycles 66, 67–7, 68, 70, 71, 72
    see also lock-in
Lifson, T. B. 182
linkages, international 76, 77, 78–9
liquidity 191, 220
List, F. 49
living standards 15, 16, 169, 169, 172–3, 175,
    176–7, 178–9
Lloyd, I. 227
Lloyd-Jones, R. 73
Lloyds Bank 210–11, 213, 215, 216
location:
    assisted regions 127**t6.1**
    of headquarters (in London) 73,
        74, 85–6
    in south-east England 119
lock-in 66, 68, 71, 74
    cognitive 8, 71, 72
    commitment and 78
    functional 71–2
    political 72
    see also life cycles
Lockyer, K. G. 139
Loft, C. 291

London 189, 207, 208
London Clearing House (LCH) 202
London Metal Exchange 20
London Stock Exchange 16–17, 29, 85
Lovell, T. 377
Lovelock, D. 377
Low, R. 307, 308, 309, 310, 311
Lowe, M. 279, 280
Ludlam, S. 163
Lupton, T. 87
Lyth, P. J. 226, 227

Mabey, C. 144
McCloskey, D. N. 15, 34, 168
McCraw, T. K. 31, 34
McCulloch, J. 375
McCulloch, R. 118
MacDonald, S. 240
McGivering, I. 139
McKay, S. 144
McKenna duties (1915) 117
McKenzie, D. 189, 200, 203, 215, 216
Mackie, R. 255, 259
McKinnon, A. 281
MacKinnon, D. 132
MacLean, M. 84, 85, 88, 89
MacLeod, K. 255
MacLeod, R. M. 255
Macmillan, Harold 271, 293
Macmillan Committee (1929–31) 189, 192,
    200
Macmillan gap 192, 193, 196
Macnab, G. 313, 314, 315, 318
Macrae, N. 340
macroeconomics 52, 53, 61, 73, 138, 162, 185,
    300
Maddison, A. 15, 33, 177
Maeda, K. 182
mail order 170, 175, 176, 183, 273
Major, J. 57
Maltby, J. 99, 111, 371
management 17, 18, 20, 31, 33, 62, 91, 116,
    119, 138
  education 367
  failure of 168, 176
  skills 118
  techniques 34–5
  UK 146–8
  USA 138, 139
  women in 100
managers:
  professional 31, 32
  salaried 84
  UK 34, 139–40, 144–7
    education 140–1; motivation in 137–8;
      training 144
Mansfield, R. 139

manufacturing industries 16, 33, 61, 86, 116,
    119, 129, 156, 158, 164
  declinism 85, 129, 159
  failure of 255–6
  industrial research 252–3
  services 60, 61–2
  tobacco 23, 24, 26
  see also employment, manufacturing;
      Germany, manufacturing
manufacturing productivity 156, 157–8
Manvell, R. 307, 308, 309
Marconi 58–9, 236, 255
Marglin, S. A. 279
Marinetto, M. 358, 368, 373
market 56, 68, 156, 240, 280
  capitalization 20, 21, 30, 85
  dynamics 73–4
  outlets 168
  size 139, 171
  world 57, 71
market orientation 170, 171–2, 184, 190
market research 171–2, 178, 180, 183
market segmentation 170, 171, 179–80, 183
marketing 17, 20, 119, 168, 170, 176,
    180, 185
marketing management 176, 181, 182, 184, 185
marketing systems 168–9, 170
Marlow, S. 103, 106, 107, 108
Marples, Ernest 293, 294
Marquese, M. 343
Marrison, A. 71
Marsden, T. 275
Marshall, A. 66, 68, 71, 75
Marshall, J. 117
Marschan-Piekkari, R. 240
Marx, K. 279
Masefield, P. 261
Maslakovic, M. 189, 200, 203, 215, 216
Mason, T. 331, 336
mass marketing 169, 185
mass media 130
mass production 30, 70, 74, 75, 118–19, 156,
    168, 169, 173, 175
Mathews, D. 139, 370
Mathews, R. 158, 164
Matthews, S. 340
Mathias, P. 111, 172, 173, 178, 271
maturity 67, 71, 73, 78
Mayer, M. 31, 33, 34, 86
merchant banks, *see* banks, merchant
mergers 17, 25, 26, 30, 52, 58, 74, 179, 261
  aircraft industries 51, 235
  banks 191, 194–5
  and Labour government 125
  retail banks 190
  retailing 273
  see also acquisitions

Merrett, D. T. 212
Michie, J. 61, 87
Mikardo, I. 147
Miles, C. 52
Miles, C. M. 120
military 231, 238, 239
Millward, R. 158, 161, 162, 288
Milmo, D. 301
Milne, A, M. 290
Ministry of Supply, *see* Supply, Ministry of
Minoglou, I. P. 84
Miskell, P. 141, 143, 314
Mitch, D. 259
Mizruchi, M. S. 86, 208
MNE, see multinational enterprises
Modernisation Plan (1955) 290, 292
Moeslein, K. 141, 143
Moir, C. 271
Monopolies and Mergers Act 1965 125
Monopolies and Mergers Commission 194,
    213, 275
Morelli, C. J. 271, 280
moral hazards 202, 376
Morelli, C. J. 271, 274, 278
Morgan, K. 76
Morgan, N. J. 180, 181
Morley, D. 147,
Morris, J. 176, 180
Morrow, S. 331, 347
Morton, R. A. 255
MoS, *see* Supply, Ministry of
Moss, M. 192, 375
Mosse, W. E. 83
motivation 106, 137–8
motor vehicles 62, 116, 117, 125, 129
    see also cars
motorways; *see* roads
Mowery, D. 16, 243, 258
Muellbauer, J. 158
Mulatu, A. 35
multinational banks, *see* banks,
    multinational
multinational enterprises (MNE) 65, 76–7,
    125, 126, 128, 129
    corporations 17, 22, 23, 65, 76
    inter-war 119
    local economy 131–2
    transient 78
    overseas 125, 133, 259
    suppliers 130
    UK 129, 130
        US entrants to 6, 116, 123, 124, 124**f6.1**,
        125
Munday, M. 128, 132
Murdock, R. 130
Murphy, R. 306, 312, 314, 315
Murray, B. G. 371

Nash, R. 348
National Bus Company (NBC) 296
national champions 48, 54, 61, 125, 226, 234,
    236, 239, 245
National Enterprise Board (NEB) 53, 56, 239
national markets 170, 171, 175, 182, 184
National Research Development Corporation
    51; subsequently British Technology
    Group
National Westminster Bank 211–12, 215, 217
nationalism, economic 259
nationality 31, 34
nationalization 50, 54, 73, 220, 365
    productivity 161–2
    see also railways, nationalization;
        transport, nationalization
NBC, *see* National Bus Company
NEB, *see* National Enterprise Board
Neely, A. 141, 143
Nelson, R. R. 120
Nenadic, S. 99, 109, 110
Netherlands 121
networks 67, 69, 74, 77
    community-rooted 69–70
    of relationships 85
    women 107, 109
Nevett, T. 170, 173, 179, 180
'New Labour' 48–9
    industrial policy 57
    transport policy 295
Newhouse, J. 54, 233
Newton, L. 191, 192, 193
niche products 24, 29, 210, 244, 275, 324, 340
Nicholas, T. 84, 92
Nichols, N. 140
Nichols, T. 145, 158
Nield, R. 160
Nohria, N. 217
Noland, M. 55
nonferrous metals industry 19, 20
Norberg, A. 238
Norman, E. R. 366
Norris, J. D. 174, 175, 176, 180
North America 120, 121
Northern Ireland 77, 127
Northern Rock 193, 198
nuclear industries 55, 225
nuclear power 61
    France 55

Oakland, J. S. 139
Oakley, B. 238
Odling-Smee, J. 164
off-shoring 65
    financial transactions 208
Offer, A. 153
Office of Fair Trading 275

O'Hagan, H. O. 375
Ogdens 26
    takeover 27
oil 126, 300, 302
    crisis (1974) 53, 294
    discrimination against US companies 121
Okochi, A. 182
Oldham, Joseph H. 366
oligopolies 34, 190, 194, 197, 201, 203, 271, 325
Oliver, J. 366
O'Mahony, M. 159
O'Neill, J. 238
OPEC 1 159, 162, 163
optical industry 77
    munitions 255–6, 257
O'Reilly, A. 145
organizations 62, 76, 132, 168
    capability 168, 171
    hierarchical 276, 277, 279
    structures 65, 66
O'Sullivan, M. 191
O'Sullivan, T. 213
Our Competive Future (White Paper, Cmd
    41/76. 1998) 57–8
output, *see* labour, output
outsourcing 62, 77
Owen, G. 60, 137, 154, 155, 156
Owen, K. 238
ownership 16, 30, 59, 62, 85, 86, 91
    control of 85, 86, 90, 91
    divorce from control of USA 34, 35, 90
    firms 280
        family firms 26, 32; private firms 86;
            public 50, 53, 86, 161, 289
    gender 102
    personal 34, 86
    women, and small business 102
ownership advantages 118
    Europe and UK 119
    USA and UK 118–19, 120
Owens, A. 99
Ozbilgin, M. 102, 109

P. J. Reynolds 30
Pack, H. 48, 55
Palmer, F. B. 364
paper:
    competition to revival 155–6
    declinism 154
Parker, R. H. 371
partial process operations 70, 71–2
Passas, N. 202
patents 62, 255
path-dependency 77–8
Pattilo, D. M. 233, 234
Pavitt, K. 228
Payne, P. L. 32, 168

Pearce, J. G. 257, 258
Perkin, H. 366
personal capitalism 69, 90
personal computers (PC) 242, 244
personal ownership 34, 86
Peters, E. 130
Peters, J. 367, 368
petrol tax 296
Pettigrew, A. M. 76, 77
pharmaceuticals 12, 50, 62, 63, 65, 124, 154,
    172, 173, 178, 245, 374
Phelps, N. A. 76, 132
Phillips, N. 99
Physick, R. 338
Pick, J. 146
Pickering, J. F. 280
Pilat, D. 62
Piore, M. J. 34, 74
Pitelis, C. N. 280
*Pitman's Dictionary of Industrial
    Administration* (Lee) 367
Pitt, S. 33
plug, *see* tobacco, chewing
Plowden Report (1965) 231
Pointon, A. C. 212
politics 72, 118, 121, 147, 219
    business and 87, 91
    Christian 357, 366
Pollard, S. 90, 274
Polley, M. 338, 340
Pontell, H. N. 358
Poole, F. 296
Poole, M. 139
Pope, D. 170, 171, 176, 180
Popp, A. 65, 67, 68, 69, 71, 72, 73, 76
Popple, S. 307
Porter, M. 60, 75, 137, 228, 276, 277
Porter, V. 306, 312, 313, 319
Powell, D. 280
Prance, G. 370
Pratten, C. F. 139, 145
predatory pricing 25–6, 27
Press, J. 84, 85, 88
Prest, A. R. 172
Prevezer, M. 67
prices 276–7
    value 277–8
private firms, *see* ownership, private firms
privatization 56, 128–9, 234
    see also transport, privatization; railways,
        privatization
procurement process 256
    aircraft manufacturing 228, 231
product development 171, 172, 176
    differentiation 118, 119, 120
    innovation 62, 185
    orientation 276

sales 170
product-oriented strategies 175, 184
production 17, 20, 67, 75, 123, 129, 170, 171,
     175, 180
  chain 66–7
  efficiency 276
  speciality 70
  techniques 119
  technologies 170–1, 172
productivity 35, 57, 63, 116, 123, 139
  declinism 153–4
  gap 132
  growth rate 162–3
     Germany and UK 157
  labour manufacturing 154**t8.1**
  performance 137, 139, 145, 154, 158, 159,
     161, 164
     West Germany 157–8
  stagnation 158–9, 162
  US solutions to 76
  US/UK gap 141, 142
professionals 86, 88
profit 26, 160
  alternatives to 97, 110
  maximimization 97, 110, 276, 279, 289,
     347, 349, 376
Progressive/Whig 31, 32, 35
property market 200–1, 277, 300
protectionism 24, 35, 117, 119, 155
Protherough, R. 146
Pryke, R. 291
PSO, *see* Public Service Obligation
public companies 19, 86, 347, 365
public flotations 26–7
public ownership, *see* ownership, public
public policy 155, 162, 300
public schools 88, 89, 90
public sector industries 128–9, 162
Public Service Obligation (PSO) 292
Public Transport Authorities 296
purchasing 15, 16, 170, 171, 175, 177
'push and pull' marketing 106, 176, 179

Raff, D. M. G. 31
Railtrack 297–8
Railway Act 1974 292
Railway Executive (RE) 289–90
railways 35, 61, 287–8, 295, 372
  and Beeching 290–1
  companies 85, 261
     and scientific analysis 254
  decline in 293
  electrification 292
  finance 289
  franchises 278, 297

freight 288, 294
investment 295, 300
nationalization 290, 297, 300
price increases 289
privatization 292, 297, 298–9, 301
productivity 161
regulatory system 297
social 292
subsidies, elimination of 297–8, 302
Ramirez, M. 144
Ramsay, Sir W. 253–4
Ransome & Marles 52, 56, 125
Raven, H. 275
Ray, G. F. 120
Rayner-Canham, G. 257
Rayner-Canham, M. 257
RBS, *see* Royal Bank of Scotland
RE, *see* Railway Executive
recession 159, 160, 162
Reed, D. 374
Rees, G. 373
regional development agencies (RDAs) 75–6,
     77, 78
regions 289, 291
  development agencies 126, 132
  industrial clusters 65
  industries 74, 168, 172
  policies 73, 74, 119, 122, 126, 127
  transfer of power to London 74
  see also clusters
Reid, M. 201, 212, 369
religion; *see* business ethics, religion
Renold, Sir C. 265
research and development (R&D) 61, 62, 123,
     132, 227–8, 238–9, 243, 252–3, 264,
     267
  conultancies 253
  expenditure 260, 260**t13.2**, 261, 263, 265,
     266–7
     government-funded 260**t13.1**,
        262, 263
  industrial research 252–3, 258, 261–3, 265,
     266–7
  planning of projects 265–6
  private industry 258, 260, 262–64,
     264**t13.3**, 264**t13.4**
     funding 264**t13.5**; government-funded
        264**t13.4**
  profits from 265
  scientists 256, 259, 266
  and small firms 258–9
  staff 262
*Research in Industry: the Basis of Economic
     Progress* (Fleming & Pearce) 258
Reshaping of Britain's Railways, The 290–1

resource:
  bases 68, 69, 70
  deficiencies 72
  dependency 68, 69–70, 71, 72, 76, 78, 130–1
  distribution 70, 71, 72, 76
  domestic allocation of 120–2
  external providers 72, 78
  reconfiguration 71
restrictive practices 145
restructuring 66, 127, 179
retail banks, *see* banks, retail
retailing 173–4, 175, 176, 177, 178, 179–80,
      181, 182, 183, 184, 273,
  competition 271–3
  development theories 275–80
  diversification 274–5
  large-scale 271, 275
  sales 273, 275, 277, 279, 281
Responsibilites of the British Public Company,
  The (CBI) 368
retail banking 190, 192, 193, 194, 199, 201, 215
  innovation 189, 195, 197, 198, 200, 203
  see also banks
Richards, H. 339, 349
Richardson, H. W. 35
Richardson, J. 293, 294, 295, 296
Richardson, R. 145
Ridley, N. 296
Ringer, F. 88, 90
Rio Tinto 19–20, 21
Rippin, T. 142
road haulage 287, 289, 294, 300, 301
roads 300, 302
  building 294, 295–6, 300–1
  lobby 293, 294, 296
  planning 293, 295
Roads for Prosperity (White Paper 1989) 295
Robb, G. 358
Robbins, K. 168
Roberts, G. 255
Roberts, G. K. 255, 259
Roberts, R. 207, 208, 211
Robertson, D. 235
Robertson, P. L. 276
rolling stock companies (ROSCO) 297, 298
Rolls-Royce 51, 53, 57, 59, 61–3, 129, 200,
      226–7, 228–9, 232, 233–4, 245
  see also Rose, Sir J.
Rooth, T. 118, 119, 121, 122
Roper, S. 77
ROSCO, *see* rolling stock companies
Rose, Sir J. 59, 61
Rose, M. B. 110
Ross, C. 276
Ross, M. 192
Rothwell, M. 236, 243
Rover 56, 58, 59

Rowe, M. 276
Rowland, T. 238
Rowntree, S. 172–3
Royal Bank of Scotland (RBS) 213, 215, 217,
      218, 220
Rubinstein, W. D. 84, 90
rugby league 338, 340, 342, 346, 348, 349
  and television 348
rugby union 330, 333, 334, 339, 346, 348
  amateurism 348
Russell, D. 334, 337
Russell, P 307
Rutterford, J. 99, 111
Ryall, T. 312, 314

Sabel, C. 34, 74
Safarian, A. E. 125, 126
Safeguarding of Industries Act 1921 117
Saggi, K. 48
sales 120, 170–2, 173, 175, 178, 181–3
  see also aircraft industries, sales; retailing, sales
Sambrook, S. C. 255
Sanderson, M. 88, 253, 254, 258
Sarbanes-Oxley Act 2002 (USA) 369, 374
SRA, *see* Special Areas Reconstruction
      Association
Saseki, J. 74
Satre, L. J. 375
saturation 67, 71
Saul, S. B. 226
Sawyer, M. 160
Saxenian, A. 240
Scale and Scope (Chandler) 20, 30, 31, 32
scale economics 19
Scandinavia 155
Scase, R. 106, 109, 148
Schaefer, N. 74
Schenk, C. R. 120, 121, 207
Schmitz, C. 30
Scholes, K. 278
Schumpeter, J. 31, 32, 33, 34, 82, 84, 276
Schuster, G. 364
Schuwer, P. 180, 181
Schwartz, E. B. 107
Schwartz, M. 86
Science, Ministry of 52
science-based industries 118–19, 123
Scientific and Industrial Research,
      Department of 50
scientific research, government funded 260,
      260 **t13.1**
scientists, *see* industrial research, and scientists
Scotland 122, 127, 131, 213, 242
Scott, J. 87
Scott, J. D. 262
Scott, P. 74, 118, 119, 121, 122, 192, 193, 201, 300
Scott, W. H. 139

Second World War 48, 49, 50, 90, 100, 105,
    108, 120, 138, 153, 169, 178, 184, 193,
    227, 230, 236, 256, 259, 261–2, 266,
    271, 273, 274, 359
sectoral distribution 85, 86
securities:
    fixed interest 26
    market 35
        Britain 16
Sedgwick, J. 314, 317
self-employment 110
    and men 103–4
    in service sector, 1984–98 104t5.4
    and women 99, 100, 102, 105, 106, 107–9
        1956–2001 103t5.3
self-service retailing 273, 274
selling 171, 177, 184
semiconductors 53, 239
Servan-Schreiber, J.-J. 237
service sector 33, 85, 86, 184
    employment by gender (1956-97) 100t5.1
        (1984–98) 101t5.2
    and innovation 62
    and manufacturing 60, 61–2
    primary producers 70
    surplus on 61
    women in 97, 99–100, 102, 103
Shackleton, L. 334
shareholders 16, 26, 29, 34
    and directors 357, 364, 366
    divorce from management 33–4
    and football clubs 347
Sharma, B. 74
Shaw, E. 98, 102, 103, 106, 107
Shaw, G. 176, 271, 273
Sheppard, D. K. 196
Sheppard, J. 281
Shimokawa, K. 182
Shimotani, M. 182
Shin, D.-H. 72
shipbuilding industries 50
    European failure 154
Shipton, H. 141, 143
Shire, K. 109
Shires, J. D. 292
Shore, E. 176, 181
Sigsworth, E. M. 174, 178
Silbertson, A. 233
Simmons, A. E. 255
Simms, A. 281
Simonson, G. 226
Simpson, A. 374
Singleton, J. 70, 71, 72
Sissons, R. 336
Sivulka, J. 175, 176, 180, 181
small and medium enterprises (SMEs) 102,
    110, 227

    and gender 102–3
    lending to 192–3, 200
Smith, A. 349
Smith, A. 276
Smith, D. 233, 234
Smithers, R. 301
Smithies, E. D. 119
smoking products 24
snooker 344
soccer, *see* football
social audit 373
software, *see* computer software
Sorrell, A. A. 310
Sorrell, T. 369
Soul of a New Machine (Kidder) 240
South East Asia 24
Southwood, R. 147
Spain 19, 21
Sparks, L. 271
Special Areas Reconstruction Association
    (SARA) 192–3
specialization 70, 71, 74, 156
    retailing 273, 278
    see also clusters
Spiegel, P. 235
spillovers 67, 130
'spin-offs' 116–17, 128, 130
sports 335, 338
    amateurism 333, 334, 335, 336, 338, 339
    business 330, 331, 332, 333, 335, 336, 339,
        340, 343, 349
    commercial sponsorship 339–46, 348–9
    competitve 332
    consumer expenditure 331–2, 338, 350
    and fashionwear 332, 349–50
    falling attendances 334, 342, 345
    goods 332, 349
    governing bodies 334
    market share 331, 332, 340, 345
    media, relationship with 331, 332, 344–6,
        349–50
    and television 341, 342, 344–5, 348–9, 350
    professionalism 333, 335, 336, 345
    recreational 332–3
    and television 331
    see also cricket; football; rugby league; rugby
        union; tennis
Staber, U. 74
stakeholding 373–4, 378
Stamp, J. C. 372
Standard Chartered Merchant Bank 212–13,
    214, 215–16, 218, 219, 220
Stanworth, P. 83, 84, 87
Starkey, K. 144
start-up businesses 53, 57, 60
    and women 107
state agglomeration economies 66

state-owned companies 56
steel industries 50, 65, 161–2
    declinism 154
        and revival 156
    nationalization 73
    and scientists 255
sterling 118, 120, 121, 122, 163, 207
Sternberg, E. 374
Steuer, M. D. 121, 123, 125
Stevens, H. 295, 297, 301
Stewart, M. 233
Stewart, R. 139, 145
Stigler, G. J. 276
Stock Exchange 208, 346
    see also City of London
stock exchange securities 26
stock exchanges 33, 201
stock markets 34, 241
    finance 33–4
stock options 59
Stollwerck 32
Stone, I. 132
Stopford, J. 116, 118, 128
Stout, D. 67
Spraos, J. 317
Strasser, S. 170, 176, 180
strategies 66, 76, 129
Strategy and Structure (Chandler) 30
Strauss, W. V. 311
Street, S. 315, 316, 317, 318, 320
strikes 145
Stuyvenberg, J. H. van 176
sub-contracting 278
sub-prime mortgages 217
Sugar, Sir Alan 330
Sunday Observance Act 19969, repeal of
    338–9
Sunderland, D. 357
supermarkets 273, 274
Supple, B. 31, 168
Supply, Ministry of (MoS) 228, 229, 262
supply chains 65, 76, 78, 132, 179, 271, 272,
    274, 278, 279, 282
supply-side policies 57, 63, 171
sustainable development 295
Swann, G. M. P. 67
Swann, K. 139
Sweden 52, 56, 59, 125
Switzerland 121
syndicates, Europe 77
Szymanski, S. 347, 348

take-offs 67, 71
takeovers 123, 129, 217
    banks 217–18
    foreign 125
    restrictions on 126

tariffs:
    car imports 129
    protection 29
    tobacco 23–4
    UK 35, 117, 118, 119, 155
tax incentives 57
Taylor, D. J. 339
Taylor, J. 126
Taylor, M. 346
Taylor, P. 332, 333, 339, 344
Taylor, R. 142
technology 70, 109, 252, 276
    changes 276
Technology, Ministry of 52, 237–8, 238–9
technology transfer 76, 118, 130, 132, 232
Tedlow, R. 170, 171, 174, 175, 176, 180, 181
Teece, D. J. 120
telecommunications equipment 58
    see also GEC; Marconi; Weinstock, Lord
        Arnold
television (TV) 313, 325, 327
    see also sports, media
Temin, P. 31
Temple, William 366, 367, 368, 378
tennis 335, 336, 338, 344 *see also* sports
Tesco 272, 274, 275, 280–2
Tether, B. 62
textiles 67
Thatcher, Margaret 48, 55, 57, 88, 126, 128,
    153, 208, 234, 238, 244, 292, 294, 367,
    373, 377
Thomas, D. 143
Thomas, H. 333
Thomas, W. A. 191, 194
Thompson, E. P. 279
Thompson, K. 311
Thomson, A. 168
Thorn 54, 56
Thornberry, J. B. 240
Tilley, N. M. 22. 278
Tillsley, C. 278
Tmmons, J. A. 241
Tiratsoo, N. 75, 76, 91, 120, 138, 144, 145,
    146, 147
Tissiere, L. S. 217
tobacco 22–4, 172, 173, 174, 175, 273, 274, 344–5
    chewing (plug) 24, 25
    cigarettes 22, 23, 25, 27, 30
        sales 24, 25, 29
    exports 24, 25, 29
    foreign subsidiaries 23
    pricing wars 28
    profits 26
TOCs, *see* train operating companies
Tolliday, S. 119, 122, 192
Tomlinson, J. 53, 75, 76, 120, 138, 145, 147,
    153, 160, 162, 164

Toms, J. S. 68, 73, 98
Toms, S. 91
Tooze, A. 35
Toulmin, V. 307
trade 23, 48, 56
    see also free trade; trade finance
Trade and Industry, Department of 52, 57, 103, 125, 126
Trade and Industry, Secretary of State for (DTI) 57, 58, 146
    see also Heseltine, M; Byers, S.
trade associations 177–8
trade finance 209, 212, 215–16
trade unions 128, 145, 146–7
trademarks 173, 182
Trades Union Congress 61
traffic 301
    congestion charge 8, 295
Traffic in Towns (Buchanan) 293
train operating companies (TOCs) 297–8
training 48, 88, 90, 154–5
    employee 142–3
    UK managers 140–1
transaction banking 191–2
transaction costs 67, 174, 272, 276, 277, 278, 279, 280
transport (since 1945):
    economic growth 299, 301
    employment in 288
    nationalization 288–90
    passenger 287–8
    privatization 287, 296
    public 294–5, 296, 301
    see also cars; railways; roads; waterways
Transport Act 1947 287, 288
Transport Act 1953 289–90
Transport Act 1962 290
Transport Act 1968 296
Transport, Minister of 293
Transport, Ministry of 300
Transport 2010 (2000) 295
Transport and the Environment (Houghton report) 295
Travers, T. 295, 297, 302
Trebilcock, C. 153, 168
Truman, C. 105, 106
trustees savings banks, *see* banks, trustees savings
Tuke, A. W. 192
Turk, J. 160
Turnbull, N. 374
Turner, F. 256
Turner, F. J. 31
Turner, L. 116, 118, 128
Turok, I. 130, 131
TV, *see* television

TV sets 54, 57
Tweedale, G. 365, 367, 368, 375, 377, 378

UK, business history 15, 30
UK Treasury 121, 191
    railways 291–2
    transport 300
Unbound Prometheus, The (Landes) 31
unemployment 53, 122, 125, 126, 160–1, 164
university education 88, 89, 90; *see also* education; public schools
Useem, M. 87
USA 15, 19, 26, 32, 86, 121, 138
    aircraft industries 50–1, 54, 228, 229, 231, 233, 235, 245
    banks 207, 208, 210–12, 213, 214–15, 217–18, 220
        purchased by UK banks 214, 217, 221
    computer manufacturers 51, 236, 244, 245
    computer software 243
    consumer goods 181
    distribution 174–5
    economic growth 16, 22, 184
    expatriate managers 18
    film industry 309, 310, 311, 313, 315, 316, 319, 322, 323, 324, 325
    foreign direct investment (FDI) 126
        in Britain 117–21
    large scale business enterprises 33, 34, 60, 168
    mail order 175
    management 138, 139
    marketing 171, 180
    mass production 30
    nonferrous metals industry 20
    productivity performance 161
    tobacco 22–3, 24
        domestic sales 24–5
    women, in business 105
    see also multinational enterprises, US entrants to Britain
Usselman, S. 237

value:
    creation 279, 282
    labour theory of 279
    price 277–8
    realization 272, 279
    in retailing 277
value added 62**t2.1**, 123, 129, 277, 278, 282
value chains 11, 74, 276, 277, 278–9
van Leeuwen, M. H. D. 259
Van Reenen, J. 142
Varcoe, I. 258
Vasta, M. 32
Vauxhall 117, 119

Veblen, T. 174, 201
venture capital 53, 57, 58, 108, 196, 241, 242
Vernon, K. 257
vertical disintegration 277, 278, 279, 282
vertical integration 70, 125, 174, 236, 276–7, 278, 282,
    film industry 312, 315, 319, 320, 323
Visible Hand, The (Chandler) 30, 33

W D & H O Wills 22, 23, 25, 26, 27–8, 30
Wada, K. 32, 34
wages, *see* income
Wagg, S. 335
Walby, S. 100, 108
Wales 19, 127, 132
Walker, A. 317, 319, 323
Wall, Sir Frederick 330
Walsh, M. 98, 102
Walvin, J. 330, 331, 346
Ward, M. 16
Ward, V. 178
Wardley, P. 33, 85
warehousing 11, 273, 274, 278, 279, 281, 282
Warren, R. C. 373, 378
Waterman, D. 321
waterways 287, 289, 299
Watkins, D. S. 102
Watkins, J. M. 102
Watkinson, H. 293, 294
Watson, C. 253
Watson, K. 192
Watson, K. D. 254
Waymark, P. 319
wealth 17, 32, 84, 107, 147, 171, 177, 299, 372
weapons 235, 236, 238, 260
Weber, J. 217
Webley, S. 369
Weinstock, Lord Arnold 52, 58
Weissmüller, A. 211
Wells, P. 236
Welskopp, T. 32, 35
Wenner, L. 331
West Europe 164, 210
Westland Affair 129
White, A. 141, 143
white collar crime 360
Whitley, R. 87
Whittington, B. 375
Whittington, R. 31, 33, 34, 86
wholesaling 174–5, 176, 177, 183
Wiener, M. 90
Wiener, W. J. 168
Wild, R. 139
Wilkins, M. 117
Wilkinson, K. 52

Williams, B. 271, 280
Williams, B. R. 265, 266
Williams, J. 331, 344, 348
Williams, J. 156, 158
Williams, K. 156, 158
Williams, R. H. 181
Williamson, O. E. 276
Williamson, P. 87
Willott, W. B. 53
Wilmot, J. 262
Wilson, C. H. 173, 178
Wilson, C. S. 87
Wilson, Harold 52, 238, 368
Wilson, J. F. 65, 67, 68, 69, 70, 71, 72, 73, 76, 168
Wilson, R. 143, 147
Wilson, R. G. 173
Winstanley, M. 271
Winter, S. G. 120
'Winter of Discontent' 163
Winton, J. R. 194, 196
Wischermann, C. 176, 181
Wiskin, C. 99
Wolmar, C. 290, 297
women:
    business/enterprise 97–9, 103, 105, 107, 109, 110–11
    career development 103
    as employees 105
    finance and discrimination 107
    industrial science 257
    investment 111
    knowledge economy 108–9
    part-time employment 100, 107
    self-employment 102, 103, 106, 107–9, 111
    service sector 102, 103
    socio-economic position of 99
    traditional roles 107–8, 109
Wood, L. 316
Wood, R. M. 226
Woodland, S. 145
Woodward, D. 349
Woodward, N. W. C. 145, 148
work place 143
    attitudes to 146–8
    women 99, 105
world markets 48, 51, 52, 57, 63
Wotinsky, W. L. 17
Wren, C. 57, 126
Wren-Lewis, S. 160
Wright, G. 343, 344
Wright, M. 91
Wright, P. 147
Wrigley, N. 271, 274, 275, 276, 279, 280
Wyatt, D, 339, 349

yachting 342–3
Yamey, B. S. 274
Yonekawa, S. 182
Yoshihara, H. 182
Yoshino, Y. M. 182

Young, P. 261
Young, S. 125, 127, 128, 129, 130

Zeitlin, J. 34, 74, 91, 378
Ziegler, P. 207